Prophetic Rhetoric
Case Studies in Text Analysis and Translation
Second Edition

Ernst R. Wendland

With a Foreword by Dr. Lynell Zogbo

"The Vision of the Valley of the Dry Bones" by Gustave Doré

Doré Bible Illustrations. Free to copy. www.creationism.org/images/

Eze 37:4–5 Again he said unto me, Prophesy upon these bones, and say unto them, O ye dry bones, hear the word of the Lord. ... Behold, I will cause breath to enter into you, and you shall live: ...

SIL International®
Publications in Translation and Textlinguistics
7

Publications in Translation and Textlinguistics is a peer-reviewed series published by SIL International®. The series is a venue for works concerned with all aspects of translation and textlinguistics, including translation theory, exegesis, pragmatics, and discourse analysis. While most volumes are authored by members of SIL, suitable works by others will also form part of the series.

Series Editors

Mike Cahill

Volume Editor

George Huttar

Production Staff

Bonnie Brown, Managing Editor
Lois Gourley, Production Director
Judy Benjamin, Compositor
Barbara Alber, Cover Design

Prophetic Rhetoric
Case Studies in Text Analysis and Translation
Second Edition

Ernst R. Wendland

With a Foreword by Dr. Lynell Zogbo

SIL International®
Dallas, Texas

© 2014 by SIL International®
Library of Congress Catalog No: 2014944671
ISBN: 978-1-55671-345-3
ISSN: 1550-588X

Printed in the United States of America

Unless otherwise indicated, English Bible quotations are taken from the Revised Standard Version, Copyright © 1946, 1952, 1971 by the Division of Christian Education of the National Council of the Churches of Christ in the United States of America, used by permission of Wm. Collins and Sons, Ltd. for the Bible Societies and the New International Version, Copyright © 1973, 1978, 1984 by the International Bible Society, used by permission of Zondervan. All rights reserved.

All rights reserved. No part of this publication may be reproduced, stored in a retrieval system, or transmitted in any form or by any means—electronic, mechanical, photocopy, recording, or otherwise—without the express permission of SIL International®. However, short passages, generally understood to be within the limits of fair use, may be quoted without permission.

Copies of this and other publications of SIL International® may be obtained from:

SIL International Publications
7500 W. Camp Wisdom Road
Dallas, TX 75236-5629 USA

Voice: +1-972-708-7404
Fax: +1-972-708-7363
publications_intl@sil.org
http://www.sil.org/resources/publications

Contents

Dedication xiii
Preface.. xv
Preface to the Second (Revised) Edition xix
Acknowledgements xxi
Foreword xxiii
1 Dramatic Rhetoric, Metaphoric Imagery, and Discourse
   Structure in Joel.. 1
   1.1 Introduction 1
   1.2 Overview: Hebrew poetic text analysis................................... 2
   1.3 The structure of Joel as a whole 5
   1.4 A literary-structural summary of two parallel pericopes 8
   1.5 Thematic image-interaction 17
       1.5.1 Image complexes in Joel... 17
       1.5.2 From image to metaphor—the stimulating blend of distinct
           "mental spaces"... 19
   1.6 Conclusion: Communicating Joel's dramatic rhetoric and imagery
       today 27
2 The 'Word of the LORD' and the Organization of Amos.................. 31
   2.1 The discourse structure of Amos: Miracle or mirage?....................... 31
   2.2 Lexical-semantic recursion: An ancient means of text processing..... 33
       2.2.1 Similarity–Contrast 35
       2.2.2 Form–Meaning... 35

    2.2.3 Linear–Concentric 37
    2.2.4 Horizontal–Hierarchical 38
    2.2.5 Scribal–Oral 39
  2.3 A structural outline of Amos 41
    2.3.1 Introduction to the prophecy (Am 1:1–2) 42
    2.3.2 Oracles against the nations (Am 1:3–2:16) 42
    2.3.3 Oracles against the house of Israel (Am 3:1–6:14) 45
    2.3.4 Five visions of Israel's ruin (Am 7:1–9:10) 55
    2.3.5 Prophecy of restoration (Am 9:11–15) 63
  2.4 The thematic implications of a structural description 66
  2.5 Controversy over 'the Word of the LORD' continues—Can a structural analysis help? 75
    2.5.1 Text criticism 75
    2.5.2 Message content 79
    2.5.3 Discourse structure 83
  2.6 Presenting 'the word of the LORD' in Amos today 93
    2.6.1 The printed text 93
    2.6.2 The performed text 96

3 The Rhetoric of Obadiah's "Day": Its Structure and Significance .. 103
  3.1 Introduction 103
  3.2 Unity in diversity: The form of Obadiah among the prophets 104
    3.2.1 Section A: 1–10 106
    3.2.2 Section B: 11–14 110
    3.2.3 Section A': 15–21 111
  3.3 The rhetorical technique of the prophet Obadiah 115
    3.3.1 A structural perspective on biblical rhetoric 116
    3.3.2 A Classical rhetorical perspective on Obadiah 120
  3.4 Levels of prophetic communication and their theological significance 121
  3.5 Implications of a text-rhetorical analysis of biblical discourse 126
    3.5.1 Some hermeneutical challenges 126
    3.5.2 Issues of methodology 128
    3.5.3 The essential message of Obadiah 133
    3.5.4 Rhetorical structure as an exegetical and communicative tool 136

4 What's the Good News? Prophetic Rhetoric and the Salvific Center of Nahum's Vision 143
  4.1 Introduction 143
  4.2 The theme of Nahum—bane or blessing? 144
  4.3 A rhetorical outline of Nahum 146
    4.3.1 Structural overview 146
    4.3.2 Structural description 148

    4.4 The principal rhetorical devices of the LORD's good-news messenger 156
    4.5 Just how "beautiful" are the textual "feet" of Nahum (cf. Isa 52:7) in another language? 171
    4.6 Conclusion 174
5 The Structure, Style, Sense, and Significance of Haggai's Prophecy Concerning the "House of the LORD" 177
    5.1 Introduction 177
    5.2 Overview of the discourse structure of Haggai's prophecy 178
        5.2.1 Structural divisions 178
        5.2.2 Discourse peaks 182
        5.2.3 Rhetorical overlay 185
    5.3 The communicative significance of Haggai's style 189
        5.3.1 Direct speech 190
        5.3.2 Purposeful redundancy 191
        5.3.3 Graphic imagery 192
        5.3.4 Larger-to-lesser progression 193
        5.3.5 Phonological pointing 194
        5.3.6 Probing questions 195
        5.3.7 Reminiscent allusion 195
        5.3.8 Supportive patterning 196
    5.4 Haggai's rhetoric: A progressive prophetic argument 198
        5.4.1 Setting 200
        5.4.2 Problem 201
        5.4.3 Situation 202
        5.4.4 Appeal 203
        5.4.5 Intentions 204
        5.4.6 Authority 205
        5.4.7 Exceptions 206
        5.4.8 Motivation 206
        5.4.9 Cotext 208
        5.4.10 Assumptions 210
    5.5 Communicating Haggai's concerns today—in Africa 212
        5.5.1 On the present religious significance of Haggai's message 212
        5.5.2 Communicative problems presented by the prophecy of Haggai 215
    5.6 Helping to bridge the communication gap 218
        5.6.1 Textual strategies 219
        5.6.2 Paratextual strategies 221
        5.6.3 Extratextual strategies 223
    5.7 Conclusion: "Rebuilding" God's Word in another language 225

6 Recursion and Variation in the "Prophecy" of Jonah: On the Rhetorical Impact of Stylistic Technique, with Special Reference to Irony and Enigma... 229
6.1 Methodology: The interaction of rhetorical and stylistic analysis... 229
6.2 Recursion in biblical Hebrew narrative discourse....................... 231
    6.2.1 Linguistic nature 232
    6.2.2 Degree of formal correspondence 235
    6.2.3 Size and scope... 236
    6.2.4 Distribution pattern 240
    6.2.5 Textual relationships... 242
    6.2.6 Plot dynamics 245
    6.2.7 Degree of subjectivity 245
6.3 Variation in literary discourse: The flip-side of recursion.............. 246
    6.3.1 Lexical-semantic variation 249
    6.3.2 Spatial-syntactic variation 254
    6.3.3 Temporal-pragmatic variation 257
6.4 Potential problems in the functional analysis of literary form........ 263
    6.4.1 Methodology... 264
    6.4.2 Genre 266
    6.4.3 Perspective.. 267
    6.4.4 Setting... 268
    6.4.5 Mode/medium of composition.. 270
6.5 The rhetorical significance of recursion and variation in Hebrew narrative discourse... 271
    6.5.1 Text organization.. 271
    6.5.2 Text demarcation.. 273
    6.5.3 Text conjunction.. 274
    6.5.4 Text projection.. 276
    6.5.5 Text characterization.. 280
    6.5.6 Text presentation.. 282
    6.5.7 Text pluri-signification.. 283
6.6 On the incisiveness and inclusiveness of irony in Jonah................. 285
    6.6.1 Textual irony 287
    6.6.2 Contextual irony 290
    6.6.3 Functions of irony.. 295
6.7 Enigma and the ever-unfolding "mystery" of Jonah 297
    6.7.1 Eventive enigma 302
    6.7.2 Dramatic enigma.. 305
    6.7.3 Lexical enigma.. 308
    6.7.4 Thematic enigma.. 310
6.8 Song from the sea: How sweet does Jonah's psalm sound? 316
    6.8.1 Introduction 316

6.8.2 An introverted textual structure to reflect a corresponding spiritual experience.. 317
6.8.3 The structural significance of Jonah's psalm 324
6.8.4 Towards a literary functional-equivalence translation of Jonah 2.. 327

7 "Can These Bones Live Again?"—Rhetoric of the Gospel in Ezekiel 33–37 337

7.1 Introduction 337
7.2 The drama of prophetic discourse in Ezekiel 339
   7.2.1 Overall plot progression.. 339
   7.2.2 Correspondence and contrast in the plot design 345
   7.2.3 The importance of discourse (structural) analysis .. 349
7.3 Chapters 33–37 as a compositional unit 351
7.4 The rhetorical purpose of the prophecy of Ezekiel 355
7.5 Summary of the literary-rhetorical development of chapters 33–37 358
   7.5.1 YHWH renews Ezekiel's call as a "watchman" for "the house of Israel" (33:1–20)................................... 358
   7.5.2 Report of the fall of Jerusalem and a twofold unrepentant response (33:21–33)................................. 362
   7.5.3 YHWH declares a woe upon negligent shepherds, but weal for needy sheep (34:1–33) 366
   7.5.4 "Edom" will be punished for its wicked attitude toward God and his people (35:1–15)........................ 371
   7.5.5 The LORD will renew the desolate mountains of Israel and its people (36:1–15) 375
   7.5.6 YHWH will vindicate his holy name by cleansing his people and their land (36:16–38).............................. 378
   7.5.7 The "Spirit of the LORD" resurrects the "skeleton" of the "house of Israel" (37:1–14) 383
   7.5.8 A prophetic object lesson in support of the divine message of restoration (37:15–28) 387
   7.5.9 Summary.. 392
7.6 "Can these bones live again"—in translation? 393
   7.6.1 An overview of the development of Bible translation in Africa 394
   7.6.2 Translation goal: A different Bible version for every major variety of user 397
   7.6.3 Principles and procedures: How is a "oratorical" version prepared? 402
   7.6.4 Illustration: A comparative stylistic-functional evaluation of translation technique 410

  7.6.5 Application: Different translation styles for different types of target group 418
  7.6.6 Conclusion: Some implications for Bible translation in Bantu Africa... 419

8 "The Righteous Live by their Faith" in a Holy God: Complementary Compositional Forces and the Rhetorical Generation of Habakkuk's Dialogue with the LORD 423

8.1 Introduction 423
8.2 How clear—the "vision" of Habakkuk? 424
8.3 Progression—the forward, climactic movement of discourse 428
  8.3.1 The overall, structural-thematic progression of the discourse .. 430
  8.3.2 The center of the macrostructure... 431
  8.3.3 The problem of 2:5 433
  8.3.4 A taunt of five "woes" against the wicked 435
  8.3.5 Chapter 3 in relation to the rest of Habakkuk 438
  8.3.6 A closer look at the prayer of Habakkuk 440
  8.3.7 Rhetorical-dramatic progression in Habakkuk's poetic-prophetic discourse 445
  8.3.8 Theodicy realized in theophany.. 451
8.4 Cohesion—the internal, connecting tissue of discourse 453
  8.4.1 Intratextual cohesion 454
  8.4.2 The "thematic polarity" of Habakkuk..................................... 461
  8.4.3 The "compositional core" of Habakkuk (2:4b) 463
  8.4.4 Intertextual cohesion 465
  8.4.5 "Mythopoetic" allusion in Habakkuk 3................................... 469
8.5 Communicating crucial aspects of the rhetoric of an ancient biblical text today 473
  8.5.1 "May the whole world hush in his presence!" (Hab. 2:20b): From silence to psalmody 473
  8.5.2 The rhetoric of discourse and performance 474
  8.5.3 Some basic issues in Bible translation................................... 475
  8.5.4 Bridging the contextual gap... 478
8.6 Conclusion—A hush in His presence... 493

9 The Drama of Zephaniah: A Literary-Rhetorical Analysis of a Proclamatory Prophetic Text 497

9.1 Introduction: What is so "dramatic" about Zephaniah's discourse? 497
9.2 Overview: The dialogic structure of the discourse 500
9.3 The rhetorical function of Zephaniah—A literary-structural analysis... 502
  9.3.1 Zephaniah as dramatic prophecy 502
  9.3.2 Discourse markers in Zephaniah 503
9.4 Overview of the L-S organization of Zephaniah............................ 505
9.5 Summary of the literary-structural analysis................................... 520

- 9.6 Deconstructing a crux interpretum—2:4 522
- 9.7 A rhetorical-argument analysis of Zephaniah 523
  - 9.7.1 The rhetorical situation 523
  - 9.7.2 A speech-act perspective 524
  - 9.7.3 The connotative aspect of the discourse 525
  - 9.7.4 Overview of the argument 526
- 9.8 Conclusion 527
  - 9.8.1 Of what relevance is this study for Bible translators? 527
  - 9.8.2 Summary of practical implications 528

10 Linear and Concentric Patterns in the Rhetorical Structure and Style of Malachi 531
- 10.1 Introduction 531
- 10.2 Aspects of Malachi's rhetorical style 532
  - 10.2.1 Parallelism 532
  - 10.2.2 Chiasmus 533
  - 10.2.3 Simile and metaphor 534
  - 10.2.4 Synecdoche and metonymy 535
  - 10.2.5 Rhetorical question 535
  - 10.2.6 Antithesis 536
  - 10.2.7 Exclamatory utterances 536
  - 10.2.8 Graphic diction 538
  - 10.2.9 Verbal shifts 539
  - 10.2.10 Closure 539
- 10.3 Aspects of Malachi's rhetorical discourse organization 541
  - 10.3.1 Linear patterning 541
  - 10.3.2 Concentric patterning 543
- 10.4 Prophetic rhetoric: On the pragmatic implications of literary style and structure 566
  - 10.4.1 Interpreting the text—exegesis 566
  - 10.4.2 Communicating the text—translation 569

11 A Case Study in Cross-Cultural Communication 573
"Do you understand what you are reading (hearing)?"—The example of Isaiah 52:13–53:12 in Tonga 573
Introduction: Proclaiming an ancient Hebrew prophecy in a modern Bantu setting 574
Hearing Isaiah's text today: How would an ordinary Mutonga respond? 577
- 52:13 577
- 52:14 578
- 52:15 579
- 53:1 580
- 53:2 581

    53:3 581
    53:4 582
    53:5 582
    53:6 583
    53:7 584
    53:8 585
    53:9 585
    53:10 586
    53:11 587
    53:12 588
  Conclusion: On the importance of a correct and convincing
    contextualization 588
12 Analyzing and Translating Haggai **595**
  Exercises—Haggai as a whole 599
  Exercises—Haggai 1:1–2 601
  Exercises—Haggai 1:3–11 604
  Exercises—Haggai 1:12–15 607
  Exercises—Haggai 2:1–5 609
  Exercises—Haggai 2:6–9 612
  Exercises—Haggai 2:10–14 614
  Exercises—Haggai 2:15–19 616
  Exercises—Haggai 2:20–23 619
13 Proclaiming Prophetic Rhetoric Today: Promoting its Potential .. **623**
  13.1 On the drama of prophetic proclamation—or is it "performance?" ... 624
  13.2 How can we proclaim the prophetic text in translation? 633
  13.3 Conclusion: Contemporizing and contextualizing the ancient
    prophets of Israel 637
References **643**
Index of Subjects **659**

Dedication

For all my Hebrew teachers over the years at Dr. Martin Luther (Northwestern) College and Wisconsin Lutheran Seminary (Mequon).

נָתַן לָהֶם הָאֱלֹהִים מַדָּע וְהַשְׂכֵּל בְּכָל־סֵפֶר וְחָכְמָה
(Daniel 1:17a)

Preface

The present book is in many respects a follow-up to my recent book *Finding and translating the oral-aural elements in written language: The case of the New Testament epistles* (Mellen Press, 2008). This becomes clearer in light of the title that I originally proposed (and still prefer) for that text, namely, "Proclaiming the Scriptures in translation: An *oral-rhetorical approach* for analyzing and communicating the Word of God, With special reference to several New Testament epistles." The main difference between these two works is their textual frame of reference; then it was the NT epistles—now it is the Hebrew prophetic literature.

The essential presuppositions of this analysis, as supported by my results from various text studies in the Hebrew Scriptures, remain the same as those of the former book:

1. The linguistic *forms* of a literary text convey important *pragmatic* (interpersonal, contextualized), and at times also *semantic*, meaning.
2. The fundamental literary/oratorical (artistic-rhetorical) character of the Scriptures is a given—in short, vital *information*, coupled with *intention* and *emotion*, that is given for the purpose of motivating *persuasion* and *acceptance*.
3. The literary/oratorical resources of any contemporary "target language" (TL) can *match* those that are manifested in the biblical text by means of a context-sensitive *functional equivalence* methodology.

4. The text of Scripture is ideally suited—in fact, most often specifically composed for—*public oral proclamation* to a listening audience.
5. Many stylistic and structural features of the original text are not readily apparent, or fully appreciated, when that text is read *silently* to oneself.
6. One creative way to bridge the communication gap between principles 1 and 2 is via an *oral-rhetorical* methodology applied first analytically to the SL text and then synthetically with regard to a TL rendition by means of an *informed-intuitive* compositional approach (carried out by competent translators and their support team).
7. Any version of this nature must first be carefully *explained* to, then *clearly* understood and *approved* by the target constituency that commissions the translation to be done, whether a full Testament, a Bible, or only a Scripture portion.

So what are the purpose and expected benefits of this type of "oral-rhetorical," structural-stylistic text analysis of the original biblical documents? Such a careful, comprehensive literary study, as exemplified in subsequent chapters with respect to a selection from among the prophetic corpus, aims to achieve the several goals listed below. Thus, it better enables the analyst to discern:

- instances of rhythmic diction and other distinctive phonological features of the Hebrew text—the primary aspects of elocutionary utterance;
- various text breaks and structural transitions, both major and minor—plus greater and lesser pause points;
- the crucial points of rhetorical emphasis and attractive artistry in the original document;
- a book's principal themes through its extensive and varied patterns of lexical recursion;
- the chief stylistic features that render the text more memorable/memorizable; and
- abundant evidence that the biblical text is semantically and pragmatically "richer" than many biblical scholars realize, incorporating additional aspects of "meaning" (in the fullest sense) that need to be conveyed—whether textually or paratextually, via translation or commentary—in order for a greater degree of communicative correspondence to be attained.

In support of the preceding assumptions and aims, I present a number of individual analytical case studies of eight works from the "minor" prophets, in the following chapter order: Joel, Obadiah, Nahum, Haggai, Jonah, Habakkuk, Zephaniah, and Malachi. In addition, the crucial chapters 33–37 of Ezekiel are investigated in detail (cf. the title page illustration of Ezek 37:4–5, a most "inspiring" prophetic pronouncement to the dead!). Various facets of an "oral-rhetorical," literary structural method of analysis are explained and illustrated during the course of these studies, each of which has a somewhat different focus and emphasis in accordance with the form, content, and communicative aim of the prophetic book being considered (e.g., the narrative of Jonah, which includes a lament psalm). To conclude each chapter, a number of pertinent implications for and applications to the practice of Scripture translation are pointed out. The set of texts included here are not the most popular of biblical books for consideration by scholars, teachers, preachers—or translators—so it is hoped that a closer look from the perspective of a more dynamic literary model of investigation might encourage a greater awareness of and more attention paid to these powerful communicators to God's people in the past. The relevance of their diverse messages rings out through the ages right up to the present day and a world much different on the outside, but just as needful on the inside, no matter what their life-setting, worldview, and cultural orientation.

As was the case with the companion volume on the epistles, so also the primary target readership of this book includes, in particular, the following groups—namely, to serve as a *resource* and *enrichment* text for:

- theological students and those in biblical (OT/NT) studies, ideally with at least one year of biblical Hebrew;
- students in translation studies, especially Bible translation, again with one or more years of Hebrew language training; and
- graduate students, teachers, trainers, consultants, and writers who are deeply engaged in the preceding studies as well as in the field of Bible translation.

In several chapters, especially those based on earlier studies, I have used a transliteration of the Hebrew text; this follows the simplified format that is used in handbooks and monographs published by the United Bible Societies (e.g., Zogbo and Wendland 2000:xiv).

The author would be grateful for any and all comments regarding this publication; he may be reached via email either at erwendland@gmail.com or wendlande@outlook.com.

Ernst Wendland
Centre for Bible Interpretation & Translation—University of Stellenbosch, RSA
Pentecost—2009

Preface to the Second Edition

This edition of *Prophetic Rhetoric* has been completely re-edited and revised in a number of places. I greatly appreciate the editorial assistance of Joyce and Jim Park when preparing this second edition. There's more that goes into this essential task than most people realize!

I have added three new chapters, one presenting a comparative discourse analysis of the book of Amos, another offering a study of some of the problems that one encounters when "contextualizing" Isaiah 52:13–53:12 in the Tonga language and culture of Zambia, and finally, using Haggai as a basis, some exercises in cross-cultural communication.

Once again, I have also appreciated the technical editorial support of the production department of SIL Global Publishing Services to bring this project to its second completion.

> Surely the Sovereign LORD does nothing,
> Without revealing his plan to his servants the prophets.
> The Lion has roared—who will not fear?
> The Sovereign LORD has spoken—who can but prophesy?
> (Amos 3:7–8, NIV)

Ernst R. Wendland
Easter—2010

Acknowledgements

I am most grateful to Dr. Lynell Zogbo, a senior Translation Consultant of the United Bible Societies (Reading, England) for taking the time from her busy schedule to review and write a *Foreword* for the present monograph as well as to suggest some corrections and improvements. I have known and worked with Dr. Zogbo for many years, and it is due to her expertise in a literary-poetic approach to the Hebrew Scriptures (cf. Zogbo and Wendland 2000) that I requested her to review my work and to write its Foreword. In addition, I wish to thank all my colleagues in the United Bible Societies, Wycliffe Bible Translators, and other translation organizations for listening to and critically commenting on various sections and segments of this work as it has developed over the years in various conferences, workshops, and journal publications.

I must once again express my deep appreciation to the many biblical scholars whom I either cite or refer to in this study as well as those with whom I have had the privilege to interact over the years (notably, Prof. Christo van der Merwe of the Centre for Bible Interpretation and Translation in Africa—University of Stellenbosch). I certainly learned a great deal from them as I wrestled with the various issues presented by my twofold topic of text analysis and translation. They have helped me to better understand the literary character of the prophetic writings of the Hebrew Bible as they were composed and enscripted for their original audiences in such a rhetorically powerful and moving manner. I also sincerely thank all of my national translation colleagues whose help has proved indispensable as we confronted together the challenge of how best to communicate these dynamic texts in a corresponding way in vernacular translation via various media today.

Finally, though in most cases I use my own translations of the original Hebrew text, I do on occasion cite one or another English version, in particular, the *New International Version* (NIV) © 1984 by the New York Bible Society. I use all of these translations within the normal guidelines by prior permission, for which I am grateful. I also express my gratitude for permission to reproduce the cover illustration by Gustave Doré, courtesy of www.creationism.org (Paul Abramson, Editor; paul@zzz.com).

Foreword

For those who have followed Ernst Wendland's career and writings, this book may not be much of a surprise. It continues in the line of detailed and fine scholarship which has characterized his long list of publications. Wendland's strong points have always been analytical accuracy and practical application.

Prophetic Rhetoric seems somehow to be the culmination of well over 30 years of life's work, much of which has concentrated on the Old Testament, beginning with his study on Malachi (1985), and moving through the Scriptures: *Discourse Perspectives on Hebrew Poetry in the Scriptures* (1994), *Analyzing the Psalms* (2002), *Translating the Literature of Scripture* (2004), including the book I was privileged to co-author with him in 2000, *Hebrew Poetry in the Bible: A Guide for Readers and Translators*, to name only a few!

In this current work, where Wendland has combined studies on nine prophetic books, eight from the Minor Prophets (Joel, Obadiah, Nahum, Haggai, Jonah, Habakkuk, Zephaniah and Malachi) and one Major Prophet, Ezekiel, each chapter could constitute a book in itself! *Prophetic Rhetoric* is not for the faint-hearted! Each chapter should be studied on its own, with the Hebrew text, an interlinear or a literal version close at hand.

Each chapter presents a discourse analysis of an individual book, showing how its structure highlights its major themes. Wendland carefully analyses and describes the rhetorical devices found in each prophetic writing: opening and closing formulas, patterns of recursion, special particles, etc., but has also "done his homework," interacting with a whole host of commentators. However, what is most interesting is that he has not used the same analytical approach in every chapter; in some, he highlights metaphor (Joel), in others, speech acts and genre (Zephaniah, Malachi), in others, more traditional discourse analysis à la Longacre (Jonah), or more pragmatic, relevance-related and *skopos*-based approaches (Jonah, Haggai). In each and every chapter, Wendland follows his analysis with a practical discussion, each chapter from a different angle, giving suggestions on how to communicate the impact and meaning of the prophetic word to modern day audiences.

In each chapter, the reader discovers something new about each book. In chapter 1 on Joel, Wendland uses "spatialized diagrams" to show that "intensification" is not just a characteristic of Hebrew poetic lines (à la Kugel), but a feature of stanza patterning (20). He suggests that Joel's message is perhaps purposely "dehistorized," so that it can be used again and again in liturgical settings (21). Using the concept of "conceptual blending," Wendland shows how Joel creates metaphor and "mental spaces," bringing to life the mixed images of locust and army, harvest and judgment.

Chapter 3 analyzes an often overlooked book, Obadiah. Wendland, not always in agreement with other Biblicists, convincingly argues that this short vision, with its typical identification-indictment-condemnation-prediction sequence, is "a model prophetic text" (39). Here careful attention is paid to conjunctions (and the lack of them), and to *hinneh*, the Hebrew marker so often overlooked in commentaries, translation handbooks and numerous Bible versions.

In chapter 4, Wendland examines the book of Nahum, trying to decide if its major message is judgment or blessing. By examining structure, Wendland discovers that at the center of this seemingly negative book, there is some "good news" for the people of God. Unlike some who minimize this book's importance and beauty, he concludes it has been written by a "master literary rhetorician," who "demonstrates his verbal craft in virtually every verse." Wendland's attention to sound effects is one of the high points of this study, along with the final discussion of how rhetorical issues can be successfully transferred into other languages.

Chapter 5 provides a study of the book of Haggai, which like Nahum and Obadiah, is little known and often not appreciated. While some belittle Haggai's "lack of literary finesse" and "stylistic clumsiness, Wendland emphasizes its literary strong points: its "textual architecture" and the role of direct speech, allusion, rhetorical questions, and irony. He carefully outlines the book's cyclical thesis-antithesis patterning, describes its rich inter-textual ties, and draws special attention to the skillful way peaks or climaxes are marked. He concludes that Haggai has a "surprising degree of literary excellence."

Profiting from his long experience in Africa among the Chichewa-speaking people, Wendland then discusses the challenges of communicating Haggai's message today, with its important points of contact as well as its "cognitive clashes." While building a "house" for a divinity is a "known," communicating certain notions of ritual impurity may prove more difficult. He suggests that the gap be bridged with glossaries, section headings, footnotes, and illustrations.

Chapter 6, treating the book of Jonah, is based on an earlier study, but is full of new and important insights. As usual, Wendland searches for and finds *recursion* and *variation* within the text. Repetition or sameness (for example, the number "three" and the sets of words repeated three times) contrasts with difference (the various meanings of the verb "call" and multiple variations in syntax and word order). He also devotes many pages to irony and enigma, surrounding characters and events. Irony is a powerful tool in Jonah, lending humor, drawing the audience into the story, and emphasizing major themes. For example, Jonah considers God ruthless for killing his plant, while all along, it is Jonah who has been "the ruthless one…and God the merciful." Breaking new ground, Wendland explores how anticipation, suspense, surprise and curiosity help convey the overall prophetic message in this book.

In chapter 7, Wendland analyzes Ezekiel, the only major prophet he considers here. After an overview of the general structure of the book, he zeroes in on chapters 33–37, which include the amazing vision of the dry bones coming to life. For Wendland, this is the "gospel" section of Ezekiel. As elsewhere, he prefers to look for answers on how the MT fits together, rather than accept arguments to emend or move verses from place to place. For Wendland, discourse structure and form are inherent parts of meaning. For example, certain themes in the book are reinforced by "parallel paneling," i.e., blocks of text which pattern each other, as when Ezekiel is commissioned (chapters 2, 3), and then re-commissioned (chapter 33). At the end of the chapter, he provides an up-to-date discussion of Bible translation in Africa, arguing that literary or "oratorical" versions are well suited to African audiences who appreciate oral-aural communication. His example of three translations of Ezekiel 37:1–10 in Chichewa (one literal, one dynamic and one oratorical) prove his point beyond all doubt. Wendland understands the challenges of trying to produce such versions, proposing a new parameter to the traditional criteria for effective translation (fidelity, naturalness and clearness): "proximity," a notion related to "appropriateness" or "equivalence," which may become key in discussions beyond this chapter and this book.

The remaining chapters are equally enlightening, as Wendland examines Habakkuk (chapter 8), Zephaniah (chapter 9), and Malachi (chapter 10). While each study is different, each one reinforces similar themes. Contra many scholars, Wendland argues that Habakkuk (in its MT canonical form) is a literary unit. He demonstrates its progression and cohesion, showing, for example, how Habakkuk's initial reactions in chapter 1 contrast sharply with his final state of mind in chapter 4. Following his linguistic and pragmatic analyses, he suggests the possibility of dramatic or audio-visual presentations.

In his study of Zephaniah, Wendland again demonstrates that a literary rhetorical analysis reveals structure which can have an important impact on this book's exegesis, the translation and typographical formatting! Again in his discussion of Malachi, Wendland uncovers intricate chiastic patterning, overlapping with a forward progression of six disputation units. Again, his discourse analysis often reveals high points or important prophetic themes carefully encoded in the middle of chiasms.

In chapters 11 and 12, Wendland offers practical examples and exercises in cross-cultural communication, using Haggai and the Tonga translation of Isaiah 52 and 53 as his models. His closing chapter deals with proclaiming the prophetic message today.

This book can be used in two ways. Readers can take each chapter separately, for the individual study of a prophetic book. Perhaps more interestingly however, the book can be taken as a whole, highlighting several important truths:

- Form cannot be separated from meaning. By studying structure and literary devices, the real message of a text can emerge.
- Faced with difficult problems of interpretation, exegetes should try to understand structure before attempting to emend a text.
- Prophetic truths have relevance for today and need to be communicated effectively in our modern world.
- There is something truly inspired and inspiring about these prophetic books. Those who think they "have no beauty" or are only a "hodgepodge" need to open their eyes. If we look hard enough, we can discover for ourselves their "beauty, power, impact, and appeal."

In this latest work of Ernst Wendland, we see the scholar of the past, with burning preoccupations of the present. He not only gives literary analyses, but never fails to provide practical discussions on how to make the prophetic message relevant and understandable for today. As he interacts with one of his true passions, poetic lines of the Prophets, Wendland is a pleasure to read. His language fluctuates from down-to-earth: "Who ever reads—or preaches from—the book of Obadiah anyway?" to poetic and playful ("the feet of messengers" of old contrasting with "the fleet" of electronic media. The many examples of excellent LiFE ("literary functional equivalence") translations of Hebrew prophetic literature are a real "treat."

Wendland notes that "people need to be educated to the nature of the Bible itself—its textual character, literary qualities, historical composition...." In this age when scholars rush to criticize and readers, to over-spiritualize, Prophetic Rhetoric is a positive and significant contribution to understanding the complexity and richness of the biblical text.

Lynell Zogbo
Abidjan, Ivory Coast

1

Dramatic Rhetoric, Metaphoric Imagery, and Discourse Structure in Joel

1.1 Introduction

This text-linguistic study focuses on a pair of particularly vivid militaristic pericopes in the prophecy of Joel, namely, 2:1–11 and 3:9–16. Both of these passages are prominent for their dynamic poetry, graphic imagery, and corresponding pragmatic function within the book, namely, as a dramatic prelude to a momentous, and at the same time thematically contrastive pronouncement by the LORD God. However, the historical setting as well as the theological meaning of these two texts, among others in Joel, is strongly debated by many commentators. After a brief theoretical introduction and summary of the discourse organization of Joel, a detailed literary-structural analysis of these pericopes is presented. Their interrelated rhetorical function within the prophecy of Joel as a whole is then investigated in somewhat greater depth from the perspective of mental space metaphoric theory. In conclusion, several salient implications of this holistic analysis for intercultural communication are discussed, with special reference to south-central Africa.

1.2 Overview: Hebrew poetic text analysis

It behooves any biblical exegete, commentator, or textual critic to clarify at the outset the particular analytical approach that s/he has adopted for the task.[1] My investigation of the literary (artistic-rhetorical) character of biblical poetry begins with the notion of *parallelism* and Roman Jakobson's familiar, albeit rather enigmatic, description of the essential parallel structure of all poetry: "The poetic function projects the principle of equivalence from the [paradigmatic] axis of selection into the [syntagmatic] axis of combination. Equivalence is promoted to the constitutive device of the sequence" (1960:358; cf. Adele Berlin's emphasis on "contiguity" as well as "equivalence" (1985:2). Hence, "[p]ervasive parallelism inevitably activates all the levels of [poetic] language" (1966:423). In short, where there is poetry, linguistic *correspondence is concentrated: similarity is superimposed upon sequence* (cf. Wendland 2007).

In other words, multiple formal and semantic resemblances are packed within standard poetic units (bicola, strophes). Thus, manifold *recurrence*—prosodic, morphological, lexical, syntactic, and as we will note especially in this study, *imagistic* reiteration—of various types, is artfully selected and harmoniously combined or condensed into line-forms, patterned sets of lines, and even larger parallel structures. The more distinct correspondences there are between the A and B segments, the more poetic the pairing normally sounds, and the more marked it is in terms of semantic and/or pragmatic significance. This is the creative motivation and compositional manner for all well-formed poetic texts, most notably in biblical Hebrew, and this feature must therefore figure prominently in any method that one uses to analyze and interpret them.

This poetic principle of *paradigmatic selection* superimposed upon *syntagmatic progression* in literary discourse may be readily illustrated from the

---

[1] In view of the systematic text studies of Joel 2:1–11 and 3:9–17 to follow, I offer a brief overview of my methodology here, rather than to simply give a cross reference to a more detailed source (e.g., Wendland 2004, 2006). Note that I am using throughout this study the verse reference system of English Bibles (Vulgate) rather than that of the Hebrew Masoretic Text (MT), merely for the sake of convenience.

1.2 Overview: Hebrew poetic text analysis

current text. Consider Joel 1:10, for example, as it has been spatialized in the following diagram:

field	it-is-destroyed	שָׂדֶה	שֻׁדַּד
ground	it-mourns	אֲדָמָה	אָבְלָה
grain	it-is-destroyed *indeed*	דָגָן	כִּי שֻׁדַּד
new-wine	it-is-dried	תִּירוֹשׁ	הוֹבִישׁ
oil	it-fails	יִצְהָר	אֻמְלַל

This passage reveals the recursion of linguistic elements as the text unfolds in time (as it is being heard) or in space (visually). The same two-word syntactic frame (V-S) is repeated, and this is filled with several interrelated sets of lexical fillers, i.e., for the subjects: field + ground, grain + new wine + oil; and for the verbs: it-is-destroyed, mourns (personification), destroyed (reiteration), dried, fails. There are also instances of phonological reduplication, namely, through alliterated pairs of predications, e.g., שֻׁדַּד שָׂדֶה, אָבְלָה אֲדָמָה and הוֹבִישׁ תִּירוֹשׁ. The overall pattern of parallelism that is produced serves to audibly underscore the speaker's point: the (once luxuriant) land has been totally depleted due to the devastating locust plague.

Thus, the feature of parallelism, as suggested by Jakobson's definition of the poetic principle above and illustrated in Joel 1:10, involves an even more basic literary device, namely, "recursion," which I consider to be the fundamental process within all elevated discourse, whether the emphasis is on form (artistry) or function (rhetoric). Such recursion may be manifested with respect to form, content, and/or function—and may involve the *exact* reiteration of elements (i.e., "repetition") or some manner of *correspondent* recycling (i.e., features that are synonymous, contrastive, logically associated, etc.).

The function of such a recursive use of poetic forms and meanings may be *pragmatic* (e.g., for topic, focus, emphasis) or *poetic* (esthetic, architectonic) in nature. In either case, there is some sort of *prominence* that is created by the recurrent elements (e.g., the command + vocative + reason syntactic pattern that is repeated at the onset of each new strophe in the first stanza [A] of Joel, 1:2–14). However, recursion can also serve as a *background* against which other, foregrounded features may be inserted (e.g., in the final, climactic strophe of stanza A [1:13–14], which now includes reference to the priests and the "house of YHWH")—or which can signal prominence when the recursive pattern is suddenly broken (e.g., the recursive pattern of strophe-initial imperatives comes to an end at 1:15 with the exclamation, "Alas for the day!").

There are, in turn, four essential architectonic, or structural, functions: *bounding*, which pertains to the segmentation of a literary work into distinct units of structure; *bonding*, which pertains to the formal (cohesion) and semantic (coherence) unity of a given text segment; *pointing*, which pertains to areas of prominence that are created by a convergence of literary features within a given text; and *patterning*, which pertains to the various parallel structures (unfolding, alternating, chiastic, introverted, etc.) that are created through recursion within a portion of text. These four structural functions are abundantly manifested in the literary-structural overview of Joel, to be presented below (cf. Wendland 1995:223–301).

However, the structural operation of textual bounding on the basis of recursion needs further explanation. This function has various manifestations in biblical discourse (in the Former as well as the Latter Testament). Its main forms are summarized by way of formula and definition below with examples given from Joel (where A, B, C, etc. = a significant instance of recursion and [...] = a distinct discourse unit; cf. Wendland 2004:123–137):

- **Inclusio:** [A...A'] – the A elements demarcate the *beginning* and *ending* of the *same* discourse unit, whether large or small, e.g., Joel 2:1, 11 (i.e., enclosing Stanza C of Oracle 2):
  For the day of the LORD is coming; indeed, it is near!...Indeed, the day of the LORD is great and very terrible...
- **Chiasmus:** [A + B +/- C...+/- C' + B' + A'] – this is a case of *inverted parallelism* within the same discourse unit, e.g., Joel 2:30–31 (i.e., delineating strophe 2 of Stanza B'):
  A "And I will give portents in *the heavens*
  B and on the <u>earth</u>,
  B' <u>blood</u> and <u>fire</u> and columns of <u>smoke</u>. (The chiastic pattern reveals the earthly location of these signs.)
  A' The *sun* shall be turned to darkness, and the *moon* to blood,
  (**Note:** B'—*blood* + <u>smoke</u>; A' <u>darkness</u> + *blood*.)
  before the great and terrible day of the LORD comes."
- **Anaphora:** [A]...[A'] – the key recursive elements demarcate the respective *beginnings* of *different* discourse units, whether adjacent or separated within the text, e.g., Joel 2:1, 15 (begin Stanza C-1; D-2):
  Blow the trumpet on Zion; sound the alarm on my holy hill. Tremble, people of Judah!...
  Blow the trumpet on Zion; sanctify a fast; call a solemn assembly!

- **Epiphora:** [...A]...[...A'] – the key recursive elements demarcate the respective *endings* of *different* discourse units, whether adjacent or separated within the text, e.g., Joel 2:17, 3:20–21 (end Part I and II):
     "Spare thy people, O LORD, and make not thy heritage a reproach, a byword among the nations.
        Why should they say among the peoples, 'Where is their God?'..."
     But Judah shall be inhabited for ever, and Jerusalem to all generations....
        Indeed, the LORD dwells in Zion!"
- **Anadiplosis:** [...A] [A'...] – the recursive elements demarcate the distinct *beginning* and *ending* of *adjacent* discourse units within the text, e.g., Joel 2:17, 18–19 (strophes 2 and 3 of Stanza D):
     "Spare thy people, O LORD, and make not thy heritage a reproach, a byword among the nations.
        <u>Why should they say among the peoples, 'Where is their God?'"</u>
     Then the LORD became jealous for his land, and had pity on his people.
     The LORD answered and said to his people, "...and I will no more make you a reproach among the nations."

(The example of 2:17 reveals that the same text can carry out several demarcative functions.)

1.3 The structure of Joel as a whole

A discourse analysis of the complete Hebrew text of Joel, of which the two pericopes examined in more detail below are a part, reveals a balanced overall structure that may be summarized as follows:[2]

---

[2] Space prevents an in depth examination of this provocative little book. My interpretation of the discourse structure, meaning, and purpose of Joel's prophecy is offered with some trepidation, in the realization that for many biblical scholars "Joel is the problem-child of Old Testament exegesis" and that "it has proved difficult for commentators to arrive at any consensus on this short and vivid book" (Barton 2001:3). Thus, as Barton summarizes the situation: "It has been dated anywhere between the ninth and second centuries B.C.E. It has been regarded as a tightly composed unity but also as an almost random collection of disparate oracles" (ibid., *loc. cit.*). In view of "the bewildering variety of scholarly interpretations of the book" (Mason 1994:98), I will certainly not be able to resolve even a fraction of the many hermeneutical issues that it raises; however, I do hope to lend support to the position that Joel is indeed "a tightly composed unity" and, further, a work that, contrary to its placement within the prophetic corpus, was composed shortly before or after the Babylonian invasions of Judah (not even an approximate date can be credibly demonstrated; cf. Craigie 1984:86). In any case, my concern is rather with form and function, namely, to call attention to the dramatic poetic character of the text and efforts to communicate it in a corresponding manner today in a contemporary setting of reception.

JOEL – Theme: RETRIBUTION, REVERSAL, AND RESTORATION IN THE DAY OF THE LORD							
Part I (1:1–2:17) – YHWH exhorts his covenant people to "return" to him in repentance				Part II (2:18–3:17) – YHWH responds by "returning" to his people to deliver them from their enemies			
Oracle 1 (1:2–20)		Oracle 2 (2:1–17)		Oracle 3 (2:18–32)		Oracle 4 (3:1–17)	
Stanza A (1:2–12) ➔ Prophetic call to lament over natural disasters	Stanza B (1:13–20) Communal lamentation to YHWH for mercy	Stanza C (2:1–11) ➔ An army of locusts prefigures the Day of YHWH	Stanza D (2:12–17) YHWH summons his people to communal repentance	Stanza A' (2:18–27) ➔ YHWH promises to restore his people physically	Stanza B' (2:28–32) YHWH promises to restore his people spiritually	Stanza C' (3:1–8) ➔ YHWH announces a time for universal judgment	Stanza D' (3:9–17) YHWH effects his judgment on all pagan nations
Conclusion – Oracle 5 (3:18–21): YHWH blesses Zion by restoring his people in the *eschaton* ("in that day")							

After the opening prophetic messenger formula (Joel 1:1), the basic bifid plan of literary construction appears to work its way throughout the text, right up to the prophecy's "Conclusion" in 3:18–21.[3] Thus, the two "Parts" feature four oracles, and eight stanzas—as displayed on the diagram above: In the case of the second (and somewhat shorter) stanza of each "oracle," there appears to be a significant "addition" or semantic augmentation in terms of the LORD's message to his people through the prophet Joel. This would be a macro-structural application of the typical poetic intensification that occurs in the second line of an A-B parallel couplet (i.e., "A," and what's more, "B"). In Stanza B, for example, the people of Judah react in lamentation to the devastating situation that they find themselves in, as graphically depicted by Joel in Stanza A. Similarly in Stanza D, YHWH himself calls for a penitent religious response to the military invasion that their covenant violation (left unspecified) has brought upon the land, as portrayed in Stanza C. Furthermore, the pair of Stanzas C-D is a clear intensification of the central message and call for repentance that is contained in A-B.

---

[3] Most commentators agree on the broad outlines of the overall discourse structure of Joel, at least in terms of the larger units (e.g., Finley 1990:11; Garrett 1997:310; Stuart 1987:226–227; Sweeney 2000a:147–185). W. S. Prinsloo proposes an interesting variant which, while largely corresponding to my segmentation of Joel, manifests an overlapping organization in which one section (stanza) builds upon another to comprise the entire text (cited in Hubbard 1989:33). However, there is much more disagreement, as might be expected, at the strophic level of textual organization. The second "half" of the book also presents more diversity of opinion. Barton, for example, considers 2:28–3:21 to be "a collection of miscellaneous oracles concerning the judgment of the nations and the future salvation of Israel" that was composed later than the prophet Joel (2001:92). My analysis and the discussion that follows do not support this conclusion about the coherence of this book or its diverse authorship (cf. Finley 1990:9–13; Garrett 1997:284–286; Stuart 1987:226–227).

1.3 The structure of Joel as a whole

Part Two of the book (2:18–3:21) consists, for the most part, of the LORD's personal reply (Stanzas A'-B'-C'-D' + Conclusion) to what has been stated in Part One (Stanzas A-B-C-D). As far as his own covenant nation is concerned, YHWH promises them both physical (A') and spiritual (B') blessings—a patent *reversal* and *restoration* of their losses as poetically delineated in Stanzas A and B—the latter (B', spiritual renewal) being a heightening of the former (A', material restitution). There will also be a righteous vindication of God's people in relation to all their ungodly oppressors (prefigured by the locust plague of Part One). These pagan forces will be summarily gathered together at the LORD's place of judgment ("the Valley of Jehoshaphat," 3:2, 12—Stanza C') and then appropriately punished at this "Valley of Decision" (3:14) on the great "Day of YHWH" (Stanza D'), while the people of Zion will live in blessed fellowship with their Lord-Deliverer forever (Oracle 5).

The prophecy's thematic peak is probably reached in 3:16–17, just prior to the eschatological Conclusion, where we find a concentration of key covenantal terms and prophetic motifs: "the LORD [your God]" (3x), "Jerusalem [holy]" (2x), "Zion [my holy hill]" (2x), "refuge for his people [the people of Israel]," "you will know…" However, this encouraging message is dramatically anticipated by several other seminal passages of semantic reversal along the text's prophetic way (2:18, 27, 32; 3:1). Thus, there is a perceptible heightening with respect to form, content, and pragmatic function as the book proceeds from one oracle and stanza, and from one reversal involving retribution and restoration to another, to reach its climactic utterance—the unequivocal proclamation on which God's covenant community ("church") forever rests, a sure foundation for the faith of all the faithful: שֹׁכֵן בְּצִיּוֹן וַיהוָה! (3:21c)

It is rather difficult to classify the book of Joel in terms of *genre*, but assuming its essential structural unity and in view of its general lack of situational specificity, I would agree with Dillard's conclusion that it is "either a liturgical text intended for repeated occasions of national lament or at least a historical example of one such lament" (1992:243; cf. Sweeney 2000a:151).[4] The latter option would of course render the text

---

[4] Joel manifests some of the important features of a typical psalm of *communal lament* (cf. Wendland 2002:34–36), though ordered and arranged differently, exhibiting different emphases, and including a great deal of divine direct speech. Among the prominent components of a lament psalm are: **appeal** to YHWH (e.g., 1:19–20), *specification of the* **problem** (1:2–12), **plea** *for forgiveness* (2:12–17), **profession** *of faith in YHWH* (3:16), **promise** *of deliverance/blessing* (2:18–27, 3:18–21). A final expression of the people's **praise** and **thanksgiving** *to YHWH* is not

useable again on similar occasions of national calamity and/or religious crisis in future. This generic feature would also account for the prophecy's "dehistoricized" nature with regard to certain crucial content, e.g., concerning which sin(s) that the people needed to repent of (1:13-14; 2:12-13); but on the other hand, it also imbues the text of Joel with "the kind of timelessness that makes it such powerful literature in our own day" (ibid., 244).

1.4 A literary-structural summary of two parallel pericopes

The following overview presents a summary of the hortatory discourse structure of two prominent passages in Joel, 2:1-11 (Text I) and 3:9-17 (Text II), which are described in terms of their major and minor textual divisions, topical organization, and principal intertextual correspondents. Both pericopes, one from each half of the book, portray the striking imagery of ANE warfare as they enunciate the LORD's righteous judgment being meted out upon his enemies. They thus enable listeners to visualize the chaotic scenes that are being depicted before their very eyes, as it were, as well as in their hearing—for the original Hebrew literally cries out for oral-aural expression (e.g., 2:1, 3:9). Noteworthy features of *artistry* (linguistic form) and *rhetoric* (communicative function) are pointed out along the way, with special attention being given to issues of topic and focus (in boxes) as the text unfolds sequentially. Both passages, which are ostensibly uttered by the prophet (with divine interjections at 3:12 and 3:17), are dramatically developed in the most forceful of terms as God's chosen messenger (1:1) continues his passionate proclamation of the punitive *justice* of Yahweh, which in each case precedes divine declarations that articulate his prevailing *mercy* towards his covenant community, i.e., 2:12-17 and 3:18-21.

---

included due to the difference in genre (but cf. 2:21-23); however, a complete psalm (e.g., Pss 66-67) could be used for that purpose if Joel (or a portion of it) were used in some type of liturgical worship.

1.4 A literary-structural summary of two parallel pericopes

TEXT I

RSV (periodically revised in favor of the MT)	MT
²:¹ Blow the ram's horn on Zion; sound the alarm on my holy hill. Tremble, all you inhabitants of the land! For the day of the LORD is coming; surely, it is near! ² (It will be) a dark and gloomy day, a black and cloudy day. Like darkness spreading over the mountains, The army, great and mighty, (advances). There has never been anything <u>like it</u>, and there never will be <u>again</u>.	¹ תִּקְעוּ שׁוֹפָר בְּצִיּוֹן וְהָרִיעוּ בְּהַר קָדְשִׁי יִרְגְּזוּ כֹּל יֹשְׁבֵי הָאָרֶץ כִּי־בָא יוֹם־יְהוָה כִּי קָרוֹב: ² יוֹם חֹשֶׁךְ וַאֲפֵלָה יוֹם עָנָן וַעֲרָפֶל כְּשַׁחַר פָּרֻשׂ עַל־הֶהָרִים עַם רַב וְעָצוּם כָּמֹהוּ לֹא נִהְיָה מִן־הָעוֹלָם וְאַחֲרָיו לֹא יוֹסֵף עַד־שְׁנֵי דּוֹר וָדוֹר:

> Oracle 2 (2:1–17)
> **Stanza C (2:1–11): An invading army announces the day of the LORD**[5]
> C, Strophe 1 (2:1–2)
> Three imperatives of alarm and the first direct mention of the "holy" city of צִיּוֹן announce the onset of this new discourse unit (v. 1). Repetition of "the day of YHWH is near" (emphasized by word order and the double כִּי) corresponds with 1:15 (beginning of the preceding stanza (B), i.e., structural *anaphora*), while "all inhabitants of the land" (כֹּל יֹשְׁבֵי הָאָרֶץ) reiterates 1:2 (beginning of Oracle I, *anaphora*; cf. 1:14, *exclusio*). A figurative unfolding of the ominous events of this dire "day" (with reiterated reference) lends cohesion to the strophe, which gradually builds to a climax in v. 2c in a pair of lengthy parallel cola (with fronted adverbial qualitative constituents). All this stresses the ominous uniqueness of the LORD's certain arrival for judgment. There was—and will be—nothing like it "throughout all generations" (דּוֹר וָדוֹר)!
>
> Stanza C features some striking images of warfare: Both the attacking army (lit. 'people') and the day of the LORD are metaphorically associated with "darkness." Short, staccato-like cola abound to verbally underscore the excitement and apprehension that is evoked by a frightful description of this relentless multitude —which plays on the imagery of the locust plague described in Oracle I to refer to a certain mysterious invading force that is under the control of the LORD (perhaps one similar to "the northern kingdoms" prophesied in Jer 1:14–15, 4:6, 6:1–2; cf. הַצְּפוֹנִי in Joel 2:20). The initial *call of alarm* (v. 2a), ostensibly uttered by YHWH himself (קָדְשִׁי - "of *my* holiness"), normally announces a *summons to battle* (Hos 8:1), but here we have an ironic reversal: this is an appeal to get ready to be battled against! The capital of YHWH's people is being attacked—not the principal city of some pagan enemy (cf. Babylon in Isa 13:1–13).
>
> This stanza also manifests a topical *chiastic* structure in addition to figurative and lexical heightening: Strophes 2 and 3 feature realistic, albeit hyperbolic, language based on military images and associations as the mighty insect army is described in graphic similes and metaphors. Both of these internal strophes present a sequence of third person plural verbs depicting warlike action. Strophes 1 and 4, on the other hand, feature the cosmic language of *theophany* (YHWH's self-disclosure in awesome natural images of the mighty forces of creation—cf. Amos 5:18–20; Hab 3:3–12; Nah 1:2–6; Zeph 1:14–16; Ps 97:2–5). The description of the attacking legions of locusts/soldiers reaches its peak as the very windows of the besieged city of Zion are breached (v. 9b). Even the great celestial lights give up hope (v. 10) as the commander of the multitudinous invaders is dramatically revealed (v. 11a). What a shock to the audience: It is none other than YHWH himself! His great "day" is one of judgment upon his unfaithful people (cf. Stanza D, 2:12–17).

---

[5] The proposed strophic structure of this stanza (2:1–11) is supported by Allen (1976:64–66). Garrett essentially agrees, but for some unexplained reason sets 2:2b off as a distinct unit of discourse (1997:334–335). Barton, too, diverges at one place within the stanza, i.e., formatting verse 3 as a separate strophe, but without explanation (2001:66–67). Several major exegetical commentaries do not demarcate this larger unit of discourse into any sub-sections at all (e.g., Finley 1990:39–40, Stuart 1987:246–247, and Sweeney 2000a:161–164), which disadvantages readers who wish to pay closer attention to these minor breaks in content and the slight shifts in the author's hortatory development that occur at such points. Dillard distinguishes 2:1–2 as a poetic segment, but then strangely does not indicate any strophic breaks in vv. 3–11 (1992:270–273). Among major English translations, only the NIV matches the stanza segmentation given above; the other versions all differ slightly, especially with regard to the arrangement of the first four verses. Least helpful (or discerning) is the REB which, like the KJV, makes no paragraph breaks at all in the entire section.

1.4 A literary-structural summary of two parallel pericopes

³ Fire devours *before them*, *and behind them* a flame burns.	³לְפָנָיו אָכְלָה אֵשׁ וְאַחֲרָיו תְּלַהֵט לֶהָבָה
The land is like the garden of Eden *before them*, but after them a desolate wilderness, *and* no survivor *escapes* them.	כְּגַן־עֵדֶן הָאָרֶץ לְפָנָיו וְאַחֲרָיו מִדְבַּר שְׁמָמָה וְגַם־פְּלֵיטָה לֹא־הָיְתָה לּוֹ׃
⁴ Their appearance is like the appearance of horses, and like war horses they run.	⁴כְּמַרְאֵה סוּסִים מַרְאֵהוּ וּכְפָרָשִׁים כֵּן יְרוּצוּן׃
⁵ As with the rumbling of chariots, they leap on the tops of the mountains,	⁵כְּקוֹל מַרְכָּבוֹת עַל־רָאשֵׁי הֶהָרִים יְרַקֵּדוּן

like the crackling of a flame of fire
  devouring the stubble,
like a powerful army
  drawn up for battle.
	כְּקוֹל לַהַב אֵשׁ אֹכְלָה קָשׁ
	כְּעַם עָצוּם עָרוּךְ מִלְחָמָה

C, Strophe 2 (2:3–5)
Keying off of the preceding all-encompassing *temporal* expressions (v. 2c), the *locative* phrases "Before them" (לְפָנָיו) along with a prophetic perfect (אָכְלָה) and "after them" (וְאַחֲרָיו - v. 3a; cf. 3b and v. 2c, *anadiplosis*) as well as "even [גַם] (no) escapee" (3b) are fronted to underscore the complete totality of the destruction being inflicted upon the country by this apocalyptic military force, again accompanied by fiery imagery (cf. 1:19–20; this passage reverses the sense of texts like Ps 97:3–5, Isa 51:3, and Ezek 36:35). "Eden" is thus transformed into "devastation" (שְׁמָמָה). The key descriptive terms "flame of fire devours" (לַהַב אֵשׁ אֹכְלָה) of v. 5b occur in inverted order from v. 1a to mark a strophic *inclusio*, while "a mighty people/army" (עַם עָצוּם) forges a link back to the close of strophe 1 (v. 2b - structural *epiphora*). The long fronted figurative description in v. 5a spotlights the locusts (plus some foreshadowed human force?), which are compared with war "horses" (סוּסִים - v. 4b), another common theophanic theme (cf. Hab 3:8; Ps 68:17). The hyperbolic language of this strophe, coupled with a stressed series of descriptive comparative expressions with כְּ, suggests that these invaders are no ordinary army, for they leap upon the mountaintops in their war chariots as they relentlessly lay waste to everything in their path.

⁶ <u>Before them</u> peoples are in anguish, <u>all faces</u> grow pale.	⁶ מִפָּנָיו יָחִילוּ עַמִּים כָּל־פָּנִים קִבְּצוּ פָארוּר׃
⁷ <u>Like warriors</u> they charge, <u>like soldiers</u> they scale the wall.	⁷ כְּגִבּוֹרִים יְרֻצוּן כְּאַנְשֵׁי מִלְחָמָה יַעֲלוּ חוֹמָה
They march <u>each on his way</u>, they do not swerve <u>from their paths</u>.	וְאִישׁ בִּדְרָכָיו יֵלֵכוּן וְלֹא יְעַבְּטוּן אֹרְחוֹתָם׃
⁸ They do not jostle one another,	⁸ וְאִישׁ אָחִיו לֹא יִדְחָקוּן
<u>each</u> marches <u>in his path</u>; they burst <u>through the defense</u> and are not halted.	גֶּבֶר בִּמְסִלָּתוֹ יֵלֵכוּן וּבְעַד הַשֶּׁלַח יִפֹּלוּ לֹא יִבְצָעוּ׃
⁹ They leap <u>upon the city</u>,	⁹ בָּעִיר יָשֹׁקּוּ
they run <u>upon the walls</u>;	בַּחוֹמָה יְרֻצוּן
they climb <u>up into the houses</u>,	בַּבָּתִּים יַעֲלוּ
they enter <u>through the windows</u> like a thief.	בְּעַד הַחַלּוֹנִים יָבֹאוּ כַּגַּנָּב׃

C, Strophe 3 (2:6–9)
This poetic unit begins with a brief front-shifted change of *focus*, from the army to those being invaded, whose "faces" (פָּנִים) overtly display their utter terror (v. 6; cf. 3a – *anaphora*; Isa 13:8). The figurative perspective immediately reverts back to that of the advancing locust troops (v. 7; cf. Isa 33:3–4), and the syntactic spotlight remains on them through constituent advancement throughout the strophe, with an emphasis on location in relation to the sacred city. The only cola not affected by this syntactic feature are the two negativized ones at the end of verses 7 and 8, each of which further stresses the *unstoppable* nature of this awesome army. Strophe 3 closes with a peak of proximity: "through the windows they enter just like the thief!" (9b, i.e., boldly, invasively!; note יְרֻצוּן + יַעֲלוּ è v. 7a, sub-*inclusio*). This unit's short poetic lines depict in rhythmic sound the persistent forward progress of the enemy as they move towards their goal—which, it must not be forgotten, is none other than "the holy hill of Zion" (v. 1a).

1.4 A literary-structural summary of two parallel pericopes

¹⁰ The earth quakes <u>before them</u>, the heavens tremble. <u>The sun and the moon</u> are darkened, <u>and the stars</u> withdraw their shining. ¹¹ <u>The LORD</u> utters his voice before his army, for his host is <u>exceedingly great</u>; he that executes his word is <u>powerful</u>. Indeed, the day of the LORD is <u>great and very terrible</u>, and who can endure it?	¹⁰ לְפָנָיו רָגְזָה אֶרֶץ רָעֲשׁוּ שָׁמָיִם שֶׁמֶשׁ וְיָרֵחַ קָדָרוּ וְכוֹכָבִים אָסְפוּ נָגְהָם׃ ¹¹ וַיהוָה נָתַן קוֹלוֹ לִפְנֵי חֵילוֹ כִּי רַב מְאֹד מַחֲנֵהוּ כִּי עָצוּם עֹשֵׂה דְבָרוֹ כִּי גָדוֹל יוֹם־יְהוָה וְנוֹרָא מְאֹד וּמִי יְכִילֶנּוּ׃

C, Strophe 4 (2:10–11)
From "the earth" to "the heavens" the scene shifts: The spatial constituent "before them/their faces" (לְפָנָיו) is again advanced to signal this new unit aperture (cf. vv. 3, 6; structural *anaphora*). The dramatic personification and hyperbole continue as the action is reported in the prophetic perfect. Now the "sun, moon, and stars" too are adversely affected—their light goes dark (10b). This familiar cosmic dimension (e.g., Exod 19:16–19; Ps 97:1–5; Hab 3:3–11, but a thematic inversion of Isa 13:10, 13) serves to introduce YHWH in the very next line (11a, subject focus)—with a certain shock effect, for the LORD, loudly thundering orders (v. 11a–b), is thus revealed to be the leader of these hordes of hostile forces! A series of three parallel כִּי noun clauses with predicate focus progressively builds up to the climax of the strophe/stanza in the concluding exclamatory rhetorical question (with a pessimistic negative answer implied): וּמִי יְכִילֶנּוּ – this awful day can be neither delayed nor endured (cf. vv. 7–8)! The emotive psychological nadir of the entire prophecy has thus been reached. The locust host (or is it now actually a huge infidel invasion?) has seemingly prevailed! The thematic expression "day of YHWH" (יוֹם־יְהוָה) forms an *inclusio* with 2:1.

TEXT II

3:9 Proclaim this among the nations: Prepare war,	⁹ קִרְאוּ־זֹאת בַּגּוֹיִם קַדְּשׁוּ מִלְחָמָה
stir up the warriors. Let all the men of war draw near, let them come up.	הָעִירוּ הַגִּבּוֹרִים יִגְּשׁוּ יַעֲלוּ כֹּל אַנְשֵׁי הַמִּלְחָמָה:
¹⁰ Beat your plowshares into swords, and your pruning hooks into spears;	¹⁰ כֹּתּוּ אִתֵּיכֶם לַחֲרָבוֹת וּמַזְמְרֹתֵיכֶם לִרְמָחִים

let the weak say, "I am a warrior!"
¹¹ Hasten and come,
   all you nations round about,
   gather yourselves there.
	הַחַלָּשׁ יֹאמַר גִּבּוֹר אָנִי:
	¹¹ עוּשׁוּ וָבֹאוּ כָל־הַגּוֹיִם מִסָּבִיב
	וְנִקְבָּצוּ שָׁמָּה

Bring down thy warriors, O LORD!	הַנְחַת יְהוָה גִּבּוֹרֶיךָ:

<u>Oracle 4</u> (3:1–17)
Stanza D' (3:9–17): The nations are summoned for slaughter[6]
D', Strophe 1 (3:9–11)

A string of commands marks the onset of Stanza D', as Joel takes over the discourse from the LORD (cf. "for YHWH has spoken—ס : כִּי יְהוָה דִּבֵּר" in 3:8c), announcing a final implementation of the LORD's prediction of 3:1–2 (thematic *anaphora*). These imperative forms (or jussives) continue throughout the unit (a prominent sequence of initial וֹ- sounds). The paired commands "proclaim…sanctify" (שׁ…קרא) pointedly recall (in reversed order) the very different scenario of 2:15, while the verb "stir up" (רוע) in v. 9 with reference to the pagan "nations" (4x in this strophe) duplicates its usage in v. 7 with reference to the Jews (i.e., all these are instances of contrastive *anaphora*). There is more powerful *irony* operating here: Instead of a "holy war" being waged against the enemies of YHWH (e.g., Isa 8:9–10; Jer 46:3–6, 9–10; Ezek 38–39), the same militaristic terminology is being used, ostensibly to rouse those very enemies to battle. The concept of reversal is further foregrounded in v. 10 as an obvious allusion to Isaiah 2:4 (Micah 4:3) is transformed into the opposite, and even the weak man (ironic new topic) is called upon (in direct speech) to be a "warrior" (predicate focus; cf. Deut 20:3–4)! Such a semantic inversion prefigures the strophe's content on a larger scale with respect to "the (pagan) nations" (גּוֹיִם) (vv. 9a, 11a; i.e., *inclusio*). The end of this strophe in v. 11c is marked *(closure)* by the prophet's personal interjection—an emotive, exclamatory plea to God for immediate judicial and punitive action: הַנְחַת יְהוָה גִּבּוֹרֶיךָ (another ironic *inclusio* with v. 9)—which YHWH forcefully and decisively responds to in the very next strophe.

---

[6] There is considerably more diversity of scholarly opinion regarding the boundaries as well as the internal strophic divisions of this stanza (3:9–17). Some commentators appear to construe the entire section as a collection of topically related group of "restoration promises, all of which in one way or another give reassurance that Israel's enemies will be dispensed with so that Israel (Judah and Jerusalem) may have peace" (Stuart 1987:265; cf. Finley 1990:93–94, and Barton, who adds, "What is not clear is where the unit ends" 2001:103). Others discern 3:9–11 as an independent strophe, but do not differentiate the following material (e.g., Dillard

1.4 A literary-structural summary of two parallel pericopes

¹² "Let the nations bestir themselves,	¹² יֵע֙וֹרוּ֙ וְיַעֲל֣וּ הַגּוֹיִ֔ם
and come up to the valley of Jehoshaphat;	אֶל־עֵ֖מֶק יְהוֹשָׁפָ֑ט
for there is where I will sit to judge all the nations round about."	כִּ֣י שָׁ֗ם אֵשֵׁב֙ לִשְׁפֹּ֔ט אֶת־כָּל־הַגּוֹיִ֖ם מִסָּבִֽיב׃
¹³ Put in the sickle, for the harvest is ripe	¹³ שִׁלְח֣וּ מַגָּ֔ל כִּ֥י בָשַׁ֖ל קָצִ֑יר
Go in, tread, for the wine press is full.	בֹּ֤אוּ רְדוּ֙ כִּֽי־מָ֣לְאָה גַּ֔ת
The vats overflow, for their wickedness is great.	הֵשִׁ֙יקוּ֙ הַיְקָבִ֔ים כִּ֥י רַבָּ֖ה רָעָתָֽם׃
¹⁴ Multitudes, multitudes,	¹⁴ הֲמוֹנִ֣ים הֲמוֹנִ֔ים
in the valley of decision!	בְּעֵ֖מֶק הֶֽחָר֑וּץ
Yes, the day of the LORD is near	כִּ֤י קָרוֹב֙ י֣וֹם יְהוָ֔ה
in the valley of decision.	בְּעֵ֖מֶק הֶחָרֽוּץ׃

1992:305, 308; Sweeney 2000a:181–182; Garrett 1997 puts vv. 9–12 together, but only loosely connects the material in vv. 13–17). Allen comes the closest to my proposed demarcation, differing only at v. 12, i.e., coherent strophes comprising 9–12, 13–14, 15–17 (1976:106–107, 116). However, Allen also considers vv. 9–12 to be the concluding strophe of the larger unit (stanza) covering 3:1–12, viz. "The last section [9–12] resumes vv. 1–3 and so rounds off the unit" (ibid., 114). This is indeed a viable alternative, including his incorporation of v. 12 into this section. But for the literary-structural reasons cited below, I prefer my own macro-segmentation, which is supported by Barton 2001:102, Dillard 2002:305, Garrett 1997:384, and Sweeney 2000a:181. Most English translations begin a new principal section at 3:9, but there is much disagreement as to where this unit ends and how it is internally segmented. A few versions like REB do not incorporate any strophes at all within vv. 9–17, while others posit as many as six (e.g., NRSV). Several popular translations (e.g., NIV and GNT) end the stanza at v. 16 instead of v. 17, as suggested above, which is possible, but as I argue below, less likely.

So, what difference does such paragraphing make within a text? If, as commonly defined, a *paragraph* is a group of sentences (or utterances) that are related by a common topic that differs in one or more respects from surrounding paragraphs, then its significance becomes clear: The paragraph is a vital element in the organization of thought and discourse, and therefore great care must be taken both when composing a text into paragraph units and also when using these units to interpret the meaning of a given text, whether oral or written.

D¹, Strophe 2 (3:12–14)
The wicked may think that they are mustering for a war against YHWH and his people "in the Valley of Jehoshaphat" (אֶל־עֵמֶק יְהוֹשָׁפָט - cf. 3:2, *anaphora*), but in fact they are gathering themselves for judgment there (שָׁם –front-shift locative focus) before the LORD, as the meaning of "Jeho-shaphat" implies (i.e., an onomastic pun with dramatic irony)! What a surprise: The pagan nations come all prepared for battle, but instead they arrive only to experience the punitive harvest of the LORD's "judgment" (a thematic reversal of passages like Isa 17:4–6; Ho 6:11; Am 8:1–3)! YHWH (apparently) shouts out commands to his warriors (perhaps in response to the prophet's poignant appeal of v. 11c) to destroy the multitudes of defeated enemies (הֲמוֹנִים הֲמוֹנִים—an onomatopoeic phrase; cf. Isa 13:4, 17:12), which alludes back to the locust hordes (e.g., 2:11). Familiar grape harvest imagery (v. 13b-c; cf. Isa 63:3; Jer 25:30; Lam 1:15) is now applied to a war scenario, as the "Valley of Jehoshaphat" (v. 12) turns out to be the "Valley of Decision" (עֵמֶק הֶחָרוּץ)—i.e., YHWH's punishment implemented (v. 14).

There is high emotive tension that accompanies this animated scene in which God has turned the tables on all the adversaries of his people. Figurative language colors the vast panorama that is being depicted, and from v. 13 a fast, two-foot meter propels the action taking place at the LORD's winepress forward to reach a thematic peak in the repetitive, judgment imagery at the end (v. 14). A strophic peak as well as *closure* is also signaled by the non-verbal utterance of v.14 with its reference to YHWH's day being near (predicate focus,14b, which is introduced by a fourth, now climactic כִּי; cf. 1:15; 2:1, 11) and "the valley of decision" (cf. 3:2, 12— double *inclusio*; cf. Obad 15). Thus, the dramatic stage has been broadly set by the LORD for the subsequent, even more impressive strophes of this prophecy-concluding stanza.

¹⁵ The sun and the moon are darkened,	¹⁵ שֶׁמֶשׁ וְיָרֵחַ קָדָרוּ
and the stars withdraw their shining.	וְכוֹכָבִים אָסְפוּ נָגְהָם׃
¹⁶ And the LORD roars from Zion,	¹⁶ וַיהוָה מִצִּיּוֹן יִשְׁאָג
and utters his voice from Jerusalem,	וּמִירוּשָׁלִַם יִתֵּן קוֹלוֹ
and the heavens and the earth shake.	וְרָעֲשׁוּ שָׁמַיִם וָאָרֶץ
But the LORD is a refuge to his people,	וַיהוָה מַחֲסֶה לְעַמּוֹ
a stronghold to the people of Israel.	וּמָעוֹז לִבְנֵי יִשְׂרָאֵל׃
¹⁷ "So you shall know that I am the LORD your God,	¹⁷ וִידַעְתֶּם כִּי אֲנִי יְהוָה אֱלֹהֵיכֶם
who dwell in Zion, my holy mountain.	שֹׁכֵן בְּצִיּוֹן הַר־קָדְשִׁי
And Jerusalem shall be a sanctuary,	וְהָיְתָה יְרוּשָׁלִַם קֹדֶשׁ
and strangers shall never again pass through it."	וְזָרִים לֹא־יַעַבְרוּ־בָהּ עוֹד׃ ס

> **D', Strophe 3 (3:15–17)**
> Eschatological "sun-moon-stars" (all darkened) imagery (v. 15, initial topic shift; = 2:10, with contrastive content and structural *anaphora;* cf. 2:31) dramatize the continued battle scene as YHWH executes (lit. "roars"- שָׁאַג) judgment "from Zion…Jerusalem" (with locative constituent focus to highlight צִיּוֹן; cf. Amos 1:2; Jer 25:30–31). This strophe's description of יוֹם יְהוָה (v. 15) echoes those found in earlier segments of Joel (2:10–11 and 30–32, now with a decidedly cumulative impact. A sudden introduction of the impressive *divine recognition formula* (וִידַעְתֶּם כִּי אֲנִי יְהוָה אֱלֹהֵיכֶם) in v. 17a forges an important thematic linkage between the deliverance (2:27) and vindication of God's people vis a vis their erstwhile enemies (topical *epiphora*). This segment of momentous direct speech by YHWH also acts as a transition to the final culmination of the prophecy (3:18–21). Verse 17 is marked by the key locative terms and their qualifiers ("Zion, my holy mountain… Jerusalem holy") to further underscore this passage (coupled with v. 16) as being the *peak,* not only of the present strophe and stanza, but also of Part Two of Joel's message. A very specific prophetic blessing concludes the strophe: "strangers" (a new topic, זָרִים), i.e., those who are alien to the LORD and his covenant community, will never again pollute their sacred space! (a thematic reversal of 2:11, 17—contrastive *epiphora;* cf. Obad 17; Isa 35:8). The personal presence of YHWH himself will forever ensure the holiness of "Zion" (צִיּוֹן)!

1.5 Thematic image-interaction

1.5.1 Image complexes in Joel

The detailed imagery of the two pericopes analyzed above has already been noted. Now it is time to view the "big picture," namely, how the central, extended metaphor of 2:1–11 is first developed on the basis of imagery that has already occurred in Joel's prophecy and is then further applied in subsequent oracles. This study thus requires some consideration of all the major *image complexes* within the book—that is, where they occur and how they are related to each other in conceptual interaction throughout the text. The following is a summary of the main imagistic combinations that are found in Joel according to their occurrence in the text's principal discourse units (i.e., oracles and stanzas as proposed above; note that corresponding image sets, whether complementary or contrasting, are marked by the same typeface/font):

Location in Joel	Image Complexes
Oracle 1	
Stanza A (1:2–12)	*locust plague* + agricultural ruin + DROUGHT + temple sacrifices
Stanza B (1:13–20)	acts of penitence/mourning + agricultural ruin + DROUGHT

Oracle 2	
Stanza C (2:1–11)	**theophany** + *locust plague* + *huge military attack* + agricultural ruin
Stanza D (2:12–17)	acts of penitence/mourning
Oracle 3	
Stanza A' (2:18–27)	agricultural bounty + *locust plague* (removed)
Stanza B' (2:28–32)	**theophany** + charismatic (Spirit-generated) renewal
Oracle 4	
Stanza C' (3:1–8)	*lawsuit: summons and judgment*
Stanza D' (3:9–17)	*huge military attack* + *judgment* + **theophany** + harvest
Oracle 5 (3:18–21)	agricultural bounty + DESOLATION

The preceding chart reveals at a glance the elaborate image interlocking which ties Joel's prophecy into a formal (structural), semantic (topical), and functional (genre-based) unity.[7] Imagery that depicts "agricultural ruin/bounty/harvest," for example, is manifested virtually throughout the text. Furthermore, we see that *contrastive* imagery occurs in the two pericopes that may be designated as thematic "peaks" within the book, namely, 2:28–32 and 3:18–21 (notably, near the middle and at the close of the text). Finally, it is interesting to observe that the *most complex* combinations of imagery are found in the two texts that were identified also as being the most "dramatic" in character, namely, 2:1–11 and 3:9–17, each one thus serving to build up to a prophetic *peak* point within the book.

In any case, it is clear that the abundant imagery to be found in this prophecy is a major contributing factor in its expression of theme. As pointed out above, the principal thematic notion of Joel is posited as "retribution, reversal, and restoration in the day of the LORD" (other expressions of these basic concepts are of course possible). The various image complexes thus line up on either side of YHWH's effecting first of all a just punishment of his people (i.e., *retribution*) on account of their covenantal infidelity in order to bring them to repentance (1:2–2:17). There is then a connotative *reversal* as some of the same, or at least similar, imagery (e.g., involving theophany, locusts, and agricultural produce) is utilized to underscore YHWH's punitive

---

[7] As Allen notes, "[Joel] is a literary tapestry covered with a host of repeated motifs...so crammed with echoed motifs that it seems impossible to reduce their crisscross patterning into a detailed structural order" (1976:39). In the present section I am simply trying to show the coherence and thematic relevance of some of the major image complexes of this book.

1.5 Thematic image-interaction

judgment of his enemies ("the nations") and his subsequent pouring out of blessings upon his now Spirit-renewed people (i.e., *restoration;* 2:18–3:21).

1.5.2 From image to metaphor—the stimulating blend of distinct "mental spaces"

An individual or compound image that is attached to some topic in the discourse at hand and used comparatively for descriptive or some other attributive purpose is termed a simile, when the comparison is *marked* (e.g., by "like" or "as"—כ in Hebrew, e.g., "like a virgin" in 1:8a), and a metaphor, when the comparison in left implicit or *unmarked* (e.g., "teeth of a lion" in 1:6b). Any simile or metaphor thus involves two primary conceptual frames, one surrounding the topic (the primary referent), the other filling out the image (the attributive referent). The more or less intuitive mental combination of these two cognitive frames, or windows, produces a cognitive blend that constitutes the essential meaning of the metaphor. However, such a semantic amalgamation is not simple, consisting of individual components of meaning (except in the case of a dead, or inactive metaphor); instead, it tends to be rather multifaceted—the more so if the metaphor happens to be novel, mixed, and/or dense in terms of its cultural associations and significance. Recently, some cognitive linguists have attempted to describe the semantic richness of metaphor by means of "mental space theory," the essence of which is outlined in the following paragraphs.

The cognitive theory of *conceptual blending* is based on the insight that true creativity of any type essentially involves bringing together elements from different semantic domains. In the words of Fauconnier and Turner (F&T), some early researchers in the field:[8]

---

[8] All the references to Fauconnier and Turner in this section come from their 2002 volume, chapter three in particular. Similarly, all the Stockwell citations come from chapter seven of his book (2002). Koops comments as follows (2000:4): "Once you see how mental spaces work and how they are connected to each other, it is not difficult to see how content from two mental spaces can combine to yield a third space. This is called 'conceptual blending.' The third space inherits partial structure from the input spaces and has emergent structure of its own.... There are also non-linguistic examples of blending, like the computer 'Desktop' interface, constructed on the basis of two conceptual units, the input of traditional computer commands, and the input of ordinary work in an office. Cross-space mapping matches computer files to paper files, directories to folders, etc., right down to the dustbin."

> Conceptual blending operates largely behind the scenes. We are not consciously aware of its hidden complexities…. Almost invisibly to consciousness, conceptual blending choreographs vast networks of conceptual meaning, yielding cognitive products that, at the conscious level, appear simple… The products of conceptual blending are ubiquitous.

Conceptual blending is the less technical reference to what F&T term the "network model of conceptual integration," which involves the heuristic notion of figurative mental spaces (2002:40). These psychological constructs may be temporal, spatial, eventive, personal, objective, circumstantial, modal, or hypothetical in nature, whether the reference is to actual or fictional settings and situations; they are activated in the mind as any perceptual, rational being moves from (or combines) one cognitive-connotative frame of reference to (with) another. In summary:

> Mental spaces are small conceptual packets constructed as we think and talk, for the purposes of local understanding and action…. Mental spaces are connected to long-term schematic knowledge called "frames," such as the frame of *walking along a path,* and to long-term specific knowledge, such as a memory of the time you climbed Mount Rainier in 2001…. Mental spaces are very partial. They contain [cognitive] elements and are typically structured by frames. They are interconnected, and can be modified as thought and discourse unfold. Mental spaces can be used generally to model dynamic mappings in thought and language. *(loc. cit.)*[9]

I now wish to apply, admittedly in a rather superficial and cursory manner, certain aspects of the theory of mental spaces and conceptual framing coupled with blending simply to suggest something of the dynamic

---

[9] This may be compared with the more literary-oriented perspective of Coulson 2001:21–25: "Mental space theory…is a theory of *referential structure*…mental spaces can be thought of as temporary containers for relevant information about a particular domain. A mental space contains a partial representation of the entities and relations of a particular scenario as perceived, imagined, remembered, or otherwise understood by a speaker…. Spaces represent such diverse things as hypothetical scenarios, beliefs, quantified domains, thematically defined domains, fictional scenarios, and situations located in time and space. As discourse unfolds, the language user extends existing spaces by adding new elements and relations to the cognitive models already evoked…. A new space is also set up when utterances concern objects or events that require different background assumptions from those of the current space…. Meaning construction thus consists of mapping cognitive models from space to space while keeping track of the links between spaces and between elements and their counterparts…. [M]eaning always emerges from understanding in a particular context." Missing, however, from this cognitive view of perception, understanding, and "meaning" construction is any substantial consideration of emotions, attitudes, values, and other *connotative* elements that characterize most communication events, certainly those found in highly literary, but also hortatory works such as Joel's prophecy (see also Wendland 2008a:ch. 3).

1.5 Thematic image-interaction

cognitive (and emotive!) activity that takes place when a biblical author is communicating his message in a vivid manner (as in Joel 2:1–11 and 3:9–17) for what he no doubt assumed would be an attentive and biblically informed local audience of Hebrew speakers.

Stockwell (2002:97–98) sums up the operation of conceptual blending as follows (original emphasis):

> This involves a [cognitive] mapping between two [mental] spaces, and common general nodes and relationships across the spaces are abstracted into a **generic space**. Specific features which emerge from this mapping then form a new space, the **blend**. Conceptual blends are the mechanism by which we can hold the properties of two spaces together, such as in metaphorical or allegorical thinking, scientific or political analogy, comparisons and imaginary domains involving characters from disparate areas…

In the evocation of new ideas then, including metaphor, four mental spaces are theoretically involved, two input spaces and another pair of consequent composite spaces (I have slightly modified the standard definitions of these; cf. Stockwell 2002:96–98; F&T 2002:41–44). These hypothetical spaces will be referred to in a specific application to Joel below):

- **Target** (base) space (**1**): the verbal or textual starting point for the construction of a conceptual network; this is the "tenor" or "topic," which is the familiar, "real-world" oriented, or literal element of a metaphor—what is being spoken about or referred to in terms of semantic sense and pragmatic significance.
- **Source** (image) space (**2**): the figurative concept(s) that is (are) used to expand and/or develop the initial conceptual space by presenting a novel, non-literal perspective; this is the "vehicle" or "image" of a metaphor—what is employed to illumine or illustrate the Target in the particular verbal cotext in which it is being used.
- **Generic** (abstract) space (**3**): formed from selective "cross-space mapping" as specific counterparts or correspondences between the two input spaces (Target + Source, 1 + 2) are initially brought together in one's mind, namely, the key cognitive elements (semantic and pragmatic "components") that they have in common or form an insightful "bond" with in the current predication (i.e., the comparative "ground" of a metaphor).
- **Blended** (metaphoric) space (**4**): specific features of the generic space (3) that become further cognitively "activated" by the

present discourse context, that is, according to the principle of "relevance" in conjunction with the wider extralinguistic, intertextual, situational and circumstantial setting; as a result a virtual "emergent structure" is formed (4) in which new relations and aspects of meaning become apparent by inference and/or intuition, often with additional connotative (emotive, attitudinal, aesthetic, etc.) overtones and rhetorical impact.[10]

The point of the preceding technical discussion is to provide a hermeneutical framework for better understanding the semantic density that confronts us when we seek to interpret the complex metaphoric imagery that Joel presents to us in 2:1–11. This passage is a *crux interpretum* for commentators in that its primary referent is either unhelpfully ignored or roundly debated. Some (e.g., Barton 2001:68–70) assert that the locusts mentioned in ch. 1 (e.g., 1:4, 6) reappear here in ch. 2, being metaphorically likened to an invading army (e.g., 2:4–9).[11] Others (e.g., Wolff 1977:41–42) claim that literal locusts have been left behind in ch. 1 and that here in ch. 2 some aggressive (super-) human, perhaps apocalyptic (e.g., 2:11) military force is being referred to instead. The prophetic poet does not seem to have typical soldiers of the day in mind, for the warlike invaders being described apparently possess powers much greater than ordinary human beings (e.g., "they leap on the tops of mountains" [GNT], 2:5). Of course, one might conclude that we are dealing here simply with hyperbolic language, but that does not help us much with 2:11 and the nature of the "army" being led by the LORD. In any case, the theophanic imagery that begins and ends this pericope further complicates its interpretation, for this clearly suggests that YHWH is in some way playing an active role in the devastation that is being portrayed. There is yet another complication that is just briefly touched upon in the present passage, namely, the possible extension of the metaphoric field to include not only the locusts but also the agricultural

---

[10] "The generic space consists of the intersection of the input spaces, that is, the conceptual structure that they share, while the blend space consists of the combination of the input spaces, where elements from each interact with each other. The result of this interaction, according to mental space theory, is that the blend space will have an 'emergent structure' with inferences not predictable from the individual source frames" (Shead 2007:55–56).

[11] Barton notes the problem here concerning our interpretation of the "locusts" in Joel: "[A]re they real or symbolic, bringers of a literal famine or harbingers of the last days, or all of these at once?" (2001:3). My "imagistic analysis" seeks to demonstrate the final option—"all of these at once"—but sequentially so, not simultaneously; that is to say, there is a progression from the literal (ch. 1, in the present or recent past), to the metaphoric (ch. 2, in the near future), to the purely symbolic (ch. 3, in the far future—the end of time).

1.5 Thematic image-interaction

produce being despoiled (e.g., the "stubble" of 2:5b). This would in turn raise the possibility of human objects of the personal army's attack—a hermeneutical option the likelihood of which is supported by the imagery of 3:9–17 (especially v. 13).

So what are we to make of this text with regard to its interpretation—can mental space theory help resolve the hermeneutical problems that we confront here? This approach cannot resolve all of our difficulties, but it can at least clarify the nature of the text's complex, interlocking chain of imagery so that it can be broken down into smaller, more manageable portions. In its simplest expression, the prophecy of Joel presents a threefold progression of adversarial activity: A. Locust attack (1:2–12) ➔ B. Locust/Military attack (2:1–11) ➔ C. Military attack (3:9–17; preceded by judicial indictment, 3:1–8). There is thus a metaphoric core in B that builds upon the imagery of A and provides a bridge to the thematically more significant imagery of C. Each of these three macro-segments is followed in turn by some significant response or result: A' Call for communal repentance (1:13–20); B' Call for communal repentance (2:12–17) ➔ YHWH's restoration, immediate (2:18–27) and subsequent (2:28–32); C' YHWH's ultimate blessing upon his land and people (3:17–21).

Stated in propositional terms then, we might express the elaborate double metaphor which underlies the book's thematic movement as follows: **The locust plague is an army sent by YHWH to devastate the unrighteous, which are like a field of grain, just waiting to be harvested**. This compound theme represents in a literary, as well as a religious, sense an authorial perceptual "blend," namely, that of the (implied) speaker, the prophet Joel, together with that of the LORD God, on behalf of whom Joel is speaking. At times these two perspectives and utterances seem to merge into one (when YHWH is referred to in the third person), while at other times they are distinct, (when YHWH speaks in the first person). In any case, the literal foundation for the *locust/army/harvest* metaphor is laid at the onset of the prophecy in chapter one; this is articulated in one direction in chapter two (the judgment of apostate Israel), and then applied within a completely different cognitive frame of reference in chapter three (judgment of the nations). Complementing the gruesome portrayal of the LORD's punishment of all pagans is the prediction of a grand reversal and great blessing for his penitent covenant people (2:18–3:21).

It is not possible to discuss all the diverse strands of this forceful divine-prophetic argument within the scope of this chapter. I will therefore consider its metaphoric development only in broad strokes, that is, in comparative juxtaposition using descriptive componential features, and with particular reference to the two dramatic texts that were analyzed above (2:1–11 and 3:9–17), along with their more or less literal foundation, which was laid in chapter one. The following chart thus constitutes a great over-simplification of the actual cognitive processes involved when interpreting complex literary texts like this and also when representing them in current cognitive linguistic literature (e.g., Semino 2002:116, 118). In this instance I considered heuristic clarity and immediate hermeneutical relevance to be more important than theoretical detail and precision.

It is important to note that the interpretive process moves backwards as well as forwards, that is, both paradigmatically and also syntagmatically. Thus, a later passage (e.g., 3:9–17) can be fully construed sequentially and as a whole only in the light of certain corresponding (similar and contrastive) information and imagery that has preceded it in the discourse (e.g., 2:1–11).

1.5 Thematic image-interaction

Target (Topic) Space (1)	Source (Image) Space (2)
Military invasion • large numbers, usually well-equipped in weaponry, etc. • the fact of their arrival may be known, but not the precise time of attack • it is difficult, sometimes impossible, for local inhabitants to repel and expel these forces • normally results in death and destruction, sometimes total in terms of the country as a whole **Judgment time** • involves a separation of morally good and bad • inevitable—it cannot be avoided by anyone • God is the sole, supreme initiator and implementer • results in dismay/despair and punishment for the wicked • results in joy/thanksgiving and blessing for the righteous • may occur in human time but most certainly in the hereafter (the eschaton) • the latter cosmic event is the occasion for great awe and apprehension on the part of all humanity	**Locust invasion** • large numbers involved, uncountable • unexpected arrival, cannot be fully predicted • impossible to prevent or expel without assistance • rapacious individuals, and devastating as a group • ruins local and/or national agriculture **Harvest time** • annual selection/collection of grapes, grains, olives, etc. • essential for an agriculturally-based ANE society • concerns domestic livestock too—cattle, sheep, goats • affects religious offerings in the regular Temple ritual • its quality is a sign of Yahweh's favor or disfavor **Natural phenomena** • thunderstorms, lightning strikes, earthquakes, floods, etc. • involving the celestial bodies: sun, moon, stars • perceived as manifestations of deity by pagans • used for divination and astrology by pagans • deviations from the norm regarded as inauspicious omens • all under the control of Yahweh in Jewish belief

Generic (Common) Space (3)[12]	Blended (Metaphoric) Space (4):
Locust-Military invasion: • large numbers of dangerous enemy • difficult, if not possible to defeat/repel • results in deprivation, death, destruction for those attacked • can only be resolved through outside intervention • natural phenomena, usually negative or adverse, are normally directly or indirectly associated with the events taking place **Harvest-Judgment:** • occurs at the end of some season/age/epoch, etc. • affects a large number of individuals, even an entire group • involves a discernment and a division between the acceptable and the unacceptable • God alone controls the entire process and its ultimate conclusion • the final outcome/result/decision normally cannot be undone, redone, or reversed	**(4a—the locust-army attack, 2:1–11)** This appears to function as a transitional text that bridges the gap between Parts I and II of the prophecy of Joel. The passage thus features a metaphoric combination of elements that characterize the locust invasion of ch. 1 (namely, the middle strophes of 2:3–5 and 6–9) as well as the worldwide punitive attack on the pagan nations of ch. 3 (namely, the external strophes of 2:1–2 and 10–11). This correspondence is strengthened by the appearance of theophanic imagery in both outer strophes (e.g., 2:2, 10). In short, the prophet rhetorically plays on the first chapter's images of agricultural destruction wrought by the locusts (and drought) in order to heighten his portrayal of the total devastation of Israel that will come at the hands of enemy forces, that is, *if* the people do not repent of their covenantal infidelity to Yahweh (or, *after* they have since come to such repentance at the prophet's urging, e.g., 2:13). This passage in turn foreshadows its correspondent in Part II, 3:9–17. **(4b—harvest-judgment time, 3:9–17)** Now the participant tables are turned and instead of Israel being the object of the LORD's punitive actions (cp. 2:11 and 3:16), the pagan nations and enemies of his covenant people (2:32) receive his righteous retribution for all their wickedness (cf. 3:1–3). Though these are evidently the "last days" prior to the universal culmination of world history, the imagery clearly reflects and builds upon that which has occurred earlier in the book—namely, harvesting action (e.g., 3:13), massive hordes (e.g., 3:14), an invincible army on the attack (e.g., 3:9)—and all this against a backdrop of the entire cosmos in distress (e.g., 3:15). Localized earthly travail and temporal turmoil thus metaphorically (or we could say, symbolically) pre-figures the universal judgment of Yahweh that will occur at the end of time—and usher in the new age of Zion, when eternal peace and prosperity for God's people will prevail (3:17–21).

---

[12] During a given text analysis the lexical and related details that pertain to this "generic space" could be readily filled out by the data provided by a good cognitive-based dictionary, like that of the *Semantic domain dictionary of Biblical Hebrew* (SDBH) of Reinier de Blois, which is available on-line at http://www.sdbh.org/vocabula/index.html.

The entire book of Joel thus consists of a repository of literal and figurative images that reverberate off one another to express as well as to enhance the prophet's essential set of warnings, admonitions, exhortations, and encouragements. The basic contrastive, covenant-centered message is simple: (a) disobedience/unfaithfulness ➔ severe punishment versus (b) obedience/fidelity ➔ superabundant blessing, plus a public vindication with respect to prior pagan foes and oppressors. Of course, in any hermeneutical exercise of this nature, it is important to establish the temporal/historical "frame of reference" for the text at hand, for this is a vital aspect of the interpretive process. In this case, the question is: Should we view Joel as being a pre- or a post-exilic prophet? The diversity and amount of intertextual references from the prophetic literature incorporated within this book, especially from the book of Obadiah, would argue in favor of a later date (Wendland 1995:242–253),[13] and I have assumed such a perspective in my analysis.[14] However, as the preceding analysis seems to indicate, the fundamental message is the same in either case, and the fabric of supportive imagery is general enough in Old Testament terms to fit both temporal scenarios. Perhaps that is the reason why there is so much disagreement regarding the dating of this book and why, on the other hand, its pressing theological and moral relevance to the people of God is essentially timeless.

1.6 Conclusion: Communicating Joel's dramatic rhetoric and imagery today

So what does Joel mean for the "modern man"? Surely a biblical book that focuses so much on locusts would seem to be quite out of touch with contemporary

---

[13] For example: "in Mount Zion and in Jerusalem there shall be those who escape"—Joel 2:32; cf. Obad. 17; "I will turn your deeds back upon your own heads"—Joel 3:4; cf. Obad. 15. Also supporting a later date is the apparent *semantic reversal* in a number of the passages that Joel has in common with other prophets, e.g., "Beat your plowshares into swords, and your pruning hooks into spears"—Joel 3:10; cf. Isa 2:4; Mic 4:3. However, it must be recognized that determining the direction of borrowing in such cases is by no means a clear-cut matter, and each apparent instance must be evaluated and decided in relation to its immediate cotext as well as that of its supposed "pre-text" (cf. Dillard 1992:241). Barton regards Joel as "a *learned* prophecy, which draws on many quotations from older works and blends them into the message that the prophet has to deliver, rather than putting forward fresh formulations of his own" (2001:19). Hubbard adds: "In a sense, Joel replete with ideas and terms drawn from many prophets, encapsulated the basic movement not only of individual prophetic books (e.g., Hosea, Isaiah), but of the prophetic corpus as a whole..." (1989:23).

[14] Garrett gives a good summary of the various controversial issues that pertain to the dating of Joel (1997:286–298), and although I disagree with his conclusion that "a seventh-century date" is preferable, I do agree that having "no clear historical context for Joel...is not a major barrier to interpretation" (ibid., 294).

reality. But is it? Just substitute for those ravaging insect swarms (still a major plague in some parts of the world, like northern Africa; cf. Prior 1998:18) a more contextualized foe with the power-potential to destroy cities, regions, and even entire nations—such as nuclear weapons, biological warfare, a SARS-like virus, or even the electronic internet type—then the threat and the prophet's urgent message strikes a bell that tolls closer to home. It all has to do with "the day of the LORD" (יוֹם־יְהוָה), an expression used more pervasively in Joel than any of the other prophets: Are we currently ready to experience that Day, or does the message of the book's opening half need to sink in first? For the LORD's faithful covenant community, all those who now live in the power of his Spirit (2:28–32; cf. Acts 2:16–21), there is nothing to fear, and everything to hope for "in that day," when the events prophesied in ch. 3 finally transpire. Craigie well summarizes Joel's ever-relevant divine message (1984:88):

> Thus Joel was a man of his own times, yet also a man for all future generations. Reading the immediate signs of his own age, he summoned his people to repentance, and they responded. Yet the threat of disaster, so vividly exemplified in the locust plague, was in a sense an ever-present threat. Wherever and whenever evil prospered, the Day of the Lord must always be at hand.... And though the Day of the Lord would be a fearful time for the practitioners of evil, both persons and nations, it would nevertheless be a time of hope. For beyond that day the prophet sees a vision, albeit distant and without clear substance, when the years lost to the locust would be remembered no more.

To be sure, Joel's message has contemporary relevance, but now the question is, How can it best be communicated to "modern man," in particular, to people who are characterized by a culture, worldview, and value system that differs greatly from that of the Ancient Near East? That decision of course cannot be made in isolation, but rather requires a careful and comprehensive study of the particular socio-religious setting and target audience to whom the text is to be communicated (Wendland 2004:369–379). In a majority of situations and in most societies, a dynamic contemporary translation is required in order to more effectively convey the dramatic, challenging character of this timeless prophecy. Eugene Peterson gives us a good example of what Joel might sound like if he were uttering his warning about "the day of the Lord" today (2:7–11, from Peterson 2000:467):[15]

---

[15] Several of Peterson's keen insights into the nature of Hebrew prophetic literature too are worth citing—with special reference to the passage given below: "If what seems like the worst turns out to be *God's judgment*, it can be embraced, not denied or avoided, for God is good and intends our salvation. So judgment,

1.6 Conclusion: Communicating Joel's dramatic rhetoric and imagery today

The invaders charge.
   They climb barricades. Nothing stops them.
Each soldier does what he's told,
   so disciplined, so determined.
They don't get in each other's way.
   Each one knows his job and does it.
Undaunted and fearless,
   unswerving, unstoppable.
They storm the city,
   swarm its defenses,
Loot the houses,
   breaking down doors, smashing windows.
They arrive like an earthquake,
   sweep through like a tornado.
Sun and moon turn out their lights,
   stars black out.
God himself bellows in thunder
   as he commands his forces.
Look at the size of that army!
   And the strength of those who obey him!
God's Judgment Day—great and terrible.
   Who can possibly survive this?

"What Joel might *sound* like" is a crucial qualification, for his prophecy, like most if not all of Scripture, was originally composed in order to be *heard* by a listening audience (cf. 1:2).[16] This is especially important in sociocultural settings that still greatly prefer oral-aural over written communication, for example, throughout most of Africa. It is only then, in actual

---

while certainly not what we human beings anticipate in our planned future, can never be the worst that can happen. It is the best, for it is the work of God to set the world, and us, right" (ibid., 8). For some suggested guidelines when attempting an "oratorical" poetic translation in a non-European vernacular (exemplified by Ezekiel 37:1–10 in Chewa, a major Bantu language of south-central Africa), see Wendland 2004:272–288.

[16] In order to gain greater insight into the intended sense and significance of some passage of Scripture along with an appropriate current application, it is most helpful to study the passage at hand along with a variety of supplementary, paratextual aids, e.g., a glossary of key terms, biblical cross references, illustrations, sectional introductions, and most important perhaps, a variety of descriptive-expository notes. For example, with reference to the portion cited above, some explanation would be necessary concerning the notion of "theophany" and its theological import when alluded to in such passages (e.g., 2:10).

speech (or better, preaching, recitation, chanting, etc.), that the intense drama of this prophetic discourse becomes fully apparent to the entire sensorium of receptors—thus enhancing the overall esthetic-emotional appeal and theological-ethical impact of its message. Ultimately, then, the ideal way to present a graphic, image-rich and metaphoric text like Joel's is via some audiovisual, including the appropriate musical, medium of transmission so that the listener's mind might be stimulated to "see" (cf. 2:4, 6) as well as to hear more of "the word of the Lord" (דְּבַר־יְהוָה–1:1) that the prophet was moved to proclaim (and have recorded for posterity). Only then can the vital, thematically contrastive, rhetorically compelling sense of a passage depicting the darkened sun, moon, and stars (in 2:10 and 3:15), for example, be adequately apprehended and appreciated, that is, emotively as well as cognitively, in the idiomatic-poetic vernacular of a living language.

2

The 'Word of the LORD' and the Organization of Amos

2.1 The discourse structure of Amos: Miracle or mirage?[1]

Due to the presence of so many instances of the 'divine messenger' and other formulas, all more or less variants announcing a prophetic proclamation of 'the Word of the Lord', the book of Amos appears to be one of the most clearly constructed of its type. For example, James Limburg calls attention to the 'sevenfold structures in the book of Amos's and concludes (1987:221–222):

> There are forty-nine divine speech formulas in Amos. These formulas occur in such a way that there are seven or, in one case fourteen, of them in each major section of the book. The distribution of these formulas is too close to the natural divisions of the book to be coincidental. Why they have been so distributed is a matter of conjecture. Could the distribution be explained on the basis of seven as an indicator of completeness, certifying each section of the book as well as the book as a whole as word from the Lord?

---

[1] An earlier version of this chapter appeared some years ago in *Occasional Papers in Translation and Textlinguistics* (OPTAT) 1988 2(4):1–51. It has been thoroughly revised and updated.

In view of the prevailing scholarly consensus which attributes the work as it stands to a corps of prophetic redactors, such significant structural unity would indeed be a miracle of composition. Coote, for example, views the book as being "the end result of a series of re-compositions of the original words of a named prophet" (1981:2). Bullock, in turn, draws attention to "the stamp of disarray that many commentators believe they see" (1986:62), particularly with respect to the numerous short, individualized sayings that exist outside the major oracles and visions which constitute the heart of the book. Most investigators would grant a certain measure of coherence to these 'oracles against the nations', found in the first two chapters, as well as to the series of vision reports that appears in chapters 7 and 8. But outside of these sections, there is considerable disagreement over how the text is formally and thematically organized and what the purpose is of this arrangement. Thus, what seemed at first to be a rather transparent, almost providential, organization of the discourse disappears like a mirage, as it were, in the heat of scholarly controversy and text-critical dispute.

In a valiant attempt to make some sense out of the plethora of conflicting proposals for structuring Amos according to some type of linear-based format, de Waard and Smalley turn to a concentric scheme of "messages and groups of messages which are balanced against each other in the first and last halves of the book" (1979:189). They advance an elaborate system of interlocking introversions alleged to span the book from beginning to end, thus representing its essential principle of organization and the primary means of articulating the prophet's message. This scheme looks quite impressive when printed on its own in outline form, but a closer examination of these patterns in conjunction with the actual text reveals some serious inadequacies along with several major problems of interpretation. These various points of difficulty, when coupled with conflicting proposals concerning even the linearly ordered arrangements, therefore serve only to raise further doubts not only about the integrity of the original discourse structure itself, but also regarding the diverse methodologies being advanced to explain it. Another problem that one often encounters in this connection when reading the scholarly literature is that the pursuit of form, or structure, seems almost to become an end in itself, and the results bear little or no relation to the theological and ethical content of the biblical text as it is rhetorically presented to the reader.

The special aim of this chapter is to explore some of the principal issues involved in the discourse analysis of prophetic literature in the Scriptures. It will be possible to take up the debate in only a preliminary sort of way as we consider primarily the matter of determining the larger discourse structure of Amos and its rhetorical implications.[2] This often involves having to make a decision among conflicting opinions and proposals regarding the text's organization. To begin with, I will focus upon the *divine speech formulas* as a means of introducing the process of demarcating the prophet's message and its persuasive organization. To what extent do these stereotyped phrases function as reliable structural, thematic, and/or motivational cues? This will lead to a consideration of some of the more detailed aspects of the book's carefully *patterned arrangement*. I will not be concerned, however, merely with form. An important part of the analysis will be an attempt to demonstrate the harmonious combination of form and content; in other words, how the formal patterns which are elucidated serve in turn to manifest key elements of Amos's provocative oracles to a largely hostile audience. In this connection I will discuss some of the chief points of tension as revealed by the text's organizational framework: topics which constituted the heart of his message and which, not unexpectedly, occasioned such bitter conflict when it was first proclaimed—a prophetic encounter graphically recorded in the midst of a series of visions (7:10–17). It will not be possible within the confines of this chapter to resolve all of the structural problems that scholars discern in the book of Amos. But it is hoped that my basic analysis will serve at least to clarify the nature of such difficulties and to suggest an initial methodology for dealing with them in a less arbitrary, more discourse-oriented and rhetorically sensitive manner.

2.2 Lexical-semantic recursion: An ancient means of text processing

The approach to discourse analysis that is being proposed here is based upon one of the most prominent features of biblical literature, namely, *recursion*.

---

[2] Although I did a thorough verse-by-verse exegesis of the book of Amos in preparation for my discourse analysis, it is not possible to present the results of that here. I can simply refer readers to some of the more helpful exegetical commentaries that I consulted along the way, namely: Anderson and Freeman (1989), Finley (1990), Mays (1969), Niehaus (1992), Smith (1989), Smith and Page (1995), and Stuart (1987). In this chapter I will focus on the discourse structure of Amos, thus interacting mainly with three studies that deal with this in detail, namely, de Waard and Smalley (1979), Dorsey (1999:277–286), and Wilson (1997:157–180).

It is no great revelation, of course, to say that these texts contain a great deal of repetition. This fact has been recognized and utilized by scholars in one way or another for centuries, no doubt since the time that the first analytical studies were made. It is also an important criterion that underlies most modern attempts to discover what arrangement of material the author (redactor) intended. Where the present method differs, in certain respects at least, from most of the others is in the complex and comprehensive role that it sees recursion as playing in the discourse. It is by no means the only literary device that these ancient authors employed to enhance the communication of their respective messages. But it is the one that definitely seems to be predominant in its overall inclusiveness, and primary in the way it organizes all of the others.

From this perspective, then, the various divine formulas that are scattered throughout the text of a book like Amos are only part of a much larger picture. Hence it is misleading to view the former in isolation from the other patterns of recursion that are manifested in the discourse, or to base one's understanding of the prophet's message solely on what significance formulas might have in the composition. These recurrent stereotyped sayings are a good place to begin the analysis since they are so concrete and obvious—well, nearly so. But one must go on to discover the other stylistic attributes of the text: those that involve repetition and those that do not (for example, figurative language, transitional expressions, vocatives, lexical and semantic shifts, etc.), in order to integrate all of these poetic components into a coherent plan of discourse arrangement and development. The goal is to determine the *rhetorical dynamics* of the original text, that is, to reveal the literary framework that best represents the way in which the biblical author (+/– redactor[s]) formulated his message so as to communicate it most effectively (that is, with relevance, appropriateness, impact, and appeal) in its initial setting.

A prior detailed examination of recursion in all of its facets and accompanying stylistic features was carried out on the book of Amos as a whole. Five principal dimensions of the phenomenon as manifested in the text were considered in particular. These may be conveniently summarized in terms of the following pairs of distinctions that served to guide the investigation.

2.2.1 Similarity–Contrast

A given text, or family of texts, may exhibit several types of recursion, which may be grouped under these two categories. *Similarity* would include the most obvious form of recursion, namely, exact repetition, as well as partial reiteration, synonymy, and complementariness. The latter refers to correspondences of a logical kind, such as means/purpose, reason/result, condition/consequence, concession/contraexpectation, and so forth. For example, many of the so-called judgment oracles of prophetic literature display a basic generic pattern of accusation or indictment (that is, reason) followed by verdict of condemnation (that is, result). Less commonly, but in many contexts more significantly, recursion is effected by means of a *contrast* either in general content or in specific motifs. This, too, may assume several different forms, such as an overt opposition (for example, positive/negative propositions), a divergence or dissimilarity with respect to a certain semantic feature, or a topical reversal. The joyous agricultural images of blessing and prosperity found in 9:13–15, for example, represent the climactic converse of the mournful scenes portrayed in 8:9–14, thus setting these two discourse segments into a clear thematic contrastive relationship with one another.

2.2.2 Form–Meaning

Within the broader distinction of similarity and contrast, recursion may be further differentiated according to whether we are dealing with textual form or content. Any message involves both elements, of course, but since in most contexts it is possible, and even necessary, to distinguish the two, this separation probably ought to be maintained. For one thing, a recursion that is based upon linguistic or literary *form,* whether phonological, grammatical, lexical, textual (involving the larger structures of a composition, and/or rhetorical (involving discourse pragmatics), is normally more perceptible to receptors, and hence more reliable as a cue or guide to the organization of a text as intended by its original author. Thus, it is both logical and practical to begin an investigation of the structure of Amos by considering the positioning of the repeated divine speech formulas.

Meaning, however, cannot be ignored when searching for significant correspondences within a discourse. Several types of meaning may be relevant in this endeavor. The most obvious is the *semantic* content or sense of a passage. Lexical reiteration will usually encompass the specific content being referred to as well, whereas the other kinds of formal recursion do not necessarily do so. Another important, but less apparent, type of meaning concerns the text's functional, or *pragmatic,* intent, whether pertaining to the book as a whole, an individual utterance, or a set of them. Amos begins, for example, with a series of oracles, each of which denounces the named addressees for their cruel, oppressive behavior and pronounces divine judgment upon them. Meaning includes the *emotive* aspect of the message, too, for the varied expression of strong feelings and attitudes may also form a deliberate pattern within the text, one that complements another of the textual dimensions. Israel's total lack of response to the Lord's measures of discipline, for example, produced a strong sense of divine regret, disappointment, and frustration (4:6, 8, 9, 10, 11)—as depicted anthropomorphically, of course, through the prophet's eyes and heart, for he undoubtedly experienced similar emotions and hoped to stir up similar feelings in the hearts (Heb 'bowels') of his addressees.

From the two primary dichotomies of form and meaning, then, there emerge a pair of important analytical principles—the first quantitative, the second qualitative in nature: The greater the number of formal and semantic elements of recursion that happen to coincide in the formation of a supposed pattern of discourse, the more reliable, or established, that particular structure would consequently be from an organizational standpoint. The *convergence* of additional poetic features at the key points of such a structural framework would obviously serve to lend support to the proposal. A corollary to the preceding is this: The structures thus revealed by a linguistic/literary investigation must be related in some significant way to the *communication* of the prophet's message, especially his major themes and emphases. The latter criterion is admittedly a rather circular proposition because structural patterns in the text are employed to discover its main thematic constituents in the first place. The point is that it is necessary to keep these two aspects of discourse analysis together and in proper balance throughout all of the procedures concerned because a consideration of form without meaning is a sterile, academic exercise, while the converse may well turn out to be completely baseless and hence indefensible. Both extremes are abundantly illustrated in the wealth of scholarly literature about Amos.

2.2.3 Linear–Concentric

The structures formed by recursion in a given text may be either linear or concentric in their arrangement. A *linear* pattern unfolds steadily forward in progressive fashion from a point of beginning to its ending, however distant this may be in the discourse. A prominent example of a linear plan of organization occurs at the beginning of Amos, where we find a series of eight oracles of judgment presented, each following basically the same sequence of generic steps as it proceeds—all except for the climactic final instance, that of Israel. Most overtly marked rhetorical structures in biblical literature are indeed of a linear variety, no doubt because they are the easiest for a listening audience to process conceptually. The development of ideas coincides with the chronological movement of the discourse. The sensory act of perceiving the message and the cognitive process of decoding it are going in the same direction, so to speak. A variety of linear patterns are possible, ranging from the simple single sequence, that is, A–B–C–D–E, to more complex types of recurrent series, such as: A–B–C; A'–B'–C', A"–B"–C"; A–B–B–C–C–D...; and so forth.

A *concentric* structure, in contrast to a linear one, features a well defined midpoint in its development as well as a sequence of semantic constituents that reverse direction at that middle juncture in order to proceed back to the conceptual beginning. In other words, there is an introversion of ideas whereby the components are manifested first from X to Y and then back again from Y to X. Temporally, of course, a concentric construction within narrative discourse moves forward just like a linear one. Conceptually, however, it does not. Once the structural center, or core, has been reached, a characteristic reversal occurs, and the basic thoughts start regressing in ordered, step-by-step fashion to return, more or less, to the starting point again. Normally, such recursion is not exact, but there is a progressive augmentation of the main constituent notions occurring at the same time, both to maintain interest and to highlight the main elements of the author's theme line. Thus, despite the correspondences which may be present, the ending of the discourse is not really the same as its beginning, either cognitively or emotively, because it has been subtly, and often substantially, modified and refined by the content that has been presented in incremental fashion between them.

The simplest instance of a concentric format is the tripartite A–B–A' *ring construction*. Several examples of this occur in the woe oracles of chapters

5–6: An idea is introduced (for example, a warning), a graphic illustration is then given, and finally the initial theme is taken up once more only to be brought to an abrupt but forceful close (see the structural outline in section 2.2). The *chiasmus* adds a fourth internal constituent, that is, A–B = B'–A'. In Amos these chiastic constructions seem to appear mainly on the microstructure of discourse, for example, in the lament that begins chapter 5:

A: *House of Israel* (1) – B: **fallen** (2) = B': Soldiers **killed** (3) – A': *House of Israel* (4).

An *introversion*, then, may be expanded to any length, though such constructions are rarely perceptible much beyond seven distinct elements, at least from an oral–aural perspective:

A–B–C–D–E ... = ... (E')–D'–C'–B'–A'.

As shown above, the middle (E') unit is optional as a correlate of E. A significant introversion of this type appears at the structural center of Amos as a whole, namely, 5:1–17 (see 2.3). In such longer compositions, the crucial concepts, those thoughts or attitudes which the poet/prophet wishes to emphasize, are normally found within the central nucleus, or alternatively, in both the middle and the ending (end stress). The process of recursion can apply also at different stages within a larger constituent structure; in other words, a particular pattern, whether linear or concentric, may occur just once, or it may itself be repeated to form a complex macro- formation, such as is evident in the series of five vision reports that distinguish the final third of the book (chs. 7–9).

2.2.4 Horizontal–Hierarchical

As already suggested in the preceding discussion, the patterns formed by recursion (and other devices) may be realized on a number of different structural levels, or degrees of inclusion. Indeed, they appear in all their diversity and complexity even on the micro-level of discourse, namely, that of individual bi- or tri-cola. Here is where most instances of the more formal type are found, such as those constructed by phonological, morphological, or syntactic means. Since we are primarily concerned with the text of Amos as a whole, our attention will be focused on the macro-level of discourse, which roughly extends from the first definable poetic-rhetorical unit above the bicolon—the 'strophe,' to give it a name—and proceeds on up through whatever intermediate strata there may be (for example, stanza, section, oracle/hymn, etc.) to encompass the entire text. *Horizontal* structures, then, are developed along a single level of formal and/or semantic organization. A *hierarchical* pattern, on the other hand, is considered more from a vertical perspective, comprising a number of included, and including, horizontal units, all arranged in pyramid-like fashion. These two types of arrangement will be illustrated in detail in the next section.

2.2.5 Scribal–Oral

The various oracles of Amos were first presented in oral form to a listening audience, being pronounced either as an independent prophetic discourse (e.g., 5:1–17); as part of an embedded narrative (e.g., 7:1–9, 10–17), or as a vision-report (e.g., 8:1–14). Some time thereafter, these distinct texts were probably gathered together, either by the prophet himself or by his scribe or a disciple, and composed in more permanent written form— perhaps in several editions before the final canonical document took shape, as it has been transmitted over the centuries. The intricately patterned discourse organization of Amos as a whole (see 2.2) would indicate that this compositional process was not the product of some patchwork redactional activity,[3] but was rather the result of careful literary construction, with a minimum of additional editing, most likely by a single hand.[4] However, these same rhythmic and recursive structures would also suggest that the text of Amos was written with oral proclamation in view so that the 'roar of the LORD' (1:2; cf. Hos 11:10) would have its full impact upon an audience (the vast majority of whom would have been non-literates). The residual orality of Amos is difficult then to perceive and appreciate when the text is read silently to oneself, especially in translation; it is really manifested,

---

[3] For example, Wolff (1977) suggests that the prophetic "sayings" found in chs. 3–6 "represent the first of six discrete layers of material in the present book. Next come the two five-part series which also stem from Amos: the oracles against the nations and the visions. There follow the early Amos school; the Bethel-interpretation of the period of Josiah; the Deuteronomistic redaction; and finally the post-exilic salvation eschatology" (Auld 1986:55). Finley offers a cogent critique of Wolff's approach and others like it (1990:110–112). I would therefore subscribe also to his conclusion: "there is every reason to suppose that the written form of the book came into existence either during the prophet's lifetime or shortly afterward. It seems best to take the statement that the 'words' of the book belong to Amos at its maximum and assume that Amos was responsible even for their organization" (ibid., 113).

[4] Good literature, in contrast to credible theology, is not composed by committee.

as intended, only in oral-aural form when performed—from memory and in the original Hebrew.[5] Of course, for the vast majority of receptors, a translation of some type is necessary to provide access to the Scriptures, but this undertaking must also give due attention to the sound-sensitive oral-aural dynamics of the biblical text and how this can be best re-presented—or re-created—in the current vernacular medium of communication. The importance of orality in the analysis of biblical texts and its special implications for my study of Amos has been well-stated by Victor Wilson (1997:55–56):

> The world of print and the oral world are configured very differently.... The oral world, and the literature it produced for oral performance, used a grammar of conventional sound markers to plot the movement and the progress of compositions. Inclusions frame portions of the text like paragraph and chapter markers in print, while refrains build repetitive patterns that create a mnemonic framework, a structure for remembering for an aurally-dependent audience. Chiasms use principles of framing and balance to build a teaching like series of nested boxes around a center, where the main point lies.

In concluding this section, it is important to note that the discourse structure of a literary-oratorical composition need not be slavishly described in terms of these five diagnostic pairs. Indeed, the proposed categories might well be rearranged to accomplish a different analytical purpose, and other features could certainly be added. But the ones outlined above do furnish at least some of the primary distinctions that need to be observed when analyzing the many intricate and interrelated patterns of textual recursion that occur in a literary work of the artistic quality of Amos, the herdsman-farmer. The purpose of such a multifaceted analysis is to observe how the

---

[5] The final requirement—the original language—is a critical factor that tends to be downplayed or even completely ignored by certain scholars who "seek to place the prophetic utterances into a context of performance criticism. We will examine the dynamics of performance—how a performer is granted social power and how that power operates on an audience. From there, we will look at changes that take place in the construction of a script and how some of those changes might be evidenced in the prophetic literature" (Doan and Giles 2005:x). While the effort to carry out such a performative effort (with reference to Amos, cf. ibid., chs. 4–6) is indeed a laudable attempt to achieve greater audience engagement, in addition to a better understanding of the prophet's message, it remains a rather speculative activity. This danger becomes apparent when certain interpretive conclusions are drawn that find no basis in the original text. For example, when considering 'the relationship between the prophet and the scribe (playwright)'—the latter designation already being problematic—Doan and Giles conclude the following: "Our investigation will lead us to suggest that what was once considered a mutually beneficial relationship between the prophet and his disciples may in reality have been a struggle in which the prestige of the charismatic prophet performer was usurped by the power of the pen" *(loc. cit.)*.

formal features of the discourse complement one another both to facilitate and to enhance the expression of its essential prophetic message from Yahweh to his wayward people. The challenge for contemporary communicators—whatever the medium of transmission used—is to reproduce more of the rhetorical force as well as the aesthetic impact of this Hebrew prophet's stirring words.

2.3 A structural outline of Amos

My overview of the discourse organization of Amos is based primarily upon the compositional technique of recursion, with special attention being paid to the devices of *inclusio* (corresponding beginning and ending of the same structural unit), *anaphora* (corresponding beginnings of different units), and *epiphora* (corresponding endings of different units). But other prominent rhetorical features (e.g., the use of a vocative, imperative, rhetorical question, word order variation, condensation, irony, personification, hyperbole, etc.) and literary processes (e.g., the use of imagery, prophetic formulas, patterns of seven,[6] shifts in poetic lineation, a change of topic/speaker/genre,[7] etc.) were also taken into account in the analysis as substantiating evidence for or against a particular interpretation of the data and consequent arrangement of the text.[8] In addition to the sequence of structural units and their designations, the outline includes some selected comments explaining, by way of summary, several of the principal criteria used in order to define a specific segment of the composition. The following proposal of Amos's five-part discourse organization was arrived at only after a detailed textual study of Amos, considering both the macro- as well as the micro-structure of the book.

---

[6] Dorsey lists 23 examples of "the prolific use of sevenfold structuring" to be found in Amos (1999:277–278). A number of these coincide with my own analysis made a decade earlier and the study of Limburg (1987).

[7] "Amos is a fine example of the melding of prophetic genres: oracles of judgment and woes, lamentations, visions, prophetic reports, and so on. Amos also incorporates the hymnic elements and doxologies that we associate with the cultic worship practices of the nation" (Wilson 1997:179).

[8] These different artistic, rhetorical, and structural features and how to study them in diverse Scripture texts are discussed in Wendland 2004:chs. 4–7.

2.3.1 Introduction to the prophecy (Am 1:1-2)

A. *Superscription* (v. 1): prophetic background—who, when, where, why, how?
B. *Prologue* (v. 2): thematic synopsis—the Lord roars from Zion (Judah) to Carmel (Israel)

Structural description: These two verses would appear to comprise a single introductory unit, the aperture to the prophecy as a whole, for the following reasons:

- *Cohesion:* 'The words of Amos…and he said' (*waw*-sequential verb form)…(shift in focus from prophet to deity) 'Yahweh will roar… He will utter his voice…' (the divine name occurs in the center of the unit)
- *Inclusio:* 'herdsmen' (v. 1a)…'shepherds' (v. 2b)
- *Key term:* earthquake—central position in the introduction; employed as a symbol of judgment in subsequent oracles, thus associated with the Lord's roaring, (that is, a significant collocation of lexical items)
- *Pattern:* 'king of Judah…king of Israel' (v. 1) 'Zion (Jerusalem)… Carmel' (v. 2)

2.3.2 Oracles against the nations (Am 1:3–2:16)

A. Damascus (Syria)   1:3–5
B. Gaza (Philistia)   1:6–8
C. Tyre   1:9–10
D. Edom   1:11–12
E. Ammon   1:13–15
F. Moab   2:1–3
G. Judah   2:4–5

Structural description of A through G: This closely knit sequence of judgment proclamations constitutes the first of the three major collections of oracles that make up the book of the prophet Amos (that is, after the introduction (1:1–2), set one (1:3–2:16), set two (3:1–6:14), set three (7:1–9:10) with the book's conclusion (9:11–15).[9]

---
[9] My proposal for the linear macrostructure of Amos agrees in large measure with that of Niehaus (1992:328) and Finley (1990:115–116), and in essence also with the chiastic arrangements of Dorsey (1999:285) and Wilson (1997:162). These structures all differ from that given in de Waard and Smalley, i.e., 1:1–5:3, 5:4–15, and 5:16–9:15 (1979:195). The obvious imbalance of the last proposal, i.e., the relatively small middle section, is an initial indication of its improbability (on this point, see further below).

2.3 A structural outline of Amos

Each of the oracles in this first section, except the last one, follows a set formulaic pattern that is enunciated in judicial style proceeding from the Lord's indictment to his verdict. The first four nations cited form a chiastic circuit geographically around Israel (that is, A (NE), B (SW), C (NW), and D (SE). The last four were all blood brothers of Israel. The point of overlap, that is, Edom (D), was an especially bitter enemy of both Israel and Judah (cf. 2 Kgs 8:22; Isa 34:5–17; Jer 49:7–22; Lam 4:21–22; Mal 1:2–5). The focus of attention is rhetorically sharpened to rest finally upon the primary addressees, the leaders of the Northern Kingdom, thus creating a powerful surprise effect to initiate the burden of Amos's message of judgment.

Every condemnatory cycle has the potential for including six constituents, or elements, which are realized in a fixed linear order:

1. **Proclamation**—divine source: 'Thus says Yahweh...' (formula)
2. **Indictment** (general): 'For three transgressions of [X] and for four, I will not withdraw it...'
   (The numerical n/n+1 formula in this case adds up to seven, which has special significance in Amos; that is, it indicates fullness, completeness, the final total, the last straw before judgment!)
3. **Evidence** (specific): 'for they...(did such and such)'
4. **Verdict of condemnation** (general): 'And I will send a fire against...'
   (Fire is a prominent image of divine punishment in Amos—cf. Am 5:6, 7:4.)
5. **Punishment** (specific): 'and I will' (do such and such)
   (The so-called Covenant curses of the Mosaic Law are here invoked even upon the pagan nations for their violation of a natural, divinely instituted international law of fundamental justice among humanity—cf. Stuart 1987:308.)
6. **Conclusion** (divine source): 'says...Yahweh' (formula)

In addition to this repeated format, which is truncated in the case of nations C, D, and G (that is, after element 4), a general coherence is created within each unit by means of the predominant battle imagery (except for nations G and H—see below). This stereotyped series of divine judgments reaches its climax in the case of the latter two, that is, Judah and Israel, and the nature of the indictment shifts as Yahweh condemns them for serious breaches of his Covenant Law in general and specific terms, respectively.[10] The principal focus of attention rests ultimately upon

---

[10] The religious dimension of covenantal violation is introduced in the oracle against Judah in 2:4 and marked by a chiastic construction: a 'because they have rejected' – b 'the instruction of the LORD' = b' 'and his statutes' – a' 'they have not kept' (Niehaus 1992:361).

the last nation mentioned, Israel (Am 2:6), which was the direct recipient of the prophet's message. Formally, then, the oracles against Judah and Israel are quite distinct, but thematically, the people are one—rebuked together, the compound seventh oracle in the sequence of wickedness.[11] Thus, the roar of the Lord, which is directed from Zion against Carmel (cf. 1:2), is a demonstration that both nations will be held responsible for their spiritual deficiency as manifested by their many crimes against both God (religious) and man (social).

H. Israel   (Am 2:6–16)

    a *Seven* socially oriented sins of Israel (2:6–8)
       b Yahweh's unfailing provision for Israel (2:9–11)
       b' Israel's faithless rejection of Yahweh (2:12)
    a' *Seven* specific personal punishments upon Israel (2:13–16)

Structural description: The preceding chiastic pattern is logically ordered, that is, (a–a'): reason–result, (b–b'): base–contrast. Once more the number seven, the biblical numerical symbol of completeness, is prominent in the overall plan of organization.

The preceding concentric structure interlocks with another which displays an alternating arrangement of key features concerning the main events and their associated agents:

    c 'I'—blessing (2:9–11)
       d 'you'—rejection (2:12)
    c' 'I'—cursing (2:13)
       d' 'he' (= you)—failure (2:13–16)

Observe the significant presence of the divine name at the heart of this whole structure, juxtaposed with an appellation the sons of Israel, which will be foregrounded in the book's third major division (see 2.2.3), and surrounded by his slighted agents in chiastic order:

---

[11] No matter what structural scheme is proposed, the last and longest judgment—against 'Israel'—is highlighted. Some commentators call attention to a '7 + 1' literary pattern in the prophets, which similarly posits a rhetorical stress point at the end of the sequence (at unit '+1') (Paul 1991:22–23).

prophets/Nazirites//Nazirites/prophets (2:11–12).[12]

The section closes with the key phrase "in that day," which previews subsequent oracles of both condemnation and consolation in the former and latter times, respectively.

2.3.3 Oracles against the house of Israel (Am 3:1–6:14)

Five collections of oracles (oracle sets) run through Amos chapters 3–6, namely, three *proclamation* sets ('Listen…') followed by two *disaster* ('Woe…') sets, all of which predict a forthcoming time of punishment for the evil nation of Israel.[13]

2.3.3.1 Oracle set 1: 'Hear this word…' (Am 3:1–15)

Cycle A: The threat of imminent punishment (Am 3:1–8)

    A Introduction: 'Listen…Yahweh has spoken' (1–2)
    reminder of the foundational Exodus salvation event; *indictment* (implicit)–*verdict* (therefore…) pattern of a Covenant Lawsuit

        B Illustration: *seven* rhetorical questions (3–6)
        all involve *cause–effect* relations with a progressive intensification of imagery which peaks in the ultimate divine Cause, 'Yahweh' (6b)

    A' Conclusion—climax (7–8)
    the *lion* (= Yahweh! – symmetrical parallelism) *roars* through his prophets, warning all listeners to 'fear', that is, hearken to the prophetic voice!

Structural description: The A–B–A' ring construction of the first oracle is readily apparent. It begins with an extended prophetic formula ('Hear this word…') and a corresponding lengthy vocative construction ('O sons of Israel…'). The outer boundaries are marked by a formulaic *inclusio* in

---

[12] "Israel's silencing of the prophets…is balanced against God's choosing the prophets…; Israel's corrupting the Nazirites…is balanced against God's choosing the Nazirites…" (de Waard and Smalley 1979: 200).

[13] De Waard and Smalley argue that 3:1–2 ends, rather than begins, a major discourse unit (1:2–3:2) (1979:193, 200). There are too many structural markers of *aperture* that contradict such a reading, however, as does the discourse organization of Amos as a whole (supported by Dorsey and others 1999:279).

chiastic order: 'he has spoken—Yahweh'/'Yahweh—he has spoken' (v. 1a/8b). A characteristic feature of the style of Amos is the formal integration that occurs between major segments of the discourse. A good example of this is found in 3:8 with the mention of a lion roaring, which recalls the prophet's opening words (1:2) and echoes a line in the middle section of this cycle (3:4).

Cycle B: The punishment is specified (Am 3:9–15)[14]

>A <u>Introduction</u> (9–11): dramatic call (imperatives) to witness Israel's judgment; *indictment–verdict* (therefore) general *socioeconomic* offenses = > destruction of military stronghold

>>B <u>Illustration</u> (12): a vivid simile with ironic reversal: Yahweh is both 'shepherd' and 'lion'—he will rescue only pieces of ravaged Israel.

>A' <u>Conclusion</u> (13–15): the call to witnesses, indictment, and judgment of A is continued; general *religious* offenses = > destruction of mansions of the wealthy

Structural description: This oracle, which features another A–B–A' structure, roughly corresponds to structural elements 3–5 in the earlier series of denunciations against the nations (2.2.2). Here the application is to Israel—the unjust, oppressive upper-class in particular. Unit A is made cohesive by repeated references to 'fortresses' (9a, 10b, 11b). Unit A' begins with a prominent anaphoric (unit-opening) motif: 'Hear!' (cf. Am 3:1). It also manifests an *inclusio* involving man-made structures corresponding to that of unit A, that is, 'house(s)' in vv. 13a and 15b, plus the formulaic 'utterance of Yahweh'. A strong ironic and judicial overtone extends throughout cycle two, with total punishment being inflicted upon the rich living in their houses of luxury and idolatry (vv. 11, 15, and Beth-el 'house of God'). This justly befits these leaders' many transgressions against both their fellow man (vv. 9b, 10b) and also their 'LORD God Almighty' (vv. 13b–14).

---

[14] Wilson (1995:166) and Dorsey (1999:280) posit an extended ring structure (introversion) covering 3:1–15, with its center situated at 3:10. This proposal puts the thematic emphasis on Israel's sin and ignores 3:8, which in my scheme highlights the 'roar of the LORD' through his prophets (cf. 3:1, 13).

2.3 A structural outline of Amos

2.3.3.2 Oracle set 2: 'Hear this word...' (Am 4:1–13)

This oracle set is introduced by the same prophetic formula that opened the preceding set (i.e., structural *anaphora*); it is comprised of four distinct sections that are arranged in an A-B=B'-A' chiastic pattern as follows:

  A Introduction (1–3): Denunciation of the oppressive wealthy women of Israel; focus upon socioeconomic oppression highlighted by sharp irony

   B Indictment (4–5): Israel's sins specified—*seven* samples;
   Cause: focus upon religious apostasy, irony again prominent

   B' Judgment (6–11): Israel's punishments specified—*seven* samples
   Consequence: seven punishments in increasing severity: no bread (6) < no rain/water (7–8) < crop diseases (9a) < locusts (9b) < plague (10a) defeat in battle (10b) < summary climax: total overthrow—fire! (11)

  A' Conclusion (12–13): Acclamation of the God who will punish Israel—
   Warning: 'Therefore...prepare to meet your God, O Israel!' (12)
   Doxology: a brief panegyric oracle in praise of Yahweh (13)

Structural description: The initial oracle of this section, 4:1–3 (A), like its concluding counterpart (A'), is clearly distinct from the paired judgment oracles that occur in the middle (B and B'). Furthermore, A also gives evidence of structural links in both directions, that is, with what has preceded and with what follows in Amos. There is an initial shift to more specific addressees, namely, the 'cows of Bashan', which might have elicited a note of surprise in Amos's audience: 'Do you mean that the (wealthy) women are as wicked as the leading men of this land?!' The *accusation–condemnation* pattern of the preceding oracles is continued (A: 1 => C: 2–3), and mention of the 'mountain of Samaria' recalls a similar reference in 3:9 *(anaphora).* On the other hand, reference to the Creator of 'the mountains' who will one day bring judgment upon the inhabitants of Samaria forms an inclusio at the end of this oracle set (v. 13). The entire section spanning Am 4:1–13 does not include the key word 'house,' which is prominent in both the preceding and the subsequent units, e.g., 'house of Jacob' (3:13), 'house of Israel' (5:1;

an instance of *exclusio*). This unit is possibly (depending on one's reading of the text) rounded out by an *inclusio* referring to 'mountain(s)': 'mountain of Samaria' (1a), and 'toward [Mount] Harmon (3b).

The second oracle (B) closes with an emphatic utterance: 'For thus you love (to do), O Sons of Israel!' (v. 5b). The set of short judgment pronouncements in B¹ then follows a similar pattern of construction: a specification of the Lord's act of chastisement followed by an emphatic *epiphoric* (unit-ending) refrain, 'yet you have not re-turned to me!' The formula 'utterance/oracle of the [Sovereign] LORD' recurs seven times in oracles A, B, and B¹ to help demarcate the section as a whole (vv. 3, 5, 6, 8, 9, 11).

The concluding combined oracle (A¹) begins with a climactic 'therefore' *(laken)* and ends (v. 13) with several important epiphoric elements: Yahweh's theophanic revelation to man (cf. Am 3:7) coupled with the formula 'Yahweh, the God of hosts, (is) his name' (cf. Am 5:27, 9:6). The doxology of v. 13 responds to the preceding challenge to Israel ('prepare to meet your God') and may, together with Am 5:8–9 and 9:5–6, form part of an ancient hymn of praise. It functions here as a transitional device in the book's larger discourse structure, being introduced, as already noted, by the stark judgment of v. 12, yet also pointing ahead to the thematic core of the book in the next oracle set (5:8c).

2.3.3.3 Oracle set 3: 'Hear this word...' (Am 5:1–17)

This collection of prophetic texts begins like the two preceding sts (3:1, 4:1; *anaphora*) Here we reach the apparent structural–thematic center of the book of Amos. It is distinguished as such by its content, a prominent (final?) call to 'Israel' to repent (5:4–6, 14–15),[15] and by its form of an extended introversion consisting of nine distinct, but interrelated segments (cf. de Waard 1977; de Waard and Smalley 1979:189–192; Dorsey 1999:281; Wilson 1997:171):

---

[15] Doan and Giles missclassify 5:1–17 as a 'Funerary dirge' (2005:107), which applies only to 1–2 and 16–17; this genre is used by Amos as an emphatic bracket around the enclosed accusations/appeals.

2.3 A structural outline of Amos

A **Lament**—part 1: occasion = Israel's 'falling' and urban decimation (1–3)
  B **Appeal to repentance:** 'seek Yahweh...*and live*' (4–6)
    C **Accusation:** against those who pervert 'justice' and 'righteousness' (5:7)
      D **Affirmation:** *doxology* lauding Yahweh's power to create (8a-d)
        E **Confessional core:** 'Yahweh is his name!' (5:8e)[16]
      D' **Affirmation:** *doxology* (continued, 5 + 2 = 7 attributes), now lauding Yahweh's power to destroy (5:9)
    C' **Accusation** (continued): against those who oppose 'truth'— a specification of the general indictment found in segment C (10–13)
  B' **Appeal to repentance:** 'seek good...*and live*' (14–15)
A' **Lament**—part 2. consequence = 'wailing' throughout the land (16–17)

Structural description: These 17 verses also exhibit the main structural features of the Hebrew (qînah) *funerary lament* genre (5:1; Stuart 1987:344), that is, a description of the tragedy (vv. 2–3; cf. 2 Sam 1:19, 23), a call to respond (vv. 4–6, 14–15; cf. 2 Sam 1:20), direct address to the fallen—or in this case those about to fall (vv. 7–13; cf. 2 Sam 1:26)—and a summons to mourning (vv. 16–17; cf. 2 Sam 1:21).

The individual components of this introversion are also tightly constructed internally, with all of them exhibiting close parallel patterning. This feature serves to artistically define the structure as a whole and give cohesion to its included segments (strophes). Several segments are concentrically composed; strophe B, for example, manifests a chiastic organization. This is based on an introductory general reference to the addressees together with a positive exhortation for a frame and an internal set of negative utterances involving shrine names:

a House of Israel
  b Seek Me and live!
    c Not Bethel
      d Not Gilgal
        e Not Beersheba
      d' Gilgal to captivity
    c' Bethel to nothing
  b' Seek Yahweh and live
a' House of Joseph

---

[16] The structural center of this extended ring construction and the religious content being expressed appears to be highlighted by micro-chiastic arrangements as well, for example, v. 7: a 'you who turn' – b 'upward' – c 'justice' = c' 'and righteousness' – b' 'earthward' – a' 'you throw'; v. 8: a 'and who turns' – b 'to morning' – c 'blackness' = c '' 'and day' – b' 'to night' – a' 'he darkens' (Niehaus 1992:418).

The significance of 'Beersheba' at the heart of this introversion may rest in the fact that it was located in the southernmost part of the southern kingdom of Judah (but apparently still frequented by northerners), as opposed to 'Bethel' and 'Gilgal', which were important cult centers of Israel in the north of the divided kingdom.

The implicit indictment of segment C is introduced in a way that corresponds formally to that of later woe oracles (cf. 5:18, 6:1). As noted above, the opposing (that is, creation–destruction) halves of the doxology (D and D'), which revolve around the name of Yahweh, are composed of seven (5 + 2) descriptive and attributive statements. In the other two hymnic excerpts found in Amos, that is, 4:13 and 9:5-6, the exclamation 'Yahweh (is) his name!' occurs at the close of the portion, whereas here, perhaps due to the larger pattern of introversion, it is placed at the center.

Segments C and C' also pattern together in a twofold terrace pattern (enveloping the central focus on Yahweh, who is about to execute judgment, D–D') as follows:

> a General accusation by Yahweh against powerful oppressors (5:7)
>   b Specific accusations, e.g., 'you trample the poor...' (5:10–11a)
>   c Consequence: 'Therefore...' (5:11b-c)
> a' General accusation by Yahweh against powerful oppressors (5:12a)
>   b' Specific accusations, e.g., 'you turn aside the poor' (5:12b-c)
>   c' Consequence: 'Therefore...' [await disaster in silence] (5:13)

A lexical chiasm within a similar linear alternating structure appears in the LORD's appeal of segments B:

> a 'seek **good** and not <u>evil</u>'
>   b 'that you may live; Yahweh will be with you...' (5:14)
> a' 'hate <u>evil</u> and love **good**...'
>   b' 'perhaps Yahweh will be merciful to the remnant of Joseph' (5:15)

At the heart of this construction (5:14c), there may be an ironic reference to the overconfident word of the apostates ('just as you say')—in contrast to the thematically central word of Yahweh (5:16a). The concept of 'remnant', which becomes the focus of the concluding oracles of the book, is here introduced for the first time in Amos (in contrast to 5:6b).

2.3 A structural outline of Amos

The closing oracle (segment A') seemingly complements the opening lament (segment A) by means of a sequence of references to mourning, presumably over the many 'fallen' in Israel (5:2-3), that is, the *effect* of a prior *cause*. The next oracle is phonologically prefigured in the interjection of direct speech: *hô-hô* 'Alas! Alas!' (5:16b), which sounds similar to the cry: *hôy* 'Woe to...!' (5:18; contra Coote 1981:18). Finally, there are also a number of intersegmental cohesive links within oracle set 3, effected by both phonological and lexical correspondences, such as: 'the house of Israel' in A/B (1a/4a, *anaphora*); a contrastive human 'turning' from justice to bitterness (injustice) in segment C, but a divine 'turning' from dawn to darkness in segment D (7a/8a); and focus on the action/word of 'Yahweh, the God of armies' in B'/A' (15b/16a).

2.3.3.4 Oracle set 4: 'Woes' upon Israel (Am 5:18-27)

There are three poetic sections (strophes) in this oracle set, the first two of which manifest a similar manner of arrangement (A-B = B'-A'). In strophe A the horror of the future 'day of Yahweh' is graphically previewed in ironic fashion for the fallen of the 'house of Israel' (cf. Am 5:1-3, 16-17), who are longing for this time (participle after *hôy*, v. 18) in the vain hope of deliverance. The reason for this terrible reversal is then outlined (B), and its implementation through the agency of 'Yahweh, the God of armies', is prophesied at the end of the unit (C).[17]

A. **Warning**: the day of the LORD will be awful! (5:18-20)

    a Darkness, not light on 'the day of Yahweh' (18)
       b Illustration: no escape (bear)! (19a)
       b' Illustration: no escape (snake)! (19b)
    a' Darkness, not light on 'the day of Yahweh' (20)

B. **Indictment**: a series of seven negatively-phrased complaints concerning the externally active, but ethically dead religious cult, which is characterized by an excess of ritualized outward formalism in worship (5:21-24).

---

[17] Dorsey (1999:282) and Wilson (1997:171-173) incorporate 5:18-27 as a tripartite portion of a larger chiastic structure that embraces chapters five and six (5:18-6:14). Dorsey's strophic structure corresponds with mine ('coming disaster', 18-20; 'what Yahweh hates', 21-24; and 'threat of exile', 25-27), but their internal organization is not discerned.

    a Religious activities (feasts, assemblies) (21)
        b Offerings (burnt, grain) (22a)
        b' Offerings (fellowship) (22b)
    a' Religious activities (songs, harp music) (23)
    CLIMAX: *Contrast*—admonition to act rather with justice and righteousness (24)

C. **Verdict:** a logical progression, grounded in Israel's history, leading to a surprising negative consequence of the people failure to act as desired by Yahweh (v. 24)—an ironically appropriate punishment for the people's apostasy; the temporal point of reference moves from past, through the present, and toward the ominous future (5:25–27)

a. *Premise:* Yahweh's covenant with Israel was not based upon ritual observances and strict cultic practices—as enumerated in vv. 21–23 (25)
b. *Contrast:* the foundation of the covenant was fidelity, which Israel has failed to fulfill, that is, instances of syncretistic worship are cited (26)
c. *Conclusion:* therefore Yahweh will reverse the Exodus—captivity is the just result (27, cf. Am 5:5).

Structural description: The notion of the 'day of Yahweh' lends cohesion to strophe A along with the incorporated rhetorical questions in a and a'. The night/day imagery recalls the theophanic core of the preceding section, a reminder that Yahweh's creative power can also be applied to destroy wickedness (5:8–9). Similarly, the day of Yahweh will turn out to be a day of judgment, instead of deliverance, for all the ungodly in Israel.

Yahweh's utter rejection of Israel's lifeless rituals gives conceptual unity to strophe B, which peaks out in the distinct antithetical exhortation of v. 24. This verse stands outside the chiastic structure for added emphasis and is the key thematic passage of the entire oracle set that spans 5:18–27.[18] Similar appeals for 'righteousness' appear at key structural nodes elsewhere in chapters 5–6 (that is, 5:7, 15, and 6:12).

Strophe C opens with another rhetorical question. Formally then, it carries on from v. 20, but thematically it stems from the argument ending in v. 23. There appears to be an ironic twist at the end, which corresponds to

---

[18] The key ethical concepts of 5:24 lie buried, unnoted, in the macro-chiastic schemes of Dorsey (1999:282) and Wilson (1997:172).

the initial irony in v. 18 (a rhetorical *inclusio*): On 'the day of the LORD' Israel will be expelled into captivity—out of the land (v. 27) that it entered many years before from the wilderness (v. 25). The people will be taken into a land 'beyond Damascus' (that is, Assyria), whose gods they were now worshipping (v. 26). The latter threat is a concluding element *(epiphora)* also in the next oracle (6:7, 14). Mention of the name of 'Yahweh, the God of hosts' (v. 27), forms another *epiphora* with 4:13 and an *exclusio* with 6:8 (that is, the two references demarcate by exclusion an intervening discourse segment, namely, 6:1-7). The closure of this oracle is thus very prominently marked by a number of literary-structural cues.

2.3.3.5 Oracle set 5: More woes upon Israel (Am 6:1–14)

Destruction of the nation and exile are predicted in a series of three A-B-A' ring structures, each of which follows a similar topical development. This 'woe'-full *(hôy,* 6:1a) oracle set, which spotlights the moral and social corruption of the rich/ruling class in Israel, complements the preceding one in which their general religious and spiritual decay is emphasized. Three specific aspects of daily life are pointed to as having lulled the land into a false sense of security:

A. Their ostentatious **wealth**—*self-indulgence* (6:1–7)
    a Condemnation: Yahweh mocks the pride of the wealthy 'men' (1–2; cf. 4:1–3)
       b *Illustration:* Seven signs of decadence (3–6)
    a' Consequence: 'Therefore...exile'! (7)

B. Their protective **security**—*self-confidence* (6:8–11)
    a Condemnation: The 'pride of Jacob' (8)[19]
       b *Illustration:* A dramatic mini-narrative (9–10)
    a' Consequence: 'For behold...!'—destruction of castles (11)

C. Their oppressive **power**—*self-conceit* (6:12–14)
    a Condemnation: Perversion of justice (12)
       b *Illustration:* Self-indictment in direct discourse (13)
    a' Consequence: 'For behold...!'—another nation will 'oppress' Israel! (14)

---

[19] Yahweh's aversion to human pride is here underscored by a chiastic construction: a 'I detest' – b 'the pride of Jacob' = b' 'and his fortresses' – a' 'I hate' (Niehaus 1992:443).

Structural description: An obvious *anaphoric* motif begins the oracle A: 'Woe to those...' (cf. 5:18). A note of irony and sarcasm prevails throughout the whole section. The first cycle is bounded by an *inclusio:* the foremost of the nation will be the 'first' (pun) to go into exile. The reference to exile is an *epiphoric* marker as noted before (for example, 5:27, cf. 2.3.3.4). Word play (on 'exile') and alliteration *(sar mirzach sirûchîm)* converge to mark the conclusion of this segment and to highlight its main ideas.

The repeated mention of 'palaces/houses'—first to denounce, and then to predict their destruction, forms an including envelope within oracle B. This pattern and theme is similar to what is found also in Am 3:9–15.

Oracle C is more conceptually diverse internally, but its boundaries are clearly demarcated as being distinct from either prior or subsequent material—that is, the proverbial statement in v. 12a, and the allusion to exile again in v. 14. The vocative, 'O house of Israel', here, reiterates a parallel reference in v. 1, thus forging an inclusive bond for the entire oracle. A distinct proclamation of judgment brings each oracle to a prominent close (*epiphora*—vv. 7, 11, 14).

It is possible to discern a chiastic ordering of thematic components extending out on both sides of the introversion that forms the heart of the central portion of the book of Amos, namely, 5:1–17. This larger ring-structure may be outlined as follows (cf. Lust 1981):

   a An enemy will oppress oppressive Israel (3:9–12)
      b Testimony against the 'house(s) of Jacob' (3:13–15)
         c Against the wealthy women of Samaria (4:1–3)
            d Against the decadent cult (4:4–5)
               e Buildup to a time of judgment (4:6–12)
                  f The dual message of Amos: Condemnation of the wicked; invitation to the penitent (5:1–17)
               e' Judgment will come on the Day of the Lord (5:18–20)
            d' Against the decadent cult (5:21–27)
         c' Against the wealthy men of Samaria (6:1–7)
      b' Testimony against the 'house(s) of Jacob' (6:8–11)
   a' A nation will oppress unrighteous Israel (6:12–14)

The unit 3:1–8, a oracle denouncing 'Israel' (following oracle set 1, 1:3–2:16) thus serves as an introduction to this entire middle section (oracle set 2) by stressing the main participants in the prophetic drama: Yahweh, the 'lion' who is roaring a message of condemnation against his unfaithful

2.3 A structural outline of Amos 55

people (3:8), through his chosen prophet(s) (cf. Jer 25:30; Joel 3:16). It corresponds then to the discourse segment that began the preceding division as well as the book as a whole, that is, Am 1:1–2 (structural *anaphora*). A powerful word of judgment from 'the LORD God Almighty' brings both 'woe' oracle sets to a dismal and depressing conclusion (5:27, 6:14—structural *epiphora*).[20]

2.3.4 Five visions of Israel's ruin (Am 7:1–9:10)

Here, at the beginning of the third and final major collection of oracles in the book of Amos, there occurs a decided shift in perspective to the prophetic 'I'. This is indicated immediately by the shift in the introductory formula: 'This is what the Sovereign LORD *showed* me [he caused be to see]...' These visions involve semi-narrative reports that convey God's messages to his people through things seen as well as heard by Amos. The prophet himself now becomes more of an active participant, as it were, in the sermons that he is delivering on behalf of Yahweh. The presence of these visionary personal experiences is perhaps foreshadowed at the very beginning of the book, where it states that the prophet 'saw' certain messages 'concerning Israel' (Am 1:2). These visions spell out in vivid visual detail the implications of the climactic prediction in Am 6:14—'I will raise up a nation against you, O House of Israel.'

Interspersed among the five visions are three distinct and diverse (genre-wise) commentaries on their content and significance of these visual

---

[20] Wilson (1997:171–173) structures 5:18–6:14 as an 8-part chiasmus as follows: A Reversal of fortunes—1st woe (5:18–20); B Displeasure with Israel—worship (5:21–25); C Threat of exile (5:26–27); D Second woe (6:1–3); D' Third woe (6:4–6); C' Threat of exile (6:7); B' Displeasure with Israel (6:8–9); A' Reversal of fortunes (6:11–14). The problem is that this proposal is rather artificial (e.g., the word 'woe' does not occur in 6:4–6) and tends to obscure other, structurally more credible discourse units, both large (e.g., the two 'woe' collections of 5:18–27 and 6:1–14) and small (e.g., the unified oracle segment covering 6:1–7).

A similar criticism could be made of Dorsey's sevenfold chiastic arrangement (1999:282): A Coming disaster (5:18–20); B What Yahweh hates and despises...(5:21–24); C Threat of exile (5:25–27); D Center—sevenfold woe (6:1–6); C' Threat of exile (6:7); B' What Yahweh *hates* and detests... (6:8–10); A' Coming disaster (6:11–14). Why the condemnation at the center (6:1–6, but delinked from the consequential 'therefore' of 6:7) should be more prominent than that of the proverbial statement in 6:12 at the end (including the key terms 'justice' and 'righteousness') is not clear. This is the hermeneutical (and often also the exegetical) problem with unitary macro-chiastic proposals: they obscure equally (if not more) important sequential arrangements. The two modes of patterning—the *linear* and the *concentric*—must function together in harmony within a hierarchical organization of the discourse as a whole.

revelations with regard to the present and future social, moral, religious, and spiritual state of the nation. The dramatic nature of this entire concluding section of the book also serves to establish both the credibility and the authority of the prophet's words, which he is uttering as a chosen, non-professional spokesman for 'the Lord Yahweh' (7:14–15). It thus augments the theological implications of the introductory motifs that lead off the prior two divisions of the prophecy as a whole, that is, Am 1:1–2 and Am 3:1–8.

2.3.4.1 Vision one: Locusts (Am 7:1–3) [follows the structural pattern of vision two][21]
2.3.4.2 Vision two: Fire (Am 7:4–6)

Structural description: Both of these two initial visions, which anticipate elements of Joel 1–2, observe a strict pattern of linear discourse development. Each sequence features the following five principal structural constituents (elements):

1. *Introductory formula:* 'Thus Yahweh showed me...'
2. *Vision:* 'And behold...'
3. *Intercession:* 'And I said...'
4. *Response:* 'Yahweh relented...'
5. *Concluding formula:* '...declares Yahweh'

2.3.4.3 Vision three: Plumb line (Am 7:7–9)

Structural description: The third and fourth visions differ from the preceding pair in that they are more complex in their structural organization and more ominous in their thematic import and implications for Israel. But, similarly, a clear set of architectural cues may be discerned—numbering seven in all:

1. *Introductory formula:* 'Thus He/Yahweh showed me...'
2. *Vision:* 'And behold...'
3. *Question:* 'Amos, what do you see?'
4. *Response:* 'And I said...'

---

[21] Anderson and Freeman (1989:619) observe that the first four visions grow ever shorter in length, *viz.,* 18 words (in Hebrew, 7:1–2a), 13 words (7:4), 8 words (7:7), 3 words (8:1). The increasing conciseness corresponds with an increasing severity in what Yahweh predicts in terms of Israel's future punishment for their chronic sinfulness. "The gradual building towards greater severity is also typical of other units (e.g., 4:6–12), and it is designed to create a desired rhetorical effect" (Dorsey 1999:283)—namely, shock and dismay among the audience.

2.3 A structural outline of Amos

    5. *Interpretation:* 'And the Lord said...'
    6. *Verdict:* 'I will not spare (Israel) any more'
    7. *Judgment specified:* 'And...' (prediction).

Elements 4 and 5 may manifest a thematic pun in Hebrew. Thus, in vv. 7–8 in the present passage it is the reiterated term 'plumb line/*tin*' *'nk* 'tin' (with reference to the LORD's justice), which sounds like the word, *'nq* 'moaning' (with figurative reference to the failure of justice in Israel and the consequent punishment of the people; cf. Landsberger 1965; Stuart 1987:372–373). Notice that the prediction of v. 9 rhetorically anticipates the two controversial issues around which the subsequent narrative portion is developed, namely, the 'holy places of Israel' and 'the house of Jeroboam'.[22]

Comment one: Dramatization of the vision's message (Am 7:10–17)

Here we have a surprising shift in genre—from a vision report to a dramatic narrative account involving two prophets/prophecies in direct confrontation. In fact, this little account brings together all the 'key players' in the book of Amos, namely, the prophet himself and the LORD whom he represents on one side in conflict with all false prophets in Israel (typified by Amaziah), who are simply sycophants of the king of Israel (Jeroboam) and the majority of people in the land. The antithetical prophetic dialogue consists of four distinct turns or units:

    1. **Accusation:**   Amaziah => Amos (7:10–11)
    2. **Prohibition:**   Amaziah =>Amos (12–13)
    3. **Defense:**   Amos => Amaziah (14–15)
    4. **Curse:**   Amos => Amaziah (16–17)

Structural description: Though regarded as a clumsy insertion by some scholars, this first 'commentary' on (or within) a divine vision of Amos fits quite naturally into the textual context. The concluding verse of the preceding vision (v. 9) presents his prophecy concerning the LORD's judgment upon the royal 'house of Jeroboam' and the false worship places that this king (Jeroboam II) has perpetuated in Israel. Verse 10 then immediately reveals

---

[22] A chiastic construction serves to mark the close of Vision 3 and the message that it conveys to Israel: a 'and they shall be desolate' – b 'the high places of Isaac' = b' 'and the sanctuaries of Israel' – a' 'they shall be destroyed' (Niehaus 1992:457).

how this divine condemnation was deliberately misinterpreted by the official religious establishment in Israel, as represented by Amaziah (rhetorically, a structural 'overlap' construction termed *anadiplosis*).

The first dialogue unit (vv. 10–11) is bounded by an *inclusio* with the dual reference to 'Jeroboam' and 'Israel'. Amaziah's report (v. 11) is an ironic reproduction of Isaiah's shocking prediction (v. 9, structural *epiphora*). The mention of 'holy place' and 'royal house' in v. 13 forms another *epiphoric* correspondence with v. 9, thus concluding unit 2 In unit 3 (vv. 14–15), Amos first of all reviews his divine commission, which culminates in a command, 'Go, prophesy...', that directly contradicts what Amaziah told him to do (v. 12) and overlaps then by ironic negation with unit 4 (v. 16, *anadiplosis*). Dialogue unit 4 (vv. 16–17) consists of two parts, which on a personal level duplicates Amos's basic message to the nation at large: *indictment*—'Hear the word of Yahweh...' (that is, *anaphora* with Am 3:1, 4:1, 5:1), and *verdict*—'Therefore, thus declares Yahweh...' The Lord's proclamation of punishment through Amos consists of a sequence of six (7-1) disasters which will befall the errant priest personally, and ultimately Israel as a whole. The climactic reference to captivity recalls similar predictions in Am 5:27 and Am 8:14 (structural *epiphora*). There was thus a total disregard for the 'word of the Lord', for which 'Israel' was going to be punished by a complete departure from the 'land' (vv. 16a/17b = *inclusio*), which was the physical symbol of their covenant with Yahweh, now irrevocably broken.[23]

2.3.4.4 *Vision four: Basket of ripe fruit (Am 8:1–3)*

Structural description: The development of this penultimate vision follows the pattern outlined above for vision three. Its opening is distinguished by a pun which fuses together the symbolic *image* 'fruit' and its topic 'end', Hebrew *qayits* and *qets*, respectively. The final word of the LORD is especially gruesome (v. 3), the broken syntax rhetorically reflecting the disaster being reported: 'Many-of the-body in-every place he-will-scatter, silence! ('The dead bodies shall be many, cast out in every place—be silent'; Niehaus 1992:466). The final word (has) appears in sharp contrast to the preceding

---

[23] As in Gen 47:27, there is a prominent pun on three senses of the key word 'land' (adama) in the concluding verse of Comment 1 (4:17): (a) Amaziah's family plot, (b) a pagan land of exile (i.e., Assyria), and (c) the home land of Israel (Niehaus 1992:465).

2.3 A structural outline of Amos

audible images of singing being transformed into wailing. But the reason for this disaster is abundantly clear: it is all due to the pervasive false religion currently being practiced in the 'temple', which may well be a figurative allusion to the nation of Israel (+ Judah) as a whole.

Comment two: Oracle of judgment on the day of the LORD (Am 8:4–14)

As was the case in comment one, so also comment two is verbally foreshadowed by a key expression in the preceding vision, namely, 'in that day...' (Am 8:3 = > 8:9, 11, 13), plus the general indictment of 'my people Israel', who were 'ripe' for destruction (8:2)—now elaborated upon in vv. 4–14. This oracle is overtly demarcated into three stanzas:

1. **Accusation:** against the wicked works of Israel, especially religious *hypocrisy* (8:4–7); there are two subunits or strophes:
    a. Seven social/moral sins outlined (4–6)
    b. Yahweh's climactic sworn response—judgment! (7)

2. **Interlude:** a brief national *funeral lament* for Israel (8:8)

3. **Condemnation:** a religious famine is predicted (8:9–14); this takes the form three distinct image sets (strophes):
    a. *Mourning*, coupled with cosmic and spiritual darkness (9–10)
    b. *Famine*—for 'the word of Yahweh', a futile search. (11–12)
    c. *Drought* and death (13–14); even the strongest faint and finally fall in the nation, from Dan (North) to Beersheba (South).

Structural description: Stanza 1 leads off with the familiar anaphoric cue: 'Listen...' (cf. Am 3:1, 13; 4:1; 5:1). The listing of seven distinct covenant/law violations gives cohesion to the main body of this unit (vv. 4–6). Closure is effected by the dramatic oath of the LORD himself (a self-imprecation, cf. 4:2) never to forget his people's chronic apostasy (v. 7). Yahweh designates himself as 'the Pride of Jacob', an ironic reference to Israel's misplaced 'pride' in 6:8 (cf. Ps 47:5[4]).[24]

The short middle stanza (2, v. 8) serves as an interlude that relates to what comes before and after it in the text. This verse takes the literary form of a *lament*—as if it were being sung by a 'chorus' in response to what

---

[24] Yahweh thus swears by the land that he swore to give Abraham's descendants, to Israel. "But he does so ironically, for they have polluted the land by their oppression and idolatry" (Niehaus ibid., 472).

Yahweh has just pronounced in v. 7 and in anticipation of the severe judgments to follow (vv. 9ff.). There is a probable allusion to an earthquake here as a physical sign of the LORD's great displeasure with the inhabitants of his land (as predicted in Am 1:1; cf. 9:5). This anticipates the cosmic signs of 'darkness' that appear in v. 9 (*anadiplosis;* cf. Isa 24:1-7; Jer 4:27-28).

The final, more lengthy stanza focuses on the national calamities that will accompany the dark 'day' of the LORD's judgment. Each of the three included strophes leads off with an explicit reference to that day (or days), thus demarking them as discrete literary units within the discourse (vv. 9, 11, 13, i.e., structural *anaphora*). It may be argued that there are seven punishments represented: vv. 9-10 [4], vv. 11-12 [2], plus vv. 13-14 [1]. The graphic imagery of each strophe, too, is distinctive, thus lending conceptual cohesion to each, i.e., (a) mourning, (b) famine, and (c) fainting/falling. The notion of a complete national demise (8:14b) is one that concludes other oracles in the book as well (an *epiphoric* refrain, e.g., 2:4, 16; 3:15; 4:3; 5:3, 17, 27; 6:7, 14; 7:9, 17; 8:3; cf. also 9:10). Once again in 8:14 the apostates are condemned by their own words (cf. 4:2; 6:13)—this time a series of futile idolatrous oaths, which contrast with Yahweh's earlier oath of judgment (v. 7, *epiphora*).

2.3.4.5 Vision five: The LORD by the altar (Am 9:1-4)

This vision begins in a different way from the preceding four, perhaps to distinguish it as the final, climactic image that Amos wanted to convey to his audience. This time, Yahweh does not 'show' Amos a vision; rather, the prophet sees Yahweh himself as the central image of his vision. Now the LORD has reached the very sanctuary of Israel's syncretistic religion, right next to 'the altar', and Amos sees directly what happens there. The unit is arranged along a linear plane in the form of a narrative dilemma in which a series of *seven* punishments is specified. Each one reinforces the other to emphasize the certainty of the calamity to come and the utter inability of the people to escape it. This vision is also organized concentrically in a way that reinforces the key conceptual elements of the horrible fate that awaits the faith-less people. This introversion is composed of the following patterned constituents:

2.3 A structural outline of Amos

    a **judgment** (general): Yahweh acts through his prophet (1a)
      b **sword:** will kill them (1b)
        c **out:** they cannot escape as 'fugitives' (1c)
          d **down:** no safety in Sheol (2a)
            e **up:** no hope in the 'heavens' (2b)
            e' **up:** no hiding atop Mt Carmel (3a)
          d' **down:** at the bottom of the sea a serpent will bite them (3b)
        c' **out:** they cannot escape in 'captivity' (4a)
      b' **sword:** will kill them (4b)
    a' **judgment** (general): 'Yahweh has set his eye against' Israel for 'evil', that is, punishment! (4c)

Structural description: The pattern of reiterated concepts that establishes the preceding introversion is quite clear, and so is the horizontal sequence of syntactic features with which the former more or less coincides. A striking image sets the sequence in motion, so to speak, namely, that of the collapse of a pillared shrine, which symbolizes the Lord's rejection of the superficial religious system that Israel had erected for itself as a substitute for a faithful keeping of the Mosaic Law. The reference to 'shaking' (9:1) may involve another allusion to the Lord's punitive earthquake (cf. 1:1, *anaphora*). The core of the chiasm (e/e') reiterates the point which is stressed on its borders, namely, that it is Yahweh himself who will initiate the just punishment of his people. The vision concludes with a vivid pronouncement of divine condemnation—the mention of 'my eye' coupled with the reference to 'seeing' in 9:1a forms a conceptual *inclusio* for this poetic unit.

Comment three: Praising Yahweh's power and condemning sinful Israel (Am 9:5–10)

There are two diverse units comprising this divinely focused comment on vision 5, as suggested by each heading below:

1. Doxology (9:5–6)

Structural description: As in the case of the two previous hymnic segments (that is, 4:13 and 5:8–9), this piece is likewise of a transitional nature and relates to the discourse units that immediately precede and follow it. All three doxologies occur in prominent structural positions: 4:13 paves the way for the book's thematic center in 5:1–17, while 5:8–9 constitutes the structural core of the preceding pericope. Similarly, the words of 9:5–6 follow a strong oracle of judgment and introduce a message that contains a glimmer of hope for the fallen nation, in this case, the remnant, which is alluded to in the subsequent oracle (9:8c).

A prominent *inclusio* frames this doxology, one that, like many of the other rhetorical-structural markers in Amos, is based on the name (person) of the LORD (of hosts). The strophe features a reiteration of the creation–destruction motif, which is the principal topic also of the hymn in 5:8–9. Here the latter idea is presented first in words that recall the close of the first stanza of comment two (that is, *epiphora* with 8:8).[25]

2. Judgment oracle (9:7–10)

There are two stanzas included within this unit (A, vv. 7–8) and (B, vv. 9–10), each of which displays the following triad of topical elements:

	(A)	(B)
a. Israel and the nations	7	9a
b. Total destruction of sinners	8a	10
c. Allusion to a remnant	8b	9.9b

Structural description: One notices a chiastic ordering of the elements (b) and (c) above, a feature which often marks a final unit in Hebrew poetic/prophetic literature. Stanza A is bounded *(inclusio)* by parallel references to: 'the sons of Israel' (7a) and 'the house of Jacob' (8b).

The *anaphoric* expression '(For) behold...' (v. 9) also initiates several of the earlier vision reports (7:1, 4, 7; 8:1) and an earlier oracle (8:11). There is another reference to 'shaking', perhaps with the notion of an earthquake in mind again (1:1). The association of 'Israel' and the 'nations' in v. 9 also establishes an internal *inclusio* with the book's opening set of judgment oracles, in which the condemnation of Israel occurred last. Notice, too, that there in Am 2:16 we find the first mention of the 'day' (of the LORD) which is a focal notion in the following stanza, the close of the prophecy (9:11–15). The prediction of the sinners of Israel being put to the sword (v. 10a) is a covenantal curse that echoes

---

[25] Niehaus prefers the term 'divine titulary' to 'hymnic fragment', although he admits that this passage is 'written in a hymnic style' (1992:483). He also draws attention to the chiastic structure of v. 6, which 'lends power to the utterance': a 'the one who builds' – b 'in heaven' – c 'his temple' = c' 'and his vault' – b' 'above the earth' – a' 'he founds' (ibid., 483).

2.3 A structural outline of Amos

the punishment decreed for Jeroboam II in 7:9 and 11 (structural *epiphora;* cf. Exo 5:3; Lev 26:25; Deut 32:25). The people's impenitent self-sufficiency is foregrounded in a direct quote that concludes this section (v. 10b; cf. 6:13, *epiphora*).

The surprising allusion to a remnant that escapes (overtly in v. 8 and implicitly v. 9) stands in marked contrast to the prevailing concept of certain and complete destruction which pervades these latter verses. The answer to this apparent paradox is given in the next strophe that leads off the final section of Amos's collection of oracles, that is, 9:12 which, in like manner, focuses upon the future transformed situation of a restored people of 'Israel' (David's fallen tent) among all the nations chosen by Yahweh.[26]

2.3.5 Prophecy of restoration (Am 9:11–15)

This final oracle of Amos is clearly distinct from all those that have preceded it in the book. And yet it is not entirely unmotivated. There are a number of explicit prior references to Yahweh's desire to forgive and renew a repentant people, for example, the oracle complex of Am 4:6–12 (with its refrain: '...yet you have not returned to me'). Other examples are the repeated invitations to 'seek the LORD and live' (5:4, 6, 14–15), the two visions in which God withholds a plague in response to his prophet's appeal (7:1–6), and most notably, the several passages which mention the possibility of a surviving remnant (5:15, 9:8–9).

The discourse-final and hence climactic oracle of blessing is divided into two strophes, each of which deals with a somewhat different aspect of restoration as it is going to affect the future remnant of the 'shelter/tent of David' (11a):

---

[26] Wilson (1997:177–179) and Dorsey (1999:284–285) posit a ring structure for the entire section covering 8:4–9:15. The latter follows this arrangement: A The land's coming destruction (8:4–8) – B Yahweh will punish Israel (8:9–14) – C Yahweh's judgment: No escape (9:1–4) – D Center: hymnic exclamation (9:5–7) – C' Yahweh's judgment: a righteous remnant will be spared (9:8–10) – B' Yahweh will restore devastated Israel (9:11–12) – A' The land's future restoration (9:13–15). This organization is certainly possible, and it corresponds in large measure with the major discourse breaks that I have proposed. There are also a number of significant differences, however, for example: not distinguishing the distinct lament of 8:8, the break at 8:11, a reduction in prominence of the break at 9:1 (vision 5), and the boundaries of the hymnic center. In order to establish the desired number of 'seven poetic lines' within the last mentioned, Dorsey must add 9:7 to the indisputable panegyric poem spanning vv. 5–6 (1999:285), thus ignoring the clear signals of *aperture* at v. 7, e.g., a pair of rhetorical questions, a shift in genre and probably in speaker as well (i.e., from Amos in vv. 5–6 to Yahweh in v. 7), and a formulaic 'utterance of Yahweh' saying in 7a.

A. Renewal of Israel among the nations (9:11-12)
B. Prosperity and permanence of the new Israel (9:13-15).

Structural description: An *anaphoric* reference to the great day(s) of the LORD leads off each of the two stanzas (9:11a, 13a). Only this time, instead of destruction, some wonderful blessings are predicted for the nation—or rather, the select group of believers (the remnant prefigured in 9:8) who have proved faithful to the Covenant of Yahweh.[27] Drastic reversals mark the content of each strophe: First of all, instead of being physically oppressed by other peoples and countries, this remnant of David will take spiritual possession of all nations on earth (as epitomized by their archenemy 'Edom', v. 12a; cf. 1:11-12), that is, through their common blessing of having the LORD's name 'called/pronounced upon them' (9:12b).[28]

In the second strophe, the material desolation of Israel which was prophesied earlier (for example, 8:9-14) will be replaced by a time of great prosperity. This is graphically detailed through concrete agricultural figures in the last of the prophet's characteristic series of *seven* (a fact, incidentally, which argues for the authenticity and integrity of this final oracle of Amos). Similarly, the sequence peaks out in a climax, this one tying all of the preceding elements together in a glorious promise of peace and stability in their land. Here, too, is a dynamic undoing of the fate that has been repeatedly predicted for the unrighteous in Israel, namely, a shameful exile to bondage (cf. 5:27; 6:7, 14; 7:17—structural end-stress, or *epiphora*). This particular emphasis would have been especially meaningful within the specific socioeconomic context of the prophet's message in view of all the gross offenses against the land that were currently being

---

[27] "Amos ends on a note of tragic-comic resolution (for the remnant). This bold affirmation and hope has troubled many scholars who find it too glaring a contrast to the judgmental tone of the rest of the book. Still, the ending agrees with the movement of Scripture as a whole, and with most of its books. It affirms the promise that God's ultimate goal is redemption" (Wilson 1997:179). Furthermore, the New Testament itself attests to the Messianic implications of this concluding oracle, namely, in the progressive growth of the Church in reaching out from the Jerusalem headquarters to embrace ever more remote groups of Gentile believers (cf. the Apostle James, who cites Amos 9:11-12 in the LXX version in application to the Gospel mission of Paul and Barnabas—Acts 15:16-17).

[28] It may be that the common imagery of a rebuilt vineyard 'booth' (A, above) and its produce (B, above) serves to link this pair of stanzas conceptually (Coote 1981:124). However, most commentators take the Hebrew sukkoth as referring to a far more substantial structure: "it is used of the Lord's heavenly pavilion (Pss 18:12[13]; 31:21[20]) and of the canopy that will cover his glory when he comes to dwell on Zion (Isa 4:5-6)" (Niehaus 1992:490).

2.3 A structural outline of Amos

perpetrated by the rich against the poor—a crime to which the preceding oracles give abundant testimony.

In closing this rhetorical-structural overview of the discourse organization of Amos, I might point out a few of the important correspondences, involving both similarity and contrast, that occur between the antithetical oracles which conclude the book (ch. 9) and its topically composite thematic nucleus of 5:1–17:

5:1–17	**Similarity**	9:5–15
8–9	creation—destruction motif	5–6
2–3	destruction of all sinners	8a, 10
15b	the remnant of Israel/nations	8b, 9b, 12b
4–6, 14–15	the hope of renewal/restoration	11–1
	Contrast	
2	the falling/raising of Israel	11
5	exile/establishment in the land	14–15
11	vineyards cursed/blessed	14

Such points of topical convergence are further evidence that would support the compositional unity of the oracles of Amos as they have been composed in writing—whether by the prophet himself or by a later associate—for repeated dramatic oral proclamation to many diverse audiences ever since.[29]

In closing this section of my study and to offer a somewhat different perspective on the construction of the book of Amos as a whole, I have reproduced a summary of Dorsey's sevenfold concentric arrangement below (1999:285):[30]

A Coming judgment upon Israel and its neighbors (1:1–2:16)
  B The prophet's compulsion: announcement of coming destruction of Israel and Bethel's cult center (3:1–15)
    C Condemnation of wealthy Israelite women: empty religious activity and Yahweh's judgment (4:1–13)
      D CENTER: call to repentance, and lament (5:1–17)

---

[29] For example, the judgment oracles against the nations in 1:3–2:16 "provide the first and easily observable instance of orality in the Amos document" (Doan and Giles 2005:109).

[30] I have not included the various verbal parallels that Dorsey has listed to support his proposal. Some of these correspondences between the posited parallel panels are quite convincing, especially between the first and last sections (1:1–2:16 and 8:4–9:16, cf. Dorsey 1999:284), others are less credible (e.g., the second layer of panels, 3:1–15 and 7:1–8:3, which are alleged to focus on 'Bethel's cult center').

C' Condemnation of wealthy Israelite men: empty religious activity and Yahweh's judgment (5:18–6:14)
   B' The prophet's compulsion: visions of coming judgment; Amos announces coming destruction of the Bethel's cult center (7:1–8:3)
A' Coming judgment upon Israel (scattering among the nations) and future restoration among the nations (8:4–9:15)

This proposed structure of Amos is intriguing but I do not find it compelling in the sense that it would override a linear perspective on the book's overall organization. I feel that a concentric arrangement like this might *complement* a sequential one, serving to help organize the latter conceptually and *reinforcing* some of the major discourse boundaries. On the other hand, a number of important linear structural units are eclipsed in this scheme, e.g., the two 'woe' oracle sets in C' (5:18–27 and 6:1–14) and the fifth 'vision' within A' (9:1–4). Finally, as in the case of all exegetical issues, it is up to each analyst to assess the evidence, thoroughly as well as independently, and then come to her/his own conclusions regarding both the text's interpretation and also how to represent it in another language via translation.

2.4 The thematic implications of a structural description

What, then, is the principal significance of the divine 'lion's roar'? Any discourse analysis of a literary text—that is, a segmentation of its verbal material into a hierarchical system of interrelated parts with varying degrees of prominence in relation to one another and to the whole—ought to contribute in some tangible way to our understanding of the author's message. Why did Amos, or a later editor perhaps, arrange the composition in the way that he did—when there are countless other formats he might have followed? What do the many patterns of recursion observed in this book, the divine quote formulas in particular, have to do with the main ideas which the prophet wished to communicate to the primary receptors of the book in its original setting?

In this section I will discuss some tentative suggestions for answering questions of this nature. These represent my own perspective on how one might view the content of Amos's various oracles within a coherent thematic framework that expresses a clear rhetorical purpose for this

2.4 The thematic implications of a structural description

collection of his prophecies. My hypothesis is based upon the foundation provided by the structural development of the text itself. Thus, my conclusions have been influenced by the particular organization which has emerged from the preceding study of the book's rhetorical form following a literary-structural analytical approach. Such an exercise serves the purpose of providing at least some measure of objectivity and a means for testing the conclusions that have been reached about the essence and purpose of this prophet's message.

First of all, the many repeated instances of the introductory *quote formula,* or 'divine messenger speech' (in its several variant forms), as they occur in key structural positions throughout the book, would indicate that the central theme of Amos has something to do with the 'word of the LORD'. However, these stereotyped expressions serve more than a purely formal purpose of marking the *aperture* or *closure* of a given segment of discourse. They perform that function, to be sure, but there appears to be something quite a bit more significant about all this recursion with reference to what Yahweh had to say, at least in the case of the present literary work. Thus, it would seem that the book's larger formal organization definitely points to the fact that the 'word of the LORD' and its specific relation to those to whom it was being directed is crucial for understanding its central message. The strong emphasis upon this divine Word—its proclamation, its reception, as well as its application in everyday life—appears throughout the prophecy of Amos, from beginning to end, as indicated by the following synopsis of occurrences:

1:2—The LORD roars out his message; it is going to shake a lot of people up!

2:11-12—Yahweh raised up prophets to preach; but the people replied, 'Don't prophesy!'

3:7-8—The LORD reveals his secrets to his chosen prophets, who are to 'roar' in turn on his behalf. People ought to take the message seriously, in fear and trembling.

3:1, 4:1—'Hear this word!' It is a divine imperative.

3:13—'Hear and testify!' The evidence is clear-cut: one can either accept the Word or reject it, and one's actions will declare the decision and determine the verdict.

4:13—The LORD reveals his thoughts and deeds to mankind; such a wonderful imparting of knowledge entails an equally great responsibility to utilize it correctly.

5:4, 6, 14–15—The message of Yahweh is founded upon his everlasting mercy; his purpose is that people repent and receive 'life', rather than punishment for their injustice and apostasy.

6:10—The failure to carry out one's obligations with regard to the Word means that in the day of judgment, one will not even be able to utter the name of the Giver; the very Name that might have brought salvation will now condemn those who refused to obey him.

7:10–17—The drama of a crisis in identity: who, after all, is a genuine preacher of the Word? The answer is simple: he who continues to proclaim the truth despite opposition, and he whose message comes true according to the will of Yahweh.

8:11–12—Persistent rejection always results in a 'famine' of the Word, when people will seek it (probably for the wrong reasons) but not find it; and when the LORD no longer speaks to people, the result is certain death—as sure as the lack of food eventually leads to starvation.

9:10—Here is another ironic instance of the fate of those who twist the Word of Yahweh in order to suit their own purposes (cf. 7:15–16)—they do so at their own peril.

9:12—The Word of Yahweh must ultimately be proclaimed to people of all nations so that they, too, can learn to 'call upon his Name'!

What, then, was that Word which Amos was chosen to announce to his cousins in the North? For all its importance, it was not really a complicated message at all. It was essentially a twofold pastoral sermon that related both to the gracious offer of the divine Source, namely, forgiveness following repentance, and, on the other hand, also to the response of those to whom this was communicated. The nature of an individual's reaction to the Word clearly divides receptors of Yahweh's message into two distinct camps, namely, those who accept the Word and endeavor to live according to it, as opposed to those who reject the Word—if not overtly, then implicitly, by

2.4 The thematic implications of a structural description

living lives that do not conform to its decrees. The Word which Amos has in mind is obviously the *Torah* of the LORD, for many of the sins which he condemns are specific violations of the Mosaic Code as set forth in the books of Leviticus and Deuteronomy. Similarly, the various judgments that are predicted in consequence are related to the so-called curses which would befall those who did willfully and persistently break this covenantal canon of religious, moral, and social precepts (cf. Deut 28–29).[31] In true inductive fashion, Amos enumerates specific crimes and punishments as stipulated by the Book of the Law in order to illustrate the general principles that he wished to impress upon his hearers. Whether they wanted to listen or not, his task was to testify to the error of their ways and to contrast this with the righteous dealings of the God whom they had in practice rejected.

But the key term *Torah* does not refer exclusively to legal regulations and requirements. It includes all the instruction of Yahweh, hence also his willing promise to forgive and to restore fallen sinners. Although this aspect of the Word is not quantitatively very prominent in the book, qualitatively it is just as important, as shown by the critical structural positions which this theme occupies. Thus, it is situated firmly within the introversion that comprises the central core of the entire prophecy—5:4–6 and 14–15, that is, 'seek Yahweh and live!' This is the heart of the message of Deuteronomy 30 also (for example, 30:2–5, 19–20). It is the gracious mercy of Yahweh that extends a message of hope to the faithful remnant of a fallen nation (5:15), a theme taken up later in the climactic conclusion of the book, first of all, by way of anticipation (9:8–9) and then by a wonderful messianic vision of future glory as the Davidic remnant opens up to incorporate believers of all nations (9:12).

So what is the Word all about? Sin and judgment, to be sure. That was the burden of the message of Amos, just as it was for all of the other Hebrew prophets. It was his thankless task as a specially chosen servant of the LORD to go preach, repeatedly, this sermon to an unwilling audience—to hostile foreigners, if not culturally foreign, then certainly foreign in a political and religious sense (1:2). The predictable response was of course complete

---

[31] Niehaus (1992:322) presents a useful intertextual summary of the way in which "[t]he phraseology of the Prophecy of Amos illustrates the covenant background against which it was written"—as indicated by references to the Pentateuch, for example, in ch. 5: 'seek Yahweh' (v. 4; Deut 4:29); Yahweh as a consuming 'fire' (v. 6; Deut 4:24); futility curses (v. 11; Deut 28:30, 39); exile (v. 27; Deut 28:36, 64–68).

rejection, as dramatized in the narrative account of chapter 7. Amos was no doubt lucky to escape that episode with his life, for he had publicly denounced Israel's central institutions of kingship and cult, the two pillars of the nation and the dual source of its current dilemma. Indeed, like many of the great men of God, he was both motivated and emboldened by the very Word which he was sent to proclaim. And in his various oracles, uttered no doubt in many different settings and circumstances, he revealed the essential aspects of that Word of Yahweh—its *authority* (which emanated from its divine Source), *potency* (power to set great events in motion), *efficacy* (capacity to achieve its intended purposes), *reliability* (genuineness and truthfulness in contrast to all counterfeit claims), and *sincerity* (demonstrating an underlying concern for the ultimate welfare of the faithful people of God).

It is this final aspect which some scholars do not fully appreciate, namely, Yahweh's boundless mercy and overriding desire that *repentance* take place so that a *reconciliation* might be effected, one which would bring about an eventual spiritual *restoration* of his people and a consequent renewal of his blessings upon them. The LORD was not only the Sovereign of all nations, as emphasized in the opening judgment oracles of the book, but he also purposed to be the Savior of all, as clearly indicated at its close. If one does not adopt this perspective, then the message of Amos becomes a predominantly pessimistic one, composed solely to announce the just punishment of an angry God upon a wicked, rebellious nation. But *Yahweh*—the very name conveys stability and a changeless devotion to his Covenant promises—had a deeper purpose in mind when he sent Amos on his difficult mission. Otherwise, why commission this novice prophet in the first place, that is, if the idea was simply to condemn and threaten his listeners in the North with a terrible fate? No, the message went much deeper than that and bore a definite implication that reform was possible, if not for the population at large then certainly for the few souls—the *remnant*—who would take the Word of the LORD seriously to heart.

Thus, righteousness *(ts-d-q)* and justice *(sh-ph-t)*, two key words that summarize what is to be the proper attitude and behavior in relation to Yahweh's Covenant, become crucial to one's understanding of the series of sermons that Amos was sent to preach. The thematic importance of these terms is once again demonstrated by the central role that they play in the overall structure of the book. They form a prominent part of the core oracle in 5:1–17, both

2.4 The thematic implications of a structural description 71

negatively through a condemnation of what should have been (that is, 5:7, 10, 12), and also by means of a positive appeal to what ought to be—which implies that this possibility for change still existed (5:15, and by structural correspondence also, 5:14, 4, and 6). Thus, the abstract admonition to 'seek Yahweh' becomes in concrete terms: Repent and receive his generous offer of forgiveness; then demonstrate this new, this right relationship with him by living a just life in keeping with his Word. What needed to be done in terms of specific behavior, especially with regard to the oppressed poor of society, is graphically exemplified in one concrete instance after another throughout the book. This sequence of social admonition then forms the vast conceptual background, one that honestly and openly represented the current precarious state of the nation, against which the carefully selected and positioned admonitions for reform stand out in bold relief.

Therefore, repentance on the part of the people, the leadership in particular, was not merely a frustrated wish being lamented by Yahweh (cf. the *epiphoric* refrain of 4:6, 8, 9, 10, 11). It was even at this late stage still his fervent desire. Consequently, a ray of hope pierced through the prevailing gloom of the prophet's many predictions of disaster for the majority who would stubbornly refuse to heed this final call to 'let justice roll on like waters, and righteousness like an ever-flowing stream' (5:24). This latter passage, which comes at the climax of a bitter message of judgment as was demonstrated earlier, makes no sense at all (and so it has been construed by many commentators) unless it is viewed as a vital component of a much larger theme complementing, even by way of sharp contrast, the obvious one of sin and judgment in Amos.

The notion of repentance according to Yahweh's explicit standards of justice in relation to both God and man is integrally related to the concept of the *remnant*. As we have seen, this is another one of those key terms which is skillfully linked to the others and woven into the underlying fabric of content, namely, condemnation for the unrighteous. The remnant motif occurs for the first time in the structural core of the prophecy (that is, 5:15), and it later appears via allusion in the book's final oracle of judgment (that is, 9:8, 9). Here it serves to anticipate the concluding vision of renewal, which encompasses all peoples (9:12) and every possible blessing (9:13–15). Indeed, there could be no restoration of this scope and magnitude without such a righteous remnant, for anything else would constitute a contradiction within the very nature of Yahweh, the Covenant God. According to this perspective, then, the final oracle of Amos (9:11–15) is neither a pious disciple's afterthought nor an optimistic redactor's post-exilic addition, as many scholars hold (for example, Mays 1969:14; Coote 1981:ch. 4). To adopt such a position is to miss the essential thrust of the prophet's message. Instead, this oracle expresses the striking consummation of a thematic potential that was already deliberately planted much earlier in the prophecy, particularly in that pivotal oracle which not only in its content (that is, 5:4, 6, 14, and 15) but also by its very structure (that is, an introversion) subtly prefigures the tremendous physical and spiritual reversal to come.

To summarize the argument thus far, it has been suggested that the message of Amos is centered in the Word of the LORD and consists of both positive and negative elements (from the point of view of those to whom it was directed). The primary constituents of this message may be expressed in terms of the five main aspects of its overall *illocutionary force,* or communicative purpose, from a speech-act perspective, as follows:

1. **Accusation**—There is a complete and specific listing of the various socioeconomic, moral, and religious sins of the nation, constituting the LORD's indictment against them for their abject failure to observe his Covenant decrees.

2. **Condemnation**—The diverse punishments that would befall the apostate people are set forth in corresponding detail. The just judgment of Yahweh was most certainly going to be inflicted upon the wicked for their willful and continual violations of his Covenant. This involved also a revelation of what the future disaster would be like.

3. **Exhortation**—The enumeration of offenses and threats of punishment did not exist for its own sake. Certainly it had little or no effect upon those who were already confirmed in their unbelief, except perhaps to incite their anger against true prophets of the Word, like Amos. Along with the accusation and condemnation was a forceful appeal to repent and return to the LORD in order to receive his promised pardon.

4. **Consolation**—Thus, the Word also included a message of hope to the penitent, who are characterized as being but a small remnant among the masses of sinners (9:9–10). However, this promise of future blessing is suddenly extended to all nations in an eschatological vision of vividly concrete agricultural imagery (9:11–15).

5. **Affirmation**—The oracles of Amos contain a number of testimonies, both explicit and implicit, to the wondrous attributes of Yahweh, his sovereign

2.4 The thematic implications of a structural description

power in particular. These are expressed most clearly in the several doxologies, or hymns of praise, which punctuate the prophecy at critical junctures as outlined on previous pages. The central characteristic of divine mercy, however, is expressed more personally, and poignantly, in the LORD's various invitations to his people to repent (for example, 4:6ff.; 5:4, 6, 14–15)—and amazingly even in his own repentance! (7:3, 6).

If we consider the collection of oracles of Amos as a whole and the socio-economic and political milieu in which they were first uttered, a possible *mimetic* function of the sequence of divine quote formulas becomes evident. Their very regularity, almost predictability (with several significant exceptions), acts as a distinctive counter-balance to the turbulent community to which these sermons and prophecies were directed. Or one might say that metaphorically they serve to symbolize the unchangeable will of Yahweh as set forth in his *Torah* Covenant in direct opposition to the fickle behavior of a people who were no longer capable of distinguishing right from wrong. In the oracles of Amos, then, the eternal stability of the Word of the LORD stands in sharp contrast to Israel's sinful and unsettled society which had been seriously fragmented due to the almost total abandonment of his righteousness by the upper classes in their proud and oppressive pursuit of personal pleasure and self-security.

On the other hand, the stabilizing force of the Word, which revolved around the basic principle of justice for all under the righteous rule of Yahweh, paradoxically served to generate severe conflict in both religious and secular circles. In fact, this overt antagonism is reflected in a long series of surprises, reversals, and even contradictions which underlie the content of the message itself. These concern the disposition of the divine Source, the characteristics of his chosen messenger, as well as the nature of the audience and their fate. In a sense Amos himself was a part of this message. In all likelihood, he was a common farmer and not a schooled prophet of the type that one would expect Yahweh to entrust with such an important message (1:1; 7:14–15). This *surprise* factor is a prominent feature of the very first sequence of oracles, when Israel, the chosen people (3:2), finds itself trapped, as it were, at the end of the line of nations that are destined to be destroyed for their wickedness. In Israel's case, though they took pride in their outward piety (5:21–23; 7:13), they are roundly condemned for the grossest of sins: their religious syncretism, social transgressions, and moral debauchery (e.g., 2:6–8). And Yahweh, too, who indicts these people with such vivid detail and pronounces the severest of punishments upon them, nevertheless seems to turn right around and offer them one last chance not only to repent (e.g., 5:4) but also to participate in the most abundant of blessings on his day (9:11–15). This apparent contradiction in his very nature—his power to create (bless) and also to destroy (curse)—is even eulogized in several of the hymnic segments of the book (e.g., 5:8–9).

Thus, the fundamental structural-thematic progression of contra-expectation, confrontation, crisis, and conflict leading to an emotive climax repeats itself time and again from the opening oracles to the close of the book. And all of this turmoil is shown to be the result of a faithful proclamation of the Word of Yahweh. Is there really a contradiction here? Only if one attempts to read Amos in isolation from the corpus of *Torah* texts upon which the LORD was basing this message to his people. These should not have been unfamiliar to them at all. What we have here is a specific application of the essential message of Deuteronomy, particularly as summarized in chapters 28–30. This was that focal 'Word of the LORD' which the ruling classes, especially, were failing to observe. The very repetition of the name of Yahweh ought to have acted like a verbal hammer to pound these truths home, to awaken a recollection of what his just requirements were within the framework of the Covenant, which he had made with their fathers—and kept (cf. 2:9–11, 3:1–2)—and to stimulate a desire to return to him in repentance (cf. 4:8, 9, etc.).

But the greatest theological paradox of all, whether for the original or the current receptors of Amos, rests in Yahweh's unfathomable nature—specifically, how his great mercy found a way to satisfy his perfect holiness and righteousness in the face of a perverse and rebellious mankind. The complete answer to that conundrum is, of course, found only in the cross of Christ. But for the faithful remnant of the prophet's time, a number of key utterances in his oracles certainly set them looking in the right direction: 'Seek me, and live...(then) Let justice roll!' (5:4, 24). As for all those who refuse to accept that simple Word of the LORD, they'd best 'prepare to meet (their) God!' (4:12).

2.5 Controversy over 'the Word of the LORD' continues—Can a structural analysis help?

The passage of time has not settled the issue of what exactly constitutes 'the Word of the LORD' in the oracles of Amos. One might argue that the controversy is of a completely different sort nowadays. But is it really? If we are talking about the genuineness of the message—did Amos really utter such and such an oracle or part of one, or how much of the book may actually be attributed to Amos?—then nothing has really changed. For as soon as we introduce the possibility of fragments, sources, emendations, accretions, reformulations, or whatever, then we are no longer dealing with an integral text or a unified message. One's interpretation will definitely be influenced by one's opinion about the state of the discourse: Is it essentially cut from a whole piece of prophetic cloth (allowing for a certain number of minor scribal/editorial adjustments), or are we instead confronted with a garment of redactional patches—each of a different age, a different style, and a different communicative purpose? A great deal has been written on this subject with regard to the book of Amos. I will not attempt to discuss all of the points which have been raised in this debate; my aim is rather to present a selection of some of the major issues in order to illustrate, first of all, some of the problems involved and then, more substantially, to indicate how a structural analysis of the discourse, as outlined in section 2.2, might help us to clarify our stand on certain key areas of interpretation.

2.5.1 Text criticism

A good place to begin is with the original text itself. How reliable is it, first of all, from a text-critical perspective, and then with regard to authorship? Though many commentators, including several fairly recent ones (e.g., Anderson and Freedman 1989:141–144; Finley 1990:111–112; Smith 1989:5; Smith and Page 1995:29), consider the text to be in relatively good shape, other scholars feel that they are in a position to freely emend the Masoretic Text in the interest of a 'better' (easier?) reading and, hence, interpretation. For example, the following is a selection of proposals for 'improving' or 'correcting' the Masoretic Text in the section 4:6–13 (Mays 1969:76–77):

v. 6   —'Omitting wəḡam, an editorial transition...'
v. 7   —'Omitting wəḡam ʾānōkî, an insertion to make v.7 similar to v. 6.'
       'MT's verb is Hiphil and lacks a sensible subject; read Niphal and omit ʿāleyhā'.
v. 9   —'Emending MT's infinitive (harbōt) to heḥerabtə.'
v. 10 —'A gloss identifying the pestilence more precisely...'
       'An addition to fill out the picture of military disaster.'
v. 13 —'Reading hāraʿam for MT's 'mountains' (hārîm)...'
       'Reading maʿaśēhū for MT's mā-śēḥō.'

The suggested revisions thus average nearly one per verse. A few of the changes and interpretations (that is, 'a gloss/addition') may be justified to a degree, such as, 'lacks a sensible subject.' But most of them are arbitrarily applied to the text as if the commentator were in possession of a special insight that indicated to him what the original autograph actually stated. Suffice it to say that this type of procedure makes light of any structural analysis, for it allows the researcher to freely alter the data as given to fit his own preconceived notion about what the Hebrew says and how it is constructed. In many cases such proposed emendations are merely an erudite way of covering up our collective ignorance concerning the object of our investigation. This is not to say that no genuine textual problems exist in the Hebrew, or that no alterations to the Masoretic Text in such cases may be considered.[32] But it certainly behooves scholars to keep these to a minimum of clearly defined and thoroughly argued instances, limited for the most part to possible variations in vowel pointing and word division. Evidence derived from a discourse analysis can and should be used to help answer questions of a text-critical nature, but the whole exercise becomes quite a dubious venture if that evidence is itself based on an emendation of the original.

Turning to the issue of the putative extent of Amos's influence on the book which bears his name, we observe that many contemporary literary experts tend to limit his authorial role considerably. For example, Mays concludes (1969:13):

---

[32] My conservative, less interventionist text-critical position is that, generally speaking, we should assume the MT 'innocent unless proven guilty'—that is, accepted as a reliable textual foundation unless unintelligible or countered at certain problem points with credible alternatives from other major sources, notably, the Dead Sea Scrolls, the LXX, and other ancient versions.

2.5 Controversy over 'the Word of the LORD' continues

> The final form of the book was thus the result of a process of formulation that reached from Amos down at least into the exilic period. A precise and detailed reconstruction of the course which that process took would have to be conjectural in large part.

Some commentators, like Wolff and Coote, go even farther. They are confident that their tool kit of assorted form- and source-critical techniques enables them to actually sort out the different strands in the redactional history of the book. Coote, for example, who feels that "it is doubtful that the first recorder of Amos's words in writing was Amos himself," posits in very specific terms "three successive stages of the recomposition of the book of Amos…A, B, and C" (1981:7). For his part, Wolff (1977) identifies "six distinct compositional layers beginning in the eighth century and concluding in the postexilic era" (Doan and Giles 2005:106). Writing from a more recent 'performance criticism' perspective, Doan and Giles seem to assume that the prophet Amos was really only the central character in a creative drama that was progressively composed by subsequent literary-minded scribes. Citing Coote (1981:3), they suggest that "[e]ach stage of recomposition represents an interpretation of Amos's words, and thus an actualization of them, a reading and understanding of them *that makes them real and important in a new and different present*" (2005:107, italics by D&G). They go on to claim (ibid., 135):

> For the scribe, the prophet Amos was a living link between the past, the present, and the future…. [A] brief summary of the performance structures we have explored to this point reveal a substantial range of techniques available to the scribe-as-actor to bring the Amos drama to life. Each contributes to the basic drama…by providing the scribe-as-actor with multiple means for representing the character of the prophet, God, and the spectators present to the prophet.

Thus, in a metaphoric sense, it almost sounds as if a modern Amaziah is still trying to tell Amos what he can, or cannot, preach! (cf. Am 7:13, 16).

The effect which this supposed long and conjectural compositional process had on the structural organization of the book is, in Mays' considered opinion, quite negative. Outside of several sections which are demarcated by obvious formulas, he reckons that "there is no demonstrable scheme to the arrangement, historical, geographical, or thematic" (1969:14). Such an evaluation, which is reiterated on numerous occasions in his commentary (and that of other scholars as well, for example, Hammershaimb 1970, Morgenstern 1961), runs directly counter to the result of my discourse analysis of the book. Granted, there are some sudden shifts in content and tone as well as several (apparent) structural anomalies. But in general, my firm conclusion would be that the book does indeed constitute a literary whole, one which is skillfully fashioned with a presiding rhetorical purpose in mind. There does appear to be a definite beginning, mid point, and climactic conclusion to the discourse, which, if not completely explainable in terms of all its internal detail, certainly does give evidence of a coherent overall plan of development which is based on an evident thematic unity that recycles the key concepts of Israel's sin, condemnation, and future punishment, coupled with Yahweh's calls to return (repent) and promises of blessing for a faithful 'remnant'.

What are the consequences, in practical terms, of a reduction of Amos's input into his book? For one thing, as was suggested above, if the received text is assumed to be the product of a joint compositional effort, then the integrity of the whole entity is thrown into question. Where, for example, does Amos actually end his words and another take over? Every verse of the book must be certified for its authenticity (Coote 1981:90)—and the crucial issue is this: if a particular passage is deemed doubtful, that is, as constituting an intrusion upon what Amos initially uttered or wrote, then it may legitimately be discarded, downplayed, or diverted in meaning as far as one's present interpretation goes. The text is thus, to a considerable degree, predetermined and shaped by what one has judged to have originated from Amos. The alleged postexilic material that one encounters here and there does not really apply to the prophet's substantive message, that is, in his own historical context and may, therefore, be ignored if necessary—namely, when it does not coincide with the views of current commentators. In this way the door is left open for present-day inspired editors and redactors to continue the process of textual growth and development which Amos and the other OT authors initiated many centuries ago. As Coote admits (ibid., 5):

> When I refer to the words of Amos, I mean the words reconstructed from later editions, but in their original context. Thereafter these same words take on new contexts and change meaning in successive editions.

2.5 Controversy over 'the Word of the LORD' continues 79

Coote goes on to give many examples of where, in his opinion, the text today, or better, the reedited document, says something quite different from what the prophet meant to say, sometimes the exact opposite in fact (ibid., 60, my italics):

> The B stage focuses squarely on the present. Whereas Amos said in effect, '*You have not set justice* in the gate; therefore, I will destroy you,' the B stage says, '*Set justice* in the gate (5:15).'

Obviously, then, where the form of the text is open to debate, so also is its content.

2.5.2 Message content

Wherever the presumed form of the text has been changed, so also the context is correspondingly modified. That is the principal danger of a fragmented, documentary approach to the interpretation of Scripture, or any other piece of literature for that matter. The meaning of specific verses or even entire pericopes are, consequently, all too often localized and viewed only in terms of their present context instead of the book as a whole. Alternatively, they may be construed as being entirely distinct from the work in which they are contained, and hence explained with reference to some different literary and historical setting from which they are supposed to have come. Take the second verse of the prophecy, for example. Many scholars consider it to be an addition, one which is completely extraneous to the message that Amos (or one of his later disciples—?) initially composed. In the words of McKeating (1971:13, emphasis mine):

> Verse 2 is a snatch of poetry. It *does not properly belong either* to the title or to what follows.... It is *probably* a fragment of a hymn used in the Jerusalem temple and *placed here when* the book of Amos was taken over for use in public worship or *reapplied* to the needs of Judah. There is no other suggestion in the book that Amos had any special attachment to Jerusalem or its temple.

Notice the circular reasoning here. Once the commentator has casually, but quite arbitrarily, concluded that the verse is a hymnic excerpt used in the worship at Jerusalem, he is free to discount its significance since he can find no other links between Amos and the temple in the book. And what evidence does he give for saying that 'it does not belong' where it occurs in the work? Nothing but what is cited above. On the contrary, a number of intricate structural connections clearly join this verse both to what precedes and what follows it in the discourse, as indicated in the earlier rhetorical-structural outline. Two further points may be added.

(1) The fact that verse two is *hymnic* in nature should not be surprising. In fact, this would be a good reason for including the passage in question as an integral part of the book, rather than excluding it. It would then form the first of a cohesive chain of similar panegyric elements which are also located at key stages both in the middle and at the close of the discourse (i.e., 4:13, 5:8–9, 9:5–6). There are topical similarities between 1:2 and 9:5 in particular. The functional importance of these other doxologies has already been pointed out. They form an important part of the book's structural-thematic framework, and this could easily apply to 1:2 as well.

(2) The second major argument for the integrity of 1:2 involves a problem of reference which occurs in v.3. There the expression *I will not withdraw/revoke it* occurs, without an apparent antecedent for the final pronoun, that is, ʾ(ă)šîben(nû). A variety of ingenious proposals have been advanced to resolve this ambiguity, many of which are hindered by the fact that by excluding v. 2 from the Amos–corpus, it is rather contradictory to look there for a possible solution. But that is the logical place to turn for a referent, and indeed one that seems to fit the context quite well is the expression ḡôlô 'his voice'. This is in parallel to the LORD's roaring and hence is most probably a reference to the judgment which he is about to pronounce upon the nations, Israel in particular, through Amos. This verdict of condemnation, then, was irrevocable according to Yahweh's own testimony in v. 3. It surely appears to be the case that one of the main aspects of the prophet's message was to demonstrate the absolute reliability of 'the Word of the LORD', whether uttered for bane or blessing. It could not be annulled.

Such a contextually immediate interpretation, based upon a holistic understanding of the text as received, obviates the need for much more elaborate, alternative explanations, such as that recently proposed by Barre with regard to this instance. It takes him twenty pages of a biblical journal to support his conclusion that "-nû does have a specific referent...the geographical name(s) in the preceding colon" (1986:613). His

2.5 Controversy over 'the Word of the LORD' continues

suggested translation is thus: 'I will not let him (that is, them—the people of Damascus, etc.) return (to me)' (ibid., 622). While certainly possible, the complexity of the reasoning that Barre offers to justify this interpretation is already a strike against its likelihood. More obviously perhaps, simple grammar would argue against it, that is, the juxtaposition of different pronouns: '...I will not revoke *it*. For *they* have...' Furthermore, with reference to Israel, which Barre too regards as the climax of the series (ibid., 630), we later encounter a contradiction when, in the book's central core, we hear the LORD appealing for just the opposite to take place: 'Seek Me, and live!...' (5:4-6). Of course, if one is not concerned about finding any sort of thematic unity in the book, then such contradictions present no difficulty.

For a second example of how a decision on authorship and discourse organization may affect one's understanding of the biblical text, we go to the end of the book and a much larger chunk of discourse. The optimistic conclusion to the prophecy of Amos, that is, 9:11-15, standing as it does in such sharp contrast to (almost) everything that he has already said, poses a great problem for many scholars. But following their customary procedure, they do not wrestle with it very long. Instead, they simply exclude it from the 'genuine' words of Amos. Thus, McKeating says (1971:9): "The hopeful prophecies at the end of the book...were added later." Mays comes up with a possible reason for this assumed addition (1969:14, italics mine):

> After the Exile, when the prophetic message of judgment *had been fulfilled,* the oracles of salvation in Am 9:11–15 *were added* to let the broken community hear the full counsel of God.

As if it were entirely inconceivable that the LORD could make his full counsel known much earlier, before the Exile—and through his prophet, Amos! But here the critic is facing somewhat of a dilemma, for if he detaches this concluding portion from the rest of the book, what is he to do with those earlier promising utterances, especially those contained in chapter 5, which allow the possibility, at least, for an optimistic outcome to occur with respect to at least a remnant in Israel? (e.g., 5:15).

Another way of dealing with such problem passages, in addition to simply deleting them from the body of 'accepted' material emanating from Amos, is to discover a way of reinterpreting them. This is what Mays does in Am 5:4, for example, when he proposes a subtle shift in tense in order to focus Yahweh's offer more on the past (1969:86, italics mine): "For this is what Yahweh *has said* (instead of says) to the house of Israel: 'Seek me and live'." This is to harmonize also with his view that what is said in v. 5 'changes the initial invitation to a message of doom for the shrines' (ibid., 87). Similarly, in verses 5:14-15, Mays makes an attempt to diminish the potential future scope of the corresponding words, for once Am 9:11-15 has been extracted from the text, Amos does not really hold out much hope at all for Israel (ibid., 102):

> *Remnant* is not so much a theme of hope for the future, like the *remnant* of Isaiah (Isa 1:24-26; 10:20f.), as a dire recognition that punishment for Israel has been decreed—that the possibility of favour can be held out only to a handful of survivors.

Compounding Mays' difficulties in this section (ch. 5) is his uncertainty over the present arrangement of the discourse. The controlling introversion (see the earlier structural description) is not recognized, and so he is forced to deal with the text as a series of fragments, that is, Am 5:4-6/7; 10-11/8-9/12-13; 16-17/14-15/18-20. Indeed, for him this entire portion of Amos is a passage 'whose unity has been lost in the arrangement and redaction of the book' (1969:96). And once the whole of the text has been lost sight of, it becomes much more difficult, if not impossible, to arrive at a correct interpretation of the remaining parts. This contrasts markedly with the results of a synthetic literary approach and a rhetorical-structural method of discourse analysis.

The notion of 'remnant' brings up another point in this connection. Just prior to the final section of the book, which Mays and others would attribute to a later author or editor, this concept reappears, that is, in the last of Amos's judgment oracles. It occurs in the form of a double allusion (9:8-9): the 'house of Jacob' will not be completely destroyed; the stones and other refuse in the wheat will be caught in the sieve and cast away—but what passes through...? The figurative implication is not pursued at this point for the 'sinners' must still be dealt with (Am 9:10). But two verses later the 'remnant' does become the focus of attention, not only as the recipient of Yahweh's bounty, but also as the core of a much larger congregation of the

2.5 Controversy over 'the Word of the LORD' continues 83

faithful, chosen from among all the nations (9:12). This mention of a group of just and righteous individuals (cf. 5:10, 13, 15) thus serves to foreshadow the climax that the book of Amos is building up to.[33] Without the glorious vision of 9:9–15 to illumine them, these references to a future remnant would fade into relative insignificance. So the matter of text and authorship, structure and function do make a difference. One's understanding of the prophet's mission as well as his message depends to a very great extent on where one stands on this issue—either with holistic, discourse-oriented interpreters or with atomizing source-/redaction critics and supposed scribal performers.

2.5.3 Discourse structure

In the final portion of this section, I will focus my attention on the more formal aspects of the discourse structure of Amos, particularly with regard to its segmentation. The first question we have to ask ourselves in this regard is: What difference does it make? Of what practical relevance to the student of Scripture is the fact that a given book is divided into [X] number of parts at points such-and-such in the text? How do we handle differences of opinion with respect to the larger organization of a given book? Hopefully, some possible answers to these crucial questions have already become apparent in the preceding discussion. But it may be useful to substantiate this with reference to a few more specific examples.

2.5.3.1 Linear

With respect to the linear, or sequentially arranged organization of the book, we might begin by considering the proposals of van der Wal in his article 'The structure of Amos's (1983). He suggests a basic twofold division of the book based on the key terms 'words' and 'he saw' in the very first verse.

---

[33] Smith offers a good summary of this text-cohesive interpretation (1989:280): "The new revelation that Amos brings [i.e., in 9:11–15] is the radical announcement of the end of Israel (8:1–3). The light and joy of divine blessings are limited to the remnant who seek Yahweh (5:14–15). Amos maintained continuity with the traditional interpretation of the blessings of the covenant, but he interposed an intermediate step of God's judgment on sinners before that day of blessing. The blessings and curses of the covenant allow for both perspectives, based on faithfulness or disobedience. Amos's eschatology was not a narrow, exclusivistic, Judean, sectarian type. He saw the doors of the kingdom spread wide open to include not just Judeans but Israelites and people from all nations."

Accordingly, the first six chapters are viewed as focusing upon the *oracles* of Amos and the last three chapters deal mainly with his *visions*. Although it does appear that a major division of the prophecy occurs between chapters 6 and 7, as also shown on the structural outline presented earlier, it is rather arbitrary to conclude that this represents the principal division of the book. Chapters 7–9 also include several oracles not unlike those recorded in chapters 1–6. One (8:4–14) even begins in a way which is similar to the onset of what might be posited as another primary section in Amos, namely, 3:1—'Hear this word...'

Van der Wal goes on to segment chapters 1–6 into five units based upon the principle of *inclusio*. His methodology here illustrates some of the problems that result from an over-reliance upon a single literary device in one's analysis. Van der Wal's first division consists of Am 1:2–3:8 (1983:109). He segments it in this way because, in both of these outer verses, the terms 'Yahweh' and 'roar' appear. That is true, and the repetition is undoubtedly significant, as noted earlier, but not to the degree that van der Wal sees here. The difficulty is that this suggestion obscures the importance of what would seem to be an even more pronounced break in the discourse, namely, the one occurring at 3:1. Thus, a careful weighing and assessment of all the available structural, as well as other literary and rhetorical, evidence is necessary in the overall evaluation process, and such a cycle must be frequently repeated, whenever alternative proposals come into conflict.

According to my analysis of the text, the reiteration of the 'lion's roar' motif serves to mark the closure of the initial stanza (or cycle) of the oracle that begins at Am 3:1. It also functions to reinforce a more immediate, and hence important, *inclusio* at v. 8, namely, the one that connects with v. 1: 'Yahweh has spoken'. By means of a prominent convergence of literary-structural markers, the opening invocation to 'hear this word' thus initiates a new series of oracles in the overall organization of the prophecy (cf. 4:1, 5:1). This is a collection of messages explicitly indicting the sons of Israel for their failure to uphold their Covenant obligations to Yahweh, the Savior-God who delivered them from slavery in Egypt after choosing them from among all the nations on earth. The significance of the content of 3:1, then, is another strong indication of its structural role as the introduction to a major discourse segment. Likewise the reference to the eschatological 'day' of Yahweh clearly distinguishes 2:16 as being the closure of the preceding unit.

2.5 Controversy over 'the Word of the LORD' continues

Similar arguments could be marshaled against van der Wal's other suggested divisions of Amos 1–6. The second section running from 3:9–4:3 is supposedly 'framed' by the single (in itself a weak criterion) key word *ʾrmwn* 'stronghold', 'fortress' (1983:109; actually, the Hebrew is *ʾarminoṯh*, '[fortified] palace'). But as the analyst himself somewhat weakly admits, 'in order for this *inclusio* to become apparent, a change of the text is necessary in Amos 4:3' (ibid.). That simply is not good enough; it is not a credible analytical procedure to emend the text in order to permit one's hypothesis concerning its organization to materialize. Besides, this proposed segment begins at an obvious subunit and also ends at one; that is to say, 4:4ff. is a continuation of the oracle that opens at 4:1. Once again, a determination of the larger pattern must decide the demarcation and interrelationship of its internal constituents. The difficulty with such morphological skewing is that it distracts readers from the intended development of the author/editor's argument. In order to correctly understand a text, it is necessary for one to process it in an appropriate manner. This involves, among other things, segmenting the message into chunks of content of various scope and relating these in turn, structurally, as well as functionally, both to one another and to the composition as a whole.

A final major methodological problem with van der Wal's system is that it is arbitrary. The data presented by the text is not analyzed consistently according to an explicit set of heuristic procedures. It is not sufficient to select and apply certain formal features while ignoring others of a similar nature in order to preserve some neat organizational model. For example, van der Wal's 'fourth part' (1983:110) comprises Amos 5:7–6:12 because it is supposedly bounded by the key (or 'catch') words 'justice' and 'righteousness'. Not only does this proposed unit cross several more important structural boundaries, that is, the 'woe' oracles that begin at 5:18 and 6:1, but it also ignores the significant *inclusio* that encloses the material between 6:1 and 6:14, namely, 'nation' and 'house of Israel'. Besides, it leaves the analyst with a final section of just two verses, 6:13–14. Van der Wal posits this segment as being the 'conclusion' of the first six chapters of Amos since 'here all the threats of disaster come together' (ibid., 111). But the latter claim is not demonstrated, and 6:13–14 is not really rhetorically marked very much at all, certainly not any more so than its counterpart at the end of the first woe oracle covering 5:25–27.

The activity of thus organizing a verbal composition into its significant units and relations needs to be guided at all times by the various linguistic and literary (artistic and rhetorical) cues built into the text by the author himself, whether consciously or not. The particular device emphasized in the procedure advanced in this chapter is lexical-semantic *recursion*—in all of its diverse manifestations in literary discourse. The point is that a different arrangement of the text will produce a different understanding of its meaning—its thematic content, emotive force, and communicative purpose. For example, by starting a major new unit at 4:4, van der Wal obscures what may be seen as the dramatic, as well as surprising, onset of a sequence of highly ironic, yet at the same time deeply moving, stanzas in which Yahweh expresses his bitter frustration over Israel's apostasy and lack of response to his appeals to 'return/repent!' (4:1–13). In this sarcastic divine complaint, the women were definitely included!

2.5.3.2 *Concentric*

As an example of a somewhat misleading concentric framework of discourse arrangement, we return to de Waard and Smalley's elaborate scheme for configuring the complete prophecy of Amos. They outline this formation as follows (1979:195):

[Part I Israel's guilt; the prophet's responsibility]		Am 1:1–5:3
A a Prologue: the prophet		1:1–2a
B b The power of God to punish [hymn]		1:2b
C c Israel's special guilt among the nations		1:3–3:2
D d The prophet's role and commission		3:3–4:2
E c Israel doesn't learn God's lessons		4:4–12
– b The power of God to create [hymn]		4:13
F a[1] Lament for Israel (conclusion)		5:1–3

2.5 Controversy over 'the Word of the LORD' continues

[Part II Possibility of salvation; Israel's peril]   Am 5:4–15

G	d^1 Seek God and avoid destruction	5:4–6
H	c^1 Warning to sinners	5:7
I	b The power of God to create [hymn]	5:8
J	e THE LORD IS HIS NAME	
I'	b The power of God to punish [hymn]	5:9
H'	c^1 Warning to sinners and righteous	5:10–13
G'	d^1 Seek good and obtain mercy	5:14–15

[Part I' Israel's guilt and punishment; the prophet's involvement] Am 5:16–9:15

F'	a^1 Lament for Israel (introduction)	5:16–17
E'	c Israel relies on false security	5:18–6:14
	f The prophet's experiences: visions	7:19
D'	d The prophet's role and commission	7:10–17
	f The prophet's experiences: visions	8:1–3
C'	c^2 The punishment of Israel	8:4–9:4
B'/B''(b the power of God to punish and create [hymn])		9:5–6
A'	a Epilogue: punishment and recreation	9:7–15

[a, a^1 = opening/closing section; b = hymn to the power of God; c, c^1, c^2 = Israel's guilt and punishment; d = the prophet's role and commission; d^1 = the prophet's positive message; f = the prophet's vision experiences]

De Waard and Smalley go to some length to justify this diagram of the organization of Amos. In the process they provide a number of other structural outlines which summarize what they see as the symmetrical (chiastic) arrangement of many of the subunits of the whole (1979:199ff.). The sections given special attention are, specifically, those in which "the discourse structure has a bearing on the recommendations to translators" (ibid., 199). Such an important application is, of course, based on the assumption that their own segmentation and arrangement of the text is correct. But what if it is not? Obviously, the possibility then exists for some erroneous advice to be given, not only to translators but also to anyone else who may be guided by de Waard and Smalley's interpretation of the organization of Amos. A quick comparison with the structural description given earlier in this chapter reveals a significant number of points of disagreement, and hence also potential areas where differences in understanding the message of Amos might arise. In the following discussion, several of the more crucial of these divergences will be compared and evaluated. Who is right/wrong?

Ultimately, the reader/exegete must carefully weigh the evidence and decide for himself. The point of this exercise is to demonstrate the importance of recognizing the various issues involved, particularly as these relate to the larger framework of the text, and to explore the implications for a more accurate, functionally equivalent communication of the original message to a contemporary constituency.

The first problem that one notices is the extreme generality of the major titles. They could easily fit almost any book either in Amos or any of the other prophets, such as, 'Israel's guilt' (and punishment) (I/I'); 'Possibility of salvation' (II). Furthermore, coupling the latter with 'Israel's peril' (II) produces an apparent contradiction, which raises the question: Is this one distinct thematic unit or two? Then, too, the difference between 'The prophet's responsibility' (I) and his 'involvement' (I') is not very clear—or is the sense intended to be the same? And what about the unique close of the book, an oracle predicting the future restoration of 'Israel'—how does this fit under the heading, 'Israel's guilt and punishment' (I')? In order to be helpful, especially for a person who is not so familiar with the discourse structure of the text, such divisional titles must be meaningful, both in relation to one another and also as designations of the sections of content which they are intended to represent and distinguish.

The second difficulty of a more general nature is the preceding proposal's lack of symmetry with respect to the actual text of Amos. The sections delineated vary greatly in size. Parts I and I', for example, cover more than four chapters each, while part II includes just twelve verses. Unit B-b applies to part of a single passage (1:2b), whereas the very next unit (C-c) incorporates thirty-one verses. Such disparities would lead one to the conclusion, whether rightly or wrongly, that certain of the smaller divisions were deliberately demarcated and introduced simply to fill out the larger predetermined scheme—to provide the necessary parts for the introversion as a whole. At any rate, it would seem that the content of such minor segments would have to be extremely important (and demonstrated thus by being formally distinguished in the discourse) in order to balance structurally with those that are much larger in size. But that does not seem to be the case, for example, with a sequence such as 'Lament for Israel' (F'-a', 5:16–17) and 'Israel relies on false security' (E'-c, 5:18–6:14). At best we are dealing here with two distinct structural levels,

2.5 Controversy over 'the Word of the LORD' continues

which unfortunately happen to be obscured in the present arrangement of de Waard and Smalley.

Next, we might examine the appropriateness of some of the smaller (enclosed), more specific segments. Unit 3:3–4:2, for instance, is labeled, 'The prophet's role and commission' (that is, D–d). But even a cursory survey of these verses reveals that this heading applies only partially, if at all, to the material it is supposed to designate. Thus, 3:3–8 does speak about the wider commission of Yahweh's prophets to announce his judgment upon the apostates in Israel. However, the larger remainder of this putative unit does not deal with 'the prophet's role and commission' at all. One can only conclude that this unit was so entitled in order to match up with D'-d in part I' where there is a clear reference to the personal experience of Amos throughout the passage (that is, 7:10–17). Yet even here, the focal conflict which the prophet's message of condemnation inspired is not really suggested by this wording. Similarly, the correspondence between C-c and E-c is by no means complete. The former unit, in fact, deals with 'Israel' specifically only at its conclusion, namely, 2:6ff. Granted, the function of the oracles against the other 'nations' is to build up to the one condemning Israel. But the point is that, as a whole, the former unit is similar to 4:4 [sic., actually 4:3]–12 only in the vaguest sort of way.

Another aspect of this same problem of overgeneralization concerns the significant material that is not given due recognition in the outline of de Waard and Smalley. For example, the unit headed, 'Israel relies on false security' (that is, E'-c, 5:18–6:14) actually includes two distinct woe oracles, namely, those beginning at 5:18 as well as 6:1. Furthermore, these deal with the designated sin of 'false security' only in certain portions. For instance, 5:21–24 and 6:3–7 present specific indictments against the people's religious and social sins respectively. The unit referring to 'The punishment of Israel' (C'-2 [sic, i.e., C'-c], 8:4–9:4) also incorporates the last of the five 'vision reports' (that is, 9:1), the other four of which were given explicit mention in the preceding pair of F units. As the arbitrariness of the system thus becomes more evident, one's confidence with regard to its reliability as an accurate reflection of the discourse structure of Amos is correspondingly shaken.

Even the overall structural arrangement may be called into question. Units F and F' (that is, 5:1–3 and 5:16–17) are positioned as the final and initial units respectively of Parts I and I'. However, both are complementary portions of the same lament, the former indicating the reason (the fall of Israel's warriors) and the latter the result (a great weeping) in terms of the song's content. And since 5:1 is a prominent aperture (for example, 'Hear this word...', cf. 4:1) and 5:17 would, by *inclusio,* be its corresponding close, it seems more meaningful to incorporate the two into part II, which would then span vv. 1–17 of chapter 5. In their effort to force the text into their expanded concentric pattern, de Waard and Smalley obliterate the prominent sectional breaks at 3:1, 4:1, 5:18, and 6:1 (the latter two being woe oracles). Similarly, their attempt to set the first two verses of chapter 3 in balance with virtually the whole of chapters 1 and 2 by means of a topical introversion is equally unconvincing (1979:200–201). The data simply cannot be stretched that far.

The problem with such proposals—and the scholarly literature abounds in them—is not only one of perspective. In other words, a discourse display that is skewed might well lead a person to forge the wrong formal and semantic relationships in the text—to see a beginning where there should be an ending (and vice-versa), to fail to recognize one part that is included within another, to miss a point of climax in the development of a section, or to follow an illusory outline of a particular topic. To a greater or lesser extent, then, these errors, when introduced into a version by way of section headings, typographical format, paragraphing, explanatory footnotes, or whatever, all serve as psychological 'noise' which interferes with the real message that the biblical author had intended to transmit. This problem does not really concern the text's original receptors, but all those contemporary readers who desire to know what the LORD's prophet had to say in his own sociocultural context and how this applies to us today.

However, that is not the greatest danger of an errant construal of a book's larger organization. Much more serious in its consequences is the effect that a flawed analysis may have on the actual interpretation of the text. This is especially true of commentators of the source, or redaction-critical, school who do not view the discourse holistically as an integral unit, but rather as some sort of composite, patchwork structure that was pieced together over a considerable period of time. De Waard and Smalley more than make up for a certain element of confusion which they impose upon the

2.5 Controversy over 'the Word of the LORD' continues

macrostructure of Amos by means of a relatively solid exegetical discussion of its microstructure. This cannot be said, unfortunately, for a number of other extensive treatments of the book's form, content, and function. A glaring example of the latter camp is Coote who, as noted earlier, has factored the text into three stages of composition (1981:7), each of which must be interpreted independently first of all, and then reinterpreted when combined in light of a supposed new editorial setting. One complex instance should serve to illustrate the adverse consequences of such an approach on one's understanding of Amos—whoever he was!

When introducing his comments on the section 3:9–6:14, Coote warns his readers that his method of sorting out the various sources of composition may have the following effect upon them (1981:73):

> You may find the literary subtleties that have so far come to light impressive or—perhaps more likely—bewildering.

Indeed, the latter term 'bewildering' better characterizes the impression that is given as Coote proceeds to apportion out the material of this pericope according to a pair of hypothetical 'editors', only stage A possibly having anything to do with the historical Amos (ibid., 75):

Samaria (stage A)		**Bethel** (stage B)
3:9–12	(1)	3:13–15
4:1–3	(2)	4:4–13
5:1–3	(3)	5:4–15
5:16–20	(4)	5:21–27
6:1–7	(5)	6:8–14

Now this division of the discourse (and its underlying presuppositions) does have some significant implications for translation. For example, the commonly accepted renderings 'winter house' and 'summer house' of 3:11 must not be correct because "they wouldn't both be at Bethel" (ibid., 77). Coote's task then is to determine "their meaning in the B stage, and thus in the oracle as presently composed" *(loc. cit.)*. Naturally, he succeeds by proposing an unattested alteration, 'autumn storehouse' and 'late summer...storehouse'—the distinction apparently being perfectly clear to him *(loc. cit.)*.

Furthermore, "vague exhortations" (ibid., 78) such as 'seek me and live' (Am 5:4, 6, 14, 15) "are inconceivable in stage A, which knows no extenuation and no remnant" (ibid., 79), and therefore they could not be found in logical combination with the lament passages of 5:1-3 and 16-20 (sic, actually 16-17). But Coote's critical eye discerns a number of inconsistencies (i.e., divergences from his hypothesis), even in the enclosed section which he has ascribed to stage B, that is, 5:4-14, and these must be sifted out. This he proceeds to do (ibid., 83-84), with an assurance that is certainly amazing, if not convincing. Coote's description of this process as it allegedly occurred at the time of stage B and of the 'artificial' structure that results might well be applied to his own handling of the text (ibid., 82-83; cf. Doan and Giles 2005:85-107):

> [The document] is intended to be magnificently artificial, devised by learned ingenuity to practice the secrets, affirm the values, and undergird the status of a limited and somewhat exclusive class of scribes who had the skill, motivation, and opportunity to pass on the prophetic voice in writing.

The problem is that erroneous assumptions about the larger organization of a discourse do have inevitable consequences upon the exegetical process. For where one finds gaps, stages, distinct structures, and different editors, there must also be diverse horizons, or perspectives and parameters, of interpretation. Strangely enough, these are often modeled upon contemporary theological theories, whatever happens to be in vogue at the time. Some years ago, it was the 'liberation' school that seemed to make the greatest impression among the scholarly 'scribes.' And so it is not surprising that Coote, too, perceives his segmentation of Amos as culminating in the notion of a 'restoration' which is to be generally understood in terms of socioeconomic class conflict and a political struggle for independence. According to him, then, the concept of '"remnant" is used by B- and C- type editors to refer to the leftover ruling elite' since it 'implies minority, even in Hebrew, and would never suit the peasantry, who make up 80 percent or more of the population' (1981:123). All vestiges of a spiritual renewal and a divinely instituted fellowship embracing all nations to be realized in a future Messianic age—and beyond in the eschaton—need to be erased in passages such as 9:11-15. They must be replaced by a more relevant, hence materialistic, conception of the ideal political state, which is typified by a 'liberation from servitude to and oppressive exploitation by the ruling elite' *(loc.*

cit.). In Coote's opinion the beatific vision of Amos—actually editor 'C'—is this *(loc. cit.)*:

> The peasantry recover their domain. The vineyards, orchards, and grain lands become theirs again, and they are the ones who reside comfortably in the cities, not their oppressors.

Thus, a combination of hermeneutical factors, notably, a disruptive, fragmented approach to the original text, coupled with an interpretive bias that is unduly influenced by current political philosophies, produces a transformation of the message of Amos into a humanistic platform that may sound more appealing to the masses. In effect, such commentators have reduced the 'roar' of the LORD to a whimper of its former self by desacralizing his Word along the lines proposed by Amaziah of Bethel. Any such deformation of the discourse structure of the biblical documents cannot help but distort the trans-linguistic, cultural, and historical communication of their intended content.

2.6 Presenting 'the word of the LORD' in Amos today

In this concluding portion of my study of the prophet Amos, I will briefly touch upon the contemporary presentation of his dynamic message via two very different media of communication—namely, the familiar printed text of our published Bibles in contrast to a personal 'live' dramatic 'performance' of the prophecy. Both modes of transmission, though dissimilar, do correspond in emphasizing the vital *oral-aural dimension* of the Scriptures and in revealing how this primary means of interacting with a target audience might be made to feature more prominently in re-presenting the 'roar of the LORD from Zion' (1:2) today.

2.6.1 The printed text

Most modern Bibles do not serve actual readers and hearers of the text very well. In fact, many typographical and format characteristics of published Scriptures detract from a ready and accurate oral articulation of what has been written. In the case of a prophetic book such as Amos, for example, we normally observe the typical two column arrangement of justified, often hyphenated lines of relatively smallish print that are not displayed on the page in a manner that clearly reflects the poetic arrangement of the text in terms of either its microstructure or macrostructure (cf. Wendland and Louw 1993). This common style of printing Bibles stems from two principal drives in the publishing industry—*tradition* (what people are used to) and *trade* (how to save money).

The following then is a sample (freely adapted from the *New Living Translation*) of what might be done in the interests of both *readability* for the benefit of the lector and also *accuracy* with respect to the rhetorical structure of the original text.

A Call to Repentance

Just listen, you people of Israel!	1
Listen to this funeral song I am singing:	
"Israel, the young maiden, has fallen,	2
never to get up again!	
She lies abandoned there on the ground,	
with no one at all to help her up."	
The Sovereign LORD says:	3
"When a city sends a thousand men into battle,	
only a hundred of them will return.	
When a town sends out a hundred soldiers,	
only ten at best will come back alive."	
Now this is what the LORD says to the family of Israel:	4
"Come back to me, you people, and live!	
Don't worship at the pagan altars at Bethel;	5
don't go to the shrines at Gilgal or Beersheba.	
For the people of Gilgal will be dragged off into exile,	
and the people of Bethel will be reduced to nothing."	
Come back to the LORD and live!	6
Otherwise, he will rush through Israel like a fire,	
devouring you all completely.	
Your so-called gods in Bethel	
won't be able to quench the flames!	
You twist justice in the land,	7
making it a bitter pill for the oppressed.	
You treat the righteous like dirt!	
But who is it that created the stars,	8
indeed, the great Pleiades and Orion?	

2.6 Presenting 'the word of the LORD' in Amos today

    Who turns darkness into morning
    and the daytime into night?
    Who draws up water from the oceans
    and pours it down as rain on the land?
    The LORD God is his name!
    With blinding speed and power he destroys the strong,   9
    crushing all their assumed defenses.

  How you hate honest judges!   10
  How you despise people who tell the truth!
  You trample the unprotected poor,   11
   stealing their grain through taxes and unfair rent.
  Therefore, though you build beautiful stone houses,
  you will never survive to live in them.
  Though you plant lush vineyards,
  you will never drink wine from them.
  For I know the vast number of your sins   12
  and the depth of your constant rebellion.
  You oppress good people by taking bribes
  and deprive the poor of justice in the courts.
  So those who are smart keep their mouths shut,   13
  for it is a most evil time!

Do what is good and run far from evil   14
so that you may live at length!
Then the LORD God of Heaven's Armies will be your helper,
just as you yourselves have claimed.
Hate everything evil and love what is good;   15
turn your law courts into true halls of justice.
Perhaps even yet the LORD God of Heaven's Armies
will at last have mercy on the remnant of his people.

Therefore, this is what the Lord,   16
the LORD God of Heaven's Armies, says:

"There will be crying in all the public squares
and great mourning in every street.
Call for the farmers to weep with you,
and summon professional mourners to wail.
There will be loud wailing in every vineyard,   17
for I will surely destroy them all!"
says the LORD.

The poeticized selection above has been formatted in parallel strophic paragraphs following the literary-structural analysis that was outlined in section 2.3.3.3. The divine formulas have been italicized, and the two divine speech segments (vv. 3–5 and 16–17) set in a different print font, as distinct from the presumed words of Amos. Finally, the verse numbers have been set aside along the right-hand margin so as not to disturb the smooth flow of the reading process. Thus, if a particular Scripture pericope can be read with more sense, forcefulness, and feeling, all listeners are bound to benefit as well. In order to increase the understanding of the silent reader of this pericope, various study notes might be added to explain various important literary, rhetorical, thematic, and format-related aspects of the discourse, for example: the central hymnic portion in praise of Yahweh (vv. 8–9); the ironic wordplays of v. 5; the significant calls of the LORD and Amos for repentance (vv. 4–6, 14–15); the intended function of the distinct type faces and styles (including the boldfaced line in the central core, v. 8c).

2.6.2 The performed text

I have already had occasion to refer to the study of 'performance criticism' as applied to the prophetic book of Amos by Doan and Giles (hereafter, D&G; 2005:chs. 5–6) on several occasions in the preceding discussion. Thus far, I have been rather critical of this approach in its effort to determine the *compositional history* of the Hebrew text. For example, having drawn attention to the essential orality of the original in its genesis, D&G correctly conclude that 'the prophets' oral performances were, in some fashion or other, transferred to writing, appearing then as literary pieces bearing the name of the orator' (ibid., 3). However, D&G mistakenly (in my opinion) go on to assert that the literary activity of writing, or recording, these prophetic works involved a prominent exercise of 'social power':

> The transformation takes ownership of the performance from the performer and gives it to the scribe.... In other words, a performance, itself an exercise of social power, became a commodity of power when transformed into written texts. But that act of writing required a new performance, and a new exercise of power, as the reader adopted the persona of the prophet to "perform" the written

2.6 Presenting 'the word of the LORD' in Amos today

> words that were uttered aloud and, in their hearing, once again became available to the nonliterate populace. (ibid., 4)

One wonders how Yahweh fits into this prophetic scenario or indeed any sort of spiritual or religious motivation. Rather, the major emphasis seems to be on this unknown sequence of nameless scribes who vied with one another in their dramatic performance of re-recording the text, regularly altering (scripting) it to suit personal preferences and pressing social conditions on each successive occasion (D&G ibid., 15, 21–22, 23–24; original italics, but my additions in brackets below):

> The scribes [certainly unlike Baruch—e.g., Jer 36:4, 27, 32] were processing the lives and acts of the prophets, creating a performance space on the written page, and contributing to the spectator / performer aggregate. The fluid nature of performance allows us to use the theatre as a hermeneutical tool for isolating elements of the theatre and drama in the Hebrew Bible while at the same time making metonymical connections between theatre practice and prophetic function. Yet it is not a straight line from prophetic performance to literate recording of that performance. The process of recording can change and even undermine the original performative intent of the prophet.... The prophetic scribe (or, perhaps better, the prophetic playwright) is dependent on the prophetic performer [i.e., the original prophet] for his inspiration [not from Yahweh?] and derives his credibility from an attachment to the prophetic performer but, nonetheless, is bent on replacing the prophetic performer. Whether intentional or not, the effect of the literature is to script the prophetic performance [actually now a 'scribal recording'] and in so doing to control the prophetic performance.... The scribes create prophetic *characters* out of the prophets themselves (prophetic actors).... The difference between character and actor resides at the crux of the struggle for power and control between the prophet and the scribe.

With specific respect to the book of Amos then, "[t]he scribe, in order to create the drama of Amos, has to appropriate Amos the prophet, both in his writing and reading of the text, if he is to achieve the power of the prophet" (ibid., 25).

The preceding should be sufficient to indicate the speculative nature of the 'performative' enterprise of D&G. The notion of an original text thus disappears, very much along the lines of source- and redaction-criticism, into a murky, albeit dramatic, succession of anonymous scribal performances—the last (canonical) one hopefully being the correct one to base all ensuing analysis and interpretation on, right up to the present day. All this is far too imaginative a venture to me, perhaps even leading some to skeptically conclude (re-phrasing the initial heading of this chapter, 2.1) about 'the prophetic *text* of Amos's—is it in fact a miracle or a mirage? Needless to say, my various literary-structural studies of this book prompt just the opposite conclusion: A document so elaborately (in terms of poetic patterning and rhetorical styling) as well as cohesively and coherently composed with respect to its compelling Yahweh-centered theme and equally focused prophetic purpose could not have been produced by committee—and a discontinuous, probably discordant group at that. It must have been generated by a single exceptional author, who not only uttered the original oracles, under divine inspiration, but who also superintended the subsequent recording and editing of the oral text in writing.

On the other hand, Doan and Giles do have some valuable insights to contribute to our current efforts in communicating the text of Amos (as well as the other books of Scripture) to a contemporary audience in a more effective, audience-sensitive manner. Thus, "…performance criticism uses insights from…other forms of criticism and combines them with an appreciation for audience response in order to present the dynamics present in a social event, namely, performance" (ibid., 105). For example, when commenting on the dramatic quality of the "oracles against the nations" (Amos 1:3–2:6), D&G offer some interesting comments on the style of performance as well as relationship that existed between the prophet and the text that he received from the LORD (ibid., 115):

> In terms of the performative context for the prophet, particularly as he moves from "Thus says the LORD," to speaking as the Lord ("I will not revoke…"), the roaring lion is a very useful image. The explicit activity of the oracles against foreign nations is clear and distinct, establishing a rhythmic pattern of exchange between the prophet and his spectators. Each oracle contains its own crux, or moment of highest intensity, as well as its own decrescence, or moment away from that intensity, punctuated by a concluding phrase: "says the LORD." The two frames of each oracle—the opening, "Thus says the LORD," and the concluding, "says the LORD," are perhaps the most significant in terms of explicit and implicit activity because they represent moments of transformation for the prophet. Each "Thus says the LORD" signifies the moment of transformation from Amos the prophet to Amos as the Lord. The concluding "says the LORD" reverses the transformation, allowing the resumption of

2.6 Presenting 'the word of the LORD' in Amos today

Amos the prophet. The prophet himself becomes the link between the real world and the performance world. The prophet becomes the performance personified.

D&G then describe the dramatic nature of this sequence of oracles as follows (ibid., 116):

> Amos's tension level is high right from the beginning: "The LORD roars from Zion." Fulfilling the activity of the prophet (Amos's project) produces the theatrical tension. The path of this tension is the action: oracles against foreign nations leading up to the oracle against Israel. The flow of this action creates the inner life of the drama: the sensations and the experiences that pass between Amos and the spectators. As Amos moves through the mounting tension of presenting the oracles, the inherent linear intensification and relaxation pattern of the drama is revealed.

D&G also offer some sample 'stage directions' which, though rather speculative, do suggest what Amos (and all subsequent performers of his text) might have done to "gain and hold the attention of his audience" (ibid., *loc. cit.*). For example, with regard to the 'Oracle against Damascus' (Am 1:3–5; ibid., 117):

> Does Amos look directly at his spectators as he speaks, "Thus says the LORD"? How long does he pause before speaking as the Lord? How does his voice change from speaking as prophet to speaking as Lord? Who does Amos look at or where does he look when proclaiming what will happen to the gate bars of Damascus?... How does Amos transition from speaking as the Lord back to a prophet: "says the LORD"?

Several additional performative directions might be suggested here—that is, not only where the speaker (prophet) looks, but *how* he looks, that is, with respect to facial expressions, e.g., to represent anger, frustration, invitation, and so forth. The quality of voice (e.g., loud/soft, fast/slow, high/low pitch, etc.), body stance as well as movements 'on stage' before the audience, and hand/arm gestures might also be considered, for example, when pronouncing a 'breaking down of the gate of Damascus' (1:5). Several of these performative dimensions are indicated in the following directions concerning the 'Oracle against Judah' (Am 2:4–5; ibid., 118):

> The oracle against Judah does not end with "says the LORD," but transitions right into "Thus says the LORD," for the oracle against

Israel. How does this rhythmic device help the audience control the attention of his spectators? How might the prophet use this as a transition? Does he intensify the pitch and volume of his delivery, preparing to reach the crux, or final climactic point, of these oracles when speaking of Israel's transgressions?... Does he use his voice and body to draw the spectators to him so that the oracle against Israel can begin at a lower pitch, with almost whispered intensity?

In conclusion, such a *performative approach* to the biblical text can be beneficial when applied to a Bible translation project in several ways:

- It can increase the translation team's awareness of and appreciation for the 'oral-aural' factor during all aspects of their work, including the selection of personnel who may be especially gifted and/or who have received special training in this field.

- They can begin by investigating the original text in order to discover its prominent features (forms) of orality and to specify how these may have functioned in the initial communication event, e.g., the use of prophetic formulas in Amos.

- Corresponding forms and functions must then be identified and described in analogous target-language (TL) genres (oral and/or written) in order to prepare a listing of possible form-functional 'matches', e.g., exact and synonymous repetition, which works equally well for similar purposes in a Bantu language.

- Next, these oral-aural structural and stylistic devices need to be applied in the process of translating the biblical text, e.g., the diverse patterns of linear and concentric recursion in Amos, so that the vernacular rendition (in addition to accuracy) manifests a similar degree of structural integrity, artistic appeal, rhetorical impact, and 'performative potential' for presenting before a typical audience.

- Preparing a translation for such a live performance and then actually trying it out, e.g., as a multi-vocal drama, a recitation, chant, musical version, etc., will undoubtedly alert the team to certain difficulties that they still have with their TL text, e.g., with respect to wording, lineation, rhythmic utterance, euphony, so that these problem points can be revised and tested again in the ongoing process of quality control for improvement.

2.6 Presenting 'the word of the LORD' in Amos today

In all of these communication-related endeavors, whether applied to SL analysis process or to various TL applications, the primary motivation is to ensure that 'the roar of the LORD' (Am 1:2, 3:8) resounds as clearly, correctly, and convincingly in translation as it did in the original event—that is, given the significant limitations that we face in determining relative equivalence in any of these respects.

3

The Rhetoric of Obadiah's "Day": Its Structure and Significance

3.1 Introduction

Whoever reads—or preaches from—the book of Obadiah anyway? What's the point when there are so many alternatives that are more familiar and seemingly more "reader-friendly"? It cannot be denied that this, the smallest book in the Hebrew Scriptures, suffers from a rather serious identity crisis, situated as it is on a single page (in most English Bibles) between Amos and Jonah in the corpus of the so-called "Minor" Prophets. But is it correct to view Obadiah as only a short and somewhat insignificant prophecy of doom pronounced against the largely unknown ancient kingdom of Edom? Did this prophecy find its way into the biblical canon simply because a number of its constituent verses happen to resemble those of Jeremiah chapter 49?

On the contrary, as we hope to show in this essay, there is considerable literary as well as theological evidence which would support the conclusion that "the vision of Obadiah" *(chazon 'ovadidah)* is actually a model prophetic text—a microcosm as it were of such literature dealing with the forthcoming momentous "day of the LORD" (*yom YHWH*). Despite its brevity (only about 70 poetic lines in the Hebrew), Obadiah is a masterfully constructed discourse in terms of its artistic style of writing. It is also one that is rhetorically motivated from start to finish, conveying a powerful message of weal as well as woe from the LORD that has just as much relevance to believers today as it did to its original receptors over 25 centuries ago. The purpose of the present study is to demonstrate this claim by means of a careful examination of the form and function of this strongly hortatory, yet beautifully poetic composition. In the process we will illustrate, at least in part, a holistic, discourse oriented approach to the analysis and interpretation of biblical texts, Hebrew prophecy in particular.

After an overview of the intricate formal organization of Obadiah, we will consider how the book's overall structure and style relate to its preeminent function as an instance of rhetorically motivated speech. In other words, we will propose a hypothesis concerning the prophecy's operation on four distinct planes of interpersonal message transmission, namely: the "surface" (explicit textual) level 1 which includes the possibility of participant "embedded" speech$_2$, and the "deep" (implicit, addressee-oriented) level$_3$—all three of which apply to the original setting of composition and communication—then also the "transferred" stratum$_4$ of subsequent application to contextually diverse sociocultural and historical situations. The latter focus on the level$_4$ of "canonical rhetoric" (cf. Vanhoozer 2002:188–199) leads to a number of concluding remarks on the enduring (if oft unrecognized) theological significance of Obadiah to contemporary Bible readers of every persuasion and degree of proficiency, in particular, all those "delivered" (*p-l-t*) members of "the house of Jacob" (*beth ya'aqov*, v. 17).

3.2 Unity in diversity: The form of Obadiah among the prophets

The prophecy of Obadiah follows the typical generic pattern of such "oracles against the nations" found in the Hebrew Scriptures. Accordingly, the text manifests four form-functional segments that serve a basic twofold purpose, namely: "to announce the enemy's defeat and to reassure Israel that God protects her security" (Klein et al. 1993:300). These four structural units are listed and briefly described below:

3.2 Unity in diversity: The form of Obadiah amongthe prophets

1. **Identification:** revelation of the foreign/pagan nation to be indicted and judged by Yahweh through his chosen prophetic messenger, often using the vehicle of divine apostrophe (e.g., Ob 1–2; cf. Jer 49:7).

2. **Indictment:** the various sins of that nation are enumerated, especially those which concern the LORD's chosen people, Israel (e.g., Ob 10–14; cf. Jer 49:16).

3. **Condemnation:** an appropriate punishment for the wicked is described very graphically in direct speech by YAHWEH himself, often colored by battle imagery (i.e., a "war oracle," Klein et al.: *loc. cit.*) and punctuated by warnings that all efforts to escape will prove fruitless (e.g., 2–9, 15–16, 18; cf. Jer 49:8–22).

4. **Prediction:** after the devastation inflicted upon the enemy, Israel (the people of God) will be graciously restored to a position of preeminence and prosperity in "the land" (at times incorporating the whole world), with certain pagan nations sometimes also sharing in these divine blessings (Ob 17–21; cf. Jer 30–31, 33, 49:39).

Characteristic of many of these judgment oracle is the radical shift in fortunes, or "turning" *(shuv),* that marks a role-reversal involving Judah/Israel and the particular enemy nations(s) in question, e.g., Ob 10, 15. Frequently these twists in divinely ordained fate are ironic in nature because the foreign oppressors will be forced to undergo the same sort of shame and punishment which they previously inflicted upon God's people. In other words, their punishment will fit the crimes that they once perpetrated: "As you have done, it will be done to you; your deeds will return upon your own head" (Ob 15, NIV). Similarly, Israel will one day rule in triumph over those who had earlier caused and/or boasted over the fall of Jerusalem: "The house of Jacob will be a fire...the house of Esau will be stubble..." (Ob 18, NIV). As will be shown in the analysis to follow, such a dramatic reversal is also typical of Obadiah's style on the microstructure of discourse organization and thematic development.

The larger formal arrangement of the book of Obadiah is delineated by a number of structural markers (SMs), which when considered in relation to one another, rather clearly demarcate the discourse into three major constituent segments: 1–10, 11–14, and 15–21, as outlined below. The interchange of speakers reveals an A-B-A' ring-construction as two complementary divine oracles having a future orientation are conjoined by a prophetic denunciation with a perspective on the past. This compositional framework is supported by the rhetorical dynamics of the text to be discussed later on. The principal portions, or "strophes" (poetic paragraphs), that comprise the vision of Obadiah may be briefly described as follows.

3.2.1 Section A: 1–10

(1) **Introduction:** The prophetic proclamation of Yahweh's punitive intention with regard "to Edom" *(le'edom)* begins. SM: The initial announcement of a "vision" *(chazon)* and its spokesman (Obadiah) is immediately followed by a dramatic revelation of its content. This is appropriately introduced by the prophetic messenger formula which indicates its divine source, i.e., "thus says the LORD...".

The second and third lines (bicola) both open with an emphatic verb-iterated construction. The third colon, a summons to battle (holy-war), features arousing assonance in *(a)*. The direct speech here giving the content of the "report" *(shimu'ah)* of the "envoy" *(tsir)* constitutes the peak (thematic nucleus) and climax (emotive node) of the introduction. It graphically foreshadows the LORD's message to follow in section one of the prophecy (vv. 2–10). The last word of the verse forms a complementary, topically related rhyming inclusio with the final word of the prophecy (v. 21), viz. *lamilchamah* ('for the battle') vs. *hamilukhah* ('the kingship').

(2–10) **Judgment of Edom:** Despite all protective measures, the proud nation of Edom will be utterly destroyed by her enemies. This will take place during the course of proximate world events and will represent the LORD's punitive justice being levied against the people of Edom for the violence that they had committed against "Jacob" (i.e., Israel, v. 10). This unit, the first of three principal sections which comprise the book, is itself composed of three distinct strophes as delineated by the SMs listed below. All of these are uttered by Yahweh (cf. vv. 4, 8).

SM (2–4): The prophetic vision of Obadiah begins appropriately with an attention-drawing *hinneh* ('look!'), which serves to emphasize the immediately following word "small" *(qaton)*. The segment ends with the common oracular formula "declaration of Yahweh" *(ne'um-YHWH),* which in its role as an utterance punctuator here forms an inclusio with a corresponding phrase at the beginning of v. 1. The logical development of this strophe

3.2 Unity in diversity: The form of Obadiah amongthe prophets

manifests a chiastic pattern which reflects the corresponding downfall (an inversion of status or belittlement) of Edom that is being predicted:

> A (2) punishment = Edom will be made small/despised
>   B (3a) indictment = Edom's deceptive pride of heart
>   B' (3b) indictment = Edom's boastful self-incriminating speech
> A' (4) punishment = Yahweh will bring Edom down to the ground

This strophe reaches its peak at the close in the LORD'S stinging rebuke: "From there I shall bring you down!" *(misham 'owridekha)*—which is a direct response to Edom's defiant rhetorical question of the preceding verse. This divine prediction summarizes in two words the first half of the prophet's message and the LORD's judicial case. It thus makes a scornful reply to Edom's arrogant boast just uttered (in a highlighted segment of direct speech): "Who can bring me down to earth?"—*miy yowrideniy 'arets* (the strophe's emotive climax).

SM (5–7): Another hypothetical construction beginning with *'im* leads off this strophe as in v. 4, but there is no connective *waw*, the asyndeton perhaps suggesting unit aperture here (Clark notes the lack of explicit opening and closing markers for this strophe, 1991:8). However, there is also an apparent shift in the semantic force, that is, from concession-contraexpectation to condition-consequence (v. 5). The strophe is tightly structured internally by means of a pair of elaborate interlocking syntactic and semantic arrangements, each of which features another chiastic pattern that mirrors the reversal in friendship, or betrayal, that Edom experienced in relation to its former allies. This sequence runs as follows:

> (5a) A: *'im* protasis
>   B: *'eykh* apostrophe
>   C: *halo'* apodasis—RQ
> A_1: *'im* hendiadys
> (5b) A': *'im* protasis
>   C': *halo'* apodosis—RQ
> (6a)   B': *'eykh* exclamation
> (6b) B'_1: extension
> (7a) D_1: act of hostility
> E_1: by allies (men of your covenant)
> D'_1: act of hostility
> (7b) D_2: act of hostility
> E_2: by allies (men of your peace)

(7c) E_3: by allies ([men of] your bread)
        D_3: act of hostility
(7d) a final short contrastive monocolon of closure makes an ironic transition to the next strophe, i.e., Edom has no understanding; even their wise men (plus national politics and foreign policy) are confounded (v. 8)!

The references to Edom's lost wisdom in vv. 7-8 along with the formally similar *'im* constructions in vv. 4-5 function as structural overlapping devices (i.e., anadiplosis) to smooth over the junctures that occur between these pairs of verses. Closure of this second strophe is formally marked by the strong sequence of word-final "you" pronominals (*-kha*, 2ms) which highlights the betrayal that Edom experienced. The peak of this strophe occurs in the middle (v. 6) with the exclamation emphasizing the pillaging of Esau, which is flanked on each side by a triad of participants, one hypothetical: "thieves...robbers...grape-pickers" (v. 5), the other real (though expressed figuratively): "men of your treaty...compact...close acquaintance" (v. 7). There is also in closing a reiteration of the verb "set" (*s-y-m*, cf. v. 4b, end-of-unit correspondence = "epiphora").

SM (8-10): The onset of this third strophe (i.e., aperture) is very clearly delineated by means of the following cluster of demarcative devices: a divine quote in the form of a rhetorical question; an anaphoric (unit-initial) link with v. 5 in the repeated negative interrogative particles (*halo'*); another instance of anaphora in the second and final mention of "Edom" (*'edom*)—cf. v. 1; anadiplosis, or overlapping, in the recursion of a word pointing to Edom's crucial lack (i.e., *tivunah* "discernment"); a reiteration of the accentuating divine oracle formula (*ne'um-YHWH*, cf. v. 4c); and an introduction of the key thematic term "day." The latter is here combined with "that" (i.e., *bayom hahu'*) to give the expression additional eschatological overtones, namely, as a prophetic reference to a future time of divine judgment.

Verses 8-9 emphasize Edom's coming doom through repeated metonymic use of the proper name (i.e., "Edom...Esau...Teman...Esau"). In that fearful day all human resources will fail—the wise men as well as the warriors. Suddenly then, at the close of the strophe and climax of the entire section, the reason for such harsh judgment is revealed: Esau had treated his blood brother Jacob with "violence" (*chamas*, cf. Deut 23:7)! This is the first time that the motivating cause for Edom's destruction is mentioned (Clark and Mundhenk 1982:19). Indeed, the nation deserved to "be cut off forever",

3.2 Unity in diversity: The form of Obadiah amongthe prophets 109

an expression referring to the awful ultimate in punishment. This ominous allusion to an eternity of "shame" *(vuwshah)*, in pointed contrast to Edom's "pride" *(zidon)* foregrounded in strophe one, rounds out the first major segment of the prophecy on a grimly negative note.

In a departure from most English versions and commentaries, I am proposing that verse 10 emphatically *concludes* this strophe and section, rather than beginning a new one as in the others (the NIV being an exception in that is does not break either before or after v. 10). There are a number of structural and thematic reasons for this decision, which are summarized below:

1. With its cluster of key terms, verse ten suddenly discloses that the great crime ("violence") of the Edomites was in fact committed against their relatives (*ya'aqov* "Jacob"), the covenant people of Yahweh. To this unexpected revelation is immediately added the appropriate divine retribution—a shameful and complete desolation. In this capacity then the verse functions as a concluding summary and peak point of the book's initial pericope.

2. The reference to "Jacob" culminates, albeit contrastively, the cohesive series of personal names referring to "Esau" that runs throughout the strophe comprising vv. 8–10.

3. In v. 11 there is a renewed reference to events taking place "on the day" *(beyom)*, a key prophetic term which was first mentioned at the beginning of the preceding strophe (i.e., similar unit openings = "anaphora"). In this instance, however, the predominant temporal setting shifts to past historical to carry on now in specific detail from the general accusation of v. 10. Verse 11, also set off by asyndeton; cf. the triad of *waw*-initial cola in v. 12), thus introduces a series of indictments concerning "the day" which runs through v. 14.

4. The last word in v. 9 *(miqatel* "from/by slaughter") is closely linked to the initial word of v. 10 *(mechamas* "from/because of violence"), syntactically, semantically, and phonologically (i.e., in the alliterative /m/ sequence). For this reason the BHS version and many commentators (e.g., Thompson 1956:863) suggest a transfer of the former to the latter verse. This makes it the longest line in the entire book and very likely terminal as well. In any case, "by slaughter" could well be a pivotal term with referential connections in both directions, thus joining the two verses within the same poetic unit.

5. The next strophe, vv. 11–14, is bounded by a prominent lexical *inclusio*, formed by the verb "you stand" *('-m-d)*, and by other external delimiting as well as internal conjunctive devices that reveal its integrity as an independent compositional unit (see further discussion below).

6. An ironic reference to "cutting off/down" *(k-r-th)* is found at the corresponding endings of adjacent strophes (= "epiphora"), i.e., Edom will be "cut off" (v. 10) because, among other things, its army "cut down" the fugitives from Jerusalem (v. 14).

7. Another epiphoric correspondence of thematic importance (depending on one's interpretation) occurs in v. 10 and the last verse of the book: In the former, Edom's complete destruction is predicted; in v. 21, however, there is another reference to "the mountain of Esau" *(har 'esav)*, this time possibly in a soteriological setting (cf. also vv. 8–9).

On the basis of evidence such as that listed above, and within the framework of the discourse design of the book as a whole, it seems likely that v. 10 functions more correctly as a highlighted bicolon of *closure,* rather than one of aperture as in most other interpretations.

3.2.2 Section B: 11–14

(11–14) **Progressive Transition:** The indictment against Esau (v. 9) is now specified in intricate poetic detail. However, in the light of history and prior prophetic messages, this passage can also be read from quite a different perspective, namely, as a review of the divine judgment meted out against the covenant-breaking people of Judah, and Jerusalem in particular. Such an interpretation is suggested, albeit indirectly, by the cohesive string of colon-final terms denoting his/their calamity, especially within the thematic peak line of verse 13 (*'edowm,* a pun on the otherwise unnamed "Edom", *'edom*).

Verses 11–14 constitute the second compositional third of the prophecy as whole. The section functions as a structural bridge to firmly establish the basis for the LORD's condemnation of Edom which is unfolded in sections one and three, i.e., vv. 2–10 and 15–21. In contrast to the latter two portions, the spotlight here is completely upon the unwarranted malevolence that Esau unleashed upon Jacob. Yahweh is very much in the background throughout, though he is of course controlling the ultimate purpose being effected by all the horrible events described. The prophet as a participant-observer (whether by revelation or actual experience) provides this damning commentary on the violence (v. 10) done to his people (v. 13a) by the Edomites.

SM: Many of the important bounding markers of this strophe were pointed out above in the discussion concerning its initial border in v. 11. In addition, the entire unit is most tightly interlocked internally by means of a strictly parallel phonological (four-beat), lexical, and syntactic sequence, which perhaps suggests the relentless course of these disastrous events. After an introduction (v. 11) which serves to specify the critical "day" as being the occasion(s) when Jerusalem was attacked, looted, and/or destroyed (= *anaphora* with the two surrounding strophe apertures in vv. 8 and 15), the accusation is dramatically made point blank: "…also *you* [i.e., Edom] (were) like one of them!" The "coming" *(b-w-')* of thieves and robbers (v. 5, *anaphora*) is here paralleled by a much more serious intrusion of strangers and foreigners (v.11).

There follows a series of eight immediate (punctiliar) prohibitions which progressively and vividly amplify the LORD's case against Esau.[1] They all follow a similar structural pattern which not only unifies the whole, but also leads one to consider them together as a single scene: i.e., *'al* "do not" + imperfect verb (= hostile action/attitude) + *beyom* "in the day of" (construct) + "their" (= people of Jerusalem) with a noun (signifying some sort of disaster). The first and last three negatives are preceded by *waw*, a feature that distinguishes them from the pair in the middle (v. 13) which is not so introduced. Verse 13 is further distinguished as the structural-thematic center through metrical irregularity (i.e., five accents instead of four) and a cluster of reiterated lexical items from the strophe's beginning in v. 11: "wealth" + "entered…gates" (in reverse order) plus the emphatic and accusatory pronominal *gam-'atah* "also you". An *inclusio* of paired antagonistic participants surrounds the entire unit, viz. "strangers/foreigners" (v. 11, i.e., the enemy) and "fugitives/ survivors" (v. 14, i.e., the prey). Verse 14 also stands out as the emotive climax of the strophe due to the particularly reprehensible actions reported there.

3.2.3 Section A': 15–21

(15–21) **Retribution and Restoration:** This third and final portion of the prophecy of Obadiah is characterized by some important similarities to, and differences from, what has gone before. The overall judgment of Edom continues, once more in the words of Yahweh himself (cf. section A), under the theme of their receiving a just punitive recompense for their traitorous

---

[1] See the discussion in Clark 1991:13–14.

treatment of Judah. Now, however, this condemnation is broadened to include all pagan "nations" (*goyim*). It is also combined with an unexpected prediction of deliverance and blessing for "the house of Jacob on Mount Zion" (vv. 17, 21). The section as a whole is composed of two distinct but closely related strophes, namely, vv. 15–18 and 19–21, the second of which specifies in detail the "inheritance" (*morashehem*, cf. v. 17) that the people of Yahweh will receive in his "kingdom" (*hamelukhah*) (v. 21). Much lexical recursion links the two strophes, notably that having a thematic import, i.e., "mountain" (*har*, = land—5x), "house" (*beth*, = people—5x), "possess" (*yarash*—5x), "Esau" (4x), "Jacob/Joseph/Israel/Jerusalem" (5x), and an important temporal indicator, "will be" (*hayah*—5x). The penultimate word features a significant seventh occurrence of *YHWH*, the Owner of the "message" (v. 1) and the "kingdom" about which it speaks (v. 21).

SM (15–18): There is a dramatic beginning to this section/strophe (including an asseverative *kiy* "surely, indeed!") as the "day" of Judah's destruction (vv. 11–14) and the "day" when Edom will be punished for its participation in that event (v. 8, i.e., *anaphora*) are both incorporated into the all-embracing judgment of "the day of Yahweh" (*yom YHWH*), which is described as being "near" (*qarov*). This apical "day of the LORD" refers to the time when Yahweh will personally intervene in human history to act in righteousness on behalf of his holy people, whom Obadiah describes as "the house of Jacob" (*beeth ya'aqov*, vv. 17–18). Its coming is as sure as the "word of the LORD" is true (the formulaic, "surely Yahweh has spoken," signals the conclusion of this strophe, with *YHWH* and another asseverative *kiy* forming the *inclusio*).

Edom's future desolation is depicted by means of a pair of conventional oracular figures: first in the imagery of "drinking" (*sh-th-h*) the cup of the LORD's wrath (vv. 15–16), and secondly as being burnt up by the "fire" (*'esh*) "of Joseph" (v. 18). Both of these internal sub-segments end on a climactic note with reference to Edom's total demise, viz. (literally): "they will become as though they had never been" (v. 16d), and "there will not be any survivor for the house of Esau" (v. 18e). The term "survivor(s)" (*sarid*) coupled with the negative and the thematic inversion (i.e., no survivor[s] for "Judah"..."Esau") is an obvious epiphoric indicator of closure (cf. vv. 14b and 18c). It would appear in the light of the following strophe (esp. v. 21) that the mention of "no survivors" for Edom should be construed hyperbolically, i.e., even Edom would have at least a small "remnant" (cf. Am 9:11–12; Mic 4:1–5; Zech 14:16–19). In conjunction with the "day" and "speaking" of the LORD, there is possibly another inclusive element in the corresponding references to "all [heathen] nations" (15a) and "house of Esau" (18c) in that the latter may act as a focused synecdochal representative of the former grouping.

Carefully situated in the middle of these two denunciatory sections is a salutary prediction of "refuge" or deliverance *(peletah)* for God's people. This particular structural position, the cluster of key terms that occur here for the first time (i.e., "Zion...holy...possess...house of Jacob...possession"), and the unexpectedness of their appearance at this point, clearly mark verse 17 as the thematic peak of the entire prophecy (though linked to the preceding by the initial *waw*). This is the essence of the message that Yahweh wanted to convey to his faithful people through the prophecy Obadiah. It is that gospel kernel which has the utmost significance and relevance to his "house" of believers throughout all generations: the LORD is most surely in control of world events and he will one day receive his household into their eternal "inheritance"!

SM (19–21): This final strophe of the prophecy serves as its denouement in a sense after the dramatic revelation of v. 17. These verses present several problems of interpretation, but the general thrust and intent of the Masoretic Text is clear as it stands. The motif of "inherit(ance)" is taken up from the preceding strophe (esp. v. 17) and developed in a twofold cycle: The people of God will one day take possession of the land—a clear Messianic notion that is expressed in two complementary ways. It will extend in all directions in a manner that approximates the territorial extent of the ancient kingdom of Solomon, i.e., south ("Negev"), west ("Shephelah"), north ("Ephraim/Samaria"), and west ("Gilead") (v. 19). Similarly then, the formerly divided kingdom will be reunited as the exiles from "Israel" assume control over the northern regions (e.g., "Zarephath"), while the exiles from "Jerusalem" take over the south (v. 20; e.g., "Negev", which we recall was the traditional territory of Edom). The underlying message here, which is figuratively (i.e., metonymically) reiterated for emphasis, seems to be that in the "day of Yahweh" and under his sovereign guidance, the "army" *(che[y]l)* of believers will cover the entire globe and ultimately incorporate all those whom the LORD himself has chosen from among "the nations".

But Yahweh, through his spokesman Obadiah, has yet another surprise for his hearers (readers) in the final verse of his prophetic vision: "deliverer" *(mosh'im),* or in this context we might say emissaries from his holy Citadel, "the mountain of Zion" *(behar tsiyon),* will go forth to govern—in righteousness *(lishpot)*—even those who were once their most bitter enemies on earth, namely, those inhabiting "the mountain of Esau" *(har 'esaw,* cf. vv. 19 = inclusio, 18 = epiphora, and 8b–9 = epiphora). Another convergence of thematically prominent items occurs in this last verse, both to mark the end of the prophecy as a whole and more importantly, to highlight the content being conveyed, in particular, that of the triumphant apothegmatic close: "and dominion belongs to the LORD!" This final line, which is exceptional in that it is half as long as the preceding five, complements the notion of "the day of the LORD" at the beginning of this third section of Obadiah (v. 15, *inclusio*). The meaning here clearly reflects and reinforces what was said at the book's peak in v. 17: One day, Yahweh's glorious kingdom of grace, centered on "Mount Zion", will incorporate as part of its "inheritance" people from the clans of all races, no matter how antithetical they may have been towards one another during certain periods of world history, i.e., those of "Jacob" as well as those of Esau. That is truly an event worth waiting for—hence the timeless significance also of the "minor" prophecy of Obadiah!

In closing this section of our study, it is necessary to point out the importance of a thorough structural analysis of the complete discourse of a given pericope. While it may be true that "more than one cogent analysis of the book (of Obadiah) has been offered," and that "its logical unity would be evident under any of a variety of superimposed outlines" (Stuart 1987:414), it is not correct to conclude that all of these proposal are of equal value or credibility in relation to one another. It *does* make a difference where the larger breaks in the text are made, for such divisions inevitably influence one's interpretation—perhaps not in a major way, but significantly so none the less. For example, the decision to segment the composition after verse 10 and to posit a structural-thematic peak at verse 17 obviously affects how one views the development of the message as a whole, not only with regard to form and content, but also in relation to the work's rhetorical motivation as well. It is to this subject of the dynamic oral-aural, verbally pointed, and personally persuasive communication of divine "prophecy" that we now direct our attention.

3.3 The rhetorical technique of the prophet Obadiah

In its Classical sense, rhetoric may be described as the *art and technique of persuasion*—a definite and definable literary strategy that aims to modify the cognitive, emotive, and/or volitional stance of the intended receptor group (whether an audience or readership). The term "art" suggests a specific ability or proficiency that one is simply endowed with as a gift of the Creator, while "technique" implies a compositional skill that can be learned and perfected on the basis of some concrete scientific principles. Though some may be reluctant to speak about the use of rhetoric and artistry in relation to the Holy Scriptures (i.e., fearing certain negative implications for the doctrine of inspiration), the obvious facts of the case still need to be dealt with. In other words, unless one is willing to either deny or downplay the patent literary-stylistic attributes of the original text (such as those mentioned above), one needs to include them in any exposition of and/or application of its intended message, for such formal features were certainly integrally involved in the overall communication process (which continues of course to the present day).

The rhetorical and poetic qualities of the composition of Obadiah in Hebrew contribute a great deal to the communicative power of the discourse as a direct prophecy from the LORD. That is, the vivid manner of writing (which no doubt reflects the features characteristic of an oral delivery) serves to enhance the clarity, definition, impact, and appeal of its specific semantic content and functional intent. Therefore, it is necessary to carefully investigate and describe these stylistic characteristics and their effect upon the activity of message reception, both in the original event as well as any subsequent reiteration in what may be a very different situational and sociocultural context. The procedure to be followed below will be simply to draw attention to the principal rhetorical intentions (or illocutions) which appear to be effected by the text's major poetic forms on several significant levels of communication. In a survey of this nature, it will not be possible to call attention to everything of interest or importance. Thus, only the high points will be considered, in particular, those which are apparent and hence manifest their functional force even in an English translation.

3.3.1 A structural perspective on biblical rhetoric

Any discussion of the rhetorical features of a given text must necessarily take the context of communication into careful consideration. In the case of an ancient document, composed in a foreign language and in a very different historical, ecological, and sociocultural setting, contemporary interpreters face some serious problems, mainly due to their ignorance of many crucial aspects of the original situation during which message composition, transmission, reception, and response occurred. For many readers or hearers of the Scriptures, these two so-called horizons of hermeneutics (Thistleton 1993:8–9), often distinguished in the terms "source" and "receptor" (or target) by translation theorists,[2] are complicated by a third, namely, the interposed horizon of a translation in a language (and culture) that is not their own, e.g., English or French for the majority in Africa.

The perception and impact of biblical rhetoric, just as the effect of its essential content, will obviously differ for current, as opposed to the initial, receptors of a given book. But while in one sense we are all "outsiders" looking in on the original text, the viewpoint of certain individuals is sharper to varying degrees than that of others due to their greater knowledge of some of the key situational factors mentioned above—plus their ability to profitably utilize the analytical techniques supplied by linguistics, literary theory, semiotics, anthropology, biblical studies, communication science, and related disciplines. It is hoped that the present study can furnish a few useful insights with regard to the ongoing process of *contextualizing* one's external (alien) horizon further along in the direction of the internal (indigenous) original.

We will begin with several observations concerning the operation of Hebrew compositional rhetoric from an alien point of view and in relation to the prophetic argument in general, excluding the stylistic details (which were partially dealt with above). Thus, if one simply takes the prophecy of Obadiah at face value, that is, reads and interprets the words naively—as they appear on the surface of the text as represented, a number of interesting features appear from a personal, interactional perspective.

At the very beginning, for example, one might ask, Why is "the Sovereign LORD" so angry at Edom—why does He want all other nations to go to war

---
[2] See, for example, de Waard and Nida 1986:11–15.

3.3 The rhetorical technique of the prophet Obadiah

against this small, seemingly insignificant mountainous state? There is some initial ambiguity in v. 2 (especially for the uninitiated, non-contextualized reader/listener of today) since the personal referents of the pronouns "I," "you," "we," and "us" are not precisely identified. The LORD God (Yahweh) is definitely revealed as the speaker of the "report" (v. 1b) at the end of verse 4. But considerable biblical background knowledge would be necessary for one to be able to link the geographical allusions of verses 3 and 4 with the mention of Edom in the first line and hence to identify the inhabitants of this rugged territory as being the ostensible addressees. Moreover, it is still not entirely clear why God is so upset with them. Obviously, their excessive pride is involved (v. 3), but that does not seem to explain the severity of the punishment that Yahweh predicts (v. 2) for the Edomites (and thereby automatically condemns them to) in a pair of progressively intensified and emotively colored judgment proclamations (vv. 5–7 and 8–10).

It is not until the final verse of the latter strophe, halfway into the book, that the reason and divine purpose are suddenly—though still somewhat obliquely—disclosed in the single word "violence". After a certain amount of background study, one would probably come to the desired conclusion that at some time in the recent past the nation of Edom had violently betrayed their closest relatives, the descendants of Jacob, who just happened to be the Covenant people of Yahweh, the Sovereign LORD (v. 1a). For such an impious and internecine crime, complete national destruction was the only just recompense (v. 10b), though to a modern reader, such an outcome might seem to be rather overdoing it, especially in this nuclear age where it would be difficult for the military obliteration of one nation to take place without affecting others, at least to some extent. In any case, this was a divinely orchestrated punishment to be meted out in turn through acts of betrayal by former friends and allies of the guilty party (v. 7)—a case of implicit or anticipatory irony that would undoubtedly be lost on the average reader the first time through.

Additional contextual information of a historical nature would surely be needed for current receptors to even partially understand and respond appropriately to the complex ethnic, political, and indeed the theological, or spiritual, dynamics underlying Obadiah's message. But assuming such content to have been supplied and the setting established as being that of the late sixth century BCE during the Babylonian invasion, destruction, and depopulation of Judah, the reader (or listener) would soon begin to grasp the gravity of the charge against Edom. The prophet himself lends a hand in his poetic elaboration of the notion of violence (v. 10) in the next strophe.

Seemingly in order to make sure that his audience gets the point, Obadiah immediately transports them verbally (and imaginatively) by way of his vision right to the very scene of the crime, as it were (vv. 11–14). He presents what amounts to a semi-narrative depiction of the military action and the treacherous behavior of the Edomites over against their kith-and-kin, the inhabitants of Jerusalem in particular (v. 11). The whole shocking tale is recounted by an apparent eye-witness, who thereby makes a convincing accusation against the guilty nation. There is a progressive build-up in dramatic tension as Edom's crimes become increasingly more heinous, moving from mere inaction (11) and gloating observation (12), through an opportunistic participation in the looting (13), to the cowardly killing of helpless refugees and the shameful deliverance of survivors to an even worse fate at the hands of a merciless enemy (14). This medial, transitional strophe thus specifies in grim and gory detail the nature of Edom's betrayal of "Jacob" (v.10) in violation of all standards of human decency and fraternal responsibility.

After the most incriminatory charges against the Edomites have been leveled by the prophet in v. 14, there is an immediately step-up to a new plane of semantic intensity and thematic significance: The "day" of Edom's betrayal of Judah becomes transformed into a prophetic, messianic-eschatological vision of the decisive "day of the LORD" (15a), a fateful date when fitting divine judgment (15b) will befall all ungodly peoples. The crucial theological import of this timely phrase would of course be lost on someone who was not well-read in biblical prophetic literature, but the rhetorical power of the language is apparent, even in most translations. Edom is once again addressed directly by Yahweh in vividly violent words of condemnation. The *apostrophe* continues right through the sudden shift in v. 17 (cf. Joel 2:32) when the peak of Obadiah's message as a whole is reached (cf. the preceding structural analysis). The prevailing tone of the prophecy perceptibly changes from negative to positive with respect to Judah in this predictive section—first in general terms and then, from v. 17 onward, as the LORD's chosen house among the nations is foregrounded on the stage of divinely controlled human history.

3.3 The rhetorical technique of the prophet Obadiah 119

The final verses of Obadiah (vv. 17–21) develop the twofold theme of deliverance for the people of "Jacob" and a complete vindication of the just dealings of Yahweh within the overall context of his judgment of all nations. The allusions and imagery here is particularly dense and difficult for alien readers, but the overall intention seems apparent: The LORD's holiness and righteousness will be abundantly demonstrated in the punishment of everyone who defiantly opposed him and mercilessly oppressed his people. The thematic reversals which characterize this book (and many other prophetic works as well—for those who have the ears to hear them! [cf. Luke 8:8b–21]) become especially prominent in its concluding verses: God's own people will now act as the mighty instrument of divine retribution (v. 18), and in the process they will journey from each of the distant regions to which they had been dispersed to take possession of (or inherit) all of the surrounding land that rightfully belongs to Mount Zion...the Kingdom of the LORD (v. 21).

Thus, the thematic correlate of v. 17 is saved for the very last, forming twin peaks of rhetorical and semantic significance as it were: From Obadiah's privileged point of view, the greatest reversal in fortunes to occur on the LORD's day will concern the unfaithful Edomites, "to (and/or) about" whom his oracle is addressed (i.e., the initial preposition on *le'edom* is ambiguous, perhaps deliberately so). God's people will most certainly repossess their divinely ordained territory, including the rocky fortresses of Edom itself. In the event, heroic "saviors" from Mount Zion under Yahweh's own direction will move out from there to invade and take control of the very mountain of Esau (v. 21). The possible ambiguities and potential theological implications of this last verse have inspired a host of commentators throughout the ages, but its fundamental significance is discernable amid the forest of interpretations: Yahweh will one day effect an amazing transformation in the physical situation and spiritual status of not only his people, but that of many other nations as well.

In sum, the LORD's initial battle cry (v. 1c) and the accompanying oracle of judgment will be realized against those who insolently dared to set themselves up in rebellion against his royal rule and sovereign will (vv. 2–4; cf. v.21). But because he is God, not a man (Hos 11: 8–9), even in righteous wrath Yahweh remembers mercy (Hab 3:2) and does not treat sinners as they deserve. Rather, he makes "deliverance" (v. 17) possible for all who heed the proclamation of his emissaries, both law (v. 1) and gospel (v. 21). The latter inclusio brings this exquisitely fashioned piece of prophetic polemic to a satisfying close. It is a short but highly significant theological composition, one that progressively engages its intended audience (those in the know) in an overtly ethno-political discourse which simultaneously articulates a much more profound and universally applicable theme.

3.3.2 A Classical rhetorical perspective on Obadiah

The book of Obadiah would seem to illustrate all three of the major types of Classical rhetoric (Gitay 1991:7): *Judicial* (or legal) speech makes "a judgment about events occurring in the past," whether in relation to accusation or defense. It is represented most clearly by the prophet's bitter denunciation of Edom's iniquitous behavior towards Judah when the latter was attacked and overrun by enemy forces (vv. 11–14).[3] Hebrew prophecy modifies Classical judicial rhetoric by incorporating a prominent future component in the punishments that are predicted for pagan excesses and covenantal violations alike, e.g., vv. 5–10, 15–16, 18. *Epideictic* (or ceremonial) discourse "celebrates or denounces some person or quality" in present time, but prophetic speech once again frequently evokes a future setting for such incisive praise or censure. It is manifested especially in the condemnation of Edom's pride (e.g., vv. 3–4) and, contrastively, in a joyful celebration of the restoration of God's people on the Day of the LORD (e.g., vv. 17, 21).

Deliberative (or conative) speech then builds upon the two preceding types to persuade the audience to either observe, or desist from, some particular action or attitude. It usually constitutes the major pragmatic purpose, or set of communicative intentions, of a given rhetorical work. In the case of most of the prophets, this might be summarized as an interrelated admonition-exhortation-consolation complex—in other words: a warning to learn from the harsh lessons of history, that Yahweh will most surely punish all wickedness; an encouragement to turn to him in repentance and faith; and comfort in the hope of a better day when the LORD will set all things right in a renewal of his gracious covenantal blessings. As far as Obadiah's message to

---

[3] Note that the prohibitions, "[and] you should not do X," are thus better rendered, "[and] you should not have done X," cf. KJV, RSV, GNT.

his primary audience was concerned, the first two elements are left largely implicit (i.e., in the negative examples of Edom immediately and all the [heathen] nations at a much later date), and attention is strongly centered in the assurance of a brighter future made possible by the vindicating intervention of Yahweh on his Day.

3.4 Levels of prophetic communication and their theological significance

The preceding was a largely surface-structure rhetorical overview of the basic thrust of Obadiah's oracle(s). But to complete the analysis, the several interlocking speech levels of communicative relevance need to be examined in somewhat greater detail. At least four strata of interpersonal interaction are manifested as the message of this compact book unfolds, both internal to and also embracing the work as a whole. The four may be viewed as being embedded, one within another that is wider in scope or frame of reference, as shown in the figure below:

$$((((S4--(((S3--((S2--(S1/S1'----R1'/R1)--R2))--R3)))--R4))))$$

There are thus four pairs of speaking (or writing) relationships, each involving a source (S) and a receptor (R), either of which may be plural. The various distinctions are as follows:

S1 = Edom (personified)	R1 = any potential enemy, even God (v. 3)
S1' = Yahweh's "envoy"	R1' = "the nations" (v. 1)
S2 = Yahweh (or Obadiah)	R2 = the Edomite nation (v. 2)
S3 = Yahweh (or Obadiah)	R3 = the people of Judah
S4 = Yahweh (or Obadiah)	R4 = any reader/hearer of the book

The first level is subdivided because it includes all embedded quotations that are employed by the author for some special stylistic effect, namely, to dramatize the message more forcefully for a (probably) listening audience. Level 2 is distinguished despite the fact that it too is a rhetorical device (i.e., *apostrophe*) because it is so prominent not only in this prophecy, but also in many of the other prophetic oracles against the nations (e.g., Jer 49). The fourth level was briefly outlined above and will be considered later within a somewhat broader frame of reference and application. That leaves level 3 and Yahweh's proclamation through Obadiah to the people of Judah. This is in fact the primary plane of communication since it engaged the prophet of God and his intended audience. It provides the essential perspective, or horizon of interpretation, according to which the rest of the message must be read and understood, both exegetically and by way of application. What are the rhetorical dynamics that motivate this transmission involving the LORD and his people, which is not explicitly marked at all in the original text?

When probing the various levels of rhetoric in a poetic discourse of Scripture, an analyst-interpreter normally moves from the inner to the outer spheres of personal interaction. The purpose is to build upon the initial contextual milieu when incorporating current receptors into the communication event by gradually merging their conceptual horizon with that presented by the original setting. As we saw, the external, hypothetical interpretation offered above was continually dependent upon the latter, in contrast to the practice of much of what is termed reader-response criticism in contemporary literary circles.[4] But it is necessary to dig back even further into the biblical scene and circumstances—as deeply in fact as current historical and literary scholarship will allow: Just how might the prophet's original audience have understood and reacted to his message? Or—to stand on somewhat safer, more textually-based ground—how may Obadiah have intended his words to be construed in a pragmatic, functional sense?

In order to fully deal with this third level of message transmission, the complete contextual background for the original communication event, its so-called rhetorical situation, would have to be known (Gitay 1991:7). Obviously, that is not feasible, especially in the case of a work such as Obadiah, for "nothing is known about the author beyond his name and that he received a prophetic revelation" (Finley 1990:339). That does not absolve us of our responsibility towards the initial setting and its prevailing world (including religious) viewpoint; it simply means that most of our information must be derived from the prophetic text itself, including a certain amount of perceptive, albeit suppositional, "reading between the lines." In other words, the best we can do at this stage is to hypothesize with regard

---

[4] For a pointed discussion and critique of the reader-response approach, see Thistleton 1993:499–508.

to such factors as date, place, scene, the immediate impetus for the oracle, its method of delivery, response, and possible reiteration on more than one occasion. The discourse in and of itself gives only a few direct clues concerning its situational and compositional context, and as mentioned, there is no certain record of a prophet named Obadiah in the historical books of the Old Testament. Nevertheless, the general contents of the book (especially the catalogue of specific sins recorded in vv. 11–14) as well as its overall style and affinity to Jeremiah 49:7–22 would lead us to posit a scene and occasion somewhat in proximity to the destruction of Jerusalem by King Nebuchadnezzar and the Babylonians in 586 BCE.[5]

As noted above, although the prophecy is for the most part addressed to Edom, it is hardly likely that any Edomite ever read or heard it. Rather, the message as a whole was initially intended for the desolate, disconsolate, downtrodden, and dispossessed people of Judah, the former inhabitants of Jerusalem in particular, wherever they may have been living at the time. It was in essence a word of comfort and encouragement to the faithful remnant that remained among God's people, those who still retained a positive theological outlook despite the almost total destruction of their nation. Though overtly a divine pronouncement of doom upon a particularly obnoxious neighbor, coupled with the distinct overtones of a lament sung over a ravaged capital, Jerusalem, Obadiah's poetic lines accomplish much more than making a superficial appeal to his people's desire for revenge—a literary means of releasing their pent-up emotions in a spirit of nationalistic fervor or *Schadenfreude*. In fact, a fully contextualized analysis would seem to argue strongly against such a perspective and would certainly eliminate the possibility of reading into this text (esp. vv. 17–21) any justification for the diabolical practice of so-called ethnic cleansing!

The prophet's words reminded his countrymen, above all, about the just Covenantal precepts of the one and only Supreme Suzerain—Yahweh, the Sovereign ruler over all nations on earth. As the oracle develops, this justice is clearly portrayed in its two central facets: All who violate the principles of the Covenant—that is, fidelity towards the LORD and mercy manifested to one's fellowman—will eventually, but inevitably, be punished. That included the chosen people of Judah-Israel, a notion expressed by the middle

---

[5] For further information concerning the historical-political background of Obadiah, see Allen 1976:135; Amerding 1985:337; Craigie 1984:197; Finley 1990:341; Stuart 1987:416.

portion of the prophecy, which implicitly, yet no less painfully, called this recent experience of divine judgment to their remembrance (vv. 11–14). In this respect, Obadiah's message stood as a renewed warning concerning the consequences of persistent sin and rebellion against the LORD's will and ways.

On the other hand, all who remain steadfast in faith-fellowship with Yahweh will receive his abundant blessing, as symbolized by the "land" and all that was associated with this in the written *Torah*—that is, spiritual as well as physical prosperity in the LORD's chosen inheritance! Thus, after the first two sections of the prophecy integrate divine object lessons from the past and near-future (i.e., vv. 1–10 and 11–14, respectively), the final pericope (i.e., vv. 15–21) comforts and assures God's people of the certain hope of restoration for the distant future, but only as holy inhabitants of Mount Zion (v. 17) and redeemed citizens of the Dominion of Yahweh (v. 21). No—the LORD had not forgotten or repudiated the house of Jacob (v. 17). But along with the glorious vision of an inheritance to come, he was also subtly, but sincerely, instructing them once more concerning the conditions under which such a possession would take place. This involved a reminder, both textual as well as intertextual, of the long-standing spiritual relationship that he had established with them (cf. Ob 17, 20–21 and Hos 1:11; 3:5; cf. also Hos 12:5, 9). This required a total commitment which they in their Babel-like pride (not dissimilar to that of their arch-enemies of Edom; cf. Hos 12:8) had freely chosen to ignore and even to desecrate in the past—with catastrophic consequences (cf. Ob 15 and Hos 12:2; Ob 16 and Jer 25:17–18, 28–29).

Would Obadiah's original audience have been able to derive that much theological content from his relatively short prophetic revelation? To this point, it is important to recall that he did not prophesy in a religious or literary vacuum. Though we cannot be sure about his exact place in the temporal continuum of the Hebrew prophets, it is almost certain that Obadiah was neither the first nor the last to carry out his divinely motivated ministry. As suggested above, a considerable overlapping with Jeremiah and his times seems likely. Thus, Obadiah inherited an active, even if officially suppressed, prophetic tradition—probably in both oral and also written, verbal and nonverbal form (i.e., symbolic action). This was the general situational environment and associated horizon of (religious) understanding within which he

3.4 Levels of prophetic communication and their theological significance 125

worked and which he could in turn assume was known by his addressees—whether or not they happened to accept its moral imperatives and put its theological implications into practice. The manifold influence of *intertextuality* is therefore a factor of utmost importance in the analysis and interpretation of any prophetic composition, certainly more so in the later works.

No fewer than six prophets dealt specifically with Edom in their oracles against foreign nations: Amos, Isaiah, Jeremiah, Ezekiel, Joel, and Malachi (for a complete listing, see Stuart 1987:405–406). On several occasions Obadiah's literary form indicates that he expected his hearers to be familiar with the particular quotation, paraphrase, figure, or allusion which he was using, for example, by means of the rhetorical particle *halo'* ("is it not so?") in verses 5 and 8. As Wolff observes, "Prophets not infrequently jog the memories of their listeners with phrases of this kind (Amos 9:7b; Mic 3:1b, 11b, Hab 1:12, Zech 7:7…)" (1986:49). Certain familiar judgment motifs are especially prominent in Obadiah, such as the wicked getting drunk on their own punishment (cf. Isa 51:17–23; Jer 25:15–29; Eze 23:31–34). The extensive affinity of Obadiah with Jeremiah 49 has already been mentioned, as has the correspondence with a number of passages in Hosea.[6]

And that was not all: another strong intertextual strand was available for cognitive accessing from within the Torah corpus, in particular, the series of Covenantal blessings and curses that would accrue to those who respectively obeyed or violated the precepts pertaining to faith and life set forth for the holy people of God. It is interesting to observe, as Stuart points out, how the Covenantal curses alluded to in Obadiah are made to fall upon the pagan nation of Edom, even as they had already been implemented against both Israel and now Judah. Edom's forthcoming decimation and degradation, for example, would fulfill the imprecations recorded in Mosaic passages such as Deuteronomy 28 (e.g., 25–27, 43–44, 62). Similarly, the wicked nation's betrayal by former allies followed the pattern of the so-called helplessness curses such as Deut 28:29 (Stuart 1987:418). On the other hand, a renewed remnant of Jacob would one day enjoy such blessings as a reoccupation of the promised land (vv. 19–21; cf. Deut 30:3–5) and a reestablishment of the sacred community of worship on Mount Zion (cf. Ex 15:17; Lev 21:11–23; Num 19:20; Stuart 1987:420).

---

[6] For a detailed listing of these parallels, see Stuart 1987:415; Clark and Mundhenk 1982:39–40; Wolff 1986:39.

We may observe in closing that such vital background information, available from the Old Testament itself, is able to furnish a helpful framework of interpretation for contemporary readers as well—provided that they know their Bibles well enough! The rhetorical impact of these interrelated passages, whether Pentateuchal or prophetic, is greatly diminished if they are not read in cotextual conjunction with one another (respecting, of course, their temporal progression, at least as nearly as we can determine it). On the other hand, recognition of their presence opens up for the careful interpreter a rich mosaic of meaning that resonates in varied degrees of amplification, shades of perspicuity, and levels of relevance throughout the Hebrew Scriptures.

3.5 Implications of a text-rhetorical analysis of biblical discourse

3.5.1 Some hermeneutical challenges

The preceding survey, which focuses a postulated rhetorical perspective on the initial communication event, leads us back once more to a contemporary setting and level four of our analytical and interpretive model. The former component would of course include the earlier text study of Obadiah. At this stage, within a complete consideration of the subject, one should really incorporate some of the main insights to be found in the many exegetical works and commentaries on this book that have appeared over the years, i.e., readings at level 4 to the nth degree. Although it would undoubtedly be enlightening to sample some of the more important of these, that will not be possible within the confines of this essay. What does need to be done, however, is to draw out the relevance of this concise and incisive prophetic work for the people of God today as they, too, live out their lives in diverse circumstances in preparation for the coming of the great eschatological "day of the LORD."

Before people can apply a given biblical pericope, they must first of all understand it—correctly, that is, on its own terms and within the horizon of its own contextual setting. However what happens in the case of the prophets, the "minor" representatives in particular? In short, they tend *not* to be taken very seriously, if at all. Why is this so often the case? The five reasons listed below may provide at least a partial explanation of this chronic state

3.5 Implications of a text-rhetorical analysis of biblical discourse 127

of affairs as it concerns not only the average lay Christian, but in many instances also the pastor, biblical scholar, and translator as well.

As was suggested earlier, it appears that the most important barrier to one's understanding these prophetic message is simply an insufficient amount of critical information pertaining to the total contextual background of the biblical composition—its *rhetorical exigency*. A knowledge of the initial setting of communication and the referential world which give the words of the text their precise semantic significance in relation to one another and the message as a whole is indispensable for interpretation—and even more so for Bible translation. We see this illustrated, for example, in the cluster of appellations in vv. 8–10: Edom...Esau...Teman...Jacob. What do these proper names have to do with one another in their original historical and religious context? Does it make any difference if the apparent referential redundancy is eliminated as in the GNT *(Good News Translation)*, for example, by merging certain occurrences of Esau with that of Edom (vv. 8–9, 19), or Mount Zion with Jerusalem (v. 21, but cf. v. 17). What effect, if any, does such semantic reduction have on the rhetoric of the text, its compositional dynamics (e.g., as markers of external boundaries and internal cohesion), or on the book's overall theological significance?

The second major problem faced by contemporary receptors is that the structural organization of these poetic-prophetic works is frequently not perceived by them, listeners in particular. If people do not discern the total discourse arrangement of a given text, then it is highly unlikely that they will be able to grasp the development of its larger argument. They cannot follow, for example, the typical progressive movement of the message to a positive thematic peak, one that features the salvific words and/or deeds of Yahweh, according to which the rest of the composition—no matter how much greater in volume or seemingly negative in tone—needs to be interpreted. It is important to see, for example, the basic tripartite structure of Obadiah, consisting essentially of a pair of divine oracles separated by an accusatory prophetic interlude, before one proceeds to analyze the microtextual details. Thirdly, as was indicated in the earlier structural analysis, the poetic style of the original Hebrew is also difficult to recognize and appreciate, especially in translation, whether literal or idiomatic. This would include such features as the many graphic but contextually specific figures of speech, the dramatic rhetorical flourishes (especially apostrophe, hyperbole, and irony), the apparent repetitiveness of the discourse in some places, or the clipped conciseness of expression in others.

On a more general level, then, there is the seemingly bitter, vindictive mood of the work as a whole, a sustained note of vengeance directed against the little country of Edom, that can put some people off. This is a quality that is more distracting, and perhaps even psychologically disturbing, the less one knows about typical Hebrew oracular style and its situation of use. And finally, the very brevity of the book of Obadiah may lead some to conclude that it is relatively insignificant within the prophetic corpus—certainly not a text worth spending much time on in comparison with a work such as Isaiah!

These some of the obstacles that one may face when considering whether or not to study—or even read through—Obadiah. A quick superficial skimming over the text may well confirm one in this unfavorable opinion. For most, if not all of the prophets, therefore, the only solution is to make an effort to carefully work through a given text from beginning to end. While the analytical approach followed in this essay is undoubtedly much too detailed for the layperson, it may be helpful in certain respects for the serious Bible student. For such individuals, there are a considerable number of practical options with regard to an operational strategy, but the following guidelines may be a useful place to begin. These observations are more or less restricted to the most significant issues as they relate to two broad heuristic and hermeneutical concerns: What can a thorough discourse and rhetorical analysis teach us about—(a) the methodology that is applied to, and (b) the message to be derived from a poetical-prophetic book such as Obadiah?

3.5.2 Issues of methodology

As far as the manner of analyzing the text of Scripture goes, there are two major points that should be made. The first principle is more general and concerns our overall approach to the original Hebrew (Masoretic) text (MT). The second then deals more specifically with our procedure for handling the discourse as a complete, unified whole.

3.5.2.1 Text criticism

It is necessary to state at the outset of any analysis the extent to which one is prepared either to deal with the Hebrew as it stands, however difficult, or to modify it where deemed appropriate through emendation. In short, the position adopted in this study is to retain the MT unless confronted with a seemingly insurmountable problem, coupled with overwhelming evidence (including major versional support) which would indicate that the original is corrupt. I have found no such instances in the text of Obadiah. Most appeals for a modification of the MT simply reveal that their proponents either have a point to prove (hence the desirability of a change in favor their particular theory, interpretation, or recommendation), or their analytical methodology is deficient. Such approaches may be incomplete in scope and explanatory power, or they are simply unable to discern other, more discourse-oriented options. Three brief examples involving alleged "transpositions" in the MT will perhaps be sufficient to illustrate this issue.

Allen (1976:137) has "reason to believe that at several places the text has suffered dislocation." First, he feels, that a displacement has taken place at v. 5, namely, that *'ekh nidmethah* ("Oh—how you have been undone!") has been moved ahead of its original position after *dayam* ("their sufficiency"). As was noted in the earlier structural analysis, however, the obvious transposition is probably intentional, the purpose being to mirror the reversal of arrogant Edom's fortunes and simultaneously to intensify the emotive level of the text as the second cycle of the judgment oracle against that nation begins (i.e., vv. 5–7).

Allen's second proposal would invert the position of the two halves of v. 15. But that would vitiate the carefully-crafted progression in the relentless build-up to "the (unique) day of the LORD" which the sequence of "days" found in the preceding (and discourse-medial) strophe (i.e., vv. 11–14) has been leading up to. This key formulaic expression therefore initiates a new strophe (and section) at v. 15 (cf. a corresponding anaphoric aperture with "day" in v. 8). Thus, the opening *kiy* is more accurately rendered in an asseverative sense (i.e., "Indeed!") than as an indicator of a strictly logical cause-effect relationship (i.e., "For...").

Finally, Allen suggests that v. 21 be placed before v. 18. But again, why should our Western logic (if we can call it that) govern—and so drastically disturb—what has been written in the original text? From a rhetorical perspective, verse 21 makes better sense (or we might say, it has a more powerful effect) right where it stands. It here functions as the structural and thematic conclusion of the prophecy as a whole (i.e., "...up on Mount Zion") and as a fitting complement to the discourse peak situated in v. 17 (also "on Mount Zion"!). Besides being stylistically inadequate in terms of Hebrew poetics, such proposals never really offer convincing reasons as to how the original text might have gotten itself so much out of kilter.

As the second procedural guideline with regard to our treatment of the original text, we can do no better than to reiterate once again that ancient principle of biblical hermeneutics: the Scripture is its own best interpreter. In other words, when faced with some difficulty or ambiguity of meaning, the exegete should always *begin* to look for an answer by carefully examining the cotext (a more precise term for the textual context) which is related to a certain problematic item, whether a single word or an entire verse. This cotext may be internal or external with respect to the document being read (i.e., *intra*- versus *inter*-textuality). It may also manifest differing degrees of "relatedness," ranging from very close parallel passages in terms of lexical, syntactic, and/or semantic similarities (or direct contrasts) to those whose association is only of a broad topical nature. Obviously, the closer the proximate or parallel expression is to the problem under consideration, the more reliability or credibility it offers in its explanatory potential.

But one must always resist the temptation to "correct" a difficult text by simply conforming to what appears to be a more straightforward parallel passage, for example, to adjust Obadiah along the lines of the corresponding verse in Jeremiah 49. As mentioned above, the present textual problem may have been deliberately introduced by the original author in order to achieve some special effect, perhaps playing his text off against a more familiar or earlier composed correspondent. The "rhetoric" which we attempt to elucidate ought to be that of the traditional Hebrew text, not our own contemporary reconstruction. Furthermore, as will be emphasized again below, a given passage always needs to be construed in light of the larger pericope in which it is contained and, ultimately, within the framework of the complete composition. That brings us to the second major aspect of a text-based methodology.

3.5.2.2 Discourse analysis

A comprehensive, discourse-oriented approach to analysis is essential if one wishes to effectively come to grips with any biblical composition as an instance of literary—as well as theological—communication. The theology of the text is paramount of course, but this divine message is always encased in literary forms, both large (e.g., a poetic genre such as the woe oracle) and small (e.g., a figure of speech like metaphor), which are specific to the language and literature concerned (i.e., Classical Hebrew and Koine Greek).[7] This thesaurus of form represents the inventory from which the inspired writer made a specific selection in order to best get his message across to the intended receptor group within a given sociocultural and religious setting. Thus, a systematic, holistic, and text/context-sensitive examination of his stylistic technique and compositional strategy will usually pay dividends as far as helping one to organize and interpret the principal ideas being conveyed by the original work.

It is not necessary to rehearse all the pertinent analytical procedures in detail here.[8] But just by way of summarizing my approach to the analysis of Obadiah, I might call attention to four basic aspects of the discourse which need to be considered, both as individual form-functional components and together as interrelated elements of a single meaning-generating process: segmentation, connection, direction, and intention. First of all, one attempts to divide a poetic discourse up into its constituent parts: the individual lines (bi-/tricola) clustering to form the smaller portions (i.e., strophes), these combining to create larger ones (i.e., sections or "stanzas"), which in turn comprise the whole. The documentation of repeated key words and phrases on structural boundaries together with all significant indicators of aperture or closure is an important factor in this delimiting operation.

---

[7] When considering the issue of genre in relation to the biblical literature, one must keep in mind the fact that "[t]he ancient genres of the Bible often exhibit differing conventions from their contemporary counterparts.... This presupposes the presence of literary counterparts; some biblical genres would seem to have no contemporary counterpart, e.g., apocalyptic literature" (Brown 2008:112).

[8] See Wendland 1995 for an explanation and application of text analysis procedures with special reference to the OT prophetic literature. As Terrance Wardlaw, Jr. has observed: "[D]iscourse analysis is capable of functioning as a hermeneutic for interpretation.... Moreover, the field of discourse analysis allows the exegete both to examine the linguistic routines of biblical Hebrew and Greek, and to examine literary and rhetorical features of the text (stylistics) in its social context" (2008:266–267).

Second, one looks for other types of verbal recursion—involving the sound, sense, syntax, or poetic structure of a text—in order to see how the various compositional components are bound together, that is, given internal cohesion, both in relation to one another and also the work as a whole. Then it is time to discover the key directive cues and stylistic clues which the author has left behind as a way of assisting his audience (or readership) to discern the high points of his message, whether emotive or informative in nature (i.e., "climax" or "peak"). Here is where we find him utilizing the special stylistic, or poetic, resources of his language, usually in marked or unusual combinations, as a means of accenting certain crucial, message-bearing portions of the text.

And finally, the analyst will take all of the preceding into consideration in order to determine the communicative significance of the entire composition in its presumed initial context. Biblical style is not merely ornamental—though it does serve to beautify the language and to increase its esthetic impact and appeal, especially in poetic discourse. On the contrary, verbal style (or artistic form) is always employed in the service of theological content to more effectively carry out any number of interpersonal objectives. Why, for example, do we find such a proliferation of rhetorical features as—to mention the most important: compaction (e.g., ellipsis), graphic imagery (including that of a military, apocalyptic, and eschatological variety), irony and sarcasm, hyperbole, nuanced and patterned lexical recursion, reversals of form and content, intertextual allusion and citation, dramatic direct address (apostrophe), intensifiers (e.g., vocatives, imperatives, exclamations), and indeed, the rhythmic and balanced line-forms of Hebrew poetry itself? Certainly, these devices do not exist in and for their own sake. Rather, they have been carefully chosen, positioned, and combined in order to make the prophet's point with greater forcefulness and/or clarity in relation to his overall theme as motivated by Yahweh.

Thus, by means of an appropriate analytical methodology, one can learn to investigate more thoroughly in order to understand the "which" and the "how" of the original text—that is, specifically which Hebrew compositional forms we are dealing with and how they communicate(d) in the way that they do. What remains to be considered is more vital and it is built upon the former procedures: namely, the "what" (content) and "why" (purpose) of the divine message—the "means" in service of the "meaning." It is to this aspect of prophecy in relation to its primary function of persuasion that we now turn.

3.5.3 The essential message of Obadiah

By means of their chosen literary-poetic style—including persuasive rhetoric—on the microlevel of discourse, the LORD's prophetic messengers were also carrying out several larger rhetorical purposes, i.e., designed broadly to influence or convince their audience to follow along the path of covenantal loyalty to Yahweh. The most important function thus was hortatory in relation to two primary and interactive motivations: (a) to give hope, encouragement, and a spirit of perseverance to the faithful remnant among God's people that a "day" of reckoning and of restoration was most certainly coming; and at the same time; (b) to offer a powerful warning to the wicked to repent of their ways before the "day of the LORD" ultimately did dawn upon them in their overt sin and unbelief. This twofold message is obviously of utmost relevance also today, and hence I wish to conclude this study of Obadiah by briefly exploring several of the crucial issues involved with regard to both the content of his prophecy and also its ongoing transmission today via translation.

Superficial readers often regard the books of the Minor Prophets as being concerned primarily, if not entirely, with the (b) element above, that is, with doom and gloom. Even a perceptive commentator like Craigie concludes: "It would be foolish to pretend that Obadiah is a pleasant book to read...(being) overcast by the dark shroud of judgment and disaster" (1984:198). However, as was suggested above, the stylistic form of these oracles (in particular, the larger organization) and to some extent also their surface content function as rhetorical vehicles in service of a much higher communicative purpose. This concerns the manifestation of a pair of theological truths which lie at the heart of divine revelation in the Scriptures: God is the King over and his Messiah (the Christ) is the Key to life—physical as well as spiritual, both now and in the hereafter. Thus, even as the graphic prophetic proclamation of woe is being pronounced upon all of Yahweh's enemies, a parallel, but frequently more subtle, message of weal is being simultaneously conveyed, either explicitly or implicitly, for the edification and renewal of all those who trust in him.

To a considerable extent, the import of Obadiah's message to the war-ravaged and persecuted people of Judah in the Babylonian era matches the significance of these same words to the believing remnant of Yahweh today, wherever they may be found in this world. The Sovereign LORD *('adonay YHWH)* is in complete—and gracious—charge of all human events, no matter how tragic, irrational, overwhelming, or contrary it may seem to the way in which we personally think things ought to be run. That was the same basic truth proclaimed by Habakkuk, a probable contemporary of Obadiah (e.g., ch. 3). The implications of the latter's last line "And the Kingship is Yahweh's (alone)!" (Ob 21), is forcefully expressed in the corresponding line of the former: "The Sovereign LORD is my *strength!*" (*cheyl;* Hab 3:19, cf. Ob 20, 13, 11).

These thematic correlates articulate a principle that "the house of Jacob" (vv. 17–18) would do well to pay more serious attention to in these troubled times. Consider once more the dominant circumscribing inclusio formed by the proper names in vv. 1 and 21: Contrary to what Edom thought, there was (and is) no military might, no physical resources, no political leadership, and no earthly wisdom (vv. 2–9) that can oppose or countermand the omniscient and omnipotent will of the God of "Mount Zion" (v. 17). Yahweh has a plan, and his irrevocable purpose is being carried out even now on the stage of human history, despite all appearances to the contrary. That plan in turn encompasses all "the nations"—each and every one included—within its merciful scope, as a messianic reading of the final strophe of Obadiah would certainly suggest (vv. 17–21). It is good for us once in a while to stop and step back from the turmoil of life just to meditate upon this immutable fact, first of all, for our own peace of mind, and then also to encourage one another with these words (1 Thes 4:18).

The second important thing that Obadiah teaches us concerns the LORD's preferred style of kingship—that is, his method of ruling or exercising his will. As the Scriptures stress from beginning to end, this is a mode of dominion (v. 21) which defies all earthly logic or understanding; it is perceptible only to those who are members of Jacob's house by faith. Yahweh's strategy, his unique manner of dispensing divine justice, is one that operates according to what from the human standpoint appears to be a reversal or even a contradiction. We noted how this motif is carried out throughout the book (and in the prophets generally), in terms of both style, or form, and also with regard to content: The high and mighty will be brought down (vv. 2–4, "Edom" is Everyman!), and the wicked will one day reap the evil that they have sown (15)—perhaps even doubly so (v. 16).

3.5 Implications of a text-rhetorical analysis of biblical discourse

Those who were once downtrodden and oppressed, on the other hand, will be raised up by Yahweh to rule over their former afflicters (v. 18; cf. Lk 1:46–55). They will be allowed to repossess the entire inheritance that Yahweh has allotted to them (vv. 19–20). In this process of divine judgment, the righteous dominion of the LORD will be completely vindicated and supremely exalted as well (vv. 17, 21). Yet, strangely enough, these astounding events will be effected through the lowly people whom He has graciously chosen to restore in blessing (vv. 11–14), that is, on the basis of the Covenant promises of his *Torah* (e.g., Deut 30; cf. its New Testament gospel reformulation, e.g., Mt 5:3–12). That is expressed in the book's final verse 21, which is essentially an elaboration of the climactic verse 17. In highly evocative fashion, Obadiah here brings the three chief participants of his prophecy back "on stage," as it were, in order to dramatize his central theme: And *saviors* will go up from (or "on") the mountain of *Zion* to establish *judgment* over the mountain of *Esau,* and *Yahweh* will rule as *king!* The Messianic implication of these words clearly stand out. The verse complements the description of the holy congregation in v. 17, but here the active aspect of "the people of God" is stressed. Missionary "saviors" will go forth from the congregation of Zion to proclaim the good news of their Savior God to people of all nations (cf. Mt 28:19)—even the iniquitous Edomites! (cf. Wolff 1986:69). In so doing they will extend the non-political "kingship" of Yahweh over all the earth and establish his righteous "judgment" everywhere.

The consummate kingship of Yahweh is a common theme of OT prophecy and poetry (cf. Ps 47:2, 7; 96:10; Isa 24:23; 33:20–22; 40:9–10; 62:3; Jer 10:10; Mic 4:7–8; Zeph 3:15; Zech 9:9). It was later encapsulated in the believers' prayer composed by the Lord Jesus himself: "Thy kingdom come; thy will be done!" (Mt 6:10). It reaches its ultimate expression, appropriately enough, in the concluding book of the "Word of the LORD": "The kingdom of the world has become the kingdom of our Lord and of his Christ, and he will reign for ever and ever!" (Rev 11:15, NIV; cf. 12:10; 22:1–5).

This brings us necessarily to the second major issue involving Obadiah's message. There is no doubt that what the prophet has to say, albeit so briefly, is vitally important. But how can the original form be best conveyed to all those for whom it is intended? Obviously, some type of translation and/or transposition of the biblical word is needed in order for it to be transmitted to others (cf. v. 1b). This requires the application of various kinds of restructuring operations in order for the essential meaning of the original message to be expressed in the languages of today. This applies also to the rhetorical features of a given prophetic text, for example. This task is nicely summarized by de Waard and Nida as follows: "What one must try to do, therefore, is to match function for function, in other words, to attempt to discover the closest functional equivalent of the rhetorical structure in the source text. The particular set of forms used for different rhetorical functions is largely language specific, but the functions…are universals, and it is for this reason that one can aim at functional equivalence" (1986:119)—including various degrees of literary correspondence (Wendland 2011:61–110). Some examples of this principle are given in the next section.

3.5.4 Rhetorical structure as an exegetical and communicative tool

The rhetorical structure has already been discussed in relation to both the overall organization and also the principal theme of Obadiah. The importance of this aspect of discourse analysis with respect to the macrostructure of the book was considered as well, especially as it concerns the controversial section break that was posited as occurring between verses 10 and 11. It may be instructive to give some attention to several examples of rhetoric that appear also on the microstructure of Obadiah. Indeed, errors of interpretation and expression are usually more obvious on this level and when compounded can seriously disrupt the intended flow of communication, with regard to function and well as form-content. Several instances of problems of a phonological, syntactic, and lexical-semantic nature will be cited to illustrate the point (for further exemplification and discussion, see the commentary by Clark and Mundhenk 1982). The particular receptor text used as the basis for these comments is a final draft of the new (but not yet published) common-language Bible in Chewa, a Bantu language of south-central Africa (Malawi, Zambia, Mozambique). A single passage is sufficient for the purposes of this demonstration, namely, Obadiah five.

The major issue as far as the phonology is concerned is of course what to do about the poetic nature of the Hebrew original. A full-scale poetic reproduction was not attempted in Chewa (i.e., as a *ndakatulo* lyric, cf. Wendland

1993a:ch. 6), at least not consistently throughout the composition, although this would have been desirable from a functional point of view. This was not possible due to limitations of time (the additional amount necessary to prepare such a version), staff (the presence of a capable poet!), and receptor-constituency (they are not yet ready for a dynamic version of this nature). However, an effort was made to render the text in rhetorically heightened "prose" so as to preserve at least some of the beauty and impact of the source text. Accordingly, the translation employs features such as the following in order to create a distinctive and functionally effective style in Chewa: parallelism (essentially as in the Hebrew) and other types of lexical recursion, a condensed, often elliptical manner of expression, graphic diction and colorful figures of speech, connotative heightening (e.g., the use of vocatives, rhetorical questions, exclamations, and intensifiers), along with selective word order variations.

Below then is the Chewa example of verse 5 as rendered in this semi-poetic form, together with a moderately literal back-translation into English

Pajatu mbala zikabwera usiku,	As you know, when thieves come at night,
zimangotengako zimene afuna.	they take away only what they want.
Okolola akamathyola zipatso,	When harvesters pluck fruit,
mwina amangosiyako zina-zake.	at times they just leave some there.
Koma inuyo adani anu	But as for you, your enemies
ha! akupululani pululu!	ha! they're going to strip you bare!

The relatively balanced lineation characteristic of a normal *ndakatulo* poem is apparent, i.e., a syllable/line pattern of 12/12/12/12/10/10. The lines decrease somewhat in length at the final bicolon as the climax is reached. The very last line is somewhat deceptive, however, in that the initial exclamation *(ha!)* and the final ideophone *(pululu!)* both generate slight pauses, the former preceding and the latter following the medial verb. The ideophone of course adds an instant dramatizing effect to the action as well as contributing to the euphony of this utterance, which suddenly reveals the total devastation that is about to befall Edom/Esau (addressed directly in the next line).

Another subtle auditory embellishment is heard in the /a/ and /u/ assonance of the first and sixth lines, which indirectly draws attention to the cause-and-effect related figures, i.e., "thieves [at] night...stripped bare!" The repeated *zi-* prefix of the first two lines closely links the subject (thieves) with the indefinite object (whatever) of this utterance. In addition, a few dummy particles (i.e., having no major referential force) were necessarily inserted to balance up the lines, e.g., *-yo* in line 5 (see below); *mwina* (i.e., perhaps or usually); *-ko* in lines 2 and 4 (i.e., an ameliorative postclitic that diminishes the scope or completeness of the verb to which it is attached).

Several other rhetorical-poetic devices are noteworthy in this Chewa version: The initial formulaic *Pajatu* ("As you really should know...") helps to mark the beginning of this new unit by indicating that a well-known piece of traditional wisdom, a generality, or some other familiar reference immediately follows. What is more, the subsequent information or advice is somehow connected with what has just been said, often for the purposes of evidence, reinforcement, or illustration. That would well suit the present context where the strophe of vv. 5–7 serves to elaborate upon the preceding, its closure line in particular: "...from there I will bring you down" (v. 4b). In the manner of poetic A-B colonic heightening, we have here an intensified specification of the meaning of being "made small" (v. 2a) and "felled," but now on the larger, strophic level of discourse.

A number of major syntactic alterations have been made in comparison with the Hebrew text: Most important is the relocation of the short exclamation of colon one to the end of the verse where it has been made a complete—yet similarly an exclamatory—utterance. Its dramatic nature is clearly indicated by the initial exclamation, *ha!* (i.e., suggesting disparagement or scorn), and the verb-cognated ideophone, *pululu!* (i.e., stripped completely bare/naked). These were not felt to be semantic additions, but merely instances of making explicit some key connotative elements that are present in the original. The penultimate line, constituting the first half of the final utterance, features an initial syntactic front-shifting operation to foreground—and here also to introduce in this strophe—the focal participant of the oracle as a whole, i.e., *inuyo* (lit.) "you [pl.]-those [whom we know about]". It thus refers back to the "you"-object of the preceding verse, and hence back to the "Edomites," made explicit in v. 1c.

Other instances of the implicit-to-explicit procedure are these: The general verb *damah* ("cut off, destroy") is sharpened in Chewa to *pululu* ("to strip/pluck off" [esp. leaves on a tree]), here used figuratively of course and complementing the preceding image of grape-picking. The verb in Chewa is also more naturally expressed in a future (for the Hebrew "prophetic perfect")

3.5 Implications of a text-rhetorical analysis of biblical discourse 139

and active construction with the subject specified as "your enemies" *(adani anu)*, who would be assumed to be the "all nations" of v. 1. The contrast between figure and fact leading up to this final utterance is made explicit in the transitional conjunction "but" *(Koma)*. On the other hand, we also have an example of seemingly extraneous information in Hebrew that is retained in the Chewa version, namely, the temporal specification of "night" *(usiku)*, though this is shifted to the first clause. Also in the realm of time is the need to pinpoint a tense/aspect in Chewa for the general actions referred to in this verse, namely, the "customary present" *(-ma-)* verb form.

Several apparent reductions were made, but in a corresponding reversal of the procedure noted above, these were regarded simply as being an implicit rendering of what was explicitly stated in the Hebrew. Thus, the "robbers" and "destroyers" of the first line are combined in *mbala,* a particularly strong term for "thieves" (since it takes a non-animate attributive and verbal concord). Also in this line, the Hebrew pronominal reference "to you" *(likha)* is omitted in order to generalize the two comparisons and build up to an emphatic "you" *(inuyo,* object) in line 5 of the translation. The Chewa also removes the two conditional-rhetorical question constructions in favor of a pair of statements expressing general knowledge. This, too, serves to highlight the final, emphatic condemnation. Although "grapes" are very important in biblical culture and known in a Chewa setting (at least in a wild form), the second comparison is generalized to "fruits" *(zipatso),* both to establish collocative congruence (i.e., with the verbal noun *okolola* "pickers/harvesters") and greater cultural relevance in terms of the receptor setting.

The extent of the preceding translational discussion of a single verse that is certainly not among the more important of Obadiah would suggest the care that needs to be exercised and the effort expended if a literary functional equivalent rendering is to be achieved in the target language. It is for this very reason that such a poetic—or oratorical—rendering is not usually attempted, certainly not in an initial version. The standard set by the original remains, however, and where it is not initially attained, translators (and perhaps also their constituency) should be made aware of the nature of the rhetorical and literary deficiency (sometimes even an impoverishment) that often results. Perhaps something more dynamic and rhetorically compelling can be aimed at in a future edition. But there is another serious barrier that needs to be pointed out in this connection, and that concerns the probable disparity occasioned by the medium of message transmission with regard to the translation.

Any attempt to deal meaningfully with the rhetoric of the biblical message in translation must take into consideration not only the form of the original text, but the form also of the original medium. The prophecy of Obadiah has come down to us (or is it "up," or "across"?) as a written composition, but as in the case of most, if not all, of the other literary prophets, his proclamation from the LORD was most likely delivered initially in oral form—an uttered oracle from Yahweh. This is suggested at the very beginning of the book in the cognate expression "we heard a report" *(shimu'ah shama'nuw)* of what the Sovereign LORD "said" *('amar)*. The various rhetorical features discussed above, especially the phonological ones, therefore have their greatest impact when they are actually heard as a corporate audience (or congregation) being spoken aloud (in the original of course), as opposed to being silently read to oneself.

This issue is of particular relevance to a target-group constituency that is still in possession of and practicing an active oral tradition and/or one that has a relatively low (-50%) level of literacy. Such a group is naturally more attuned and accustomed to appropriating messages, notably religious ones, via the aural mode. I need not repeat here what I have said elsewhere on this point,[9] except to emphasize the need for giving this factor the amount of attention it deserves, for example, in the preparation of exegetically faithful, but medium-sensitive, audio "transpositions" of the Scriptures (cf. Sogaard 1991).

And finally, we must recognize that the resource of rhetoric, in and of itself, in relation to the source as well as the target language, is not sufficient to guarantee an effective communication of the message of Scripture. It represents a major segment, but certainly not the only one, contributing towards a fuller comprehension of the biblical text from the perspective of the hermeneutical horizon of either the original setting or that of any subsequent translation. Rhetoric deals largely with matter of literary form, but there remains the more important factor of conceptual, notably theological, content to consider, as was pointed out earlier. The fact is that when Obadiah reports, "We have heard a message from the LORD" (v. 1b), the message that comes across is quite different, sometimes radically

---

[9] See for example, Wendland 1993a:ch. 7; 1993b.

so—depending on the particular historical, sociocultural, and spiritual environment in which it is articulated. Just who is "the LORD" (*YHWH*), for example, and what is his "dominion" *(hamilukhah)* like (v. 21b)? If that was true even in the prophet's own times (e.g., v. 3), how much more so is it applicable nowadays—for example, to a member of the rebel group "Lord's Resistance Army" as opposed to someone belonging to the ruling political party of Uganda? What are some of the crucial characteristics of this divisive communication gap and how can they either be bridged or detoured around (i.e., compensated for)? This is a topic which has also been taken up elsewhere with respect to Bible translation,[10] and so it is necessary only to reiterate the conclusion: the preparation of contextually conditioned explanatory notes—"relevant" (Gutt 1992:67–74) to both the prophetic and also the contemporary contextual settings—would seem to be the only viable answer.

Such situationally selective commentary, whether conveyed personally (i.e., human instructors) or via some mediate pedagogical device—aurally, electronically, in written form, or by audio-visual means—provides the only reliable vehicle for transporting receptors today back to the biblical life-world so that they can determine the value (i.e., sense and significance) of at least part of the conceptual "currency" which they have inherited (i.e., the essential message of Scripture in whatever linguistic form they possess it). Once the original conceptual "exchange rate" has been determined, it will be possible to return as it were to their native land and re-convert those same "funds" (biblical knowledge) into something of functionally equivalent value in local currency (i.e., through various processes of message contextualization, as appropriate) so that this resource can be effectively utilized to satisfy their various personal or societal wants and needs. It may then also be "invested" (through further concentrated study and use) so that the initial capital sum might increase in value and pay even greater dividends in terms of future spiritual growth within the Christian community at large.

---

[10] See the various essays in Stine and Wendland 1990, e.g., 119–122.

4

What's the Good News? Prophetic Rhetoric and the Salvific Center of Nahum's Vision

4.1 Introduction

The "vision" (1:1) of Nahum is generally not very highly regarded among the books of the Minor Prophets. Perhaps the main reason for this is the seemingly negative nature of the message, which appears to concentrate on the ruthless destruction of the city of Nineveh. However, there is much more to this little prophecy than meets the eye/ear. It majors in fact on "good news" (1:15) for the faithful people of God—then and now. A careful study of the book's discourse structure reveals this prominent evangelical emphasis in Nahum's proclamation. This is complemented by a survey of some of the text's principal rhetorical devices, which serve to highlight the encouraging word that the prophet brings to Judah. The present study concludes with an overview of several of the chief implications of this sort of text-rhetorical analysis for contemporary Bible translation and a meaningful presentation of the prophetic message today in both oral and written form.

4.2 The theme of Nahum—bane or blessing?

So, what is the book of Nahum all about? If you ask the average Bible student such a question, s/he will probably give as a standard answer something like this: "the LORD's judgment of Nineveh." One usually cannot probe too much farther, however, because Nahum is not one of the better known books of the Scriptures, nor is it a common subject of biblical studies.[1] Thus, queries like, "Who [or what] is Nineveh?"—or "Why was Nineveh judged?"—are likely to go unanswered. If one turns to a more scholarly source of information about this book, one generally finds its message summarized for the most part in connotatively negative terms. The following overview, for example, is what the inquirer will read about Nahum in at least one edition of the Good News Translation (GNT):[2]

> The book of Nahum is a poem celebrating the fall of Nineveh, the capital city of Israel's ancient and oppressive enemy, the Assyrians. The fall of Nineveh, near the end of the seventh century B.C., is seen as the judgment of God upon a cruel and arrogant nation.

This version goes on to posit a two-part Outline of Contents: "Judgment on Nineveh 1:1–15 [and] The fall of Nineveh 2:1–3:19." It is no wonder that many readers, having glanced at an introduction of this nature, will be only to happy to move on to some other book, especially if they do not know a great deal about ancient Bible history. Why risk becoming depressed by such an apparently gloomy prophecy of punishment upon some obscure pagan city and nation?[3]

But is this being fair to Nahum and his vision (1:1)? Is it indeed all bane—bad news—with no blessing interspersed somewhere within? More experienced students of Scripture will know in advance that the answer to both questions is "No." All biblical books, the fierce Old Testament prophets included, incorporate some rejuvenating "gospel" for God's people as well.

---

[1] Achtemeier adds: "...the book has been almost totally ignored in the modern church" (1986:5).
[2] Published by the Bible Society of South Africa, 1977 edition, page 906.
[3] Robertson, for example, complains that one "can hardly lift the bleak cloud of negativism that provides the substructure for this prophetic word" (1990:57). Such a conclusion is unavoidable if one views the book as declaring an "unbroken note of judgment" (ibid., *loc. cit.*). But as I hope to demonstrate, an evaluation of this nature rather misses the prophet's point and hence also his relevance today.

In Nahum's case, of course, the entire book is in a certain sense good news because the destruction of Nineveh and the Assyrians meant immediate release from one of Israel's most ruthless oppressors. Thus, Assyria's bane automatically becomes Judah's blessing. But even taking the notion of gospel in a stricter, salvific sense as a passage in which is concentrated a message of divine deliverance and future restoration for the people of God, we find that all the books of Scripture qualify to a greater or lesser, more or less overt, degree. What many texts, including those of most of the prophets, lack in *quantity* with regard to this gospel, they make up for in *quality*. In other words, while the obvious good-news passages may not be nearly as long or as many, they are generally rhetorically crafted and positioned in such an excellent manner as to make the essential evangel component clearly stand out, that is, to be highlighted within the discourse on both its larger and its lower levels of compositional organization.[4]

In this chapter I will outline some of the principal ways in which the prophet Nahum[5] structures his discourse and rhetorically shapes it in order to foreground a positive, persuasive message of comforting hope for his people.[6] I view the crucial core of this proclamation as being situated on the boundary which divides this prophetic work into two major sections, namely, at the close of part one (1:15). Here we see—and hear, as it were—through the mouth and eyes of the LORD's chosen messenger, the "bringer of good news" *(mebaser)*, a most astonishing prediction. This textually borderline passage is artfully interlocked by corresponding segments into both of the book's primary divisions, the initial dramatic announcement of God's just control of world events (1:1–15) followed by a longer, reinforcing response of confirmation (2:1–3:19). The stylistic devices manifested here in Nahum are characteristic of the passages of prophetic rhetoric found in similar works of the Hebrew Scriptures.[7]

---

[4] These upper and lower levels are sometimes termed the "macro-" and "micro-structure," respectively.

[5] In view of the lack of any convincing alternative, I will throughout this chapter refer to the author of this book as "Nahum" despite the fact that many scholars doubt the historicity of an OT prophet by this name. For two somewhat different perspectives on the prophet's probable historical and socio-political setting, see Armerding 1985:449–451 and Smith 1994:158–160.

[6] The name "Nahum" is based on the Hebrew verb meaning "compassion" or "comfort" (Smith 1984:71). Thus, the prophet's message is one of comfort for Judah (a manifestation of the LORD's compassion), but just the opposite for "Nineveh"—i.e., a terrifying judgment!

[7] Nahum's inventory of rhetorical-stylistic techniques is similar to those described by Gitay in his detailed examination of Isaiah 1–12 (1991). Accordingly, Nahum "does not appeal to reason but to the emotions. He does not present bare facts, but colors reality. His descriptions

Typically, however, Nahum personalizes these general features to suit his particular communicative purpose, which is to exhort and encourage the people of God (including those of anywhere and anytime), in particular, those who are living during a period of great external threat to their way of life and indeed their very existence. The closing portion of this chapter is devoted to a brief survey some of the main implications of rhetorically oriented discourse studies for effectively conveying the prophetic good news in this present era of multifaceted message transmission, where the "feet" of messengers are more often than not completely replaced by the fleet output of sophisticated electronic machines.

4.3 A rhetorical outline of Nahum

4.3.1 Structural overview

The larger textual organization of the book of Nahum is briefly described below. It is not necessary to go into detail regarding the various analytical procedures that produced these results.[8] Thus, the compositional and thematic structure of Nahum is simply outlined and formatted with a minimum of expository comment. This "panoramic" perspective will be followed by a more "scenic" summary in which the significant rhetorical devices are described in terms of both form and function with reference to the prophet's dynamically presented oracle. The figure below simply shows how this tripartite announcement of "good news" to the people of Judah (i.e., 1:12–13, 1:15, 2:2) serves to tie Part I of the declaration of judgment against Nineveh (Assyria, ch. 1) textually into Part II (chs. 2–3):

|| *I.* | 1:1.............1:11–[**1:12–13**]–1:14–[**1:15**] || *II.* |2:1–[**2:2**]............3:9 ||

The overlapping gospel core of Nahum

---

seek to win the hearts of his audience" (ibid., 8) in order to persuade them to adopt his (Yahweh's) view of religion and reality.

[8] The methodology underlying this study is presented in chapters 2–3 of Wendland 1995 (cf. Christensen 1989). Although I disagree with Christensen's interpretation in a number of significant ways, his careful study forced me to examine the text in much greater detail than I might have done otherwise.

4.3 A rhetorical outline of Nahum

In the following spatialized diagram, different levels of indentation are used to indicate the various kinds of discourse that are distributed within the text of Nahum. It is a rough way of illustrating how the diverse *types* (or genres,—listed beside the capital letters) and *topics* (listed vertically below the types) are carefully interwoven to complement one another in a cohesive composition of the whole.[9] What may appear to be jarring interruptions on the surface of the text turn out to be the manifestation of an expert strategy of integration and opposition. One discourse segment is played off of another to rhetorically focus upon particular theological concepts and themes, yet all in service of the primary message of religious well-being (*shalom*, 1:15) in relation to both God and one's fellow worshipers. The internal diversity of content and purpose may be summarized in terms of the following general categories:

    A. Prophetic messenger speech introduction
    B. Eulogy in praise of the divine attributes of Yahweh
    C. Descriptive theophany of the LORD's coming as a Warrior for judgment
    D. Prophetic indictment against Nineveh and a prediction of her overthrow
    E. Prophetic revelation of blessing for Judah (* = gospel core)
    F. Dramatic visual portrayal of the scene of battle at Nineveh
    G. Direct divine announcement of Nineveh's destruction
    H. Mock lament/dirge decrying the demise of Nineveh/Assyria and her king
    |A |B |C |D |E |F |G |H
I. |General announcement of the oracle concerning Nineveh (1:1)
        |The LORD's righteously motivated wrath (1:2–3a)
            |A vivid depiction of the LORD's power in natural imagery (1:3b–6)
           |A panegyric summary of divine mercy contrasted with just anger (1:7–8)
                |All who plot against the LORD will be punished (1:9–11)
    |Introduction to a divine oracle (1:12a)
                  |Judah will be delivered from her enemies (1:12b–13)*
    |Introduction to a divine oracle (1:14a)
                      |God will bury Nineveh's dead gods (14bcd)
                  |The good news of future peace for Judah (1:15)*

= =

    |A |B |C |D |E |F |G |H
II. |Warning to the defenders of Nineveh (2:1)
                |Promise of restoration for Israel (2:2)*
                    |Chariots enter the city, the defenses collapse,
                    and the pillage begins (2:3–4, 5–7, 8–10)
                        |Song eulogizing the "lion" (2:11–12)

---

[9] There are different ways of classifying the various genres of prophetic discourse. The types listed here are largely descriptive and not necessarily specific form-critical categories.

|Introduction to a divine oracle (2:13a)
　　　　　　　　　　　|God will destroy Nineveh's lions (2:13)
- -
|A |B |C |D |E |F |G |H
　　　　　　　　　　　|Woe to the city of blood and witchcraft (3:1–4)
|Introduction to a divine oracle (3:5a)
　　　　　　　　　　　|God will expose Nineveh's shame (3:5–7)
　　　　　　　　　　　|Nineveh will be destroyed like other pagan empires (3:8–12)
　　　　　　　　　　　|Fires of war will consume Nineveh (3:13–15b)
　　　　　　　　　　　|The locust-like hordes of Nineveh will disappear (15c–17)
　　　　　　　　　　　　　　　|Fall of the cruel king! (3:18–19)

From the preceding rough, generic spreadsheet of the text of Nahum we can discern some of the primary differences between the two larger portions of the book as well as several prominent correspondences that interconnect them.[10] Part I (covering chapter one in most English Bibles)[11] manifests a more diverse set of discourse types and is more directly focused upon Yahweh as the supreme agent of retribution upon Nineveh and of rescue in relation to Judah. Part II provides a more detailed application of divine judgment to the evil empire of Assyria, but the same essential thematic elements occur, namely, a mixed proclamation of indictment and judicial verdict which builds up to some significant human communicative response (or the lack of one), i.e., in 1:15 (Judah), 2:13 (Nineveh), and 3:19 (all people). The basic theme of the LORD's justice in relation to those who trust him as well as those who oppose him (1:7) is viewed from three somewhat different (but closely related) perspectives in each chapter: 1—Yahweh, the Sovereign Judge (1:2); 2—his earthly surrogate, the "scatterer(s)" (2:1); and the city condemned for its deceit and wicked atrocities (3:1).

4.3.2 Structural description

The LORD, who is the primary participant and thematic subject, whether overtly or implicitly, throughout the entire text, is given an appropriately rousing welcome on the stage of poetic action. He is introduced in a "divine warrior hymn" (1:2–8; cf. Ps 19:7–15, 98)[12] by an impressive catalogue

---

[10] For a summary chart of the main lexical correspondences between Parts I and II, see Armerding 1985:453.

[11] The Hebrew Masoretic text begins its chapter two with what is 1:15 in most English translations.

[12] In this instance, "the victory is celebrated before the battle is actually waged" (Longman 1993:788). Smith correctly observes that "the psalm is not a typical hymn of praise because

4.3 A rhetorical outline of Nahum

of divine covenantal attributes (1:2–3a, 8) which lays the dual thematic foundation for the entire prophecy. Thus, the first segment stresses the sovereign right of Yahweh to exercise judgment, but there is a sudden shift in verse 7 where we have a reassuring reference to his goodness and providential care (highlighted by the vivid contrast of v. 8; cf. Ex 34:6–7; Num 14:18–19).[13] This eulogistic recital is interrupted for the sake of emphasis by an awesome theophany that figuratively describes the LORD of all creation vigorously engaged in punitive action (C, vv. 3b–6, with strong allusions to the Exodus deliverance and the divine display at Sinai). "Yahweh" *(yhwh)* is mentioned both before (v. 3a-b) and after (v. 7a—i.e., *exclusio*) this panegyric depiction of his primeval, but also protective, "anger" *('ap)* and "wrath" *(chemah,* cf. vv. 2–3a and 7). The close of the first major section of Part I culminates in a prediction of the "end" *(kalah)* of all his "enemies" *('oyebayw,* v. 8; cf. 2b),—but this is judgment tempered by mercy (v. 7; cf. 3a—a double topical *inclusio*).

A thematically prominent "tail-head" lexical construction *(anadiplosis)*[14] distinguishes the onset of the seemingly antiphonally arranged second half of Part I (1:9–15), which presents a divinely focused judicial response to the preceding hymn in his honor. This leads off with a declaration of judgment directed against Nineveh: "he will make an end of [his enemies]"—*kalah ya'aseh,* vv. 8b/ 9a), for those who make "trouble" for his people *(tsarah,* vv. 7a/9b). This is the book's first official indictment against the evil city, which is left unmentioned for the sake of suspense in the text. *Strophe* (= poetic paragraph) D1 (vv. 9–11) reverses the order of a typical prophetic crime-and-punishment pronouncement. This segment, which presents the logical, contextualized outcome of the theological hymn of vv. 2–8, is bounded *(inclusio)* by a phrasal summary of the divine accusation: "you (sg/pl) [are] plotting against Yahweh" *(ch-sh-b 'al-yhwh;* note the emphatic shift to direct speech at the close of this unit, v. 11).

---

it lacks the imperatives which are usual in the call to thanksgiving in Israel" (1984:67). Longman points out the possible prophetic polemic (e.g., anti-Baal imagery) in these verses (ibid., 789–90), and Chisholm does the same in the case of "several typical ancient Near Eastern warrior motifs" (1990:168–169).

[13] As Achtemeier observes, "we have here only little less than a complete presentation of the biblical witness to God's person" (1986:8)—though this divine characterization properly ends at v. 8, not v. 11.

[14] For a further description of "anadiplosis" see Wendland 1995:69–70.

The second strophe (1:12–13, E1) begins with a typical marker of aperture in the formula of divine proclamation: "Thus says the LORD..." *(koh 'amar yhwh)*. In this incisive verdict of judicial reversal, Yahweh takes up where he left off in v. 11, but Nineveh (and allies) are now referred to in the third person. In the middle of this strophe, the focus is unexpectedly changed again to a word of comforting release for the afflicted penitents of Judah (v. 12b).[15] Then as the rapid-fire alternation of unnamed, but contextually implied addressees continues,[16] the focus returns to vile Nineveh (v. 14, G1), its monarchy in particular, as implied by the singular pronouns (cf. 3:18). The initial formal pronouncement: "And Yahweh has commanded [this] concerning you..." features more, typically prophetic *enallage*—a double pronominal shift this time (vv. 13–14), i.e., from a first-to-third person reference to the speaker, Yahweh, and from a third-to-second person masculine direct speech to the condemned addressees of the oppressor, Assyria, most notably its royalty and pantheon of pagan deities. All of these are condemned in a diverse set of imprecatory utterances most appropriate for the occasion (Chisholm 1990:173).

With the familiar emphatic discourse deictic "Look!" *(hinneh,* v. 15), Nahum begins the final strophe of Part I by announcing the welcome arrival of a messenger of good news, one who proclaims "peace!" *(shalom)* to the downtrodden people of God. This second explicitly gospel segment (E2) brings the first, and shorter half of Nahum's message—the "oracular" *(masa')* portion (cf. 1:1a)—to a climactic, strongly optimistic close: The city of wicked/worthless ones from which all "wickedness" *(beliyyal,* vv. 11b, 15b—i.e., *epiphora*)[17] "came out" *(y-ts-')* and whose army had "invaded" *('-b-r)* Judah would be "completely" *(kulloh,* v. 15b, which sounds like *kalah* "end" in vv. 8–9, = *inclusio)* destroyed. In other words (characteristic of Hebrew recursive poetry), it would "pass away" *['-b-r,* v. 12] according to prophetic prediction (i.e., by means of a catastrophic, divinely directed "overflowing *['-b-r]* flood," = *epiphora,* v. 8)!

---

[15] The people were "chastised" in order to lead them to repentance; cf. Deut 8:2–3; Ps 90:15; 119:71, 75.

[16] This use of second person pronominal forms, though exegetically problematic at times (e.g., 1:11), helps to distinguish the second half of Part I (vv. 9–15) from the first (vv. 2–8). Generally speaking, 2ms pronouns refer to the Assyrian king (1:14; cf. 3:18), while 2fs forms refer either to Nineveh or to Judah as dictated by the context.

[17] A significant lexical correspondence, whether by synonymy or antithesis, at the concluding boundaries of distinct compositional segments (strophes and up) is termed "epiphora" (Wendland 1995:50–51), while at the respective opening boundaries it is called "anaphora" (ibid., 37–38).

4.3 A rhetorical outline of Nahum 151

The "event vision" *(chazon)* section (Part II, cf. 1:1b) leads off with the first of a series of graphically descriptive, rhythmically gripping passages (F1–3) which provide an on-the-scene commentary on the futile battle for the defense of Nineveh. It almost seems as if the visionary prophetic watchman has suddenly shifted positions, namely, from high up on Jerusalem's wall (1:15) to the fallen ramparts of Nineveh (2:1; cf. 3:12–13). Three sensually evocative, semi-narrative segments of three verses each act as the cohesive backbone for this expansive reinforcement of the general judgment oracles uttered in Part I, i.e., 2:1 + 3–4, 5–7, –10). The first two strophes each begin with a mention of the military action of the enemy agent (3ms)—the "scatterer" (i.e., to slavery and exile—*mepits*), while the third focuses the poetic-narrative spotlight upon the plundered city of Nineveh, here (v. 8) named explicitly for the first time since 1:1. That these first three visionary strophes function together in the discourse is indicated by a chiastically ordered *inclusio,* i.e., pre-attack: faces + loins affected (2:1), post-attack: loins + faces affected (2:11c-d). Another, more subtle *inclusio* is formed by the fourfold description of the anguishing physical effects of the overwhelming invasion upon the inhabitants of Nineveh (v. 11) and the set of four futile commands to defend the city which began the chapter (2:1).

The initial cycle of this dramatic depiction of the ignominious defeat and devastation of the world's most powerful city (and nation) reaches its peak with the LORD's punitive decree in 2:13 *(ne'um yhwh* "oracle of Yahweh"). This single-versed strophe (G2) corresponds to a similar segment (G1) encoded as divine direct speech in Part I (1:14)—the former dealing with a spiritual-religious downfall, the latter with military-political defeat. Mention of the preeminent war-machine of that age, the "chariot" *(rekeb),* and its purpose, namely, to "cut off" *(k-r-th)* the foe, serve as compositional markers of final closure, i.e., *inclusio* (cf. 2:3) and *epiphora* (1:15), respectively. The consequent silence of Nineveh's heralds (2:13d) pointedly contrasts with the joyous shouts of victory and peace in Judah which conclude Part I (i.e., conceptual *epiphora*).

Two additional, quite distinctive poetic pieces appear in this first half of Part II. One is the third occurrence of a contrastively worded good-news passage, which interrupts the first battle strophe to tie the entire passage into Part I, i.e., 2:2 by means of this structural-thematic overlap *(anadiplosis)*. The internal logical sequence of concession-contraexpectation (even though...nevertheless) found in 1:12–13 (E1) is reversed here in 2:2 (E3). The other rhetorical novelty is an ironic poem, or taunt, in mock praise of the proud lions of Nineveh (H1), the entire pride of which will soon be wiped out, leaving only a desolate den (2:11–12).[18] This penultimate strophe is linked up with the final one by several key lexical items, for example, "young lions" (*kepirim*, vv. 12b/14c) and "prey" (*terepah*, vv. 13c/14d).

"Woe!" *(hoy)* marks the dynamic onset of the second, recycled portion of Part II.[19] 3:1–4 (F3) is of special significance due to its central position and function within the final two chapters. It announces the resumption of the scenic but gory commentary on the sack of Nineveh. Much as in the case of lineal parallelism, i.e., "A and what's more, B" (Kugel 1981), there is a perceptible step-up in the intensity of action depicting the city's downfall begun in 2:1.[20] This graphic, descriptive-poetic montage quickened the imagination and no doubt also the hope of the prophet's discouraged and doubt-ridden compatriots. He begins with the LORD's case against "bloody" Nineveh (v. 1) and concludes with a figurative indictment of this nation's seductive deceit and sorcerous paganism (v. 4), which expands on the characterization "full of lies" in verse one (thematic *inclusio*).

Such gross wickedness summons forth as it were a new strophe and another word of direct denunciation by the LORD (G2, 3:5–7). The similarities between this latter judgment oracle and the earlier one of chapter two are indeed striking, both in their respective beginnings, i.e., the exact repetition of vv. 2:13a and 3:5a (= *anaphora*), and at their accented endings, i.e., the topical correspondence of silent accusatory "speech" in vv. 2:13d and 3:7bc (= *epiphora*). Such obviously patterned textual features are a rhetorical indication that these portions are not only to be paired within the overall structural organization of the discourse, but must also be interpreted together. The divine, first-person centered oracle of condemnation begins (3:5) with an emphatic *hinni* ("behold/listen to me!"—cf. 1:15, 2:14, 3:1, i.e., *anaphora*). This dramatic demonstrative is followed by a direct

---

[18] The royal art of Assyria frequently depicts the power and prowess of the king and nation through the use of leonine imagery. The city's patron goddess, Ishtar, is similarly portrayed (cf. also Isa 5:29; Jer 50:17).

[19] This initial word corresponds by way of connotative likeness with the hinni of the preceding verse (i.e., anadiplosis) and contrastively with the structurally similar word *hinneh* at the opening of 1:15 (i.e., anaphora; Wendland 1995:37–38).

[20] The second cycle of Part II (ch. 3) is also characterized by more incisive satire and a more caustic degree of *sarcasm* directed against Nineveh and the entire Assyrian empire.

4.3 A rhetorical outline of Nahum

reference to the villain ("against you"—*'elayik*), and the unit ends with a similar word, one of mock address, i.e., "to you"—*lak, inclusio.*

Yahweh's sardonic double rhetorical question of 3:7c–d is followed by another one in 3:8, a long and ironic introduction to a graphically expressed taunt poem (vv. 8–12), one based now on historical precedent. This is the lone prophetic denunciation (D2) of Part II (see the spreadsheet diagram on page 147) which corresponds to 1:9–11 (D1) in Part I, e.g., in the analogous imagery of debilitating drunkenness and the contrast between thorns or dry stubble (1:10) and ripe figs (3:12). It is possible to divide 3:8–12 into two strophes at verse 11 where the judgment of Nineveh is stated directly and sarcastically in the twofold emphatic *gam-'at* "also you!" Yet another visualizing *hinneh* "behold!" signals the start of two final poetic vignettes which delineates the complete wasting of Nineveh, first by "fire" (*'esh*, probably literal—F4, 3:13–15b) and second as if by hordes of locusts, the most destructive biological enemy of the ancient Near East (probably figurative—F5, 3:13–17). The reiterated action of "devouring" (*'-k-l*) lends cohesion to F4, while a string of references to "multitudes" of various types of locusts interlocks the various semantic constituents of F5. The latter strophe closes with another "where?" of despair (cf. 3:7, *epiphora*).

A mock lament in "honor" of the "king of Assyria," who is addressed for the first time by way of apostrophe, brings the dual prophetic "vision" and "burden" of Nahum to a triumphant conclusion (H2, 3:18–19). Here a thematically significant instance of lexical correspondence occurs in the verb *sh-m-'* ("hear"), which links the book's final verse with both the close of the first portion of Part II (2:13) and also the evangel ending and climax of Part I (1:15): The people of Judah would one day hear the good news of "peace" (1:15), while the warlike messengers of Assyria would be silenced (2:13)—and instead, the happy news of the mortal wounding of this world oppressor would reach the ears of all people (3:19).[21] Four additional markers of (final) closure are (a) the mention of no "gatherer" (*meqabets*—3:18d) which contrasts with the "scatterer" (*mepits*) of 2:1a (*inclusio*); (b) the concluding accusation in the form of a rhetorical question (3:19c, cf. 3:7c—*epiphora*); (c) a negative combined with the key verb *'-b-r* ("come upon," 3:19,

---

[21] The close of Nahum's oracle-vision also resonates epiphorically and by way of contrast with the conclusion of the other Old Testament "prophecy" devoted to Nineveh, namely, Jonah. These are the only two books of the Bible to end with dramatic rhetorical questions.

cf. 1:15—*epiphora*); and (d) the final phrase "your endless evil" (cf. "the one plotting evil *[ra'ah]* against Yahweh"—1:11, *epiphora*).

The following is a *structural-thematic outline* of Nahum based on the preceding discourse analysis, providing a summary of the prophet's rhetorically shaped argument. It provides another, perhaps more traditional perspective on the book's overall compositional organization. The segments that are designated by the Arabic numerals represent distinct strophic units, and all those encoded as direct address have the explicit or implicit addressee indicated in brackets.

Part I: The Destruction of Nineveh Means Deliverance for Judah (1:1–15)

   A. Prophetic aperture (1:1)

   B. Recital of the chief covenantal characteristics of Yahweh (1:2–8)

        1. The righteous vengeance of the LORD against his enemies (2–3b)
        2. A natural theophany describing the awesome anger of Yahweh (3c–6)
        3. The LORD is either a protective "refuge" or a punishing "flood" (7–8)

   C. Alternating proclamation of doom [Nineveh] versus deliverance [Judah] (1:9–15)

      x   1. [Nineveh]: All your rebellion against the LORD will be ended (9–11)
      y   2. [Judah]:   Your oppressor's "yoke" will be broken (12–13)
      x' 3. [Nineveh]: Your people and their gods are doomed to the "grave" (14)
      y' 4. [Judah]:   A messenger will bring you the "good news" of "peace" (15)

Part II: A Vision of the Final Battle for Nineveh (2:1–3:19)

   A. The first cycle—Nineveh is invaded by a powerful military force (2:1–13)

      x" 1. [Nineveh]:   Prepare for a final defense! (1)
      y" 2. The ravaged splendor of "Jacob" + "Israel" will be restored (2)
          3. The sight of the attacking army is fearsome (3–4)
          4. Nineveh's defenses fail and the city falls (5–7)
          5. Nineveh is sacked (8–10)

6. A flashback to the good life of the lions [Ninevites] (11–12)
7. [Nineveh]:Your young lions will become prey for the LORD (13)

B. The second cycle—A fitting fate for a bloody kingdom (3:1–19)

1. Inhabitants of the seductive city of sorcery are slaughtered (1–4)
2. [Nineveh]: Yahweh will transform your city into a spectacle of shame (5–7)
3. [Nineveh]: You should have learned a lesson from Thebes! (8–10)
4. [Nineveh]: Your forces and fortresses will drop like overripe figs (11–12)
5. [Nineveh]: You will be eaten by fire (13–15c)
6. [Nineveh]: Your locust-like hordes will all fly away (15d–17)
7. [the king]: Your wound is fatal—you will die! (18–19)

Structural-thematic outline of the oracle-vision of Nahum

Another way of viewing the larger organization of Nahum is within the framework of a "prophetic disputation speech."[22] This generic form consists of three principal elements, which would apply to Nahum as follows: *thesis* (implied) = Yahweh is an impotent, ineffectual god [so counsel the plotters (vv. 9–11) due to the Assyrian invasion of Judah]; *counter thesis* (ch. 1) = Yahweh is the almighty, supreme ruler of heaven and earth; *refutation* (evidence, chs. 2–3) = the imminent defeat and destruction of Nineveh and the great Assyrian empire. It is interesting to note some of the general structural and thematic correspondences between the two complementary cycles of Part II (the "refutation" portion), for example: in the overall number of

---

[22] Sweeney (1992) provides a good study of this possibility. It is not easy, however, to discern "a pattern of theme, development, and reaction" running in a clear-cut manner throughout the "bifid structure" of Nahum (Patterson and Travers 1988:48–49). Similarly, Armerding's arrangement of chs. 2–3 into four unequal sections, each consisting of five parallel topical segments and "all building on the pattern set forth in 2:1," involves an interesting, but rather arbitrary interpretation of the discourse structure (1985:470–471). Somewhat more credible, though only at a general, topical level of organization, is to view the text after the introductory portion as manifesting a chiastic formation: A—Celebration of the fall of Assyria and her king (1:12–15//3:18–19); B—Sounding of the alarm (2:1–10//3:13–17); C—Taunt song (2:11–12//3:8–12); D—Declaration of judgment (2:13//3:5–7); E—Woe oracle [the structural center] (3:1–4; judicial indictment = vv. 1/4) (cf. Chisholm 1990:166–167).

strophes (7, perhaps suggesting the complete-ness of the city's demise), the similar beginnings (i.e., dramatic scenic vistas of the battle for Nineveh) and endings, i.e., mock laments for the lions [= the nation's leaders] (A5) and their chief "shepherd," the cruel Assyrian king (B6). This matched portion of the book is similar in turn to some of prophetic "oracles against the foreign nations," to Jeremiah 46 [against Egypt] in particular, e.g., 46:2–5, 27–28.[23]

The dominant rhetorical feature of the entire discourse arrangement is the contrapuntal set of three paired poetic segments in the structural center which overlaps at the boundary between Parts I and II: The strophes marked by an [x] denote direct oracles of judgment against Nineveh (the first two including an *indictment* of the nation's crimes along with the expected divine *verdict*), while those marked as [y] announce a message of deliverance and, by implication, also forgiveness for the "afflicted" faithful of Judah (1:12–13, i.e., the people were punished for their prior disobedience of the LORD's covenantal obligations; cf. 1:3, 7–8). As the preceding organizational overview would suggest, this prophecy is clearly not a patchwork piece of literary composition![24] Such a positive evaluation is reinforced by a closer look at some of the outstanding poetic features of the Hebrew text.

4.4 The principal rhetorical devices of the LORD's good-news messenger

A preliminary identification and description of some of the noteworthy rhetorical features of Hebrew "prophecy" was already begun in the preceding discussion of the macro-structure of Nahum. The most important of these stylistic devices, namely, (a) linguistic, primarily lexical, *recursion* was utilized in particular to help *demarcate* the boundaries and internal contours of major compositional units within the book. The reiteration of certain key terms and expressions from both within and without the text (i.e., the process of "intra-" and "inter-textuality") also gives a certain conceptual depth, or resonance, to the discourse that contributes to the richness of the overall theological message conveyed. Other significant formal features of this nature involve the use of: (b) *figurative language,*

---

[23] Sawyer finds chs. 2–3 "comparable with the Song of Deborah (Judg 5) in its vivid imagery and dramatic power" (1987:117).

[24] For some arguments against the basic unity and integrity of Nahum, see for example, Smith 1911:268–270; Mason 1991:62–63.

4.4 The principal rhetorical devices of the LORD's good-news messenger

analogy in particular (metaphor, simile, and anthropomorphism), along with *graphic imagery* to assist the audience in visualizing key aspects of the message, notably the destruction of Nineveh; (c) *direct discourse,* including vocatives, imperatives, etc., and *rhetorical questions* to render the prophecy in diction that is more immediate, engaging, and impactful for the audience;[25] (d) *phonological punctuation* through rhythmic patterning, punning, alliteration, and assonance, to give the message a greater auditory impression; and (e) periodic *condensation* of the text, e.g., by means of ellipsis, asyndeton, and syntactic shifts (especially nominal advancement) to render selected passages with heightened urgency and excitement as a complement to their semantic content.[26]

Having taken a bird's-eye view, so to speak, of the larger construction of Nahum, we will now proceed through the text again, this time with a particular view toward locating those points on the microstructural level of discourse which are distinguished by some special usage in terms of either *quantity* (concentration) or *quality* (uniqueness) with respect to the five rhetorical characteristics mentioned above. The aim is to see how these features reinforce one another to further establish the compositional boundaries posited earlier and also to highlight certain *peak* passages in the book, that is, in addition to the mountain top of 1:15. But one must also ask why the latter passage is considered to be to be the structural-thematic summit of the entire book, and how is it related in turn to the lesser peaks. Furthermore, how does a detailed investigation of these literary devices help us to better understand the content and intent of the prophet's message? It will not be possible to discuss each and every stylistic gem that is manifested in the work of one who has been rightly designated as the "poet laureate" of the minor prophets (Patterson and Travers 1990). But the following summary should suffice to demonstrate Nahum's divinely inspired gift of poetic diction which he effectively utilizes to communicate a vital word of encouragement to his spiritually debilitated religious community.

---

[25] Baker takes special note of the different functions of rhetorical questions in Nahum (1988:29).

[26] I agree with Phillips that the prophetic literature exhibits "primary rhetoric" that was not practiced as a "theoretical art" form, and thus, "we do not have the specific categories to name the commonplaces, devices or tropes, or to analyze whether they conformed to any putative standards" (2008:252). However, we have to use familiar literary concepts to describe what we find in Hebrew literature, recognizing in this process of analysis that some measure of analogizing and approximation is always involved (cf. ibid., 253).

This selective description will proceed diachronically, that is, following the sequence of primary poetic text segments which were identified in the preceding figure of the book's structural outline.

I. A. (1:1)

This short introduction to the prophecy of Nahum is distinguished by three distinct references to the nature of the discourse: "oracle" *(masa')*, "vision" *(chazon)*, and "book" *(seper)*. This combination is unusual in that the first two terms denote oral works and the third a written text. "Yahweh" *(yhwh)*, the primary source of the prophetic communication, is only implied here, but he is abundantly specified in the opening strophe (vv. 2–3a). It may be that this concentrated, threefold reference to the work's text-type is a subtle foreshadowing of its peak passage in 1:15, which conveys a manifold "peace"-bearing "message" *(b-s-r)* or "announcement" *(sh-m-')* for the people of God.

I. B. (1:2–8)

The overt theme of "Nahum" *(nachum)* is emphatically introduced in v. 2 by a triple recursion of the phonologically similar key verb "avenge" *(n-q-m)*, set each time in parallel with its divine subject, Yahweh. But this verb is semantically polar in that it entails a pair of opposing participants in addition to its agent, namely, those who are "avenged" as well as those upon whom "vengeance is taken." Less obvious then, but far more important overall, is the book's covert theme, i.e., the faithful remnant of Judah will be vindicated—in this case, also delivered—even as their oppressors, Nineveh, are totally defeated. Indeed, the covenant LORD "will by no means leave the guilty unpunished" *(n-q-h*, with strong emphasis!)—whether those who violate his revealed will *(Torah)* or who unjustly persecute his people.[27] The phonologically similar but semantically polar forensic verbs, *n-q-m* and *n-q-h*, together with the near-initial and final references to *yhwh* form an *inclusio* around the opening strophe (vv. 2–3a).

Verses 3b-6 present a vivid theophanic description in praise of the righteous "wrath" *(chemah*—i.e., "judgment" by metonymy; v. 6; cf. v. 2) of

---

[27] It is important to stress "the covenant background [for] a proper understanding of the use of this term in the OT" (Smith 1984:73). We also note that the business of avenging evil in the world belongs to the LORD alone, not to those who are wronged, no matter how unjustly (Ex 34:6–7; Deut 32:34–43; cf. Ro 12:19; Hb 10:30). The prophet Jonah, along with many like-minded individuals in Israel (and else-where), had a serious problem with Yahweh's manner of dealing in justice with Nineveh (Jon 3:10, 4:2).

Yahweh, the Divine Warrior, who is mentioned just before and after the hymn, but not during (i.e., *exclusio*). The climax of the piece occurs in the chiastically arranged, double rhetorical question at the onset of v. 6, a verse that is intensified by various expressions denoting the LORD's anger. Cohesion throughout the strophic unit is maintained by means of the varied, nature-based (e.g., volcanic!) imagery, including metaphor [3b], personification [5], simile [6] and a string of locative references to what is before him on "his path" (*darko,* 3a).[28] The brief following strophe (vv. 7–8) leads off with the second of two prominent theological predications, based on his gracious covenant, which frame section B: "Good is Yahweh..." (cf. v. 3a: "Yahweh [is] slow of anger...", i.e., full of "mercy" –Ps 106:1). This segment proceeds to conclude B with an emphatic pronouncement of his contrastive, saving behavior with regard to those who trust him as opposed to all his enemies—the implicit "Nineveh" being preeminently in mind (cf. the prophetic heading in 1:1).[29] Much of the epic, Yahweh-focused wording and imagery found in vv. 2–8 reproduces, modifies, or alludes to similar panegyric discourse in Israel's rich religious-literary tradition, to the Psalter and Isaiah in particular.[30] Several key covenantal terms also appear in the conceptually focal verse seven (e.g., *y-d-h* "know," *ch-s-h* "seek refuge") to further establish this scenario as the primary contextual background for interpreting the entire section.

I. C. (1:9–15)

Mention of the LORD's "enemies" (*'oyebayw,* vv. 2b, 8b) prods the prophet into a denunciation in direct address (strophe C1, vv. 9–11). Whatever "evil" (*ra'ah,* 11a) "you [= they] plot against Yahweh [front-shifted]" (9a),

---

[28] Evidence for a half-acrostic arrangement of the verses covering 1–10 is scanty, at least in the Hebrew text as it now stands. For a conservative (non-emendational) attempt to defend the presence of such an elaborate literary device, see Patterson 1991:18 (for a counter argument, see Bullock 1986:219–20). Due to the irregularity of the pattern that is posited, it is highly unlikely that this feature would have any impact or effect on the oral-aural communication of the discourse. Longman suggests that "the partial acrostic is a poetic device for communicating the message that God, the Warrior who melts mountains and dries up seas, is present" (1993:775).

[29] The parallel term to "enemies," i.e., *meqomah,* allows for two vocalizations and meanings: "to her place" (MT) and "to those who rise against him" (LXX), either of which fits well in this context. Concerning the sharp contrast between the LORD's "wrath" and his "goodness," Armerding notes: "as long as evil exists, his judgment is an inevitable expression of his goodness on behalf of the victims of evil" (1985:465).

[30] For details concerning these prominent lines of intertextuality, see Patterson 1991:28–30 and Armerding 1985:196.

"he" (emphasized) will bring it to an "end" (*kalah,* note the rhyme; cf. v. 8a). These plotters are in for big "trouble" (*tsarah,* v. 9c) because of all the "trouble" they caused for his loyal people (v. 7). Despite the fact that verse 10 "must be one of the most difficult texts of the Old Testament" (Cathcart 1973:60) its rhetorical means and ends seem clear: A series of three, possibly proverbial images, sharpened by rhymed alliteration (e.g., *s, k, b, m*) and introduced by a climactic *kiy* "surely!," combine to highlight the threat of a complete punitive consumption for those who are "trapped" by the consequences of their active promotion of "lawlessness" [LXX] *beliyya'al* (i.e., by "thorns," "wine," and "fire" [implied, cf. v. 6c]).[31] Verse 11 makes Yahweh's indictment against Nineveh clear: it summarizes the deliberate, rebellious sort of attitude and impious behavior that moves a "jealous" God to "take righteous vengeance" (v. 2) against them—and all evildoers.

At last Yahweh himself speaks after the familiar prophetic messenger formula: "So says the LORD" *(koh 'amar yhwh).*[32] He begins with a reference to the wicked of verse 11, but his words are really intended for the oppressed people of Judah. The LORD's judicial sentence here manifests a logical semantic sequence (i.e., a paired positive-negative, concessive-conditional construction) and is a bit irregular in its syntactic rhythm (especially at the end of the strophe in v. 13). Nevertheless, the poetic nature of the discourse is still evident, namely, in the abundant repetition, parallelism, and figurative language that is present.[33] As in the preceding strophe, so this one culminates toward the end in a rhetorically "step-up" device, the transitional "and now" *(we'attah),* which leads to a concluding chiastic construction (a common marker of *closure* in Nahum) that increases the impact of the thematic reversal being formally proclaimed.

The rapid shift in addressee(s), shown in the personal pronouns, continues in verse 14 as Yahweh now "commands" *(ts-w-h)* a prophecy of judgment

---

[31] Though the meaning may be somewhat unclear, the figures of v. 10 are perceptibly interconnected by soundplay such as consonance [e.g., *k, b, s, m*] and rhyme, i.e., *sebukim* "entangled"//*sebu'im* "drunken." On the important intertextual semantic implications of "Belial," see Achtemeier 1986:16. The particular "one counselling worthlessness" (v. 11) may well be a pointed reference to the "king of Assyria" (cf. 3:18; Robertson 1990:75), "who represented the Assyrian goddess of the underworld, Belili" (Smith 1994:162).

[32] This being the only occurrence of this formulaic expression in the entire book may mark it as having a foregrounding function here, that is, to signal the onset of the first distinct "good news" message for Judah, especially in v. 13 (cf. vv. 15, 2:2).

[33] This is hardly an example of "narrative" (Patterson 1991:43; cf. Patterson and Travers 1988:50).

to fall upon the unnamed potentate of Nineveh ("he who plots evil against Yahweh," v. 11; cf. 3:18) and, by implication, all his perverted subjects—their pagan deities in particular. Reference to *'eloheyka* "your gods," which rhymes with "upon you" *('aleyka),* is spotlighted in the lexical center of the strophe. The LORD's metaphoric condemnation (e.g., the king/city's "name will not be sown again") concludes with another emphatic two-word utterance: "...for/indeed you are vile" (cf. the close of vv. 11, 13, 15, i.e., structural *epiphora*).

The book's major thematic peak point is suddenly reached "on the mountains" of verse 15 (2:1 in the MT). A dense concentration of poetic devices converges here to formally mark the spot, as it were—from the initial *hinneh* "behold/listen-up!" to the final "he will be cut off." This inventory includes such rhetorical features as: consonance (e.g., the sequence of /m/ and /sh/ sounds in the first line),[34] metonymy (i.e., "the feet" = a swift herald), internal rhyme (e.g., *shalom* "peace"//*shallemi* "carry out [vows]"),[35] the medial pair of imperatives in parallel syntactic constructions, the book's first overt mention of "Judah," the recursion of several key lexical items from preceding strophes (e.g., *'-b-r* "pass through or away" [cf. 1:8, 12], *k-r-th* "cut off" [cf. 1:12, 14], *beliyya'al* "worthlessness" [before God]), the colon-penultimate emphatic *ki,* and a final condensed utterance of closure, which formally reflects the action that it describes: "his all will be cut short!" *kulloh nikrath.* The central commands "celebrate!" and "carry out!" refer by synecdoche to the re-establishment of public worship practice and personal piety in Israel, and they forge a significant contrast with the fate of official religion in Nineveh (v. 14c).

II. A. (2:1–13)

Once again there is an unexpected shift in the ostensive addressee of the discourse as Nahum leads off the second (and larger) "half" of his prophecy with a dramatic warning to the citizens of Nineveh—a (satirical) call to battle to its army in particular. In the interest of greater suspense, the city is not mentioned by name, but there can be no doubt as to who the "you" (lit. "your face") refers to. The mightiest military machine in the world

---

[34] This soundplay is not merely decorative, for it serves to foreground the "messenger"—*mebasser + mashmia'*.

[35] This rhyme is interlocked with another, i.e., *chaggayik* "your festivals"//*nedarayik* "your vows."

is summoned to marshal its "strength" *(koach)* and match it with that of Yahweh (cf. 1:3). In marked similarity-with-contrast to the preceding strophe (1:15), there is an invitation (here implicit) for the populace to "look" and see their imminent destiny (but now it is war instead of peace). The threat of a force powerful enough to "scatter" *(mepits)* them all (perhaps an indirect reference to Yahweh himself; cf. 1:2–8, 2:2) is reinforced by the continuing alliteration of the /ts/ sound. A series of four brusque commands (probably intensive infinitive absolute forms) punctuated by asyndeton ironically sets the scene of the impending disaster with a drill-like staccato beat. It is as if Nahum has set his feet right there on the stage of action and is reporting the events as they occur before his very eyes.[36] The whole of Part II then acts as a realistic recital of its ostensive theme—the overthrow of Nineveh—in order to stress the certainty of this profound prediction. But at the same time it celebrates the book's deeper, more substantial message, namely, the righteousness of the LORD operating inexorably through the events of world history for the good of his faithful, penitent flock (cf. 1:12; contrast 3:19).

The prophet's on-the-scene report is suddenly interrupted by a brief parenthesis (v. 2), introduced by a deictic *kiy* "surely!" The passage functions to remind listeners of the real significance of the battle commentary that has just begun (v. 1). It is all part of Yahweh's plan to ensure that justice is done in relation to his Covenant people, who are metonymically referred to as a totality by the epochal pair of Patriarchal names "Jacob" and "Israel"—and perhaps also indirectly by the metaphoric symbol of the grapevine (designated by synecdoche under the term "their branches"—*zemorehem*). Internal lexical recursion (i.e., *ga'on* "splendor" + *b-q-q* "lay waste") and mention of the divine agent, Yahweh, further heighten the importance of this verse as a preview of eschatological "restoration" *(shuv).*[37] It is the third element of the gospel trio that forms the heart of God's message for his people through the prophet Nahum: 1:12–13 + 1:15 + 2:2—which is the gracious outcome of his essential "goodness" *(tov,* v. 7). In each case there is a reference to blessing for God-fearing Judah in the first part of the strophe and to bane for her God-defying enemies in the second part. If the three segments were

---

[36] Indeed, "as [Yahweh's] inspired poet," Nahum here composes "some of the most vivid war poetry ever written" (Achtemeier 1986:18). Perhaps it was even "designed to be sung" (Smith 1984:82).

[37] See Deut 30:3; Jer 16:15; Ezek 38:8; Joel 3:1; Zeph 3:20.

4.4 The principal rhetorical devices of the LORD's good-news messenger

conjoined, they would form an effective instance of alternating parallelism, i.e., A-B, A1-B1, A2-B2. As it stands, this partially dispersed pattern of joyous proclamations serves as the theological foundation of the book of Nahum and the structural bridge that firmly links Part I of the prophecy into Part II.

The prophet's semi-narrative account of the attack against Nineveh continues (from v. 2:1) in verse three,[38] which leads to a series of three strophes (vv. 3–4, 5–7, 8–10) that progressively builds up in dramatic suspense and intensity to a pathetic expression of anguished emotion in v. 10: melting hearts, weak knees, shaking limbs, and pale faces (these physical symptoms being an overt reflection of the terrified psychological state of the city). This moving description of the horrors of war is introduced by a powerful image of doom: blood-red shields and scarlet uniforms (2:3). The spotlight is upon the destructive "chariots" (*rekeb,* mentioned twice) racing back and forth on the conquered city's streets. The confusion being poetically recounted seems to be mirrored by the broken style of discourse, e.g., rapid shifts of person and perspective, few finite verbs, rare vocabulary and morphology, and the lack of clear pronominal antecedents. In verse 4 for instance, three distinct Hebrew verbs in different and uncommon conjugations serve to augment the intensity of the action being portrayed, while their placement in a double chiastic construction mimics the criss-crossing military movement involved.

Another apparent reference to the leader of the invading enemy forces (2:5) begins the next strophe (vv. 5–7), highlighted by alliteration in /k/ and /h/. The enigmatic verb *k-sh-l* "stumble" (v. 6) turns out to be a grotesquely picturesque summary of the battle scene, for it is clarified by its "parallel" passage in 3:3: the advancing infantry of the attackers are tripping over corpses![39] Next, the means of Nineveh's downfall is figuratively alluded to, namely, the flooded "river gates" which led to a "melt-down" *(m-w-g)* of much of the city's protective wall (2:6—just like the hills under the feet of the Warrior LORD, 1:5).[40] The ominous consequences (according

---

[38] There is some disagreement among commentators over whether verses 3ff. refer to the Ninevites scurrying about in an effort to defend the city, or to the incursion of the invading army. I prefer the latter interpretation simply because that provides a referent for the pronoun in "*his* soldiers" (*gibborehu,* v. 3a, cf. v. 6a), i.e., the "scatterer" of v. 2a, and a more logical sequence of events between vv. 5 and 6.

[39] Most commentators point out the referential difficulty here, and some feel that it is the Ninevites who were "stumbling" on their way to defend the city's walls (e.g., Achtemeier 1986:20–21; Smith 1984:82).

[40] For details on the strategy whereby the supposedly impregnable Nineveh was conquered, see Maier 1980:250–255; Achtemeier 1986:18–20.

to divine decree [n-ts-b, niphal], cf. 1:14) for those inhabitants who survived is immediately evoked (v. 7) by one of Nahum's most pathetic scenes (Patterson and Travers 1988:53), that of the grieving slave girls, the lowest of the low, who under the figure of synecdoche represent the entire population.[41] This strophe-concluding passage features two lines of assonance that first—in /a/—emphasizes the coming exile, i.e., '-l-h "go up," and then the widespread "sound" *(qol)* of mourning in /o/, like "doves" (*yonim,* cf. Ezek.7:16).[42]

Nineveh, introduced by a waw of specification (i.e., "as for N."), is at last mentioned by name (cf. 1:1) to lead off the next strophe (2:8–10).[43] Cycle A reaches its dramatic peak in this unit as a cluster of rhetorical devices converge to foreground the hopeless plight of the Ninevites. Too much water (*mayim,* accented by the surrounding alliteration in /m/), formerly their surest line of defense, has produced an outpouring ("flight" *n-w-s*) of its population (v. 8).[44] Conflicting commands ring out—"stop!" [to defend the city], "plunder!" [the city's wealth]—as the prophet masterfully (and no doubt ironically) conjures up a scene of mass pandemonium with a paucity of words. Phonological underlining reappears at the thematic center of the strophe in the assonance and alliteration which characterize the three juxtaposed verbal derivatives that cumulatively summarize the sad state of the formerly "glorious" [*kabod*] Nineveh: *buqah umebuqah umebullaqah* "devastated, and destroyed, and denuded!" (v. 11a—i.e., a just reversal of what the Assyrian destroyers did to the "splendor" *[ga'on]* of Judah, cf. 2:2). Reiteration of the word "all" *(kol)* stresses the totality of the catastrophe, which is given concrete expression in the series of physiological, synecdochial (i.e., a part for the whole) images that conclude the strophe (cf. Isa 13:7–8).

The nature of the discourse abruptly changes with the onset of a pair of rhetorical questions in verse 11 where the prophet takes up a so-called

---

[41] Perhaps *'amhotheyha* "her slave girls" refers to the sacred cult prostitutes of the defeated goddess Ishtar, designated by the verse-initial, sarcastic term "beauty" (from *tsebi;* cf. Longman 1993:806).

[42] Is it mere coincidence that at the lexical center of his prophecy Nahum should use the word *yonim,* which sounds like "Jonah," the former prophet to Nineveh, whose book ends similarly with a pointed, thematic rhetorical question?

[43] Longman may well be right in suggesting that "this delay of precise identification causes the reader [and listener!] to be more attentive and also produces a dramatic sense of suspense" (1993:769). It further "opens up the book to much broader application" (ibid., 795).

[44] For an explanation of the rather ambiguous "liquid" imagery, see Armerding 1985:485–86.

4.4 *The principal rhetorical devices of the LORD's good-news messenger* 165

"taunt song" at the expense of the ravaged Assyrian metropolis. The lyric satirically bewails the loss of a powerful pride of lions which metaphorically represent the greatness and glory that once was Nineveh.[45] The strophe (vv. 11–12) is very tightly knit semantically by a string of references to various types of lions and related terms, e.g., "den" (*me'on*, which begins and ends the unit), "cub/s," and "lairs." It concludes with a repetitive and chiastic focus upon the feature that makes lions so fearsome—their habit of "tearing up" *(torep)* their "prey" *(merepah*, v. 12). But all this lies in the past as far as Nineveh is concerned (Where has it all gone?!—v. 11), and the reason for this surprising reversal of fortune is the theme of the concluding strophe of cycle A of Part II (v. 13).

Another emphatic *hinneh* initiates this prominent judicial "declaration of the LORD of Hosts" *(ne'um yhwh tseba'oth*, cf. 2:1, 3:5)[46]—this time coupled with a pronominal self reference in opposition to its offensive predicate: "Look-*I* [am] against-*you!*" The "sword" *(chereb*, i.e., war = metonymy) will "devour" *('-k-l*, cf. 1:14, 3:15) the "young lions" (cf. 2:11) of Nineveh, and all their "prey" *(tarpek*, cf. 2.12) will be "cut off" *(k-r-th*, a euphemistic metonymy [= death!], cf. 1:15). Several other key terms (or close synonyms) from Nahum's prior prophecy are also found in this climactic verse, which arranges military [M] and lion [L] imagery in chiastic fashion [M-L=L'-M'], e.g., "fire" (lit. "smoke," cf. 1:6, 2:4), "no...more" (cf. 1:15, 3:19), and "chariot" (cf. 2:4). But the *intra*textual recursion of greatest significance lies in the unit-final messenger-motif, here appearing in dramatic negative contrast to its earlier joyous occurrence in 1:15 (another instance of unit-final *epiphora*, cf. 3:19), and perhaps also as an ironic reversal of a humiliating episode of Judean history (cf. Isa 36–37:20; 2 Kg 18:17–19:7).

II. B. (3:1–19)
The second structural-thematic cycle of Nahum's message of reproach against Nineveh begins (3:1) appropriately with a word of genre characterization: "woe!" *(hoy)*. This highly emotive interjection was taken over from funerary

---

[45] "The lion was the favorite animal for artistic and decorative purposes in Assyria; hence the figure is particularly fitting" (Smith 1911:324). There may be an ironic reference to a traditional prophetic motif in 2:11: "there was no one to frighten [them]" (cf. Mic 4:4).

[46] This prophetic "messenger formula" functions to highlight the divine source of a prophetic message (e.g., Jer 9:22, Ezek 20:30, Zech 12:1, and Amos *passim*).

laments and applied in prophetic invective or imprecatory against some reprehensible national and religious foe (cf. Am 5:18-20; Isa 5:8-24), here specified as a "city of bloods" (*'ir damim,* the latter being an intensive plural). A further figurative, greatly condensed depiction of the murderous and rapacious character of Nineveh follows in summary form, ending with a term that echoes (by *anadiplosis*) the preceding taunt song—e.g., *tarep* "prey" (= innocent victims, 2:13c; cf. also "full" *mele'ah,* 2:12).[47] In the present strophe a topical intensification of the battle report found in chapter two (cycle A, 3:2-3) builds up to a gruesome indictment of the surpassing wickedness of the Assyrian nation (vv. 1, 4). Her crimes were moral (v. 1) as well as political and spiritual (v. 4) in nature, the latter being stressed through recursive metaphoric imagery—"harlotries" *(zenuth)* and "sorceries" *(keshep,* a pair of augmentative plurals).[48]

Thus, in between a structural enclosure of accusation is sandwiched a continuation of the graphic, seemingly on-site vision of the retributive slaughter of Nineveh, carrying on from the scene ending in 2:10. In fact, a number of terms (or their synonyms) found in the battle scenario of 2:3-10 are reiterated in 3:2-3. This passage is again "characterized by a staccato style and filled with alliterative words that take on an almost onomatopoeic quality,"[49] for example, the *shott* "crack" of a whip (v. 2). One can easily visualize and almost hear the "sound of" *(qol,* 2x in v. 2, cf. 2:13) the bloody military action that is taking place, e.g., the "jolting chariots" *merkabah meraqedah* or the "flashing sword" *lahab chereb* (cf. 2:13). A grim instance of macabre synonymy (v. 3) heightens the impact of the immediate outcome: the collective silence of a city of "slain one[s]" *(chalal),* "corpse[s]" *(peger),* "cadaver[s]" *(gewiyyah,* also in the plural). The pointed irony is that "endless" *('en qetseh)* "wealth" *(kavod,* 2:9) has been transformed into a "countless" *('en qetseh)* "pile" *(koved)* of bodies (3:3)! A repetition of the adjective "many/much" *(rov)* subtly links the judicial effect (many dead) with the criminal cause (v. 4): too much abhorrent "harlotry" (an intensive

---

[47] For some historical background concerning the murderous cruelty of Nineveh, see Maier 1980:292.

[48] "...the city was a center of the cult of Ishtar—herself represented as a harlot...and society was dominated by magic arts..." (Armerding 1985:481).

[49] Patterson 1991:88. In the absence of any explicit indication, it is doubtful that this passage (3:2-3) recounts "an example [ironic flashback] of Assyria's military conquest of a foreign city" (Achtemeier 1986:23)—though the use of such a sophisticated literary device, an unmarked illustrative intercalation, would not be beyond the scope of Nahum's considerable literary skills.

infinitive absolute verbal construction) coupled with diabolical "witchcraft" (both figures suggesting an illicit, captivating control of mind as well as body). And there is yet more woe to come in the next strophe.

"Look, [it is] I [who is] against you!" *(hinni 'elayik)* thunders "the LORD of Armies" (i.e., the invincible heavenly forces) once again for good measure (v. 5, cf. 2:13). In this confrontational judgment oracle (3:5–7), which may reflect the wording of an ancient "treaty-curse" (Hillers 1964:59), Yahweh himself announces his shocking verdict upon a totally degenerate nation. He utilizes a series of highly evocative images that express their punishment in words appropriate to the nature of their previously announced transgressions (3:4, i.e., endemic prostitution coupled with widespread practice of the occult).[50] Before all nations, especially those who had experienced her brutal, often deceptive, military and political oppression, there will be a public "display" (*r-'-h,* hiph.—v. 5, the root being reiterated in vv. 6 and 7 for emphasis) of the end result of Nineveh's moral bankruptcy—her nakedness, shame (v. 5), filth, and contempt (v. 6). All people (v. 7) will view the divine reprisal that will befall the city on account of "all" *(kol)* her wickedness (v. 1, *inclusio*). On a final sarcastic note, the LORD cites a hypothetical dirge over the destruction of Nineveh (last mentioned in 2:9), which expands upon the implication of the section-initial "woe" of v. 1 (inclusio): Who will mourn her loss?! (the rhetorical query is reiterated synonymously for impact). Of course, nobody will; in fact, just the opposite will occur: No one will be there to "comfort" (*n-ch-m,* in a play on the prophet's name) any survivors. The pathetic lack of response here anticipates by way of contrast the resounding roar of the world's applause that greets the announcement of Assyria's demise (3:19). The messenger motif, here implicit, again rounds out a major unit of discourse (cf. 1:15; 2:13: 3:19).

The next strophe (vv. 8–10) leads off with another analogy-introducing rhetorical question (cf. 2:11, *anaphora*) and the LORD's satiric rebuke of Nineveh for her overweening pride.[51] The initial utterance hums with /m/ alliteration, as if to stress the "waters" (*mayim,* i.e., of her surrounding rivers) upon which both the cities of Nineveh and Thebes depended for their

---

[50] For a detailed study of this "law of retaliation" and the correspondence between sin and judgment, crime and punishment in the Hebrew prophets (cf. Ob 15), see Miller 1982 (cf. Jer 13:25–27).

[51] Jemielity discusses the "satiric" nature of much Hebrew prophetic invective, including certain passages in Nahum (1992:46–47, 89–90).

defense (lit. "rampart" *chel,* i.e., synecdoche).⁵² Similarly, alliteration at the end of the unit may serve to emphasize the central notion of "captivity" *(laggolah)* into which "all her great men" *(kal-gedoleyha)* "went" *(halkah)*. This, and a more horrible punishment inflicted upon the young of a fallen Thebes, took place (in contrast to Assyria) despite (*gam* "yet" suggesting a logical contradiction) a powerful protective circle of allies—S: "Cush" *(kush)* "and [Lower] Egypt" *(wemitsrayim);* N: "Put" *(put)* "and Libya" *(welubim).*⁵³ This strophe manifests a considerable number of lexical and topical matches that correspond with the battle report segment of 2:5–10, a rhetorical feature which reinforces the prophetic application of the present example (Thebes) to its referent (Nineveh), e.g., the cause of defeat: "water" *(mayim,* 3:8/2:8), and its consequence: "captivity" (*galah,* 3:10/2:7).

The point of Yahweh's comparison from history is made specific in verse 11: "You too!" *gam-'at.* This short strophe of judicial application (vv. 11–12), though clearly related to the preceding (e.g., via direct speech and lexical recursion, especially the progressively intensive *gam* + *kol* sequence), is also distinct with regard to the nature of discourse, i.e., heavily figurative as opposed to largely literal as in vv. 8–10. The literary device of intertextuality is also operative, for example, in the use of metaphors and similes such as drunkenness (Isa 49.26; cf. Na 1:10), ripe fruit (Am 8:2), and eating (Isa 28:4; cf. Na 2:14) to refer to the LORD's righteous judgment. There is also a surprising reversal evoked through a reiteration of the key terms "refuge" *(ma'oz,* i.e., for Judah, excluding Nineveh) and "enemy" (*'oyeb,* i.e., against Nineveh, sparing Judah, 1:7–8). This immutable verdict is also foregrounded phonologically by means of the corresponding rhymed terms *yinno'u wenophlu* ("they are shaken and they fall!") in the last line. As Nahum (Yahweh) approaches the end of his word of judgment against Nineveh, he becomes more insulting and derisive in tone: the formidable fortresses of the city will fall like overripe figs into the mouth of her famished foe (v. 12)!

The next closely linked pair of strophes (vv. 13–15c and 15d–17) are similar in their overall sarcastic tone, internal lexical repetition, and a large concentration of figurative language, which overlaps in the dominant image of the "grasshopper" (*yelek,* 15c/15d). Nahum demonstrates his literary

---

⁵² Armerding provides a good description of the "watery" defense of ancient Thebes (1985:484).

⁵³ These two pairs of proper names feature phonological parallelism in assonance.

4.4 The principal rhetorical devices of the LORD's good-news messenger

virtuosity by using this figure with two different, almost contrasting, senses (and "grounds" of comparison): In the first the voracious appetite of a swarm of locusts is the point as this "eating" is predicted as being the ultimate fate of Nineveh (15a, c). In the subsequent strophe the sudden, often mysterious disappearance of such an all-consuming horde is likened to the mad rush by the city's upper classes to desert their doomed capital, which was once the locative source of all their ill-gotten wealth and prestige (16–17).

One more *hinneh* marks the onset of an exclamation that scornfully juxtaposes its subject (the impotent Assyrian army) with its predicate (women).[54] The prophet appears to resume his role as a news commentator (instead of a "watchman") stationed on the soon-to-be demolished wall of Nineveh (cf. 2:1–10). This strophe (vv. 13–15c) is also lexically interlocked with the preceding unit, for instance, by the terms "eat" (*'-k-l*, 12/13), "enemy/ies" (*'oyeb*, 11/13), and "fortifications" (*mivtsar*, 12/14). Nineveh's dire straits are grammatically foregrounded: "to the enemies" (syntactic advancement) the gates "are completely open!" (infinitive absolute verbal combination). The prominent figure of a "conflagration" (*'esh*, cf. 1:10, 2:4, 2:13, 3:13) surrounds the strophe's central core. The latter consists of a satiric set of ineffectual imperatives (v. 14, cf. 2:1), which features both chiastic and analogous parallelism plus the reiterated verb "strengthen" (*ch-z-q*, cf. Isa 41:25).[55] It is ironic that right "there!" (*sham*, v. 15a), at the very point where Nineveh's defenses were shored up, (v. 14b) the enemy would break through to "cut down" (*k-r-th*, cf. 1:15, *epiphora*) her inhabitants with the sword and devour the city with fire (cf. 2:13, more structural *epiphora*).[56]

Another mocking command initiates the following and companion strophe (vv. 15d–17; cf. 2:1): "multiply!" (2x—the first masculine, the second feminine to indicate everyone; cf. the five ironic orders of v. 14). The figurative locust family is clearly in focus as a quarter of the total number of the strophe's vocabulary is selected from this semantic domain in a string of vivid similes that stress the solitary exposure of the now defenseless city. The hasty flight of all those who had the means to do so

---

[54] Apparently, this utterance is based upon a conventional "treaty curse" (Longman 1993:823).
[55] For a good summary of the three major satiric segments in Part II, see Patterson 1991:109.
[56] The images of "fire" and a "sword" are often used in OT judgment passages, e.g., Isa 9:19, 10:17, 27:1, 34:5–6, sometimes together, cf. Isa 31:8–9.

is stressed by several lexical and syntactic parallels, as well as in sound:[57] *wenodad welo'-noda'* "and it [the locust swarm] flies away and it is not known" where it now is. Yahweh/Nahum closes with an evocative (but progressively satiric) appeal to the imagination in the compound particle "where [are] they" (*'ayam*, v. 17), which rhymes with the corresponding "there" *(sham)* of v. 15—the place of national destruction (cf. 3:7c = double *epiphora*).[58]

A sarcastic *apostrophe*, disguised as a lament and addressed to "the king of Assyria" *(melek 'ashshur)* brings the book of Nahum to an emotively ironic, yet comparatively quiet, close, i.e., sad for Nineveh but glad for Judah (cf. Jer 51:57).[59] The guilty (*ro'eykha* "your shepherds," i.e., the nation's leadership) and their reprehensible guilt (*ra'athekha* "your evil") begin and end the strophe (vv. 18a/19c), which resounds with the accusatory pronoun "you" (2ps) i.e., with reference to the king (for similar judgment imagery, see Isa 13:14; Ezek 34:11–10).[60] A complex, contrastive play on sounds phonologically seals the empire's fate; there is no "gatherer" *(meqabets)* to retrieve all those dispersed by the "scatterer" (*mephits*, 2:1a = *inclusio;* cf. *naphoshu* "scattered," also in 3:18). Nineveh was as good as dead (for similar judgment imagery, see Isa 17:11, Jer 10:19, 30:12–15; Hos 5:13; Mic 1:9). As was observed in the earlier structural analysis, this "oracle-vision" finishes with a number of prominent *epiphoric* lexical-thematic links with earlier material, most notably, the "all"-inclusive *(kol)* messenger motif (with emphasis: *shome'ey shim'akha* "those hearing your report"; cf. 1:15, 2:13, 3:7) "on the mountains" (1:15), telling about "your wound" (*lishverekha;* cf. *shalom*

---

[57] For an explanation of the connection between the "merchants" (v. 16a) and the "guards" (v. 17a), see Patterson 1991:110. Armerding's observation is also appropriate: "[The Assyrian] empire was to succumb as a victim of the self-interest it had promoted—eaten away from within no less than it was devoured by the sword from without" (1985:489). We note the importance of Nahum's incisive and artful use of figurative language in forging an overt thematic linkage between these two judicial notions.

[58] A case can be made for interpreting the interrogative *'ayyam* as a pivotal, double-duty transitional that functions also to initiate the strophe beginning at v. 18, i.e., "*Where* are your shepherds sleeping…" This poetic device is typical of Nahum's condensed, often elliptical style (e.g., the colon-final vocative).

[59] Given Nahum's obvious familiarity with Isaiah, it is highly possible that these references to a dispersed and dormant leadership represent a reversal of the dynamic imagery with which the Assyrian (implied) host is prophetically portrayed in Isa 5:26–27.

[60] The strong intertextual resonance of this final pair of verses reinforces not only the punitive side of Nahum's message (judgment), but its converse as well (mercy), e.g., Num 27:17; Isa 40:11; Jer 23:3; Ezek 34:13.

"peace," 1:15) with "unending" consequences (*tamid,* cf. 1:7, 15; 2:13).[61] The final lines then lengthen into an indicting rhetorical question of closure, a query that will likewise ring for eternity in the ears of all evil doers who will one day stand in judgment before their avenging LORD (cf. 1:2–3; also the direct accusation of 1:11). But the end is not all black: in graphic contrast to the destiny of the ungodly, we have juxtaposed a dramatic audio-image of the oppressed people of God of every land clapping their hands in joyful approbation (3:19b).

4.5 Just how "beautiful" are the textual "feet" of Nahum (cf. Isa 52:7) in another language?

In this concluding portion of our study, it is necessary to address the inevitable "so-what?" factor: Of what practical benefit or relevance is a rhetorically oriented discourse analysis like the preceding as far as contemporary communication is concerned?[62] How can we achieve a greater semblance of dynamic, functional equivalence in the interlingual transmission of the essential biblical message, whether that of Nahum or any other book? It may be helpful to outline five particular areas of significance or implication with respect to the translation and transmission of Nahum's prophetic oracle-vision today:[63]

- **Demarcation:** This factor concerns the determination and marking of the discrete units of discourse and also their principal interrelationships with one another as well as the composition as a unified, hierarchically organized whole (based on concrete textual evidence).[64] There is a need then to read and understand a given biblical pericope as a complete message, a total communication event having a specific ideological purpose, rhetorical structure, and micro-aesthetic

---

[61] For a survey of how the LORD's judgment upon Nineveh and the Assyrian empire was fulfilled in world history, see Maier 1980:104–139; Patterson 1991:105–107.

[62] A thorough discourse analysis of any text of Scripture also has important exegetical and wider hermeneutical implications. These have been left more or less implicit in the preceding discussion and will not be taken up here due to the limitations of space.

[63] For a similar survey in relation to the book of Obadiah, see chapter one.

[64] A literary-structural study, as exemplified in this essay, may serve to support the unity and integrity of a particular composition, whether large or small. In Nahum, as in many of the other prophetic works (e.g., Hosea and Joël; cf. Wendland 1995), the text has been demonstrated to be arranged and to function as a complete literary whole, not as a patchwork of heterogeneous units fortuitously (or awkwardly!) stitched together to form a single received text.

form along with its expected theological content. Any meaning-based translation must therefore strive to utilize the corresponding signals for aperture and closure in the "target language" (TL) to mark the text's constituent segments and to link these up by means of natural transitional devices.[65] In many cases, this will involve the technique of recursion so characteristic of Hebrew poetry (thus favoring a more concordant style of translation). In addition, it is helpful to visually display the main outline of the book's overall structural organization through the use of its printed format (e.g., paragraphing, indentation, spacing, varied typefaces, etc.) in order to increase the text's legibility, readability, and hence also its overall comprehensibility.

- ***Disambiguation:*** In a poetic work, this aspect primarily concerns the need to clearly identify the probable "speaker," "addressees," and/or "referents" of adjacent compositional units, especially in cases where these participants are not explicitly indicated in the literal text (e.g., by means of a vocative or descriptive characterization), or where there is a sudden shift with respect to either option. In Nahum, this factor is of paramount importance in the second portion of Part I (vv. 11–15), where the LORD alternatively addresses or refers to the two protagonists of the discourse—to Nineveh, which is sharply condemned, and Judah, which is strongly encouraged. Such clarification in a translation may be achieved through the setting off of separate strophic units accompanied by either identificational section headings or explicit nominal forms in the text to designate the correct addressee/referent(s). In some cases, it will also be necessary to disambiguate places in the text where *enallage* (pronominal shifting) has occurred, e.g., in 1:9–11 where Nineveh is the implicit antecedent of a series of 2mp, 3mp, and 2fs pronominal forms.

- ***Definition:*** This feature involves the textual highlighting of certain thematically crucial elements of the message. In Nahum such literary marking is particularly necessary in the book's tripartite salvific cen-ter, or "gospel core," namely, 1:13, 1:15, and 2:2, but other important junctures in the discourse should also be similarly distinguished, for example, the points of appearance of the

---

[65] A literary-structural analysis also provides a concrete means for evaluating and choosing between alternative proposals for demarcating the text, for example, against a decision to separate 1:7–8 from 1:2–6 (Chisholm 1990:166); to extend the first half of the discourse (i.e., Part I) to 2:2 (Longman 1993:795); to eliminate any structural break at all between chs. 1 and 2 (Evans 1992:140); to designate 2:13 as a major independent compositional unit (Mason 1991:62, 67); to include 3:1 as the final element of the first "cycle" of Part II (Armerding 1985:479); to mark 3:11 as a passage of closure (Patterson 1991:101), or to distinguish a fourth main section within the prophecy, i.e., 3:12–19 (van Gemeren 1990:164–165).

central "messenger motif," i.e., 2:13b, 3:7, and 3:19. The devices used for poetic definition are of course specific to each language, but there may well be some general stylistic correspondences to biblical Hebrew, e.g., with respect to: verbal recursion, figuration, word order modifications, phonological intensification, and formal-semantic condensation (as illustrated in the earlier text analysis). Over and above such internal definition of peak passages within a given Scriptural composition, external marking is needed with regard to prominent intertextual quotations, adaptations, or allusions (i.e., in addition to the usual footnoted cross references, perhaps a device like italicization might be used for close, coherent citations). The book of Isaiah seems to have been a source of special significance for Nahum throughout his message, most notably its focal proclamation of "peace" for the people of God (1:15; cf. Isa 52:7).[66]

- ***Dramatization:*** In this instance, the question is: how can the dynamic rhetorical aspects of a text such as Nahum—in terms of persuasive impact, appeal, and relevance—be reproduced in a functionally equivalent manner by means of corresponding features in the TL? It is clear that the prophet's message is intended in many places to be an audio-stimulated visual display, that is, in the imagination of his audience, especially the periodic "battle scenarios," e.g., 2:1, 3–6, 9–10; 3:2–3, 13–17. How then can the same effects be duplicated in another language and perhaps also a different literary genre (e.g., prose versus poetry—or something in between, such as "oratory")? Is it possible to activate the prominent oral-aural aspect of the discourse by means of some musical text-type, or one that is declamatory in nature, having poetic features such as rhythm, rhyme (perhaps), alliteration, paronomasia, ideophones, and measured lines?[67] Perhaps even more of the text needs to be recast in the form of direct speech in order to dramatize the discourse to a sufficient degree—yet selectively and appropriately so in order to avoid "overdoing" the message and thereby obscuring its primary theological point and pastoral purpose.

---

[66] In his commentary (1993), Longman pays special attention to the Isaianic connection as the principal focus of intertextuality in Nahum. Armerding also gives a valuable overview of this feature of literary interdependence (1985:453–56), which he calls "an outstanding example of OT prophetic interpretation and application within the OT itself" (ibid., 456; cf. also Smith 1994:160).

[67] Longman concludes that "the poetical and literary effects on which the book is based are most notable on a written, not an oral, level" (1993:768). But why then would the text include so many important phonological features to help emphasize certain aspects of its message? It would seem more likely that the work was deliberately composed with oral articulation in mind. This might also explain the partial (or "broken") acrostic of 1:2–8: the text was intended primarily for *auditory,* not visual, consumption.

- **Decoding:** The various books of Scripture, the prophetic works in particular, communicate in a very concrete, culturally specific way. They are not written in the form of abstractly worded, complexly constructed, and rationally argued dogmatic treatises. Their diverse messages strike directly at the hearts and lives of the people for whom they were initially intended and in their specific historical and sociocultural setting. This emphasis on meaningfulness in context, while of utmost importance in the original event, presents problems of varying proportions today, due to the situational gap that separates two very different sets of receptors—those of Bible times and people today. As a result, many of the key aspects of the message of a prophet like Nahum sound rather strange, senseless, or even repulsive in a modern, twentieth-century setting, e.g., an avenging, angry God (1:2, 6); the annihilation of a nation (1:14); the importance of festivals, vows, and vines (1.15, 2.1); the apparent glorification of warfare (2:3–10); the significance of "lions" and "loins" (2:11–13); the association of "prostitution" and "witchcraft" (3:4); the fall of Thebes (3:8–10); the scourge of locusts (3:15–17); and the nature of an unspecified "fatal injury" (3:19). Some of these conceptual conflicts, contradictions, and conundrums can be effectively clarified right within a dynamic, meaning-oriented translation itself. But the majority will have to be handled by means of a "paratext" that accompanies the biblical text, consisting of a priority-rated selection of appropriately worded and contextually relevant footnotes, glossary entries, and cross references.[68]

4.6 Conclusion

We began this study with a brief allusion to the figured "feet" of LORD's chosen herald of "peace" (1:15). Is this perhaps a covert reference to the prophet Nahum himself? That question of course cannot be answered, and it is not really important, for the entire "book" is his personal "vision" from the LORD for the people of Judah (1:1, 15). And what an exciting and stirring panorama he presents—today too—as one soon discovers, once the twin barriers of the original text (language) and context (life-setting) have been adequately bridged. This inspired spokesman is undeniably a master literary rhetorician, as he demonstrates his verbal craft in virtually every verse. The text was composed as a powerful proclamation of "comfort" *(n-ch-m)* and

---

[68] Smith calls attention to the need for detailed knowledge about biblical culture in relation to the process of communication in order to better understand the intended message of the OT prophets (1994:10–13; cf. Wendland 1987).

4.6 Conclusion

encouragement to his fellow countrymen and women, in particular, those who had learned to depend on Yahweh as their refuge and strength (1:7)—those who knew what it meant to faithfully serve him in a covenantal relationship (1:15) based on his unfailing mercy and goodness (1:7). It gave them a new, revitalized perspective on life, their relationship to the LORD, and the eventual destiny of the wicked in the world.[69] Nineveh and its king are often addressed directly in words of righteous condemnation, but this is more than a mere rhetorical device.

The prophet's announcement of avenging judgment (1:2), of which the greater portion of his message is composed, stands as a lasting testimony to God's immutable justice and his resolve to punish all "Ninevites" of every generation who oppose his gracious will—those impenitent transgressors from among his own flock (1:12) as well as the tormenters of the people whom he has chosen (1:2–3, 13; 3:19). On the other hand and at the same time, Nahum's gospel includes a wonderful promise of vindication, deliverance, and blessed restoration for those who revere and trust in Yahweh *(yhwh)* as their Savior and LORD (2:2)—the awe-inspiring Creator God who, as a good "Shepherd" (contra 3:18; cf. Jn 10:15, 27), knows each of them in person (1:7).

---

[69] "A more immediate purpose was to encourage [the faithful of] Judah that the tyranny under which [they] lived would have an end" (Baker 1988:22). So Nahum's powerful message concerning divine vindication can function for the unjustly oppressed among God's people also today.

5

The Structure, Style, Sense, and Significance of Haggai's Prophecy Concerning the "House of the LORD"

5.1 Introduction

This chapter presents a detailed structural and stylistic analysis of the relatively short prophetic book of Haggai, which is then complemented by a general text-rhetorical overview. The goal is to bring to light some of the main themes, formal features, and interpersonal dynamics of the urgent divine proclamation that the prophet initially conveyed to a rather disheartened post-exilic Jewish community living in the environs of Jerusalem. This study suggests that, contrary to much scholarly as well as popular opinion, the prophecy of Haggai manifests a surprising degree of literary excellence whereby the form of the text both establishes and also enhances its content to reveal a message that is considerably more significant than its surface structure would at first indicate. Some salient implications of these findings for Bible translators and other contemporary communicators will be considered in the final section of this chapter.

5.2 Overview of the discourse structure of Haggai's prophecy

The aim of this opening section is to reveal some of the principal features of compositional form that have thematic importance in terms of the prophet's central message as well as rhetorical significance with respect to the skillful manner in which the original text has been fashioned to create its special persuasive impact and appeal. Such discourse artistry is not only functional, but also constitutes a vital part of the total reservoir of 'meaning' that Yahweh wished to convey to his people in the initial setting and hence a factor that adds a further dimension to the challenge of communicating his Word effectively in a different language and culture today. The following survey examines the text of Haggai in terms of its broad structural contours, its special areas of topical emphasis, and the general rhetorical development of the divine argument conveyed through his prophet.

5.2.1 Structural divisions

Five explicit time designations coupled with traditional prophetic formulas of aperture function to demarcate the distinctly narrative-framed text of Haggai into its larger discourse segments.[1] This is by no means a mechanical procedure, however, for enough variety in selection, arrangement, and secondary marking technique is present to make for a rather interesting compositional structure overall. Furthermore, within the six larger discourse units, or sections, some carefully patterned semantic formations divide each

---

[1] I use the following designations for the common prophetic formulas found in Haggai: 'messenger formula' = הָיָה דְבַר־יְהֹוָה בְּיַד־חַגַּי; 'divine announcement formula' = כֹּה אָמַר יְהוָה צְבָאוֹת לֵאמֹר; 'oracle punctuator' = נְאֻם יְהוָה צְבָאוֹת; 'divine speech formula' = אָמַר יְהוָה. The first two are most diagnostic for the purposes of discourse demarcation; the latter two help to indicate the close of paragraph units within a section (see further below). In addition to indicating that the 'source and authority [of his message] were rooted in God' (Craigie 1985:139), the repeated formulaic references may well have a thematic implication: 'Haggai's desire to stress the time factor...derives from the imminence of the termination of the seventy-year period referred to in the prophecies of Jeremiah (25:11–12 and 29:10).... A people could not resume self-rule, which was really rule under divine sovereignty, without also restoring the home—the temple—in which that sovereign's presence might reside and give sanction and guidance to his revitalized earthly territory...' (Meyers and Meyers 1987:20). One temporal formula naming a specific, present 'day' is given in each of the six major structural units posited: 1:1, 15; 2:1, 10, 18, and 20, while an indefinite, future 'day', along with its associated eschatological events, is anticipated in the ultimate seventh reference (2:23; cf. 'in a little while'—2:6).

5.2 Overview of the discourse structure of Haggai's prophecy

unit into two major portions. These structures also serve to lend cohesion to the text and to highlight certain important themes and rhetorical motives. The following summary outlines the main stylistic features that function to distinguish the principal discourse units as they relate to one another in sequential order within the book:

Extent of unit	Principal indicators of aperture, closure, cohesion, and continuity
A. 1:1–11	Three juxtaposed formulas announce the onset of Haggai's prophecy (1:1–2): a temporal frame formula ('In the second year of King Darius…'); a messenger formula ('…the word of the LORD came through the prophet Haggai…); finally, a divine announcement formula ('So speaks the LORD Almighty'). This impressive beginning stresses the divine origin of Haggai's message and is addressed specifically to the political and religious leaders of the community, Zerubbabel and Joshua. The LORD's rebuke concerning misappropriated 'time' (עֵת), reinforced by a repeated messenger formula, is extended to all the people in v. 3–4.ª Section (and 'oracle') **A** may be divided into two parts at the midpoint of the unit, where Yahweh begins the exhortation for his audience to do something about their problem (v. 7–8). It ends at the close of his condemnation of their neglect for his 'house' (the word בַּיִת is mentioned 7x in this opening unit, also in contrastive reference to the people's 'houses'), the divine censure being stressed by means of a rhythmic series of prepositional (עַל 'upon') phrases that specify the earthly objects of the LORD's wrath (manifested in 'drought' חֹרֶב and its devastating consequences).
B. 1:12–15	A distinct *narrative* passage begins here (1:12), a reaction to the text act enunciated in **A**, as indicated by the sequence of *wayyiqtol* (wc + imperfect) constructions. The pair of addressees mentioned in 1:1 (Zerubbabel and Joshua) reappears at the onset of this unit (1:12). A subtle pattern of recursion segments this section **B** into two parallel, nearly synonymous panels, or paragraphs: vv. 12–13 (the latter verse closing with the oracle punctuator formula) and vv. 14–15. Verse 14 reiterates the essential content of 12–13, and v. 15 concludes the first half of Haggai's prophecy. In v. 15 the order of the main temporal frame formula is reversed in Hebrew from that of v. 1 (from year/month/day to day/month/year), thus forming a prominent *inclusio* for this major unit. Verse 15ab, though ending the unit, functions as the temporal frame for vv. 12–14 (**B**), while 15b does double duty (*Janus* function) to serve also as an aperture for the temporal frame of the next section (**C**) in 2:1.

C. 2:1–9	This oracle begins in a similar way to section **A** (2:1–2), suggesting that the book may be partitioned into two parts at this juncture; the relative length of **C** also corresponds to that of **A**. An *inclusio* containing the thematic key words 'glory' (כָּבוֹד), 'this house' (הַזֶּה הַבַּיִת), and 'former' (הָרִאשׁוֹן) demarcates the unit of direct discourse: *'this house in its former glory'* (v. 3); *'the glory of this house… more than the former'* (v. 9). In unit **C** the LORD encourages his people in their task of building by enunciating a speech that spells out the implications of his crucial assertion in **B**: 'I [am] with you' (אֲנִי אִתְּכֶם—i1:13; cf. the repetition in 2:4). It may be divided into two portions at the emphasized divine announcement formula in v. 6 where the temporal scope also shifts from a rather tenuous present perspective to a much more confident *future*: 'Surely…as for me, I am going to shake' (וַאֲנִי…כִּי מַרְעִישׁ— a participial *futurum instans*).
D. 2:10–14	An initial time frame formula, followed by a messenger formula plus a divine announcement formula (2:10–11a), signals the beginning of this section. Like **B**, unit **D** is distinct from the surrounding oracular discourse, being articulated in the generic form of a rabbinic *disputation* speech. This pertains to cultic *halakah* precepts of purity which acts as a deliberate point of disjunction within the book's development, thus creating an effective pause for spiritual and moral reflection. Like **B**, unit **D** is also clearly segmented into two, in this case contrastive, sub-sections (10–12, 13–14). Closure is marked by an emphatic utterance: '…and whatever they offer *there* defiled it [is]!' (טָמֵא הוּא וַאֲשֶׁר יַקְרִיבוּ שָׁם—v. 14b; see also below).
E. 2:15–19	This unit follows closely upon **D** as a divine response to the preceding disputation—but it also presupposes the content of, and continuity from sections **A-C** (i.e., in 2:15 the LORD resumes the message concerning his 'house', v. 9, but now refers to it as a 'temple' הֵיכָל; cf. v. 18). **E** is addressed to all the people, not just to the priests as in **D**. Unit **E** is also divided into two parallel panels, this time by means of the repeated initial imperative clauses: 'set [your] hearts, I urge you (נָא), from this day and onwards…' (וְעַתָּה שִׂימוּ־נָא לְבַבְכֶם מִן־הַיּוֹם הַזֶּה – vv. 15a and 18a, which forms an *exclusio* around the brief, rhetorically digressive glance back at the people's unproductive past in vv. 15b–17). The beginning of the first paragraph is further distinguished by the initial temporal and logical marker 'now' (וְעַתָּה), while the onset of the second paragraph is extended by a subsequent temporal frame formula (v. 18b, which reiterates that of 2:10, thus forming an approximate *inclusio* delineating sections **D** and **E**). The close of section **E** is clearly signaled by the third occurrence of 'from this day' followed by the unexpected, emphatic divine declaration: 'I will bless [you, implied]!' (אֲבָרֵךְ – v. 19c, contrasting with v. 14b).

5.2 Overview of the discourse structure of Haggai's prophecy 181

F. 2:20–23 Section F begins with an abbreviated reversal of the prophetic formulas that initiated section D (an instance of structural *anaphora*). Just as unit C elaborates upon the divine assertion of B, 'I am with you!', so also F enlarges upon what Yahweh promises at the end of E, 'I will bless [you]!' The emphasis is upon a future messianic-eschatological setting that also implicitly develops in the theophanic imagery of an earthquake what is predicted in oracle C (2:6–9 = > 2:21–22), now with a negative rather than a positive implication for world powers when the LORD 'shakes (מַרְעִישׁ) the heavens and the earth' (cf. Joel 3:16). Oracle F is, like the preceding sections, divided into two portions at v. 23 by means of a sudden shift 'On that day' (בַּיּוֹם הַהוּא) to unexpectedly throw the prophetic spotlight upon a single person, namely, 'Zerubbabel' (v. 21a). Closure of this climactic segment and the book as a whole is marked by the thrice-reiterated oracle punctuator formula 'declares Yahweh of Hosts' to emphasize who will bring all these things to pass.

ᵃThe literary parallelism between v. 2 and v. 4 would suggest that we are dealing with essentially the same oracle, not necessarily that 'the two messages presuppose a time lapse' (Verhoef 1987:57; cf. Boda 2004:159). A chiastic interconnection is thus formed: *this people + time to build // time to live + this house.*

There are several problematic aspects about the discourse organization of Haggai. We have noted, for example, the difficulty concerning the division of 1:15 where we find a distinctive date formula that apparently operates in two directions: Thus, v. 15 as a whole applies to the unit (B) starting in v. 12, while the latter portion (15b) functions also to open the second half of the book and unit (C) beginning in 2:1. While this may be unusual, it is certainly not an unknown prophetic technique. Rather than a stylistic aberration, it is more likely that this is just another indication of the author's literary creativity, manifested in subtle, diverse ways and for which he has not often been given much credit by scholars in the past.

A greater obstacle for many scholars and text critics, however, also involves 1:15. Some feel that the entire section covering 2:15–19 (E) does not fit well content-wise with its cotext and belongs instead after 1:15a; others proceed to reverse the excision operation and shift 1:15a to a position before 2:15–19.[2] Besides having no manuscript support, such proposals actually create more problems of interpretation than they solve (e.g., what

---

[2] These alleged 'improvements' to the text of Haggai are discussed in Baldwin 1972:43, Boda 2004:142–143, Coggins 1987:36–37, and Motyer 1998:983–984; such emendations are also summarily dismissed by Smith (1984:149, 159). For references to several other prominent scholars who support the general reliability of the MT, consult Holbrooke 1995:3 (see also Meyers and Meyers 1987:lxvii; Verhoef 1987:18–19).

to do with the initial sequential conjunction וְעַתָּה 'and now' in 2:15) and thus only manage to distort a text that may be understood perfectly well as it stands. Why should the LORD not employ a vivid object lesson to remind 'this nation' (הַגּוֹי הַזֶּה) and its priestly leaders (הַכֹּהֲנִים) about their negligent *past* (D, 2:10–14)? The next unit (E, 2:15–19) then follows this up with a gradual transition to a much more optimistic outlook as the LORD responds to their new initiative regarding his 'temple'. In v. 19 Yahweh focuses the attention of his people on the hope of a blessed *future* ('from this time on' מִן־הַיּוֹם הַזֶּה)—if they would only remain faithful to the life-related implications of his sacred presence among them. The concluding key verb 'I will bless [you]' (אֲבָרֵךְ) thus serves as a conceptual bridge that links the parallel prophetic portions 2:6–9 and 2:20–22.

5.2.2 Discourse peaks

Exploring the internal (e.g., paragraph) organization of Haggai's principal sub-divisions is an interesting study in itself, but due to space restrictions will not be carried out here (see, for example, Clark 1992). Worthy of note, however, is the fact that the first two sections demarcated above (A–B, ch. 1) appear to build up to a minor *peak* of thematic significance towards the middle of each unit, while the last four (C–G, ch. 2) do so either at or near the close, with the prophecy's major emotive climax coming, appropriately, at the very end of the book. The following chart summarizes these observations, and also suggests how the prophet's style of writing admirably complements the main aspects of the message that he so vigorously conveyed to the people of God:

Unit peak:	Thematic content that is highlighted:	Marked by these literary features:
A. 1:8	This verse, the structural core of section A, expresses the central *appeal* of ch. 1 (go build the LORD's house!) and its *motivation* (for the 'glory' of the LORD—in contrast to self-centered human 'ways').[a]	Verse 8 features two balanced lines in terms of syllables, a series of three staccato imperatives followed by a pair of climactic cohortatives, and concluding reinforcement by means of the divine speech formula.

5.2 Overview of the discourse structure of Haggai's prophecy

B.	**1:13**	Records the *resolution* of the problem enunciated in section **A** in response to the people's obedience to the LORD's command (v. 12, cf. 1:8). Their *fellowship* with Yahweh has been restored! אֲנִי אִתְּכֶם	What more satisfying 'message from the LORD' could a 'messenger of the LORD' deliver than 'I [am] with you!'? In addition to these key thematic terms, three references to the act of speech are given in this short verse.
C.	**2:9**	There is a special semantic focus on God's 'house': it is more than a building, for it reflects the 'splendor' of its Owner (cf. 1:8). 'Peace' (שָׁלוֹם = total well-being, abundant life) applies only to people, not a place. It is brought about by Yahweh's presence (2:4) which guarantees both his future irenic intervention (2:6–9) and contrastively also his all-encompassing judgement, which is highlighted in the dramatic, militaristic close to this book (vv. 21–22).	The 'greatness' (גָּדוֹל) of the present temple's 'glory' (כָּבוֹד) is highlighted through syntactic fronting and by additional attribution ('the present...the former'). An implicit pun, perhaps a touch of irony too, appears in the unexpected utterance of closure: after the divine Warrior imagery of vv. 6–7 (e.g., Jdg. 5:4), there will be 'peace' (שָׁלוֹם) in this place ['Jerusalem'] (יְרוּשָׁלַםִ), specifically, in the rebuilt temple of 'Solomon' (שְׁלֹמֹה)!
D.	**2:14b**	Here is a strongly contrastive *negative* peak and a motive for continual vigilance: A lack of total devotion to the LORD inevitably brings a debilitating *defilement* on the people at what should be a holy site![b]	The point of the object lesson developed in the preceding verses is forcefully revealed, with emphasis: 'this people'—'this nation'; parallel closing utterances culminate in: '...there defiled it [is]' (שָׁם הוּא טָמֵא...)!![c]
E.	**2:19c**	The book's central thematic *reversal* is succinctly pronounced: It has moved from complete desecration (a curse on the land and its inhabitants—v. 14b) to a promise of unlimited 'blessing'. Thus the people's perspective progressively shifts from their bitter past (vv. 15–17), through an uncertain present (vv. 18–19b), and on to a divinely confirmed, hope-filled future (v. 19c).	This short utterance-final declaration is quite unexpected, hence foregrounded in relation to the preceding discourse: '...from this day [onward] I will bless [you]' (אֲבָרֵךְ).[d] This notion *contrasts* markedly with the close of the preceding unit, 'desecrated!' (טָמֵא), while a third mention of 'this day' (הַיּוֹם הַזֶּה) in v. 19c brings to climactic completion the temporal sequence begun in v. 15a and continued in v. 18a.

F. 2:23 | The entire paragraph F constitutes the book's eschatological climax. Yet it too peaks in an astonishing salvation oracle that stems from v. 19c. This amazing promise dramatically narrows in thematic focus from a cosmic vista to a solitary, but divinely 'chosen' (בָּחַרְתִּי) messianic 'servant' (עַבְדִּי) from among God's people—'Zerubbabel, son of Shealtiel' | Typical eschatological and military prophetic imagery highlights the first two verses, while the final verse is further distinguished by a singular, yet allusive and symbolic figure 'like the signet' (כַּחוֹתָם) to foreground its personal referent. An unusual concentration of three prophetic formulas also serves to signal the book's close, from 'On that day...' to '... declares Yahweh of Hosts'.

ᵃ"Everything in this brief prophecy hangs on this one imperative—build God's house (1:8)" (Alden 1994:1507). But one cannot go on to conclude categorically that "[c]entral to Haggai's theology was the temple" (ibid., 1508). Rather, Haggai as a whole foregrounds the great God of the covenant, Yahweh, whom the temple represents only by way of an elaborate locative symbolism (cf. Mal 1:10–14).

ᵇFishbane (1985:427) concisely describes the rhetorical dynamics of this section, which peaks out at the end of v. 14: "[A] prophet may involve his addressees in a question-answer scenario in order to establish a certain objective logic of inference or possibility—only to redirect the topic to the subjective condition of the listeners in order to shock them into new realizations and attitudes."

ᶜRonnie Sim (1992:33) and I (1992:44) argue that the demonstrative 'there' (2:14) refers to the neglected, hence defiled temple site. Taylor sees a reference rather to "the specific site of sacrificial offerings, namely, the altar of the unfinished temple building" (2004:178–179). In favor of the former interpretation is that fact that no 'altar' at all is mentioned in the book of Haggai; 'temple' ('house'), on the other hand, occurs repeatedly, including in the very next verse (2:15). Moreover, Haggai's first question of the priests figuratively concerns the temple: 'Does the very act of rebuilding the temple make the Judeans a morally pure, acceptable community in the eyes of God?' (i.e., 'not at all!' Achtemeier 1986:103; cf. Bullock 1986:307). This prepares the way for the second, the crucial indictment: the unbuilt 'house of the LORD', like a corrupting corpse, spiritually pollutes the people and all their religious service carried out 'there'. On the other hand, one referent here does not necessarily exclude the other—i.e., the sacrificial altar being piously utilized by priests (Ezra 3:2–6) on the premises of a disregarded temple. "Similar to the preceding scenarios, this application sets up three levels of contact as a defiled people have defiled the altar and in turn defiled the sacrifices they offer there" (Boda 2004:146).

ᵈ"The prophet...predicts a bumper harvest of crops and fruit at a time in the agricultural year when no sensible agronomist would risk his neck.... [H]e firmly predicts a bountiful harvest, not because he has inside knowledge on future weather conditions or special means of blight control, but because the conditions in the community are now appropriate for the experience of divine blessing" (Craigie 1985:150–151).

The structure of the book of Haggai thus moves progressively towards its impressive conclusion: The LORD's message starts off on a sour note, namely, rebuke concerning a corporate *negative* religious, social, and economic situation (pessimistic, depressing, deprived), but it moves progressively towards a *positive* personal prediction (optimistic, encouraging, confident) about a single individual. The two unequal divisions of the text assume the general shape of a contrastive thematic chiasm, with the second, forward-looking portion developing oracular material from the first at greater length and with a higher level of intensity:

    a The past and present *negative effects* of the Lord's unbuilt house (section **A**, 1:1–11)
        b The people's obedient response summons the Lord's *immediate empowering presence* (**B**, 1:12–15)
        b' The Lord's *continued presence* in his house guarantees a promising *future* for his people despite the circumstances (**C**, 2:1–9)
    a' The *positive effects* of the Lord's rebuilt house will be fully realized in messianic times (**E–F**, 2:10–23; including an initial warning against the attitudes condemned in oracle **A**)

5.2.3 Rhetorical overlay

Overlapping with and complementing the preceding *topical* structure is a threefold *rhetorical* arrangement that is based upon the so-called 'disputation speech' pattern. This is comprised of three essential elements: 'a statement of the *thesis* to be disputed, a statement of the *counter-thesis,* and the *argumentation* itself' (Sweeney 2000b:537, italics added). In fact, the book of Haggai as a whole may be viewed as consisting of three disputational cycles, each embedded within a narrative framework as outlined below (cf. the book of Malachi):[3]

Cycle ↓	Thesis	Counter-thesis	Supporting argument
A (1:1–11)	1:3–4 + 7–8	1:2	1:5–6 + 9–11
B (2:1–9)	2:4–5	2:2–3	2:6–9
C (2:10–23)	2:12c + 13–14	2:11–12ab	2:15–19 + 21–23

We observe that Haggai (or the book's final editor) does not present any of the three disputations (A-B-C) in a mechanical, unimaginative manner. For example, each cycle begins not with its primary 'thesis' (a proper covenantal viewpoint), but with an oblique expression of the 'counter-thesis' (a false religious premise, potential or actual, on the part of the people). The climactic cycle C is further complicated by its metaphorical, dialogic overlay, which requires the correct interpretation before the argument can be processed and applied (see below). This cyclical pattern of disputation revolves about a

---

[3] Each one of the three structural units formed thereby (1:1–15, 2:1–9, 2:10–23) begins with a different date. Furthermore, "[t]he third section (2:10–23) draws together...various motifs from 1:1–2:9 into a final message of the prophet, focusing on past, present, and future" (Boda 2004:38). With reference to 1:2, Verhoef correctly notes: "What [the people] said is represented in an abridged form. The prophet refers only to the very essence of the argument. It may be considered a summary of the people's case in court" (1987:54). On the rhetorical pattern of disputation in Malachi, see chapter 9.

consequential narrative core. Thus, the text of 1:12–15 recounts the outcome of the central problem specified in the LORD's case against this people in cycle A and further motivates its prophetic 'resolution' in cycles B and C. In each cycle then the three constituent disputative elements are interwoven into an intricate structural design and presented in a rhetorically varied manner. The respective interlocking arguments may be summarized as follows:

A   **Thesis:** The people must rebuild the temple for the glory and good pleasure of the LORD (expressed by ironic implication in 1:4 and by direct command in v. 8).
    Counter-thesis: It is not the right time for building the LORD's house (v. 2).
    Supporting argument: The Law's curses for covenant-breaking have befallen the people for their negligence and misplaced priorities (vv. 9–11 intensifying the initial indictment of vv. 5–6).

B   **Thesis:** The LORD's house is worth building as an expression of covenantal solidarity and as a manifestation of his presence (2:4–5).
    Counter-thesis: It's a waste of time to build this house (implied) because it will never be as glorious as the former temple (expressed indirectly by the RQs of v. 3).
    Supporting argument: Yahweh himself will glorify his house by 'shaking' the universe so that 'the nations' bring their 'wealth' to it (vv. 6–9).

C.   **Thesis:** Neglect of God's house demonstrates an irreverent heart-attitude that pollutes the people along with all their offerings (2:12c—an explicit 'no!' to the counter-thesis + 2:13–14, which is contrastively conveyed by means of a metaphoric priestly 'case study' in a manner parallel to the initially-stated counter-thesis).
    Counter-thesis: Simply worshiping in the ritually correct manner at the temple site can purify the people and their offerings before Yahweh (vv. 10–12ab, expressed metaphorically through the scenario of a hypothetical ritual *torah* ruling).
    Supporting argument: This develops the arguments of cycles A and B in heightened fashion:
    (a) The people should keep in mind their former state of deprivation due to disobedience, even as they look forward to the LORD's blessings as a result of obedience (vv. 15–19).
    (b) Yahweh will 'shake' the universe and destroy all powers opposed to his rule, which will be epitomized in a future messianic 'servant' who shall come forth from the Davidic line—the ideal 'Zerubbabel' (vv. 21–23; cf. 2 Sam 7:11–16; Mal 3:1).

Observe that the first disputational discourse (A) involves a strong *reproof* of the people for their indifference to the LORD's covenantal obligations. The second (B) unfolds an equally forceful *encouragement* to persevere in their newly reformed attitude and actions. The third pattern of disputation presents reinforced aspects of both prior communicative goals, i.e., (a) *warning*: remember your past and (b) *encouragement*: look forward to a blessed future. The book's narrative framework comes to the fore in the remaining portion of the text (1:12–15)—a medial passage that expresses the essential ideals of the Mosaic covenant: fearful *obedience* on the part of the people, coupled with an assurance of the gracious *presence* of Yahweh in their midst.

The preceding discussion concentrated on the major theological nodes in the thematic organization of Haggai. However, a strong case could be made, based on our discourse analysis of the text, for one additional peak, namely, the LORD's personal, paraenetic and pastoral expression of encouragement to his people (i.e., the 'thesis' of disputation cycle B). This is located in the approximate verbal center of the book (often a significant structural location), that is, in 2:4 (there are 264 words preceding and 257 words following this passage).[4]

And now take courage, Zerubbabel, **says the LORD;**	וְעַתָּה חֲזַק זְרֻבָּבֶל ׀ נְאֻם־יְהוָה
and take courage, Joshua, son of Jehozadak, the high priest;	וַחֲזַק יְהוֹשֻׁעַ בֶּן־יְהוֹצָדָק הַכֹּהֵן הַגָּדוֹל
and take courage, all you people of the land, **says the LORD;**	וַחֲזַק כָּל־עַם הָאָרֶץ נְאֻם־יְהוָה
and act, <u>for I am with you</u>, **says the LORD of hosts,**	וַעֲשׂוּ כִּי־אֲנִי אִתְּכֶם נְאֻם יְהוָה צְבָאוֹת׃

The artistically balanced iterative symmetry that is displayed in this verse serves to underscore its powerful hortatory import and impact; indeed, it closely resembles a traditional salvation oracle (e.g., Isa 41:10, 13; 43:1, 5). Strong intertextual resonance with a momentous historical parallel passage, namely, King David's encouragement of son Solomon to build the first Temple (1 Chr 28:20), adds to the significance of Yahweh's promise to Zerubbabel here. The concluding causal clause of this reassuring word of confirmation recalls the LORD's earlier message to the people (cf. 1:13), while its distinctly covenantal language "I—with you!" anticipates what is said in the next verse (2:5a; cf. the prophet Nathan's declaration to David

---

[4] Taylor (2004:71–72) draws attention to the detailed study of D. L. Christensen (1992) which analyzes the entire book of Haggai as manifesting a symmetrical and rhythmic poetic structure throughout the text. Christensen views the imperative verb 'and do [work]' (וַעֲשׂוּ) in 2:4 as being the centrally placed 'summary of the book's essential message' (ibid., 72).

in 2 Sam 7:3).[5] In addition, the threefold repetition of the oracle punctuator formula foreshadows the only other time that such reinforcement occurs in the book, namely, at its climactic close in 2:23:

On that day, **says the LORD of hosts,**	בַּיּוֹם הַהוּא נְאֻם־יְהוָה צְבָאוֹת
I will take you, O Zerubbabel my servant, the son of Shealtiel, **says the LORD,**	אֶקָּחֲךָ זְרֻבָּבֶל בֶּן־שְׁאַלְתִּיאֵל עַבְדִּי נְאֻם־יְהוָה
and make you like a signet ring;	וְשַׂמְתִּיךָ כַּחוֹתָם
surely I have chosen you, **says the LORD of hosts.**	כִּי־בְךָ בָחַרְתִּי נְאֻם יְהוָה צְבָאוֹת׃

There are some intriguing formal and semantic parallels between these two passages which, together with their demonstrated structural significance, suggest a possible thematic linkage between them. This appears to be especially pertinent in their respective endings. The clear correspondence between "surely I am with you (pl.)" and "surely I have chosen you" may extend to the immediately preceding words, thus favoring a more substantial interpretation of the enigmatic metaphor, "signet [ring]" (חוֹתָם), e.g., the dynamic leadership qualities and rule of the future divine servant, 'Zerubbabel', rather than simply his worthy status or intrinsic royal (secular) power.

As in the case of 2:4, there is also a prominent instance of intertextual relevance that augments the interpretation of 2:23. In this instance, we have

---

[5] Many scholars dispute the authenticity of 5a. Baldwin, for example, comments: "The Hebrew...is not the usual idiom, and, moreover, the clause interrupts the sense, separating the parallel statements 'I am with you' and 'My Spirit abides among you.' A scribe's marginal reference to Exodus 29:45, 46 may have become incorporated into the text" (1972:47; cf. Smith 1984:156). Such objections may be countered, however, and the MT read meaningfully as written (cf. Motyer 1998:988–989). The alleged infelicitous separation of related concepts may, on the contrary, be shown to fit a meaningful chiastic pattern of arrangement, a familiar construction in Haggai, viz.: **A** *And do [*מְלָאכָה*] work, cf 1:14]!* – **B** *for I am with you* – **C** *a declaration of the LORD of Hosts, [do] the very thing that I covenanted [lit, 'cut'] with you when you came out from Egypt* – **B'** *and [= for] my Spirit abides among you* – **A'** *do not be afraid! [an imperative, as in A].* The core of the chiasm (C), an allusion to the covenantal basis for the divine imperatives, could itself function as the object of the initial command in A ('do!'). Thus, the separation between the verb and its object "can be an intentional displacement of the object to heighten the authority of the command and to include citation of Yahweh's involvement" (Meyers and Meyers 1987:51; cf Sweeney 2000:547; for a somewhat different proposal, see Verhoef 1987:98–100; Taylor 2004:156–157). This example further illustrates the potential utility of adding available *literary* arguments when debating such text-critical and interpretive issues (cf. Davis 1999:316).

an apparent reversal of the curse that was placed upon Zerubbabel's infamous ancestor, King Jehoiachin, to whom Yahweh announced: "As surely as I live...even if you...were a signet ring (חוֹתָם) on my right hand, I would still pull you off!" (Jer 22:24). In a sense then, Zerubbabel became God's personal representative, guaranteeing that one day there was going to be a great shaking and shattering among all nations (vv. 21–22). This divinely decreed, punitive shock-wave, to be presided over by a future descendant of the 'house' (lineage) of David (cf. 2 Sam 7:5–16), would figuratively begin at the locus of the LORD's presence in Israel (hence Haggai's emphasis on the 'house' of God in Israel) and ultimately extend throughout the world. In addition to the allusive messianic and eschatological implication of this passage, these words also attest to Yahweh's individualized concern for all those servants who are currently facing the challenges of his calling in uncertain, turbulent times.

5.3 The communicative significance of Haggai's style

In the preceding sections we have noted how the author's style enhances the book's structure in order to highlight the essential aspects of his message.[6] In other words, the main artistic features, operating both individually and also in concert, serve to reinforce the hierarchical discourse organization of the text as a unified whole, along with the central thematic argument that this structural framework articulates. Below I summarize a selection of these different literary devices and point out some additional aspects of their communicative significance for an undoubtedly depressed audience that surely could use some spiritual enlivening. This is the task that Haggai, chosen spokesman for Yahweh, masterfully accomplishes by means of a formally varied and composite prophetic sermon that often stylistically reflects its oral origin and a vividly expressive manner of proclamation. The LORD's

---

[6] My opinion of Haggai's literary style thus differs from that of George Fohrer, who opined that 'Haggai is no more than an epigone of the prophets' (cited in Craigie 1985:137). Other commentators too see "a lack of literary finesse in Haggai's style," for example, "the narrative is hurried, abrupt, without introductions and transitions. It is not a literary composition..." (Verhoef 1987:54). "His language is relatively unadorned and straightforward; it is not ornate from a literary standpoint" (Taylor 2004:66). In this chapter, I offer some varied evidence in presenting a perspective on the text that contrasts with such negative evaluations. Indeed, Haggai would appear to be a creative communicator and composer who "draws on older forms of prophetic speech, using them in new ways while also devising new forms and style" (Boda 204:86).

urgent message not only speaks directly to his people's faults and needs, but it does so in an attractive, yet forceful and compelling way that captures their cognitive attention, moves their emotions, and motivates their corporate will.

5.3.1 Direct speech

As to be expected in a prophetic book, direct speech predominates in terms of *quantity* (the amount of text incorporated), but these personal quotations also distinguish the text with regard to their relative *diversity*. "Articulated speech, that uniquely human ability, provides a ubiquitous means in the Bible for defining alternatives and expressing realities" (Meyers and Meyers 1987:57). Major discourses of judgment alternate with those of blessing, including many different speech acts and associated sentiments, as the guiding prophetic perspective ranges from past to present and forward into the near and far future.[7] The central exhortation of 2:4, for example, which underscores the LORD's own words ("I [am] with you [people]!"), also features these illocutions in rhetorical combination: encouragement, motivation, consolation, and unification (namely, of the leadership and common community with their covenantal Lord).[8]

Haggai's message begins with a self-incriminating popular saying (1:2), and a distinctive, hence highlighted, section of the book features an embedded rabbinic disputation that requests a specific *torah* ruling (termed a *pesaq din*, 2:10–14). This figuratively dramatizes the book's initial and motivating problem, one brought about by the ritual defilement of a dead body—i.e., the neglected temple site, which symbolically reflected the dismal spiritual condition of an unconsecrated people. The strong contrast between the two answers to the corresponding pair of embedded direct questions

---

[7] "Typically the prophets announce words of judgment or vindication, doom or comfort. These are pronouncements with intended effects, as declared by Yhwh through Isaiah..." (55:11) (Briggs 2008:79).

[8] Briggs distinguishes between "strong" and "weak" illocutions as follows: "A weak illocution, then, is one that requires only linguistic functions in order to function. This is the case with many assertions. A strong illocution (such as a promise, curse or confession etc.) requires certain non-linguistic conventions to be in place before it functions" (2008:99). In other words, the more extralinguistic, sociocultural background information that is necessary in order to conceptually process and respond to an illocution, the "stronger" it is, thus constituting a contextually shaped implicature.

> ...allows for the lesson of analogy to be drawn for the second question in verse 14...to impart an unstated analogy with the first question.... Haggai therefore regards the people as "unclean" or "defiled" because the temple is not yet completed and because the uncleanness that abounds cannot yet be restrained. (Meyers and Meyers 1987:57)

5.3.2 Purposeful redundancy

There is a great deal of exact and synonymous repetition in Haggai. Most prominent and rhetorically significant of course are the many speech formulas, which render the book so 'self-consciously prophetic' (O'Brien 2004:133) in stressing its divine source as well as endorsing its human spokesman and addresses, Zerubbabel in particular.[9] The succession of temporal openers, in general similar to, but in specifics different from one another, function cumulatively to emphasize the progressive fulfillment of the LORD's purposes in historical time, and also to distinguish the final, foregrounded margin by virtue of its indefinite eschatological reference, "In that day..." (בַּיּוֹם הַהוּא, 2:23).

Furthermore, the iterative style of the book renders many passages rather poetic in nature—rhythmic *poetic prose* at least—which at the same time lends an authoritative prophetic tone to the discourse (e.g., 1:6–11; 2:4, 6–9a, 21–22). A number of poetic chiastic constructions appear within this lexical redundancy, e.g., to indicate totality (1:10); to forge emphatic cohesion (2:7b–9a: this house—glory—Yahweh of hosts :: Yahweh of Hosts—glory—this house); or to create topical focus (2:23—'Zerubbabel' sandwiched between two synonymous verbs).[10] The same expression may be

---

[9] The text's twofold context needs to be remembered in this connection—namely, that of the discourse itself in its recorded historical setting (*intrinsic*) as distinct from that of subsequent audiences (*extrinsic,* see further below). This dual perspective would call into question present-day assertions such as the following: "The great stress that the book places on the prophetic credentials of Haggai and of the prophetic legitimation of the building project, then, serves not to encourage Temple rebuilding but rather to address issues of a later date" (O'Brien 2004:133). Why do these illocutionary goals have to be mutually exclusive, granting that one may be primary, the other secondary?

[10] This is the last of seven occurrences of the name 'Zerubbabel' (וְזְרֻבָּבֶל) in the book of Haggai, a significant symbolical number in itself; the repetition creates a cohesive strand throughout the text as well as an inclusio with 1:1 where the patronymic also appears in the full *plene* form (שְׁאַלְתִּיאֵל). 'Haggai, by using a living individual in his future vision, bridges the gap between present and future...he presents a view of time in which eschatology is not distinguished from history' (Meyers and Meyers 1987:84; cf. ibid., 67–68).

employed to introduce contrasting perspectives, e.g., a single word: 'house' (בַּיִת) in 1:9 referring to a human dwelling as opposed to God's residence; a phrase: 'from this day and onwards' (מִן־הַיּוֹם הַזֶּה וָמָעְלָה), used retrospectively in v. 15 and prospectively in v. 18. Such recursion may evoke a sense of pressing urgency in direct speech, e.g., "consider your ways" (שִׂימוּ לְבַבְכֶם) at the beginning and end of 2:18. Even lowly prepositions and particles are pressed into the service of the prophet's rhetoric, for example:

- to inject sudden emphasis, as at the onset of the LORD's initial indictment of his people in 1:4 (לָכֶם אַתֶּם "for you yourselves");
- to create a meaningful verbal cadence, like the long series that ends the first major discourse unit (1:11), consisting of natural items which the prevailing drought lies heavily upon;
- to add a cohesive, theological flavor to the discourse, as in the repeated (8x) reference to Yahweh (+ *'their* God' אֱלֹהֵיהֶם – 3x) in 1:12–15, i.e., the people now recognize their covenantal obligations;
- or to develop an impressive climax, as in the dynamic trio of consequential (כִּי) clauses that concludes Yahweh's minatory reminder in 2:14.

5.2.3 Graphic imagery

The images and scenes depicted by Haggai are varied, vivid, and veracious, that is, intensely life-related. They are also thematically significant—from the holes in the pockets of a disobedient people (1:5) to the consequent punitive winds that puffed away their expected profits (1:9); from completed, well-appointed personal houses to the desolate house of Yahweh (1:4); from the sight of a new temple that pales in the shadow of the old (2:3) to the vision of that same "house" glorified with the silver and gold of the world's nations (2:7–8); from the choicest sacrificial meat (2:12) to a stinking polluted corpse (2:13). The prophet's main scenes are reinforced by a succession of picturesque, often contrastive vignettes of current human experiences or representative listings of familiar items, e.g., 1:4, 6, 11 (grain – new wine – oil); 2:12, 15 ("one stone upon another"), and 16–19. These all climax in a twofold graphic appeal to the imagination involving a profound terrestrial and celestial 'shaking' that will result in blessings for God's house (2:6–9) but judgment upon all his enemies (2:21–22).

This local imagery is punctuated by periodic, colorful figurative language, for example (the Hebrew text is translated literally):

5.3 The communicative significance of Haggai's style

- metaphor/simile, e.g., 2:6 ('shake'—earthquake), 2:14 ('defiled'—like a corpse);
- metonymy, e.g., 1:4 ('house'), 1:14 ('spirit'), 2:7 ('desired thing'), 2:8 ('silver/gold'), 2:11 ('torah'), 2:22 ('throne');
- merismus, e.g., 1:10 ('heavens—earth', 'men—beasts', cf. 2:6);
- personification, e.g., 1:10 ('the heavens/earth have held back [from you people]');
- anthropomorphism, e.g., 1:11 ('I called for a drought'), 1:12 ('[they] heard the voice of ... God'), 1:17 ('I blew it away'), 2:22 ('I will overturn');
- euphemism, e.g., 2:13 ('the unclean thing of a life' = dead body);
- hyperbole, e.g., 1:9 ('each person running to/for his house'—also metonymic);
- various idioms, e.g., 1:12 ('feared from before the LORD'), 2:3 ('is not like it like nothing in your eyes?'), 2:6 ('yet once, it [is] a little'); 2:15/18 ('from this day and upward').

Some imagery is extended into a deeper level of symbolic import and implication, from the divine abstract (e.g., 'glory' – 2:7) to the highly specific (e.g., 'signet seal' – 2:23). Such deeper, more elaborate figuration would include the thematic temple symbolism that underlies the disputational dialogue with the priests in 2:10–14.[11]

5.3.4 Larger-to-lesser progression

In an interesting study of the textual organization of Haggai, Holbrooke reveals a "general-to-particular ordering of the themes of the book and the expanded-to-contracted size of the discourse markers" (1995:1). Thus, the thematic scope of the four primary oracles progressively narrows from a focus upon creation (1:2–11), to all nations (2:2–9), to the people of Israel (2:10–19), and finally to the Davidic kingship (2:21–23), while the size of the formulaic opener as well as the body of each oracle is correspondingly reduced as follows: (a) 50 (or 33 words, depending on whether 1:3 is included) + 126 words; (b) 29 (including 1:15) + 115 words; (c) 23 + 92 words; and (d) 16 + 43 words (Holbrooke 1995:8). This noticeable pattern

---

[11] That is to say: the consecration normally associated with service at the temple is not mechanically transferred to people *ex opere operato;* on the other hand, the defilement being occasioned by the unbuilt temple is generally contagious. There may be some symbolism also associated with the name of Haggai himself (חַגַּי): "The name is derived from the Semitic word for 'feast' *(hag),* an appropriate name for a prophet focused on rebuilding the temple... [E]ach of his messages is delivered on a day associated with a festival or liturgical event..." (Boda 2004:32–33).

of discourse development brings considerable natural prominence (plus cumulative end stress) to the last and shortest oracle of the book, which spotlights an individual: "my servant Zerubbabel" and the future Messianic descendant whom he (as a divinely chosen "signet ring") prefigures.

5.3.5 Phonological pointing

Though not written in the typical forms of classical Hebrew prophetic poetry, as noted above, Haggai does evince a demonstrable "poetic prose" style in which the sonic force of the text is periodically focused in order to stress selected aspects of its variegated message. In addition to the prominent examples of choppy, excited cadences (1:6, 9—featuring short nominal clauses comprised of infinitives and participles; cf. Verhoef 1987:69; Taylor 2004:70), expanding verb parallels (2:4), and paronomasia (2:9) already mentioned, we might add a few more to show that the preceding are not isolated cases.

A prominent similarity of sound draws aural attention to an impious adage that incriminates all who utter it (לֹא עֶת־בֹּא עֶת־בֵּית יְהוָה לְהִבָּנוֹת— 1:4). Thus, the people expected 'much' (הַרְבֵּה —1:9a) from their various life enterprises, but by leaving the LORD's house a 'dried-out' ruin (חָרֵב —1:9b) in their midst, they summoned his punishment upon themselves in the form of a devastating 'drought' (חֹרֶב —1:11a, which is a phonologically foregrounded cause-effect relationship and an incisive instance of *lex talionis*).[12] The alliterative reference to Haggai as a "messenger of YHWH" (מַלְאַךְ יְהוָה) "with the message of YHWH" (בְּמַלְאֲכוּת יְהוָה) about "work" (מְלָאכָה) occurs in the middle of a narrative segment (B) that rhythmically highlights the favorable presence of the LORD in a report about the obedient response of his people (1:12–15). Finally, we observe another set of cadenced utterances that heightens the aural impact of Yahweh's eschatological threat at the prophecy's penultimate portion (2:21b–22); notice again the progressive narrowing of scope and size in these allusive expressions as they reach a climax at the very end, thus setting the stage for the crucial personalized conclusion of v. 23:

---

[12] The adverse outcome that the people brought upon themselves is highlighted by another play on words at the beginning of 1:10: 'Therefore against/on account of *you*...' (עַל־כֵּן עֲלֵיכֶם), which features an emphatically fronted personal pronoun.

5.3 The communicative significance of Haggai's style

I will shake the heavens and the earth:	אֲנִי מַרְעִישׁ אֶת־הַשָּׁמַיִם וְאֶת־הָאָרֶץ׃
And I will overturn royal thrones,	וְהָפַכְתִּי כִּסֵּא מַמְלָכוֹת
and shatter the power of the foreign kingdoms;	וְהִשְׁמַדְתִּי חֹזֶק מַמְלְכוֹת הַגּוֹיִם
and I will overthrow chariots and their drivers,	וְהָפַכְתִּי מֶרְכָּבָה וְרֹכְבֶיהָ
and horses and their riders will fall,	וְיָרְדוּ סוּסִים וְרֹכְבֵיהֶם
each by the sword of his brother.	אִישׁ בְּחֶרֶב אָחִיו׃

5.3.6 Probing questions

A key feature of the direct discourse that animates the entire book of Haggai is the occurrence of periodic rhetorical questions—a total of seven in all. Such probing, often ironic, queries are "intended to bring his audience to certain conclusions…[and] to awaken in [them] an awareness of conditions the asker knows all too well" (Taylor 2004:69). Each of these thus fulfills some important illocutionary purpose in the speeches in which it occurs: the opening *rebuke* (1:4—with a foregrounding of the pronoun 'you' [pl] and the thematic word 'time' עֵת, cf. v. 2); *indictment* (1:9—'why?!'); *specification* (2:3a); *confirmation* (2:3c); *reorientation* (2:19a). Alternatively, the RQ performs a distinct compositional role, such as: to highlight a subsequent accusation (1:9b—the shortest, most concise query: יַעַן מֶה 'because of what' = 'why!?') or a following question (2:3b); to create a climax (the 3 RQs of 2:3); or to emphasize the negative or affirmative response being called for by a legal inquiry (2:12b and 2:13b, respectively). Questions of any type also perform the general rhetorical functions of attracting the attention of the current listening audience (or readership), of drawing them experientially into the prophetic message, and of encouraging them to answer these same interrogatives for themselves, whether overtly during a public preaching of the text or when reading it silently to oneself.

5.3.7 Reminiscent allusion

Undergirding the overt discourse of Haggai from beginning to end is an extensive covert text—a manifold implicit corpus that is formed by the intertextual web of allusions to and citations of a host of pre-texts found in the Hebrew Scriptures and in the oral teachings of Israel's priests and sages. They are obviously presupposed by the author to be well enough known by his intended audience to be left unexpressed, without explicit marking. These sub-texts do not merely contribute a level of stylistic embellishment or enrichment to the book; more importantly, they serve to support the prophetic theme and to shape the current argument that is being articulated—in particular, key terminology that harks back to Yahweh's fundamental spiritual covenant with Israel, e.g., 1:12–13.

The oracular dates, for example, carried both religious and also social significance, eg, 'the 21st day of the 7th month' (2:1), which was the last day of the Feast of Tabernacles, when the summer harvest would normally be celebrated (Exo 23:16; Lev 23:34–43). Yahweh begins his word of reproof with a pointed vocative that telegraphs the confrontational tone of his subsequent address: 'This people' (הָעָם הַזֶּה –1:2a; cf. 2:14; Isa 6:9–10, 8:6–12; Jer 14:10–11).[13] Housing construction that involved 'paneling' (סְפוּנִים –1:4) was associated with royalty (1 Kgs 6:9, 7:3, 7) and had rather recently been sharply criticized by the prophet Jeremiah (22:14–15). The people's negligent behavior towards the LORD and his house was an overt act of disregard for their covenantal obligations, and hence the whole land experienced the designated chastisement in so-called 'futility curses' (1:6, 10–11—cf. Deut 28:15, 22–24, 38–40; Lev 26:18–20; Jos 2:20; Hos 4:10–11; Am 4:9; Mic 6:13–15). Yahweh could not be pleased or honored unless they changed their ways (1:7–8—cf. Isa 1:11; Jer 13:11). But when they did, the divine assertion "I [am] with you" (אֲנִי אִתְּכֶם —1:13, 2:4; cf. Gen 17:7, 26:3; Num 14:9; Jos 1:5; Isa 41:10; Jer 1:8, 19) graciously assured the Jewish community, the remnant, that they would again be blessed in keeping with the covenant (1:12–14, 2:15–19; cf. Isa 10:20–22, 28:5, 37:31–32; Jer 23:3–8; and especially Zech 8:11–13). The people were not sufficient of themselves, but they depended on "my Spirit remaining among" them (2:5). This allusion would have undoubtedly called to mind the great empowering presence that motivated Israel's early leaders (e.g., Num 11:16–30), providing an infusion of inspiration that they also needed now in order to get the job done (cf. 1:14; Ezr 1:1).

5.3.8 Supportive patterning

In addition to the strong linear progression that the time-marked oracles establish throughout the book of Haggai, plus a number of minor structural

---

[13] Contrast 'my people': Ex 6:7; Lev 26:12; 2 Sam 7:10; Isa 52:6; Jer 30:3; Ezek 37:13, 39:7; Hos 2:23; Am 9:14; Zech 8:7, 13:9.

arrangements created by lexical recursion (noted above, e.g., chiastic constructions), there are two larger, less apparent patterns of special thematic significance. These extended instances of reversed parallelism are also delineated by means of a reiteration of key concepts and related expressions; they serve to complement the syntagmatic structures that have already been discussed, their central segments in particular. The first chiastic formation embraces the LORD's *rebuke* that motivates chapter one (1:2–11), and the second is manifested in his message of *support* that begins chapter two (2:3–9). Each parallel structure is anchored by significant instances of exact repetition (underlined below), while the rest of the pattern is filled out by less precise conceptual correspondences. The two structures may be diagrammed as follows (cf. Dorsey 1999:316):

  A *Complaint* by the people: No time to build the house of Yahweh (1:2)
    B *Rhetorical question* concerning the complaint: 'Is it a time for you yourselves to be living in your paneled <u>houses</u> while this <u>house</u> remains a <u>ruin</u>?' (1:3–4)
      C *Contra-expectation*: 'You planted <u>much</u> but are <u>bringing</u> in <u>little</u>...' (1:5–6)
        D *Command*—solution to the problem plus motivation:
          '...build the house...that I may be honored in it.' (1:7–8)
      C' *Contra-expectation*: '[You] expect <u>much</u> but look, <u>little</u> you have <u>brought</u> home...' (1:9a-b)
    B' *Rhetorical question* concerning the consequence: 'Why?... Because of my <u>house</u>, which remains a <u>ruin</u>, while each of you is busy with his own <u>house</u>.' (1:9c-d)
  A' *Consequence* for the people: The land is under the LORD's curse 'because of you'. (10–11)

  E *Complaint* (implied) by the people: The <u>former</u> <u>splendor</u> of <u>this</u> <u>house</u> was much greater than the one being built now (2:3)
    F *Encouragement*: Take courage and get to work! (2:4a-c)
      G *Assurance*: 'Indeed, I am with you!' (2:4d)
        H *Fact*: The covenantal foundation that unites Yahweh and Israel: Act (cf. F) in keeping with your promise as a people after I had delivered you from slavery in Egypt (implied)—including the construction of a house for my worship and to manifest my presence among you (2:5a)!
      G' *Assurance*: 'My spirit is abiding among you!' (2:5b)
    F' *Encouragement*: The LORD will get to work, as it were, and reveal his majesty! (2:6–8)
  E' *Consequence* of Yahweh's intervention: The <u>splendor</u> of <u>this</u> present <u>house</u> will be greater than that of the <u>former</u> house (2:9)

Such patterned symmetry is both forceful and functional. Notice, for example, how the central cores of these structures are linked to one another by a relationship of *imperative* (D) and *incentive* (H—the ostensive reason for the Exodus, Ex 10:25–26). The preceding survey would surely confirm the fact that Haggai's powerful prophetic proclamation is strongly supported by a corresponding rhetorical manner of composition that not only complements his message but, indeed, also helps to constitute it.

The excellent verbal construction of the text in terms of literary structure and style thus enhances its content in a way that subtly suits both the explicit subject of rebuilding Yahweh's house and also the implicit theme of rebuilding the 'house' (lineage) of David. The implications of such artistic textual architecture for communicating the book of Haggai today will be more fully explored in the following sections.

5.4 Haggai's rhetoric: A progressive prophetic argument

We move now from a consideration of *form* to a study of *function*—from discourse structure and style to a closer look at the interrelated rhetorical significance of literary form. To provide a framework for this discussion, I will use an expanded *speech-act model* which helps one to systematically survey some important textual and contextual considerations that come to mind when analyzing Yahweh's twofold message to the political and religious representatives of his people (i.e., Zerubbabel and Joshua, 1:1). Unfolding his message in the form of a 'progressive prophetic argument', the LORD strongly reasons with his addressees through the voice of the prophet Haggai, exhorting them to adopt a major change in perspective, one that would in turn radically transform their 'heart' relationship with him (cf. 1:5, 7; 2:15, 18). This radically altered point of view involves several different facets, which are treated sequentially in separate oracles, one building upon the principles already taught, and hopefully accepted, during the course of an earlier divine pronouncement.

The earlier structural and stylistic overview (Part One) has revealed the principal textual contours and thematic peaks of the book, but Yahweh's rhetorical intentions need to be further explored: What goals did God wish his message to accomplish in terms of conscious reflection and behavior with respect to his addressees? Stated differently, what did the prophet

5.4 Haggai's rhetoric: A progressive prophetic argument

want to persuade his audience to think or to do, and which are the main contextual factors that most likely influenced the composition of this close-knit series of oracles? Second and more speculatively, how was the content and style of the book as a whole intended to function in relation to later generations of reader-hearers? Its rhetoric must therefore be analyzed in terms of at least two different contexts, namely, *intrinsically* (the initial setting) and *extrinsically* (any subsequent setting) in relation to the historical, social, moral, and theological situation described within the text itself.

In order to understand and interpret the rhetorical dimension of a biblical text more completely and correctly, one must thoroughly investigate its *extralinguistic background*—that is, the sociological, cultural, and religious environment, or milieu, of the text in its original Ancient Near Eastern environment. A detailed examination of this nature would take us well beyond the scope of the present chapter, so I will merely offer an outline of how this manifold contextual factor may be combined with a co-textual and a textual study within the scope of a single, more comprehensive analytical framework.[14] I will also limit myself largely to an overview of Haggai's *intrinsic* rhetorical situation and exigency (Kennedy 1984:34–35).[15] A factored, 'argument-structure analysis', as outlined below, is especially helpful when dealing with the largely *paraenetic* (hortatory-admonitory-minatory) texts to be found in the Hebrew prophets (as well as the apostolic epistles), because it takes into consideration a relatively large number of verbal, interpersonal, and situational variables.

The key structural and pragmatic elements that are explicitly or implicitly involved in the formal presentation of a major *argument* text-type are displayed below. This diagram reveals how these features exist in dynamic interrelationship with each other and with the central nucleus of the whole composition, namely, the core constituents *PROBLEM—MOTIVATION—APPEAL*. All ten contextual factors develop our understanding of the basic, or generic 'speech act' of making a reasoned and revelatory *exhortation*, whether to admonish or encourage, in favor of a significant attitudinal and behavioral change, in this case, one involving the Sovereign Lord with the

---

[14] The following outline is a slight modification of Wendland 2004:218–224, applied here specifically to the book of Haggai.

[15] For some stimulating scholarly speculation on the *extrinsic* rhetorical situation, see for example: Coggins 1987:34–35; Gowan 1998:164–165; O'Brien 2004:133–136; Petersen 2002:206–207.

Jewish nationals who had returned to Jerusalem immediately after their Babylonian exile. The basic outline is as follows:

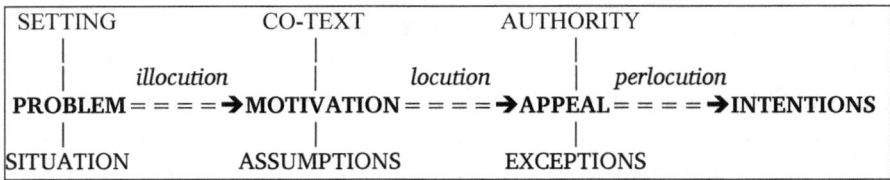

According to this approach, the ten crucial aspects of an argument, here a primarily hortatory discourse, operate as an integrated communication system. They thus manifest the internal framework of the broader pragmatic theory of speech (and text) acts, which focuses upon *interpersonal discourse action*—that is, what words (oral or written) actually *do* as distinct from what they overtly *say*. A 'speech act' then may be defined as a combined sequence of three basic constituents: an *illocution*, or underlying utterance intention, a *locution*, the concrete verbal representation in a given language, and finally, a *perlocution*, which designates the desired (or realized) consequence or outcome of a certain speech act from the point of view of the original speaker.

The larger *argument structure* of Haggai may be progressively described in terms of this model and with reference to the biblical text according to its ten distinct, but overlapping elements. This serves as a rhetorical summary of Yahweh's urgent 'wake-up call' to his lethargic covenantal 'remnant' (1:12; all English citations are from the NIV).

5.4.1 Setting

The "setting" encompasses the general historical, cultural, social, political, religious, and environmental milieu in which the written act of communication takes place, as this concerned both the author and his addressees/audience.

The book of Haggai provides us with one of the most explicitly delineated compositional settings in Scripture. Four precise dates spanning nearly four months anchor the text firmly in its specific historical context, namely, from August 29 to December 18, 520, during the reign of Darius I ('The Great') of Persia. These were times of severe trial and constant uncertainty for those Jews who had been brave, or desperate, enough to return to Palestine

5.4 Haggai's rhetoric: A progressive prophetic argument   201

following the emancipation edict of King Cyrus in 538 BCE. Indeed, would they even survive as a nation having a distinct ethnic and religious identity? Were they in fact, and in view of their lowly circumstance, worshiping the right God? The disaster that had befallen them under the Babylonians would have generated this latter query of worried reservation, or even rank skepticism, one that undoubtedly grew in their minds with every passing day without a central place of worship and a locus of national character.

But from Haggai's perspective, there was more to it than that: In the ANE setting of that time, "Temples were intimately bound up with the founding or legitimatizing of nations.... Building a temple in which the god [of a people] took up residence was a powerful symbolic statement meaning that the god sanctioned the dynastic power.... [T]emples were not simply religious institutions in the ancient world but rather were components of a religio-political entity. Erecting a temple in an administrative center was an integral part of the process of establishing the authority of the political regime.... The decision to build, or rebuild, a house for a deity was one of the most important decisions that a community could make in the ancient Near East" (Meyers and Meyers 1987:21–22, 64). The repeated specific mention of both Zerubbabel (political sphere) and Joshua (religious realm), i.e., 1:1, 12, 14; 2:1, 4, would seem to underscore this dual concern over divine credibility and authority that underlies the prophet's urgent message.

5.4.2 Problem

"Problem" refers to the particular critical spiritual or moral lack, fault, failing, need, test, or trial that the author wishes to bring up and to deal with in his text.

There are two major problems addressed in Haggai—one more immediate and evident, the second less obvious but more important for the nation as a whole. The first problem is clearly stated in the LORD's own words as recorded in Haggai 1:4—'Is it a time for you yourselves to be living in your paneled houses, while this house [i.e., the Temple] remains a ruin?' In other words, the Jewish returnees had failed to complete the task that they had committed themselves to (Ezra 3:11), a house-building exercise that the Great King, Cyrus himself had commissioned them to do on his royal behalf (Ezra 1:2–3). It was a matter of ethnic pride as well as religious honor and solidarity that the Jews have a central place of worship to serve as both the focus of their identity as the community of Yahweh and also the mark of his abiding presence among them (1:8b, 13b; 2:4c—אֲנִי אִתְּכֶם 'I [am] with you!').

The second and related problem, one of general morale, concerned the house of Israel as the chosen people of Yahweh. This matter comes to the fore in chapter 2: A deep religious malaise had set in, one that had some serious, long-term implications for the Jews as a worshiping covenant community. They were spiritually demoralized, and this was reflected in their corresponding disobedient, indifferent attitude towards their God. They were strongly tempted, it seems, to equate their low standing among the nations with the correspondingly limited power and honor of Yahweh. Such a pessimistic outlook is not overtly expressed by either the people, their leaders, or Haggai himself, but it is clearly implied in the depressed view attributed to them in 2:3 (retrospectively also in 2:17), which in turn motivates the LORD's subsequent exhortation (2:4), reassurance (2:5), and glorious prediction that he controlled the destiny of 'all nations' for the sake of his 'house' (2:6–9) and his chosen 'servant' (2:21–23).

5.4.3 Situation

In "situation" we consider the collateral human events or external circumstances that provoked or exacerbated the central 'problem'; it is the provocative state of affairs (the so-called 'rhetorical exigency') that calls for a verbal response from one or more of the parties concerned.

The immediate situational setting is revealed in Haggai's first oracle, which describes in vivid, life-related terms the local drought and accompanying natural disasters that had befallen the land (1:5–11; cf. 2:16–17) as well as their current precarious economic circumstances (2:19). Why did these calamities occur to aggravate their state of humiliation in the eyes of 'the nations'? The LORD was evidently indicating to his people that their values and priorities were all wrong. The Jews had swiftly laid the foundation for a new Temple (Ezra 3:8–11), but almost immediately, the work stalled and ultimately stopped due to the vigorous opposition of their neighbors to the north, the Samaritans (Ezra 4:1–5, 2–24). After that, it seems crass materialism and pure lethargy set in to quench their noble cause (Hag

5.4 Haggai's rhetoric: A progressive prophetic argument

1:4), coupled with the constant struggle to survive in a physically harsh environment. As a result, all planning to rebuild the Lord's House apparently ceased, and the site became little more than a local shrine for the faithful few to maintain their tenuous ties to Yahweh by means of offerings made at an un-housed altar. In fact, the question of skeptic materialists may have arisen: Why do we even need a Temple at all—have we not survived well enough on our own without one?! In effect, these cynics were in danger of cutting themselves off from their covenantal relationship with Yahweh; thus, instead of 'I—with you' (2:4), the situation was quickly becoming 'not you—with me' (אֵין־אֶתְכֶם אֵלָי— 2:17)!

5.4.4 Appeal

"Appeal" designates the central exhortation, command, admonition, rebuke, or warning (perhaps pluralized) that either promotes or prohibits a certain way of thinking and/or behaving in keeping with biblical (prophetic) teaching and its associated consecrated lifestyle.

Haggai's concisely worded appeals on behalf of Yahweh to the people are expressed in rather general terms, but the full implication of each command is crystal clear. With regard to their first major problem (the temple), the people are sternly commanded to consider their situation (1:5, 7; lit., 'Set your hearts upon your ways!' שִׂימוּ לְבַבְכֶם עַל־דַּרְכֵיכֶם) and then to get on with their assigned task (1:8—to 'build [my] house!' וּבְנוּ הַבָּיִת). As for the second (their attitude), they are more gently, yet insistently (3 times) urged to 'Be strong [in your faith]!' (חֲזַק; 2:4). In fact, these seemingly disparate entreaties, which synopsize the text's basic argument, are integrally and expertly interconnected: *attitudes* (get serious—be strong!) must be manifested in *actions (build—don't give up!)* The great temptation was to give in to spiritual as well as psychological doubts and dismay (2:3) even concerning their covenant with Yahweh (2:5). Hence the prophet's rhetoric is concentrated in the longer second half of the book, for this is where the heart of the matter had to be dealt with (2:15), no doubt on repeated occasions during the course of the rebuilding project as well as thereafter.

This was, in short, a crisis concerning the 'word of Yahweh' (a fact reiterated in varied forms throughout the book)—how credible and reliable were his prophetically mediated utterances? Could the verbal promise ('I am with you'—2:4) guarantee God's immediate personal presence? The divine appeal to faith was at the same time an exhortation to 'fear not!' (אַל־תִּירָאוּ; 2:5); it also assumes a timeless character that transcends generations: Yahweh had obviously been there to deliver his covenant people in the *past* ('when you came out of Egypt'); his 'spirit' (רוּחִי) was even now at *present* 'in their very midst' (בְּתוֹכְכֶם) (2:5); as for the *future*, Yahweh promises to bring about a worldwide 'shaking' מַרְעִישׁ that would result in great 'glory' (כָּבוֹד) for 'this house' (הַבַּיִת הַזֶּה) (2:6–9), thus also confirming his exhortation to remain fearless and strong in their trust.

5.4.5 Intentions

"Intentions" summarize the author's desired results in terms of new, reinforced, or altered thinking and actions that may be expected to materialize, sooner or later, if the addressee(s) fully comprehend and comply with the appeal.

The LORD's message, as passionately expressed through his courageous prophet, manifests an overt desire that his people should, by means of the appropriate behavior, be released from the physical economic chastisement that had been levied upon the land due to their allowing the overt 'problem' (the Temple 'corpse') to fester among them. But more, Yahweh wanted to be 'pleased' with his people's devotion to him and thereby also to manifest his 'glory' in and through them (1:8). This desired 'perlocution' did in fact occur: the leaders and the people wholeheartedly responded to the initial appeal with action, namely, with a resumption and eventual completion of the Temple building project; Yahweh in turn assured them of his personal beneficial presence among them (1:12–15; cf. Ezra 6:15).

The LORD also earnestly wished to deal with the second and more critical psychological 'problem', that is, to reduce the people's doubt and discouragement resulting from a worldly perspective on their religious worship and its central locale. Spiritual devotion is not, after all, predicated upon a place, but rather a person—not where adherents worship, but whom they serve! The success of this second communicative 'intention' is not revealed anywhere in the text of Haggai, but if the book of the later prophet Malachi is anything to go by, this reformative goal was not successfully realized in the long run, neither among the laity nor the religious leadership (e.g., Mal 2:10–16, and especially the final verse of the Hebrew Bible, 4:6; cf. Ezra 9–10; Neh 13).

5.4.6 Authority

The "authority" factor includes all explicit and implicit references or allusions to the author's perceived, ascribed, or actual status, prestige, authority, etc. (ethos), which supports the present 'appeal' (or command) that he is making. Also considered here is the relative degree of linguistic and emotive forcefulness with which the text's major appeal and supporting motivation(s) are expressed (i.e., its apparent level of directness, urgency, strength, and authority) or the relative degree of *mitigation* and *amelioration* manifested during the overt or covert line of argumentation. An imperative verb, for example, would exhibit the greatest amount of verbal potency while an indirect request would convey the most mitigation.

All of the characteristic formulae referring to the 'word of the LORD' (or something similar) being transmitted by the prophet clearly establish the divine authority that is backing up Haggai's oral and written words. The repeated references to precise historical dates throughout the book further underscore the author's assumption of factuality and credibility with regard to his message. More specifically, Yahweh's opening imperative to his people is blunt and reiterated for emphasis, that is, in 1:5 and 1:7. The discourse initial position within each paragraph also serves to underscore the Yahweh's insistence on this matter: There can be no more delays, let alone a refusal to get to work! This overt command is accompanied by an implied threat that the current adverse ecological situation will remain in force until some positive action is taken (1:5–11).

The second problem addressed by Haggai is handled in a more deliberate and extended fashion—at first, in a similar way through a direct command (2:4a), now coupled with a reassuring promise (2:4b–5). The latter is supported in typical prophetic terms by a pair of vigorous oracles of divine blessing, the second more potent, particular, and personal than the first, i.e., 2:6–9 and 2:20–23. Sandwiched in between these two optimistic salvation oracles is a sober, symbolically expressed object lesson that vividly reminds the people of where they have come from in their spiritual journey, namely, their past failure with regard to God's house (2:10–14) and its punitive covenantal consequences (2:15–19; cf. 2:5). In one sense, this is also a covert warning that such moral 'pollution', occasioned through religious lassitude, must not be allowed to occur among them again.

5.4.7 Exceptions

"Exceptions" encompass any potential objections to the central appeal or imperative. Exceptions are conveyed by such devices as contrast, antithesis, a counter-case, opposing evidence, or a hypothetical rebuttal. They are generally anticipated by the author and dealt with in the discourse, whether overtly or—to avoid drawing too much attention to them—indirectly. Since exceptions are often implicit rather than fully stated, their postulation in the analysis must be tentative.

In contrast to Malachi (later in time), there is no impudent response to Yahweh's rebuke on the part of the priests being addressed as representatives of the people. In Haggai's discourse-central dialogue with them (2:11–14), they reply truthfully, if not with much apparent enthusiasm for the lesson that they are being taught by the Lord's prophet (at least as the interaction is reported by Haggai). But since we do not have access to the entire dialogue which took place on that 24th day of the ninth month in the second year of King Darius, we cannot really conclude for sure how the priesthood in general reacted to Haggai's initiative on behalf of the building project. The words attributed to the priests neither condemn nor commend them for their present response.

There is, however, a more subtle exception that is expressed in an implicit and hypothetical manner with respect to Yahweh's dealing with the people's second and more serious problem: their ostensible religious indifference towards or lack of concern for respecting the LORD's glory. Yahweh himself puts their consensus opinion into words in 2:3—'Does it [the new Temple] seem to you as nothing?' The implied answer to this rhetorical question is a definite affirmative. It is this underlying attitude, whether motivated by pure and honest discouragement or a more critical cynicism regarding the utility of worshiping Yahweh, which is effectively countered by the various discourses that comprise the second and major portion of the book (2:4–23).

5.4.8 Motivation

"Motivation" specifies the various types of reasoning offered in support of the author's appeal(s). These may be either deductive (e.g., cause-effect,

5.4 Haggai's rhetoric: A progressive prophetic argument

general-specific, lesser-to-greater) or inductive (e.g., proofs, maxims, syllogisms, testimonies, examples, analogies, role-playing). Both kinds of reasoning involve content *(logos),* emotion *(pathos),* and/or the speaker's personal credibility, reliability, and authority *(ethos).*

The LORD motivates his message largely through obvious inductive means: the concrete example of the effects of the drought that the nation was currently experiencing (1:5–11); vivid contrasting images of the people's houses in comparison with the desolate House of Yahweh (1:3), or the envisioned new Temple in comparison with the glorious memory of the former place of worship (2:3); eschatological visions of world warfare culminating in the LORD's victory and a glory-filled new Zion (2:6–9, 20–22); a graphic case study involving positive and negative contagion, consecration versus pollution (2:11–14). Underlying these strongly visual techniques, however, is a powerful logical development of the LORD's argument: from *cause* (sin, repentance) to *effect* (punishment, blessing), a focus on key events in the history of God's people that coincides with a progression in the national ethos and outlook from the greater (past Solomonic temple) to the lesser (present pathetic replica) and on into the much greater future (the glorified divine dwelling). This further corresponds with a lesser-to-greater movement in the main argument of the book as a whole: a resolution of the present problem (the unbuilt Temple—ch. 1) leads to a revelation that creates hope for a richly blessed spiritual future in the messianic personage who will one day bring the surpassing glory of the LORD to this very place (the antitypical Davidic descendant of 'Zerubbabel'—2:23).

What is noteworthy, though certainly not unique, about the various oracles that comprise Haggai is the passion that is expressed by Yahweh in these vibrant messages to his people. The divine emotions seem to move quickly from anger and frustration in the warning of 1:5–11, to sympathetic concern in the encouragement of 2:2–9 including several expressions of personal presence ("I [am] with you...my Spirit is standing [!] among you"—vv. 4–5), to a more subdued, reflective tone in the reminder of 2:15–19, and finally, to the seemingly animated predictions of 2:20–23. Such an appeal to *pathos,* in the Greco-Roman rhetorical sense (i.e., a God who cares!), serves to reinforce both the credibility of the speaker *(ethos)* and also the reliability of the divine message being articulated *(logos).*

5.4.9 Cotext

"Cotext" identifies all texts that are semantically related to the discourse under consideration, whether syntagmatically (i.e., intratextually, as part of the same document) or paradigmatically (i.e., intertextually, from an extant, different but somehow related discourse—oral or written). The more exact this correspondence of meaning, the more important it is to the development of the author's argument.

The issue of intratextual influence within the book of Haggai occurs with specific reference to corresponding passages within the book, such as the crucial assertion 'From this day on I will bless you' in 2:19c, which can be understood only with reference to the preceding discourse. Similarly, the lexical parallels and 'holy war' imagery linking 2:6 and 2:21 also invite a hermeneutical linkage between the prophecies that they introduce, i.e., 2:6–9 and 21–23. The importance of intertextuality, though less noticeable perhaps, is also considerable: Such verbal resonance is both extensive and essential to the development of Yahweh's argument. However, one cannot be certain as to which related oral or written texts the communication participants, including Haggai himself, had direct access. These concern, in particular, the works of Ezra and Zechariah, e.g., Zech 4:7–9 and Ezra 3:8–9; 6:14–15 with reference to the Temple rebuilding project, including the disheartened reaction on the part of some to the envisaged outcome of this endeavor (Hag 2:3; cf. Ezra 3:12–13).

A striking case of altered allusion for the purposes of sharp rebuke is found in the LORD's opening words 'these people' (lit. 'this people' הָעָם הַזֶּה), which replaces the affectionate 'my people' in covenantal language (cf. Hos 1:9; 2:5, 23). This reference shifts more optimistically to 'remnant of the people' (שְׁאֵרִית הָעָם) after they demonstrate their penitent obedience (1:12–15; cf. Isa 1:9). Yahweh's sacred testament with Israel is also in the immediate background of several passages that describe the ecological results of the current famine, being a fulfillment of the curses specified for disobedience (e.g., Hag 1:6, 11; 2:16–17; cf. Deut 28:22, 38–39). On the other hand, the promise of Yahweh's immediate presence 'with' his obedient people at the site of his 'house' (Hag 1:13; 2:4–5) harks back to the founding of Israel as a nation at the time of the exodus from Egypt (e.g., Ex 29:44–45) and explicitly recalls King David's encouragement to Solomon to build the first Temple

5.4 Haggai's rhetoric: A progressive prophetic argument

(1 Chr 28:20). This magnificent edifice was dedicated during the days of the Feast of Tabernacles (1 Kgs 8:2), some four centuries before Haggai preached his second oracle in the seventh month, but both the date and that former place was surely still in the memory of many (2:1–3).

The admonitory object lesson of Haggai 2:10–14 obviously recalls the original command concerning ritual defilement through contact with a corpse (Lev 21:11, 22:3–8; Num 6:6), and this principle of positive or negative contamination is reinforced by many similar regulations set forth in the ceremonial law (e.g., Lev 6:27; Num 19:11–13:22). The specific 'request' for a priestly 'ruling' (lit. 'ask...instruction' שְׁאַל־נָא...תּוֹרָה in 2:11) is also provided for in the Mosaic Torah (e.g., Lev 10:8–11; Deut 17:8–11; cf. Jer 18:18; Mk 1:44). That this little didactic deliberation had deeper implications for the relationship between the people and their God, Yahweh, is intimated by an unusual reference to their need for repentance in 2:17b (אֵלַי אֵין־אֶתְכֶם – lit., 'there is not you unto me'). The sense of this latter expression is clarified, however, by the LXX reading (καὶ οὐκ ἐπεστρέψατε πρός με) as well as by intertextual comparison with the earlier prophetic reproof of Amos (וְלֹא־שַׁבְתֶּם עָדַי; 4:6b). In addition, the minatory implication of this serious prophetic vignette is implicitly expressed by the forceful term 'polluted' (טָמֵא)—a word summarizing the sinfulness of Israel that had summoned the LORD's punishment upon their ancestors, including the recent Exile. (e.g., Ezek 22:3; 20:30–3; 23:17; 44:25; Jer 7:30; 32:34; cf. Hos 5:3; 9:4; Ps 79:1).

The degree of messianic allusion or implication in Haggai 2 is of course debatable. However, in view of the more obvious passages in Zechariah, especially with reference to Joshua and Zerubbabel (e.g., 3–4; 6:9–15), one might be led to see more of such theological influence and import rather than less. In the rather gloomy situational setting being referred to, would this not be a logical prophetic strategy? For example, the expression 'desired one of all the nations' (חֶמְדַּת כָּל־הַגּוֹיִם) used in close conjunction with Yahweh's *shekinah* 'glory' (כָּבוֹד) in 2:7 might possibly recall Isaiah's earlier visions of a worldwide attraction to the righteousness and light of the LORD (e.g., 40:5; 60–61; cf. Mal 3:1).[16] Apocalyptic language and

---

[16] Such a messianic interpretation construes the 'wealth of the nations' (Isa 60:5, cf. also 6–7) to be an underlying metonymic allusion to either the Gentile peoples themselves or their manifold possessions being brought to the Lord's worldwide covenant community. A more immediate and material fulfillment of this prophecy in 2:7–8 may be seen in the decree of Darius

traditional battle terms (e.g., Deut 2:20–23, 9:1–6) with reference to 'that day' (בַּיּוֹם הַהוּא), coupled with an allusion to both the 'overthrowing' of Sodom (הָפְכִּי—Gen 19:25, 29; Isa 13:19) and the equally dramatic Exodus deliverance at the Red Sea, is found in Haggai 2:22 (Eze 38:21; Zech 14:13; cf. Ex 14:23–25; 15:1, 4, 19, 21).

The strongest intertextual connection with Isaiah occurs at the end (2:23) as Zerubbabel is given the messianic title 'my servant' (עַבְדִּי; e.g., Isa 41:8; 42:1; 49:5–6; 50:10; 52:13; 53:11), the significance of which is further confirmed and reinforced by Yahweh's 'choice' (בָּחַרְתִּי) of this Davidic descendant, who is also given the royal designation 'signet ring' (חוֹתָם).[17] Thus, the curse placed many years earlier on King Jehoiachin is patently reversed (Jer 22:24–30; cf. 1 Chr 3:17–19), and the people's hope either renewed or restored in a future Messiah arising from the 'house' of David (Jer 23:5–6; 2 Sam 7:11–16; Mt 1:6, 11–-12; cf. Mt 3:27).[18]

5.4.10 Assumptions

"Assumptions" indicate the various ideas, values, attitudes, and feelings that an author shares with his readership. A speaker also takes it for granted that his own presupposed viewpoint (including a wider worldview) will be understood and applied to the text at hand by his audience according to the pragmatic principle of relevance (processing cost versus cognitive-emotive gains). When they share such knowledge, it does not need to be made explicit in the text, though it may be stated for special impact or appeal.

the Persian monarch to open the royal treasury of the satrapy of Trans-Euphrates in order to provide the necessary funding to complete the temple for 'God' in Jerusalem (Ezra 6:6–10). In later years, 'this temple, expanded and adorned by Herod, was indeed of greater splendor than the contemporaries of Haggai could have imagined' (Mark 13:1)—also in terms of welcoming many more proselytes and indeed, 'the Lord himself' (Verhoef 1987:109; cf. Wolff 1976:37). A more immediate, Darius-based scope for the prophetic vision of Haggai is also proposed by Sweeney (2000:530–531).

[17] Meyers and Meyers call attention to the literary and thematic importance of this juxtaposition of key terms: "'Signet' is therefore a marvelous metaphor for the concept of Yahweh's cosmic and supreme rule being effected on earth through a designated 'servant' who would be his signet, assigned to carry out the divine will" (1987:69; cf Verhoef 1987:147–148). Furthermore, the verb "*lqh* is found in contexts in which Davidic kings are anointed for kingship (2 Sam 7:8; 2 Kings 14:21; 23:30)..." (Boda 2004:163). There is undoubtedly also a deeper messianic implication here (cf. Isa 42:1; Zech 3:8–9), and it must have been understood in that sense from the beginning, "for the Persians would not tolerate a man laying claim to the promises here stated" in these closing verses (Alden 1994:1513).

[18] So, in a symbolic sense, the prophecy of Haggai is about the rebuilding of two theologically interrelated 'houses'—that of YHWH, the temple, as well as that of David, the messianic dynasty.

5.4 Haggai's rhetoric: A progressive prophetic argument

Some of the basic assumptions of this series of divine oracles, plus the historical interlude, are quite obvious, and these are based upon the previously announced word of the Lord, as exemplified in the preceding section. Thus, Yahweh's reminder to his people that the primary purpose of the Temple was to 'honor' him (1:8) is so obvious that it becomes in effect an indictment against them. Another key assumption underlying the argument of Haggai was that the prior Temple, the one constructed by King Solomon, was indeed a most 'glorious' edifice. It was a temple worthy of the LORD's worship and one that could not be physically replicated even by the best efforts of his remnant people (2:3). On the other hand, the important thing was that the people reverence the LORD with their hearts (2:17b), not with mere ritual action (2:14b)—they should have known that. Yahweh is not just a national or regional deity, but he exercises sovereign control over the entire universe and all nations on earth, including their political and military might (2:6–7, 22). The LORD's gracious choice of a 'servant' is always effective and will inevitably be realized in that person's life and work (2:23—with reference to 'Zerubbabel', prototype of a future messianic figure who is suggested by the immediate cotext as well as the book's overall cumulative discourse structure). Finally, the prophet's own divine credentials and authority are presupposed, being just briefly alluded to in the reported reaction of the people to his initial oracle—immediate obedience (1:12).

In the unfolding dramatic sequence of oracles that comprises the book of Haggai, the LORD develops a powerful rhetoric that contrasts the prevailing stark physical realities on the local Palestinian scene (2:15–19) with a grand, albeit allusive vision of future cosmic transformation that will lift God's people into a completely new experience of his universal rule (2:21–22). The viability, or credibility, and integrity of this amazing divine argument stands or falls according to the degree of one's acceptance of the reliability and authority of the prophetic word ('utterance') of Yahweh that announces it (a point reiterated thrice in 2:23 as well as throughout the book). The 'remnant' of Israel could—or should—'be strong' in both faith and life because the LORD Almighty had personally promised them, several times, that: 'Indeed (כִּי), I [am] with you!' (2:4; cf. 1:13). Thus, "[w]e continue to live, though, in faith as Haggai's audience of old, awaiting the ultimate shaking of the cosmos, the overthrow of all earthly power through the arrival of the divine warrior in the last days (Rev 19)" (Boda 2004:171).

5.5 Communicating Haggai's concerns today—in Africa

Space precludes an adequate treatment of any particular conceptual 'domestication' of the book of Haggai,[19] but I will briefly address two important issues that relate to the subject of communicating the contemporary significance of the Scriptures in an African context. The first challenge has to do with a general evaluation of the current relevance of LORD's message regarding his 'house' for people who live in a very different religious and sociocultural setting. Several illustrative points of possible identification and application will be discussed in this connection. The second and related matter involves a consideration of some of the specific hermeneutical problems that these divine oracles pose for a particular target group, namely, a rather diverse audience residing in Zambia.[20]

5.5.1 On the present religious significance of Haggai's message

Haggai's first oracle is of the utmost concern to virtually every listener in southern Africa. People, especially subsistence peasant farmers, are able to identify at once with the adverse, *drought*-related scenario that has been so vividly portrayed—not only in respect to the effects being described (especially in vv. 6 and 11; cf. 2:16, 19), but also with the ultimate cause (the divine 'I', who 'blew away' all their agricultural profits, v. 9; cf. 2:17).[21] Similarly, the intervening, secondary cause of such a disaster is familiar to the life and religious beliefs of this region of Africa—namely, some individual or corporate fault or failure in the community ('on your account', v. 10) that has dishonored or angered God and consequently brought his punishment upon them all via the current ravages of 'nature'. The necessary remedial,

---

[19] For some penetrating thoughts on the 'contemporary relevance' to the Church of the messages of Haggai (and Zechariah), see Boda 2004:65–68. I should perhaps specify my frame of reference more precisely as south-central Africa (Zambia—Malawi—Zimbabwe).

[20] These opinions represent the combined perspectives of a class of third-year Lutheran seminary students on the one hand (who come from many different parts of Zambia and Malawi), and the reflections of several semi-literate rural groups of ordinary congregational members on the other (located in the vicinity of Lusaka, capital city of Zambia). This point of view is relatively homogeneous, though it was naturally expressed with more sophistication and supporting details by the seminary students.

[21] Even as I write this chapter, many parts of Africa (especially in the Horn) are currently experiencing another severe drought and its disastrous aftermath: famine, sickness, debilitation, suffering, death. These afflictions are accompanied in many places by political instability, military conflict, and hence also social disorientation.

communal response is also quite natural: 'Give thought to your ways!' (vv. 5, 7)—that is, find out what the offense was/is and deal with the offender(s) so that the curse may be lifted. Of course, here is where some diversity enters this picture: the adherents of traditional religion will seek an answer, a psychic revelation of the cause (e.g., the breaking of some major taboo or the wicked machinations of a sorcerer, 'someone who binds up the rains') from a local renowned diviner or medicine (wo)man. Christians, on the other hand, will appeal to God for a solution, but in some denominations will also endeavor to identify the human source of the calamity.

The problem for God's people in Haggai's time sounds somewhat strange but it is not completely unimaginable. The incongruity in this case concerns not the Lord's punitive response, but the unseemly popular attitude that had provoked it in the first place: People dare not act so casually about such religious affairs, especially if they had already been explicitly warned by God's chosen 'prophet' (cf. 1:1–2)! In the practice of traditional African religion, a local or regional rain *shrine* is either natural (an isolated shady grove of trees) or temporary (a small grass-stick shelter). In any case, the site is not regularly maintained or expanded; it is simply renovated or rebuilt in honor of the deity and the great ancestral spirits at the time of major planting and harvest festivals which feature prescribed ritual offerings and prayers. However, in the dynamic Christian tradition that has grown up in the last century or so, building a suitable 'house' for God is an issue of considerable urgency and often also a source of pride for the entire worshiping community. Therefore, a separate 'church' structure is erected as soon as the congregation is able, and this will normally be upgraded—from poles and a grass thatch roof, to mud block and tin, to some modern style of construction—when the group finds the resources necessary to do so. Producing a subsequent, inferior place of worship (say, after the original structure had been destroyed by a bush fire or annual flooding) would indeed be a cause for shame and chagrin (cf. 2:3). The LORD's appeals to build a house for his 'glory' (1:8, 2:7) thus strike a very responsive chord in the hearts of most African Christians, and Haggai's words often serve as the source-text of many a local fund-raising drive.[22]

---

[22] However, this is not to claim that any contemporary Christian, whether African or Western, can fully understand or "appreciate the pivotal role of the temple in ancient society" (Meyers and Meyers 1987:66)—or, more importantly, to comprehend the central place that Yahweh had in the hearts and lives of his faithful 'servants' in Israel.

The ceremonial case study involving matters of *consecration* and *defilement* (2:10–14) captures African listeners in a web of intertwined similarities and contrasts. There are differences concerning many of the details, in particular, the limited positive contagion that is brought about through contact with offerings designated for the Lord (2:12), which is not a familiar notion. The general concept of ritual pollution, on the other hand, is widespread, including that occasioned by contact with a corpse (2:13), as well as the general harmful contamination that has been caused either directly or indirectly by the people's neglect or misuse of a sacred site (2:15). Such customary beliefs and taboos, extending from pre-birth to post-burial personal states and physical conditions, were common in the traditional way of life, and many of these persist to the present day, especially in a time of crisis or calamity. Similarly, in cases where some sort of major sin or violation was discerned through divination to have provoked a disciplinary response from the ancestors, it would not be enough simply to acknowledge the deity (cf. 2:17), but specific, concrete acts of penance and atonement would have to be carried out. However, these would normally involve prayers, laments, outward ritual demonstrations, and designated offerings—that is, over and above a major communal activity (like rebuilding the Temple, 1:8, 12–15) designed to set matters right and to obtain a divine 'blessing' (2:19).

Finally, we might by way of contrast note Haggai's record of the active and pervasive *immanence* of Yahweh in the lives of his people, from establishing his personal dwelling place among them ('I—with you', 1:13, 2:4), to ruling kingdoms and shaking cosmic powers in order to carry out his will and rule among them (2:6–9, 22–23). This is not a common theological concept in the tenets of central African traditional religion. On the contrary, 'God' (e.g., *Mulungu, Leza, Chauta, Nyambi*), though still ultimately responsible for the overall governance of the universe, is thought to have delegated the authority for regulating the world's day-to-day operations to recognized ancestral representatives *(mizimu)* and to certain charismatic mediators whom the great spirits have mystically empowered (e.g., paramount chiefs, diviners, ritual specialists, and periodically 'possessed' persons). Thus, in a pre-Christian religious setting, it would not seem reasonable, or even possible, for the Creator to specifically address and interact with a mere mortal, like Zerubbabel (2:23)—or even the prophet Haggai for that matter. Rather, this duty would be carried out by an appropriate ancestral emissary, specially

5.5 Communicating Haggai's concerns today—in Africa

'chosen' for such a mission (often a departed relative). The Christian (biblical) message thus provides a radical alternative, which remains for many also a controversial option, namely, the promised Messianic descendant, who is arguably prefigured in the Davidic line of Zerubbabel (2:23; cf. Mt 1:12–13). From a New Testament perspective, he is the 'Servant' whom the heavenly Father-God has chosen to efficaciously mediate on behalf of his people (= 'the desired/precious [ones] of all the nations' – 2:7?), thus also maintaining the saving covenantal relationship, which continues to be guaranteed by the presence of the divine Spirit (2:5).[23]

As we have seen, there are a number of important contact points that relate the message of Haggai to the lives, interests, fears, and concerns of people living in Zambia today. Evaluating the relative prominence of these different themes and their various interrelationships and connections with other aspects of Old Testament theology (or theologies), however, is not an easy task. And this conceptual element is just part of the problem, for it is mediated, or verbally conveyed, by a style of discourse that is rather difficult for many to interpret. It is to this challenging subject that we now direct our attention.

5.5.2 Communicative problems presented by the prophecy of Haggai

In the preceding section, several potential conceptual barriers in Haggai were noted, in particular, those concerning the immanent, personal character of God, coupled with occasional cognitive clashes generated by implicit ideological interference stemming from the ancient traditional, but still persistent religious belief system. However, the real difficulty of Haggai's message for ordinary lay text consumers lies, not so much in the individual details on the paragraph and sectional level, but rather in the way that the book as a whole has been composed and arranged. In other words, it is the discourse organization as a whole that does not always seem to cohere logically—a complaint that is raised by some modern scholars as well (hence their efforts to reorganize the text).

Any current attempt to make sense of this book, to get Haggai to hang together as it were, is hampered of course by our great distance from

---

[23] For a thorough overview of the major difficulties of communicating the biblical concept of 'covenant' among an east-central African people, see Foster 2004.

it—historically, culturally, linguistically, philosophically, and in other respects as well. Nevertheless, despite the lack of a fully complete or documented hermeneutical framework in which to operate (a situation that pertains also to many other OT passages), it is possible to reconstruct the primary sociocultural setting and religious situation of this prophetic message to a sufficient degree to permit a fairly reliable, and generally agreed upon interpretation of the text to be made. Furthermore, critics who conclude that 'stylistic clumsiness is predominantly responsible for awkward passages in the Hebrew text' (Harrison 1969:947) perhaps ought to reexamine the discourse using a literary approach, as summarized in Part One of this chapter. However, it cannot be denied that a number of difficulties do confront contemporary African readers (and more so, hearers) of Haggai.[24] In this section, I will simply point out several of these obstacles according to the arbitrary categories of structure, style, and rhetoric as a prelude to making several concrete proposals for dealing with these matters both within and alongside a given Bible translation.

The overall *discourse structure* of the book of Haggai is problematic for many receptors—at least for those who have occasion to read the book straight through, or in chronological sequence from one reading to the next. The first chapter does not present much difficulty, for the two major sections (vv. 1–11 and 12–15) progress in a rather straightforward narrative fashion. However, chapter two is a different story: After the people's positive response to the prophet's call to action (1:13–14), God himself appears to put a damper on their optimism by calling attention to their new temple's substandard character (2:3). The subsequent divine word of encouragement (vv. 6–9) sounds rather too general and visionary to be much of a present help to them. Furthermore, this latter prophesy is resumed via reiteration more than two months later (vv. 21–22), but why the long intervening break? The remaining, internal sections of ch. 2 do not fit well into the ostensible framework at all, and people today struggle to make sense of them, either as individual portions or in combination. This would include the seemingly irrelevant dialogue over specific issues of consecration and defilement (10–14), the apparent historical flashback that concludes with a sudden flash-forward (15–19b + 19c), and the final figurative blessing

---

[24] Taylor's assertion that in Haggai "[p]roblems of text and translation are few" (2004:28) may be true for the scholar or trained exegete of Scripture, but it is not generally applicable to the target audience that I have in mind.

of just one man, Zerubbabel, the LORD's special agent, 'chosen' for some unspecified mission or responsibility (v. 23).

What then is the real purpose of Yahweh's message to the repatriated residents of Jerusalem—the *rhetorical point* that his prophetic spokesman Haggai wants to make? The overt appeal to get them moving on the central building project is clear enough in terms of both motive and means, that is, the line of argumentation is designed to achieve this goal (reinforced by some serious ecological persuasion). But is there not more to the divine proclamation than that? How clear are the allusions to the people's religious covenantal obligations, which they had been grossly neglecting, but which are foregrounded, for example, by the LORD's words in 1:13 and 2:4 ('I—with you!'), followed by reference to the great Exodus (2:5)? How does this reflective glimpse of salvation history jibe with the forward glance into the eschatological future (2:6–9, 21–23), when God will manifest great glory in his house and transform a mere man, a servant, into his "signet ring"?

These allusive details are inaccessible to virtually all members of a contemporary audience simply because they lack the necessary cognitive frame of reference and a contextualized point of view for interpreting them. The same goes for the underlying significance of the priestly *torah* disputation (2:10–14) and the accompanying references to the futility curses of the Mosaic law (vv. 15–19; cf. 1:6). Without the *hermeneutical key* provided by the considerable measure of information that is presupposed by this discourse, derived from both its Ancient Near Eastern setting and basis in the Hebrew Scriptures (e.g., Lev 10:10–20), most people are lost with regard to the relevance of what is being said. The LORD obviously wishes to teach his people something more about their relationship with him, but the somewhat cryptic, allusive rhetoric of the text remains a largely impenetrable barrier. The problem is compounded then when teachers today proceed to misconstrue the message and provide an alternative, erroneous interpretation, eg, by viewing the hypothetical object lesson of 2:10–14 as an actual historical narrative report of an incident that occurred 'on the 24th day of the 9th month in the 2nd year of Darius'.

We have noted the formally skillful, semantically layered manner in which the text of Haggai has been constructed in terms of its macro- and microstructure. However, these compositional details are not readily apparent to those people are reading the book in translation, and certainly not to those who are only hearing it being read. The problem of comprehension is compounded due to certain aspects of the prophet's *style of writing*, which is rather difficult to perceive and interpret in places. This difficulty presents itself especially when the text is more or less literally reproduced in another language and with special reference to the many local images, figures of speech, and Hebrew idiomatic expressions that flavor Haggai's message. For example we find the following expressions in the first chapter alone: 'LORD of *Hosts*' (1:2), 'your *paneled* houses' (1:4), '*set your hearts upon* your ways' (1:5), 'I *blew* it away' (1:9), 'the heavens withhold *dew*' (1:10), 'the grain, *new wine,* and *oil*' (1:11), 'the whole *remnant* of the people' (1:12), and (especially from a African perspective) 'stirring up the *spirit* of Zerubbabel (Joshua, the people—2:14)'.

Thus, the main hermeneutical difficulties in Haggai are primarily conceptual in nature, being generated by a distinct worldview and way of life as expressed via a very different linguistic system. On the other hand, it must also be said that the affinity for direct speech and the recursive nature of analogous genres of Bantu oral argumentative discourse allow corresponding features of Haggian style to sound quite natural in translation. This would include, for example, the repeated hortatory imperatives of 2:4, the elaborate divine threats of 2:22, and the reiterated temporal introductions to the text's major text divisions, punctuated by accompanying prophetic message formulas, which, when idiomatically vernacularized, are most appropriate in terms of both form and function. However, to a typical Western (English-speaking) readership, unfamiliar with an oral-aural rhetoric and manner of composition, these same stylistic qualities may seem rather awkward and unsophisticated.

5.6 Helping to bridge the communication gap

What can be done then to overcome the great cognitive disparity that considerably hinders, or even prevents, an adequate understanding of the original text by a contemporary audience? The prior analysis has suggested the rather large amount of extratextual and intertextual data needed to properly 'frame' the text conceptually. But how can this essential background knowledge be imparted—what are the most effective methods? This clearly depends on the target group involved, namely, what they desire, expect, and can reasonably handle in the primary setting of use (which of course varies from corporate public worship to individual private devotions). Three areas of possible strategy implementation are briefly overviewed below. Not one of these is sufficient on its own; indeed, each method has its own strengths and weaknesses. But when each technique is suitably contextualized for the principal target group, and they are all then coordinated into a comprehensive, communication-oriented program of Scripture translation and audience engagement, then some measurable beneficial results can be expected in the related areas of biblical literacy as well as personal life application.

5.6.1 Textual strategies

The most fundamental way to enhance communication via Bible translation is to begin with a *meaningful* version—one that reflects an accurate exegesis of the original text, yet also conveys its sense and significance in a natural, intelligible speech style in the target language. This fact might be illustrated best through a sample comparison of translations, namely, the old (1923) missionary version of the Chewa Bible ('Sacred Book') over against the recent (1998) popular language edition ('Holy Book').[25] Below I have set out relatively literal English back translations of each of these versions (as punctuated) with reference to the rhetorically crucial, centralized passage presented in Haggai 2:4–5:

Buku Lopatulika (1923)	*Buku Loyera* (1998)
But be strong now, Zerubabbel, says Jehovah; also be strong, Joshua, child of Jehozadak, the chief priest; and also be strong all you people in the land, says Jehovah, and do; because I am together with you, says Jehovah of multitudes; just as I agreed with you at the time when you went out from Egypt, and my Spirit stayed in your midst; do not fear.	Nevertheless I *Chauta* the Almighty I say, Don't be discouraged, Zerubbabel, don't be discouraged, Joshua, child of Jehozadak, the chief priest, don't be discouraged all of you. Begin to work, for I am with you for sure. Don't be afraid, since my spirit is in your midst, just like I promised when you went out from Egypt.

The greater difficulty of the older Chewa Bible is readily apparent simply from these two back translations—in particular, the extreme sentence length (due to the excessive use of semicolons), the lack of

---

[25] A survey of the many differences between these two translations is provided in more detail and by means of numerous examples in Wendland 1998.

an obligatory object for the key verb 'do', the misleading divine title 'Jehovah of multitudes' (or 'mobs'!), use of the wrong verb 'agree' (as if between equal parties), and the confusing past reference to 'my Spirit'. In contrast, several noteworthy idiomatic features of the newer version are manifested: beginning this little exhortation with a single identification of the authoritative divine speaker, *Chauta* the Almighty, expressing 'be strong' (חֲזַק) from a figuratively negative perspective ('don't throw away your heart' in Chewa) to harmonize better with the preceding verse (2:3), breaking the discourse at the crucial verb 'Begin to work' for emphasis, foregrounding the divine-human relational correlate (כִּי־אֲנִי אִתְּכֶם) by means of an intensifier 'for sure', and clarifying the ever-present function of Yahweh's 'spirit'.

The first major barrier then that readers (hearers) of the old version have to contend with is a foreign-sounding, hard-to-understand text. This is not to say that the newer version cannot itself be enhanced (along with most English translations), for example, by explicating Joshua's attribution to 'the chief priest, child of Jehozadak' (the present word order implies that the latter is actually the high priest). Moreover, the especially difficult passage in 2:10–19 could be more clearly marked linguistically to cue readers regarding the most likely intended meaning (along with an explanatory note to spell out a possible interpretation of the underlying symbolism). For example, the following textual adjustment strategies (underlined) would help to clarify the development of the discourse in Chewa (given below in a literal English back-translation):

- 2:10 – '...Chauta [Yahweh] gave the prophet Haggai a message <u>that killed the priests with a parable</u> *(wophera ansembe fanizo)* saying...' This slight addition (underlined) would clue readers (and hearers!) in to the fact that there is an underlying symbolic meaning to the overt 'disputation' that follows in the text. Such figurative and/or allusive indirection is a normal, and much appreciated technique in the rhetorical arsenal of recognized debaters in a Bantu vernacular.

- 2:14 – 'Everything that they do and everything that they offer as a sacrifice <u>at this very place</u> *(pa malo anowa)* is defiled!' The original locative adverb is made more specific and highlighted by means of idiomatic demonstrative pointing in Nyanja in order to draw attention to the importance of the crucial location being referred to.

5.6 Helping to bridge the communication gap 221

- 2:15 – "'<u>Likewise</u> *(Moteromu)*, <u>you people (anthu inu),</u>" so speaks Chauta *(akutero Chauta)*, "think about what used to happen to you..."' An inserted vocative at this point clarifies for the TL audience that all the people are being addressed again (as in 2:1, 4), not just the priests as the text of vv. 10–14 seems to imply. This vocative, coupled with the verb 'think about' and the comparative transitional word 'Likewise' also suggests that a break in the text has occurred and the discourse is shifting from a parabolic riddle (vv. 10–14) to an explanatory application to their life-situation. An indication of the current speaker (Chauta/Yahweh) also helps to mark this crucial conceptual movement.

- 2:16, 18, 19 – '<u>Formerly</u> *(Kale)* when a person... Just give some careful thought to <u>what is the situation now</u> *(chimene chilipo)*.... <u>Nevertheless</u> *(Komabe)*, starting from <u>this very</u> day *(lero linoli)* I will <u>surely</u> be blessing you! *(ndidzakudalitsani<u>tu</u>)*'. The three distinct time settings referred to in vv. 15–19 (i.e., past, present, and future) need to be more clearly indicated and interrelated in the translation so that people can more readily perceive the text's internal progression and grasp its concluding climax.

In general then, the new *Buku Loyera* (BL) does provide its audience with a highly readable text in a natural style of speech that is easy to perceive and comprehend. However, some important improvements could still be made in terms of a more accurate representation of content and a more polished expression of form.[26]

5.6.2 Paratextual strategies

Nowadays there are a wide variety of paratextual features, or supplementary helps, that both individually and in tandem serve to enhance the communication of a modern Bible translation. These auxiliary devices help create a contextual background, that is, a hermeneutical frame of reference, for interpreting the vernacular language text from the perspective of a particular target audience, as specified by the project's job description and

---

[26] Several excellent examples of idiomacity occur in the *Buku Loyera*, such as the graphic depiction of drought through the use of ideophones in 1:10: *Nkuwonatu mvula yati zii! nthaka yati gwa!* 'One could see it [the result of v. 9], rain ALL GONE! the soil ROCK HARD! However, more polishing could have been done to 'poeticize' the translated text in keeping with power and beauty of the original (cf. Wendland 2004:304–307). To give one example: *Alliteration* and *assonance* highlight the book's first quotation, namely, the people's self-incriminating declaration, 'The time has not yet come for the LORD's house to be built' – לֹא עֶת־בֹּא עֶת־בֵּית יְהוָה לְהִבָּנוֹת (1:2b). The current BL rendition could easily be modified to reflect a similar phonological effect and rhetorical impact: '<u>Ayi</u>, ntha<u>ŵ</u>i s<u>ii</u>na<u>f</u>ike <u>yoti</u> <u>i</u>fe nkumanganso N<u>y</u>umba <u>y</u>a Chauta<u>yi</u>.'

primary goal (e.g., a popular-language devotional/study Bible intended for a mature, literate Chewa readership).[27] I will simply mention seven of the more important of these paratextual techniques, along with an illustrative reference or two from the book of Haggai:

- *Glossary entries* – to briefly define and concisely cross-reference key terms or technical vocabulary items that appear in more than one biblical book, e.g., from ch. 1:1–2, 11, 14: 'high priest' (הַכֹּהֵן הַגָּדוֹל), 'Sovereign LORD' (יְהוָה צְבָאוֹת), 'new wine' (הַתִּירוֹשׁ), 'remnant [of the people]' (שְׁאֵרִית הָעָם).

- *Cross references* – to suggest pertinent (not trivial, ambiguous, or controversial) passages that need to be consulted in order to bring contextually related information to bear on the text at hand, or to indicate the probable source of a present quotation or allusion, e.g., revealing the vital intertextual connection between 2:4 and David's similar encouragement of Solomon in 1 Chr 28:20, or the similarly vital linkage between the promise made to Zerubbabel in 2:23 and the cursing of his royal ancestor Jehoiachin in Jer 22:24.[28]

- *Section headings* – to synopsize the primary content and/or purpose of the integral unit (pericope) that follows, as well as to indicate where a major discourse boundary occurs, e g, to help distinguish the break between chaps 1 and 2, that is, after v. 15a and before 15b (cf. NRSV, although a structural footnote will also be needed here to point out the bridging, or transitional function of 1:15b); before 1:12 to help mark the major shift in genre, topic, and tone that occurs at that point, and similarly, prior to the climax of the book in 2:20.

- *Sectional introductions* – to furnish by way of a summary overview a conceptual entry-point to a certain chapter or major section unit as a whole—prior to 2:10, for example, to suggest how the paragraphs 10–14 and 15–19 relate to one another (the latter text implicitly commenting on the former) and they, in turn, to the surrounding discourse (as a subtle admonition, reflecting back upon ch. 1, warning people not to take the LORD's person, place, and provisions for granted).

---

[27] For further information concerning the functionalist translation notions of a project job description *(Brief)* and principal goal *(Skopos)*, see Wendland 2004:291–293.

[28] In his excellent discussion of intertextuality in Haggai, Taylor rightly observes that "it is assumed that the reader of Haggai will be familiar not only with the citation [or allusion] itself, but also with its context in the original setting. That assumed context will be important for understanding the use Haggai is making of the earlier biblical text" (2004:84). One example of such intertextual reflection occurs in 2:22 where the 'language calls to mind certain Old Testament scenes that provide the poetic imagery and visual backdrop for this oracle' (ibid., 193). The pertinent hermeneutical questions then are: What if the language of a translation *does not* have a similar evocative effect for contemporary readers and hearers? How can this loss of conceptual significance be counteracted or compensated for?

- *Marginal notes* – to concisely explain or describe (whether as a footnote or a side note) some important, difficult, or potentially misleading element of the biblical text as translated, or to make a relevant application to, or comparison with, the local target language setting, e.g., in 1:11 to point out that in Palestine even certain 'mountains' (or 'high hills') were cultivated through terracing techniques; that 'the grain, new wine, and oil' were three main representative items of agricultural produce, often used in passages of blessing or cursing (Deut 7:13; Joel 1:10); or that a 'chief's walking stick' *(ndodo yachifumu)* would be a weak, partial cultural equivalent to the 'signet ring' (2:23) in terms of symbolizing authority and reliability (cf. also *chidindo cha boma* 'official government stamp').

- *Illustrations* – to depict or reveal certain strange, foreign, or unusual aspects of the discourse (from the perspective of the target audience), especially those that are difficult to visualize or conceptualize on the basis of the information provided by the text alone, e.g., the scene described in 2:12 of a male worshiper walking along while carrying something 'in the fold of his garment'.

- *Formatting* – to plainly indicate the boundaries of major and minor text units (sections and paragraphs) as well as any special compositional arrangements that help to reveal the development of a particular discourse segment, using devices such as a single column of print, unjustified right margins, variable left-hand indentation to indicate semantically parallel utterances, the judicious use of white space, special typefaces to highlight keys words, etc., e.g., the series of four sets of positive-negative contrasts which unfold Yahweh's assessment of the people's plight in 1:6; perhaps also the larger chiastic structural arrangement of 1:2–11.

Any of these auxiliary aids may be elaborated upon and given more of a didactic structure in the third type of strategy for bridging the communication gap in Bible translation, namely, using an expository *extratextual* publication or a corresponding electronic resource.

5.6.3 Extratextual strategies

In an ideal situation, a Bible translation, the text along with its paratext, is never received, interpreted, and applied individually in total isolation—that is, without reference to other persons or other texts. The Church, however defined, has always played an essential role by providing a localized supportive environment in which believers may assist one another to facilitate and maintain the hermeneutical process, and also to establish the basic principles and parameters according to which it takes place for a particular faith-community. I do not have space to develop the implications of this vast and vital interpretive resource, which is variously manifested in diverse forms—oral (e g, preaching, teaching), written (publications), and mass-media (radio, video, TV).

My primary concern in this section is to draw attention to the increasing importance for today's Bible consumers of more substantial extratextual aids that are geared specifically towards elucidating in greater detail the different aspects of a given translation of Scripture. I have in mind here more generous portions of the many different facets of Bible interpretation than can be dealt with through paratextual means. To begin with, there is a great need for situating Haggai more securely within his immediate temporal, sociocultural, and religious setting: When did he appear on the scene of Israel's history? It makes a great difference to how people approach this text if they know that Haggai appeared *after* the Babylonian captivity—an earth-shaking, heart-rending event that rocked his nation to the core of its ethnic identity and spiritual relationship with Yahweh (cf. Hag 2:6-7, 21-22). What was the nature of life then in that backwater province of Persia for a greatly demoralized and doubtful people (cf 2:3)? How did Haggai relate in terms of time and message to Israel's other prophets, past and present (Isa 14:1-2/Hag 2:6-7; Zech 4:6-8/Hag 2:4-5)?[29] Despite the fact that we are living in an age of instant, manifold global communication and mass methods of education, the level of biblical literacy does not seem to be increasing much, if at all, for the majority of churchgoers. In fact, in many areas concrete knowledge about the Scriptures appears to be diminishing as people get involved with so many other captivating everyday pursuits; as a result, just like their ancient counterparts, they have 'no time' for the Lord's business (Hag 1:2) and little concern for his presence ('house') among them (Hag 1:9).

In addition to well-prepared, culture-, language-, and audience-specific Bible background commentaries (e.g., Walton, Matthews, and Chavalas

---

[29] For example, House presents an interesting theological overview of "the character of God in the Book of the Twelve" (2000:125). This could be expanded or simplified as needed and developed into a useful extratextual resource for the study of Haggai. More specifically, Coggins (1987:85) points out a significant connection between the message of Haggai and "the hymnic passage in Zephaniah which immediately precedes it, promising a great festival in the temple on Zion when God himself would be in the midst of his people (Zeph 3:17f.). In just the same way Haggai's community could look forward to God's presence with them when all his commands had been carried out (Hag 2:5)."

2000) and study editions, people need to be educated as to the nature of the Bible itself—its textual character, literary qualities, historical composition, process of author- and editor-ship, canonical development, major intertextual connections, and principal theological as well as ethical themes. Another critical topic for learning concerns the history and nature of Bible translation, including the process of preparing a translation and evaluating the diversity of versions that are now available in print, in audio or visual form (e.g., *The Jesus Film*), and elsewhere (even online, e.g., the *New English Translation,* www.netbible.com). But as noted above, providing extratextual information of high quality solves only part of the critical communications problem: This must be accompanied by more effective methods of 'Scripture engagement', which are aimed at assisting and encouraging people both to actively utilize these supplementary tools to their full potential and also to apply them more meaningfully in terms of their own personal needs and life setting. These diverse issues are very capably addressed and illustrated in the recent practical study by Harriet Hill and Margaret Hill (2008): *Translating the Bible into Action.*

5.7 Conclusion: "Rebuilding" God's Word in another language

There are some interesting analogies that may be drawn between several key aspects of the message of Haggai and the task of Bible translation today. A major *rebuilding* project is involved in each case—the *house* of Yahweh in the original scenario, the *Word* of the LORD in a contemporary application. The goal of a translation of the Scriptures is to reconstruct, as it were, as much as possible of the *meaning*, both expressed and also directly implied by the original text, using the forms of a different language and the cognitive framework of another cultural world. This task of verbal communication is every bit as challenging as the physical and material Temple-building operation that faced Zerubbabel, Joshua, and 'the whole remnant of the people' in 520 BCE. Thus, there is also an equal need for a *total* community involvement (1:12a), consecration to the LORD (1:12b), commitment to the cause (1:14), and confidence in an ultimate, divinely enabled outcome (1:13; 2:5–9).

Translators must deal with the 'structure, style, sense, and significance' *(SSSS)* of the original text (as reads the title of this chapter). What a creative, but demanding exercise this is, to access the meaning of Scripture through careful textual exegesis, to conceptually 'carry this across' to another thought world, and then to re-formulate it again appropriately in another language! In addition, a proficient translation team may take communication to the next level and adopt the ideal objective of completing their assignment in such a way that the resultant target language text will match not only the content and intent, but also more of the *beauty, power, impact, and appeal* of that original verbal edifice. However, experienced translators also realize the practical impossibility of this goal, as would be the case in any effort to reproduce a momentous corpus of thought that is also expressed in the architecture of a great work of art. Any such endeavor is doomed to failure from the start *(tradutore, traditore!)*. Thus, it is not surprising that the reaction of skilled readers of the original text, who seriously reflect upon a certain translation of the Scriptures, often parallels the unexpressed thoughts of those old-timers of Jerusalem as they considered the sacred site of the second 'house' of Yahweh: What a disappointment—*'Does it not seem to you like nothing?'* (2:3).

Indeed, no Bible translation can ever duplicate its source text in every respect for the duration of the document, even one as short as the book of Haggai. Only varied degrees of *approximation* are possible. The more a person examines the Scriptures and realizes what is really there in terms of form, content, function, and implication, the more hopeless or impossible the task may seem to her/him. But the fact of the text's multifaceted, multidimensional literary character does not relieve people of the *obligation* to communicate the Scriptures in their language, and to do the best that they can, whether they are engaged in a first translation, its revision, or some newer contemporary version.

So, after all the skilled vernacular text-builders have been mustered and trained, a group that in one respect or another should embrace the entire language community (cf. Hag 1:12), the work begins: First, a comprehensive and credible exegesis of the biblical text must be produced, as partially exemplified in the first part of this chapter, in order to determine as precisely as possible the essential scope of the *SSSS* presented by the original. Second, this essential meaning-package must be appropriately expressed in

5.7 Conclusion: "Rebuilding" God's Word in another language

the target language, again, as *accurately, idiomatically, and acceptably* as possible, in accordance with the project's job commission *(Brief)* and primary communicative goal *(Skopos)*. Finally, translation specialists must seek to convey a selective representation of other important and useful background (presupposed) information—that which could not be incorporated within the TL text itself—through some of the paratextual or extratextual means and methods that were surveyed in the second part of this chapter.

Yahweh's stirring words of encouragement ring out just as loudly today to all those who are currently engaged in this exacting, but also exciting textual re-construction work. We are communicating ('re-presenting') the Hebrew and Greek Scriptures in a different language, culture, and situational setting: '"Be strong…for I am with you!" declares the LORD Almighty' (2:4). As for those especially perceptive and sensitive individuals who realize the greatly diminished outcome of this enterprise, he tells them not to worry or get overly upset, for 'I will fill this house *(indeed, this lowly translated text)* with my glory!' (2:7).

6

Recursion and Variation in the "Prophecy" of Jonah: On the Rhetorical Impact of Stylistic Technique, with Special Reference to Irony and Enigma

6.1 Methodology: The interaction of rhetorical and stylistic analysis

This study is based on a prior text analysis and translation of the entire book of Jonah (Wendland 1996). The methodology involves a systematic investigation of such macro-structural properties as *demarcation* (an internal segmentation of the text), *conjunction* (textual cohesion and coherence), *projection* (the foregrounding or highlighting of focal information), *progression* (the development of syntagmatic sequences and paradigmatic sets), and *inclusion* (the hierarchical integration of all discourse constituents into a unified whole). The result provides one with an overview or exposition, depending on the degree of detail, of a given biblical text's larger organizational framework and, perhaps more importantly, its associated (albeit assumed) functional operation as a unique instance of theological *and* literary communication, whether in the original event or during subsequent oral and written rehearsals in different contextual settings.

In this chapter, I will focus on the form and function of what appear to be the two most prominent stylistic techniques in the Jonah text, namely, *recursion* and *variation*. These two are of course related by mutual complementation. Both similarity (recursion) and difference (variation) are necessary for the production of verbal meaning in general and poetic effect in particular. "Style" concerns the *how* (or manner/means) of transmitting the content (the what) of a certain message. It refers to the sum of all those literary and linguistic characteristics that serve either to distinguish one text (or related corpus) from another or to relate one text to another. Two other important, and closely related, artistic devices in Jonah (as in other biblical Hebrew narrative works) involve the use of "quotation" (i.e., inter- as well as intra-textual citation) and "interrogation" (i.e., both real and rhetorical questions), but these will be treated under the more general categories of recursion and variation. The use of any given stylistic feature will normally not be textually distinctive in itself. But the total inventory and placement of such items (their selection and arrangement) as they interact with one another within a single composition and situational context will inevitably be text-specific in terms of both form and function.

Any consideration of functional significance will normally engage an analyst with the rhetorical dimension of discourse. A study of "rhetoric" investigates the why (or aim/intention) of a certain text in relation to both the primary as well as any secondary receptor group. Rhetoric (in the narrower sense as used here) is the art of argumentation. It takes up where stylistics (the art of composition) leaves off and examines the utilization of a specially shaped and organized ("styled") verbal composition for the purposes of receptor persuasion. How did the original Hebrew author (whoever that happened to be, a unified text being presupposed) endeavor to employ a considered selection of content coupled with a skillful manipulation of form in order to direct the thinking, mold the opinion, move the emotions, and motivate the will of his audience—in short, to adopt a divinely shaped ideology and point of view? Following this discussion of function, I will focus upon the diverse operation of two prominent rhetorical techniques in Jonah, namely, irony and enigma. These effects are frequently (but not always) generated by, or we might say—embodied in, the pair of stylistic means mentioned above, recursion and variation.

The present chapter consists of several major sections. In sections 6.2–6.4, I will survey the major formal features which distinguish the text of Jonah, with special reference to *recursion* and *variation,* which are key characteristics of Hebrew narrative style. In section 6.5, I consider the wider *functional* dimension of this type of discourse—though it is impossible to completely separate form and function during any meaningful analysis. In 6.6 and 6.7, *irony* and *enigma* specifically are described and illustrated from the text of Jonah. The four poetic and rhetorical resources of recursion, variation, irony, and enigma are crucial components of the "artistic code" (Long 1994:35) in which the book was first written and hence they are also keys to its contemporary interpretation. In the course of this investigation I hope to demonstrate why the short narrative work of Jonah has often been characterized as a "masterpiece of rhetoric" (Brichto 1992:68)—an excellent example of artful, affective religious communication. The principal reason for paying such careful attention to artistic form has been well-stated by V. Philips Long (ibid., 42):

> An increased appreciation of the literary mechanisms of a text—*how* a story is told—often becomes the avenue of greater insight into the theological, religious and even historical significance of the text—*what* the story means. A brief overview of Jonah's main theme(s) or "message," validates in turn the book's classification as a "prophetic" discourse; that is, it manifests a similar generic (hortatory) purpose to other texts found in the corpus of the so-called "minor" prophets.

Finally, in section 6.8, I present some thoughts on the practical implications of this study, Jonah's psalm of chapter two in particular, with reference to Bible *translation*—communicating the "word of the LORD" persuasively (i.e., rhetorically) to God's people today in an appropriate genre and an idiomatic style.

6.2 Recursion in biblical Hebrew narrative discourse

The abundant recursion of linguistic form in terms of both quantity (i.e., the sheer amount and variety of it) and quality (i.e., in elegantly constructed patterns and combinations) is perhaps *the* most important attribute of artistic rhetorical discourse in literary traditions, both oral and written, the world over. In biblical Hebrew poetry such restatement is manifested most clearly and distinctly in the multifaceted technique known as "parallelism," which normally permeates all verbal levels of a given text. Formal recursion is not quite so obvious in biblical works that are more "prosaic" in nature, but this difference is in the final analysis more a matter of degree than of kind, for beneath the apparent surface of most narrative discourse, for example, there exists an elaborate virtual edifice of iterative construction just waiting to be concretely realized, or "activated," by the attentive ear or eye and profitably applied to the message at hand.

The superficially simple story of Jonah's mission to Nineveh furnishes us with an outstanding instance of this, as has been noted in a number of literary-oriented commentaries and monographs.[1] In the following discussion I will summarize and develop some of the principal insights of these studies, with a particular emphasis upon those features of recursion that are of special significance in conveying the book's essential aspects of "meaning" (formal significance + semantic content + pragmatic intent). This presentation is arranged according to an eclectic set of primary analytical distinctions that can be made during the study of recursion in any literary discourse, but Hebrew "theological-prophetic" narrative in particular.[2]

6.2.1 Linguistic nature

The linguistic nature of recursion is most evident in the kind that features a reiteration of either phonological and/or lexical material. The latter category would of course manifest the former along with morpho-syntactic reduplication, which is not nearly as apparent to the average listener unless it actually incorporates some prominent similarity of sound or corresponding vocabulary, as in the cognate accusative (better: adverbial complement) construction, e.g., "And it *was evil* to Jonah a great *evil*" (4:1), which is balanced by a similar form having the opposite meaning near the onset of the next narrative sub-unit (scene): "And Jonah *was happy* over the castor-plant a great *happiness,*" for it helped to ameliorate his "evil" (i.e.,

---

[1] Three prominent examples are Magonet 1983, Sasson 1990, and Trible 1994.

[2] All of the cited English translations are my own rather literal renderings, unless indicated otherwise.

discomfort, 4:6; cf. also 1:10, 16; 3:2). Since there is so much extended lexical recursion in Jonah (to be illustrated in most of the examples that follow), it is not necessary to point out instances of the less conspicuous morpho-syntactic variety. It is sufficient simply to note that this stylistic resource too is present to augment the overall repetitive nature of the text as a whole and to enhance its larger rhetorical function.

A number of examples of *phonological* recursion appear to operate either independently or in conjunction with instances of lexical correspondence. Most subtle and hence easy to miss are the occasional rhythmic-accentual patterns which serve to reinforce the content that is being conveyed. Sasson, for example, points out that in addition to a reiteration of vocabulary, Jonah's "angry" reiterative reply to God's question in 4:9 reproduces its basic "punctuation" (i.e., accentuation) as well, thus highlighting the ironic contrast between the two utterance-final phrases, viz., "over the castor plant" and "unto death" (Sasson 1990:307). Wolff observes that Jonah's optimistic psalm of chapter two "consists exclusively of five-stress lines," thus rhythmically unifying the entire piece.[3] The repetition of selected vowels ("assonance") and/or consonants ("alliteration") in certain words functions to foreground the concepts concerned. For example, a sequence of /a/ vowels in 1:2b seems to extend from the initial command *qera'* "cry out," intensifying the solemn import of the LORD's message. In 4:6 a string of /l/s is intertwined with /o/ vowels to reflect the "shade" *(tsel)* of "deliverance" *(lehassil)* that Yahweh "caused to grow over" *(wayya'al me'al)* his irate messenger. A little later, however, a renewal of Jonah's feeling of "anger" *(charah;* 4:9) is preauditioned, as it were, by a series of terms that feature the sounds /ch/ and /r/: "dawn," "on the next day," "as its rising," "wind," "scorching" (vv. 7–8).

Similar examples serve to punctuate selected moods and meanings throughout the book. In addition, there are several instances of evocative onomatopoeia, for example, *chishebah lehishaber* in 1:4, which "captures the sound of planks cracking when tortured by raging waters" (Sasson 1990:96). There is also some rhyming, such as the commonly co-occurring pair *chanun werachum* "gracious and compassionate" in 4:2 (cf. the subsequent *wenicham* "and relenting"). The existence of rhyme in Hebrew verse is a debatable issue due to its ubiquitous pronominal suffixes, but certain concentrations

---

[3] Wolff 1986:129. Ironically, this so-called *qinah* meter [3 + 2] in often found in psalmic laments.

seem more than fortuitous. As Jonah and the sailors dialogue in 1:10–13, for example, "the sounds, positions, juxtapositions, and preponderance of twelve pronominal objects dot the wordscape as they interrelate the characters" (Trible 1994:145). Just the opposite is the case in Jonah's complaint of 4:2–3, however, where only a single pronoun reference is devoted to God ("you"), whose merciful attributes—now so obnoxious to Jonah—are surrounded by two strings of self-centered personal references (*-i* "I/me/my"). A similar denotative disparity characterizes Jonah's song of thanksgiving in the second chapter, e.g., v. 3: "I called out *(-ti)* in [the] distress of mine *(-li)* unto YHWH, and he answered me *(-ni)*; from the belly of Sheol I cried *(-ti)*, and you heard my cry *(-li)*."

But most important of all (thematically) are the various passages in which a significant sound pattern is utilized to play one sense against another to rhetorically heighten the discourse. Such punning, or "paronomasia," periodically appears to artistically unify the account and to accent its essential content. For example, the sudden and unexpected "believing" of the people of Nineveh *(wayya'aminu)* in 3:5 calls to mind what in 1:1 seemed to be the extraneous name of Jonah's father *('amittay)*. Thus, "the unstable 'calling' of the son of Belief (Amittai) elicits belief in God" (Trible 1994:181). Much more elaborate phonological linkage helps to bridge the transition from chapter three (scene 5) to four (scene 6):

> When God saw *(wayyar')* their deeds, that they turned from their wickedness *(hara'ah)* way, God had compassion concerning the disaster *(hara'ah)* that he said [he would] do to them, and he did not do it. And it was displeasing *(wayyera')* to Jonah a great displeasure *(ra'ah)*, and it burned *(wayyichar)* to him. (3:10–4:1)

There is another prominent play on words at the end of the book which spotlights the contrast between Jonah's incongruous, "pitiful" attitude towards the castor plant, which he did "not cause to become great" [i.e., to grow] *(lo' giddaleto,* 4:10), as compared with the "great" *(haggedolah)* city of Nineveh (4:11). To be sure, "Nineveh—the great city" is much "greater" now in the ears of the listener than it was, either at the beginning of the story, or at the onset of its second "cycle" (1:2/3:2—a double *inclusio*), for a strongly favorable divine perspective has been superimposed (cf. 3:3). In addition to underscoring key aspects of the message, such deliberate phonic

6.2 Recursion in biblical Hebrew narrative discourse 235

enhancement, a feature that pervades the Jonah text, also acts to augment the dramatic impact or the ironic effect that is being created (see further examples below).

6.2.2 Degree of formal correspondence

The degree of formal correspondence that is involved in any instance of recursion ranges between the two poles of verbatim repetition and the loosest type of synonymous paraphrase. In Jonah the *exact* form of reiteration is predominant, especially in the sets of corresponding verbs and related qualities that carry the action forward from beginning to end.[4] A skeletal summary of the entire narrative plot may be derived from this sizeable corpus of lexical duplicates alone, for example: *arise, go, call out, [be] great descend, fear, perish, throw, appoint, say, know, [be] angry, turn, do, have pity, [be] evil, be good, die.* As the three main paradigmatic participant groupings (i.e., YHWH < = Jonah = > pagans) interact via these concepts, the crucial twofold conflict of the central story line is developed, and the book's thematic nucleus is correspondingly formulated: merciful YHWH judges/delivers pagan peoples through his unwilling messenger, Jonah.

The feature of *lexical* synonymy is foregrounded most notably and noticeably in the several expressions that are used to refer to the deity: god[s], [the] God, YHWH, and YHWH God. The variation here appears to be significant in terms of the divine relationship to Jonah as well as to the heathen peoples with whom this reluctant prophet comes into contact. Thus, by means of these designations the narrator would suggest, on the one hand, different degrees of "knowing" the true God (YHWH), and on the other (especially in chapter four), God's manifestation of mercy coupled with discipline in relation to his offended (and offensive) ambassador. The most concentrated instance of synonymy in the book is realized in the "covenantal catalogue" of 4:2 where Jonah finally acknowledges the divine attributes which apparently drove him to distraction upon receiving the "call" of the LORD to Nineveh: "gracious, and compassionate, slow of anger, and abundant [in] steadfast love, and relenting over evil [i.e., a just punishment]." In this case, a collection of significant theological designations that fall within the same semantic domain are utilized in concert by way of analogy to give the fullest

---

[4] Magonet provides a sorted listing of these verbs in Hebrew (1983:14).

(the only?) possible description of a personal Being who is fundamentally indescribable in human language and categories of thought. Coming from the lips of Jonah, however, this apparently admirable profession of faith is contradicted by the incredible irony of his present situation: he could simply not bring himself to apply these wonderful words to the willing masses all around him.

6.2.3 Size and scope

The size and scope concerns the relative amount as well as the extent of lexical material that is reiterated. This may range from a single root, such as *g-d-l* "[be] great," to full clauses or even complete utterances, e.g., "And the word of the LORD came to Jonah..." The former appears in all four chapters (for a total of 15 times) while the latter is found only twice, i.e., in 1:1 and 3:1. As Timothy Wilt points out in his helpful study of "lexical repetition in Jonah," which focuses on the individual word level of recursion (verbs and adjectives): "the repetition of phrases and clauses is [a] feature that has not been given much attention" (Wilt 1992:260).[5] In my own examination of discourse-level restatement in Jonah (Wendland 1996:17), I draw attention to the several specific, compositionally related functions that these larger sequences perform in the narrative (cf. also below). I will not go into detail on this aspect of recursion, but will just mention a few interesting features that are associated with it.

As far as the repetition of individual words is concerned, one observes a number of distinctive *triadic* occurrences, that is, lexical and syntactic reiteration in closely spaced sets of three. Such patterning, like all of the recursion in Jonah, does not appear to be especially symbolical in import (e.g., "three days and three nights" 1:17; cf. "a journey of three days" 3:3), nor is it some stylistic quirk or merely a literary embellishment. Rather, the device is purposeful; in other words, on one level of the discourse and its telling or another, the several clearly functional examples would suggest a specific rhetorical intent underlying each instance. A triple reference to Tarshish within the single sentence of 1:3, for example, progressively heightens the disjunction between Jonah's intended destination and where

---

[5] However, Magonet (1983) and Sasson (1990) do include considerable treatment of this subject in their respective commentaries on the book of Jonah.

the LORD actually wanted him to be. An opening parallel set of three *waw*-initial action clauses in 1:5a acts to reinforce the contrast between the sailors' strenuous activity (cf. that of the Ninevites in 3:5) and Jonah's seemingly oblivious lack of it, summarized by a closing trio of verbs (5b). Somewhat later, three *ki* ("because/that/indeed") clauses at the end of 1:10 serve to emphasize the *cause-effect* relationship that is uppermost in the mariners' minds as they interrogate their suspicious shipmate.[6] A triad of verbs extolling Jonah's acts of "thanksgiving" (2:9) ironically echoes three adverbial complement constructions that recount the pagan crew's pious acts of devotion (1:16). The antanaclastic usage of a lexical triad occurs at the close of the king of Nineveh's proclamation (3:8b–9): Here the verbal root *sub* ("turn") is first employed with reference to the people's repentance and then in terms of the hoped-for response from the LORD—a turning towards compassion and away from anger. These outstanding divine attributes, as ruefully recalled by Jonah, are typical of YHWH, whom Jonah bitterly addresses three times in his confessional complaint of 4:2–3. A threefold mention of "city" (*'ir*) in 4:5 no doubt reflects the chagrined prophet's obsessive preoccupation with Nineveh's fate. A threesome of divine appointments triggers the temporary rise and subsequent fall of Jonah's spirit (4:6–8) and leads up to the LORD's final lesson for him, expressed, appropriately, in two syntactic sets of three (4:10–11). These are just some of the more obvious examples of meaningful recursion in terms of three, that is, over and above its possible numerical signification in the Scriptures, i.e., "to enhance [some noteworthy act] or to bring it to full effect" (Sasson 1990:153).

Another important effect of such exact lexical recursion may be seen in the diachronic bands of *resonance* that develop synchronically as one "repetend" echoes off of another during the story's forward progression in plot and time. This is not a matter of deficiency, of lacking an adequate vocabulary either with regard to the language as a whole or the author of this particular narrative. Rather, it is the product of deliberate choice and the adoption of a rhetorical strategy best suited for accomplishing his didactic-hortatory purposes. The scope of this cohesive reiterative technique may be limited to a single verse as we see in the threefold use of the verb root

---

[6] A similar sequence motivates Jonah's lament in 4:2–3. Causal relationships, both fulfilled and frustrated, permeate the discourse and give it a progressive, but not necessarily a predictable, character.

n-p-l in 1:7. The first two instances (formed from the causative *hiphil* conjugation) refer to the mantic practice of "casting" lots. On the third occurrence, however, the chosen form (i.e., over several other possibilities; cf. Wilt 1992:253) shifts to *qal* and the climactic outcome is reported: "...the lot *fell* upon Jonah!" Several other key verbs having a special theological significance but a relatively restricted spatial range appear in peak positions in the second half of the book, e.g., *n-h-m* "have mercy on" (3:9–10; 4:2), *sub* "[re]turn, repent" (3:8–10), and finally *hus* "have pity on" (4:10–11) to underscore the correspondence between Nineveh's hope (as expressed by her king) and the LORD's response. Thus, the dynamic interaction among the narrative's major participants is highlighted as they are brought into syntactic contact via such marked verbal correspondence.

But the Jonah text is permeated by several, much longer single-word sequences as well. Naturally, these have a proportionately greater semantic (if not always a corresponding thematic) effect in terms of the meaning field that is thereby generated. Such a resonant string of signifiers is created because every time the term in question appears, it is cumulatively imbued with additional semantic overtones which accrue from its new lexical collocation and plot-related context. The scope of a word like *q-r-'* "cry/call out," for example, extends through the first three chapters and accentuates the contrast between Jonah's two missions—the first undone, the second undertaken—but both having ironically similar results as far as the surrounding heathen were concerned.

Thus, Jonah is sent by YHWH to <u>call out</u> against Nineveh (1:2). He flees on a ship destined for Tarshish, but is discovered by its captain during a severe storm and is told to <u>cry out</u> to his god (1:6). Before casting the peccant prophet into the raging sea, the sailors "<u>cry out</u>" to YHWH for forgiveness (1:14). Later, in the belly of the great fish (and in the midst of the two panels of penitentially-oriented repetition), Jonah too <u>calls out</u> to the LORD for help (2:2). The second series occurs in chapter three: once again YHWH sends Jonah to <u>call out</u>—now *unto* Nineveh (3:2). This time he obeys and <u>cries out</u> his short sermon of doom (3:4). The conscience-stricken Ninevites <u>call</u> for a fast (3:5) and their king commands them all to <u>cry out</u> to God for mercy (3:8). In this transparent but highly effective manner, the divinely initiated means-result process, which underlies the overt side of the central message of Jonah, is both unified and foregrounded: Sinners invariably verbalize their repentance in prayer as they respond to a prophetic testimony and proclamation of judgment, no matter how grudgingly delivered.

There are a number of recursive phrases and constructions of larger scope that also play an important part in the author's rhetorical strategy. In the first chapter, for instance, the incongruity, impropriety, and impossibility of Jonah's flight is tacitly stressed by means of the repeated expression, "away from the face of YHWH" (1:3). It is only fitting therefore that this phrase should figure prominently in the case that the ship's crew had against Jonah—in fact, the guilty prophet indicted and clearly condemned himself by these very words (1:10). Jonah's persistently ambiguous relationship to the LORD comes to the fore in the closing stages of the story through the emphasis created by another sequence, this one exhibiting a "mixed" [exact + synonymous] sort of iteration. In 4:6 it is reported that <u>YHWH-God "provided"</u> (*m-n-h*) some welcome relief for Jonah in the form of a castor plant. Shortly thereafter, however, [*the*] *God* provided a worm to destroy that same plant (4:7). Then, to add insult to injury as it were, God provided a scorching sirocco corresponding to the psychological heat that his prophet was feeling (4:8). These variations in the divine name may reflect the decreasing relative proximity in their personal relationship and/or the nature of God's dealing with Jonah, whether in compassion (as *YHWH,* cf. also 2:1) or in chastisement (as *'elohim*).[7]

Another interesting instance of mixed (mostly synonymous) recursion occurs in chapter one with reference to the increasing intensity of the life-threatening storm: First, we hear of YHWH hurling <u>a great wind upon the sea</u> (1:4). This terrifying phenomenon is later described in personified terms as <u>the sea getting rougher and rougher</u> (1:11, NIV; lit., the sea walking and raging), and then when almost all hope was lost, as <u>the sea getting rougher and rougher against them</u> (1:13). The ultimate instance is paradoxically used for contrastive effect when all of a sudden it is reported that <u>the sea ceased from its furious raging</u> (1:15, *z-'-p* being more graphic than *s-'-r* [vv. 11, 13]) as it receives the body of Jonah in apparent appeasement. In this example of the so-called "growing phrase" in Jonah (Magonet 1983:31), the effect of the iteration is probably both qualitative (intensive) as well as quantitative (augmentative) in character.

As is stylistically typical of this narrative, the repetitive sequence just described is complemented by another, diachronically parallel pattern which

---

[7] For further discussion on this issue, see Sasson 1990:291 and Magonet 1983:37.

serves to enrich its thematic implications in terms of both character and event. Thus, in a progressively perceptive response to the LORD's revelation of himself by means of the storm and also the words of his prophet, the sailors are said to manifest a growing reverential "fear" *(y-r-')*: First they feared [and proceeded to cry out to their god/s] (1:5); then they feared with a great fear [upon hearing about "YHWH" from Jonah] (1:11); and finally they feared YHWH with a great fear [as they observe the word of his prophet come true before their very eyes] (1:16). All this stands in ironic contrast to the pious, but perfunctory, fear that is professed by Jonah himself (1:9) after being indicted by lot. A second, less overt parallel to the raging storm sequence occurs in the final chapter where we hear about the increasing "anger" *(ch-r-h)* and "evil" *(r-'-h)* of Jonah (the former is a visible manifestation of the latter) in reaction to the LORD's compassionate sparing of Nineveh, i.e., 4:1, 4, 6, 9.

6.2.4 Distribution pattern

The kind of distribution exhibited by any set of recursive items may be either significant or random. A *significant* mode of repetition develops when the various repetends are positioned in such a way that a key spatial pattern or focal point in the discourse is highlighted. A structural "pattern" results from a placement of the reiterated words on two or more boundaries such that a larger compositional unit is formed. The most obvious instance of this device is the division of the text into two halves by means of the extensive lexical recursion found in 3:1–3a (cf. 1:1–3), a pericope which accordingly leads off the second portion with a *re*-commissioning of Jonah by the LORD. Emphasis upon a particular "point" in the text is the product of a special concentration of repeated elements which thereby helps to mark a thematic and/or emotive peak of some type. The climax of chapter one (scene two), for example, occurs near its close in v. 16, a passage that is distinguished by four pairs of exact reduplication that links "YHWH" (2x) with the "fear" (2x), "sacrifices" (2x), and "vows" (2x) of the heathen, foreign sailors. The latter are referred to simply as "the men" *(ha'anashim)* and the collocation of this word with "fear" *(y-r-')* in turn forms a structural *inclusio* with v. 10, thus delimiting the second half of scene two. Similarly, the high point of chapter three is reinforced as God "repents" *(n-ch-m,* 3:10) in terms that

6.2 Recursion in biblical Hebrew narrative discourse

echo the king of Nineveh's indirect appeal for forgiveness (3:8–9; cf. also 1:6). Several more examples of such a significant distribution of lexical items are given below under a discussion of the compositional function of recursion.

A *random* dispersion of repetends includes all those that do not give evidence of performing any special demarcative (syntagmatic) purpose in the discourse, though they do of course contribute greatly to its overall cohesive quality (see below). Their importance is thus primarily thematic (paradigmatic) in nature, that is, to cumulatively outline or underscore a certain theological or moral point. We have seen several instances of this already (e.g., in the sharp contrast between the sailors' "fear" of YHWH in ch. 1 and Jonah's "anger" against God in ch. 4), but it may be helpful to mention another noteworthy example, just to reinforce the functional significance of such usage: The prophet's professional and spiritual descent from the LORD is metaphorically reflected in a deliberate repetition of the verb *y-r-d* "go down" at the beginning of the account: Thus, after receiving the initial command from YHWH, Jonah immediately goes down (and in the opposite direction) to the port of Joppa (v. 3b), and upon finding a suitable vessel, he proceeds to go down on board it (v. 3c). Sometime later then he went down into the very bottom of the boat, perhaps so that he would not attract undue attention to himself (v. 5c), and soon thereafter fell [down?] into a deep sleep (*yeradam*; v. 5d).

The *y-r-d* lexical set is artistically overlapped with another random sequence in chapter one, namely, a fourfold reiteration of the verb *tul* "throw, hurl." This may be regarded as being semantically supplementary to the preceding in that it further stresses the prophet's continual downward descent: Accordingly, YHWH hurls a storm down (from heaven, cf. 1:9) upon the sea (v. 4), and the sailors in turn try to save their ship by hurling its wares overboard (v. 5). Later, after the "falling" *(n-p-l)* of the lots has fallen upon him (v. 7), Jonah reveals that the only way to ensure deliverance was to hurl him down into the raging waters (v. 12). Finally, when all else has failed, the crew acquiesces and prayerfully hurls the LORD's prophet into the sea (v. 15). Jonah ultimately (but now figuratively) bottoms out on the ocean floor, and his pathetic plight—internal as well as external—is accentuated in the words of his psalm by yet one more occurrence of *y-r-d* (2:6). This final appearance stands out by virtue of its contrastive juxtaposition with the word "bring up" (*'-l-h*, 2:7).

6.2.5 Textual relationships

The final set of recursive distinctions to be made involves their pertinent textual relationships. These may be either "intratextual" or "intertextual" in nature. All of the previous examples as well as most of those which follow are instances of the *intratextual* variety, so nothing more needs to be said about them, except to call attention to one further qualification made by Meir Sternberg, namely, the difference between "verbal" and "non-verbal" repetition (Sternberg 1985:402): *Verbal* recursion, as the term suggests, is that which is constructed out of actual speech acts, whether direct or indirect, external or internal (i.e., cognitive discourse), individual (i.e., a monologue) or dialogic. *Non-verbal* recursion, on the other hand, consists of repeated references to some object, entity, event, happening, situation, or circumstance. This category includes the occurrence of "significant silence," i.e., a place where no report of either speech or action is given when it might reasonably be expected (e.g., Jonah's lack of a verbal response to God in 1:2–3, 3:2–3, and 4:4–5; cf. 4:2, 9b). Mixed discourse forms are also possible where, for example, a certain segment of direct speech is later reflected in the corresponding narrative action (e.g., God's reaction to the king of Nineveh's prayer, 3:8–9/10), or vice-versa (e.g., Jonah's subsequent complaint about YHWH's compassionate and forgiving behavior, 4:2). The significance of this twofold distinction, according to Sternberg, concerns the expectation that one has about the nature of the recursion that follows: a verbatim repetend in the case of human speech but a variable one elsewhere (Sternberg 1985:402, 406). Any variation that occurs, especially in direct discourse, usually introduces the additional important hermeneutical factors of a different thematic perspective and possible personal bias.

Divergences (or variations—see 6.3) from the verbal/non-verbal principle may also be utilized as a means of creating some special literary effect. For example, a shift in character viewpoint (e.g., his/her insight, awareness, attitude) and/or the narrative tone or point of view (e.g., its source or degree of subjectivity) may be intensified by the appropriate form of recursion—or the lack of it. Normally, when a real (as opposed to a rhetorical) question is asked, a certain amount of reiteration is expected or desired in the reply, that is, to fully explain the answer that is required. In his response to the anxious queries of the sailors (1:8; note the insistent *mah* + /m-/

alliterative alternation), however, Jonah seems to evade the issues that they demanded clarification about (1:9). He directly answers only their last question—concerning his ethnic origin, "a Hebrew." His subsequent formulaic creedal confession sounds somewhat out of place, although it was in fact an indirect way of replying to their first question, i.e., who was responsible for causing the storm. Jonah's solemn invocation of "YHWH," the "God of heaven" *(hashamayim),* "maker of the sea" *('asah 'et-hayyam),* whom he feared, however, reflects back ironically upon the last mention of the divine personal name—a non-verbal narrative statement of Jonah's plan to flee (by sea) to "Tarshish" *(tarshishah),* far away from YHWH (1:3d).

Intertextual recursion is a stylistic feature of paramount exegetical importance throughout the Hebrew Scriptures, no less so within the book of Jonah. In form, such text-amplifying and illuminating reiteration ranges along a continuum starting from a more or less exact reproduction of direct speech (i.e., citation), through a partial reduplication of either verbal or non-verbal material (i.e., paraphrase), to a covert, but still recognizable, reference to some important event or situation (i.e., allusion). In the passage referred to above (1:9), for example, Jonah paraphrases a number of passages that laud the LORD's creation of and sovereign control over the heaven, the earth (or dry land), and the sea (e.g., Pss 69:34; 95:4–5; 146:6). In a similar coerced confession after the Ninevite episode, Jonah utters a much more extensive listing, this time of YHWH's gracious attributes (4:2). While not an exact citation of any specific biblical text, this passage does pull together a great many of the items included in similar covenantal catalogues, e.g., Ps 86:5, 15; Ex 34:6–7; Deut 4:31; Ne. 9:17 (Sasson 1990:280).[8]

The various *allusions*—or "reminiscences" as Magonet terms them (1983:65)—are much less conspicuous (hence often debatable), but there are a number of rather obvious instances: The predicted "overturning" *(h-p-k)* of Nineveh (3:4) for its "evil" *(ra'ah)* and "violence" *(chamas,* 3:8), for example, harks back to Genesis and the evil coupled with violence of the wicked pre-flood generation (Gen 6:6, 11, 13) and the later archetypal overturning of a corrupt Sodom and Gomorrah (Gen 19:25). The LORD's subsequent "relenting *(n-ch-m)* from the evil he said he would do" to Nineveh (3:10) is strongly (due to the amount of lexical recursion) and (now also) ironically reminiscent of YHWH's similar relenting in relation to his own

---

[8] The wording in Jonah appears to provide the basis for Joel 2:13 (cf. Wendland 1995:326–327).

people, Israel (Ex 32:14). The point of the correspondence here underscores a basic similarity in the lost human condition and a universal spiritual need that Jonah, as a man of God and a representative of the people of God, should have been keenly aware of and sensitive to, but which he (also they) was apparently not the least bit interested in or concerned about.

The mother lode of intertextual citation and paraphrase is found of course in the psalm of Jonah.[9] Just about every verse (except for v. 6) incorporates a key reference or two, with varying degrees of precision, to create an interwoven poetic tapestry of panegyric theological language. The very first line, for example, finds close parallels in two different psalms:

> I called in my distress unto YHWH and he answered me… (Jonah 2:3a)
> In my distress I called YHWH and unto my God I cried… (Ps 18:7)
> Unto YHWH in my distress I called and he answered me. (Ps 120:1)

This correspondence and many other instances like it, are indeed noteworthy.[10] Jonah—or whoever composed/compiled this song—was certainly familiar with his Psalter. Some commentators doubt the appropriateness (even the genuineness) of the psalm in its present co-textual (literary) and contextual (situational) setting. However, current hermeneutical interest centers not so much on such likenesses, the many cross-textual echoes and verbal recurrences, but upon the crucial disparities, both great and small, that are often manifested in this "Jonahic version." Is there any significance, for example, to the fact that Jonah begins with a personal reference to his own petitionary action—"I called"—thus inverting the order of Psalm 120? One reason may be intratextual: a closer contrastive parallel is thereby formed with the introduction to the sailors' prayer in 1:14—"And they called unto YHWH…" (cf. the king's decree in 3:8b). The two passages are quite different of course: the latter is a passionate appeal for help and forgiveness, with a special focus upon the fate of poor Jonah and a pervading emphasis upon the pity of YHWH. Jonah, on the other hand and incongruously perhaps, utters a song of happy thanksgiving that highlights a distinctly personal perspective on his rapidly changing fortunes and what he piously intends to eventually do for God. There is a tangible irony here, that is, in the pitting

---

[9] This psalm also contains many intratextual correspondences; cf. Trible 1994:166–171.

[10] For a full listing of citations, paraphrases, and allusions, see Magonet 1983:44–49; Sasson 1990:168–215; Limburg 1993:63–64.

6.2 *Recursion in biblical Hebrew narrative discourse* 245

of pagan versus prophet. Further aspects of this vital rhetorical dimension will be more fully explored in Part Three along with a number of additional important intertextual "deviations" with respect to citation, paraphrase, and allusion that make this psalm as well as other key passages of Jonah semantically unique and emotively compelling.

6.2.6 Plot dynamics

Several other of the distinctions that Sternberg makes in his important study of the structure of repetition in Hebrew narrative discourse (esp. in ch. 11) may enable one to make an even more detailed analysis of the form and function of recursion in Jonah and other biblical texts. The categorization of such iterative instances in terms of the plot dynamics, for example, is particularly useful. Thus, a <u>forecast</u> stimulates an expectation about the narrative future; an <u>enactment</u> involves a focus on the narrative present; and a <u>report</u> produces a retrospection on the narrative past (Sternberg 1985:376). An example from Jonah, one based upon general intratextual synonymy, concerns the eventual fate of the great city of Nineveh. The sequence begins with this command of the LORD: "Cry out against it because its evil has come up before me!" (1:2 [cf.3:2]; i.e., forecast). We hear about its delayed enactment in 3:4: "He [Jonah] cried out and said, "Yet forty days and Nineveh will be overturned!" A summary report of what eventually took place is given in 3:5: "And the people of Nineveh believed in God...," and more specifically in the king's command: "...let them cry out unto God..." (3:8). The ultimate report then is found in 3:10: "And the LORD saw their doings (including a fervent and reverent crying out unto him)—how they turned from their evil way—then he relented from the evil that he said he would bring upon them..." Extensive recursion of this nature provides fertile ground for the creation of message-enhancing irony and enigma (see sections 5.6–7).

6.2.7 Degree of subjectivity

Another distinction that allows for these and other rhetorical effects to be more fully explored concerns the particular source of any given instance of recursion (a *repetend*) and the degree of subjectivity or objectivity that is represented in his/her point of view (Sternberg 1985:380). The thoroughly objective and omniscient narrator reports, for example, that "Jonah arose to run away to Tarshish away from Yahweh" (1:3), and as readers we have no cause to doubt that this really was the man's precise intention. Later, however, it comes as somewhat of a surprise to find out that the men [sailors] knew about Jonah's religious predicament, namely, that he was running away from YHWH (1:10). But in this case the transmitter of the information was the prophet himself (i.e., "for he [had] told them"). Consequently, considering the source, we may be excused for being at least a little suspicious—as well as curious—about how much and how accurately the situation was presented to these foreign mariners and why this news had such a great impact (fear!) upon those who did not even know YHWH. No doubt the great wind (1:4) that was growing in intensity (raging, 1:11) upon the sea, coupled with Jonah's own theological testimony (1:9), exerted considerable influence upon their response!

In the preceding discussion I have merely been able to scratch the surface of repetition within the book of Jonah. But hopefully this survey has demonstrated that this is a literary-rhetorical feature whose manifold complexity not only enriches the beauty of the Hebrew narrative, but which also taxes the insight and ingenuity of all those who endeavor to probe beneath the artistry to more fully investigate the depth and diversity of the original author's message.

6.3 Variation in literary discourse: The flip-side of recursion

As has been suggested above, large-scale or extended recursion in literary discourse normally appears in exact form (i.e., repetition) only in a limited number of cases in order to achieve certain special aesthetic, rhetorical, or structural effects. In fact, along with the formal sameness or similarity (synonymy), as the case may be, there will always occur a definite difference to some degree—certainly so with respect to the literary co-text and situational (often including the locutionary, or speech-event-related) context in which the reiterated items are placed. Furthermore, all of these differences, large and small, are somehow significant, for:

6.3 Variation in literary discourse: The flip-side of recursion

> ...there is no randomness or free variation in the [narrative] surface structure. Any morphosyntactic form in a text represents the author's choice whether conscious or automatic; we may not know the whys of all such choices, but we may speculate on them as implementations of differing discourse strategies. (Longacre and Hwang 1994:337)

Even more basic is the fact that meaning in any conventional system of signs, language in particular, is generated as the product of both similarity and difference, continuity and discontinuity, recursion and variation. This principle is the fundamental basis for productive signification on both the paradigmatic and the syntagmatic axes of verbal organization—from the phonological on up to the highest generic levels of composition. In literary works, additional meaningful types of likeness-with-contrast in the form of varied sequences and patterns are typically incorporated to augment the total signaling potential of the discourse in both denotative as well as connotative terms.

In many cases where some distinctive intratextual poetic effect is created in a literary composition, a basic structure of recursion is utilized to establish the necessary backdrop (ground) against which—or a fixed frame of reference within which—a certain *deviation* (figure) can be introduced. This sort of variation is occasioned by a marked deflection from a norm that has either been deliberately or unconsciously built into the text, notably by means of some form of repetition, or that is inherent in the language code itself, e.g., the order of syntactic elements (see 6.3.2). Such a disjunction—whether subtle or pronounced, overt or inconspicuous—serves to highlight specific aspects of the overall organization of the discourse and/or its central theme (motifs, sub-topics, etc.). Any departure from some recursive pattern then would be one way in which an author more or less defamiliarizes his account to force listeners (or readers) to take notice. According to the Russian Formalist school of literary criticism, such *defamiliarization* functions to "transfer the usual perception of an object into the sphere of a new perception—that is, to make a unique semantic modification" and thereby "to create the vision which results from that deautomatized perception" (Shklovsky 1995:21–22). However, as far as the Scriptures are concerned, the purpose of this technique is not merely "an aesthetic end in itself" (Shklovsky ibid., 12). Rather, it is invariably connected with a more effective communication of the intended message, whether that be primarily informative, emotive, volitional, and/or mixed in nature.

The best example of pointedly contrastive deviation within a framework of recursion in Jonah occurs at the beginning of the second half of the narrative, namely, 3:1–3a. The adverb *shenit* "a second time" formally announces the pattern and a likely parallel to 1:1–3. The wording of these two opening pericopes is largely the same, a fact which is significant in itself: YHWH is hereby giving his prophet another chance to fulfill his office according to divine expectation. But the real impact of the second episode is conveyed by its several key differences from the first. At that time Jonah was told simply to "call out against [Nineveh] *('aleyha);* now the LORD commands him to "call out unto [Nineveh] *('eleyha)* a calling [i.e., proclamation] which I am giving unto you." In chapter three then, the assignment to Nineveh is given in much more personal terms, that is, with respect to Yahweh in relation to Jonah. In addition, there is no explicit mention of Nineveh's flagrant "wickedness" *(ra'ah),* though this might reasonably be assumed. From the plot perspective too, the outcome is drastically different: This second time Jonah arises and does not try to run away from the face of YHWH, but rather he travels to Nineveh "according to the word of YHWH." The alteration here—along with the recursion—is carefully selected and situated both to inaugurate this major recycling of the account and also to suggest a change in the nature of the interpersonal dynamics that is now operating among the narrative's chief participants and groups.

Variation in literary discourse may take the form of a deviation from some established pattern or norm as illustrated above, or it may be realized in the *diversity* that results when a paradigmatic set of synonymous or contrastive items is created within the text. The classic example of this technique in Jonah occurs in the catalogue of YHWH's covenantal attributes in 4:2, all of which complement one another (ironically so in this instance) to present the fullest possible expression (humanly speaking) of undeserved divine mercy. A similar specific, but less concise and spatially concentrated, picture is given of the "greatness" of Nineveh. This city was not just "great/large/important" (i.e., the simple adjective *gedolah,* 1:2/3:2) in the abstract, but it was "great [i.e., important] to God" (3:3), a journey of three days in magnitude (3:3), a city consisting of both "great and small ones" socio-economically (3:5) and of urban and rural dwellers (i.e., man and beast, the herd and flock, 3:7), numbering more than 120,000 people (4:11), who in their spiritual-religious naïveté do not [even] know the

6.3 Variation in literary discourse: The flip-side of recursion

difference between their right hand and their left as far as YHWH was concerned (4:11). By means of such lexical diversity attached to a single referent, the odious, alien metropolis of Nineveh is given "a human face" (cf. *'adam,* 4:11), as it were, hence every bit as worthy and needy of the "piteous concern" (*chus,* 4:11) of YHWH as were the original Jewish hearers of this prophetic message.

Three overlapping types of variation, involving both *deviation* from a norm and also *diversity* in form are prominently manifested in the book of Jonah: lexical-semantic, spatial-syntactic, and temporal-pragmatic. Certain aspects of these have already been exemplified in the previous discussion, but it may be helpful to describe and illustrate their nature and function somewhat more precisely as distinct stylistic and rhetorical categories:

6.3.1 Lexical-semantic variation

Lexical-semantic variation is undoubtedly the most recognizable and commonly found type of modification, one that is used in conjunction with recursion to create some special semantic effect in relation to a given narrative plot and/or theme. This primary category can best be surveyed in terms of Sternberg's five "forms of physical deviance in repetition," namely: "expansion or addition...truncation or ellipsis...change of order... grammatical transformation...[and] substitution" (Sternberg 1985:391–392).

Of these, the first—*expansion/addition*—would appear to be the most important or productive narrative technique as far as the book of Jonah is concerned. As was noted earlier, the growing "fury" of the storm at sea and the resultant "fear" of the sailors in chapter one is mirrored in the steadily augmented qualifiers that are used to describe these interlocked natural and human phenomena. There is an expansion from "a great storm on the sea" (1:4) to "the sea continued to rage [ever more] against them" (1:13) as the overt cause. As for its consequence, there is a corresponding progression from "the sailors feared" (1:5) to "the men feared YHWH with a great fear" (1:16). The final addition of "the LORD" highlights the awe-ful demonstration (1:15) of his ultimate power over what had previously been their greatest fear! Thus, in this case, as Magonet observes, "in the form of writing is reflected its content" (Magonet 1983:32)—and we might add, also its underlying thematic (theological) implications. Perhaps the most interesting variations of this kind, not surprisingly, occur in the last chapter to dramatize the contrast between the respective attitudes of Jonah and YHWH over against Nineveh. When the LORD interrogates the prophet concerning his burning anger about the plant (4:9a; cf. 4:4—i.e., an explicit expansion) and whether this was a good idea, Jonah insolently replies that his ire is "good" enough even to die for (4:9b). YHWH goes on to point out that Jonah's indignation stemmed from his (previously undisclosed) pity over the passing of this transient plant (4:10; cf. 4:7). God, on the other hand, was anxious not only about [the people of] Nineveh, but also [its] many cattle (4:11; i.e., an emphatic ironic addition in ultimate syntactic position).

Jonah 4 also contains several outstanding instances of *truncation/ellipsis*: In the very first verse, for example, it is easy to miss the fact that the construction of the original text appears to deliberately leave implicit the specific cause of Jonah's great displeasure, namely, the repentant deeds of the Ninevites which led to the LORD's relenting (3:10). Perhaps this was done to give a somewhat closer and hence more dramatic impression of what Jonah's actual perspective was. In the event, he did not even want to think about such an offensive outcome (i.e., to him), though indeed he had already anticipated it (4:2). This indicting cause-effect connection is brought out more clearly in a rendering such as, "But *this* was very displeasing to Jonah, and..." (NRSV)—in contrast to a more literal and equivocal, "But Jonah became greatly displeased and..." (NIV). Another self-incriminating omission occurs in Jonah's complaint when he leaves out from the revelation of "his word" (4:2; cf. YHWH's word in 1:1; 3:1) the fact that his attempted flight to Tarshish was directed away from the presence of YHWH (cf. 1:3; a truth that he had apparently revealed to the sailors, 1:10). Perhaps the prophet finally realized that this was a physical and spiritual impossibility!

Closely related to the preceding point is the subtle intertextual "truncation" that also occurs in Jonah's confessional lament of verse two, an utterance which clearly recalls the LORD's own revelation of his essential nature ('name') to Moses in Exodus 34:6–7. Significantly, however, Jonah leaves out the original mention of "faithfulness" (*'emet*, NRSV), perhaps because this would have reflected badly on his own name (*'amittay*, 1:1) and the servant he should have been (Sasson 1990:69). More importantly, Jonah omits the last part of the divine saying: "[He] fails to cite God's

6.3 Variation in literary discourse: The flip-side of recursion 251

rewarding of grandchildren for their ancestors' merit...and totally ignores the concluding note of retribution" (Brichto 1992:85), i.e., about the punishment that will befall the descendants of iniquitous ancestors. Instead, Jonah substitutes the exact opposite idea: "...ready to relent from punishing" (NRSV)—which is, of course, a reinforcement of this crucial attribute of YHWH as expressed in the very words of the heathen king and the LORD alike (3:9–10). Another major omission distinguishes Jonah's earlier prayer of chapter two: Although the confession of sin is an optional constituent element of the individual psalm of praise and thanksgiving,[11] it certainly would have been appropriate in Jonah's composition (cf. Ps 32:5), that is, if he had recognized any personal wrongdoing at all in his relation to YHWH.

A *change of order* is most evident in the series of urgent questions that the sailors ply Jonah with after he has been implicated by the lot. It appears as if there has been some sort of a reversal in the normal sequence (Brichto 1992:70) which begins with the interrogative climax: "Who is responsible for all this?" (1:8a) and works down to the general issue of nationality. But then again, perhaps this is merely an indication of their great distress and an anxious desire to discover the deity responsible for the calamity surrounding them so that the appropriate supplication could be made (cf. vv. 6–7). In any case, Jonah's evasive reply features another significant spatial displacement or *hyperbaton* (literally): "A Hebrew [am] I and YHWH, God of the heavens *I [am] fearing*, who made..." Lexically, Jonah tries to "box" his God in (i.e., by the repeated emphatic pronoun "I"), but in doing so "YHWH" is put into a syntactically prominent position and hence dominates the entire utterance (*contra* Trible 1994:141). Such unexpected grammatical shifts (i.e., from the usual V-S-O word order) often serve a compositional function to mark a new juncture in the discourse (to be discussed further below). This may also involve lexical recursion as we observe at the onset of the second scene: "... to sail with them to Tarshish away from *YHWH* (1:3) = > (1:4) And *YHWH* hurled a great wind on the sea..." This stylistic transposition plus the accompanying repetition effectively highlights the theological fact that "man proposes, but God disposes!"

A recursive change in order is formally characteristic of the chiasmus construction, which performs a number of functions on both the macro- and also

---

[11] For a further description of this particular psalmic genre, see Gerstenberger 1988:140–141; Westermann 1980:72; Wendland 1994a:394.

the micro-structure of Hebrew discourse, in prose as well as poetic texts. At the beginning of the story, for example, there is an ironic reversal of events on board ship (i.e., A-B—B'-A') that serves to highlight Jonah's failure to carry out the LORD's explicit command as earlier enunciated: After receiving the divine command to "get up...and call out against [Nineveh]" (A: v. 2), Jonah <u>gets up and goes down</u> to Joppa to <u>go down</u> on board a ship bound for Tarshish (B: v. 3). But then, having gone down into the very heart of that vessel and <u>lain himself down</u> to sleep (B': v. 5b), Jonah is discovered by its captain and told to <u>get up and call out</u> unto his god[s] (A': v. 6) in the hopes of averting the disaster that he himself had brought down upon everyone present.

Later on, after the dramatic events of chapter one, we hear that YHWH provides a great fish to deliver his guilty prophet from a just drowning in the sea. In grateful response, Jonah prays to the LORD (2:1), the correspondence between these two verses being heightened by the reiterated phrase "from the inside of the fish." The change of order here serves to foreground the close interrelationship between Jonah and "his God" (2:1)—the God from whom he had been trying so hard to flee. The sovereign transcendence and intimate immanence of Yahweh is stylistically suggested by the fact that he stands both "outside"—and "inside"—a much longer double chiasmus that conjoins Jonah and the great fish that had swallowed him:

(1:17)	**YHWH**	*fish*			<u>Jonah</u>	
			<u>Jonah</u>		*fish*	
(2:1)			<u>Jonah</u>	**YHWH**	*fish*	[prayer]
(2:10)	**YHWH**	*fish*			<u>Jonah</u>	

However, Jonah's self-centered attitude does not seem to have changed much, as evidenced by his first-person oriented song of thanksgiving (i.e., 27 references to "I/me/my" as opposed to 15 second- and third-person [including nominal] references to the LORD). This predominantly personal orientation is given its cue in the reordering that is implicit in the prayer's very first word, "I called" (2:3). The closest psalmic parallel to this initial line begins instead with a focus upon YHWH: "To the LORD in my distress I called" (Ps 120:1; cf. Ps 18:7—"In my distress I call, 'O LORD!'..."—the vocative here placing the emphasis again upon YHWH).

Certain *grammatical transformations* (perhaps "morpho-syntactic" would be a better designation so as to distinguish this from the preceding category)

6.3 Variation in literary discourse: The flip-side of recursion 253

may be utilized in conjunction with their co-text to produce a wide range of interesting semantic implications. Naturally, these are not always evident in a translation, hence the importance of a thorough examination of the original Hebrew text. The guilt of Jonah is revealed, for example, when the mariners decide to "cause the lots *[object]* to fall *[hiphil verb]*"—and having done so, when "the lots *[subject]* fall *[qal verb]*" upon Jonah (1:8). The righteous (divinely-directed), cause-effect nature of this divinatory procedure is thereby implicitly underscored. Jonah opens his thanksgiving prayer to YHWH by referring to the latter in the third person (2:2a). In the very next line (2:2b), however, there is a transformation to the second person which remains in force throughout the rest of the poem, indicating perhaps a (temporary) rapprochement between him and his God.

The contrast between the past evil doings of the Ninevites and YHWH's present merciful activity is foregrounded in 3:10 by a reiteration of the root *['-s-h]* in three different forms: a participle, an infinitive construct, and a perfect finite verb (the last emphasizing the LORD's decision not to destroy the city). After this extraordinary sparing of infamous Nineveh, Jonah complains that it is "good" (adjective) for his life to be taken away (4:3). Yahweh's rhetorically barbed response is sharpened by his ironic use of the same root *[tob]*, but now as a verbal (infinitive): "Is it good [this] anger of yours?" (4:4). The underlying correspondence here might emphasize the very fact that Jonah's anger could one day cost him his life! Finally then, in the book's closing passage there is a prominent transformation with respect to the initial personal pronoun, set within a recursive frame begun in the preceding verse, which functions to intensify a profound "perspectival clash" (Sternberg 1985:398): "As for *you* [Jonah]," the LORD said, "you were concerned about that plant..." (v. 10)—"But as for *me,* should I not be concerned about Nineveh...?" (v. 11). Of course the respective objects of the verb are foregrounded at the same time (i.e., by positioned parallelism and attribution) for additional contrastive effect.

The category of *formal substitution* is probably second only to the first one mentioned above (expansion) in importance. The effect of this device is heightened in an ancient (literary) language like biblical Hebrew which is characterized by so much overt repetition. When a synonym is used, therefore, or where there is an obvious change with respect to one element, such as placement, within a sequence of recursive constituents, this will invariably carry with it some special semantic (including thematic) and/ or pragmatic (sociolinguistic) significance. For example, in the reiterated [verb + cognate noun] syntactic frame of 1:16, the three actions referred to typify a cause-effect (internal/external) relationship that encompasses the ultimate in religious devotion, i.e., "fear" = > "sacrifice" + "vow." A good example of lexical substitution occurs at Jonah's recommissioning, as it were, when "the word of the LORD comes to [him]"—not as "the son of Amittai" (i.e., "faithfulness," 1:1), but simply "a second time" (3:1). In other words, the prophet's fidelity remained to be proved as he is told once more to "call out"—now "unto Nineveh" (3:2), not "against [it]" (1:2). Indeed, at this stage in the narrative, it is debatable as to who was more "evil" and accountable in the eyes of YHWH, the bearer of the divine message or its delinquent addressees?

Does Jonah pass the LORD's overt test of his character? The issue is very much an open question at the end of the account (4:11), as we witness the man "rage with a great raging" (cf. NJB) when the teeming city of Nineveh is spared (4:1), but "rejoice with a great rejoicing" (4:6) over the appearance of a transient plant, whose demise he later mourns in trenchant anger (4:7–8). This emotive and attitudinal contrast is associated with the clearest instance of synonymic "substitution" in the book, namely, that involving the divine name: It is the "LORD God" who graciously provides the castor-bean plant (4:6) to "deliver [Jonah] of his discomfort [lit. 'evil']," just as he planted a garden for the benefit of the first humans in Eden (Gen 2:8). However, it is simply "God" who subsequently provides the means of the plant's destruction and then reproves an unrelenting Jonah for his introverted response. All this is in obvious contrast to God's "repenting over the evil" (3:10; 4:2) he had intended for the now transformed Nineveh (3:8–9)—a city in which each one [had] turned from his way of evil, and from the violence that was in *their* hands (3:8b). The synonymous, complementary parallelism of the preceding expression emphasizes both the individual and the corporate guilt and responsibility of all citizens in this salvific, life-changing event (cf. Trible 1994:186).

6.3.2 Spatial-syntactic variation

Spatial-syntactic variation could perhaps be classified under a "change of order" as discussed above, but in this case the crucial shift occurs, not so

6.3 Variation in literary discourse: The flip-side of recursion 255

much in terms of a proximate group of *lexical* items (i.e., diversity—though this may still be involved), but rather with respect to the usual arrangement of *syntactic* elements in the Hebrew verbal clause, namely, [verb => subject => object; i.e., deviation], especially in relation to "the sequence of *wayyiqtol* clauses that occur throughout the story from beginning to end" (Longacre and Hwang 1994:345). For this reason, outside the original text, the critical movement is not perceptible in any but an interlinear translation. Such a departure from the norm is utilized to foreground the noun (phrase) involved for the purposes of focus or emphasis. Such an item is put into *focus* in order to mark it as the new principal topic or agent in the discourse. This will often coincide with a major compositional boundary, e.g., a paragraph or episode unit in narrative texts, but only if reinforced by some other prominent signaling device, such as those mentioned above in connection with recursion. *Emphasis*, on the other hand, is more restricted in scope, i.e., to a single clause, sentence, or utterance (if in direct speech). It serves to intensify the semantic significance of or to call special attention in terms of thematic and/or plot-related importance to the noun (or qualifier) so displaced. Most commonly the movement of the item is to the *front* of its regular position in the clause (i.e., front shift), but on occasion the displacement is in the other direction, that is, to the *back* of the clause/sentence ("back shift"). The operation of focus and emphasis as well as the distinction between these two functions are illustrated in the following examples:

As was pointed out above, the nominal "(And) YHWH..." begins verse four, but since the divine name has just been mentioned at the end of verse three (in the iterated, stressed phrase, "from before YHWH"), this does not seem to be simply an instance of special emphasis (as stated, for example, in Sasson 1990:93). More precisely, we have here the onset of a new stage (episode) in the action, which coincides with a dramatic revelation of (and a focusing upon) the principal divine character who is acting behind the scenes, as it were, to control all subsequent events upon the sea. An emphatic front-shift does occur in the last clause of this verse as the narrative spotlight shifts to the ship, which was threatening to break up. A similar sort of thing occurs in 1:5c. "(And) Jonah..." appears at the head of the clause, but this personage is not necessarily being "emphasized" thereby (e.g., Limburg 1993:50). Rather, the spotlight is shifting back to him by means of a narrative flashback to an earlier point in time. Thus, the function of the syntactic deviation is global, not local, in nature—a product of the author's selective staging of crucial events in the story.

The norms of syntactic ordering are quite different in Hebrew poetry as distinct from prose, but it is apparent that the fronted pronoun "I" in 2:4 is distinguished for some special reason. Although there may be an element of "emphasis" here (Limburg 1993:67), the introverted structure of the complete psalm, coupled with the contrastive content of this very utterance, would indicate that it may play a more important role in the poetic discourse, namely, to signal the compositional core of the chiasmus. We observe a similar sort of thing in 2:9 where a corresponding front-shifted emphatic pronoun is also utilized to mark the close of the song as well as to suggest its singer-centered focus.

Another example of such structurally-related foregrounding—or in this case, backgrounding—is found in 3:3b, where the initial "(And) Nineveh..." is not really given any particular referential "emphasis" per se (*contra* Limburg 1993:77). Instead, the complete clause is marked as being an explanatory "aside," one that occurs "off" the event line and is intended to highlight the city's great size and significance to God. A final instance of this sort of discourse focus may be observed in the last verse of the text. Presence of the separable pronoun "I" is no doubt emphatic, i.e., in contrast to the corresponding "you" (sg.) of the preceding passage. But its frontal position in the Hebrew word order (Limburg 1993:97) serves primarily to highlight the important shift in the LORD's argument at this stage, that is, to its climactic second half, which of course concludes the adventures of Jonah with a challenging comment by its divine author.

A good example of utterance emphasis was observed earlier in Jonah's confession of 1:9. Here a front-shift of the object phrase, "Yahweh the God of heavens," though surrounded by Jonah's obtrusive "I"s, places the appropriate thematic prominence where it belongs, not only with respect to this particular juncture in the account, but also within the entire second episode, and even the book as a whole. Similar emphatic syntactic advancements appear in Jonah's song of thanksgiving—first as a series to progressively stress the depths to which he felt he had sunk (i.e., "from the belly of Sheol," 2:2b; "all your breakers..." 2:3b; "the deep" 2:5b; "to the roots of the mountains" 2:6a; "the [lower] earth" 2:6b). A second set of front-shifted

6.3 Variation in literary discourse: The flip-side of recursion 257

elements then serves to contrast himself (i.e., "I," 2:9a) and his promised ritual actions with the disparaged behavior of those who cling to worthless [idols] (2:8a).

The relative significance of syntactic position in non-finite clauses is based more on percentages and what the more usual order of components in similar expressions would be. For example, "by reversing the more normal phraseology [in 1:12b], *"ani yodea'*, the narrator stresses Jonah's awareness of his role" (Sasson 1990:125), that is, in relation to the maritime disaster that has befallen the crew. This interpretation is reinforced by a subsequent advancement of "on account of me" in the verbless object clause that follows, which is neatly balanced by "upon you [sailors]" at the end.

Back-shift displacement in the syntax is not nearly as common as front shifting, but the impact is as great, as we observe in the initial clause of 1:16, literally: "And they feared, the men, with a great fear YHWH." This verbally mimics the profound realization that these heathen sailors had been inevitably led to by the awful sequence of events at sea. The gradually unfolding revelation surely confirmed for them Jonah's prior (1:10b) and latter (1:9) public testimony (in both of these instances, YHWH is front-shifted). Later, the miraculously saved singer's realization of his utter dependence upon God is reflected syntactically by means of a retrogressive movement of two self references, i.e., "my life" and "my soul" in 2:6b–7a, and their juxtaposition with "YHWH." But the most obvious and dramatic example of emphatic back shifting is found—appropriately—right at the very end of the discourse. In this case, the second, and thematically surprising, half of a compound subject is positioned as the concluding climax of the utterance and the entire book. Indeed, YHWH is concerned *"even [w-]* about Nineveh's many animals" (4:11b)! Thus, "syntax has distorted a desired link between the vocabulary of God's lesson and that of the king's edict [in 3:8]" (Sasson 1990:315)—the purpose being to accent the inability of man to limit the magnitude of the LORD's mercy by means of humanly based rational and religious categories.

6.3.3 Temporal-pragmatic variation

Temporal-pragmatic variation in Hebrew narrative discourse involves a disruption or displacement in the normally strict diachronic flow of events.

In other words, the progressively unfolding and forward moving verbal event-line is interrupted and there is a shift in time, usually backward (i.e., flashback), but sometimes forward by way of prediction or a more covert foreshadowing to a new and distinct temporal and situational setting.[12] In this connection, Sternberg observes, "Within his generally reticent discourse, *fore*telling would yet seem the least congenial form of telling, expositional *back*telling definitely included" (Sternberg 1985:268). Such retrospective deviation may vary according to quality (i.e., perspicuity) and/or quantity (i.e., the degree of chronological separation, that is, relatively near to or far from the current setting). Due to its deliberately disjunctive effect, however, it is always functionally significant in terms of general or specific character representation and motivation, (sub-) thematic expression, and/or the pragmatic (interpersonal/audience-related) intent of the message.

The problem confronting analysts of Hebrew narrative is that these points of temporal discontinuity are not always unambiguously marked in the original text. In an English story, for example, a flashback is often indicated by the presence of a pluperfect ("had") tense and/or the use of a temporal adverb (phrase), e.g., "at that time," "the previous day," "the week before." In Hebrew, however, such verbal-based differentiation is simply not available (on its own) and the adverbial cue is much less common in occurrence. The primary marker is a shift in word order (coupled with an obligatory non-narrative verbal tense sequence, i.e., N + *qatal* (Longacre and Hwang 1994:347), but as we have seen this device is also used for other purposes (e.g., to indicate emphasis or to distinguish a compositional boundary), and hence it is a rather ambiguous signal. One is thus left to rely upon the co-text and the structure of the narrative as a whole to make a decision with regard to any given (possible) instance of such temporal disjunction. It is in this light then, namely, the larger discourse style, that I would propose chronological displacement as a feature of considerable rhetorical importance in the story of Jonah.

In order to support such a claim, it is necessary to begin with the most conspicuous, least controversial cases—not that one will be likely to achieve complete agreement with regard to any individual instance, but simply to try and develop an argument that will take into consideration the greatest

---

[12] I have not yet made a study of possible "parallel," or simultaneous, event sequences, e.g., "Meanwhile back at the city,..."

6.3 Variation in literary discourse: The flip-side of recursion 259

amount of evidence, whether strong or weak. At the top of such a scale of certitude would surely be the flashback that is found in 4:2. There can be no doubt about this instance because it is explicitly stated to be a reference backward in time, that is, back to the very beginning of the narrative: "Is not this what I said while I was still at home? For this reason I hurried to run away to Tarshish..." The important functional implications of this temporal reordering, dramatized in the form of direct speech, will be considered more fully in section 5.6. For the moment, it is sufficient to note its unambiguous presence in the story, suggesting at least the possibility that other examples of this device remain to be found.

Several other possible instances of flashback construction have been noted in Jonah. This first occurs in the second half of 1:5: "As for Jonah [i.e., initial syntactic front-shift], he *had gone down* (lit., "he went down") below deck..." (cf. Magonet 1983:116, n. 20). Wolff observes: "Before the narrator can bring him into the scene (v. 6) he has to catch up with what has been happening to the Hebrew ever since he went on board at Joppa (v. 3)" (Wolff 1986:112). Another likely example comes shortly afterwards in 1:10: "...because he [Jonah] *had told* them." In this case, the flashback may be marked by being the third in an unusual (for narrative) series of three *ki* "for, that" clauses. Once again the narrator intentionally omits "certain events from their proper chronological sequence in order to introduce them later for greater impact" (Allen 1976:185). In other words, "Biblical narrative often withholds pieces of exposition [or in this case, conversation] until the moment in the story when they are immediately relevant" (Alter 1981:66).

An interesting and debatable instance of such reordering appears in 4:5. A number of commentators[13] have suggested that immediately after Jonah's climactic prediction of disaster (or so he thought) in 3:4, i.e., "Yet forty more days and Nineveh will be overturned," there is a bifurcation, or "literary forking," in the narrative: One line reports the dramatic and turbulent events within the city itself, which ultimately lead to its receiving a saving reprieve from the LORD, i.e., vv. 5–10. The other line, beginning at 4:5, follows Jonah outside the doomed city to a place where he awaits its downfall since he is "still not certain of the outcome of his warning" (Stuart 1987:504). This is not a matter of dealing with a clumsily misplaced piece

---

[13] For example, Allen 1976:231; Brichto 1992:78; Wolff 1986:163; Stuart 1987:504.

of text as some older commentators have suggested (Wolff 1986:163). It is rather the display of a deliberate, artistically fashioned (e.g., the lexical overlay in 3:10 and 4:1), "cut-and-paste" technique whereby the actual events, whether parallel or overlapping in nature, are reported in a way that best suits the author's didactic and admonitory intentions. In this instance, the inexcusable, prejudicial anger of Jonah, which ends the narrative proper (4:3-4), is placed in the background, while the unmitigated mercy of YHWH is highlighted and allowed to bring the story to a more positive, theologically centered close (4:11). The message-reinforcing ironic and enigmatic aspects of this textual movement will be discussed in sections 5.6-7 of this study.

However, the narrative can also be interpreted as it stands in strict chronological sequence. This indicates the potential problems involved when a temporal (versus a textual) displacement is posited for there is admittedly a rather large disjunctive gap involved in this instance. It also illustrates the need for a careful weighing of all available evidence for the move, both cotextual (linguistic) and contextual (situational). The flashback approach to 4:5, for example, i.e., "And Jonah *had gone out* from the city and established himself..." is supported by the following pieces of textual evidence:

- the obvious emphasis upon "city" that follows naturally from the prediction of Nineveh's "overturning" in 3:4;
- the provision of an explanation for the phrase "to see what will happen to the city" (4:5), which would otherwise seem to contradict Jonah's knowledge of its deliverance and his consequent "anger" in 4:1-2;
- the presence of other, less ambiguous flashbacks in the book (e.g., 4:2); and
- the rhetorical advantages of this perspective on the text as outlined above.

Finally, we should take note of a probable retrospective reference at the onset of the LORD's concluding speech in 4:10, namely, his mention of Jonah's "pity" *(ch-w-s)* in 4:10. Nothing was said about this earlier in the narrative, but it would seem to refer back to the powerful, but unexpressed, sorrowful reaction that Jonah experienced when his shady plant dried up and died (4:7b).[14]

On the other hand, commentators have also proposed a number of what may be termed "false flashbacks" at different places in the book. The psalm of Jonah in chapter two, for example, is sometimes construed as a later

---

[14] This interpretation is convincingly argued by Trible 1994:219-223.

6.3 Variation in literary discourse: The flip-side of recursion   261

reflection (a conceptual flashback as it were) upon the events recorded in 1:17 and 2:1 in support of erroneous conclusions such as these: "the *situation* of the psalm [and its language] does not fit the context" (Wolff 1986:129); or the psalm "disrupts symmetry...and introduces perspectives at variance with the narrative" (Trible 1994:173). Therefore, it is not necessary to use a pluperfect to translate the verbs of "descent" (i.e., recounting Jonah's predicament, e.g., v. 3) because it is supposedly "the appropriate tense in light of the logic of the chronology of events" (Stuart 1987:469). Actually, this song of grateful thanksgiving is very suitable right where it occurs within the structural framework of the book as a whole. For one thing, it could be a response to YHWH's act of delivering Jonah from death by drowning (1:17), whereas his subsequent rescue from the sea/great fish itself (2:10) goes unthanked (which would not be a surprising [non-]reaction for a fickle character like Jonah). Furthermore, this psalmic *genre,* i.e., "an individual song of thanksgiving," does not invariably celebrate some specific personal salvation event in the past. Due to its functional affinity to the individual lament, the temporal orientation could possibly be *future,* namely, a strongly anticipated deliverance based upon YHWH's prior acts of preservation (Wendland 1994a:390–394). This would fit the setting quite well in the case of the passage at hand, i.e., 2:2–9 in response to 1:17 and in confident hope of 2:10.

A few other examples of such chronological over-(or mis-)interpretation may be noted: A pluperfect rendering of the event of 2:1 (had appointed) (Stuart 1987:468), for instance, is quite unnecessary and even counter to the Hebrew narrative perspective and style. First of all, there is a relatively insignificant gap in time involved here. Moreover, use of the "*waw*-consecutive" construction along with a following explicit noun subject would simply represent the least disruptive way of indicating concurrent actions being carried out by different agents, that is, "YHWH" and "the men" (1:16). It is thus misleading to claim that "as far as events are concerned, this goes back in time, catching up with what has already happened" (Wolff 1986:126). Similarly, it is not quite accurate to view verses 6–9 of chapter three as being "a kind of flashback."[15] Instead, this would appear to be a significant example of the Hebrew narrative technique of "summary-and-scene" whereby a

---

[15] Wolff, for example, renders the verbs of vv. 6–7a by an awkward string of pluperfects (1986:144–145).

general synoptic overview of a some important pericope (v. 5) precedes a more detailed telling of what happened (vv. 6–9). Thus, having heard of the divine proclamation (v. 2) that Jonah was currently announcing throughout his city (v. 4), the Ninevite king responds by issuing a royal proscriptive and prescriptive edict to apply to all his subjects, including the livestock (3:7). This is similar to what happens in 1:17, a summary statement which leads to the psalm of 2:1–9, and also the preview-and-quotation sequence that occurs at the end of 4:8, i.e., "...[Jonah] asked that he might die. He said, 'It is better for me to die than to live.'"[16]

It is a sign of our author's considerable narrative skill that along with the several passages involving a temporal displacement backward, there are also a few cases where a definite future orientation is suggested, again inserted for apparent rhetorical reasons. Meir Sternberg provides a useful classification of such "foreshadowing" (to be distinguished from more direct narratorial foretelling) by proposing three main types: "analogy, paradigm, and dramatic forecast" (Sternberg 1985:268). *Analogy* entails episodic similarity, that is, a series of events experienced by one biblical personage that corresponds in certain significant respects to what later happens to another. Such "analogical organization [is] designed to launch inductive reasoning from known precedent(s) to some present counterpart facing an uncertain future" (ibid). Thus, the completely unexpected conversion of the Tarshish-bound mariners gives an unobtrusive hint that if and when Jonah ever does make it to Nineveh with his "word of the LORD," the outcome for them might not be as bleak as first indicated at the start of the story (1:2). The several important parallels that materialize to link the two accounts (i.e., in chs. 1 and 3) later confirm this divinely planted intuition. An instance of *contrastive* analogy pertaining to the same personage[17] would of course be that which is played out in the re-sending of Jonah to Nineveh (cf. 1:1–3 and 3:1–3).

A *paradigm*, which operates now with more influence from the principle of deduction, is the product of a recursive series of such analogies. It is "a general rule...which grows in predictive determinacy and ideological force with each new successful application" to enhance a greater awareness of "God's controlling design" in biblical history (Sternberg 1985:269). The

---

[16] Cf. NRSV; *contra* Brichto 1992:269, n. 20.

[17] These are not necessarily different characters as Sternberg seems to imply (1985:268–269).

outstanding example of this phenomenon in Jonah—arguably the thematic point of the entire book—is embodied in the prophet's ironic testimony of the benevolent divine character in 4:2. It was the paradigmatic—indeed, the axiomatic—nature of this theological proposition that, in fact, motivated Jonah's fateful flight in the first place and which, paradoxically, had also made possible the gracious experience of divine deliverance (cf. 2:9) that his erstwhile shipmates enjoyed.

Most obvious on the continuum of revelation that ranges between implicit analogy and overt narrator, prediction is realized by some manner of *forecast* by a character (including, most reliably, God himself). Such "deductive prospection," designed to "catch the eye [and the ear] of the most dim-sighted [and hard-of-hearing]," is normally reserved for "vital matters of doctrine" (Sternberg 1985:270). Thus, Jonah's capsule sermon, "Yet forty days and Nineveh will be overturned" (3:4), at first seems to be an application of the divine principle of retribution that serious (chronic) evil will be punished, a notion that is implicit in the words of Jonah's first commissioning (1:2). However, this forecast leads to an expectation that is counteracted both by prespection in the analogy of the sailors' salvation and also by postspection in the stated paradigm of God's essential goodness. The theologically grounded punitive proposition is not thereby compromised in the process; it is simply superseded by its larger, contra-rational correlate, namely, the fact that YHWH prefers to relent and to respond in compassion to penitent hearts and concrete acts of repentance (3:9–10). This hope-generating possibility, which is undeserved and contrary to all human logic, lies semantically implicit within the key verb itself, *h-p-k* "over-turn/turn-over," i.e., respond in repentance (cf. Hos 11:8, in which the latter verb also co-occurs with "relent" *n-ch-m*).

The wider *functional* and *theological* implications of the Hebrew narrative stylistic techniques of recursion and variation as well as their specific manifestation in the rhetorical devices of irony and enigma will be considered in subsequent sections of this chapter.

6.4 Potential problems in the functional analysis of literary form

No study of literary form is satisfactory or complete in and of itself. It must always be accompanied by (or better, integrated with) a study of the specific *communicative functions* which the formal features—in this case, recursion and variation—were selected to carry out in the discourse. In his extensive treatment of the poetics of biblical Hebrew narrative, Meir Sternberg periodically emphasizes "the limited value of the formal typologies that so often pass for the business of literary theory and analysis" (Sternberg 1985:392). He goes on the point out the need for an integrated methodology, one that combines a careful description of form—and, we should add, content as well—together with a related discussion of authorial intent (ibid., 393):

> [T]his two-way divorce [i.e., between form and function] establishes the need for a properly communicative approach, one that will accommodate the interplay of means and ends in sophisticated art and relate the principle of repetition to the working of the narrative whole.

But the domain of function is considerably more difficult to handle with certainty during the process of text linguistic-literary investigation. Five noteworthy problem areas that may arise in this endeavor pertain to methodology, genre, perspective, setting, and the mode or medium of message composition. Each of these factors, operating either alone or in conjunction with one or more of the others, can seriously affect one's assessment of role or purpose in the case of any given stylistic technique, whether major or minor in terms of the overall development of a particular plot or story.

6.4.1 Methodology

The matter of general methodology is the first issue that comes to the fore in connection with the functional analysis of biblical literature: Should the Scriptures be regarded and treated like ordinary written (literary) discourse in terms of analytical and evaluative procedure, or is there a *qualitative* difference between the Bible and any other text or corpus—whether religious or secular, historical or fictional, informational or aesthetic (primarily) in nature—which would call for a different approach to the task of investigation and interpretation? Obviously, one's particular theological presuppositions (with specific reference to the "Word of God") will determine any decision

6.4 Potential problems in the functional analysis of literary form 265

which is made in this regard. That issue cannot be taken up here.[18] Suffice it to say that my basic assumption, that is, concerning the reality of the influence of divine inspiration in the composition of the Old and New Testaments, inclusively governs my perspective on both the nature of the original text and also my mode of hermeneutical inquiry with respect to it. Accordingly, I view the fundamental nature of biblical narrative as being definable in terms of the following four characteristics, in descending order of importance, but nevertheless all carefully integrated:

(a) **theological** in relation to overall content, i.e., thoroughly God (YHWH/Christ)-centered, motivated, directed, fulfilled, and empowered;

(b) **historical** in relation to quality, i.e., on the whole (except for clearly marked and included sub-genres, such as parables) a reliable, factual representation (including author-determined selection, sequencing, shaping, summarization, shading, and stylization) of the events reported as having taken place;

(c) **rhetorical** in relation to purpose, i.e., aimed at "persuading" receptors to accept an all-governing divine perspective and imperative on their prevailing worldview and way of life; and

(d) **artistic** in relation to means, i.e., utilizing a wide range of Hebrew (or Greek) literary-poetic devices and compositional techniques according to the specific context and co-text to generate the appropriate volitional motivation, emotive involvement, cognitive impact, and esthetic appeal with regard to the essential message being conveyed.

Some, more conservative scholars might object to the relative importance attached to—or even the inclusion of—features (c) and (d) in my analysis of biblical texts. But in general I think the abundant textual evidence speaks for itself in this regard. To be sure, one must always guard against the danger of "overinterpretation" (Stuart 1987:456), that is, rhetorical overreading and/or creative artistic "enhancement" with respect to the original text and the author's intended objectives. But one must not go too far in the other direction either and discourage, discount, or disparage attempts to probe the depths of communicative potential in these areas. To conclude, for example as Stuart does in relation to Jonah, that "most of the repetition of vocabulary that does exist in the chapter [one] and in the book as a

---

[18] See the valuable discussion in chapters two and three of Long 1994.

whole is due to a single factor: the desire for simplicity," or that "the narrative bears no hint of humor" (ibid., 457, 485), would appear to be contradicted by an honest and open analysis and assessment of the text itself. Such an evaluation is also countered by his own characterization of Jonah as being "*sensational* literature," that is, "composed with a high concentration of elements designed to arouse the imagination and emotion of the audience..." (ibid., 435—original emphasis).

6.4.2 Genre

The term *genre* may be defined as "a socially defined constellation of typified formal and thematic features in a group of literary works, which authors use in individualized ways to accomplish specific communicative purposes" (Brown 2008:122).[19] The importance of genre to the functional analysis of literature is aptly summarized by David Clines as follows: "literary works... generate meaning [over and above lexical and grammatical means] through their overall shape, their structure, and their dominant tendencies, that is, through their identity as wholes."[20] The identification of a work's overall macro-genre and constituent sub-genres enables one to better understand not only how a story is told (in terms of its stylistic features) and what it tells (i.e., the nature of its content in relation to reality), but also why the story is told (i.e., its interactional purpose in relation to the assumed intended audience). I have elsewhere described Jonah as being generically (and uniquely) complex, that is, a dramatic, didactic, factive, typological narrative with a significant underlying hortatory (prophetic) character.[21] Such a comprehensive perspective on the text helps to define the principal parameters within which one might carry out the manifold hermeneutical process of analysis, interpretation, and contemporary application—including idiomatic, but accurate, Bible translation.

---

[19] Genres may thus be individualized, or stylistically manipulated, with reference to "the arrangement, priority and coherence of these features" that happen to be characteristic of a given genre (Brown 2008:122). An "emic," or indigenous (Hebrew), classification of genre proves to be problematic because "some ancient contexts have no explicit genre theory, as in the case of the ANE" (ibid., 129). Therefore, an "etic," or externally derived, classification cannot really be avoided, although it must not be applied too categorically in any given case

[20] This quote from Clines is cited in Long 1994:47.

[21] Support for this rather complex genre description of Jonah is detailed in Wendland 1996:191–206.

6.4.3 Perspective

The issue of message perspective, including the associated factor of the degree of pragmatic intentionality, is a crucial one in contemporary literary and theological hermeneutics. It is particularly relevant in any discussion of literary (or communicative) function. There are four basic stances possible—with many different modifications and combinations in between.[22] One may have an orientation from the point of view of the *source* (or implied author) of the work, or from that of the intended *receptors* (implied audience) of the *initial* communicative event. Alternatively, the perspective adopted may be that of the real audience *today*;[23] or even that of the linguistic *text* itself (i.e., in such a way that it supposedly speaks for itself without being tied to the original author or any particular audience).[24] It is not possible in the present chapter to consider the relative pros and cons of these diverse positions. I will simply concur with that of Sternberg (1985:69) who stresses the need for adopting the standpoint of the assumed *authorial source* when undertaking the initial phases (at least) of any exegetical and/or literary study of the Scriptures. I do so despite the likelihood of being accused by some of committing the alleged hermeneutical error known as "the intentional fallacy."[25]

My reason for choosing this perspective is that "communication presupposes a speaker who resorts to certain linguistic and structural tools in order to produce certain effects on the addressee" (Sternberg 1985:9)—and, it may be added, to most effectively convey the full extent of the desired

---

[22] For an overview of these different methodologies, see Longman 1987:ch. 1 and Osborne 1991:ch. 6.

[23] These two receptor-oriented settings and their associated hermeneutical approaches need to be distinguished due to the radical difference between them. A concern for the original audience and context will often manifest itself in a study that has great affinities to one in which the author (or redactor/editor) is the focus of attention, as in traditional evangelical biblical criticism or, by way of contrast, typical "source criticism." In the case of modern reader-centered theories, on the other hand, the situational context is largely irrelevant, for "the reader creates the meaning of the text" or "in interaction with the text," an approach that ultimately leads to a "deconstruction" of the discourse (Longman 1987:38, 41).

[24] Since a completely neutral, unbiased interpretation is impossible, the fourth, supposedly "text-oriented" approach often merges in practice with the third, which is sometimes termed "reader-response" criticism. On the other hand, a focus on textual form in relation to the postulated original setting of use and composition is characteristic of traditional "form criticism." Thus, the overlapping nature of any proposed system of hermeneutical classification is evident.

[25] This supposed fallacy is outlined (and to some extent supported) by Trible 1994:96; a good refutation of the misuse of this criterion is found in Osborne 1991:405–406, 414–415.

message to him/her/them. Such tools may be overt (we might term them "cues") or covert ("clues") in relation to the textual surface, and they are situated on both the macro- as well as the micro-structure of discourse organization. Explicit statements of a writer's attitude and intent are comparatively rare in Hebrew narrative, but not entirely absent, e.g., Judg 21:25; 2 Kgs 17:7-23; 2 Chr 36:14-21. Other comments that presuppose authorial purpose and perspective are less direct, such as the epilogues of Deuteronomy (34:10-12) and Joshua (especially 34:21); the genealogy of Ruth (4:17-22); the autobiographical report of Ezra (9:1-2); and the prayer of Nehemiah (1:4-11).

In any case, the principal guide in any attempted functional reconstruction is inevitably the text itself and how it is rhetorically shaped through formal means such as recursion and variation (plus interrogation, the use of intensifiers, etc.) and semantic techniques like irony and enigma (plus figuration, hyperbole, etc.) to effect certain basic communicative objectives. It all sounds rather subjective, but the alternative is much more so, for as far as procedure and perspective are concerned, "the choice turns out to lie between reconstructing the author's intention and licensing the reader's invention" (Sternberg 1985:10). Advocates of the latter option would include notably "the rhetorical critic [who] can find structures and meanings in the biblical text apart from the intention of the implied much less the real author" (Trible 1994:229). To be sure, "author intentionality cannot be assured," but at least it is a reasonable goal to shoot for in order to help "control interpretation of the text" (*contra* Trible 1994:230)—its originally intended meaning, that is, but not necessarily also its contemporary application and contextualized extension.

6.4.4 Setting

The problem of interpretive viewpoint is integrally related to that of the original situational setting, for the question of "who?" cannot be satisfactorily determined in isolation from others, such as "where?" and "when?" (i.e., "what?" then pertains to content, "how?" to form, and "why?" to function). Again, Sternberg offers several important observations in this regard (Sternberg 1985:11): "[T]he text has no meaning, or may assume every kind of meaning, outside those coordinates of discourse that we usually bundle

6.4 Potential problems in the functional analysis of literary form 269

into the term 'context'." And having decided in favor of a *source*-oriented perspective, it remains for one to vigorously pursue every analytical means and resource available for ascertaining the closest possible approximation of the original compositional milieu, for: "...the more complete and reliable our knowledge of the world from which the Bible sprang, the sharper our insight into its working and meaning as text" (ibid., 16).

The problem is that the bare text of Jonah does not give us a great deal of information concerning the background of its literary origin. No dates are mentioned, and the general geographical references to "Nineveh," "Tarshish," and "Joppa" (1:2–3) do not help much in terms of fixing a precise historical setting. In this case, about the best we can do is to adopt that which is suggested—intertextually—by the Scriptures themselves, namely, the only other passage where a "prophet" named "Jonah, son of Amittai" is mentioned. This textual setting is found in 2 Kings 14:25 where there is a rather cryptic reference to the work of a seer who ministered in the land of Israel during the relatively prosperous reign of Jeroboam II. This passage does not say anything about the city of Nineveh and their king, but obviously the nation of Assyria was a subject of considerable current concern since it was either the dominant or at least a major threatening world power in the Middle East at that time.[26] Therefore, the book about the prophet Jonah must be set and is best interpreted in the light of the tragic events that overtook Israel in the eighth century B.C.E. just a few short decades before the ruthless Assyrian armies overran the Northern Kingdom, destroyed its capital Samaria, and deported its people en masse (cf. 2 Kgs 17). Additional support for such an approach comes from the wider canonical context and the editorial fact that a "...linking of Jonah with Hosea, Amos, and Micah in the Book of the Twelve indicates that Jonah ought to be understood as a story about a person from the eighth century B.C." (Limburg 1993:22).

The prophetic surroundings (i.e., cotext) of the book of Jonah also has an important bearing on the nature of its message as was suggested earlier: It is not merely the history of a particular prophet; it is "prophetic history," that is, paraenetic (admonitory and hortatory) as well as hagiographic (biographical) in nature. Thus, Scripture interprets Scripture also with regard to its larger compositional organization and constitution.

---

[26] For a helpful summary of the political situation of this age, see *The NIV Study Bible*, 550–551.

6.4.5 Mode/medium of composition

This factor is presented last because it is probably the most nebulous and open to debate. The pertinent issues revolve around various efforts to identify the particular manner of message production in the original event: Did the complete text exist initially only in *oral* form, was it first presented as a *written* document, or did some *combination* of influences characterize a longer compositional process in relation to a particular biblical book? It would seem that the third possibility is the most likely in the case of Jonah, as for most of the prophetic works.[27] In other words, the text was probably formulated in the final instance on the basis of one or more spoken (or proclaimed, recited, chanted, etc.?) versions that were already in circulation. The precise degree of influence of the oral upon the written is of course indeterminable, but the audio medium has clearly left its mark on the discourse in the form of such devices as recursion (the large amount of exact repetition in particular), phonological accentuation (e.g., paronomasia, alliteration), direct speech, sharp character contrasts, and graphic diction—to mention just some of the more obvious features—and of course the distinct thanksgiving prayer of chapter two.

What influence then does the medium of composition have upon the message and its interpretation? In the case of Jonah, the fact of an extended oral prehistory certainly helps to account for some of the stylistic devices listed above (e.g., repetition/recursion in particular). This mode of communication also supports the supposition (explored in 5.6–7) that the literary-rhetorical techniques of *irony* (creating an implicit level of critical significance) and *enigma* (introducing motivated hermeneutical gaps and queries) both play an important role in the hortatory development of the account—yet without necessarily compromising its basic historicity. Literary-narrative strategies of such relative sophistication as irony and enigma would tend to be more effective—and indeed perceptible—in the case of a story and context that were well known, that is, in contrast to one which was newly created (if fictitious) or being reported or recorded for the first time.

A traditional oral-based text also frequently manifests the device of *hyperbole* (deliberate exaggeration for rhetorical impact), but since the effect of this particular feature would detract from the fundamental facticity of

---

[27] For an analogous approach to the NT epistles, see Wendland 2008b:ch. 1.

6.5 The rhetorical significance of recursion and variation in Hebrew narrative

the narrative, I do not see it as being operative in Jonah, for example, with regard to the account of the great <u>storm</u> (ch. 1), the <u>great fish</u> (ch. 2), the <u>great conversion</u> of the <u>great city</u> of Nineveh (ch. 3), or the <u>great anger</u> of this prophet of the LORD (ch. 4).[28] This is a rather controversial issue in past and present Jonahic studies and obviously one that is very closely connected to any consideration of genre (see above).

A final point to note in this connection is the mode (intended medium) of *performance*. All factors being considered, there can be little doubt that the narrative of Jonah was set down in writing in such a way as to preserve its essential orality. In other words, it was composed in a natural style that would make it relatively easy to "re-oralize" the discourse in dramatic fashion during any subsequent public reading or recital. This important factor will be further considered under the topic of "text presentation" in section 6.5.6.

In the discussion that follows I will present a brief (and incomplete) overview of seven generic (macro) communicative purposes that pertain to the functioning of recursion and variation in narrative. Several additional examples are included to show how these principles apply to Jonah in particular. More specific (micro) poetic motives and moves are presented in association with the treatment of selected illustrative passages, especially during my survey of the rhetorical operation of irony and enigma in sections 6.6–7.

6.5 The rhetorical significance of recursion and variation in Hebrew narrative discourse

Seven major pragmatic (i.e., rhetorically motivated) aspects of a discourse-based functional approach are posited, namely, those that relate to a text's larger organization, demarcation, conjunction, projection (accentuation), characterization, presentation, and pluri-signification, i.e., semantic/thematic diversity (cf. Wendland 1996).

6.5.1 Text organization

Repetition and variation play an important role in the overall organization of narrative discourse, with specific reference to the creation of a design that

---

[28] My approach contrasts in this regard with that of Edwin Good, for example, who feels that "everything about Nineveh is exaggerated…to highlight the irony of the peevish prophet's totally unexpected success" (1981:49).

renders a certain text attractive and hence appealing in terms of its artistic form and aesthetic effect—but also including such features as temporal ordering, content proportioning (i.e., a detailed *scene* vs. a sketchy *summary*), and information selection. Why should this be a factor of note where religious—yes, strongly theological—and what is assumed to be "historical" literature is concerned? Are these crucial notions not mutually exclusive or at least quite unrelated, i.e., artistry, theology, morality, and history?

In short, I would say no—not necessarily, at least not with regard to the diverse narratives found in the Hebrew Scriptures. In fact, I would go so far as to claim that the four aspects stand or fall together, that is, in the case of a text that is believed to have originated from God himself. Such divine "inspiration" obviously (according to present perspective) controls the *factuality* of biblical history, the truth of its *theology,* and the validity of its *morality,* but I would add that it also makes possible the excellence of its literary *artistry.* Thus, the Bible is literature that stands supreme in every respect, not only in terms of its multiple divine purposes (expressed in relation to many different authors and settings)—that is, in comparison with any other religious book or corpus—but also with regard to its compositional quality and "poetic" craft.[29] This fact does not contradict or detract from its historical character; rather, it only enhances it. To this point, J. Philips Long writes in his helpful survey of "the art of biblical history": "To be sure, there is often an element of patterning in the Bible's portrayal of people and events, but this does not disprove the essential historicity of those portrayals" (1994:114).

A number of examples have already been cited (in sections 6.2–4) to demonstrate that Jonah, like any other biblical work, evinces a text that is highly organized according to its genre and permeated with manifold literary patterns. Sternberg refers to this as its "analogical design" and mentions such typical instances as "parallelism, contrast, variation, recurrence, symmetry, [and] chiasm" (Sternberg 1985:39). Undoubtedly a texture so obviously, yet also skillfully, structured was more easily and effectively conveyed (articulated, apprehended, and remembered) in an oral-aural setting of communication—which was, and still is, the principal mode of Scripture transmission.

---

[29] "Poetics" is "the science of literature," especially with regard to its artistic qualities and rhetorical effects (Berlin 1983:15).

6.5 The rhetorical significance of recursion and variation in Hebrew narrative

But performance-related factors provide only part of the answer as far as the Bible's popularity is concerned. The structural symmetry that is inherent in Jonah—not only as expected in the "psalm," but throughout the book— also contributes to a more effective (informative, affective, and imperative) conveying of the diverse aspects of its theme. Thus, we move from the problem of how to deal with the gross sinfulness of a thoroughly pagan society, which is emphasized in the point-for-point paneling of the first three verses of chapters one and three, to the contrastive and critical "from minor to major" *(qal wachomer)* manner of reasoning in the book's final two verses, which foregrounds the prophet's moral and spiritual problem in relation to his LORD. Throughout this development the reiteration of linguistic and literary form plays an indispensable part in the multifaceted transmission of a multifarious message centered upon divine mercy. But complementing this overarching theological perspective are periodic, carefully placed ruptures of the anticipated cause-effect progression of the narrative surface, each of which act as a subtle reminder that the grace of God does not operate according to human norms, mores, desires, or goals.

6.5.2 Text demarcation

From the larger organizational design of discourse we move to its internal demarcation, in which recursion and variation also perform a leading role. This comes about through the application of a number of important text-defining principles as noted earlier. The obvious lexical correspondence at the respective beginnings of chapters one and three (i.e., anaphora), for example, signals the onset of these two major divisions of the book as a whole and also delimits the extent of their initial episodes (1:1–3 and 3:1–3). Similarly, the two halves are each divided by means of the "prayers" *(p-l-l)* that initiate and set the tone for chapters two and four (2:1; 4:2). Jonah's promise to "offer sacrifices" *(z-b-ch)* and "fulfill vows" *(n-d-r)* at the close of his psalm (2:9) ironically echoes the analogous actions that the sailors are reported to have actually carried out at the ending of chapter one (1:16; i.e., epiphora). The subsequent report of "Yahweh providing a great fish to swallow Jonah" (1:17) is neatly paralleled by "Yahweh's telling the fish to vomit Jonah out" in 2:10. Thus, the prophet's song of thanksgiving is completely enclosed by its occasion, namely, the LORD's salvific action (i.e., inclusio).

The book's last major transition, that is, between chapters three and four (3:10–4:1), is marked by extensive verbal overlap (i.e., anadiplosis) involving both similarity (a play on the root "evil," *r-ʽ-h*) and a striking contrast, i.e., YHWH's all-embracing "compassion" *(n-ch-m)* versus Jonah's inveterate, prejudicial "anger" *(ch-r-h)*. These two chapters are segmented internally by the prophet's contrastive movements, i.e., into the city (3:4) and later exiting it (4:5, i.e., anaphora). Finally, the divine-human disputation of chapter four is bounded by a pair of important position statements which are strangely synonymous: Jonah's reluctant and perfunctory enumeration of the merciful attributes of the LORD (4:2) is applied specifically by YHWH himself to the case at hand, namely, the needy inhabitants of Nineveh (4:11). In this way all of the text's principal boundaries may be established, appropriately dividing the narrative into a "perfect" sequence of seven episodes, or scenes: 1:1–3, 1:4–16, 1:17–2:10, 3:10–3, 3:4–10, 4:1–4, 4:5–11 (cf. Wendland 1996).

6.5.3 Text conjunction

Hand in hand with the syntagmatic demarcation of a given discourse goes its internal conjunction, that is, a consideration of those devices that contribute to its essential characteristics of unity and harmony. Such a conjoining is one of two principal kinds, namely, that based upon textual form (i.e., cohesion), and that which pertains to its overall sense and significance (i.e., coherence). These two types of linkage are often, but not necessarily, effected together, and their primary purpose is to interrelate the principal parts of the composition both to one another and also to the complete text as an independent unit of literary communication. All types of lexical recursion, whether exact or synonymous [+/– deliberate variation or direct semantic contrast], naturally contribute to this quality of connectivity, but some sets are thematically more important than others. Of the terms reiterated in all four chapters, for example, *g-d-l* "[be] great" (15 occurrences) is clearly more significant than '*-m-r* "say"(21 times). As Wilt observes, "a thing is spoken of as *gdool* only because of its direct relationship to God" (1992:259). Similarly, the different references to Israel's deity (39 times in 48 verses), especially YHWH as distinct from '*elohim,* are far more consequential for the message than the recurrence of Jonah's name. Some iterative sequences are

6.5 The rhetorical significance of recursion and variation in Hebrew narrative

much more restricted in scope and thereby serve to unify smaller segments of the discourse, e.g., "fear" *(y-r-')* in 1:4–16 (scene two) or "[re]turn" *(sh-w-b)* in the king's proclamation and the LORD's response of 3:8–10.

Two other, less obvious types of conjunction need to be mentioned. One of these linking techniques, intertextuality, has already been illustrated (6.2.5). Its importance lies in tying the book of Jonah as a whole into the textual tradition as well as the canon of the Hebrew Scriptures. The many varied, seemingly deliberately positioned and/or modified citations, paraphrases, and allusions that are present would suggest a rather late (postexilic) date for the work's composition. But on the other hand, all these references firmly situate this story within the mainstream of traditional Yahwistic theology (e.g., 4:2, 10), with special reference to his compassionate regard for all those, including foreigners, who penitently and devotedly enter into a covenantal relationship with him by grace (cf. Deut 10:18–19; 24:14–22; 26:10–13; Isa 2:2–4; 42:1–9; 56:1–8). The fact that Jonah ministered (albeit grudgingly) on behalf of YHWH to pagan peoples strikes a strong resonant chord with many prophetic oracles (e.g., Am 9:11–12; Ob 20–21; Mic 4:1–4; 7:15–17; Zeph 3:9–10; Zech 8:20–23; 9:9–10; 14:16–19; Mal 1:11; 4:1–3). This ancient corpus of divine truth needed (and still needs) to be recalled and reinforced within the prevailing setting of a lukewarm religious society and a threatening world age when most of the people of God had either forgotten or were determined to ignore the fact that YHWH had ordained that a regenerated Israel and his chosen servant, the Messiah, were to be "a light to the nations—so that all the world may be saved...and praise [him]" (Isa 49:1–7).

Then there is another important kind of formal cohesion which recursion, usually coupled with variation, effects (along with demarcation) in Hebrew literary discourse, and that is by means of a chiastic construction—or as it is more commonly known when extended beyond the typical four terms (A:B::B:A), an *introversion* or *palistrophe*. In this case the principle of deviation is actually built into the compositional pattern as the second half of the structure reverses the sequential order of significant elements of the first. Jonah incorporates several good examples of this symmetrical sort of inverted formation, all of which have been documented elsewhere (Wendland 1996). They serve by way of literary analogy to underscore the predilection of the LORD to "turn *(sh-w-b)* whenever possible—even in the most unexpected of human circumstances—in order to exercise his manifold "compassion" (*ch-w-s;* 3:9–10).

As a partial illustration of this device, I might draw attention to the key junctures of the elaborate introversion that unifies the form and highlights the semantic significance of the narrative's second scene (1:4–16): At the beginning (vv. 4–5) we are told of the vague but powerful "fear" *(y-r-')* that the mariners felt when YHWH "hurled" *(tul)* the great wind against them on the sea. They react appropriately (that is, for pagans) by "crying out" *(z-'-q)* in disparate and desperate prayer to their various tribal "gods" *('elohim)*. At the end of this pericope (vv. 14, 16), on the other hand, having heard and believed Jonah's revelation, the sailors "call out" *(q-r-')* for forgiveness for "hurling" the LORD's prophet overboard. Here they experienced a specific kind of religious fear, one directed solely towards YHWH (as named now by them) and which motivated them to perform very focused types of reverential ritual action. At the foregrounded central core of this introverted structure then (vv. 9–10a), we have Jonah's surprising and somewhat strange profession of faith (literally, his "fear"). It is verbally pointed to YHWH, and yet at the same time rather vague (perhaps deliberately so) in terms how the LORD actually related to the serious situation at hand. The theologically perceptive sailors, however, immediately realized what was going on and were struck with an overwhelming sense of fear—a sacred awe that Jonah himself should have experienced if he really believed the words he had just uttered.

6.5.4 Text projection

The preceding passage also illustrates the role of recursion and variation in effecting discourse projection, that is, in helping to distinguish and to display the diverse areas of special semantic importance within the narrative. Obviously, not all of the persons, places, objects, events, and circumstances in an account are of equal prominence. Therefore, a good narrator will always verbally spotlight the selected items that he wants his audience to pay special attention to if they wish to perceive the point of his message— *why* he is telling them this particular story. Reiteration is one of the most common and effective literary tools in this regard. In chapter one it serves to highlight the peak in the *narrative* action that occurs in the final verses of

6.5 The rhetorical significance of recursion and variation in Hebrew narrative

the second scene, for example, through the mention of YHWH (5 times in vv. 14–16). As suggested above, the repetition of key theological terms also functions to emphasize the *thematic* nucleus that is situated in the center of this pericope (v. 9), a proposition that is significantly amplified later in 4:2. One more locus of special significance that is sometimes distinguished in literary discourse (whether prosaic or poetic) is that of climax. This refers to a certain apex of emotive intensity and/or dramatic tension that appears to be marked in the text. Again in chapter one, we might note the battery of /m-/-initial questions that the sailors bombard Jonah with both before and after the nucleus of v. 9. The climactic query is rhetorical in nature (as is often the case) and is set off by itself: "What have you done?!" (v. 10a).

Frequently, of course, one or another of these three areas of projection will coincide, with consequently greater import in relation to the author's main message. The thematic nucleus and emotive climax of Jonah's psalm, for example, converge in the final two words: "Salvation [belongs] to the LORD!" (2:10). Its contrastive, action-centered peak, on the other hand (indeed, many psalms give evidence of such a semi-narrative progression), occurs a few lines earlier in the sudden shift from downward (death) to upward motion (life) in relation to the sea (and psychologically, if not spiritually, to YHWH as well): "And you, O LORD my God, brought my life up from the Pit!" (2:6b). In these two passages then a repetition of the divine name helps mark the crucial points of projection, thus continuing an emphasis that was initiated in both the introduction to and the first line of the song (i.e., 2:2–3a). Intratextual recursion also functions to spotlight the close of the book where culminating repeated references to both the size ("more than two hundred thousand"; cf. 3:3b) and the nature ("humans," "those who do not know ...," "beasts"; cf. 3:5b, 8) of those living in "the great [now saved] city of Nineveh" (cf. 1:2; 3:2), coupled with a semantically reduplicative, ascensive manner of argumentation on the part of the LORD (4:10–11), would seem to indicate a final grand convergence of peak, climax, and nucleus.

The notion of discourse projection may be associated with that of semantic accentuation, a term that is normally applied to text segments of a more restricted co-textual range or scope. Thus, the author utilizes some form of repetition, deviation, and/or defamiliarization to *foreground*, to *emphasize*, or to *intensify* specific aspects of the message that happen to be uppermost in his thinking—or narrating—at any given stage of the story's development. These three notions are very closely related of course, and it is not always possible to differentiate between them in relation to the particular passage at hand. Nevertheless, the distinction does seem to be valid, one that has some basis at least in the way in which we both prepare and process narrative texts, and probably other types of discourse as well.

Foregrounding (highlighting) involves the use of repetition to focus upon and/or to attract the listener/reader's attention to certain noteworthy aspects of the narrative event progression *(plot)*. One of the most diagnostic ways of marking (hence also of recognizing) the central storyline in Hebrew narration, for example, is to string together a series of verbs in the so-called *waw*-consecutive *(wayyiqtol)* construction. We see an instance of this sort of sequence immediately after the LORD's initial command to Jonah: "*and* he arose...*and* he went down...*and* he found...*and* he gave [paid]...*and* he went down..." (1:3—all in the space of a single verse, so quick was Jonah to leave the scene!). This would be a type of low-grade foregrounding, for though important to the development of the story, it constitutes the default mode of Hebrew narrative style and consequently is not a very prominent or attention-grabbing focusing technique.

Other poetic devices capitalize upon some form of variation to create a more conspicuous sort of foregrounding, such as the introduction of syntactic front-shifting, a full noun phrase, a (rhetorical) question, or a segment of direct speech. Nominal advancement to first place in an utterance (before the verb) is often employed, for example, to indicate the onset of a new compositional unit, i.e., paragraph/episode/section/etc. (e.g., "And Yahweh..." in 1:4) or the insertion of a parenthetical remark and/or temporal displacement (e.g., "And Jonah..." in 1:5b). General repetition is also used to spotlight the central character(s) of a story or a given episode/scene in the account. The different references to the deity, for example, clearly designate "YHWH-God" as the chief participant in the book as a whole (occurring almost three times more often than "Jonah"). On the other hand, the multitude of personal references in the psalm of chapter two suggests that the prophet was clearly preoccupied with himself, despite the fact that the text was ostensibly addressed to the LORD. A similar personal bias is evident in his complaint-prayer of 4:2–3. Characters that are foregrounded over the span of a paragraph unit are normally introduced by a full subject

6.5 The rhetorical significance of recursion and variation in Hebrew narrative 279

noun phrase in the first clause (not necessarily in sentence-initial position) and thereafter continue to occupy center-stage in the subject slot (usually in bound pronominal form) for a majority of the action utterances that follow. Alternatively, or conjunctively, they provide most of the direct speech within a particular segment of discourse., e.g., "the sailors" in 1:7–8 and "the men" in 1:13–16.

Emphasis in verbal discourse (narrative or otherwise) is generated through the use of recursion to accentuate some particular aspect of a text's *theme*. The different semantic facets or components of "great"ness *(g-d-l)*, for example, tend to merge and resonate with respect to one another as they reappear in different settings throughout the text as a way of emphasizing the book's main *chesed*-centered message, which is concentrated in passages such as 3:9–10, 4:2, and 4:11: What-(who-)ever is great in the eyes of Yahweh as far as their need of a merciful deliverance is concerned (2:9) ought to be equally important in the thinking of his people, and it should govern their behavior accordingly. The scope of this gracious concern includes everyone, even Israel's great heinous, implacable foe, i.e., Nineveh (3:3; 4:11). That was the crucial theological point which an ardent, ethnocentric nationalist like Jonah could not seem to grasp in spite of the LORD's patient instruction, indirectly (ch. 1) or overtly (ch. 4), whether by way of physical chastisement (4:8) or verbal rebuke (4:4, 9–11). As a result he fell, and his "descent"—psychological (in relation to himself, what he knew to be right), moral (in relation to the ship's crew), and spiritual (in relation to Yahweh)—is aptly emphasized by the repetition of *y-r-d* "go down" in chapter one (plus once more for good measure in 2:7). Similarly, but on a much smaller scale, certain reiterated terms are utilized to suggest what is topically central, either wholly or in part, within the scope of a specific (sub)paragraph, Jonah's "flight to Tarshish away from the presence of the LORD" in 1:3, for example, or the unknown "god[s]" in 1:5–6, or the "casting of lots" in relation to "the cause of this calamity" in 1:7–8, or the "calming down of the sea over against" the mariners in 1:11–12.

Finally, *intensification* involves the reduplication of a particular *lexical* item, whether a root, word, or phrase, to increase its particular semantic scope or force, e.g., size (large, small), quality (good, bad, etc.), diversity (many different kinds), and so forth, usually within the span of a single utterance or clause. The outstanding instance of this device in Jonah is manifested in the verbal cognate construction, as noted in section 6.3.1. Thus, the expression "the men feared a great fear" in 1:10 means that they were utterly terrified (cf. 1:16). Similarly, in the latter verse the "sacrificing of sacrifice[s]" and the "vowing of vows" may accentuate the nature of such reverent action in terms of quality (e.g., thoroughly committed vows, the best available sacrifices) or quantity (e.g., repeated sacrifices, reiterated vows). It should be noted that repetition may also be involved with the generation of emotive intensity as shown, for example, in the series of interrogatives of 1:8 (indicating an extremely agitated, irritated, and impatient [collective] frame of mind), or in Jonah's (angry) reiterative response to God's probing inquiry (4:9). The phonological recursion that is characteristic of alliteration and punning may also serve an intensifying purpose, as we see (hear) for example in the description of the amazing *qiqayon* plant which the LORD causes to grow so quickly over *(wayya'al me'al)* Jonah *(yonah)* to provide immediate shade *(lihyot tsel)* over his head *('al-ro'so)* and to give him some relief *(lehatsil lo)* from his physical and psychological discomfort (*mera'ato;* 4:6). Obviously, a certain auditory focusing effect is also active in this entire passage.

6.5.5 Text characterization

Participant characterization pertains to the manner in which the various personages (including God) mentioned in the story are portrayed and evaluated by the author—whether positively, negatively, or in a (relatively) neutral light. This feature is of course related to the overall narrative purpose and perspective as well as to the (implied) narrator's contextually specific point of view. In biblical literature the norm is for this general viewpoint to be objective (third-person), subdued (unobtrusive), reliable (with regard to the facts being reported), and omniscient (concerning the breadth and scope of knowledge available), which is of course in keeping with its "inspired" authorship.

But strangely enough, despite his potentially infinite knowledge, the narrator does not usually indulge in or interject much personal description, opinion, or commentary on the various characters and their actions. He prefers to allow individuals (and corporate groups, such as the Ninevites) to reveal positive and/or negative beliefs, values, attitudes, motives, and goals

6.5 The rhetorical significance of recursion and variation in Hebrew narrative

of and for themselves. This may be effected both in what they actually do and by what they say, perceive (e.g., "And God saw...," 3:10), or think, i.e., interior monologue, which in Hebrew narrative is not always clearly distinguished from actual articulated speech (e.g., Jonah's thanksgiving prayer in the belly of the great fish). Furthermore, what personal description there is, whether physical, psychological, or—most important—ideological, is typically provided "not to enable the reader to visualize the character, but to enable him to situate the character in terms of his place in society...to tell what kind of a person he is" (Berlin 1983:36). Such a characterization is always made, I might add, from the perspective of Yahweh and in relation to his divinely instituted instructions and associated covenantal obligations (torah), both religious and interpersonal.

In any case, the twin techniques of recursion and variation are also prominent in the development and definition of character—as far as this is allowed to go in a given account. In other words, the process of biblical characterization is highly selective in what it reveals about a person, whether hero or villain, and is generally kept subordinate to the controlling plot—which, in turn, serves the larger theological purpose of the work as a whole. As far as the book of Jonah is concerned, the nature of the central human character, namely, the prophet himself, is revealed primarily through repetition (+/- variation) coupled with the principle of contrast. According to Adele Berlin (1983:40):

> There are actually three types of contrast:
> 1) contrast with another character,
> 2) contrast with an earlier action of the same character, and
> 3) contrast with the expected norm.

All three varieties of contrast occur with respect to Jonah. The second type is most prominent in the parallelism that is manifested in his two commissioning accounts (chs. 1 and 3). The second time Jonah sets out and goes to Nineveh, that is, after doing the exact opposite on the first occasion and having experienced near disaster. Does this then suggest a change of heart or character? Not necessarily, for again the absence of any overt verbal response (3:3; cf. 1:3)—in contrast now to both the verbose psalm of praise to YHWH in chapter two and also to his vigorously expressed original objections to the LORD's mission (left implicit until 4:2)—would seem to imply that his fundamentally self-centered, antithetical attitude had not changed. The second time around he simply acquiesced, or worse, was sullenly forced along in the LORD's direction.[30]

Similarly, recursion with variation also highlights the contrast between Jonah's lyric promise to offer sacrifices and vows to the LORD (2:9), which to our knowledge he never fulfilled, and the pagan sailors' reverent completion of these same worshipful activities, whether right on board ship or once they finally reached safety on shore (1:16). A similar antithesis appears between the conspicuous penitential activities of the Ninevites (3:5–9) and Jonah's obstinate refusal even to admit that his attitude was wrong, or at least mistaken (4:9).

Finally, direct contrast with an expected prophetic norm is foregrounded intertextually in the fourth chapter as Jonah angrily exclaims his fervent desire to die (4:3, 8)—all because the foreign Ninevites, including their king, thoroughly repented (at least in terms of the divine knowledge that was available to them) and were consequently spared by YHWH. The prophet Elijah, on the other hand, also expressed such a morbid death wish (1 Kgs 19:4), but his plea was uttered in response to widespread apostasy among God's own people, including their reigning king and queen (1 Kgs 19:1–2, 10, 14). In sections 5.6–7, several suggestions will be made as to how plot-related characterization is integrally connected with the rhetorical devices of irony and enigma to enhance the expression of theme in biblical narrative and Jonah in particular.

6.5.6 Text presentation

Discourse presentation has to do with the presumed initial mode and medium of narrative transmission. As was suggested earlier, there can be little doubt that Jonah was specifically composed with a performative oral recital in mind. This would surely be (both then and now) the most effective way for its dramatic, didactic, declamatory, and (probably also) debatable point to be brought home—that is, with its diverse repetitions and its dynamic contrasts forcefully ringing in the ears of every listener. James Limburg suggests that "the repetition of words in written material quickly becomes monotonous, but in oral discourse the speaker can play upon the

---

[30] For this reason, the word "obeyed" (e.g., NIV, REB) may be a somewhat misleading translation in 3:3.

6.5 The rhetorical significance of recursion and variation in Hebrew narrative

repeated word or words, varying pitch, volume, and tempo for dramatic effect" (Limburg 1993:27).

Several other prominent qualities of this text would promote its suitability for public oral performance, in particular, the proportionately large amount of direct speech (i.e., nearly half of the total number of words) which features a relatively heavy concentration of questions (14 in all). There is also a great deal of intensive, graphic, rhythmic, and frequently emotive diction, as expressed especially in the picturesque figurative language of the psalm and the several heartfelt prayers for mercy—or death. Would the original audience have been able to recognize and interpret the significance of the many subtle deviations from the norms established by recursion? Certainly so, if the experience of contemporary oral-aural oriented societies is anything to go by, such as those found in many parts of Africa. In these situations, most if not all verbal communication takes place via the spoken word, and therefore the trained ears of those addressed are able to perceive the minute distinctions and precise phonological devices (e.g., alliteration and paronomasia) that would easily escape most modern-day, video-biased "listeners." The point is that more effort must be made to render the abundant, functionally significant rhetoric of the biblical message more ostensibly by increasing not only a translation's level of stylistic naturalness (in indigenous literary terms) but also the physical "readability" of the text itself (in terms of its published format).[31]

6.5.7 Text pluri-signification

The final general function of recursion and variation that is prominently exhibited in the book of Jonah relates to what I have termed discourse "pluri-signification." This refers to a characteristic "double-articulation" of sense and/or significance that is realized in most, if not all, instances of outstanding and memorable traditional oral art. In other words, the lexical and grammatical surface of the text conveys an overt, obvious, or literal meaning and, in addition, one or more levels of deeper, less apparent, nonliteral meaning. The latter in turn may represent simply a more effective (dynamic, graphic, idiomatic, forceful, etc.) way of expressing the thoughts and emotions of the manifest discourse. Alternatively—more importantly

---

[31] For some suggestions in this latter regard, see Wendland 1993b.

and probably also more commonly—the underlying level of semantic reference may extend throughout a given pericope (e.g., a parable), or even the composition as a whole, thereby transmitting a distinct message, one which reinforces, complements, augments, or contrasts with that of the narrative surface. This is of course the great hermeneutical question of Jonah: Is there just one main message, and if so, where does it reside— in the narrative surface, on some deeper level, or simultaneously on both planes of communication? This question will be taken up in subsequent sections of this chapter.

A more obvious and limited instance of such pluri-signification occurs where so-called figurative language is involved, e.g., metaphor, metonymy, hyperbole, and so forth. Poetry is the preferred domain of these figures of speech—for example, "the *heart* of the seas" (v. 3) or "the *bars* of the earth" (v. 6) in chapter two. But such semantic embellishment is by no means absent from skilled prose writing, e.g., "*the ship thought/planned* (i.e., threatened—personification) to break up" (1:4), but later "the *sea stood still from its raging*" (1:15) at the covert command of YHWH.

Distinctly rhetorical figures are often comprised of a secondary level of meaning that is quite different from that which the surface textual forms would imply. In the case of a rhetorical question, for example, the intention of the utterance is not so much semantic as it is pragmatic in nature. In other words, the point is not to elicit information from the addressee, but rather to convey something to him/her in a more emphatic, yet tactfully indirect, way, e.g., "Is it right for you to be so angry?" (4:4) = "Surely you have no right to be so angry!" Thus, the ending of the book is not as "open-ended," "incomplete," or "improperly" closed as some commentators have concluded.[32] Indeed, by the very nature of this sort of question, YHWH has emphatically— and we might add, convincingly—concluded his case. It remains for the obedient reader/hearer to trustingly accept the LORD's theological position and with that also to faithfully put into personal practice the implied divine evaluation and imperative. Disagreement can only lead to disaster, as evidenced by the unhappy experience of Jonah. Douglas Stuart has nicely summarized the pertinent implications on the negative side of the issue: "Anyone who replies 'Why is this such an important question?' has not understood the message. Anyone who replies 'No!' has not believed it" (Stuart 1987:435).

---

[32] For example, see Crouch 1994:106–107, 110.

In the next two sections of this study I focus upon a pair of non-literal rhetorical devices that seem to be particularly important from a functional perspective in the book of Jonah and which are generated primarily by the artful interaction of the two stylistic techniques of recursion and deviation as described in sections 6.2–4, namely, irony and enigma. Indeed, a major part of the enigma of Jonah lies in the many instances of irony that it manifests: Why is this particular rhetorical feature so prominent in the text and how is it effected? On the other hand, one of the prominent ironies of this narrative is its polyvalent—hence generally "enigmatic"—expression of theme. In fact, a certain receptor constituency might be in total agreement with one possible expression of the book's message (e.g., the need for a universal, cross-cultural communication of the necessity of repentance before Yahweh), but find themselves in either overt or implicit conflict with an important corollary (e.g., this life-saving message is for everyone, even your greatest national/ethnic/religious enemy!).

6.6 On the incisiveness and inclusiveness of irony in Jonah

There is no doubt among most commentators that irony does occur in the book of Jonah. The debate rather concerns the extent to which this device is manifested—in a relatively few isolated instances or virtually throughout the text.[33] Of course the issue of occurrence and distribution cannot be decided without first determining a definition for the term "irony," and here one encounters additional difficulty because there are a number of proposals to consider in relation to several posited sub-types.[34] But in general we can say that irony typically involves some critical conflict, contradiction, incongruity, contrast, or contra-expectation, whether overt or covert. Such a focal disjunction pertains to two (or more) distinct levels of knowledge, speech, or behavior, and with respect to two (or more) individuals or groups.

Concerning its rhetorical operation then, we note that irony usually functions to convey—either explicitly, or more commonly, in an implicit

---

[33] As representatives of these two extremes, we have respectively Stuart 1987:437–438 and Good 1981:41.

[34] These cannot all be discussed and evaluated here (cf. Wendland 1995:ch. 6) Useful definitions and biblical illustrations of related literary tropes (e.g., sarcasm and satire) are found in Good 1981:26–28.

manner—a certain measure of criticism that may or may not be perceptible or even accessible to the one(s) being criticized (or as it were, "ironized"). However, the "burden of recognition," as Edwin Good puts it, rests with the primary receptor(s) of this barbed form of pluri-signification, that is, "the discovery of the relation between the ironist's 'is' [i.e., pretense] and his 'ought' [i.e., reality]" (Good 1981:31). Thus, the crucial implication for effective literary communication and analysis is that a partial or complete "failure of this recognition" will lead to a "misunderstanding of the ironist's criticism" (Good *loc. cit.*) and the point s/he was trying to make, whether major or minor in relation to the intended message as a whole.

For the sake of classification, I will distinguish between two general types of irony, namely, textual, which places special emphasis on some incongruous or contrastive use of language, and contextual, which deals with the unexpected import of events in general or the inappropriate, incriminating, or self-destructive behavior of certain narrative participants in relation either to each other or to the larger plot (story line). *Textual* irony, in turn, may be either "verbal" or "evocative" in nature: The *verbal* variety is grounded in the discourse itself (direct or indirect speech) and a double meaning (one sense being critical or foregrounded) that is conveyed by what one character says to another, whether deliberately or in ignorance. *Evocative* irony, on the other hand, is effected by a certain prominent opposition or antithesis that becomes apparent as a result of what is said (or narrated) at a given point in the account as distinct from a later (intratextual) citation or some familiar intertextual reference.

Similarly, *contextual* irony is twofold: It may be *dramatic* where a sharp contrast is drawn between two (or more) characters, or when there is a significant discrepancy between what a certain character supposes reality or the truth of a matter to be and what the enlightened audience knows it actually is by virtue of what the narrator (or implied author) has revealed to them. *Situational* irony, on the other hand, occurs when there is presented a sequence of events, a combination of circumstances, or a final outcome that is the opposite of what might be expected or considered just and/or appropriate in relation to some conventional pattern or accepted standard (including a moral or religious norm). The four sub-categories proposed above (i.e., verbal, evocative, dramatic, and situational) are not necessarily mutually exclusive, and there may well be a certain amount of merging or overlapping with respect to their concrete realization within a given story. Moreover, differences in the details of classification will inevitably arise depending on one's point of view and the particular nature of the analysis that was carried out. The purpose of these four distinctions is simply to sharpen one's perception of the great depth, diversity, and multi-functionality of the operation of irony in biblical narrative, with the book of Jonah being the particular focus of attention.

6.6.1 Textual irony

6.6.1.1 Verbal

In the case of verbal irony, one individual communicates an element of critical dissatisfaction, disapproval, rebuke, or censure to another person (or group) by means of some overstatement or understatement. This discrepancy between what is said (i.e., the ironic *vehicle*) and what is actually meant (i.e., the *tenor*) is invariably marked, that is, overtly "cued," within the textual surface (or the contextual setting) in some way—gesturally (e.g., by a distinctive facial expression), phonologically (e.g., through vocal modulation or intonation), lexically (e.g., by selective reiteration or punning), semantically (e.g., use of an incongruous collocation of terms or hyperbole), and/or morpho-syntactically (e.g., by means of a rhetorical question or a shift in word order). Verbal irony is most prominent in the pair of dialogic confrontations involving YHWH and Jonah recorded in chapter four. The ironic sequence begins with a reversal of the divine messenger formula: Now, it is "the word of Jonah [that comes] unto YHWH" (4:2; cf. 1:1; 3:1). Later, when the LORD responds to Jonah's request for death (4:3–4), he ironically foregrounds the impropriety of his prophet's attitude and value system by reiterating the root "good" (*tov*) in an emphatic, compound verb construction:

> **Jonah:** "My death is good…" (i.e., because you spared Nineveh)
> **YHWH:** "Is your burning [anger] good?" (i.e., since I spared Nineveh)
> The obvious answer to the LORD's rhetorical question is emphatically "no!"
> This ironic interchange continues in chiastic sequence in verses 8–9:
> **YHWH:** "Is your burning [anger] good?" (i.e., since the plant was destroyed)
> **Jonah:** "My burning [anger] is good, (especially if it leads to) my death"
>   (i.e., because of the plant).

The LORD's reiterated query might be more pointedly rendered: "What right do you have to be angry?" (Stuart 1987:435)—i.e., "You have absolutely no right at all!" since you are in effect presuming to sit in judgment over the Supreme Judge and "the LORD God of heaven who made the sea and the dry land" (1:9) and who even saved you from the sea by causing the fish to vomit you out onto dry land (2:9–10). Thus, the tragic irony of Jonah's inconsistent loyalty to *his* God (2:1; cf. 2:8) is made abundantly clear.

Jonah's unrepentant and hyperbolic response then leads up to the LORD's final word on the matter—a devastating, albeit generally-stated, rebuke which in addition to the *a fortiori* mode of argumentation also features another prominent instance of "verbal" irony (God—4:10; **YHWH**—4:11). This usage, in contrast to Jonah's approach, is based rather upon subtle iterative understatement: Jonah "pitied" *(chus)*, i.e., was deeply grieved about, the plant; YHWH, on the other hand, "pitied," i.e., relented and did not destroy, the entire city of Nineveh. It is possible, as Wolff suggests,[35] that another level of irony is also present in the LORD's initial reference to Jonah's "pity": In fact, the man was not really sorry about the fate of this puny plant at all; instead, he was extremely bitter because of his frustrated hope of seeing the great city destroyed and was perhaps also upset over his potentially ruined prophetic reputation. According to this viewpoint, Jonah's self-pity extended to a sense of shame and apprehension over a likely loss of prestige when it would become known back home that he had been God's chosen instrument in bringing about a deliverance of his nation's worst enemies!

6.6.1.2 *Evocative*

Textual irony of the evocative kind, namely, that which is based on a prominent correspondence or a distinct contrast in relation to some other passage of Scripture, is generated on a number of occasions throughout the book. There are both intratextual and intertextual instances of this, many of which have already been commented on above. Virtually all of the repeated sequences of lexical items involve two levels of meaning at some stage or another depending on which words they happen to be collocated with. The irony that is inherent in the illogical reasoning concerning Jonah's "anger" *(ch-r-h)* as contrasted with his "pity" *(chus)* in the preceding example is of manifest thematic relevance.

---

[35] Wolff 1986:173; this interpretation is disputed by Trible 1994:218.

6.6 On the incisiveness and inclusiveness of irony in Jonah

Use of this device becomes apparent at the very beginning of the narrative as Jonah's continual physical "going down" *(y-r-d)* in flight from the command of YHWH—first to Joppa (1:3), then into a ship (1:3), and finally down "below deck" (1:5)—may be viewed as a parallel to his moral and spiritual descent away from positive fellowship with his God, as he himself suggests, but does not openly admit, in his psalm (2:6). Jonah's estrangement in this regard is intimated by his self-(I)-centered confession of 1:9, i.e., *'anoki*...YHWH...*'ani*. Even a common adjective like *gadol* "large/great/important" is skillfully incorporated by the author into his all-embracing ironic network. Everything characterized as "great" in the account becomes so only by being directly or indirectly associated with the purpose and activity of YHWH, who does not himself require any such augmentative attribution (Wilt 1992:259). Even the fish, once it has completed its divine mission, is no longer termed great (2:10). The only exception to this pattern is negative (and verbal) in nature, occurring with reference to what the rebellious and irreverent Jonah was not able to do—that is, he could not even "make great" an insignificant and helpless plant (4:10)!

Evocative irony of an *inter*textual type is also quite prevalent throughout the story, as we have seen. Several important instances involving the nature and role of the prophetic office were noted in Part One. For example, the expected response to the divine command "Arise and go..." (1:2) is immediately "And he arose and went" (e.g., Elijah—1 Kgs 17:9–10; Jeremiah—Jer 13:4–5). To be sure, Jonah "arises" (1:3), but the audience may well have been shocked to hear that he does so only "to flee ... from the presence of YHWH!" The surprise and potential significance of that initial reaction is underscored later when on the second occasion Jonah dutifully (but also silently) obeys "according to the word of YHWH" (3:2). He preaches the divinely assigned message (at least the choicest part from his point of view): "Just forty days and Nineveh will be overturned. "Here the key verb *h-p-k* evokes a strong intertextual reminiscence of the fate of Sodom and Gomorrah (e.g., Gen 19:25, 29; Deut 29:23; Isa 13:19; Jer 49:18; Lam 4:6; Amos 4:11), yet it also semantically embraces within itself "the irony of reversal" (Trible 1994:190). Thus, contrary to all (certainly Jonah's) expectation, "the men of Nineveh believed in God" (3:5), and the verbal phrase found here *('-m-n b-)* is used elsewhere in the Hebrew Scriptures only with reference to God's people Israel. The outcome for Jonah was a great personal tragedy and a psychological disaster, one that left him longing for immediate death at the hands of his LORD (4:3). The horrible experience was exactly like that of his illustrious predecessor Elijah (1 Kgs 19:4)—but ironically, for just the opposite reason: Jonah desired self extermination on account of the tremendous success of his testimony—Elijah, on the other hand, due to the apparent lack of it (1 Kgs 19:10).

6.6.2 Contextual irony

6.6.2.1 Dramatic

Turning now to contextual (eventive, stative, circumstantial) irony of the dramatic variety, we take note of several of the thematically pertinent character contrasts that develop as the story unfolds. These examples, all of which spotlight Jonah's actions and attitudes in relation to that of the other narrative participants, are usually reinforced by textual irony as described above. But there does seem to be an added dimension present that serves to enhance the book's overall message, particularly its ideological import. Jonah refuses to go and "call out" *(q-r-')* to despicable foreigners God's message of judgment (1:3), but a friendly pagan sailor has to encourage him to "call out" to his God for deliverance (1:6) along with all his heathen shipmates (1:5):

> Thus the call words are repeated, but in an ironic fashion, meaning...different things to Jonah (and the reader), who hear in them God's original command repeated, and to the captain, who intends only that Jonah pray to his God. (Magonet 1983:17)

Similar instances of the language of traditional Israelite religious piety emanating from the lips of heathen speakers occur elsewhere in the book. The mariners, for example, later call out to the LORD (now) to forgive them for putting into effect the judicial decision of the lot they believed to be divinely inspired, as attested to by the guilty party himself (1:7, 12, 14). The sailors' reverent demeanor and worshipful behavior (1:16), no matter how ignorantly motivated in relation to YHWH's full covenantal requirements, certainly contrasts with the words and deeds of the LORD's chosen prophet, who knows the right answers (e.g., 1:9), but seems so oblivious to their pragmatic implication that he apparently cannot put them into meaningful

6.6 On the incisiveness and inclusiveness of irony in Jonah

practice in relation to his fellow human beings anywhere in the account. As Good observes (1981:54):

> [Jonah] congratulates himself that it is no idol to whom he prays (v. 9), for idolatry would be the abandonment of covenantal loyalty (*chesed*, v. 8). Yet that loyalty is precisely what Jonah abandons...

In case anyone did not get the point, it is reiterated even more forcefully through Jonah's subsequent interaction with the inhabitants of Nineveh. His utmost desire is to see God punish them with complete judgment and destruction (3:4), while they wish only the bare minimum of divine mercy (3:8-9). Accordingly, the great king penitently humbles himself by "sitting down" *(y-sh-b)* in the dust (3:6) and fervently pleads to God to "turn [from] his anger" *(shub...'appo*, 3:9), whereas Jonah self-righteously sits down (4:5) for the sole purpose of watching God bring "evil" *(ra'ah)* upon the whole city (3:10). In his opinion, therefore, it was a great evil that the LORD did not act according to his prejudicial personal will (4:1-2). An ironically trenchant transformation has thereby taken place: The evil that is offensive to the LORD is no longer that of Nineveh (1:2), but rather that exhibited by his own petulant prophet! Accordingly, Jonah's subsequent prayer over the city bitterly laments the fact that YHWH actually did see fit to "take compassion" *(n-ch-m)* upon its people. The king, on the other hand, like the captain before him (1:6), can only bring himself to appeal very indirectly to God to take compassion so that "we (himself included) are not destroyed" *(lo' no'bed)*. The monarch fears an outpouring of the "wrath" *('ap)* of God (3:9), but Jonah complains when the LORD's great "wrath" is withheld (4:2). Indeed, Jonah appears not to fear the punitive displeasure of God at all, but peevishly demonstrates his "anger" *(charah)* over the loss of a divinely provided plant and what he felt was some well deserved physical comfort (4:8-9). One contrast thus resonates with the next to highlight the tragic irony of a man (in fact, a whole class of like-minded individuals) who had already graciously experienced the abundant mercy of God, but who would selfishly begrudge it to others who were not in his (their) favor.

Contextually based dramatic irony may also be generated by a selective lack of knowledge attributed to certain characters within the plot. According to Webster's Dictionary[36] there is a fundamental contrast "between what a

---

[36] Victoria Neufeldt, ed. *Webster's New World Dictionary of American English*, Third college edition (Cleveland and New York: Webster's New World, 1988), 714.

character thinks the truth is, as revealed in a speech or action, and what an audience or reader knows the truth to be." Throughout the first half of chapter one, for example, the audience—as well as Jonah—know the reason for the terrible storm, but the mariners do not. This irony (and partial enigma; see below) is resolved in an emotionally pleasing manner (for those who do not have the same racial or religious bias as Jonah) as the crew gradually comes to a realization of the ultimate divine cause and then make an appropriate heartfelt cultic response. The case of Nineveh is somewhat different, but as suggested above, the positive direction in which events are headed is clearly indicated (to the Scripturally literate) by the elaborate, evocative penitential terminology that is used in the summary of 3:5. In both instances, Jonah's problem does not really involve any ignorance on his part; it is rather a basic misunderstanding of (or a refusal to understand) the central theological principle concerning the operation of divine *chesed* "steadfast love" (2:9). YHWH was desirous of demonstrating his gracious deliverance to all individuals and peoples (4:2); his mercy was not ethnically restricted to members of the long-favored nation of Israel.

The final example of dramatic irony is foregrounded by means of the text-temporal displacement proposed in chapter four (should this hypothesis be accepted; cf. the argument in 6.3.3). Thus, Jonah camps just outside the city (4:5) after preaching his short sermon of judgment (3:4) in hopeful anticipation of a positive result—from his jaundiced perspective, i.e., "to see what would happen to the city." The audience already realizes that the eventual outcome has turned out to be contrary to his wishes (3:10)—ironically even Jonah himself knows, that is, if the literal surface sequence of the narrative is followed (4:1–4). This makes his subsequent behavior sound even more irrational (4:5ff.) and serves to heighten the unrighteousness of his unacceptable moral and religious position in that he would drastically limit the LORD's expression of saving mercy.

The temporal displacement manifested at 4:2 makes possible an interesting reversal of the device of dramatic irony. In this case it is the audience who lacks a vital piece of information which is available to a narrative participant (cf. "enigma" below). They did not realize that Jonah had actually protested quite vigorously to the LORD about his mission to Nineveh at the very beginning when he received his call (1:2). That explains his subsequent un-prophetlike behavior—at least partially, for Jonah never comes right out and says that he hated the Ninevites (or their doings) so much that he did not want YHWH to give them even a chance to repent (knowing that if they did, they would receive forgiveness according to the divine nature). The withholding of this vital speech act until the latter portion of the story gives listeners a more positive picture of Jonah throughout—and the impression that he was acting more by natural instinct than deliberate prejudice. This effectively keeps the Jonah-vs.-YHWH conflict more in the background until it can be highlighted later by way of contrast, once the Ninevite issue has been happily resolved. The tragic nature of Jonah's fundamental character "flaw" (*hamartia*, i.e., proud, ethnocentric prejudice) is also dramatically heightened and given such prominence that it becomes the basis for the book's central message. The didactic irony underlying much of what he has spoken previously in the narrative is therefore emphasized through retrospection. For example, "his complaint about Yahweh's sparing the city suggests that his earlier confession was mere heartless orthodoxy, intended only to appease God" (Woodward 1993:353). Furthermore, his enumeration of the (now) offensive attributes of YHWH in 4:2 only magnifies his own guilt, for he himself had already been a happy beneficiary of the LORD's lovingkindness *(chesed)*, a fact which he lauded so poetically (yet superficially) in his psalm (2:9).

6.6.2.2 *Situational*

The situational variety of contextual irony is the most general perhaps, and hence also the potentially most inclusive category. It is activated, so to speak, whenever a "character reacts in a way contrary to that which is appropriate or wise" (Preminger and Brogan 1993:635) or when there is "a combination of circumstances or a result that is the opposite of what is or might be expected or considered appropriate" (Webster 1988:714). Jonah's playing the role of the prophetic antitype in such a blatant manner is an obvious case in point: After receiving the characteristic divine call, he promptly heads off in the opposite direction—to Tarshish, the virtual end of the world—without so much as a word of protest, explanation, or argument (thus, the account is constructed to sound, 1:2–3). While on his contrary way then, he receives a lecture on personal piety from a pagan sea captain (1:6), a character who would not normally be known for religious reverence. Shortly thereafter, this poor excuse for a man of God sanctimoniously proclaims his faith in the LORD of creation, who made the [very] sea that he is presently utilizing in his vain bid to escape (1:9). Having transformed the ocean into an awesome instrument of punishment, YHWH turns right around and appoints one of its mysterious creatures as a vehicle for effecting a divine rescue operation (1:17).

There Jonah sits—"for three days"—the same amount of time it is estimated that his Nineveh crusade would be expected to take (3:3). Yes, he does "pray," but his is a prayer that manages to avoid the real theological issue as far as he personally was concerned—namely, his obstinate rebellion against the LORD. Instead, he blithely speaks about the public performance of ritualized religious service (2:9) in the "holy temple" (2:4), which he had just recently been trying to get as far away from as possible! Even Jonah's poetic technique fails him, for he intones his exultant song of thanksgiving in the [3+2] rhythm of a lament (which is also suggested by the *hithpa'el* form of the introductory verb *p-l-l* "pray" (4:2) (cf. Trible 1994:162).

One can proceed in this manner throughout the entire narrative; just about anything Jonah says or does has some subtle ironic and an associated thematic implication, one (or more) that is based on a crucial textual or intertextual contrast or incongruity. The same is true of a number of quotations which emanate from other members of the cast. For example, in their desperate prayer to the God whom they now know as "YHWH," the mariners "reveal a theological good sense and a moral scrupulousness that provides a sardonic contrast to that of YHWH's prophet" (Brichto 1992:71). They optimistically refer to Jonah as being a "man...[of] innocent blood"— when everyone hearing the story knows that just the opposite is the case (i.e., a certain measure of dramatic irony is also involved here). Similarly, the pagan king of Nineveh interceedingly—and also "prophetically"—prays for compassion using language (3:8–9) that God himself later seems to indirectly appropriate in appointing a complete reprieve (3:10).

The result is an underlying accumulation of ironic signification that progressively builds to a peak of incisive intensity in the final chapter: God spares the great city of Nineveh and thus provokes Jonah to a great anger (3:10–4:1). His subsequent prayer is another incongruous antitype: Although he uses all the right words, Jonah does not praise YHWH's all-encompassing merciful attributes; on the contrary, he critically laments them (4:2). He does not thank the LORD for saving so many lives (as he did when his own *nepesh* was at stake, e.g., 2:8); instead, he asks for immediate death to end his sense of shame, misery, frustration, and failure (4:3). According to the book's present arrangement, Jonah later goes into a peevish funk over the scorching of an ephemeral plant (4:9-10), whereas he could not give the slightest care about the thousands of ignorant human beings clinging to worthless idols (2:8) whom the LORD himself was greatly concerned about and had given Jonah the privilege of ministering to in their tremendous spiritual need (4:11).

The superfluity of irony in the book thus makes it virtually impossible for concerned receptors today to hear/read Jonah as a mere story, or more significantly, as a simple historical account only. Rather, this prominent rhetorical device acts as a continuous cue that the narrative is meant to be understood on another, a more deeply personal level—namely, as an incisive *prophetic preachment*: What about that germ of "Jonah" in me—or in my society? To what extent does his tragedy reflect a similar state of affairs in my/our own thinking, speech, and behavior?

6.6.3 Functions of irony

There are three special purposes of irony that may be briefly noted in addition to the more context-specific instances noted above. They operate in rhetorical concert to enhance the author's principal didactic and paraenetic purposes in bringing his prophetic message more forcefully home to the hearts and minds of all listeners (and readers). First of all, irony appears to lend a perceptible element of *humor* to the account. Though some commentators do not see this (e.g., Stuart 1987:438), it seems apparent—at least to most modern critics—that the narrative does have its lighthearted moments. There is Jonah's ignominious exit from the great fish (2:10), for example, in immediate answer, or so it sounds, to his solemn declaration that "salvation belongs to the LORD!" (2:9). Jonah's all-too-typical angry reply to YHWH's ironic inquiry about his anger over the desiccated castor-bean plant adds a humorous touch to an otherwise emotively heavy concluding chapter (4:9). While one would perhaps hesitate to go far as to characterize Jonah as "a laughable figure...[who] is held up to scorn by being rendered ridiculous" (Ryken 1992:337), the poetically astute and literarily aware listener does sense a subdued, gentle sort of wit that contributes to this tragi-comic account a perceptible element of both human interest, appeal, and realism (Brichto 1992:73).

This carefully controlled humorous tone serves to render the character of Jonah in more natural—hence believable—terms. His soul-searching experience therefore becomes more universally and personally applicable, and cannot be simply dismissed as a figment of the fantastic, the parabolic, or the esoteric. This is a feature that concerns the second general purpose of irony in the story, namely, to encourage a fuller *psychological engagement* of the audience as part of a total, rhetorically conditioned communication event. In other words, the restrained, alternating satiric and tragic tone that unobtrusively colors this historical narrative tends to "criticize [Jonah's] failure to reach high but reachable ideals, involving the reader in a moving story that mixes scornful looks and smiles" (Woodard 1993:357). Jonah's failure and frustration thus becomes potentially (or actually) our own as the flashes of his down-to-earth, fallible human nature periodically shine forth throughout the account: his headstrong desire for independence, his deeply set but thinly disguised ethnic prejudices, his self-righteous questioning of the specific plan and purpose of God, his fickle and situationally determined religious moods, and above all, his predominantly self-centered perspective on life—and death.

And finally, pervasive irony such as we have in Jonah is used for the purpose of *foregrounding* key aspects of the book's message as a whole. This becomes evident in the sequence of contrasts and incongruities that Jonah leaves in his wake as he is swept from one unhappy narrative experience to the next. It is his perverted attitude towards the LORD's ideal of *chesed*-love which is thereby made prominent as part of the overall didactic intention. God is speaking to his people in and through the person of his chosen prophet. Even that portion of the text most disputed as to its originality and appropriateness may be vindicated with reference to this fundamental thematic principle. Stuart explains (1987:473):

> Far from being extraneous, therefore, the psalm is actually pivotal. The hypocrisy of Jonah's attitude in ch. 4 is muddled without the psalm. The psalm celebrates Yahweh's deliverance (cf. Exod 15; Judg 5), and thus fixes an ironic contrast: Jonah's obedience (3:3) is won by mercy; but Jonah cannot abide the thought that Nineveh's obedience could be won the same way!

Just as Jonah had greatly rejoiced to be himself a partaker of YHWH's wonderful act of merciful deliverance (2:9), he should have been overjoyed to see an entire city-state repent and receive new life (3:10), even its lowly livestock (3:8, 4:11)! But his reaction was the polar opposite, manifested in brutish, racist, irrational (i.e., for any follower of the LORD) pique (4:9, 4). Irony thus heightens the impact of the double-standard of judging that Jonah would impose upon the world at large—the magnanimous divine will being rendered subservient to his own introverted perspective.

6.7 Enigma and the ever-unfolding "mystery" of Jonah

Recursion and deviation in narrative discourse are utilized in the creation of irony, as we have seen, and also a closely related device designated here as "enigma." I am using this word in a somewhat wider sense than its popular (dictionary) reference to a certain phenomenon (speech, behavior, natural state, or set of circumstances) that is distinctly ambiguous, perplexing, surprising, and seemingly inexplicable—or at least so it appears based upon one's initial and/or superficial sensory perception. I thus employ enigma as sort of a cover term to refer to the various *questions* and cognitive *cracks* which a skillfully composed narrative text (as opposed to one that is mediocre, or worse) deliberately creates in the listener's/reader's mind as s/he goes along. Such points of interrogation or disjunction are stimulated by the selection and arrangement of content as well as by the diverse literary and linguistic forms that are chosen to convey the message. They are intended to be "answered" or "patched," at least tentatively, by inference and anticipation, based upon what the text has already said and where it seems to be heading with regard to plot and theme. The importance of the opening scene in setting the stage for what follows and in shaping the initial expectations of the audience cannot be overestimated, for it is "the first step in the intentional production of meaning."[37]

It should be noted that these author-implanted gaps and queries are always related somehow to the point and purpose of his intended message *in its initial setting* (as closely as this may be determined on the basis of reliable research). The preceding contextual specification and its goal, although quite impossible to fully achieve in practice, is necessary in order to

---

[37] Edward Said, cited in Crouch 1994:104.

limit the scope of possible textual inquiry to that which is most relevant in terms of so-called "speech-act" theory—that is, to the primary "illocutionary" functions of a specific rhetorically governed discourse, plus any desired "perlocutionary" effects that are made explicit, either in the text itself or in some related (biblical) co-text.

It is clear that the less current receptors know about the original author, his envisaged or implied audience, the setting of communication, and of course the text itself, the *more* serious breaks in knowledge they will undoubtedly experience. As a result, there will be certain important thematically related questions that they will not even realize are implicit in the biblical text. On the other hand, they may seek answers to a number of queries that are either irrelevant to or not derived from the source-intended message. The larger the number of these conceptual lacunae, therefore, the greater the likelihood (albeit unintentional) of faulty exegesis and misinterpretation—that is, the lack of an acceptable or appropriate hermeneutical "closure" (Sternberg 1985:199). However, one must distinguish between those "gaps" which an author deliberately leaves in the text to create interest and to effect other rhetorical purposes (see below) and accidental "blanks" which are quite irrelevant to the telling of a story and the conveying of its intended message (ibid., 235–237).

In this connection it is important to distinguish also between a text's author-intended meaning (including content, connotation, impact, import, and purpose) in the initial event and its possible significance today, that is, in terms of contemporary relevance and practical application. The former, as noted earlier, is never completely determinable, but that is quite different from being open-ended as Jonah is often claimed to be.[38] The criterion of compositional intention, although to varying degrees hypothetical from a present-day perspective and therefore imperfect, is nevertheless the best basis or norm that we have for controlling the level of intrusive and potentially distorting subjectivism during the process of analysis, interpretation, and qualitative assessment. Certainly, the analytical tools at our disposal are inexact and our knowledge of the initial biblical context is inadequate, but at least these can provide some general parameters within which the missing pieces of the complete communication puzzle can gradually be filled in as new discoveries are made and as current studies build upon earlier ones to modify, correct, reinforce, or augment our overall understanding.

---

[38] One proponent of such "open-endedness" is Trible (1994:227).

6.7 Enigma and the ever-unfolding "mystery" of Jonah

Despite that fact that in the case of biblical literature we are dealing with a divinely inspired, omniscient author, we must also recognize that he never tells us the whole story, as it were. The information that he presents is always highly selective in terms of both form and content in the service of his higher communicative objectives. This situation is well described by Sternberg as follows (1985:186):

> From the viewpoint of what is directly given in the language, the literary work consists of bits and fragments to be linked and pieced together in the process of reading: it establishes a system of gaps that must be filled in. This gap-filling ranges from simple linkages of elements, which the reader performs automatically, to intricate networks that are figured out consciously...and with constant modifications in the light of additional information disclosed in later stages of the reading.

In the case of complex literary works and/or those that are contextually remote in terms of time, place, culture, and setting, this functionally important gap-filling process—or multiple system of processes (ibid., 222)—becomes much more tenuous in nature and dependent upon various text-analytical procedures for execution, evaluation, and validation. Such procedures would normally include a comprehensive discourse (generic, structural, lexical-semantic, propositional, and rhetorical) analysis of the larger macrotext (cf. Wendland 1996), complemented by a detailed stylistic and semantic close reading of the microtext (e.g., Trible 1994). These would naturally have to be coordinated with a careful study of the situational context that pertains both to the participants and events depicted within the narrative account and also to the (postulated) original author and his intended addressees in their distinct setting of inter-communication.

Before I discuss some of the prominent text-based queries that appear in Jonah, it may be helpful to draw attention to the following aspects of enigma. These are four partially overlapping distinctions that may be made with respect to its possible manifestation in narrative discourse. *Anticipation*, or "foreshadowing," is generated when a specific future outcome or turn in the plot's development is suspected, expected, or even more strongly looked forward to. It is set up or encouraged by something that is either said in the account (e.g., a veiled forward allusion) or done (e.g., a reiterated sequence or pattern of events). Jonah's blatant disobedience to the LORD's command

(1:3) introduces an obvious complication into the story. It produces a clear expectation that the book is dealing not only with the problem of manifest corporate "wickedness," i.e., that of Nineveh (1:2), but with two crises, including now also the silent individual rebellion of Jonah. Somewhat later, the communal conversion of all the heathen sailors on board Jonah's Tarshish-bound ship (1:16) at least hints that the fate of similarly pagan Nineveh might somehow be not as severe as originally suggested in the LORD's first commission. This anticipation is reinforced by the minor but significant changes in wording found in the second sending (3:2).

Suspense involves a much vaguer sort of anticipation. Some sort of resolution or outcome is awaited—accompanied by a greater or lesser level of interest, emotion, and/or excitement—but one does not know for certain what that will be, whether good or bad in relation to some major participant or enterprise. When Jonah is cast into the sea, for example, there is absolutely no clue concerning his present and future fate (1:14). The sudden calm that follows (1:15) only increases the suspense—or in this case, apprehension, for it definitely does not look good for Jonah! Not until "the LORD provides" (1:17) is this tension at least partially resolved—then held that way until Jonah finishes his song of thanksgiving and God decisively acts again (2:10). Later, when the prophet finally does preach his message of doom, one wonders what the effect is going to be on the Ninevites. However, his words certainly do not offer much reason for hope for the city (3:4).

Surprise occurs when there is an unexpected outcome or result, that is, when one's prior anticipation is either denied, contradicted, or altered (i.e., when a significant variation takes place instead). This usually stimulates varying degrees of worry, awe, or wonder in the listener or reader. The swallowing of Jonah by the mysterious great fish (1:17) is an obvious case in point. That is of course preceded by the extraordinary prayer meeting at sea, one which was organized by a foreign ship's crew but dedicated to the worship of Israel's God, YHWH (1:16). Similarly, though possibly anticipated by those who know the LORD, the complete conversion of the great pagan metropolis of Nineveh certainly comes as no small surprise to the audience (3:10). How could all this happen—indeed, so fully and so fast? But the important fact is that each of the unexpected eventualities just referred to could only have occurred as a result of determined divine intervention.

6.7 Enigma and the ever-unfolding "mystery" of Jonah

Finally, *curiosity* looks backward, whether near or far, instead of forward in time to something that does not quite make sense in the account due to insufficient evidence or information. It therefore arouses a certain amount of interest, attention, and the desire to know more because of the questions it raises in the listener's mind. Why, for example, do the sailors try their best to row back to shore even after they have learned by infallible lot that Jonah is the cause of the storm (1:13)? Surely this serves to highlight the contrast between their behavior and Jonah's even more, but their motive is not entirely clear—not until their subsequent prayer for forgiveness for committing the sacrilege of taking a human life at sea (1:14). Why does Jonah apparently proclaim his abbreviated message for merely a single day (3:4)? Is this yet another indication that he was performing his loathsome mission only with the greatest reluctance and an ongoing attitude of willful rebellion? Most important perhaps, why does God deal so patiently with such an unfaithful and disagreeable servant as Jonah? Certainly, he knew what the man said in his heart (4:2) at the very beginning, so why does the LORD wait so long to explicitly (verbally) teach him a lesson? That delay of course is just as much for our benefit as for Jonah's since we too are expected to learn from this report of his chastening experience.

To summarize: *surprise* involves definite contra-expectation while *curiosity* evokes a certain measure of ambiguity in relation to how things are turning out in a given story. *Anticipation* and curiosity, on the other hand, are related by virtue of the fact that they both stimulate the process of active hypothesis-formation in the listener's mind—the former in relation to what will happen; the latter in relation to what is or has already taken place. Another possible difference between the two is that, whereas anticipation is mainly concerned with future events, "most of the curiosity gaps bear on [character-related] internals—motives, schemes, personality..." (Sternberg 1985:284). *Suspense* differs from the other three in that it is derived from a relatively greater amount of uncertainty in the account, a lack of knowledge that is correspondingly of greater significance to the eventual outcome of the story. It is an innocent ignorance that often "escalates into a clash of hope and fear" which keeps the audience more physically attentive and emotionally involved (ibid., 264). Suspense, however, is always carefully held in check within Hebrew narrative, e.g., through a divine prophetic (hence certified and certain) prediction, in order to preserve the divine order of things, that is, "God's [sovereign, controlling] involvement in the world and the overriding need to publish his supremacy" (ibid., 267). That is the fundamental presupposition which guides both the author's presentation of the story of Jonah and the expected response of any audience or readership.

I will not attempt to sort out the preceding four distinctions in the overview and exemplification below. They have been introduced simply to indicate the relative complexity and also the importance of enigma as a narrative concept and an analytical tool. Taken together, the enigmatic elements of anticipation, curiosity, suspense, and surprise function in three closely related ways:

(a) **structurally,** to lend additional cohesion to an already tightly constructed account;
(b) **semantically,** to enhance and to emphasize certain key features of the book's multifaceted theme; and
(c) **rhetorically,** to add a greater measure of interest, impact, and appeal with respect to both the surface narrative and also its underlying message.

In the following discussion I organize the illustration of enigma in Jonah according to four principal (but not necessarily the only) areas of its possible realization within a biblical story, namely, in relation to plot, character, vocabulary, and message—or eventive, dramatic, lexical, and thematic enigma respectively. The four are interconnected and mutually impacting of course, but for the sake of this presentation they will be treated more or less separately.

6.7.1 Eventive enigma

Plot-related, or eventive, enigma is the most general, and therefore also the most inclusive in nature. It involves major uncertainties concerning the sequential, incident-based development of the narrative. The first and seemingly most important question pertaining to plot in Jonah is raised by what is reported in the book's opening verse: What will happen to Nineveh—or more specifically, how bad is its definitely implied punishment going to be (cf. Gen 18:21; Lam 1:22)? The suspense stimulated over this issue is renewed (after the shift in spotlight to Jonah in chapter two) and

6.7 Enigma and the ever-unfolding "mystery" of Jonah

heightened in more personal terms as the king of Nineveh utters his indirect but poignant plea: "Who knows ...?" (i.e., whether God will relent and spare his city or not, 3:9; cf. the captain's corresponding hope expressed in 1:6).

Notice that many issues relating to the cultural and historical background of the text are not included in this exegetical stage of analysis, e.g., What did the people of Nineveh do wrong? Or: why pick on the city of Nineveh? Such questions may well occur to an audience today (and thus have to be answered as the book is made contextually relevant and applied), but they would not have been necessary from the perspective of the original hearers/readers. Contemporaneous receptors would have known all too well about the wickedness that characterized Nineveh, the "great," and why it justly deserved its punishment, whatever that might turn out to be.

The narrative's second principal question is provoked by Jonah's unexpected behavior in 1:3: Why did he act in the way he did, to think he could run away from the LORD? And to leave without even a proper word of protest or complaint—what kind of behavior is that? Now what is going to happen to him as a result? How will he be divinely disciplined (which is surely a strong anticipation at this stage)? Here is where the device of textual displacement operates, i.e., the forward movement of Jonah's reply, which should have occurred at the end of verse two but is relocated for rhetorical effect to 4:2. This quote clarifies the query concerning Jonah's character (see below), but its removal from 1:2–3 also renders subsequent events in a somewhat more enigmatic light than they would otherwise have been. This reordering along with the palliative psalm of chapter two also serves to keep the YHWH-Jonah conflict in the background and subservient to the Ninevite issue until it suddenly resurfaces in the final chapter. The fact that the LORD's second call to Jonah with respect to Nineveh features so much lexical recursion suggests that the relationship between the two crises is still of major concern to the narrator—but how so, and what is the significance of Jonah's obedience on this occurrence?

Several other important eventive enigmas function to develop the primary pair just mentioned. The first chapter is especially suspenseful in this regard as the dramatic tension elicited by a relentless succession of plot-initiated interrogatives sweeps listeners along from start to finish: For example, what will happen to the ship in the storm (v. 4)? How long can Jonah keep silent about his guilt (v. 6)? Will the lot operate effectively to expose his deception (v. 7)? Will Jonah finally come clean when confronted with his crime (v.

8)? Would the sailors by force of might and sheer willpower be able to save their own lives—and Jonah's too (v. 13)? Will the casting of Jonah into the sea mark the end of his role in the narrative about Nineveh (v. 15)? What effect will the solemn "fear of the LORD" have upon the lives of the crew (v. 16)? This last question remains an enigma to the end, but its positive outcome as far as the sailors were concerned hints at a similar conclusion for the parallel episode in chapter three. Finally, what will happen to Jonah after he is swallowed by the great fish (v. 17)?

The suspense which has peaked by the close of the second scene is greatly relieved by the revelation that Jonah is only going to spend three days and three nights in submarine transit. But how was he going to escape this divinely appointed vessel of deliverance? And what would happen to him then? It is now clear that the respective fates of Jonah and the inhabitants of Nineveh were closely intertwined—but how, and to what end? The psalm of chapter two lessens the prevailing tension considerably, but this is only a lull in the storm of the story's persistent forward progression. It serves to intensify the presence of an increasingly important enigma concerning Jonah's character: what kind of messenger of the word of the LORD is he? How should he be assessed in personal, moral, or spiritual terms?

Before dealing specifically with this apparent prophet's character, it is necessary to mention what is undoubtedly the central *utterance*-related enigma in the book. This crucial speech act by Jonah is preceded and prepared for by two others which also have a certain enigmatic quality about them, namely, YHWH's command to "call out *against*" (1:2)/"call out *unto*" (3:2) the city of Nineveh. As argued earlier, the shift in preposition from *'al* to *'el*, coupled with the altered narrative/ plot setting, i.e., before and after the "storm" with Jonah, would suggest a change in both connotative tone (from negative to positive) and communicative intent, that is, from complete condemnation (1:2) to the possibility of a reprieve (3:2)—if true and total repentance would be forthcoming. In any case, the critical question is: What message did Jonah actually preach to the Ninevites? Did it faithfully represent what YHWH told him to say? Was it limited to the concise, rather cryptic, clause (four words) recorded in 3:4, or was there more? His proclamation does not indicate either *how* or *why* Nineveh was going to be "overturned," *who* was going to do this, and *what* the people could do in order to avoid this threatened catastrophe (the verb itself is suggestively

6.7 Enigma and the ever-unfolding "mystery" of Jonah

enigmatic in this regard. At any rate, circumstantial evidence derived from what is reported about Jonah in the rest of the story would indicate that he preached only the bare minimum of the message he was entrusted with and hoped for the worst. Nevertheless, ironically—and providentially—his words, whatever they were, had the effect of instigating a mass public display of repentance and a consequent divine pardon of the entire city.

6.7.2 Dramatic enigma

Character-based, or dramatic, enigma is naturally very closely related to the eventive variety since biblical personages are always strongly characterized by their actions and by their reactions in turn to what is done or happens to them. But their respective natures are also made manifest by what they are reported as saying and, less commonly, by what the narrator reveals about their thinking and feeling as well. In some cases there is an apparent dual level of enigma: This occurs when certain crucial information is disclosed to the audience, but not to the participants concerned. Thus, while the protagonists may experience certain doubts and queries about their present situation and/or the future course of events, the audience already knows what is going on, as least in part. This is of course the basis for dramatic irony as earlier described. It also provides the foundation for the dramatic nature of narrative itself. In summary, where there is "no ignorance," there can be "no conflict"; and if "no conflict" occurs, there cannot be a plot—at least not in the normal narrative sense (Sternberg 1985:173).

Certain well-known characters, or character types, may be endowed with a specific reputation—good, bad, or indifferent—as the story begins. It is based upon the historical and literary tradition which the audience or readership has come to know through enculturization, including religious indoctrination, and which they consequently bring with them conceptually to the narrative event in the form of underlying presuppositions, attitudes, judgments, and opinions. The nature of such character assessment of course varies according to the audience, but our concern must always be directed initially toward that of the assumed original receptor group, as difficult and hypothetical as such a contextually-related designation may be.

This matter is of considerable importance as far as the content and significance of the book of Jonah is concerned, for on it depends the magnitude of impact in relation to the great reversal in thinking which this seemingly unsophisticated narrative ultimately effects. If, as it is reasonable to suppose, the didactic-hortatory purpose of the story is aimed primarily at those whose theological orientation would be similar to that exhibited by Jonah, then there would be the greatest possible divergence manifested in relation to their initial estimation of character: Jonah, first introduced as a genuine messenger of the LORD (1:1), would probably be viewed in highly positive terms. The foreign (gentile) mariners, on the other hand, and particularly the pagan, politically and militarily hostile people of Nineveh would evoke an intensely antithetical connotative reaction. The first major enigma for this audience would likely have been *why* does the narrator depict these characters in such an unexpected, un-conventional, and culturally contradictory light?

The second, even more important question then follows. It is one that, considering the sacred nature of this text, borders upon a critical dilemma, for upon it the book's central message depends: Would the intended recipients (and ultimately you or I) finally have accepted the tremendous, anti-traditionalist shift that occurs in the book and accept its new moral vision and religious perspective—or would the psychological jump be too great? This point is dramatically summed up in the divine rhetorical question that serves to conclude the narrative proper, but the issue has been fully anticipated by the pair of chiding queries of 4:4 and 9. This trio of seemingly Jonah-specific utterances at the same time ironically initiates a demand that each receptor personally resolve the enigma involved, not only conceptually, but more concretely, also in their associated behavior towards ethnic outsiders as well. Who really is my spiritual neighbor (cf. Lk 10:29, 36)—does this category of interpersonal relationships actually include such characters as the king of Nineveh? It may be noted here that the final question does not appear to be a free invitation to the audience simply to "Choose sides, [and pick] who is right in this conflict, YHWH or Jonah?" (Crouch 1994:106). Being rhetorical in nature, the interrogative embodies its own (intended) answer, i.e., surely the LORD—and his perspective or decision alone—is completely correct! Being ideologically biased, the Scriptures also presuppose the essential justice of YHWH (1:2), as well as his steadfast mercy (2:8, 4:2), in all his dealings with humanity. Thus, the only question for the current audience concerns the nature and degree of their commitment

6.7 Enigma and the ever-unfolding "mystery" of Jonah

to what they know to be right. In that sense then, "Will you choose to side with the LORD or not?"

Meir Sternberg considers Jonah to be "the only biblical instance where a surprise gap controls the reader's progress over a whole book," one that is based upon a "false impression produced at the start."[39] He begins with the assumption noted above that the LORD's called prophet would be viewed initially in a very positive light. However, he follows this up with the claim that Jonah's subsequent contrary response would be interpreted in like manner—not as an act of rebellion against a mission that might just allow the mercy of YHWH to be manifested towards Nineveh, but "because Jonah is too tender-hearted to carry a message of doom to a great city." The prophet thus acts in protest "against a wrathful God" whose "image grows more and more forbidding as he pursues Jonah with relentless violence." In other words, YHWH initially appears to be the true villain of the story, and "it is fear alone that he inspires in the dramatis personae." It is not until the general repentance of Nineveh is matched by "the surprise of God's repentance" that this erroneous "model of the narrative world and world view" is shattered, and the reader "discovers that his reading of the past [has been] turned upside down." This realization is reinforced by the revelation of 4:2, and when "this master gap [is] disclosed in closure, God and Jonah prove opposites indeed," and it is shown that "of the two Jonah has been the ruthless one all along and God the merciful."

While I cannot deny that such a reading of the account is possible, I do not think that it is very probable in terms of the book's original religious setting and initial audience. For them the very mention of Nineveh at the beginning would amount to a raising of the proverbial red flag, connotatively that is, and it is not likely that anyone would be very upset at all to hear of the city's forthcoming judgment. Jonah is ruthless all right, but the narrative's elaborate recursions, subtle variations, and sharp contrasts in relation to the heathen with whom he comes into contact all serve to highlight his impious and implacable behavior from the very start. The story's principal enigma rather concerns why Jonah behaves the way he does, and this question is not fully clarified until the fourth chapter where it is foregrounded throughout—its inevitable sequel, however, is not. What does Jonah (or

---

[39] Sternberg 1985:318; all the citations in this paragraph are taken from pages 318–320 of this important study of biblical narrative.

you/I) finally decide to do? This example illustrates the potentially equivocal quality of literary enigma and also points up the need for grounding any hypothesis concerning its supposed operation in biblical narrative as firmly as possible upon the original text, context, and Scriptural cotext.

6.7.3 Lexical enigma

"Lexical" enigma in Jonah may also involve an element of irony in cases where one sense is played off another. It is occasioned by a use of the same word or root either with essentially the same semantic significance or with a somewhat different meaning in disparate narrative settings. This feature is generated by the text's generous amount of verbal recursion, a process that forces the reader/hearer to question whether a given term is being used as before, or whether some new sense, connotation, or implication is intended. As was pointed out in section 5.2, the associative "resonance" of a particular term automatically increases as a narrative develops by virtue of the fact that it is inevitably either collocated with different words, or it is contextualized in new dramatic settings. For example, in what sense was Nineveh "great" *(gadol)*? There is a gradual shift in both denotation (i.e., from size to importance) and connotation (i.e., from negative to positive) as the account proceeds, and finally "great" ends up being connected with the gracious "concern" *(chus)* of the LORD (4:11).

In such instances, we are not dealing with an obscurity, or unclarity, of lexical usage, nor is it vagueness (imprecision) either. The author is too skilled a narrator to allow that to happen (at least in relation to his initial receptors). Rather, he occasionally introduces a deliberate ambiguity into the account, where *either* of two or more different, but definite, senses are possible—but probably *not both* at once. The word 'elohim in 1:5–6 is an example, i.e., either "god" or "gods" would fit (though the latter may be preferable to accent the heathen nature of the mariners more strongly). Stuart feels that the noun ra'ah in 1:2 is another instance of such ambiguity, that is, either "wickedness" or "misfortune," but with an emphasis on the latter (1987:437, 449). Again, however, such equivocality does not seem to be very likely if evaluated with respect to the book's original setting, where "evil/wickedness" would seem to be the sense most perceptible (and desirable) to the intended audience.

6.7 Enigma and the ever-unfolding "mystery" of Jonah

Lexical enigma is also involved more commonly (and importantly) in cases of what I have elsewhere termed semantic density, that is, where two or more senses are not only possible, but *both* are probably intended in a particular textual context (Wendland 1990:304). In other words, several meanings are appropriate and also mutually reinforcing or complementary at that specific point in the discourse. The vital conjunction *ki* in 1:2, for example, which "performs a major role in Hebrew rhetoric" (Trible 1994:126), is a likely candidate: It may be rendered causally (since/because), objectively (that), or asseveratively (surely/indeed), and all of the options happen to fit here, though most commentators and versions prefer the first: "...because their wickedness has come up before me." But an intensive construal (i.e., obviously) is also attractive (Sasson 1990:3, 75), for this would stress the LORD's indignation over the issue at hand. Not often considered is the possibility of an object clause because, according to Wolff, "this is not the message which Jonah is supposed to convey according to 3:4..." (1986:95). But what if it were—the utterance of 3:4 being an obvious truncation? Certainly the two segments harmonize well together, e.g., "In forty days Nineveh will be destroyed [because] YHWH/God is faced with its wickedness!" True to his character then, Jonah would prefer to accent the negative (3:4) and leave a (potentially merciful) Lord out of the message as much as possible.

Chapter three appears to illustrate a number of other instances of semantic density. Here Nineveh is described as a "city great to God" (v. 3), that is, not only large in size, but also of considerable concern to him in his abundant grace. Accordingly, Jonah is commissioned to "cry out" *(q-r-')* both in denunciation of its evil (cf. 1:2) and also as a proclamation that saving repentance was still possible. Hence Jonah's short message was twofold in implication: if no genuine penitence occurred, the city would surely be physically "overturned" *(h-p-k)*; on the other hand, God might just perform a mighty saving work there, in which case the city would be spiritually "turned-over," i.e., in a mass conversion event. As it turned out, the latter option was realized, and the LORD relented concerning the "destruction" *(ra'ah)* he had determined to carry out upon the city—which of course would have been a tragic "calamity" (or "evil") from their unfortunate perspective. The frequency with which such pluri-signification and punning occur in the text contributes a great deal to the overall lexical resonance, the emotive richness, and the ideological scope of this brief, but profound narrative.

6.7.4 Thematic enigma

By virtue of the preceding three categories, enigma is also vitally thematic in nature, that is, it has a definite bearing on the total message that is conveyed—not only in the original situation, but also with respect to captivated listeners (and readers) ever since. This applies in a specific way to the many plot-related, character-based, and lexically significant questions that the text generates as noted above. All of these engage the audience in a search for clues and ultimately answers to the strange and wonderful things that are taking place within the narrative. As Magonet observes (1983:88):

> This anticipating of events is one of the thematic and structural keys of the book itself. Jonah himself states that he fled from God's mission because he "anticipated" (4:2) (*qiddamti*) God's compassionate response.

The irony here is that even at this late stage in the action Jonah did not realize or even anticipate the fact that he himself was the first—and most personally touched—recipient of the LORD's manifold mercies. It was all still a tragic puzzle as far as he was concerned. A further thematically relevant irony associated with an enigma involves Jonah's incongruous pitying of a dried up plant when a great thriving metropolis was in grave danger of being struck down dead before his very eyes (4:5b)! The revelation of this paradoxical attitude is effectively delayed (i.e., from its logical location in 4:7) until a point where it can be contrastively juxtaposed with the ideal and ultimate pity of God (4:10a/11a).

In a more general sense too the text of Jonah is enigmatic—or we might say, evocative, or even provocative—in relation to its manifestation of theme. The question here is: What then *constitutes* its principal theme? Is it A, B, or C? The answer simply is "yes"; it is all of these and more. Thus, Jonah is a book that appeals to a wide range of receptors, certainly because it presents an interesting, action-packed account of divine intervention in the affairs of human beings, but also due to the potential diversity of its thematic expression and the consequent depth of its overall communicative significance. Not all of the possible themes may be recognized by every reader or hearer, but they do appear to be

6.7 Enigma and the ever-unfolding "mystery" of Jonah

conceptually accessible, that is, to all those who possess the competence and put forth the effort to perceive them.

In this process of thematic extraction and critical assessment it is again important to distinguish between the two so-called "horizons" of interpretation (Thistleton 1980:16), namely, that of the *original* text (i.e., where the analyst is concerned with intended *"meaning"*) and that of the *current* exegete (i.e., who is concerned with contemporary *"significance"* (Hirsch 1967:255). In short, not all interpretations, hence also themes and associated functions, are valid or credible in relation to the initial biblical setting of communication. Relative validity and credibility must therefore be determined by a joint consideration of text, cotext, and context as these interrelated perspectives pertain to the assumed rhetorical intention of the inspired author. Our consideration of theme within this general framework will have to be brief and limited to the bare essentials, namely, a viewpoint governed by the interaction of the major plot participants and key terms. These perspectives are summarized in the two figures shown below:

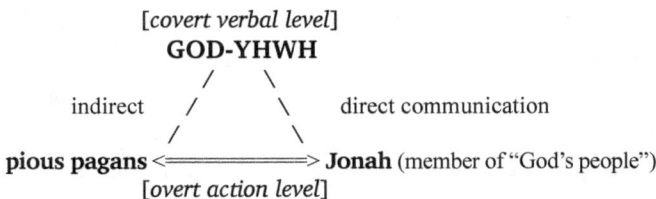

Triangle of participant interaction in Jonah

This "triangle" is articulated synchronically with what we might posit as a "circle" of central semantic significance. In other words, as the various participants interact, sooner or later they confront the issue of the LORD's "steadfast love" *(chesed)* in one dimension or another. We thus have a sequence of associated key terms that cluster around this central notion as the events move from the beginning to the end of the account, as schematized (in part) below:

'-s-t (1:6)   *'al-titten 'alenu* (1:14)

m-n-h (4:6)   *chus* (4:10)   *m-n-h* (1:17)   *'-n-h* (2:2)

rab chesed (4:2)   *n-ch-m* (4:2)   **CHESED**   *'-l-h* (2:6)   *chesed* (2:8)

r-ch-m (4:2)   *'erek 'appayim* (4:2)   *y-sh-'* (2:9)   *shub* (3:9)

ch-n-n (4:2)   *n-ch-m* (3:9–10)

Circle of semantic-thematic significance in Jonah

The concentration of YHWH's covenantal qualities in 4:2 clearly represents the point of greatest emphasis in relation to the book's overarching theme, and it is highly ironic that Jonah himself is forced to make this revelation even as he reluctantly (and angrily) fills the principal narrative gap or plot-related enigma.

Jonah interacts with several sets of pagans on the overt level of the narrative surface. He also inter-communicates directly with YHWH (he knew the "name"), that is, via verbal messages, formal as well as informal, which flow in both directions—though in isolation from the story's other participants. The pagans, on the other hand, communicate only formally with "God" (one of many?) and receive verbal messages from him solely through his prophet, Jonah. The personage of YHWH-God is manifestly the central participant throughout—occasionally in the foreground, but always in the background of virtually everything that takes place. He actively impinges upon the entire story, controlling its action (but not necessarily its outcome), to an extent that is reminiscent of the momentous Genesis and Exodus accounts.

Thus, one way of generating a set of the various relevant themes of this narrative is to list the principal oppositions or contrasts that are possible between any pair of participants (or participant types) as they relate to God and/or interact with each other. One side of the antithesis is emphasized and/or encouraged as a principal part of the message (symbolized by +), while the other is downplayed and/or discouraged (–). Jonah himself may be taken as representative of an outwardly "religious" but inwardly self-righteous class of Israelites living at the time of the book's writing. The

6.7 Enigma and the ever-unfolding "mystery" of Jonah

application to similar hypocritical individuals who regard themselves as being charter members of the select "church" of God is not difficult to make; it is in fact encouraged. The following listing provides a sample (only) of just five of the comparative possibilities in this regard; it is intended to be merely suggestive of what would need to be done in a complete, integrative thematic analysis.

Note: [+] = a positive, foregrounded, and/or promoted attribute, attitude, or action
[–] = the negative, backgrounded, and/or condemned counterpart
[J] = self-righteous "Jonah" type   [P] = pious "pagan" type

a. Certain individuals [J] have considerable religious knowledge [+], but they fail to put it into practice (i.e., *chesed*) in their everyday lives [–], or they do so in a strictly tradition-bound, stereotyped, or limited sort of way [–]. Others [P] with little or no knowledge of the LORD of Scriptures [–] can sometimes teach the "enlightened ones" [J] a lesson or two in relation to spontaneous personal piety and public obedience to their professed religious principles [+].

b. Ethnic or any other type of prejudice [J] has no place among the people of God [–], for it is the very antithesis of the *chesed* principle [+]. YHWH is the only universal God and the divine embodiment of *chesed* [+]. He wants all peoples [P] to come to know and worship him aright [+]. Many pagans [P] put self-professed "believers" to shame by their "fear" of God [+] and their consequent behavioral acknowledgment of his ever-present immanence and his immediate relevance to their everyday lives [+].

c. Repentance before God and man is an obligation that applies to all people [+], especially the self-righteous [J], who do not think that they need it [–]. Moreover, it must be total, involving one's whole being [P]—with a manifestation of: genuine sorrow over sin, a confession of one's iniquity, and an appeal to and trust in God for forgiveness [+]. A repentant heart is further confirmed by a willingness to publicly demonstrate one's conversion in a new life of worship and complete obedience (*chesed*) in keeping with the revealed will of YHWH [+], be that extensive [J] or limited [P] in any given case.

d. God is holy and righteous [+], and is therefore bound by his essential nature to punish all sinners [+], whether they wrong him [–] willfully [J], hypocritically [J], or in blind ignorance [P] and pagan idolatry [P]. However, YHWH in his grace and mercy [+] is ever desirous of finding ways to manifest his forgiveness [+] to those who respond positively to his initiatives [+] at whatever imperfect level of recognition this may be [P]. Similarly, he continues to seek [+] the sinner [J], trying to get him to see [+] the error of his rebellious way [-]. God's patient and steadfast love (*chesed*) for the lost [+] should in turn be a model [+] for all those who claim to be his people [J].

e. YHWH is the sovereign Creator and almighty Ruler over the entire universe [+]. Human beings cannot resist the punitive judgment of God [P], nor can they escape his enjoined will [J], no matter how hard they may try [-]. However, they may indeed reject [-] his unchanging love (*chesed*) and his gracious purpose [+] for their lives [J], especially as this relates to their obligation to witness for him [+] and reveal to others [P] the fact that "salvation belongs to the LORD" alone [+]!

Of course, these are not the only themes possible for Jonah, nor are they necessarily stated in the most relevant or appropriate way. But they do serve to illustrate the point that even with reference to its original biblical setting, this book generates a multitude of potential themes, statable with varying degrees of generality or specificity in relation to the nuclear core of *chesed*. The complex construction of the narrative, involving recursion and variation on all possible strata of form and meaning, structure and style, creates manifold possibilities of semantic significance and pragmatic relevance along many different planes of implicature. Magonet comes to a similar conclusion after his own useful thematic survey (1983:112; cf. Trible 1994:108):

> Different emphasis on any single element or group of elements can result in quite different readings. That such ambiguity exists and that no single reading is the "true" one, is no more, and no less, a problem than the attempt to recognize and understand the word of God itself at any given time.

However, instead of "ambiguity," a better term might be "polyvalency" or even "thematic density."[40] That is because these themes are not vague, contradictory, or mutually exclusive, nor do they result in any confusion or uncertainty of meaning, with regard to either the nature of God himself or his enscripturated Word. Rather, they are all (the correctly "contextualized" ones that is) quite definite and serve to complement one another in relation to the unifying conceptual force of *chesed* to convey a message that is not

---

[40] The latter by analogy with "semantic density," as in Wendland 1990.

6.7 Enigma and the ever-unfolding "mystery" of Jonah

only very rich in theological and moral significance, but one which also has many different levels of practical implication and possible application.

Perhaps this enigmatic, irresolvable aspect of the book's thematic potential is an implicit lesson to all listening "Jonahs": Do not assume that you know God and his *chesed* (cf. 4:2) simply because you are able to quote a few creedal and confessional statements about him (e.g., 1:9; ch. 2, 4:2) and can carry out the requisite public acts of ritual worship (2:9). To be sure, YHWH is fundamentally unfathomable with respect to his being (essence), nature (attributes), behavior (actions), and purposes (or decisions). However, he condescends to meet people where they are in their individual religious understanding, general morality, inner spirituality, and personal devotion. He thereby expects and encourages them to continually probe more deeply so that they might derive ever greater blessings as a result of their fellowship with him—and with all fellow seekers along the way, no matter what race, culture, language, political persuasion, or socio-economic status they may represent. In short, the LORD "is concerned" about, or "pities," us all (4:11), and he wants us to feel the same way about each other!

A final question that somehow seems pertinent: Why "is Jonah also [included] among the prophets?" (cf. 1 Sam 10:11–12). The answer—still debatable perhaps due to the book's largely narrative format—should hopefully be more apparent now: Like the other prophetic texts of the Hebrew Scriptures, the function of Jonah is not primarily informative (in this case, a dramatic Bible history lesson), though it does also include this particular communicative function. It is rather preeminently *hortatory* (i.e., commending the right, condemning the wrong in relation to God) and also a *didactic* (i.e., an instructional, faith-building) literary composition. Similarly, its message is stylistically complex, strongly critical, morally challenging, and contextually related to the lives of its intended receptor constituency. It is also firmly founded upon the principal covenantal attributes of YHWH—his omnipotence, omniscience, immanence, holiness, justice, mercy, fidelity, and (especially in relation to Jonah) his patience. By means of the poetic techniques of recursion, variation, irony, and enigma the text is rhetorically crafted to convey its pluralistic, multipurpose theme in a manner most likely to *persuade* its audience to move mentally and physically in a positive direction. That is, through the impelling force of "the Spirit *(ruach)* of YHWH" (cf. 1:4) we are all encouraged to recognize the error of Jonah's perspective (4:4/9), the rightness of God's position (4:11), and the need for actively applying this highly relevant, prophetic Word of the LORD to and in our own lives.

But before one can apply the Word, one must first understand it, and this, for most hearers or readers, first requires a meaningful *translation*. I will conclude this chapter with a summary of the analysis and transmission of Jonah ch. 2 in a contemporary Bantu language.

6.8 Song from the sea: How sweet does Jonah's psalm sound?

6.8.1 Introduction

Jonah's psalm is not a very highly regarded example of its genre for both textual and contextual reasons. Purportedly original in composition, it is actually a *pastiche* consisting of bits and pieces of many psalms. It is also sung, or prayed, by a prophet whose genuineness in terms of spiritual motivation is questionable at best. We will now take a closer look at the literary qualities of this passage (Jonah 2), pointing out certain aspects of its structural arrangement and artistic style, irony in particular, that are not so obvious on the surface of the text. The importance of Jonah's prayer within the organization and development of the surrounding discourse is also noted.

Our focus then shifts to the present day and various options for conveying this song of thanksgiving in a functionally equivalent manner for a contemporary constituency. The *ndakatulo* genre of Chewa lyric poetry has been selected to illustrate the potential for a correspondingly literary mode of translation. The aim is to re-present certain salient aspects of the overall communicative relevance of the original message—that is, its rhetorical impact, aesthetic appeal, and thematic significance—for a specific, youth-oriented target audience in a more oral-aurally sensitive media environment.

It is not my intention to present a detailed discourse analysis of the book of Jonah as a whole (cf. Wendland 1996). I will rather focus my attention on the prophet's psalm of chapter two in order to identify some of the important Hebrew structural and stylistic features of this poetic text as they interact in relation to each other and within their compositional context.

6.8 Song from the sea: How sweet does Jonah's psalm sound?

These crucial textual elements must form the foundation of any attempt to communicate the song's significance today in a completely different situational setting—one that encompasses time, place, language, culture, and religious background.

This contemporary scenario is set among the Chewa-speaking peoples of east-central Africa. The specific project *Skopos,* or communicative goal, is to produce a "literary functional equivalence" *(LiFE)* translation that will foster a dramatic oral recital or choral rendition of this prophetic narrative (cf. Wendland 2011), which is intended to augment the repertory of a Christian young people's organization or choir group. A linguistically more dynamic version of this nature is deemed especially appropriate in view of the particular target audience envisioned and also to adequately reflect the dynamic nature of this psalm in terms of its original textual setting within the narrative prophecy of Jonah.

The goal is not necessarily to get this petulant Hebrew prophet to "sing" more sweetly in the vernacular (in comparison with how he currently sounds in existing translations). One could in fact argue that this seemingly pious prayer actually lends an additional "sour" note to our overall evaluation of Jonah's unhappy missionary experience. Rather, the aim is to recreate his poetic discourse in a way that better reflects one credible interpretation of its *rhetorical function* in the Hebrew text as it has been so dramatically composed and presumably also articulated in the original event of public religious proclamation.

6.8.2 An introverted textual structure to reflect a corresponding spiritual experience

To a great extent the organizational structure of a literary text is created by the macro-compositional techniques of verbal *recursion* and selective *variation* (see 6.2–6.3). These strategies operate in conjunction with one another to segment, solidify, and shape the composition as a whole, thus establishing its internal demarcation, cohesion, and points of prominence respectively. This is well illustrated by Jonah's prayer from the belly of the great fish (2:2–9, Heb 2:3–10), which takes the generic form of a typical "psalm of (individual) *thanksgiving*" that responds, in this instance by way of anticipation, to a specific act of deliverance on the part of YHWH. The abstract sequential structure of this pericope is shown in the figure below (verse numbers follow the English text):[41]

A. **Introduction** [2]: the psalm is summarized (problem => prayer => provision => praise)
B. **Lament** [3–6a]: the psalmist's problem/crisis is poetically described
C. **Appeal** [7]: Yahweh was called upon for help in the pressing distress
D. **Proclamation** [6b]: the LORD's mighty deed of deliverance is lauded
E. **Testimonial** [8]: a recital of the LORD's greatness and glory (here altered to a condemnation of the ungodlyy
F. **Thanksgiving & Vow** [9]: praise of God and a promise to carry out some concrete act of worship/devotion

As is characteristic of many of the laments and individual eulogies, a broad semi-narrative sequence is evident in the text as it moves progressively from an initial problem (v. 3a) through a point of ultimate personal crisis (6a) to a final resolution (6b–7). Several minor variations from a strictly conventional sequence appear, thus serving to highlight the content that is being enunciated. We note in particular the appearance of an unexpected confession of hope (4b) within the lament portion; a forward displacement of the psalmist's proclamation (front-shifting, 6b), and a subtle modification of the panegyric testimonial (8) to heighten the irony of Jonah's admirable *words* in contrast to the actual righteous *deeds* of the heathen sailors (1:16). These all serve to illustrate the importance of certain deliberate alterations with respect to basic generic patterns as a means of augmenting the artistic appeal and rhetorical impact of a given discourse. In the skillful hands of the Hebrew composers (cf. 1 Chr 6:31), religious literary structure was never a straitjacket, but was always a flexible tool whereby subdued as well as more obvious communicative effects could be achieved when the need arose.

A carefully crafted graphic design utilizing the spatial layout of the printed page may be employed in order to display more precisely some of the larger symmetrical patterns to be found in an artfully composed poetic text such as we have in Jonah's song. This applies in particular to its major formal parallels and introversions as well as to its crucial semantic correspondences and contrasts (cf. Wendland and Louw 1993:ch. 2). An illustration is

---

[41] Westermann concludes that "it is in this [thanksgiving] psalm genre that the solid structure of a genre can be seen by anyone..." (1980:73).

6.8 Song from the sea: How sweet does Jonah's psalm sound? 319

given below; for the purpose of this exercise, the New International Version (with its versification on the left) is used with a few alterations, but in a greatly modified format. The parallel lineal couplets (cola, or half-lines, as the case may be) are designated by means of capital letters and numbers along the right margin:

---

[2] In my distress I called to the **LORD**,	A1
and he answered me.	B1
From the depths of the grave I called for help,	A2
and you listened to my cry.	B2
[3] You hurled me into the deep,	C1
into the very heart of the seas,	
and the current swirled about me;	D1
all your waves and breakers swept over me.	
[4] I said, "**I have been banished from your sight;**	A3
yet I will look again toward your holy temple."	B3
[5] The engulfing waters threatened me,	D2
the deep surrounded me;	
seaweed was wrapped around my head.	
[6] To the roots of the mountains I sank down;	C2
the earth beneath barred me in forever.	
But you brought my life up from the pit,	B4
O **LORD**, my God.	
[7] When my life was ebbing away,	A4
I remembered you, LORD,	
and my prayer rose to you,	B5
to your holy temple.	
[8] *Those who cling to worthless idols*	E
forfeit the grace that could be theirs.	
[9] But I, with a song of thanksgiving, will sacrifice to you.	A5
What I have vowed I will make good.	
Salvation comes from the LORD!	B6

As befits this grateful song of thanksgiving, there is a special emphasis upon the [B] elements, which state in both general and specific salvific terms what the LORD has done for the psalmist (i.e., his timely saving response to a prayerful plea for help). The parallel [A] segments indicate the divine Source of the singer's strength, to whom he accordingly appeals in his deep distress. The [C] constituents portray the low point of his personal crisis in graphic imagery of the dangerous depths of the sea (*physical* setting), while those of [D] describe in corresponding figures his associated emotional experience (*psychological* setting). One notes the chiastic arrangement of these two sets ([C] and [D]) around the central [A3-B3] pairing, which would suggest some special significance for the latter. Indeed, this core element, functioning as part of the general introverted construction of the whole, represents the only citation of embedded speech (bold print) in the entire psalm. It also incorporates a rather distinct semantic conjunction of concession with contra-expectation (surprise), as marked by the exclamatory and/or restrictive particle *'ak* 'surely' and/or 'however' in Hebrew (cf. van der Merwe et al. 1999:309, 313).

[B3], the compositional midpoint, is closely matched conceptually by [B4] after the [D2-C2] reiteration. As marked initially in Hebrew, utterance B3 appears to anticipate B4 in the text, thus giving further intimation of a positive outcome for Jonah's precarious position (cf. B1 and B2). Element [B4] then occurs as the most specific of the [B] deliverance motifs; it is also thematically and structurally climactic, a status that is signaled stylistically by several features that are combined in an alliterative double mention of the divine name: *chayyay yhwh [adonaiy] 'elohay*. This is followed by a segment that appears to be rather detached from the rest of the composition, namely, the psalmic denouement, as it were [A4-B5], which leads to a formal pronouncement of the vow [A5]. The latter is linked by way of a strong contrast (*wa'aniy* 'but I'; cf. A3) to element [E], in which Jonah rather self-righteously comments disparagingly upon what he views as hopeless pagan piety. The latter, which evidently reflects back upon the sailors' religious rites as narrated at the close of the preceding narrative segment (i.e., 1:16), almost seems out of place in the psalm in terms of both content and tone. This serves to highlight its ironic contrastive thematic function: Who were the ones who wanted to show grace to Jonah by saving his life? None other than those "lost" idol worshipers! A final epigrammatic reminder of the deliverance motif concludes the song on an exultant note [B6] and probably expresses the divinely-orientated theme of the entire composition, despite the proliferation of first-person forms (including several that are especially emphasized, as already noted).

6.8 Song from the sea: How sweet does Jonah's psalm sound?

Certainly, this is a masterfully composed poetic piece, one that is most appropriate to both its contextual and co-textual settings, namely, the dramatic narrative plot development as well as the discourse organization of the book as a whole. A patterned, "isomorphically equivalent" (de Waard and Nida 1986:63–65) transposition of its compositional arrangement to the printed page, as illustrated below, helps to reveal to readers (not necessarily hearers) today how effectively the text has been verbally shaped in order to convey its message more forcefully in the original. The following format, which is more viewer-friendly than the one displayed earlier, includes several adjacent verses to show how the Jonah's psalm has been carefully woven into the fabric its textual co-text. The general introverted arrangement functions both as an ironic reflection of the disturbed spiritual state of the singer and also as a means of drawing attention to the text's key thematic components (the English is again that of the NIV):

[1:16]	At this the men greatly feared the LORD, and they offered a sacrifice to the LORD and made vows to him.				[A]
[1:17]	But the LORD provided a great fish to swallow Jonah, and Jonah was inside the fish three days and three nights.				[B]
[2:1]	From inside the fish Jonah prayed to the LORD his God. He said:				
[2:2]	"In my distress I called to the LORD, and he answered me. From the depths of Sheol I called for help, and you listened to my cry.				[C]
[2:3]			You hurled me into the deep, into the very heart of the seas,		[D]
				and the currents swirled about me; all your waves and breakers swept over me.	[E]
[2:4]				I said, 'I have been banished from your sight; ================ YET I WILL LOOK AGAIN TOWARD YOUR HOLY TEMPLE.'	[F] [F']
[2:5]			The engulfing waters threatened me the deep surrounded me; seaweed was wrapped around my head.		[E']

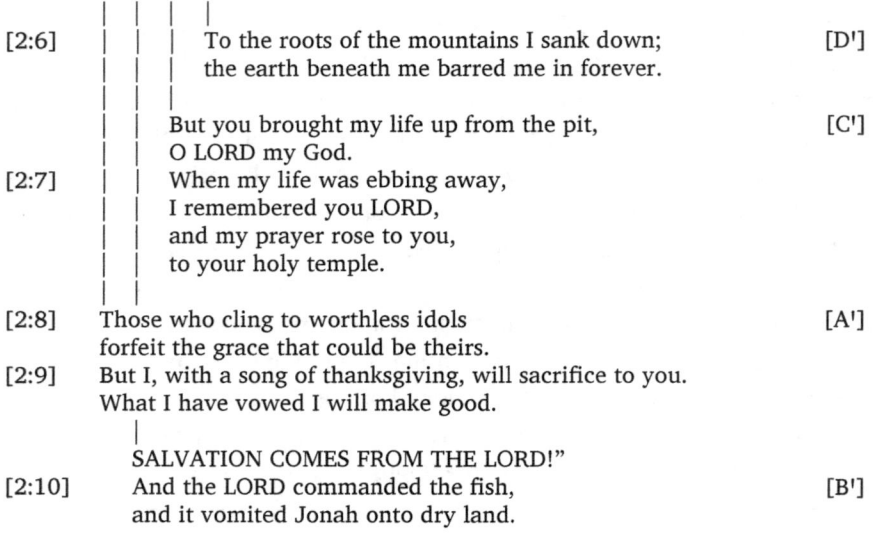

As indicated on the preceding diagram, the psalm of Jonah, which is a mixed composition, made up of various excerpts from the Psalter,[42] forms only a part of a more elaborate and extensive structure, namely, its medial quotative portion (2:2–9). It is enclosed by two obviously corresponding narrative frames that describe the prophet's initial predicament (B: being swallowed by a great fish) and his later deliverance (B': the fish deposits him on dry land). In between, Jonah's cited song of thanksgiving first portrays in graphic poetic detail his progressive descent into the depths of the sea—moving farther and farther away from Yahweh—and then lauds his divinely initiated resurrection from "the pit" (C'; cf. "Sheol," C). Verse 4 constitutes the nucleus of the introversion, expressing in emphatic direct (included) speech the essential content of verse 2, on the one hand, and verses 6b–7 on the other (the mid-point of the entire book in terms of word count occurs in the immediately preceding bicolon, 3b). On one side of the poetic structural break (F), shown by the double dashed line, Jonah

---

[42] For a listing of the intertextual parallels, see Limburg 1993:63–64. Due to the heavy *ironic* overlay of ch. 2, from a rhetorical perspective I would prefer to call it an "Anti-Peak" rather than a "Peak episode" Longacre and Hwang 1994:342). Accordingly, I do not discern any special "height of tension" here because the psalmic genre itself (i.e., an individual thanksgiving) has implicitly resolved the issue of "Jonah's fate" (ibid 344). Furthermore, within a wider literary-structural framework, Jonah's psalm corresponds only with his disputatious "prayer" to the LORD of 4:2–3, not the entire chapter (ibid 342; Wendland 1996:374).

laments his removal from the LORD's benevolent presence. On the other side (F'), he confidently looks forward to entering that same presence again through prayer directed to the "holy temple" of Yahweh—its earthly locus (4b) as well as its heavenly epitome (7b).

Verses 8 and 9 express Jonah's joyous reaction to his miraculous rescue and bring his hymn to an end in a triumphant shout of victory: "Salvation belongs to (i.e., is the prerogative of) the LORD (alone)!" This acts as the song's thematic peak and emotive climax, being an instance of the literary device of "end stress." At first glance this final segment (A') does not appear to fit the overall structural pattern, that is, not until one observes the artful manner whereby it is linked, both lexically and semantically, with the closing narrative portion of chapter one (A, 1:16).[43] Jonah's ethnocentric prejudice seems to shine through even his pious prayer as he cursorily dismisses all "those who cling to worthless idols," contrasting their fervent religious behavior (actual) with his own righteous acts of sacrifice and vows (anticipated). His ritualized words recall, with considerable irony, the reverent response of the heathen seamen as they fearfully witnessed YHWH's impressive dealing with his unwilling messenger. So thematically important is this contrast that the structural pattern is reversed at the end in order to draw attention to it, i.e., A' and B' (cf. A and B). In addition, this second scene of the drama is effectively tied into the first by means of the correspondence between verses 2:8–9 and 1:16, a masterful compositional interlocking device. The final, soteriological line of the song is followed by the subtly satiric anticlimax: Jonah's salvation was effected by a shameful expectoration. Not even the good fish could stomach this contrary prophet of God and was therefore compelled to throw him out (as the sailors also had done, cf. 1:15).

The discourse structure of this, and any other, biblical book needs to be clearly marked in translation, especially in terms of its key transitional points and peaks. This may be done formally within the text by means of natural target language (TL) mediating and focusing expressions, e.g., Chewa at 2:1—"So it was that while Jonah was inside the belly of that big

---

[43] To designate such subtle structural modifications by the term "symmetrophobia" (Trible 1994:117) seems to suggest a certain artificiality or undue arbitrariness in ancient Hebrew compositional strategy. On the contrary, such slightly "imperfect" discourse may just as well have been deliberate and intended to accomplish specific rhetorical objectives within the text. For example, a formal variation from the norm or an established pattern may be used as a focusing devise to draw attention to that particular point in the text.

fish, he began to pray to the LORD. He said..." The larger compositional organization may be also manifested typographically through the use of judicious paragraphing procedures (along with carefully worded section headings at crucial sectional divisions, e.g., at a new "scene"), or by varied stages and levels of indentation to display structural breaks and general thematic correspondences (as illustrated above). Furthermore, it is necessary to pay attention to points of special significance within the whole, for example, 1:17 and 4:1. In this case, one would want to somehow distinguish these passages with respect to their parallel transitional function as "hinge" verses that effectively divide each half of the book (i.e., chs. 1–2 and 3–4) again into two. The text's central and principal break of course occurs between 2:10 and 3:1, as shown by the extensive recursion—along with selective and contrastive variation—that occurs at 3:1–3 (compare 1:1–3).

6.8.3 The structural significance of Jonah's psalm

One of the major controversies in modern Jonahic studies involves the scope of the text itself—the discourse as originally composed, that is. The reliability of the Hebrew Masoretic Text *(Biblia Hebraica Stuttgartensia)* is not at issue, for this seems to be comparatively well preserved, and the variants are not all that significant.[44] Rather, the question concerns whether the unexpected psalm of chapter two is original or not. In other words, was it composed by the author of the rest of the book, or was it incorporated at some later stage of textual transmission?[45] The following are several macro-textual principles that would argue for the retention of this poetic pericope as an integral and important constituent of the complete book:[46]

- The citation of poetry within a narrative prose co-text is a regular features of biblical literary style (e.g., Gen 49; Exod 15; Num 21:27–30; Deut 32–33; Judg 5; 1 Sam 2:1–10; 2 Sam 1:19–27; 22; 2 Kgs 19:21–28; 1 Chr 16:8–36).

- The finely wrought symmetrical organization of the book as a whole would be undone were the psalm to be excluded, in particular, the structural correspondence

---

[44] The integrity of the Hebrew text is supported by commentators as diverse as Allen 1976:191, Ellison 1985:365, Limburg 1993:33, and Sasson 1990:10.

[45] For a survey of the opposing opinions on this particular issue, see Alexander 1988:63–69.

[46] There is no evidence that the text "ever circulated without the psalm" (Landes 1967:10). For additional support in favor of this position, see the discussion in Stuart 1987:470–473; Brichto 1992:73; and Limburg 1993:32.

6.8 Song from the sea: How sweet does Jonah's psalm sound? 325

(and ironic contrast) between the two "prayers" of Jonah, i.e., 2:2–9 and 4:2–3.[47] These two antithetical pericopes even begin in exactly the same way: "And he [Jonah] prayed to the LORD…and said." Furthermore, both units incorporate traditional religious ("cultic") diction (Landes 1967:17–18)—with this fundamental difference: "The themes that drew forth Jonah's praise in the psalm are ironically the very ones that cause him grief in his second prayer" (Allen 1976:199).

- There is a major, and deliberate, intratextual contrast developed also between Jonah's self-centered prayer of thanksgiving in chapter two and the surrounding appeals of the pagans with whom he comes into coerced contact, notably, the fervent exhortations of the captain in 1:6 and the Ninevite king in 3:7–9. For self-righteous Jonah, on the other hand, no act of penance or confession of sin or guilt was apparently required to repair his supposed standing before the LORD.

- Brichto also notes the psalm's function as the narrative's "peripeteia," that is, "the hinge, the point of change or reversal in the drama's action" (Brichto 1992:74). In this case, it provides a dramatic pause (in addition to the character contrast noted above) before the onset of the second and climactic half of the story.

- The narrative development of 1:17 and 3:1 is not properly motivated and executed if the psalm is excised. Thus, the LORD "appoints" the great fish to swallow Jonah in the former passage and "tells" the fish to expel Jonah in the latter, but what is the point? Jonah simply becomes a passive participant having no interaction with Yahweh, which is such a crucial aspect of the final stages of the book in terms of both plot and theme. Besides, without the words of the psalm ringing in the background, the subsequent obedience of Jonah to the divine commission (i.e., "paying his vow"—cf. 2:9b) seems quite arbitrary and out of character.

- There are a surprising number of topical and plot-related motifs that link Jonah's song *intra*textually to the rest of the text.[48] This is significant because it is characteristic of the psalms of Scripture to be rather general in their reference and hence universal in their potential applicability. The concluding utterance, "Salvation belongs to the LORD," is especially noteworthy in this regard. Indeed, it is highly ironic that Jonah did not realize the full implications of what he was praising God for here—whether with regard to a sinking ship, a transient plant, or a teeming metropolis (4:10–11). This short exclamation of closure, which occurs near the book's structural center, summarizes the entire narrative, and "being an apt commentary on the significance of the adjacent narrative…is basic to the meaning of the book (Allen 1976:185).

---

[47] This has also been noted by Ackerman 1987:238. Trible arrives at quite a different evaluation: "[my] analysis supports source critical findings that deem the psalm a secondary addition to the narrative" (1994:172). Even in terms of her own study, however, it is difficult to see how "the psalm disrupts symmetry…(etc.)" (ibid., 173). On the contrary, a careful reading of her work would lead one to just the opposite conclusion (e.g., ibid., 110–111), namely, that Jonah's prayer of 4:2–3 is "juxtaposed to the psalm in the external design" (ibid., 199).

[48] For a summary, see Stuart 1987:471–472 and Limburg 1993:32. Trible too points out many of these correspondences in her analysis (1994:160–171).

To summarize: while "excisability has never been a legitimate criterion for questioning the integrity of a pericope" (Stuart 1987:470), the extensive compositional compatibility as outlined above is valid evidence for *supporting* such textual integrity. Thus, I would disagree with the suggestion that "interpolators also have strong stakes in neatly balanced books" (Sasson 1990:203). Such a hidden agenda on the part of a biblical "interpolator" (perhaps the interpolating "scribe/copyist" is a better analogy) is much more likely to be theological and explanatory in nature rather than artistic and/or compositional as in this case with Jonah's psalm.

Several aspects of the structural significance of Jonah's psalm with specific respect *ironic intertextuality* (cf. section 6.6) are listed below:

- In the highly emotive prayer of the pagan sailors, which initiates the climax of scene one (1:14), the words they use call to mind the prohibition concerning "innocent blood" found in Deut 21:8 and Jeremiah's warning about the taking of his life in Jer 26:15. Furthermore, in this prayer we have "almost a miniature *cento*, that is,...a composition that draws together, if not always known biblical passages, at least perfectly recognizable Hebraic sentiments" (Sasson 1990:136). It thus sets up a poignant contrast with the personally introverted thanksgiving prayer of Jonah soon to follow.

- As has already been noted, the psalm of Jonah is permeated with near (for the most part not exact) quotations from the Psalter (cf. Alexander 1988:113; Ellison 1985:364; Magonet 1983:50). Among other things (e.g., contributing to the general contrastive irony of the text), such a concentration of traditional and undoubtedly well-known religious language would suggest the importance of this pericope (2:2–9) within the overall structure and thematic purview of the book. It helps to portray the fickle character of Jonah as a person who is thoroughly cognizant of the immutable "word of the LORD" that came to him, but who is reluctant, if not most unwilling, to put it into practice in trying or unwelcome circumstances (that is, from his biased perspective). Scriptural citation and paraphrase also serve to highlight critical topical elements within the song, notably its final exultation: "Salvation [is] to/for the LORD!"—a close echo of Psalm 3:8, which also stresses the ultimate salvific activity of Yahweh.

- In a literary piece such as Jonah's thanksgiving that is characterized by so much intertextuality, any perceptible lapse in the pattern or procedure may be significant. Thus, just after the poem's structural-thematic midpoint in verse 4 (cf. the diagram above), as Jonah apparently experiences his deepest psychological and spiritual demise (going down), there are no psalmic citations evident in the text. This may be an indication that "Jonah's descent from conventional experience is matched by a move beyond conventional language" (Limburg 1993:68).

How can the rhetorical dynamics of Jonah's psalm be conveyed in another language-culture? This vital aspect of Scripture communication is considered in the next section.

6.8.4 Towards a literary functional-equivalence translation of Jonah 2

6.8.4.1 Overview of LiFE translation

It is generally recognized nowadays that any type of translation is a very specialized and complex act of communication, one which involves an interpersonal sharing of the same text (an integrated, significant systems of signs) within two different systems of language, thought, and culture. In other words, translation—especially that of a literary nature and desired quality—requires the *re-signification* and *re-conceptualization* of one text in another linguistic and sociocultural setting.[49] This multilingual, inter-semiotic, cross-cultural process of textual representation and cognitive reference may be variously defined and described in greater or lesser detail, depending on a number of important factors, for example: the underlying theoretical model that one adopts; the designated purpose, or *Skopos*, of the translation in relation to the target audience; and the style or manner in which the re-composition is carried out (e.g., relatively literal versus idiomatic in quality).

In the light of a "frames of reference" model of communication (Wilt 2003:ch.1, Wendland 2008a:ch. 1), and in keeping also with the distinctive nature of Scripture as a source text, we might describe the nature and purpose of translation in general as follows:

---

[49] A translation of the "holy" Scriptures imposes a greater constraint, obligation, and/or responsibility upon translators to preserve the "meaning" (however defined) of the original text. This is due to its perceived divinely generated, hence determinative and authoritative, nature for a particular religious community as well as for individual users. The religious nature or constitution of the biblical text thus greatly affects the expectations of a given target audience about its translation into their language, including the level of verbal creativity that they would like to see or are willing to allow in their version of the Word of God. It needs to be pointed out, however, that most societies with a long-established Christian and biblical tradition tend to be initially rather conservative with regard to their acceptance of any new translation of the Scriptures, especially one that is linguistically more free in comparison with the version that they have become accustomed to. In such situations, which would include the older generation of Chewa speakers, a significant amount of *preliminary* education regarding the nature and possibilities of Bible translation needs to be undertaken. The aim is to enable the target audience (all segments of society, not merely the church leaders) to make an informed, intelligent decision concerning the style of the new version that is to be prepared for their use.

> TRANSLATION involves the mediated verbal re-composition of one contextually-framed text within a different setting of communication in the most relevant* manner possible in keeping with the overall Brief and Skopos of the specific TL project concerned.
> [* "functionally equivalent" or selectively "marked" both artistically and also rhetorically]

A few explanatory comments may help to clarify the scope, implications, and options that pertain to the preceding descriptive summary. To begin with, it is obvious but nevertheless important to note that translation of any sort is different from monolingual communication in that at least two distinct cognitive settings, external environments, and interpersonal situations are involved. In the case of Bible translation, there is often a third set of circumstances as well, if the translators cannot access the original text directly. In any case, they must act as conceptual mediators to bridge the great linguistic and cultural gap that exists between two very different texts and contexts.

The formal and semantic distance between these two (or three) settings of message transmission is of course quite variable, depending on the general relatedness of the languages and societies concerned. Generally speaking, the greater this disparity, the more difficult the translation task and more proactive mediation on the part of the translator is required—particularly if a complete, literary-equivalent version is being prepared.[50] Thus, the translator can never really remain communicatively neutral, for even a very literal rendering conveys significant textual (semantic) and contextual (pragmatic) implications, including various types and degrees of misconstrued meaning, depending upon the expectations, experience, education, and ethos of the target audience.

Each of the distinct communication settings that are activated during translation incorporates several interacting levels or dimensions of

---

[50] A more SL form-oriented, "foreignized," translation of the Scriptures may be preferred for various reasons that pertain to the specific communicative situation and/or interpersonal setting concerned. For example, certain churches may wish to promote the tradition-based *ritual* function of communication, while other interest groups would like to expand the literary categories or stylistic features of the TL by incorporating those of the SL text. Still others may desire to retain a certain amount of formal similarity in the translation with respect to some familiar existing version in the TL or a major world language (e.g., French, Spanish, English, etc.). The focal text of my study also emphasizes *form*; however, in this case it is the *literary* forms of the TL that are resourced and capitalized upon during the production of a poetic rendering. The degree of textual domestication is therefore considerable, but so are the potential positive contextual effects that an artistically aware and appreciative audience may derive from such an idiomatic manner of expressing the Word of God in their mother tongue.

extratextual influence which together affect all aspects of text representation—its production, transmission, and processing. There are thus cultural, institutional, religious, physical (environmental), interpersonal (sociolinguistic), and personal (psychological, experiential) factors that pertain with varying degrees of impact to the overall context of message transmission. These all merge to form the respective collective "cognitive frameworks" of the source language or receptor language communities (as well as the individuals of which they are composed).[51] The current, audience perspective and prevailing opinion, as determined by appropriate research methods and sampling techniques, must therefore inform the committee of program managers. These are the persons who have been charged with the task of drawing up an explicit *Brief* that defines the specific communicative purpose *(Skopos),* principles, and procedures of a given Bible translation project for a particular target constituency, medium of transmission, inventory of resources, and socio-religious setting.[52]

In terms of the outline above, translating with a specifically "literary" version in mind is carried out according to the *principle* of communicative "relevance." The aim is thus to achieve a greater amount of cognitive-emotive-volitional effects despite the possibility of requiring a larger measure of processing effort on the part of the audience. This general principle of communication is here coupled with the *Skopos*-specific *practice* of functional equivalence (FE). The latter refers to the goal of achieving an appreciable, yet also an acceptable and appropriate, degree of "similarity" in terms of literary (artistic and rhetorical) "likeness" with respect to the meaning variables of pragmatic intent, semantic content, and textual-stylistic form.[53] Another type of translation—for example, a more literal version for liturgical purposes—would fit under the same

---

[51] I am here distinguishing between the notion of "context" as an external, perceivable "reality" and "frame," which is one particular *cognitive* organization or representation of that reality. The sum of frames that are relevant to the interpretation of a given text constitutes its conceptual "framework" (this perspective stems from Gregory Bateson, as explained in Katan 1999:34).

[52] The terms *"Brief"* and *"Skopos"* are being used more or less as defined according to the functionalist approach to translation—that is, *Skopostheorie* (cf. Nord 1997:137, 140, ch. 3; Fawcett 1997:ch. 9).

[53] For a handy survey of "relevance theory" (RT) as applied to Bible translation, see Gutt 1992; the theory of "functional equivalence" (FE) is described and applied in de Waard and Nida 1986. I thus view RT as offering a useful way of conceptualizing the process of communication in general; however in my experience, an FE approach, worked out within a broader sociological, text-linguistic framework, provides a more practical model for teaching mother-tongue translators the basic principles and specific procedures of Bible translation (cf. also Nord 1997; Hatim and Mason 1997:ch. 11).

definition as that proposed above, except for placing more of a formally oriented restriction on the scope of the crucial qualifier relevant. In such a case, the goal would not be full functional equivalence, but a more limited category of this—thus specified as equivalence in certain, specified relevant respects.[54] The translation would still be stylistically marked in terms of the rl, but not on all linguistic levels of the text and only in some discernable and appreciable manner. Certain phonological distinctions would be the very minimum, for this is perhaps where the style of a given translation is most immediately perceptible. How does the text read aloud and sound? That is a criterion of utmost importance in any Bible translation.

My primary, indeed ultimate, point of reference in the present study is a translation that is literary throughout.[55] In other words, such a version aims to manifest a harmonious coordination of artistic qualities on all levels of linguistic structure in the TL. This would normally be effected within the formal framework of a particular TL *genre,* one that is the closest functional equivalent of the SL discourse that is being rendered. It would also be characterized by its own set of distinctive stylistic features that operate in conjunction to effect the principal communicative purpose(s) of the original text. However as noted above, varied levels of artistic involvement are possible—depending, it must be emphasized, on the target-specific *Skopos* that has been decided upon. Even a single literary technique, such as rhythmic alliteration or some other phonological embellishment, may be applied in a more or less restrained manner. This would concern the degree of markedness that is manifested and/or its extent of realization within the translation—normally limited to the microstructure of discourse organization. This possibility for allowing varied strategies of application with regard to a literary methodology results in the availability of a wider range of translational options, which would be determined by the project *Brief.* Such flexibility of usage would be reflected in turn by a number of potential translation

---

[54] "It is in finding the appropriate level of adjustment that so much of the translator's art resides" (Boase-Beier and Holman 1999:13). The term "art" here is significant: the complex juggling act involving inter-textual form, content, and function where literary translation is concerned requires a corresponding artist in the TL for success to be attained.

[55] Ryken and Ryken discuss five "fallacies about a literary approach to the Bible" (2007:xiii-xiv):
1. Viewing the Bible as literature betrays a liberal theological bias.
2. The idea of the Bible as literature is a modern idea that is foreign to the Bible itself.
3. To speak of the Bible as literature is to claim that the Bible is fictional.
4. To approach the Bible as literature means approaching it only as literature.
5. To say that the Bible is literature denies its divine inspiration.

6.8 Song from the sea: How sweet does Jonah's psalm sound? 331

types, a provision that has not been sufficiently explored and exemplified in previous works on Bible translation theory and practice.

From a theoretical perspective, it may be argued that a well-prepared *communicatively* equivalent translation of the Bible will normally turn out to be a recognized *literary* text in the target language, whether on an elaborate, common, or some specialized level of linguistic formality. Thus, if the original document, at least certain recognized portions/pericopes, has been determined to be literature,[56] then its corresponding interlingual representation should ideally be so too, as defined in accordance with recognized standards of verbal excellence in the vernacular.[57] A great deal of formal correspondence with the original text will undoubtedly be lost in this effort to gain pragmatic resemblance—"a [perceptible] similarity of communicative functions" (de Beaugrande 1968:94). But this may be compensated for through the attainment of a high degree of situational "relevance" for the intended audience, to be accomplished as the result of a creative, but disciplined exercise in artful text reconstruction.[58] The particular approach to translation being proposed here is clearly *functional* in nature and purpose, but of a specific sort, namely, "*literary* functional equivalence" *(LiFE)*, in explicit recognition of both the high literary character of the original

---

[56] The latter is a contentious issue in biblical studies. My own research (cf. Wendland 2002) indicates that it is much safer to assume *more* literariness than less with respect to a given biblical book. Recent studies seem to regularly push the general assessment of overall quality higher rather than lower in this regard, even when applied to the "less honorable" books of the Bible, for example, Leviticus or Revelation.

[57] "Thus, the translator creates a new text…the text is not new in meaning, for the semantic features and relationships will be as close as possible to those of the SL text. But the form and structure of the translation will be those of the TL…. This has the further implication that a translator must be a reasonably good writer in his [her] own right. Translation, far from being a mechanical process that might eventually be done by a machine, *is a creative literary activity*" (Stine 1980:18, added italics).

[58] "Relevance" here refers to a balanced, situationally determined appropriateness with respect to *efficiency* on the one hand (not requiring too much conceptual "processing" effort for the audience) and *effectiveness* (attaining sufficient cognitive gain or communicative impact) on the other. Both of these receptor-oriented aspects of relevance are rather difficult to identify and apply in any given speech event because the act of assessment tends to be subjective in nature and itself contextually influenced. This perspective therefore needs to be supplemented and used in close conjunction with what may be termed the "principle of *reliability*," that is, communicative relevance evaluated also with respect to the original SL text-context. In this case, the criterion of "functional equivalence" or "parity" in terms of *semantic* content and *pragmatic* intent, including the discourse-determined features of impact and appeal, continues to be a useful heuristic tool. Thus, the concerns of both relevance and reliability, applied in complementary conjunction within a given translation setting, need to be considered in the establishment and execution of a given project *Skopos*.

(biblical) text and also of our translational goal as we attempt to convey the Scriptures today in a version of similar literary quality.

This is not to suggest, however, that a complete literary version is the only valid option. There is rather a hypothetical *continuum* of translation types or styles from which to choose, ranging from a relatively literal formal reproduction to a rendering that is much more idiomatic and dynamic in both style and structure. A literary functional equivalence approach may thus be applied in a fuller or a more limited way during a given translation project, beginning with the immediately perceptible phonological and lexical levels of discourse structure (e.g., rhythmic, alliterative, euphonious TL wordings). Local figures of speech, idioms, and even genres are applied in a more intensive formal re-conditioning, as long as the essence of the original denotative and connotative meaning is preserved. In this connection, we might recommend that such a literary translation be ideally accompanied by a generous array of descriptive and explanatory notes in order to comment on certain important aspects of the biblical text that may have been lost in the message transfer process. Depending on the specific need at hand, different sizes of text may be chosen for this exercise, from an individual selection (e.g., the book of Jonah) or pericope (e.g., Jonah 2) to the Bible as a whole. As already noted, the portion to be translated and the appropriate methodological approach will be influenced by many local situational factors, including the principal medium of transmission.

Before any translation project is undertaken, therefore, the overall communication context must be thoroughly researched and an appropriate *Skopos* formulated with regard to guiding principles and practical procedures. This needs to be done in consultation with a broad spectrum of representatives of the target language community. Where the pertinent circumstances allow (e.g., the time available, suitably qualified translators, a supportive potential user group), a greater measure of *literariness*—that is, *literary* functional equivalence in terms of artistry and rhetoric—may be considered as a possible goal for which capable and creative translators may aim. They would thus utilize all the verbal resources at their disposal in order to render the Scriptures as recognized literature (or *orature*) in a fully accessed—and hopefully also accessible—vernacular style.

6.8.4.2 Jonah's song poeticized as a lyric in Chichewa

In this section I present a sample of the attempt to put several of the principles discussed above into practice in a Chewa translation of Jonah 2. This prayer pericope is reproduced below in a more vigorous lyrical style (i.e., *ndakatulo;* cf. Wendland 1993a:ch. 3), which puts special emphasis upon the text's oral-aural properties, e.g., through the use of local figures and idioms, ideophones, deictic and asseverative suffixation, rhythmic utterance, and alliterative diction. The specific *Skopos* for this project may be summarized as follows:

> This lyric (*ndakatulo*) translation is intended to serve as a base text for a Chewa youth group which is interested in preparing a dramatic performance (*sewero* 'play') of the narrative of Jonah in the vernacular, including a musical rendition of his prayer-song, set to the tune of a popular contemporary melody.

This new Chewa composition is in many respects similar to, yet also quite distinct from, the Hebrew original. Both texts capitalize on the macro-techniques of recursion and variation, but the micro-stylistic features of the vernacular version are noticeably distinct. An ironic tone is maintained in the latter, being manifested in the bold, somewhat self-centered style of this composition. A subtle enigma is simultaneously generated: What would YHWH think of a prayer like this, which even sounds a bit boastful at times, especially towards the end? The formal poetic properties of the text in translation certainly give the audience some cause for reflection: What sort of a prophet could sing like this to the LORD after behaving the way he did? The formal layout of poetic lines (though the print size has been slightly reduced) is designed to facilitate a dramatic oral elocution of this hymn, just as if the prophet himself were happily singing (or chanting) it there in a fish's belly at the bottom of the sea.

---

[2] *Inu Chauta, ndidakuitanani,*   O Chauta, I called upon you,
    umo ndikali m'mavuto akulu,   while I was there in big troubles,
    apo mudandiyankha inetu.   then you answered me indeed.
    Ndisanalowe m'malowaakufa,   Before I entered into the place of the dead,
    ndidalirira lanu thandizo,   I cried out for your, your help,
    ndipo liu langa mudalimva.   and my voice you did hear

[4] *Mauwo anali odandaula oti,* *"Nanga ndidzalowanso bwanji* *m'nyumba yanu yopatulika ija?"*	My words were complaining to say, "So how will I ever enter again into that holy house of yours?"
[3] *Ndinu mudandiponya phi!* *ine n'kuti lowu! m'nyanja.* *Muja mozamamo akuda bi!* *mweza udandizunguliradi.* [5] *Mafunde adandiyesa m'khosi,* *udzu wam'madzi wakayandeyande* *udandikwidzinga m'mutu monse.*	It was you who threw me, right out! as for me I was down! into the sea. There in that deep dark place, so black! currents kept swirling round about me. The waves reached up to my neck, the grass floating in the waters there was wrapped tightly around my whole head.
[6] *Ndidatsikira m'nyanjamo mwaa!* *m'tsinde mwa mapiri muja, inde—* *kudziko kumene maunyolo ake* *amanga nji! mpaka muyayaya.*	I descended into that sea—out of sight! at the base of the mountains, yes indeed— in the land where its chains and fetters bind so tightly! until forever-and-ever.
Koma inu Chauta Mulunguwanga, *mudanditulutsa uko kumandako* *ndili moyo gwa! mwamphumphu!*	But you LORD God of mine, you brought me out from that grave I am alive, just fine! completely.
[7] *Poona kuti,"Maayo ndikufa inedi!"* *kuganiza inu kudadza pha! m'mutu.* *Bas! pemphero la inelo lidachoka,* *lidati fiku! kwanu koyera kuja.*	On seeing that, "Mother, I'm dying I am!" the thought of you entered fully! my mind. That did it! that prayer of mine departed, it arrived right there! at that holy place.
[8] *Ha! iwo opembedza zacabecabe* *amangosiya kukhulupirika kwao* *n'kutaya cifundo mukadawacitira.*	Ha! those who worship worthless things they simply desert their faithfulness and throw away the mercy you might've shown them.
[9] *Koma ine, sindingalephere konse* *kupereka nsembe zonse kwa inu* *poyimbadi nyimbo zokuyamikani.* *Indetu, zonse zija ndidalonjeza,* *ndidzazicita ndithu mosakaika!*	But as for me, I cannot fail at all to offer all sorts of sacrifices to you while singing songs of praise to you. Yes indeed, all those things I promised, I will really do without a doubt!
N'thu, cipulumutso ca onse anthu *n'cocita inu Chauta, inu nokha!*	Truly, the salvation of people all is done by you O LORD, you alone!

6.8.4.3 *Evaluation and conclusion*

A vernacular text in a foreign language is very difficult to read, let alone appreciate, even when translated, and so my personal assessment of the preceding Chewa rendition will necessarily be brief. Both stylistically and structurally, it would seem to be a fair functional equivalent of the Hebrew text. The poetry is a fairly dynamic match—that is, forceful, graphic, expressive—hence much more effective artistically than any of the three existing Chewa Bible translations, including the recent "popular language" version. From a functional perspective, the *ndakatulo* lyric genre is especially suited for reproducing, or at least suggesting the bitter-sweet irony of the original, including the sarcastic overtone that appears to be present in verse 8. There is some structural loss in the reordering that was carried out to produce a smoother narrative flow; thus the psalmic midpoint (4b) has been shifted ahead in the text. In my opinion, there is also a minor semantic loss that occurs due to the translator's following the NRSV's more pessimistic interpretation of verse 4b rather than that of the NIV (i.e., in rendering the particle '*ak*). However, the relative significance of this passage within the development of the entire passage is retained due to the text's representation in Chichewa as a rhetorical question in direct speech. The climactic segment of the prayer (6b) is similarly highlighted by devices such as these: alliteration, a vocative expression of the divine name, a double ideophone, and separate text formatting.

The ultimate test of any translation is of course that which is furnished by public opinion and usage—in particular by the intended target group. It remains to be seen therefore how various audiences will react to a production that has been specified by the guiding *Skopos* of this project, namely, a youth-based dramatization of Jonah's turbulent, ethnocentrically colored mission to Nineveh. How, for example, will younger listeners respond to a poetic, and possibly also musical, rendering of Jonah's song from the seabed? On the other hand, how will an older, more conservative audience react? Will this interpretive reading and intuitive re-writing effectively express the prophet's surprisingly optimistic perspective on his personal situation—especially the spiritual proximity that he apparently feels in relation to a God whose "presence" he had so recently been trying to distance himself from? Hopefully the rhetorically motivated translation style will also help to suggest the ironically sour note in Jonah's attitude towards the Lord, thus reinforcing the underlying implication of his prophetic narrative as a whole. Certainly the need for combating the insidious dangers of social and ethnic prejudice is a message for the people of God that is just as relevant today as it was in the days when this book was first composed and transmitted.

To sum up, the preceding hermeneutical and translational experiment ultimately has a practical motivation and goal. It is intended to encourage similar poetic and oratorical efforts in the production of additional, more specialized, audience-specific and setting-sensitive versions of the Scriptures—texts that capitalize on the full oral and literary resources of a Bantu language, whether Chewa or any other member of this illustrious African linguistic family. How artistically "sweet" (or rhetorically "strong") does Jonah's song sound in your language? If you are not a Bible translator, it might well pay to put forth the effort to compare several popular versions in your mother-tongue in order to find out—and also to discover in this contrastive process what difference it makes.

7

"Can These Bones Live Again?"—Rhetoric of the Gospel in Ezekiel 33–37

7.1 Introduction

The book of Ezekiel can probably lay claim to being the most minor among the Major Prophets as far as recent scholarly interest and output goes.[1] Journal articles on this text tend to appear with relative infrequency, and Ezekiel is certainly never the first to be treated in any given commentary series or prophetic anthology. The situation may be changing with regard to available source material, however, since several notable, first-rate commentaries on Ezekiel, or a portion of it, have recently been published,[2] and these will probably give rise to an appreciable increase in journalistic activity as scholars react to and supplement the larger studies. My own delay in dealing with

---

[1] For a brief, albeit somewhat dated survey of the field, see McKeating 1993:chs. 4–5. "Ezekiel" can mean "God is strong," "God strengthens," and/or "God makes hard" (cf. 3:8, 24:24); thus, the prophet's name summarizes the twofold thrust of his message—whether "gospel" or "law."

[2] See, for example, Allen 1990, Blenkinsopp 1990, Block 1997a, 1998, Cooper 1994, Greenberg 1997.

the book stems from several reasons: a certain amount of apprehension concerning its anticipated difficulty, that is, due to the sheer size of the composition; its diversity in terms of genre and relative disproportion of prose; the hermeneutical problems occasioned by certain figuratively fantastic or apocalyptic passages (e.g., chs. 1, 38–39); as well as a relatively large number of lexical and textual uncertainties.[3] However, I have also experienced a rather strong attraction to Ezekiel on account of the drama and dynamism of the prophet's discourse, which arguably includes some of the most vivid and evocative, hence memorable, pericopes in all of Scripture.

In view of certain limitations with respect to both time and space, I have selected a smaller portion of Ezekiel to focus upon in the present study. This integral text segment, which includes chapters 33 to 37, is especially appealing because of its gospel emphasis and consequent relevance to the entire message of the New Testament. In these five chapters most of the "good news" of Ezekiel's prophecy to Israel (actually Judah) is concentrated, and this gives the unit a theological significance that goes far beyond its actual size in relation to the rest of the book. My attention will center on the general and specific compositional techniques that are manifested by the prophet as he endeavors to verbally persuade his compatriots to adopt a new attitude to go along with a new heart and a new spirit (36:26). This concerned their covenantal bond (past, present, and future) with their sovereign yet merciful Lord, *YHWH*, a relationship that needed to be transformed into action in keeping with their holy status as his select people living in a pagan world.

After an overview of the book's overall arrangement as an artfully constructed dramatic prophecy in defense of the justice of God ("theodicy"), I will describe some of the major literary markers that serve to delineate chapters 33–37 as a cohesive and coherent text segment within the book. The second half of this chapter is then devoted to an examination of the salient structural and stylistic properties of this thematically central pericope. This survey includes a

---

[3] The nature and scope of my analysis does not allow me to deal substantially with the outstanding lexical or textual problems to be found in Ezekiel. In any case, these do not affect my presentation in a significant way. As far as the textual difficulties are concerned, I would subscribe to the position taken by L. Allen in his helpful commentary: "In the quest for an eclectic text MT is of such importance that very strong grounds are needed to substantiate other readings.... The principle of the harder reading will often induce the retention of MT…" (1990:xxvii-iii). The differences between the MT and the LXX are probably best explained as a reflection of the translation process itself or perhaps different underlying literary traditions; thus the latter probably utilized as a variant translational "base text" (*Vorlage*; cf. Cooper 1994:36; see also Dillard and Longman III 1994. For brief, critical comments on the LXX translation, see Alexander 1986 and Taylor 1969.

description of some of the principal literary features that play a prominent role in the prophet's gospel-based rhetorical strategy. It will also consider their chief pragmatic functions as these relate his twofold message of comfort and hope to a receptive minority, coupled with a stern warning and rebuke for a rather hardened and hostile audience living in justly deserved exile.

7.2 The drama of prophetic discourse in Ezekiel

7.2.1 Overall plot progression

The following diagram is a crude two-dimensional attempt to depict the larger organizational and connotative "plot" design of the complete prophetic work known as "Ezekiel,"[4] with special reference to the crucial kerygmatic core comprising chapters 33–37 (marked by **).

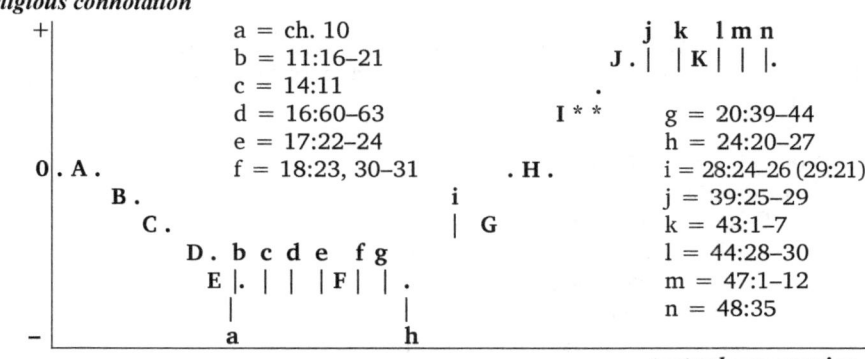

A schematic depiction of the macrostructure of Ezekiel 1–48
(X = main compositional units, x = focal internal pericopes/passages)

---

[4] Evidence in favor of the essentially unitary authorship of the book of "Ezekiel," namely, a text produced (orally and/or in writing) by a 7th–6th century BCE Judean prophet by that name, to my mind far outweighs the various arguments adduced against such a position. This includes such factors as: the book's well-organized and balanced overall structure; a general uniformity of language and style (also certain linguistic anomalies that reflect great emotional agitation and possibly an in-group, "priestly" register); its strongly autobiographical nature; its extended sequence of dated prophecies; the content progression moving conventionally from mainly condemnation (judgment) to largely blessing (restoration); and the relatively consistent reflection of a single "implied author" in terms of character and personality. For further discussion in support of this position, see Cooper 1994:31–37; Greenberg 1997:396; Taylor 1969:14–16; also Greenberg 1986; Greenberg 1987:215, 219, 222; Rosenberg 1987:194–195.

On a deeper level of textual organization, Ezekiel also manifests a rather more detailed architectonic design, one that assumes the shape of a semi-narrative, "dramatic" macrostructural (plot) development as shown below (the letters A-K correspond on these different displays):[5]

A. Ezekiel's vision of the glory of the LORD in exile! (ch. 1)
| B. The LORD calls Ezekiel to be a prophetic "watchman" announcing a message of judgment (2–3)
| | C. Prophetic symbolic actions and their significance with respect to the judgment of Jerusalem (4–5)
| | | D. Oracles of judgment against the "house of Israel" (6–7)
| | | E. Visions of a defiled Temple and a corrupt leadership (8–11)
| | | F. Various symbolic acts, oracles, laments, legal addresses, disputations, parables, allegories of judgment, and priestly regulations—all condemning "Israel" (12–24)
| | | |G. Oracles of judgment against surrounding pagan nations (25–32)
| H. The LORD renews Ezekiel's prophetic commission as a "watchman" for the "house of Israel" (33)
| I. Messianic oracles, parables, and a vision of the return, renewal, and restoration of Israel (34–37)
| | J. Oracles of judgment concerning the pagan prince Gog of Magog (38–39)
K. Ezekiel's vision of the new Temple and the glory of the LORD, living among his people (40–48)

A. *initial situation* (ch.1) =>
  B. *problem* (2–3) =>
    C-D. *complication* (4–9) =>
      E. *crisis* (10, the LORD's glory leaves the temple!) =>
        F. *deepening* crisis (11–24) =>
          G. *interlude* (25–32) =>
            H. *turning point* (33) =>
              I. thematic gospel **peak** (34–36) =>
                I'. emotive **climax** (37) =>
                  J. *reinforcement* (38–39) =>
                    K. *denouement*/resolution (40–48, the LORD's glory returns to the temple, thus residing once more among his people!)

---

[5] P. R. House has similarly, but with considerably more detail, analyzed the book of Zephaniah as "a prophetic drama" on the basis of these criteria: "It has a structure of alternating speeches between characters, a plot construction around a distinct conflict and resolution, a set of developing characters, and a dramatic point of view" (1988:106). The text of Ezekiel manifests these same basic features, but in a considerably more complicated manner of construction, as would be expected in a work that is over ten times as long. The "character" of the Ezekiel prophet, for example, is developed through actions (his own and what happens to him)

7.2 The drama of prophetic discourse in Ezekiel

The book opens on a religiously neutral (0), albeit emotively shocking, note with a graphic, attention-attracting vision of the four living creatures (cherubim, cf. 10:9–14) that attend the glory of the LORD (1:26–28). After this appropriately awesome introduction to a great and glorious God, the prophetic problem is immediately introduced as Ezekiel ("God is strong"), the watchman, is divinely commissioned for his challenging task, namely, to testify to the stubborn rebels of the house of Israel (= the chosen people of *YHWH*) (chs. 2–3). The difficulty of this assignment is underscored (the plot's complication) as the various, serious covenant-violating sins of Israel are exposed through both prophetic symbolic action and also judicial accusation (idolatry, sacrilege, immorality, social oppression, foreign alliances; chs. 4–9). Along with this graphic indictment are specified the fitting punishments that have been predicted in Scripture for such religious failure and moral wickedness (e.g., famine, death, destruction, imprisonment, and exile; i.e., the so-called "covenant curses"; cf. Lev 26 and Deut 28).

The psychological and spiritual low-point (–) of Ezekiel's prophetic corpus is probably reached with his vision of the desecrated and now disgusting Temple scene (chs. 8–11), which provokes a departure of the LORD's *shekinah* glory (10:18–19 [passage a]) as a prelude to a prediction of its ultimate destruction (24:20–27 [h]). This would indeed be a severe crisis of faith for the people of God, especially the faithful few who constituted the marked remnant (9:4, 8). The diverse literary forms that comprise chs. 12–19 serve to spotlight different aspects of the spiritual calamity that had befallen all Israel, its capital Jerusalem in particular (e.g., chs. 15–16). In the seven-stage unit sequence of pivotal ch. 20, the LORD himself outlines for the elders of Israel the despicable nature of the people's sin and their need for punishment (*past*: 3–7, 8–12, 13–20, 21–26; *present*: 27–31), but he follows this with his divine program for purification and restoration (*future*: 32–38, 39–44). God's pronouncement of absolute judgment and the reasons for it are reiterated in chs. 21–23, and this leads to the peak (or pit) of depressing intensity found in the climactic ch. 24, at the book's structural midpoint. Here the siege and sack of Jerusalem is announced, Ezekiel's wife dies, and a complete ruin of the LORD's sacred house is foretold. Thus, the four great pillars of traditional Israelite faith will have been destroyed, that

---

as well as by his words, which generally express some message from the LORD. The nature of his opposition among the people, on the other hand, is usually revealed by means of a short, internal, characterizing quotation, e.g., 33:24, 30.

is, as seen from the people's cynical perspective: land, temple, Davidic kingship, and covenant. That this is not really the end of it all is demonstrated by the predictive words of *YHWH* through his prophet in the second half of this prophetic compilation.

There follows a series of judgment oracles (featuring the accusatory conjunctive pairing יַ֫עַן...לָכֵ֫ן "because" [indictment]..."therefore" [verdict]) against the surrounding nations (chs. 25–32), which features an important cross-over linkage with ch. 24 through reference to the LORD's now "desecrated sanctuary" (24:21/25:3). This distinct section, which contains some of Ezekiel's most forceful and colorful poetry,[6] acts as a gradually rising thematic "interlude" (i.e., emphasizing divine retribution upon Israel's arrogant enemies) in preparation for the connotatively positive message that is announced in the book's final third portion. Periodically piercing the psychological gloom that accompanies the prophetic account of the downward spiritual spiral of Israel and its neighbors is a sequence of relatively short good-news passages that encourage the faithful with a reminder of the LORD's covenantal mercy. These reassuring textual precursors anticipate, or "foreshadow," their full compositional realization in chs. 34–48 (note that the first passage, 11:17–20, is topically reiterated by the last in 28:24–26, which divides the section denouncing the nations (chs. 25–32) structurally into two balanced halves).[7]

Another major turning point is reached with chapter 33 [H]. This transitional and resumptive unit (i.e., following from 24:27) reiterates a number of the images and topics that appeared in first half of the book (e.g., Ezekiel's call as "watchman"; cf. 3:17–21/33:2–9 [B]), with a special concern for a linkage with autobiographical elements in the text-framing chs. 3 and 24.[8] The fugitive who had escaped the devastation of

---

[6] My position on the compositional integrity of this unit differs from that of Boadt 1990:5. For a general overview of its literary-poetic beauty, see Rosenberg 1987:199.

[7] For the details of this symmetrical division, see Block 1998:4–5.

[8] The corresponding segments in chs. 24 and 33 that refer to the destruction of Jerusalem and its "sanctuary," the Temple, are an illustration of the structural bounding device of *exclusio*, i.e., they serve to *externally* bracket the enclosed foreign judgment oracles section (chs. 25–32). The operation of *exclusio* is thus similar to that of *inclusio*, except that the former is constituted by a pair of passages that lie just *outside* the initial and final borders of the demarcated unit. Other salient structural evidence must of course be evaluated in order to determine precisely which marking device is present in any given instance. Parunak, for example, regards the correspondences in chs. 24 and 33 to be an instance of *inclusio*, thus enclosing the single discourse block covering chs. 24–33 (as cited in Allen 1990: xxiii, who disagrees). In this connection it may be noted that it is both structurally and thematically inaccurate to regard 33:1–20 as the "latter half of Ezekiel's concluding prophecy against Egypt" (Alexander 1986:904).

7.2 The drama of prophetic discourse in Ezekiel

Jerusalem according to divine prediction (24:25–27) arrives in Babylon to report that "the city has fallen!" (הֻכְּתָה הָעִיר, 33:22). The preceding evening in a special visitation, God restored Ezekiel's voice (cf. 3:26/24:27/33:22) so that he was ready to utter an appropriate prophetic response to the tragic news—that is, he can now speak words other than those expressing primarily condemnation and woe in conjunction with a message of righteous judgment from the LORD (2:9–10).[9] In short, he is able to resume a much more positive pastoral role among his people.

Thus, the first half of ch. 33 (vv. 1–20) functions like a formal recommissioning of Ezekiel as a prophet among God's flock in parallel with chs. 2–3 (2:5/33:33, cf. Jonah 3:1–2; see also the medial segment of 18:21–32).[10] He begins his work anew in the next discourse section (33:21–33), that is, *after* the cataclysmic fall of the sacred city of *YHWH* has been announced. Ezekiel now acts primarily as a messenger of *good* news (of "sweetness," cf. 3:3) and a spokesman of the Shepherd-LORD's future program of gracious restoration (ch. 34). But first, the still outstanding sins of the nation need to be punished in order to lead people to a complete repentance, especially with regard to the sordid moral and spiritual corruption of idolatry and adultery (33:25–26; cf. 22:1–16). We notice how these spaced autobiographical references (chs. 3, 24, 33) serve to highlight the tripartite division of the book into its foundational beginning (1–3 + 4–24), which covers the Babylonian period prior to the destruction of Jerusalem (586/7 BCE); a temporally diverse, topical bridge (25–32); and a triumphant ending that presents a revelational post-586 perspective on the rejuvenated, reconstituted people of God (33–39 + 40–48).

After ch. 33, Ezekiel's message is one of progressively increased blessing for the LORD's followers concerning both the near and the distant future. The former setting undoubtedly has reference to a return of the Jews to Palestine after their period of captivity in Babylon. The latter age, however, may be posited

---

[9] Alexander does not regard v. 22 alone of ch. 33 to be a flashback in time and thus interprets the entire discourse from v. 23 to 39:29 as being uttered by Ezekiel the night before the messenger arrived with his sad report concerning Jerusalem (1986:909). Though possible, this does not seem to be a very logical perspective on these passages, which follow more naturally upon the news of the city's fall (cf. Allen 1990:151; Greenberg 1997:681–682). For some pertinent remarks on Ezekiel's divinely imposed "silence," see Rosenberg 1987:200 (cf. Taylor 1969:27 for further thoughts on his "ritual dumbness").

[10] Although it is "not cast in the form of a call narrative" (Block 1998:235), 33:1–20 clearly corresponds to 3:17–21 in both form and function.

on the basis of earlier prophets such as Isaiah as a prediction of the incorporation of individuals from all nations into the holy people of God, that is, "Israel" of Messianic (neo-"Davidic") times (e.g., 34:11–16; 36:24; 37:21–23—cf. Isa 11, John 10; see also 39:25–29; cf. Mt 25:31–46; Rev 7:9–17, 20:11–15). The generally optimistic atmosphere of Ezekiel's all-encompassing "gospel" is occasionally interrupted by retrospective judicial reminders of the nation's apostate past and present state, giving detailed reasons why a complete renewal and divine restoration were necessary (e.g., 36:16–23).[11] The different aspects of the broken covenant needing repair are summarized in 37:12–14, 21–28 (cf. 18:30–32, 20:32–44). These involved, for example, a penitent recognition of the absolute sovereignty of Yahweh, a complete religious transformation and purification of the people, an empowering outpouring of the divine Spirit upon them, and the return to a blessed state of fellowship with the LORD. Such a miraculous change would be effected through the ministry of the future divine Shepherd-King. The central edifying and encouraging truths contained in chs. 33–37 (to be examined in greater detail below) are prophetically heightened (but not necessarily clarified) in terms of their temporal as well as spatial scope by means of the militant, apocalyptic, battle imagery of the paired judgment speeches found in chs. 38–39.[12]

Within the book's final third portion, important backward and forward references function to demarcate its dynamic good-news nucleus. For example, the prophecy concerning the LORD dwelling in his sanctuary at the

---

[11] The universalism of a prophet like Isaiah is often contrasted with the alleged ethnic "parochialism" of Ezekiel who is viewed as focusing his hope "on peace for the restored nation of Israel" (Cooper 1994:43; cf. Block 1997a:47). Such a contrastive hermeneutical perspective depends of course on one's interpretation of the reference underlying the key term "Israel" in Ezekiel, that is, whether broader or narrower in scope. I adopt a wider accommodative, "Messianic" viewpoint based on Ezekiel's assumed familiarity with the prophecies of Isaiah and their incorporative nature, e.g., ch. 56; see Ezek 47:22–23 (cf. Taylor 1969:253, which reflects Young 1960:247–248. This position is echoed in turn by Bullock 1986:249; see also the relevant remarks by Van Gemeren 1990:335–337). For a theological summary of my perspective on the relationship between "the new Israel" and "the [NT] Church" in relation to Ezekiel 33–37, see Clowney 1989: 214–216. Therefore, it is my belief that although Ezekiel's gospel offers "hope" to believers of every age, it was (will be) ultimately fulfilled in the Messiah who became the Gospel personified and in his Church (*contra* Block 1998:367). He will one day come again to make the fact of total salvation, renewal, and restoration a concrete personal reality in the experience of all the faithful.

[12] The structure of chs. 38–39 is well outlined in Block 1998:431–432. Although Block does not consider these chapters as being an instance of "apocalyptic" writing (or reference; ibid., 428), it would appear that many of the characteristics of this literary-religious genre are present. For example, "in Ezekiel 38, the end of days is the time when Gog invades Israel, and so it is a time of distress, but one that culminates in the distruction of the invader" (Collins 1997:56; cf. also 91–92).

7.2 The drama of prophetic discourse in Ezekiel

end of its climactic segment (37:28; cf. 24:21) anticipates the temple vision of chs. 40–48 (note 48:35), hence function also as an externally defining *exclusio* for the eschatological overview and powerful divine warrior scenery of chs. 38–39. There is also a double reference to Meshech and Tubal (38:2; cf. 32:26), which serves two purposes. Thematically, these names incorporate Japhethites together with the previously mentioned Shemites and Hamites into Ezekiel's expansive revelation of the future of all nations, and structurally they create another *exclusio,* this time around the dramatic peak of chs. 33–37. The book's concluding section recounts an architectural vision of the holy perfection of the restored Temple and its sacred precincts (chs. 40–48). This includes several strong, intertextually resonant depictions of salvation (e.g., 44:28–30 [priesthood]; 47:1–12 [river of life]) plus a vital image of reversal as the LORD's radiant glory is seen to reenter the Temple (43:1–7; cf. 10:18–19).[13] The Ezekielian prophetic corpus now comes to a most satisfying narrative close (thematic resolution) as *YHWH* is once more portrayed as tabernacling there in peace among his obedient people and for their eternal well being (אֶשְׁכָּן־שָׁם; 43:7; 44:28–30; 47:9–12; 48:35b; cf. 37:26–28; Ps 46, esp. vv. 7, 11).

7.2.2 Correspondence and contrast in the plot design

There is an overall recursive balance in the construction of Ezekiel with respect to the book as a whole and also in relation to many of the constituent sections. The serene vision of the LORD dwelling harmoniously and benevolently among his people in a Temple-dominated realm at the end of the book (K, on the figure above) contrasts markedly with the turbulent, theophanic depiction of God's kinetic glory being manifested to Ezekiel in their place of exile at the beginning (A). The prophet is divinely commissioned twice as it were: first for a ministry of condemnation (B) and then, once the judgment has taken place, to deliver a message of consolation and hope for the future (H). Thus, the various oracles, symbolic actions, and visions (etc.) of indictment,

---

[13] The two dominant pericopes of this final unit, namely, the vision of the return of God's glory to the temple (43:1–9) and that of the river of life (47:1–12) appear to divide chs. 40–48 into three sections: 40:1–43:9; 43:10–47:12; 47:13–48:35 (for a different structural perspective, see Block 1998:498). Block notes some interesting parallels between chs. 40–48 and the "Exodus narratives" on the one hand, and Revelation 21–22 on the other (ibid., 499–503). Ezekiel's priestly role in relation to the crucial manifestation of the "glory of the LORD" is considered in Sweeney 1998:91–92.

disputation, and reproach that appear in sections C-F correspond by way of reversal to those of comfort, hope, and encouragement in the dual apical portion of I-I'. Finally, the sequence of standard judgment speeches against seven representative foreign nations (G) is both balanced and rhetorically enhanced by the epiphanic sevenfold prophecy against the alien alliance of Gog et al. in J.[14] In short then, within the inclusion formed by segments A and K, we observe a general unfolding (terrace) pattern of elements that repeats itself in terms of a basic thematic polarity of similarity and contrast, i.e., B + C (D-F) + G :: H + I-I' + J. Obviously, Ezekiel is no hodgepodge collection of oracles; it is rather an artfully and purposefully constructed prophetic compilation that brings "the word of the LORD" to its addressees of all ages in a most convincing and convicting manner.[15]

A summary of the dramatic plot of Ezekiel's prophetic work may be stated along the following lines: He was called to serve the disconsolate community of God's people in exile (1:1–2). Their forced exodus from the land had been brought about by profound and prolonged covenantal violations (ch. 2). As a result of the disaster that had devastated their nation, these people were undoubtedly both psychologically and spiritually depressed—but many defiantly so (3:7). They had not yet learned the LORD's punitive lesson from history despite the loss of the chief corner stones of their culture

---

[14] Each of the seven constituent units in chs. 38–39 is introduced by the citation formula: "Thus speaks the Sovereign LORD" (כֹּה אָמַר אֲדֹנָי יְהוִה); 38:3–9, 10–13, 14–16, 17–23; 39:1–16, 17–24, 25–29. There are other ways of segmenting this section (e.g., Block 1998:431–432), but the emphasis, especially in ch. 39, is upon manifesting the LORD God in his great glory and holiness (cf. 38:23; 39:7, 21–22, 27).

[15] For a somewhat different view of the symmetrical macrostructure of Ezekiel, see Van Gemeren 1990:326. It may be noted that the seemingly sequentially disruptive oracles against the nations (i.e., segments G and J) are interposed between the two distinct periods ("dispensations") of YHWH's dealing with "Israel," namely, for judgment: 1–24 | 25–32 | 33, and for blessing: 34–37 | 38–39:20 | 39:21–48. Thus, the larger discourse structure itself suggests that God both reproves and restores his people as a testimony also to the surrounding nations—"so that they will know that I am the LORD!" (36:22–23, 36; cf. Van Gemeren 1990:333). Certain aspects of this work that may make it sound redundant, bombastic, contrived, or clumsily redacted to the modern reader and critic were undoubtedly evaluated quite differently by those who were receiving the prophet's message aurally and in the original language—whether first or second-hand, e.g., with regard to the sometimes shocking imagery (e.g., in ch. 16) and the many punctuating discourse formulae. The latter in particular serve to stress the divine source and authority of Ezekiel's oracles and other speech forms—the reiterated prophetic content of which had once been thoroughly ignored and transgressed by the ancestors, a fateful choice that inevitably led to their downfall and the destruction of their nation. The eloquence and well-formedness of Ezekiel as a whole leads some scholars to conclude that "much of his prophecy…is likely to have been *conceived* as literature from the beginning" (McKeating 1993:13)—of *oral* literature (orature), that is (e.g., ch. 37).

7.2 The drama of prophetic discourse in Ezekiel

and religion: their land, capital city, temple, and its ritual. Perhaps the pious among them were now asking themselves: Has *YHWH* now revoked his eternal covenant with Israel? Is he really inferior to the gods of the nations? Has he finally left us for good? Is this exile the end?

It was Ezekiel's unenviable task to explain—and to justify—why the answer was a definite, divine negative to questions such as these. His message was in essence a dramatic *theodicy* in defense of the justice of Yahweh—of God's right to punish all unfaithful desecrators of his covenant, yet also of his prerogative to show mercy to those who were truly penitent. Ezekiel would thus minister to this largely hardened and bitter group of deportees in essentially a twofold manner, speaking as the LORD's chosen mouthpiece to proclaim a message of strong reproof combined with reassuring consolation concerning: (a) why this terrible calamity had occurred and what they needed to do about it, namely, repent (16:59–63; 33:11) and trust in the LORD's future deliverance (28:25–26; 34:11–16); (b) why there was no need to despair, for *YHWH* had great plans in mind for his people, but only for the righteous among them (3:21; 18:30–32; 43:7–9; note how this divine caveat covers the complete text).

For half of the book (chs. 1–24), with brief respite (e.g., 11:16–20), the LORD thunders against "the house of Israel" through his long-suffering prophet. These were harsh messages of condemnation, conveyed both verbally and in nonverbal symbolic action, that were intended to break down their hard hearts and obstinate spirits (e.g., 17:21). Nevertheless, these diverse pronouncements are occasionally interrupted by poignant appeals for repentance (e.g., 18:3–32). God makes it crystal clear in the revelatory visions and condemnatory parables of Ezekiel just exactly who he is ("and they will *know* [= recognize/acknowledge/confess]…!")—namely, the holy Sovereign LORD of all who is in total control of earth's events, religious as well as secular (e.g., the removal of his "glory" from the temple, ch. 10, and unfaithful Israel from their land, ch. 11). Furthermore, his absolute holiness will not be compromised by the cheap harlotry of his people (as emphasized in the jarring allegories of the prostitute and the two adulterous sisters, chs. 16 and 23). The predicted downfall of the city (24:20–27) is held in suspenseful abeyance throughout the series of declarations of righteous punishment upon every nation that refuses to acknowledge Yahweh (chs. 25–32)—right up until the stark and unexpected announcement of its fulfillment (33:21).

By then (as the linear plan of this dramatic prophetic plot unfolds), Ezekiel had already been re-authorized to preach the same sermon of rebuke (33:2–9; cf. 3:17–21) and repentance (33:11–20; cf. 18:21–32). Now, however, there was a decided difference: the glorious results of the return of a remnant to the LORD (cf. 11:13, 16–21; 14:22–23) are revealed in a manner that impressively reverses the former images of death and devastation. God's re-gathered, chosen people will receive a new land, a new Shepherd, a new sanctuary, a new heart and spirit, and a new covenant (chs. 34–37). However, *YHWH* stresses that fact that his merciful acts of restoration and renewal are effected solely for the sake of his "holy *name*" (= the divine ethos/personality/character) and to manifest his glorious omnipotence before all nations (36:22–23), as notably expressed in the book's reiterated leitmotif, e.g., "Then you will know that I am the LORD" (36:11). This divine recognition formula, which underscores the fundamentally *theodicidal* character of Ezekiel's message, occurs in this or some variant form 66 times throughout the text (note especially 20:5, 7, 12, 20, 26, 38, 44; cf. Ex 6:2, 7:17, 10:2, etc.).[16]

A concluding complex proof oracle of apocalyptic judgment is progressively developed in two stages (chs. 38–39).[17] It shows via some vivid, panoramic (at times grotesque and subtly ironic) imagery that Yahweh in his supreme sovereignty also controls the distant, unforeseeable future and will most certainly defeat even the most formidable foe of his faithful flock in order to allow his manifold promises to be realized. Thus, Israel's hope was assured in the final extended vision of a new country, city, sanctuary, and cultus of the LORD (chs. 40–48). This quartet of powerful traditional symbols stood as God's guarantee of all his covenantal commitments, made on behalf of a renewed community of faith among whom his glory forever dwells (43:1–7) and from whom the river of lasting life is dispensed (47:1–12). It is an ideal place where everything is in order and every person has his/her place—with the LORD (47:13–48:35). Thus, the prophecy concludes on a familiar note, with some powerful consolatory imagery which

---

[16] For this reason too the following conclusion by McKeating concerning the LORD's motivation would seem to be very much in error: "The origins of the Lord's interest in Israel are in the book of Ezekiel left totally unexplained" (1993:80). Then, as now, God's manifestation of saving mercy to his people is motivated solely by grace (cf. Rom 1:16–17, 3:21–26).

[17] Block argues against an "apocalyptic" interpretation of chs. 38–39 (1998:427–28); he prefers to understand this text as "a satirical literary cartoon" (ibid., 431).

7.2.3 The importance of discourse (structural) analysis

The preceding overview of the larger compositional organization supports Joseph Blenkinsopp's contention (with specific reference to Ezekiel) that "since the way a text is structured is an integral part of the total meaning, it is important in the first place to understand how the book [or any major pericope] is put together" (Blenkinsopp 1990:3). This is because meaning is always construed in terms of units and relationships that are either similar or different both qualitatively and quantitatively. A variation in one's hypothesis regarding the total discourse organization of a given passage will inevitably juxtapose correspondingly different segments and linkages, thus providing an alternative perspective on the text's constitution, one that may be more—or less—correct and complete. In isolation on its own, a given difference of opinion with regard to textual arrangement may not matter too much. But the combination of a number of such divergences will undoubtedly affect one's overall interpretation and application of the data to a greater or lesser extent.[19]

On the other hand, the search for structure and a unity of discourse form (whether explicitly or implicitly expressed) is an essential analytical exercise, for in the case of Ezekiel (as with the entire prophetic corpus), "the unique style and use of structuring devices (especially the recognition formula) so permeate the book...that it cries out for the commentator to discern an overarching theological conception behind it" (Boadt 1990:21). In

---

[18] As the dramatic plot of Ezekiel unfolds, we find—in addition to an ever-present emphasis on the divine word (e.g.,....שִׁמְעוּ דְבַר־יְהוָה: כֹּה אָמַר אֲדֹנָי יְהוִה..., 36:1b–2a)—a continuous recycling of the "seven common [thematic] components of prophetic writing" (House 1988:113): election/covenant => sin/unfaithfulness => judgment/punishment => mercy/recalling => repentance/recommitment => redemption/restoration => testimony/praise. Considered individually and together, these concepts serve to foreground Ezekiel's primary concern, namely, to describe, to vindicate, and to magnify the awesome grace, glory, and holiness of the LORD YHWH.

[19] This may be observed, for example, in the editorial decision to group chs. 33–34 together under the heading "True Shepherd," 35–36 under "Land," and 37–39 under "People" (La Sor, Hubbard, and Bush 1982:466); in the opinion that ch. 33 "interrupts" the basic tripartite structure of the book (Rofe 1997:41); in a compositional arrangement based on only two major "parts" and which leaves ch. 33 completely detached from chs. 34–37 (Block 1997b:617–618); or in a "grand apologetic scheme" that omits any reference to Yahweh's essential Spirit-directed action of purifying his polluted people (Block 1998:272; cf. 36:24–27, 31, 33; 37:23, 28).

this case, the reiterated declaration of divine revelation ("then you/they will know that...") reinforces the basic nature of the work as a theodicy. Furthermore, the highly organized arrangement of the discourse on all levels of composition attests to the surpassingly upright character of the God it proclaims (as epitomized in the prolonged Temple vision, chs. 40–48). Finally, the book's graphic, often shocking and/or surprising imagery intimates both the seriousness of the message being conveyed as well as the perfect holiness (complete "otherness") of its divine Author (e.g., ch. 37).

From a macro-stylistic perspective, we note in the textual outline of Ezekiel as it has been described above the prominent features of <u>significant segmentation</u> and <u>parallel paneling</u>. The former refers to the compositional technique whereby many of the larger compositional components of the book are either unexpectedly interrupted or forcefully concluded by some dramatic passage of special importance, which is thereby emphasized (e.g., 3:24–27 [Ezekiel stricken with selective dumbness]; 10 [the divine glory departs]; 16:59–63 [covenant renewal]; 20:39–44 [land restoration]; 28:24–26 [return of the people]; 35 [judgment of Edom; cf. 25:12–14]; 43:1–7 [the divine glory returns]). Perhaps this too is a subtle literary means of reflecting the manner in which the almighty LORD God suddenly intrudes upon the seemingly relentless cycle of this world's principal events to demonstrate both his supreme righteous sovereignty in relation to human history (e.g., by bringing disaster upon a wicked Gog, 39:1–20) as well as his constant and abundant mercy with reference to his people (e.g., by undoing their foreign captivity, 39:21–29).

In the case of parallel paneling,[20] we observe how one integral portion of text is later reflected upon in another section, that is for the purpose of thematic contrast, reversal, reinforcement, and/or expansion (e.g., the prophetic commissioning of Ezekiel, 2–3 => his recommissioning, 33; the mountains of Israel ruined, 6 => they are restored, 36:1–15; the LORD's glory departs from the Temple, 10 => it returns again, 43:1–5; prophecy against the nations, 25–32 => against Gog and allies, 38–39; the sheep scattered by their shepherds, 34:1–10 => gathered by their divine Shepherd, 34:7–16 (note the overlapping segment, 7–10). So it is that the competent and attentive reader or listener encounters many welcome surprises in the

---

[20] Block calls this stylistic feature "halving" (1998:310), and he points out many instance of the device in Ezekiel, both large and small in terms of textual extent.

form of theological insight and practical life-application as s/he apprehends the intricately patterned organization of the lively prophetic message of Ezekiel, whether as a whole or within any of the carefully positioned parts.

The structural study of a complete text, as outlined above (i.e., from the top down), is generally carried out prior to a corresponding, more detailed examination of any of its included compositional sections—a constituent pericope (bottom up) analysis. The latter is what is presented in Part Two of this study, that is, in conjunction with a survey of some of the main (not all) stylistic features of the discourse, for example: its prominent inventory of graded prophetic formulae pertaining to direct speech (i.e., to indicate an oracular unit beginning, ending, or peak);[21] evocative, memorable, message-reinforcing imagery and symbolic actions; different literary genres in artful combination; topical (more or less lexical), intra-textual recursion; plus many noteworthy inter-textual citations of and allusions to other works of the Hebrew canon or its related religious tradition. Our primary aim in this respect is to determine the various ways in which the overall form of the book as a unified literary composition contributes to a fuller communication of its intended meaning, especially with regard to significant levels of thematic content or rhetorical intent that may not be immediately apparent on the verbal surface of the text.

7.3 Chapters 33–37 as a compositional unit

The section covering chapters 33–37 includes numerous structurally cohesive and thematically emphatic reiterations of sayings that occur earlier in the book (i.e., *intra*textual recursion—that is, along with the numerous consequential *inter*textual allusions, especially to prominent covenantal passages such as Lev 26). There are a number of demarcative features, however, in addition to the semantic focus on return, renewal, and restoration that function to set this portion off as a distinct compositional unit within Ezekiel as a whole. The principal division that precedes it, a series of oracles against the nations, for example, obviously ends at the close of ch. 32. There is an elaborate structural pattern that functions to reinforce this major break in the text: Seven distinct nations are included in this ethnic catalogue, or religious rogue's gallery (Ammon, Moab, Edom,

---

[21] See, for example, Parunak 1994:485–519.

Philistia, Tyre, Sidon, and Egypt; cf. Deut 7:1); the last is clearly divided (especially by *apertures* of time setting) into seven segments (29:1–16, 29:17–21, 30:1–19, 30:20–26, 31, 32:1–16, 32:17–32); the final oracle against Egypt manifests (by key repeated opening and closing expressions) a further seven strophes, namely, 32:17–21, 22–23, 24–25, 26–27, 28 + 31–32 [a disjunctive judgment against Pharaoh], 29, and 30. The recursive number seven in this section appears to emphasize the completeness of the LORD's condemnation of *all* possible forces of wickedness in the world that would oppose the execution of his gracious covenantal plan (cf. 28:24–26).

It is clear then that at 32:32 the discourse section covering chs. 29–32 (the composite oracle against and lament concerning Egypt and its Pharaoh) comes to an end. The onset of Ezekiel's gospel-oriented kernel in ch. 33 is marked by a key-word overlap (i.e., *anadiplosis* with חֶרֶב "sword," 32:31–32/33:2–3; cf. also 24:21)[22] plus several initial markers: the word-event [prophetic word] formula (i.e., "And the word of the LORD was to me saying…"—which usually begins a high-level discourse unit; cf. 33:23; 34:1), a vocative of address, and the command to "speak!" (33:1–2). The expected date notice, which normally signals the beginning of a significant segment of text, is rhetorically postponed for special effect to 33:21, where it is especially relevant, and there is not another temporal setting of this nature given until the book's final constituent (chs. 40–48), that is, at 40:1. The section covering 33:1–20 reiterates and reinforces God's call to Ezekiel to be a prophetic "watchman" for his people (cf. 3:16–27); it thus serves as a transitional introduction to the main division that follows.

The close of the unit spanning chs. 33–37 is also quite patently indicated in the text. After its dramatic and distinctive opening vision (vv. 1–14), the climactic ch. 37 concludes (vv. 15–28) with the last, and only connotatively positive, in the series of twelve prophetic symbolic actions which are scattered throughout primarily the first half of the book, namely, that portraying two sticks of wood (Judah + Ephraim) joined together to form one. It is compositionally significant that the preceding picturesque narrative event of this type occurs way back in 24:15–24, at the conclusion of the

---

[22] For a definition and illustration of some of the major demarcative devices of Hebrew literary discourse, e.g., "anadiplosis," see Wendland 1995:ch. 2.

7.3 Chapters 33–37 as a compositional unit

book's first principal division (an instance of structural *epiphora,* or similar discourse unit endings).

Commentators differ over whether or not the twofold prophecy concerning Gog (divided roughly in the middle by analogous discourse openings, 38:1–4 and 39:1–2, i.e., structural *anaphora*) should be included as an integral part of the section beginning in ch. 33.[23] On the one hand, there are several clear ties between chs. 38–39 and 33–37, for example, in the several references to the metonymically symbolic mountains of Israel (e.g., 38:8; 39:2, 4; cf. 36:1, 4, 6, 8, etc.); the mass judicial slaughter that will take place there (e.g., 38:22; 39:4; cf. 37:1–2); the need for a similarly great purging and cleansing of God's people (e.g., 39:12–16; cf. 36:25, 33; 37:23); and particularly the words predicting a return and spiritual restoration of the house of Israel (39:25–29; cf. 34:13; 36:24, 27; 37:12–14, 21). We also note that the next major dating formula occurs at 40:1 (cf. 33:21).

However, there are also a number of important distinguishing features and supporting evidence that would justify a decision to retain chs. 38–39 as a separate and discrete compositional unit. Among them are, for example, the previously noted *exclusio* involving the LORD's sanctuary/temple, where he will dwell among his people forever (37:26–28/40:2, 5; cf. 43:7); the prominent, repetitious sectional aperture that includes names mentioned nowhere else in the book (38:1–3); the exaggerated, apocalyptic and mythopoetic imagery, which is "unlike anything else in [Hebrew] prophecy up to the exilic period" (e.g., 38:4–9, 19–23; 39:17–20);[24] an apparently different, eschatological temporal setting *after* the initial restoration of Israel (38:8, 11–12, 14—a time frame which varies in turn from that suggested at the end of the unit in 39:22–29, which harks back to the Messianic temporal setting featured in chs. 33–37); the distinct possibility that the prophecy against Gog in chs. 38–39 also represents a "heavily coded message predicting the demise of the Babylonian power,"[25] which is surprisingly not included in the catalogue of nations denounced in chs. 25–32; the depiction of a complete destruction and burial of the enemy (Gog's forces) *within* the land of Israel (38:16; 39:2–4, 11); and finally, the fact that chs. 38–39 occur

---
[23] For example, Cooper (1994:291) and Block (1998:273) do include chs. 38–39 in the section beginning at ch. 33 (or 34), while Allen (1990:xxiv) and Greenberg (1997:760) do not.

[24] McKeating 1993:114; see also Boadt 1990:17–18 and Russell 1994:30–32.

[25] McKeating 1993:122; see also Craigie 1983:266–267.

in a displaced position in some LXX manuscripts (i.e., after ch. 36).²⁶ Thus, according to the panoramic Gogian vision, *YHWH* will mightily reveal his holiness and omnipotence in the eyes of everyone on earth, that is, "Israel" (the people of God) and all heathen nations in the world (38:23; 39:27; as metonymically represented in geographic relation to the land of Palestine: Meshech and Tubal + Gomer = N, Persia = E, Cush = S, and Put = W; 38:2, 5–6).

In addition to the boundary markers listed earlier, the composite pericope of chs. 33–37 is set apart by means of a major *inclusio* through its topically contrastive beginning and ending. In 33:2 *YHWH* instructs Ezekiel to tell "[his] countrymen" (an expression of interpersonal estrangement) that he is about to bring destruction upon the land (of Israel) and its people as their righteous Judge (cf. 33:20). In 37:27, on the other hand, the word of Yahweh is transformed into one of blessing for "[his] people" (personal fellowship), namely, that he will be their God and will settle among them (in the land) as their benevolent covenantal Lord. The coming "sword" of the LORD (חֶרֶב, 3x in 33:1–3) will one day—and "forever" (לְעוֹלָם, reiterated 3x in clause final position for emphasis, 33:26, 27, 28)—be replaced by his divine "sanctuary" (מִקְדָּשִׁי, 3x in 37:27–28). Then there will no longer be any need for a prophetic "watchman" (צֹפֶה, 33:2); instead, the Davidic (Messianic) servant of the LORD will be their protective "monarch" (מֶלֶךְ) and guiding "shepherd" (רוֹעֶה, 37:24).

The solemn warning in 33:4–6 enjoining each individual to watch out for his/her "life" (דָּם + נֶפֶשׁ) is topically counter-balanced by the obvious stress throughout ch. 37 upon a harmonious "living" (חיה) and "dwelling" (ישׁב–with *YHWH*) on the part of the entire resurrected community (e.g., vv. 5–6, 9–10, 14, 25, 27). In this connection we observe the alternating pattern of judgment and blessing that runs throughout chs. 34–37 (extending also into 38–39) and indicates the two possible consequences of the human response to the LORD's call to "repent" in 33:11. This contrastive sequence, as shown below, begins after Ezekiel's own commission has been renewed (33:1–20) prior to an announcement of the fall of Jerusalem (33:21–22) as a testimony to God's people "that a prophet has been among them" (33:33).

---

²⁶ See Taylor 1969:241; Allen 1990:xxviii.

JUDGMENT	DELIVERANCE
33:23–33	
34:1–10	
	34:11–16
34:17–21	
	34:22–31
35:1–15	
	36:1–15
36:16–21 (22–23)	
	36:24v38
(37:1–3)	
	37:4–14
(37:15–18)	
	37:19–28
38:1–16	
	38:17–23
	39:1–29

The alternation of judgment and deliverance speeches in Ezekiel 34–39
(Debatable texts are indicated in parentheses.)

These and many other subtle, less apparent literary features lead us to read and interpret chs. 33–37 as a consciously composed (or compiled) unit of prophetic discourse and hence also to discern its crucial thematic and rhetorical function as an integral part of the complete text of Ezekiel.

7.4 The rhetorical purpose of the prophecy of Ezekiel

A closer look at the "texture" of chs. 33–37 (section 7.3) enables one to determine how its diverse stylistic devices coupled with significant theological content function together in elegant combination to promote the practical "rhetoric" of this section as a discrete unit within the book as a whole.[27] It

---

[27] A detailed textual study also leads to an evaluation concerning the book's style that is very different from the following: "As a writer Ezekiel is often ponderous and repetitive...for the most part he writes in prose; not a colorful, descriptive prose, but a sombre prophetic prose..." (Taylor 1969:28; cf. also McKeating on the "wordy and repetitive" prose style of Ezekiel [1993:17]). Indeed, the man seemed to have been one of the most popular litterateurs of his day—but sadly to little religious effect (cf. 33:30–32). In those places where the text may sound relatively "stiff, if not monotonous" (e.g., ch. 45), there is usually some generic explanation, such as, discourse that is "characteristic of formal ritual prescriptions" (Block 1998:660).

shows how the prophet (possibly along with a close associate-disciple-redactor), acting as a spokesman for the LORD, strategically shaped the central argument of his momentous message in order to perform a number of closely related communicative functions in relation to its presumed initially intended audience, e.g., reproof, warning, appeal (for repentance), instruction, revelation, exhortation, and encouragement. It is clear, however, that such a specification of illocutionary aims is only as valid as the degree to which the analyst is able to posit a plausible hypothesis concerning the original setting of message transmission and reception. In the case of much of the literature of the Scriptures, this is a task that is not always easy to accomplish with much certainty due to the lack of reliable information regarding the initial circumstances surrounding a particular text and subsequently brought it into circulation among the religious community.

As far as the book of Ezekiel is concerned, there is not much to go on other than what is stated in the text itself. However, in contrast to Jeremiah, his prophetic contemporary, there are many precise dates and a number of diachronically arranged narrative segments included that enable one to make a fairly accurate guess as to the external historical setting in which the prophet was working, namely, shortly before and for some years after the fall of Jerusalem to the Babylonians (587 BCE). Such contextually related information, when linked up with various other current sources, makes it possible to assume a "rhetorical situation" ("exigency") that involved, among other tensions, a severe crisis of faith for all Jewish survivors of the national calamity, those who remained in the land, but especially those who were taken captive into Babylon (Ezekiel focuses upon the latter group, where the spiritual future of Israel lay; 11:14–21; 33:23–29; cf. Jer 24:1–10). There were five main options open for enabling people to deal with this overwhelming threat to their conceptual worldview and religious perspective (cf. Butler 1988:982):

> a) **Accommodation**—the pragmatists would swiftly shift their fickle allegiance to the seemingly more powerful Babylonian gods and serve them, either instead of, or syncretistically alongside YHWH (e.g., 8:14–15).
>
> b) **Nationalism**—the radicals maintained that their recent defeat and exile was only temporary and that God would soon act to miraculously overthrow Babylon and enable them to return home to their former lives (cf. Jer 28:1–4).

7.4 The rhetorical purpose of the prophecy of Ezekiel

c) **Resistance**—the fanatics were convinced that their future lay in the eyes of optimistic magicians and diviners who were urging them not to submit to Babylonian rule, but rather to resist and seek freedom through military means (cf. Jer 27:8–15).

d) **Fatalism**—the pessimists concluded that all was lost, that there was no hope left for either the people or their religion; they were all as good as dead and may as well be buried—along with YHWH, their God (37:11).

e) **Reformation**—the penitent among the people were moved to take Ezekiel's message to heart, acknowledge their sins, and return to a renewed commitment to serve YHWH, their covenant LORD (36:26–28), trusting that He would one day work saving wonders on their behalf for the sake of his holy name (36:22–23).

It was Ezekiel's divinely-given task to stimulate and to encourage in particular this last, distinctly minority, position. As for the rest, it seemed as if they could not get the point of his message, or even if they did, stubbornly refused to accept its pressing import and implication—despite the indisputable correctness of the prophet's argument (theodicy) regarding the reason for their national disaster and current slavery. For the faithful remnant, however, Ezekiel sought to promote a clear understanding of, and a total commitment to, the LORD's desire for a restored spiritual relationship with a cleansed covenantal people: "Then [everyone] will know that I YHWH am the One who makes Israel holy…" (37:28).

This was the central focus of Ezekiel's twofold, mutually-interactive prophecy—an announcement of God's just judgment ("Law," foregrounded in chs. 1–32) coupled with promises of providential blessing ("Gospel," chs. 33–48). This longsuffering spokesman for the LORD faithfully carries out his challenging mission—exalted (with respect to YHWH), but humbled (with respect to himself)—under the inspiring guidance of the Spirit of God (2:2; 37:1), who activated and animated all the verbal (homiletical and visionary) as well as non-verbal (representational) rhetoric at his disposal (3:1–3). Ezekiel proclaims an intensely dynamic Word from Yahweh concerning his surpassing glory and perfect holiness. It is a message that needs to be preached and applied in all the fullness of its rhetorical vigor and religious vitality also to many believers today who have been overly caught up in the pressing concerns of their present political, social, or economic circumstances.

7.5 Summary of the literary-rhetorical development of chapters 33–37

The constituent structure of Ezekiel's evangel core found in chs. 33–37 as a cohesively arranged, progressively developed, and rhetorically shaped compositional entity is overviewed below according to its sequence of principal discourse units. Only the most salient thematically related aspects of a given structural and stylistic segment are included for mention. Each pericope is entitled, delineated, and then further elucidated in relation to its ostensive pragmatic, or interpersonal, communicative function. My purpose is to demonstrate how the main literary features manifested in this text serve to enhance the *persuasive* impact and appeal of the prophet's overall message. It is directed not only to the original "dry bones" audience of Jewish exiles, but also to all members of the elect people of God who live as exiles in this world (cf. 1 Pet 1:17, 2:11), even as they prepare for the new life so vividly promised by Ezekiel in this dramatic portion of Scripture. This exercise also serves to illustrate how a close, text-rhetorical analysis may contribute to a greater understanding of the artistic form and oratorical technique of any biblical pericope—whether prophetic or some other genre.

7.5.1 YHWH renews Ezekiel's call as a "watchman" for "the house of Israel" (33:1–20)

The boundaries of this introductory compositional unit are sharply demarcated on the one hand by the close of the mock lament of condemnation against Egypt (and similar pagan nations) in 32:32 and, at the other end, by a final impassioned vocative exclamation ("O house of Israel," v. 20b) along with the onset of a dated narrative segment in 33:21. The divine oracle covering vv. 1–20 presents a carefully crafted combination of instructions previously given to the prophetic watchman (33:2; cf. 3:16) on the point of individual responsibility (the corporate dimension being also implied, e.g., in the expression "house of Israel," v. 11). The message is presented with an emphasis upon righteousness (or wickedness) in relation to the all-discerning judgment of the LORD and on the basis of his immutable, authoritative word.

In keeping with its judicial nature, this section consists of a combined divine casuistic + disputational speech that is reinforced with a certain measure of divine *irony*, e.g., the particular danger that the chosen lookout must warn his people about originates from YHWH himself, not some foreign enemy (v. 7). This closely knit piece may be divided on the basis of introductory formulae of prophetic address and parallels in content into the following five topical-structural units. These may in turn be arranged in two primary divisions, each dealing with a serious pastoral problem: I—pertaining to the prophet, and II—pertaining to his people. These are linked by a transitional bridge, which presents the only possible solution for both prophet and people as far as the LORD is concerned, namely, sincere repentance and steadfast obedience to God's merciful call:

I.	

	a) **General task**: the responsibility of God's prophet to warn his people (2–6)
	    A: the watchman *does* warn (2–5) + B: the watchman *does not* warn (6)
	
	b) **Specific task**: the responsibility of Ezekiel to warn "the house of Israel" (7–9)
	    B': the watchman *does not* warn (7–8) + A': the watchman *does* warn (9)
	
	➔c) Hinge: *question*—How can we live? *answer*—Repent! (10–11)

II.	

	d) **General principle**: both the "righteous" and the "wicked" need to repent (12–16)
	    C: the righteous sins/dies (12a) + D: the wicked repents/lives (12b) +
	    C': the righteous sins/dies (13) + D': the wicked repents/lives (14–16)
	
	e) **Specific principle**: the justice of the LORD in relation to Israel (17–20)
	    E: complaint (17) + C'': the righteous sins/dies (18)
	        + D'': the wicked repents/lives(19)
	    E': complaint (20a) + divine *conclusion* (20b)

Structural Outline of Ezekiel 33:1–20

The structural and topical symmetry manifested in this oracle, made apparent by the abundant lexical recursion (in varied, intricate, incrementally overlapping sequences), is clear from the preceding outline.[28] The formally

---

[28] See Greenberg 1997:676. Observe that Ezekiel seems to favor compositional patterns based on segments of two, three, and/or four.

balanced, topically measured discourse represents a literary reflection of its judicial content—a *theodicy* which concerns the perfect justice and righteous equity of *YHWH*'s judgments and dealings with Israel. Neither the people, who are punished for their sins, nor the unfaithful messenger, have any cause for complaint. They had been duly warned by God's chosen prophets of the dire consequences of covenantal disobedience—from the very beginning of their initial, divinely worked establishment as a nation (Lev 26:14–44). This constructive rebuke had to be penitently understood and acted upon before there could be any hope of an optimistic word concerning future restoration. The several chiastic formations that occur within the text are typical of such contrastive, antithetically-phrased, forensic discourse in Hebrew literature.

The key element in Ezekiel's prophetic message, which pointedly mimics the priestly case-law legislative style of Deuteronomy (e.g., ch. 13), is situated in its center (segment [c], v. 11; cf. 18:23, 32; 14:6), which is thereby structurally and hence also topically highlighted. Here in the midst of his dispute with the house of Israel, the LORD himself plaintively calls his wayward people to spiritual life, through repentance, rather than death on account of their continued rebellion. This is in response to their confession of sin and anguished plea for a way out of their misery (v. 10b)—in words that fulfill God's prior predictions through Ezekiel (e.g., 4:17; 24:23). They were afflicted with a progressive rotting away on account of their sins (cf. Lev 26:39). This was a spiritual problem that could be divinely addressed only if they received the correct message from *YHWH* through his prophet (cf. vv. 7–9) and they in turn adopted the proper attitude towards him/Him (cf. 17–20).

This medial passage is further viewed as a compositional hinge because of its reversal from the order of appearance of the parallel verses in ch. 18, i.e., 33:10–11 = 18:30–32; 33:12–20 = 18:21–29 (no inversion appears in part I, 33:2–9, from the corresponding text in 3:17–21).[29] This arrangement therefore functions to focus one's attention on what occurs in the middle (v. 11), namely, the boundless mercy of *YHWH* in relation to both prophet (1 + 2) and people (4 + 5). His pastoral appeal is sealed, as it were, by a personal oath, which itself expresses the key concept of "life" (חַי־אָ֫נִי

---

[29] For a helpful synopsis of the various intertextual correspondences between 33:1–20 and the precedential texts in 3:7–9 and 18:21–30, consult Block 1998:242, 247, 249, 251.

7.5 Summary of the literary-rhetorical development of chapters 33–37

"As I live!"), coupled with the emphatic divine appellation "[oracle of the] Sovereign LORD" (or "Lord Yahweh"— נְאֻם ׀ אֲדֹנָי יְהֹוִה ׀) at the very midpoint of the pericope (11a). Such an obvious textual foregrounding of God's intense desire to deliver his people (of every age and place) underscores the fact that "this cardinal feature of Ezekiel's theology needs to be written underneath every oracle of judgment that his book contains" (Taylor 1969:215).

The thematic center is complemented at the conclusion of this section by a parallel, rhetorically constructed disputation (i.e., thesis + dispute + counter thesis) which dramatizes (through the use of hypothetical quotations), and thus accentuates, a related "wisdom" debate concerning the "way" (דֶּרֶךְ) of God's justice (cf. 11 and 17–20). This judicial message was not really new to the people, for Ezekiel (the LORD) was simply reiterating the covenantal principles given to them through Moses in the *Torah* (e.g., as stated in Lev 26 and Deut 30, an instance of authoritative intertextuality).[30] They therefore had no excuse for their wickedness, and the only option for the reasonable among them (the leadership in particular, to whom this didactic discourse appeals) was a complete turn-around with respect to heart and life.

In this incontrovertible, either-or way, despite the impious "protest" that is rhetorically allowed (vv. 17, 20, i.e., as an additional instance of human self-incrimination), the LORD's proclamation is set forth by Ezekiel as he is about to begin a new tack in his prophetic ministry. It was a course during which the related threats of indifferent accommodation, blind nationalism, fanatical resistance, and/or demoralized fatalism on the part of his congregation(s) had to be firmly, but gently, combated in order to prepare the ground for a genuine religious reformation and spiritual renewal. YHWH needed to be recognized, revered, and trusted not only as a willing Savior (v. 11) but also as the supreme, righteous Judge of every human being (v. 20).

---

[30] We may also discern here an allusion to the Noahic covenant through a repetition of the key term "blood" דָּם (cf. Gen 9:5–6 + 9–17).

7.5.2 Report of the fall of Jerusalem and a twofold unrepentant response (33:21-33)

This is a distinct compositional division as indicated by the new temporal setting in v. 21 coupled with the dramatic quotation recorded there ("The city has fallen!"). Another section begins in 34:1 where we find an *anaphoric* reiteration of the prophetic reception formula in 34:1 (cf. also 33:1, 23), the command to "prophesy" (הִנָּבֵא, = "say unto"), and the distinct content of the following passage (shepherd - flock). The present unit ends with a climactic word of warning to all the impenitent with regard to their impending judgment (v. 33a): "Now when it comes [and] behold it is coming..." (וּבְבֹאָהּ הִנֵּה בָאָה), which puns on the people's complacency concerning their ominous future; cf. vv. 30b-31a). The punitive events of world history serve to confirm the prophetic word as well as to vindicate both the LORD and his faithful preachers of repentance (cf. 2:1-3:11, *inclusio*).

In addition to some obvious lexical links (e.g., "blood" + "sword" in 25-26; cf. vv. 4-6), there are several notable literary-structural features that tie this unit into the preceding pericope, thus welding ch. 33 into a coherent segment. The whole discourse functions as a transitional bridge that leads off the larger rhetorical-thematic portion covering the book's remaining chapters. Before the blessed promises of chs. 34-48 can be appropriated, a complete change of heart and life on the part of the recipients is necessary (cf. vv. 11, 32). In very general terms with respect to the prevailing *connotative* progression of the book as a whole we have:

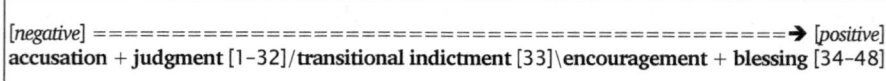

The overall movement from judgment to blessing in Ezekiel

Fundamental then to ch. 33 as an integral unit is the referential *inclusio* that ties in Ezekiel's vocal restoration by the LORD (v. 22) with his certification as a true prophet (v. 33) and a moral-religious watchman (v. 2; cf. 2:1-5). Within this wider framework a basic topical chiasmus is formed that incorporates the larger textual segments of the chapter, which assume the following, centrally spotlighted pattern:

7.5 Summary of the literary-rhetorical development of chapters 33–37

> **A** Judicial dialogues that emphasize the <u>importance of obedience</u>, of heeding the LORD's warnings—focus on the faithful *prophet* (2–11)
>
>   **B** Legislative discourse regarding the need for "righteous" <u>behavior</u> and the consequences of "wickedness"—focus on the *people* (12–20)
>
>   **C Report of Jerusalem's fall**—the LORD's judgment upon the people's sin; focus on the faithful *prophet* (his "mouth is opened," 21–22)
>
>   **B'** Disputation highlighting the judgment that will befall the non-exiles on account of their "detestable" <u>behavior</u>—focus on the *people* (23–29)
>
> **A'** Judicial indictment of the people for their <u>lack of obedience</u> for not paying attention to the LORD's words—focus on the faithful *prophet* (30–33)

Rhetorical arrangement of Ezekiel 33

This structure may help to explain the present arrangement of the chapter, that is, with the spatial displacement of the important (and relatively rare) autobiographical narrative away from what might seem to be a more logical or expected location at the beginning (or ending) of the pericope. It is now situated in an equally prominent position at the center of the larger chiastic arrangement, which balances messages of divine warning (1–20) with those of condemnation upon the people for not listening to the present word of the LORD (23–33). Neither the Babylonian exiles (30–32) nor those lesser folk who remained in the land of Israel (24–29) appeared to have learned their shocking lesson from history, as epitomized in the formally medial exclamation "The city has fallen!" (21). The validity and authority of the word of the LORD, as faithfully proclaimed by his chosen messengers, is thereby vindicated structurally as well as semantically in ch. 33.

Turning then to the internal construction and rhetorical style of this chapter's second half (vv. 23–33), we note its clear twofold, mutually complementary division, i.e., 23–29 and 30–32 (v. 33 acts as a summary conclusion for both portions). First, there is a well-formed judgment oracle, beginning with the reception [or prophetic word] formula ("Then the word of *YHWH* came to me," 23).[31] This is pronounced against a group of arrogant, impenitent boasters who were left in Judah and had smugly concluded

---

[31] For a handy survey of common prophetic discourse formulas, see Sweeney 1996:544–547.

that the land was still theirs by divine right no matter what had happened to Jerusalem, their nation, or indeed, to their fellow countrymen who had been exiled to Babylon (cf. 11:15). It is cast in the form of another judicial disputation speech: *thesis* (a self-indicting utterance, 24) + *dispute* (accusation, 25–26) + *counter thesis* (= condemnation, 27–29). The latter is a characteristic instance of *lex talionis*—a punishment being molded to fit the crime.[32] To be specific: a spiritual desecration of the land + relying (lit. "standing") on the sword = > physical desolation of the land + falling by the sword (26–27; cf. chs. 5–6, Lev 26:14–39).

This is followed by a "unique passage in the prophetic writings" (Boadt 1990:7), a stinging divine indictment of the many hypocrites living within the current community of Babylonian exiles. Like many contemporary church-goers, these fickle folk (cf. v. 30b) were superficially enthralled with or entertained by Ezekiel's dramatic prophecies of word and deed, but they failed—or rather, refused—to take his clear moral admonitions to heart. The prophet could draw a large, enthusiastic crowd, but like many worshipers at such rallies today, they were not coming for the right reason and they had no intention of "putting his words into practice" (v. 31–32).[33]

As in virtually all of Ezekiel's oracles, the two constituent pieces of this pericope (23–29/30–33) are very clearly demarcated structurally both internally and externally by some key elements of lexical recursion. These embody crucial aspects of the LORD's urgent message to his people, both near (in Babylon) and far (in Judah), for example: the initial *anaphoric* vocative "son of man" (24, 30; cf. 33:2, 7, 10, 12); the concluding *epiphoric* recognition formula ("Then they will know that…;" 29, 33); accompanied by paired occurrences of the messenger formula ("This is what the…LORD says…;" 25, 27) and popular sayings (24, 30) along with other thematically prominent expressions, e.g., the accusatory rhetorical question, "should you then possess the land?" (25, 26); its negative response, "I will make the land a desolate waste" (28, 29); and its incriminating reason, "they hear your words but do not put them into practice" (31, 32). What happened to the land of Israel was a concrete symbolical index of an inner spiritual reality,

---

[32] See Miller 1982:*passim* and Fishbane 1987:170–187.

[33] I do not think that Ezekiel's problem of communication was that the "rhetorical form [of his message] has overshadowed rhetorical function; [or that] artistry has interfered with communication" (Block 1998:267). It was rather that unbelief had so blinded the majority of his audience that they were unable to penetrate this prophetic form in order to perceive its divinely intended function.

namely, the relative health of the covenantal relationship between Yahweh and his people.[34] When they violated the LORD's trust by their repeated acts of infidelity, his last resort was to startle them into a recognition of his righteous, holy nature, will, and purpose by despoiling the politically unstable piece of territory in which they had placed their vain earthly hope.

The rhetorical effect of such carefully placed and interconnected reiteration is to reinforce the validity of the punishment that this insolent and ungrateful people deserved for their repeated covenant violations (cf. Deut 28:58–68). The only cure for a stubborn and rebellious attitude such as theirs (cf. 2:4–5) was a judgment so shocking and pervasive (i.e., the total destruction of Jerusalem and Judah, 33a; cf. 21b, 24a) that as many as possible would hopefully be driven to contrition (if not complete repentance, 33:10). Then even the most skeptical in their ranks would be forced to admit that a prophet has been among them (33b). The purpose of this chapter is to emphasize the concrete "coming" (בּוֹא) to pass of this potentially demoralizing prediction (33a; cf. 31b–32a and 21b).[35] Such a ruinous realization was nothing less than a cathartic preparation, as it were, for the new message of spiritual life, restoration, and reconciliation (between YHWH and his people) to follow. However, the latter would make sense only to those who had truly "turned" (שׁוּב) from their wickedness to the LORD in sincere penitence and with faith in a future under his merciful, sovereign rule (33:11 => chs. 34–37).

The subtle *irony* (cf. section 5.6) that now closes this section, i.e., in the image of a popular singer of lustful (possibly erotic) lyrics that everyone listens to but nobody takes seriously,[36] highlights the point that the repentance being demanded would have to be a matter of the heart, not only of the mouth (33:31–32). The present, un-religious and un-knowing people ("my" = more bitter *irony*) would surely get to know by personal experience the LORD (and his messenger), whether in the day of their destruction (33:28–29) or through their eventual deliverance (34:29–30). Indeed, such

---

[34] As Block observes, "The integrity of the tripartite deity-people-land relationship depended on covenantal fidelity" (1998:262).

[35] The absolute certainty expressed by the divine assertion here at the end may constitute an implicit indictment of a possible earlier reference to the illicit use of "blood" during certain Near Eastern divinatory procedures (v. 25; cf. Greenberg 1997:684).

[36] See Greenberg 1997:686–687. Even their seemingly pious exhortation, "Come now, listen to the message that has come from the LORD" (v. 30) is probably sarcastically or insincerely meant (ibid., 685).

a renewal of divine knowledge was "the aim of classical prophecy (e.g., Jer 31:34; Hos 2:8; 4:1) (cf. Bullock 1986:251). It constituted the pathetic dimension" of *YHWH*'s message via Ezekiel, namely, his fervent longing to be recognized and revered as the covenant Lord by a heretofore faithless people (cf. Ex 6:7; 7:5; 14:4, 31).[37]

This entire concluding segment (vv. 30–33) acts also as a sad commentary on and a serious warning to our own age of popular megachurches. All too often it would appear that although their plush auditoriums abound with eager and excited participants, many of those present are, as in Ezekiel's time, there simply for emotional gratification or psychological affirmation, rather than being motivated by an genuine longing to learn how to use the Word of God more effectively as a guide for their everyday lives (v. 31).

7.5.3 YHWH declares a woe upon negligent shepherds, but weal for needy sheep (34:1–33)

This relatively long unit is bounded by a reiteration of the "prophetic word saying," which also occurs *anaphorically* at the start of the next compositional section in 35:1. There are multiple instances of closure, including a variant of the divine recognition formula coupled with covenantal terminology (30), a double occurrence of the accentuating signatory formula (נְאֻם אֲדֹנָי יְהוִה, 30–31), and an *inclusio* formed by the "sheep/flock—shepherd" metaphor (cf. vv. 2/31).[38] The latter figure also provides a perceptible cohesive unity to the entire pericope (obviously related intertextually to Jer 23:1–2). The chapter may be divided into three principal portions as shown below on the basis of thematic focus coupled with the usual delineative discourse markers (i.e., for Ezekiel: *recursion* patterns + topical *shifts* + prophetic speech *formulas*):[39]

---

[37] On this point, see Fishbane 1987:186.

[38] For an overview of the complex mixture of prophetic formulae that appear in this chapter as well as the "oral quality" of its discourse, see Block 1998, 273–274. Block also provides a useful listing of the "strong semantic and formal links" that ch. 34 has with Jer 23:1–6 (ibid., 275–276).

[39] Block offers a rather different perspective on the larger construction of this chapter (1998:274). We appear to use similar criteria for demarcating the salient units of prophetic discourse, but interpret the textual evidence somewhat differently.

7.5 Summary of the literary-rhetorical development of chapters 33–37

Sheep-Shepherd oracle one (1–16)
    a) *Indictment*: of the rapacious shepherds (1v6)
    b) *Verdict*: against the shepherds (7–10)
    c) *Deliverance*: of the Lord's flock (11–16)
Sheep-Shepherd oracle two (17–24)
    a) *Indictment*: of the fat oppressive sheep (17–19)
    b) *Verdict*: against the fat oppressive sheep (20–21)
    c) *Deliverance*: of the Lord's flock (22–24)
Covenant of Peace oracle (25–31)
    a) *Promise*: removal of wild animals (enemies) (25 => a' 28b)
    b) *Blessing*: upon the whole land (God's people) (27a => b' 29a)
    c) *Deliverance*: from the pagan nations (enemies) (27b => c' 29b)

In the first two sections (1–16 and 17–24) the prophet's message mainly concerns the unjust socio-religious conditions that pertain within the flock of Israel. The third unit (25–31) adopts a global perspective, as foreign enemies are also included within the divine judgment. As a rhetorical whole, the role of the Shepherd-LORD as the faithful Protector, Provider, and Peace-Maker for his faithful flock is foregrounded throughout, that is, with respect to all their internal and external enemies.

It is common in Ezekiel (and the prophets generally) for there to be a sudden shift in perspective as the discourse develops. So here, grim descriptions of the current adverse situation—defenseless sheep scattered in exile (vv. 5–6, evoking the sorry scene portrayed in 1 Kgs 22:17)—are later transformed into glorious promises of salvation under the leadership of the saving Shepherd (e.g., vv. 11–16). Thus, the overall thematic movement is in a positive direction, giving the section as a whole strongly optimistic overtones as the temporal setting moves from the past (vv. 1–10) through the present (17–21) and on to a predicted future of great blessing (11–16, 23–24, 25–31). Certainly, this glorious outlook should have given much encouragement to the displaced and, for the most part, leaderless Jewish refugees who were languishing with little hope in a foreign land—if only they would listen (cf. 33:31–32)!

Another typical feature of Ezekiel's literary style is evident in this chapter and that is the complex thematic interweaving that we find linking the several distinct, internal subsections. This promotes an essential *unity in diversity* that appeals to listeners (readers) in that the main point of his message becomes crystal clear, but not at the expense of boring his audience. Certainly, no faithful preachment of the basic law-gospel truths of God need become monotonous or wearisome. Complementing the prophet's powerful diction and colorful depiction (featuring connotatively effective sensory evocation, with imagery that is both negative [e.g., v. 18] and positive [e.g., v. 26]) is a great deal of strategically placed *repetition* (e.g., the symbolic expression "mountains of Israel" אֶל־הָרֵי יִשְׂרָאֵל (note the soundplay) in vv. 13–14; cf. ch. 36). Such lexical-semantic recursion renders the text in a rhetorically very persuasive manner, even on the micro-textual level of pronominal usage (e.g., the ironic contrast between *my flock* and *my shepherds* in v. 8). The discourse thus captivates its receptors on several communicative strata (including such important inter- and intra-textual resonances as Jer 23:1–4 and Ezek 20:40–42).[40] We see this illustrated, for example, in the diversely picturesque pastoral scenes, set within a temporal framework of Jerusalem's judgment ("a day of clouds and thick darkness," v. 12; cf. Joel 2:2, Zeph 1:15), which are graphically depicted in each of the three oracles that comprise the first section (vv. 1–16).

Just before an announcement of the divine verdict—in this case condemnation—the initial accusation against Israel's exploitative leaders is reiterated in summary fashion (v. 8, cf. vv. 2–6), thus reinforcing the magnitude of their crimes of commission and omission against the political and religious community that they were given charge of. Accordingly, in another instance of the ironic principle of corresponding retributive justice, the Defender-LORD deprives the greedy shepherds themselves of "food" (אָכְלָה) in the end (2–3/10, an obvious *inclusio*). The earlier calamities that had befallen the defenseless sheep (4–6) are then wonderfully undone, both denotatively and sequentially, in the closing passage of divine restoration (11–16).[41] The unit concludes with contrastive emphasis upon the LORD's "shepherding" (רעה) with beneficent "judgment" (מִשְׁפָּט, 16c—cf. 2, *inclusio*) and a mirrored reversal of the internecine crimes recorded in v. 4.[42]

---

[40] Lemke calls attention to the subtle nature of Ezekiel's intertextual irony: The rare expression "you ruled harshly" (בְּחָזְקָה רְדִיתָם; 34:4) with reference to the iniquitous "shepherds" of Israel is used to describe how the Egyptians treated their Hebrew slaves (Ex 1:13–14). Thus, "he accuses Israel's rulers of doing what their own history should have taught them to abhor and what the law of Moses [Lev 25:43, 46] expressly forbade" (1987:207).

[41] For the details, see Greenberg 1997:706; McKeating 1993:913. The expressions of divine deliverance in v. 13 reflect "new exodus terminology," i.e., to "bring out from" [הוֹצֵאתִים מִן], "gather together from" [קִבַּצְתִּים מִן], and "bring to/into" [הֲבִיאֹתִים אֶל] (cf. 20:34–35, 41–42; Micah 2:12, 4:6–8; Block 1998:286).

[42] "By inverting the sequence, Ezekiel emphasizes that with Israel's restoration the tragedies of the past will be reversed. By recasting negative statements as positive affirmations, he deliberately portrays Yahweh as a good shepherd, the antithesis of the earlier evil shepherds" (Block 1998:291).

7.5 Summary of the literary-rhetorical development of chapters 33–37

The transitional middle segment (34:17–24) begins with a direct address by *YHWH* to his entire flock (especially the unrighteous oppressors among them). It is also clearly divided into three sub-sections (17–19, 20–22, 23–24) by a complex of literary devices:
- first, the prophetic message formula (*anaphoric* aperture at 17 and 20 [+ "therefore" לָכֵן]);
- by a sequence of accusatory rhetorical questions (18–19) which end with an *inclusio* in the striking expression my flock (17a–19a);
- by another internal *inclusio* ("I will judge between…," 20b–22b);
- by the sudden introduction of the foregrounded Messianic "single shepherd" motif (23; cf. Ps 78:70–72; 2 Sam 7:12–16; note the verb "I will place" and the stressed pronoun "he" הוּא);
- and finally, by an emphatic utterance of *closure*—"I [אֲנִי] the LORD have spoken" (24b), which matches the initial accented "but [and] you" וְאַתֵּנָה (17a).

This pericope clearly culminates in its stylistically distinct third paragraph,[43] which proposes a divine substitutionary solution for ineffective human leadership. In addition to being explicitly Messianic (נָשִׂיא = the "exalted," ideal intercessor and sin-bearer; cf. 4:4–6), these words are also topically pivotal. That is to say, they look backward by means of the ongoing shepherd-sheep imagery, but also forward through citation of the correlative interpersonal language of the "covenant" (בְּרִית, cf. v. 25): "I [אֲנִי] the LORD will be their God." The other half, "they…are my people" occurs *epiphorically* at the close of the next compositional unit, vv. 30–31.[44] As

---

[43] *Contra* Boadt 1990:9. Note, for example, the repeated stress upon the key notion of "servant-shepherding." In a significant reversal of 17:11–21 we have here a prediction of the coming of a divinely endowed "David" who would accomplish what all the human "davids" in Jerusalem manifestly failed to do in their role as covenant leaders, guides, and models (cf. Jer 30:8–9).

[44] In a patent example of circular reasoning, McKeating asserts that "the figure of the messiah is not prominent in the book of Ezekiel" (1993:105) and then concludes that "in each case the messianic oracle looks like an addition….[and] that the messianic ideas present in the book have entered the Ezekiel tradition at a later stage of development" (ibid., 108–109). The hermeneutical problem arises here because in the case of such key theological notions, it is not necessarily *quantity* which counts or makes the case one way or another. Rather, it is *quality*, that is, how and where a particular passage containing such a concept is utilized in the text as a whole. Thus, by virtue of its reiterated occurrence in climactic positions (34:23–24 = > 37:22, 24–25) in the thematically focal section of chs. 33–37, the messiah motif is clearly *one* prominent feature of Ezekiel's overall message (cf. also 17:22–24, 29:21). Similarly, in view of what he regards as Ezekiel's "narrowly nationalistic" vision of the future, Block argues that his "messiah" is correspondingly only a "national ruler," for such a construal would seem to be at "home in the ideological and cultural milieu of ancient Mesopotamia" (1997b:625–626). A more immediate and hence relevant context for interpretation, however, would be the writings of earlier prophets, who surely had a much greater, yes divine, figure in mind (e.g., Isa 9:1–7,

in the preceding section, there is an emphasis upon YHWH's simultaneous "salvation" (יָשַׁע) and judicial "vindication" (שָׁפַט) of his faithful "flock" (22), but without the ominous word of punishment for any guilty offenders.

The concluding salvation oracle of wholesome "peace" (שָׁלוֹם, vv. 25–31), which strikingly reflects the earlier or contemporaneous prophecies of Jeremiah (e.g., 30:8–10; 31:8–14), sounds a joyous note throughout, with unmistakable echoes of the salubrious promises recorded in Leviticus 26:4–13 (cf. Ezek 20:33–44).[45] This segment is given cohesion and is at the same time roughly divided into two by a reiteration of the integrated motifs of wild animals (25a/28a), agricultural fertility (26–27/29), and deliverance from pagan nations (28a/29b). Intertextual allusion, periodically woven into the discourse, adds much to the richness of the verbal tapestry, e.g., "and no one will make them afraid," v. 28 (cf. 39:26; Lev 26:6, Jer 30:10, Mic 4:4). There is thus a sustained focus on the symbolical blessings of the covenant which reach their climax in the twofold, literal and metaphoric articulation of the LORD's providing, protective presence with his people in vv. 30–31 (with YHWH once more suddenly addressing [his] flock/sheep directly as in v. 17; = *inclusio*). These two verses, taken together with the preceding primary pair of 23–24, effect a *means* + *result* relationship as well as an implicit theological identification of the Messianic shepherd (23) with the LORD himself (31; cf. 37:24–28).[46]

This comforting passage represents what is surely a major point within the larger division covering chs. 33–37, and indeed in the book of Ezekiel as a whole. It is a thematic peak that anticipates the climactic, triumphant close of the entire unit in 37:21–28. The house of Israel will one day live again; the Sovereign LORD would mercifully see to that according to the outworking of his covenant of peace (34:25; cf. 37:26; = the "new covenant" of Jeremiah 31:31–34).[47] The pronounced covenantal perspective is

11:1–16 + 12:1–6; Mic 5:1–5a; Hos 3:5; Zech 9:9–10; Jer 23:5–6; 30:8–9, 21–22; 33:15–16, 26).

[45] For a synoptic comparison of Lev 26:4–13 and Ezek 34:25–30, see Block 1998:304.

[46] *Contra* Lemke 1987:208. This would appear to be a deliberate fusion of theological concepts, not some sort of compositional inconsistency or infelicity. Thus, "...every new paragraph of this chapter opens out the analogy [of the Messianic Shepherd] still further...if each section is taken separately it will be obvious that new ideas are added all along" (Taylor 1969:222), that is, in order to build up to a culmination in which the "servant shepherd, David" (v. 23) and "the Sovereign LORD" are viewed as being one.

[47] *Contra* Alexander 1986:914. This "new" covenant foregrounded in Jeremiah may itself be a divine restatement of an ancient salvational "covenant of peace" (Ezek 34:25–30; cf. Lev 26:3–6; Isa 54:7–10): "Understood in terms of ancient Near Eastern symbolism, planting

emphasized at the very end of the section by means of a chiastic expression of its two fundamental correlates, that is, concerning: A = "the LORD their God" (30a) + B = "the house of Israel...my people" (30b); B' = "the sheep of my pasture...[my] humanity" (31a) + A' "your God...the Sovereign LORD" (31b). Such evident reinforcement surely stresses the all-inclusive promise that the Church of God today has graciously (i.e., without merit) been made heir to through its great Messiah-Shepherd (cf. Luke 19:10; John 10:1–18). But this passage, both directly and by way of contrast, also underscores the LORD's trenchant warning (woe!) against any arrogant pastoral abuse (vv. 2/10; cf. Jude 12) and the selfish, discriminatory affliction of weaker members of the flock by the strong (18, 21; cf. Jn 10:27–29), especially in view of the universal judgment to come (17, 20; cf. Mt 25:17–22).

7.5.4 "Edom" will be punished for its wicked attitude toward God and his people (35:1–15)

After the preceding gospel peak in 34:30–31, there is a sharp contrast in topic and tone as the discourse unexpectedly reverts as it were by means of its opening formulas (vv. 1–2; cf. 25:1–2) to another one of the oracles against the nations which had seemingly terminated with ch. 32. This one in fact sounds as if it were a continuation or a reiteration of the short oracle against Edom found in 25:12–14. Thus, the vengeance (5x) that is so prominent in the former text is satisfied by the desolation which characterizes the latter (9x). This intratextual structural connection aside, there is another, rhetorical reason for the inclusion of this judgment pericope at the present juncture. That is to serve as a sharply contrastive backdrop to the following salvation oracle proclaimed to the mountains of Israel (ch. 36). In other words, a deliverance of the righteous is often coupled in the prophetic literature with an announcement of their express vindication in the face of their enemies (hence the device of direct address, vv. 2–3). Edom, the

---

peace was a powerful statement about divine rule and its implications. Set in the context of human rebellion against divine authority, the planting of peace in the earth was a statement of confidence in divine mercy to forgive human offenses and to take the initiative in bringing peace and harmony to a world disrupted by sin and violence" (Batto 1987:211). Jeremiah of course put proper emphasis on the inward, spiritual nature of this "peaceful," covenantal relationship (e.g., Jer 31:31–34), while Isaiah focused upon the essential divine motivating factor of "unfailing love" חֶסֶד (Isa 54:10). Taylor proposes a more dynamic interpretation of this notion: "The word *peace* is used to describe the harmony that exists when covenant obligations are being fulfilled and the relationship [between parties] is sound" (1969:224).

brother nation which played such an inimical role in the dramatic history of God's people (cf. Obadiah), serves that very purpose here as the extreme negative, hence also an accentuating counterfoil, to Israel within the larger divine message of encouragement to his faithful remnant. Accordingly, the LORD's vengeance would find a definite fulfillment in the disastrous fate of their supercilious neighbor to the southeast, "Mount Seir" (2–3).

There is another prominent connection with the cotext, in this case, the prior passage in ch. 33 that explained the reason for the fall of Judah and the transformation of the land into "a desolate waste" (שְׁמָמָה וּמְשַׁמָּה, vv. 28–29; this emphatic alliterative expression becomes a key motif in the condemnatory oracle of ch. 35; cf. 6:14). As with "the mountains of Israel" (33:28), so also with "Mount Seir" (35:2), a complete devastation is destined for all people, even those who think they are specially chosen, whose wickedness is characterized by sins involving "blood" and the "sword" (i.e., gross immorality and callus oppression, 33:25–26; cf. 35:5–6). It may be that ch. 35 and the doom of Edom is chosen to stand as a vivid object lesson and an obvious warning to any other inimical or iniquitous nation that would have contact with God's chosen community of faith. First, they are liable to the same just judgment for similar evils, but more importantly, when the LORD graciously decides to defend and restore his people, no enemy dare object, deride the decree, or endeavor to stand in the way (35:5, 12; cf. 36:3–4).[48]

The respective oracles "against" (עַל) Edom and "unto" (אֶל) Israel (35:1–15 and 36:1–15), are obviously interrelated although it is appropriate to view them as distinct, but parallel and contrastive literary units. As for their connection,[49] we note several significant correspondences (e.g., in selected terminology, such as the correlative condemnatory conjunctives "because… therefore," 35:5–6, 10–11/36:2–7) and the lack of a prophetic "reception formula" between them. However, they may also stand as independent pericopes. This is indicated by the strongly disjunctive formulaic aperture at the onset of ch. 36, which is indeed quite conspicuous (or audible!) in itself. It leads off with an emphatic "now [and] you" (וְאַתָּה), followed by no less

---

[48] This comforting promise extends in amplified fashion also to the Church of God in New Testament times (e.g., Rev 19:11–21, but with an entirely new significance for shed "blood" and the sharpened "sword," vv. 13–15).

[49] See, for example, Greenberg 1997:710; Lemke 1987:209; Allen 1990:169.

7.5 Summary of the literary-rhetorical development of chapters 33–37

than four conventional *anaphoric* elements (vv. 1–2, two of which are reiterated in v. 3).

While 36:1–7 evinces much topical overlap with ch. 35, the second half of the section (vv. 8–15, beginning with "mountains"; cf. v. 1, *anaphora*) is distinct due to its concentration of restoration imagery. It also has many features that anticipate the *next* compositional pericope in 36:16–38, especially vv. 33–35. Just as ch. 35 may be viewed as a renewal of the oracle against Edom in 26:12–14, so also 36:1–15 functions as a prominent reversal of the oracle *against* the mountains of Israel found way back in ch. 6.[50] Thus, all nations will *know* [i.e., personally experience for sure just exactly who] the LORD is when he vindicates his people and testifies to his own supreme power and authority by bringing a devastating judgment upon all their adversaries (cf. 34:30).[51] The same principle of divine justice and righteous reversal has been manifested, time and again, in some of the major historical events of the recent present world age. There is simply no escaping the "living" (= eternally active) God who is always there (vv. 10b–11a), both to witness the crimes committed against his people and also to avenge them.

The Yahwistic recognition formula referred to above occurs four times in ch. 35, three times *epiphorically* to conclude a prophetic paragraph, that is, in vv. 4, 9, and 15 (the compounded oracle as a whole). This designative expression appears to be displaced for special rhetorical effect to emphasize the act of divine "judgment" (11b), that is, up from the close of the unit ending in v. 13 (where an iterative "tag" remains, "I heard" שָׁמָעְתִּי) and to its compositional center at the beginning of v. 12. In its place we find the *anaphoric* "prophetic messenger" formula—"So speaks the Lord *YHWH*" (כֹּה אָמַר אֲדֹנָי יְהוִה)—in contrast to the blasphemy of Edom, vv. 10–13)—at the start of the final sub-section (14). There are thus four balanced paragraphs of structure in ch. 35, namely, 2–4, 5–9, 10–13, and 14–15,[52] and the entire passage is bounded by an *inclusio* based

---

[50] For a listing of some of the chief similarities, see Greenberg 1997:723.

[51] Block attempts to demonstrate a "close structural parallel" between 35:1–36:15 and ch. 34 (1998:310). His scheme is marred, however, by a certain reductionistic tendency, for example, excluding 34:17–21 as an instance of a "judgment oracle" pertaining to the "old order" of leadership in Israel. Similarly, 34:25–29 concerns "the land of Israel" just as much as 36:1–15 does.

[52] Block also indicates four internal segments, but corresponding to verses 3–4, 5–9, 10–12aa, and 12ab–15 (1998:314). In a later schema, however, he proposes four that correspond to those listed above, based on the difference between "absolute" and "motivated" declarations of judgment (ibid., 324).

on the crucial terms "Mount Seir" (the accused) and "desolation" (the punishment) (vv. 2–3, 15). These segments combine to form the following chiastic topical pattern, which reinforces the measured, immutable nature of the LORD's righteous retribution:

> A **Result**: Focus on the "desolation" wrought by YHWH [*inclusio* of the divine name] (1–4)
>
> > B **Reason**: Specification (because יַעַן) of the iniquity and punishment of Edom (5–9)
> >
> > B' **Reason**: Specification (because יַעַן) of the iniquity and punishment of Edom (10–13)
>
> A' **Result**: Focus on the "desolation" wrought by YHWH [*inclusio* of the divine name] (14–15)
>
> Structural outline of the double doom oracle in Ezekiel 35

In addition to the various markers already mentioned, the two internal paragraph units are also defined by the device of *inclusio* (i.e., "forever" עוֹלָם, vv. 5/9 + references to Seir's speech, vv. 10, 12–13) and by the prophetic "inversion (crime => corresponding punishment) sequence" (also exhibited in vv. 14–15). Several specific wordplays also appear to highlight the "calamity" (אֵידָם, v. 5) that will befall "Edom" (אֱדוֹם, v. 15, as the epitome of every subsequent, ungodly corporate villain) and to demonstrate the absolute righteousness of "the Sovereign LORD" (אֲדֹנָי יְהוִה, v. 6). Indeed, he is the ultimate "kinsman-redeemer/vindicator" (גֹּאֵל—cf. Isa 41:14, 43:14, 44:6) of his chosen people, who is referred to metonymically under the graphic, personified figure of the "blood[shed]" דָּם (reiterated 4x) which according to the levitical principle of *lex talionis* relentlessly "pursues" (רדף) all their former "Edomic" persecutors (v. 6; cf. Num 35).[53]

---

[53] The fact that no similarly proud, impious, or oppressive nation during the course of human history has ever escaped Yahweh's eventual punitive justice is a serious warning to the many hostile governments and regimes today who feel that they can flaunt God's laws and persecute his [true] covenant people with impunity.

7.5.5 The LORD will renew the desolate mountains of Israel and its people (36:1–15)

The prominent formulaic opening of this section, in which the topic of discourse shifts to Israel, has already been noted. Even the obvious emotional agitation with which this oracle begins (יַעַן בְּיַעַן...יַעַן "because...because, yea because," vv. 2–3) would suggest a new text unit here (cf. the opening exclamation of the initial quotation: הֶאָח "Aha!"—v. 2). Continuity with the preceding pericope is established, however, by an overlapping reference to the people in focus and their land, i.e., "house of Israel" (35:15) and "mountains of Israel" (36:1, an instance of structural *anadiplosis*). We also hear another derisive and boastful, but in effect self-incriminatory, speech by "the enemy" (36:2, הָאוֹיֵב; cf. 35:10, 12–13), not revealed as Edom until v. 5. They wanted to permanently expropriate the eternal highlands given by *YHWH* (my land, v. 5) to his chosen people (cf. Deut 32:13, 33:15). But an angry (burning, v. 5; cf. v. 6) God would "assuredly" (אִם־לֹא, v. 5; cf. v. 7) intervene for the sake of his honor, that is, to put an end to the scornful calumny of the heathen (vv. 6–7).[54]

Indeed, it is clear that the present pericope, considered by some to be "misplaced,"[55] is intended to be foregrounded by way of thematic contrast to the one just concluded. The punishment that is inflicted upon the erstwhile persecutors of *YHWH*'s covenantal community (a rhetorical extension from Edom to all impudent adversaries) will be complemented by a dramatic reversal in the status of Israel. All her trials and tribulations (35:1–15 + 36:1–7) would one day—"soon" (v. 8, that is, according to the LORD's reckoning, i.e., initially at the time of Cyrus the Persian)—be transformed into a new era of prosperity and plenty (ch. 36:8–12; cf. Lev 26:1–13). The prevailing "desolation" (שְׁמָמָה, 10x in ch. 35) would be the fate of Edom (36:5), and the land would be returned as a divinely worked "possession" (נַחֲלָה) for God's people (36:12; Greenberg 1997:724)—in marked contrast to the punitive judgment that was predicted for these same "mountains of Israel" in ch. 6.

Whether or not the horror of intervening events had worked some salutary effects upon at least a remnant of the nation is not revealed (cf. 36:22–23). In any case, the LORD here promises with uplifted hand (v. 7, i.e., under a self-imposed divine oath) to reactivate his covenant with them—and

---

[54] This passage is a solemnly sworn warning (v. 7) that all contemporary revilers of the LORD of Scripture also need to hear.

[55] See, for example, the discussion in Wevers 1967:186–188.

with their subsequent spiritual descendants—first of all, with respect to the abundant blessings promised for faithful obedience.

The prophecy of 36:1–15 is a divine address to the personified, symbolical "mountains of Israel" (a natural representation of God's everlasting protective and purifying presence among his people, e.g., 20:40, 28:14, 39:17, 40:2; cf. Ps 48:1, Mic 4:2, Zech 14:4, Mark 9:2, Acts 1:11–12). It may be divided into three portions, that is, in the form of an A-B-A' ring construction having a parallel beginning and ending which surround a distinctive, and thereby foregrounded, middle section as shown in the following figure:

A Woe oracle (לָכֵן...יַעַן) against Edom and other pagan "nations": These enemies will be punished for their malevolent behavior and scornful speech against the land/mountains of the LORD (1–7)

   B Salvation oracle–contrast ("But you" וְאַתֶּם):
   Messianic/eschatological blessings are predicted for both the land/mountains and the people of Israel (8–12)

A' Woe oracle (לָכֵן...יַעַן)—continued:
The scornful talk against the land/"nation" of Israel on the part of hostile "nations" will be completely silenced by YHWH (13–15)

Structural outline of Ezekiel 36:1–15

In the first segment, vv. 1–7 (A), the basic thrust of which is resumed in vv. 13–15 (A'), the abundance of explicit references to the LORD's speech (e.g., כֹּה אָמַר אֲדֹנָי יְהוִה—v. 2, 13; = *anaphora*) is meant to counteract the blasphemous and threatening talk of all of Israel's pagan adversaries. This rhetorically motivated verbal superfluity may render the piece "form-critically less coherent,"[56] but it is nevertheless an effective device that stresses the powerful performative authority of God's efficacious word in contrast to the empty, malicious slander of these impious, but comparatively petty, human enemies. It also emphasizes the fierce protective "zeal" (קִנְאָה) of *YHWH* for his land (5)—his divine patriotism.[57] Thus, again according to the LORD's retributive justice (*lex talionis* again), their hateful "scorn"

---

[56] Allen 1990:169. Block refers to 36:1–15 as being very "repetitive" and "disjointed" (1998:322).

[57] J. Skinner, cited in Greenberg 1997:724.

(כְּלִמָּה) would one day be undone and heaped upon their own heads (6–7 + 15, = *epiphoric* closure).

In addition to the wicked speech motif (cf. 35:10–13), there are a number of noteworthy lexical correspondences—often involving some dramatic reversal—that tangibly link this prophetic passage directed against "Edom and the rest of the nations" (36:5) to the preceding one. These include, for example, "enmity" (אֵיבָה, 35:5) and "enemy" (אוֹיֵב, 36:2); "ruins" (חָרְבָה), predicted for Edom (35:4) but now the current condition of Israel (36:4), which the LORD will in future reverse (36:10); YHWH's restored "humanity" (אָדָם) filling the very "land" (אֲדָמָה) that the oppressors of "Edom" (אֱדוֹם) greedily aspire to (35:15; 36:6, 10–12).[58]

There are surprisingly no references to speech at all in the contrastively marked (וְאַתֶּם "but [and] you [pl.]") medial segment (36:8–12), where we find the only occurrence of the divine name within the recognition formula that appears near its close (11b), just prior to the summary and hinge passage of v. 12. The latter reiterates the essence of the LORD's wonderful promise for [his] people (vv. 8/12, *inclusio*) and looks forward to the negation of Israel's status as a nation deprived of children (vv. 12/13, *anadiplosis*). This eschatological piece both amplifies its precedent in ch. 34 (e.g., vv. 14–15, 26–27, 29) and also anticipates its further elaboration in the next literary unit, especially in 36:33–36, where the land once despised yet also desired by "Edom" (אֱדוֹם, v. 5) will be transformed into an "Eden" (עֵדֶן, v. 35) for God's "my [YHWH's] people" (עַמִּי, vv. 10–12). The unexpected revelation of the LORD's mercy upon unworthy recipients, begun back in ch. 34, is thereby expanded to highlight his goodness and glory as he graciously showers manifold blessings upon them. Thus, we see here both "continuity and development in the gospel of salvation for the shell-shocked exiles" of every world age[59]—manifestly including the multitudes that stir the emotions of our own supposedly enlightened times, over two and a half millennia later. Ezekiel's pastoral rhetoric of reassurance is progressively and impressively building up to a thematic and emotive climax, also for those of us who are reading/hearing it, as it were, from a more distant vantage point.

---

[58] For other items of similarity, see Allen 1990:170–171; cf. Greenberg 1997:724.

[59] Allen 1990:174; Allen helpfully provides a list of the key correspondences between chs. 34 and 36.

7.5.6 YHWH will vindicate his holy name by cleansing his people and their land (36:16–38)

The *anaphoric* prophetic reception formula reinforced by the vocative "son of man" indicates in typical fashion the start of this new structural division (36:16), which closes with the *epiphoric* divine recognition formula in v. 38, just prior to another principal sectional opener, the revelatory formula of 37:1. A minor *inclusio* is formed by the reference to the "house/people of Israel" in marked relation to "the nations" (vv. 17–19/36–37). The former group is spoken of in the third person throughout the respective bounding sub-sections, i.e., 16–21 and 37–38 (in contrast to the medial portion, vv. 22–36).

The second pericope of ch. 36 develops in particular one important aspect of the rhetoric of the preceding unit (36:1–15) and takes it to an even higher, more intense affective plane. This issue concerned the divine honor of *YHWH*—"my name of holiness" (שֵׁם קָדְשִׁי, e.g., v. 20)—which the nation of Israel had horribly "profaned" (חלל, e.g., v. 20) by their persistent rebellion and wickedness (most notably "bloodshed" and "idolatry," v. 18), leading to the disaster of their national "judgment" (שׁפט, v. 19b). This had in turn provoked the scornful ridicule of all surrounding pagans in mockery of both the LORD and his now exiled people (due to their ignominious exit from his land, v. 20; cf. 36:6, 13, 15). So what was God going to do about this sacrilegious behavior on the part of the house of Israel, which elicited such public vilification from all observing nations? Contrary to all human expectation—but according to inviolate, irrevocable prophecy—he himself would bring about their miraculous return, renewal, and restoration as a covenant community by means of his chosen Messianic servant-shepherd (34:12–16, 23–24).

This gracious divine action was not in the least a result of any virtue or value to be found in the human objects of such mercy, as might be suggested perhaps by the preceding oracle (vv. 1–15). It was due solely to the LORD's righteous concern for [his] holy *name* (v. 21), a synecdoche which denotes the whole ineffable being, nature, person, and purpose of God. Here, in contrast to the supremely sacred excellence of *YHWH*, we have yet another prominent instance of "the stress in the book of Ezekiel on Israel's unworthiness to be chosen" (McKeating 1993:80), or indeed, to be shown any sort of

7.5 Summary of the literary-rhetorical development of chapters 33–37

special favor at all. The shocking imagery of menstruation dispels all such illusions (vv. 17–18). Certainly a passage of divine direct speech such as this forcefully articulates a needed warning to the many so-called people of God nowadays who also profane [his] great name (vv. 22–23), whether through pronounced infidelity or pure laxity with respect to both word and deed.

Most of the essential elements of this vital God-centered aspect of Ezekiel's message to the mountains of Israel have already been introduced within the current macrotext (chs. 34–35), and even earlier in the book, ch. 20 in particular (Boadt 1990:13). But here once again they serve in the distinct context of *theodicy,* demonstrating the absolute justice and perfect wisdom of *YHWH*'s dealings with humanity in the world—the good as well as the evil—and now in relation to the righteousness of his own inviolate character. Indeed, "Ezekiel's [vigorous] apologetic for the nature of God can be traced throughout the book" (Bullock 1986:251), but the issue is expressed with particular clarity and conviction in this pericope (e.g., vv. 20–21, 22–23, 32).[60]

Another critical feature of the inclusive benevolent design for the future of the LORD's people (in keeping with his holy name) is prominently foregrounded in the present section. This concerns his provision for the house of Israel of that crucial dual internal component consisting of a "new heart and a new spirit" (לֵב חָדָשׁ וְרוּחַ חֲדָשָׁה, v. 26; cf. 11:19; 18:31). This refers to a life-giving, God-effected resuscitation involving a person's whole morality as well as her/his spirituality, an event which is powerfully dramatized in the next unit (37:1–14). The reassuring promise of a regenerated total personality to go along with a "new covenant" as foretold earlier by Jeremiah (31:31–34; cf. also Ezek 16:60–63) is here reinforced and significantly expanded upon,[61] namely, by explicit mention of the animating "Spirit" (רוּחַ) of Yahweh, the dynamic divine agent of the people's repentance and renewal (cf. 37:14).

Three occurrences of the prophetic messenger formula (כֹּה אָמַר אֲדֹנָי יְהוִה, vv. 22, 33, 37) function to divide the section covering 36:16–38 into four segments, namely: 16–21, 22–32, 33–36, and 37–38). The first two antithetically expressed units are interlocked by means of the following inverted topical pattern:

---

[60] This awesome emphasis on the utter and total "holiness" (קֹדֶשׁ) of God needs to be impressed upon people today who casually, or even indifferently, approach "the Sovereign LORD" (אֲדֹנָי יְהוִה, v. 23) in prayer and worship as if he were as down-to-earth and secular as the next-door neighbor

[61] Taylor 1969:232; *contra* Boadt 1990:14.

A **Defilement** of the people and their land—*Means* (16–19)

B Consequent **pollution** of YHWH's holy name—*Result* (20–21)

B' Revelation of the **purity** of YHWH's name—*Reason* (22–23)

A' **Cleansing** of the people and their land—*Result* (24–32)

Structural outline of Ezekiel 36:16–32

Thus, the central problem of desecration that is brought out in the first part of the section (A-B) finds its divinely occasioned resolution in the second portion (B'-A'). Segment A is clearly demarcated by the *inclusio* forged by the chiastically arranged reason-result judicial sequence: "they defiled [the land] by their conduct and by their deeds" (17b) = > "according to their conduct and according to their deeds I judged them" (19b). Another patent *inclusio*, one that highlights the public shame of Israel's offense, bounds paragraph B: "among the nations, wherever they went [there]" (20a/21b). A prominent iterative overlap *(anadiplosis)* involving the latter expression, coupled with the repeated antithetical key terms "profaned" + "name of holiness," accents the point of structural and thematic transition (22b).

The focal majestic name "Sovereign LORD" (אֲדֹנָי יְהֹוִה) encircles the B' element (22a/23b), which is given strong internal cohesion through the mention of either "Israel" or "the nations" in every line, with an emphatic pronominal juxtaposition at the very end: "in *you*, to *their* eyes" (23c). These continuous references to the mutually contrastive (but purposefully interrelated) pair of human participant-groups in the soteriological drama of judgment and restoration are reiterated in reversed order to sharpen the outer borders of segment A', i.e., "from the nations" (24a) and "house of Israel" (32c). The close of this composite unit is further marked by three elements: the "oracle formula" (נְאֻם אֲדֹנָי יְהֹוִה), an imperatival rebuke in direct speech, and an *inclusio* (i.e., for the B'-A' resolution portion) "it is not (emphatic לֹא) for your sake that I am doing [this]" (22b/32a).

The thematic core of A' (in the preceding figure), and correlate of the "great/holy name" notional peak of B', is distinguished by a concentrated reiteration of primary terms and imagery that stresses divine initiative *(means = > result)* in the process of corporate (and by way of implication also personal) regeneration. The effect is heightened by means of a

7.5 Summary of the literary-rhetorical development of chapters 33–37

repetition of selected terms and concepts from A-B (vv. 16–21), but with a reversed reference and connotation.[62] This message is intricately patterned for additional emphasis by means of parallel as well as chiastic phrasing and set off within the discourse by a twofold surrounding internal *inclusio* (frame a/b), as synopsized in the following figure.

Thus, the blessed result of YHWH's motivating action (the "means," repeated for emphasis) is a renewal of the covenantal correlates: (a) the people's faithful *obedience* (27) and (b) the LORD's *promise* to protect and provide for his adopted people (28). Further benefits for the elect (i.e., "taken" and "gathered" from among all the nations on earth, v. 24) are revealed in the surrounding frame: (a) a home-"land," and (b) spiritual "cleansing."[63] The close connection between these latter concepts and the ideational core is suggested by the intercalation of frame-a before the occurrence of result-b in the expected sequence. In this masterful way,

frame-a: divine restoration of Israel to "the[ir] land" (24)
frame-b: divine spiritual "cleansing" of the people (25)

   means-a: YHWH "gives" [A] the people a "new heart"[B]
       and a "new spirit" [B'] he "puts" [A'] inside (26a)

   means-b: YHWH removes their "stony heart"
       and he "gives" [A] them a "fleshy heart" [B] (26b)
       and the divine "spirit" [B'] he "puts" [A'] inside (27a)

   result-a: "my decrees [C] you will follow [D],
       and my judgments [D'] you…will do [C']" (27b)

frame-a: divine restoration of Israel to their "land" (28a)

   result-b: "you will be [X] to me [Y] as a people [Z],
       and I will be [X'] to you [Y'] as a God [Z']" (28b)

frame-b: divine spiritual "cleansing" of the people (29a)

Compositional emphasis on divine initiative (36:24–29)

---

[62] For a summary of these topical inversions, see Greenberg 1997:734. Greenberg also draws attention to certain "unusual vocabulary [in this section that] injects freshness into what otherwise might have been only an anthology of Ezekielian speech and is now a vehicle for a new idea" (ibid., 738). Some of this diction undoubtedly stems from the prophet's priestly background, for example, a cleansing that reflects the rituals performed on the Day of Atonement (v. 25, cf. Lev 16; ibid., 731).

[63] Block helpfully elaborates upon this "new exodus motif" (extraction from exile => gathering as a nation => return to their land); cf. Deut 30:1–5 => Ezek 11:17; 20:34–35, 41–42; 28:25; 29:13; 34:13; 36:24; 37:12, 21; 39:27 (1998:353).

Ezekiel has stylistically shaped his message in order to foreground its principal restoration themes of *renewal* for God's people/nation (A', = the initial purpose) and *reverence* for God's person/name (B', = the ultimate purpose). In the process he also rhetorically underlines its dramatic (emotive-volitional) implications for all to hear (primarily) and to see (when reading the text). Indeed, a powerful scriptural preachment such as we have here needs to be forcefully and competently read, and re-read—aloud—and just as carefully listened to in order for the desired verbal-religious impact to be felt.[64]

The two final oracles of this major section serve to emphasize by way of recursion some of the main motifs of the prior messages of salvation, just to keep them current as it were in the minds and hearts of Ezekiel's audience. The first (36:33–36) leads off with a citation formula followed by a reminder of the people's moral "cleansing" (טהר, 33a; cf. 25) and by implication, its marked opposites, "defiled" (טֻמְאָה, vv. 17–18) and "polluted" (חלל, vv. 20–23).[65] Then the land-based, physical notions—as an extended metaphor for underlying spiritual realities—of rebuilding ruins (prosperity) and replanting wastelands (productiveness) are highlighted (cf. 34:27; 36:10, 29–30) in a graphic reversal of previous judgment passages like 5:14–17. These "golden-age" prophetic concepts (Taylor 1969:233)—in essence, Paradise regained in "the Garden of Eden" (גַּן־עֵדֶן, v. 35; cf. Isa 51:3)—give cohesion to the unit as an integral compositional segment. They also act as the evidential background for a variant of the divine recognition formula in v. 36a (cf. 23c)—significantly manifested on behalf of the "remnant" (שְׁאָר—of believers?) among the nations.[66]

---

[64] For some helpful comments concerning these fast fading faculties in the contemporary church, see Rang 1994. I would certainly agree with the assertion that the "exalted literary style" of 36:16–38 stems from the fact that here "the theology of the book reaches its zenith," especially in the segment covering vv. 24–30 which "contains the most systematic and detailed summary of Yahweh's restorative agenda in Ezekiel, if not in all the prophetic books" (Block 1998:340, 352–353).

[65] On the importance of such "priestly/cultic language" in Ezekiel, see McKeating 1993:86–88.

[66] Although there is certainly room for debate on this issue, I feel that such expressions of testimonial, when read in the mutually reflective light of similar passages, e.g., the final two (Hebrew) words of v. 23 (i.e., literally, "in you to their eyes") convey a definite *missiological* implication.

Other OT passages also reflect on this issue, most notably, in the Psalter (e.g., 22:27, 47:9, 66:8, 67:1–7) and Isaiah (e.g., 42:6, 54:17, 55:4–5. The individual books of the Holy Scriptures, of both the Old Covenant as well as the New, were not composed, communicated, or canonized in a vacuum. Therefore, due to the ever-present influence of the literary principle of *intertextuality*, they cannot correctly be interpreted or applied nowadays in isolation either from one another or from the main hermeneutical tradition of the Church throughout the ages.

A rhetorical procedure similar to the preceding is observed in the final paragraph (36:37–38), except that here the key recognition formula occurs as a marker of discourse closure (38c). Now the reiterated ideas of this restoration oracle ("again this" זֹאת עוֹד; cf. "never again" לֹא...עוֹד, v. 30) suddenly reintroduce the metaphor of "sheep" and "flocks" (along with associated imagery—cf. 34:11–16 + 31)[67] which are endowed with numerical increase (cf. 36:11, 30). In this picturesque, poetic manner the great Shepherd-LORD is memorably depicted as both vindicating his name (22–23) and vivifying his people (26–28, with a further emphasis upon divine instigation) in a God-established realm of future glory. Furthermore, YHWH will once again allow himself to be appealed to [by name!] on the part of his penitent people (37, a notable *niphal* use of the verb דרשׁ). The essential thematic concerns of theodicy and theocracy are thus forcefully combined. And so the literary stage is set for the onset of the grand climax of this prominent gospel portion of Ezekiel's prophetic collection (ch. 37; cf. 11:19–20).

7.5.7 The "Spirit of the LORD" resurrects the "skeleton" of the "house of Israel" (37:1–14)

The twofold announcement of visionary reception, in which divine impression (his hand upon me) is coupled with a reference to spiritual inspiration (v. 1), replaces the usual prophetic word formula as an *anaphoric* signal of a primary textual aperture (cf. 1:3, 8:1, 40:1). This expression reappears at the onset of the next pericope in 37:15, while the divine utterance formula marks the close of the present unit, as does an *inclusio* formed by the pair of similar-sounding terms "spirit" (רוּחַ) and "settle" (נוח) in vv. 1 and 14. It is also noteworthy that the setting specified here ("the valley/plain"—בִּקְעָה) appears to be the same as that of Ezekiel's initial vision of the glory of the LORD, i.e., in exile (cf. 3:22). Thus, God is viewed as being powerfully operative in the whole wide world, wherever the objects of his merciful action may happen to be.

The dramatic depiction of a divinely inspired life-infusion with respect to a vast landscape of dry bones is undoubtedly one of the best known (and perhaps also most misunderstood) of Ezekiel's prophecies (cf. the possible

---

[67] For a discussion of this figurative usage, see Allen 1990:180.

allusion to vv. 10–13 in Mt 27:52–54).[68] Moreover, it is, like many of the others, very tightly and symmetrically constructed by means of parallel patterns of lexical recursion, both synonymous and contrastive in nature. The present pericope is once again chiastically arranged, perhaps as a further literary reflection of the spiritual *reversal* that is being revealed with regard to God's people. This dialogic and autobiographical vision-report also exhibits a progressive, semi-narrative, plot-like development as shown in the figure below:

> A *Problem*: YHWH shows Ezekiel a scattered multitude of human bones (1–3)
>
>> B *Complication*: the dry bones are raised up and embodied, but still no life (4–8)
>>
>> B' *Peak*: the bodies are infused with the breath of life, and an army arises (9–10)
>
> A' *Resolution*: YHWH reveals to Ezekiel his plans for the resurrected bones (his people) (11–14)

Structural Outline of the "Drama" of Ezekiel 37:1–14

Many lexical correspondences and formulas serve to demarcate these four sub-sections and also to interrelate them into a tightly integrated rhetorical unit. The purpose of the whole is to spiritually inspire the disoriented, displaced, and depressed exilic community of Israel (the immediate referent of the "dry bones," v. 11; = "my people," vv. 12–13). The initial compound speech-opener "And he [*YHWH*] said to me…, 'Prophesy unto…and say to… "Thus says the LORD…"'" *anaphorically* occurs at the beginning of each paragraph (vv. 4, 9, 11–12). The variation, or deviation, evident in the final instance, which includes the transitional double quotation of v. 11, i.e., with reference to both (a) 1–10 and (b) 12–14 (Fensham 1987:59), functions to distinguish the last segment (11–14) as the *thematic* climax of the entire passage—as distinct from the *dramatic* peak which appears in vv. 9–10. Thus, the physical resurrection of a sea of scattered skeletons captures the imagination of the audience, while the spiritual resurrection of a dead and buried people conveys the main religious import of this passage.

---

[68] Why have all these bones not been buried? Block plausibly suggests that "Ezekiel probably viewed the present scene as evidence of Yahweh's own covenant curse in Deut 28:25–26" (1998:378; cf. Jer 34:17–20). But the LORD is about to graciously undo his punishment—for the glory of his name/person (v. 14).

7.5 Summary of the literary-rhetorical development of chapters 33–37

A number of other artistic touches highlight the prophetically delivered, but divinely authored, message that is being conveyed within this vision (1–10) and the subsequent interpretive comment (11–14). The latter begins with Israel's complaint, which leads to a divine salvation oracle that predicts the rejuvenation of God's people and a restoration to their land, i.e., their undeserved place of eternal fellowship with YHWH (cf. 37:27–28). The apparently doubtful (from a human perspective) rhetorical question of v. 3a (A, coupled with Ezekiel's ambiguous reply) is balanced by the hope-less communal lament of v. 11b (A').[69] Similarly, the emphatic divine recognition formula that is situated in the middle of the section in v. 6b is reinforced by its corresponding expansion in vv. 13–14 at the close of the unit. The sequence of words and actions that comprises the LORD's command to the bones in B is basically duplicated in B' with his summons of the breath/wind/spirit. However, there is a characteristic inversion that takes place at the respective endings of each unit: Bodies appear in v. 8 but with no breath in them. In v. 10, on the other hand, breath enters them and the bodies come to life—"a very very (מְאֹד־מְאֹד) great host,"[70] which is the result of the Spirit-ually effected transformation of the "very many...very dry" heaps of bones in the vision's opening scene (2). The redundant qualifier "very dry" (יְבֵשׁוֹת מְאֹד) serves to emphasize the stark and utter deadness of the individuals concerned.

A string of deictic "behold"-s (הִנֵּה + an emphatic אֲנִי when Yahweh speaks) punctuates the discourse throughout (vv. 2, 5, 7, 8, 11, 12). It brings the audience—including the prophet himself—sensorially into the very heart of this amazing, cinematic revelation (its sounds as well as sights, cf. the "clattering" רַעַשׁ of v. 7). The graphic discourse thus invites all subsequent receptors "to look in on the theater that is going on inside the prophet's head" (McKeating 1993:14). Certainly it is true to say that "as one reads [or hears such] an apocalyptic vision, he feels as if he is there, for the details are given in the first person by the recipient" (Alexander 1986:924). The dramatically prolonged, two-staged resurrection of the bones—first embodiment (8), then em-*breath*-ment (10, paralleling the account of man's creation in Gen 2:7)—is reproduced in the non-symbolic expression of the vision's meaning. First there is a predicted exit of the people from their

---

[69] Cf. Lemke 1987:212; for some psalmic parallels, see Allen 1990:186.
[70] Note one of a number of significant word/soundplays in this section: וַיִּחְיוּ...חַיִל (v. 10).

metaphorical graves, then an Exodus-evoking transfer to their land (12–14, another dual sequence of corresponding events). The great army left standing at attention at the end of B' is finally brought home to their God-given rest at the conclusion of A', where the "doing" of the LORD is foregrounded at the very close (14c; cf. 36:32, 36; = structural *epiphora*).

This inspired and inspiring spectacle is a vivid, visual and verbal reaffirmation of the reliability of *all* the LORD's predictions or promises given in the preceding oracles of the book, as well as those still to come. Indeed, the same basic hope-filled theme of renewal and restoration (following punitive punishment or disciplinary chastisement, as the case may be) is being recycled throughout these pericopes, but from varied viewpoints and with differing emphases each time. This recursive feature serves to further demonstrate the authenticity, veracity, and authority of God's chosen mouthpiece, the human vehicle for his holy word (note the repeated נבא 'prophet'). Everything thus comes meaningfully together in this potent depiction of an entire "people" resurrected, beginning not from lifeless bodies, but from the ultimate proverbial negative—dry, desiccated bones scattered about in the dust. So also the repentant among Ezekiel's discouraged addressees should know that they most surely did have a happy future in store. They may look and feel quite dead in a religious sense, but they had only to depend on the energizing Breath of *YHWH*, and new life would one day be theirs:

> The despondency of the exiles, betokened by their drastic death and burial metaphors, is met by the prophet's stunning counter-metaphors of resurrection and disinterment [vv. 11–12].[71]

"Will these bones live again?" (v. 3): The Sovereign LORD (v. 5) answers his own provocative question in a vision so life-like, albeit surrealistic, that it must have seemed as if it were taking place in the very imaginative presence of the prophet's audience. The distinctive mode of message transmission served to highlight the fact that this highly memorable, beatific event of revitalization was as good as done. God's own indwelling Spirit is the unfailing guarantor (14; cf. 10 and 36:26–27), and God himself is the

---

[71] Greenberg, 1997:47. For some helpful "background to Ezekiel's notions of resurrection," see Block 1998:383–387. Block's comments on the gospel significance of this pericope are especially appropriate: "As in his earlier representations of the netherworld, Ezekiel's vision of the resuscitated dry bones offers his compatriots powerful declarations of hope. The gospel according to Ezekiel affirms that there is life after death, and there is hope beyond the grave. Yahweh remains the incontestable Lord not only of the living but also of the dead" (ibid., 392).

gracious initiator of the entire process (note the strong first person focus in vv. 12–14).[72]

7.5.8 A prophetic object lesson in support of the divine message of restoration (37:15–28)

After the drama of the preceding inspiring revelation in support of his message, what more could Ezekiel say? In short, just about everything positive that he has already proclaimed as an authoritative word from the LORD (37:15; cf. its next announcement in 38:1) in earlier passages of his collection (e.g., 11:17–20; 16:60–63; 20:40–44; 28:25–26), but especially from the immediately antecedent selections in 34:11–31; 36:5–15, 24–38; and 37:12–14. Thus, after the initial object lesson (37:15–19), which is an effective symbolical follow up and scene-setter,[73] what we have in vv. 21–28 is a cohesive pastiche of prophecies that review and thereby reinforce virtually every one of the principal components of Ezekiel's gospel message to the house of Israel—here now specified as the whole, *unified* "nation" (לֹא יֵחָצוּ עוֹד lit. 'they will not be divided again', v. 22), namely, Joseph (Ephraim, = N) as well as Judah (S, v. 19).

There is, however, a pair of significant new elements that are added to increase the impact and implication of the LORD's words in the final portion of this pericope. First is the notion of *permanence*: This manifold promise of salvation is good—guaranteed by YHWH himself—"forever" (עוֹלָם, as stressed in vv. 25–28). Second, we have the crucial concept of covenantal *presence*: The concrete symbol of "my dwelling place" (מִשְׁכָּנִי) or "my sanctuary" (מִקְדָּשִׁי) is here introduced (vv. 26–28; note the distinctive alliteration—cf. the contrasting "their idols" גִּלּוּלֵיהֶם and "their detestable things" שִׁקּוּצֵיהֶם in v. 23). The Sovereign LORD is present with, indeed residing in the midst of, his people—in anticipation of

---

[72] This same resurrection promise (cf. Isa 26:19) also has the divine power and potential to renew and restore the flagging hearts and minds of his faithful saints today—no matter how "dead" they may feel, or how deeply they might be psychologically, socially, and perhaps even spiritually, "buried" (12–13).

[73] McKeating makes the following pertinent observation: "Ancient Israel never, as far as we know, produced any drama or developed a theater, as did the Greeks. Any drama which did take place was probably confined to the liturgy, and the cult may well have satisfied any dramatic urge which Israelites may have felt. It is significant that it is from a cultic background that Ezekiel, the priest, emerges.... His parables are essentially dramatic, and his visions are pure spectacle" (1993:14)—with a divinely motivated, religious-moral purpose of course.

the last major compositional division of the book (its heavenly denouement, chs. 40–48).

Another patterned architectonic structure is manifested in this section. In contrast to the framework that defined the first half of ch. 37, however, this one is not chiastic in nature. Rather, it is sequential and conceptually overlapping ("terrace-like") in its overall organization, as outlined below:

A Command: God tells Ezekiel to take two enscripted sticks and join them into one (15–17)

A' Explanation: The preceding prophetic sign-act is transformed into a divine metaphor (18–19)

    B Interpretation: Basic renewal of the LORD's covenant blessings ("one king," 20–23)

    B' Interpretation: Elaborated renewal of the LORD's covenant blessings ("David," 24–28)

Parallel patterning of the conjoined sticks passage (Ezek 37:15–28)

Both the A' and B' paragraphs serve to restate, expand upon, sharpen, and intensify the semantic material that is contained in the corresponding A and B segments—with reference to the singular solidarity of God's regenerated people (stressed also in the earlier resurrected bones vision). The paired units thus function here as discourse level equivalents of the technique of parallelism, or seconding, which is so characteristic of biblical Hebrew poetry (i.e., on both the macro- and micro-structure of a given text).[74]

The same principal set of symbolic actions concerning the "stick/tree/wood" (עֵץ) is reiterated in A and A',[75] each of which ends with an emphasis upon the divinely desired outcome of indissoluble "one"-ness (אֶחָד, vv. 17, 19c). Note the reversal in the order of eponymic names: Judah-Ephraim-Joseph [A] :: Joseph-Ephraim-Judah [A']; thus any way we look at it, the two become one. Similarly, paragraphs B and B' are formed within the thematic framework provided by promises regarding the <u>land</u>, <u>one king</u>, divine

---

[74] On Hebrew parallelism, see Kugel 1981:51–52 and Wendland 1995:266–268; 2007.

[75] Cf. Greenberg 1997:758–759. Block presents a strong case for understanding עֵץ as a "wooden writing table" (1998:399–401, 409; cf. Isa 30:8; Hab 2:2). This would certainly make the action of "writing" (כְּתֹב, vv. 16, 20) more plausible, though the possible royal allusion (of "stick/scepter") would be lost.

7.5 Summary of the literary-rhetorical development of chapters 33–37

cleansing, and an expression of the divine-human covenantal correlates. The latter concludes each portion--but in a reversed order to further underscore the envisioned harmony between the people(s) and their Lord ("they will be my people, and I will be their God," 23c – "I will be their God, and they will be my people," 27b). A noteworthy variation in the divine recognition formula brings the pericope as well as the larger section (chs 33–37) to a prominent close: "Then *the nations* will know that I, YHWH, make *Israel* holy" (v. 28). Hence in addition to his own person (name, 36:20–23), the LORD will also graciously make his chosen people holy, hence worthy to dwell in his presence—in contrast to all outsiders who witness purifying divine operation, but do not discern its spiritual implications (e.g., 36:23, 36).

Significant areas of conceptual overlap (*anadiplosis*) function to progressively tie one discourse unit into the next within the complete composition. Thus, the query of the curious exiles in v. 18 links A with A¹; YHWH's command to hold the two sticks (tablets) together before the people's eyes (20) acts as a transition between the two halves of the text, A-A¹ and B-B¹; and reference to the single Davidic-Messianic king (24) binds the initial divine prediction in B to its expansion in B¹ and back again to A-A¹ by virtue of the fact that the stick is a symbol of kingship (scepter) as well as of undivided nationhood (cf. 19:10–14; Gen 49:10). The prophetic object lesson also reflects the preceding visional report through the reiterated notion of attaching or joining—'bone' (עֶצֶם) to bone and 'stick' (עֵץ) to stick (37:6/19; 37:7/17). This leads in turn to the Exodus-evoking prediction that the people will be brought together from all points of the world compass to be reunited in their "own land" (vv. 12, 14, 21–22).

A less overt, but equally eminent manifestation of *intra*textuality, as already noted, is the concentration of citations, allusions, and reminiscences that appear in this section, especially the B-B¹ constituent. This significant topical recycling acts as a climactic summary of the preacher's urgent message of encouragement to his fellow exiles on behalf of the LORD (cf. in any Bible version with cross references).[76] In short, this stirring recapitulation "combines the promise of purification of the people with restoration of the land, under a new David, in a covenant of peace, when God's dwelling is reestablished in their midst" (Boadt

---

[76] Greenberg 1997:758. Allen advances the suggestion that "37:1–13 seems to have been intended as a commentary on 36:27a...and likewise 37:15–24a as a commentary on 36:27b" (1990:192). Such an argument is rather too intricate to be credible. Besides, what is one to do then with 24b–28, where we have an equally impressive convergence of prior primary "salvation" terms and texts?

1990:15). Using the Scriptural symbolism and concrete imagery from past salvation oracles and promises, Ezekiel thus proclaims a gospel message of hope in the LORD for all obedient members of the flock of the royal Shepherd (v. 24).

Such an evangelical rehearsal naturally—for Ezekiel—includes many prominent instances of *inter*textuality with reference to such primary covenantal text precursors as Ex 6:7, Lev 26:4–13, Deut 28:4–13, 2 Sam 7:11–16, and 1 Kgs 9:4–5, along with historically more immediate passages like those of Jeremiah (especially chs. 30–33). The recurrent, theophanic refrain ("then you will know that I [am] the LORD...") is itself a constant reminder of the supreme archetypal instance of divine deliverance (37:6, 13–14, 8; cf. Ex 6:2, 7:17, 10:2, 14:4, 16:12). The result is an expertly fused, scripture-packed prophetic kaleidoscope that fairly bristles with denotative import and connotative impact. It is indeed a nuclear prophecy that resonates with the heart of Old Testament theology, yet one which is stamped with the unique perspective and experience of its human mouthpiece, the pastor-prophet-priest Ezekiel.[77]

Obviously, this entire section covering chs. 33–37 presents us with a very carefully and consummately crafted compositional whole. It is indeed a prophetic sermon that is admirably suited to perform its primary rhetorical purpose of highlighting key aspects of the intended message, while at the same time it also incites the emotions and captures the imagination of its audience.[78] It does this through the heart-inspiring "hand of the LORD"

---

[77] The validity of his glorious vision of future everlasting fellowship with the LORD dwelling amid his "people" (יִהְיוּ־לִי לְעָם —37:27) is certified at the very end of the sacred canon in the reaffirming vision of the Apostle John in Rev 21:3. The essential unity in ethnic diversity that John seems to emphasize by his choice of terms in this passage is perhaps an interscriptural commentary on the intended interpretation of Ezek 37:27.

[78] The preceding analysis of the topical *selection* and structural *arrangement* of Ezekiel, both internally and in relation to the work as a whole, has furnished us with a broad perspective on how and why the discourse has been organized as it stands. Certainly, there is no need for apologies on account of any supposed infelicities in terms of either compositional artfulness or rhetorical effectiveness (for an overview of such alleged textual discontinuities and disruptions from the point of view of many older Ezekiel scholars, see Cooper 1994:32–35.

In "classical" rhetorical terms, the book evinces a convincing combination of *ethos* (e.g., through the constant involvement of the authorial "son-of-man"), *pathos* (e.g., in the many striking, emotionally touching, evocative images), and the preeminent *logos* (i.e., the dominant, authoritative "word of the LORD"). Similarly, we have an engagingly varied mixture of the three basic functional types ("species") of *epideictic, judicial,* and *deliberative* rhetoric, that is, passages expressing praise or blame with respect to the basic nature of some character, event, or situation; that which is right/just or wrong/unjust with respect to some legislative norm or juridical case; and discourse that pertains to what is advantageous or harmful with respect to some behavior, which is correspondingly either encouraged or discouraged (cf. Kennedy 1991:48–49). In view of all of the stylistic features which the author seemingly puts to good rhetorical use in the text of Ezekiel, it is difficult to see M. Zulick's point that Hebrew

7.5 Summary of the literary-rhetorical development of chapters 33–37   391

(37:1) by means of the various parallels, correspondences, and contrasts that are manifested simultaneously on several conceptual and affective levels in such a compelling, yet also appealing, manner. In the end, the thematic spotlight is fixed once more upon the text's central character—*YHWH*, the sovereign, holy God who will inevitably demonstrate his integrity (note the periodic divine "I" אֲנִי appearing emphatically throughout the text, e.g., 37:19, 21, 23, 28) by establishing both a people and a place that are completely holy unto himself (27–28; cf. 23bc and 36:23, 26–28).[79]

What remains in the following text is to demonstrate this divine motive and mandate also on a cosmic scale and within an eschatological framework at the expense of Gog and all other godless, antagonistic nations on earth (chs. 38:1–39:20). This penultimate passage foregrounds the holiness of *YHWH* (38:16, 23; 39:7, 27) even further as it demonstrates his omnipotent power and sovereign control over the entire universe. The almighty LORD is in complete charge of this world's events, and he will surely see to it that the ultimate victory is won over all the forces of evil and enemies of his people (Rev 20). As "was common in the judgment-speech literature of the sixth and fifth centuries BC" (Alexander 1986:929), this section includes a reiterative recycling to heighten the drama of God's revelation (i.e., 39:1–8 basically repeats the sense of 38:1–23). It then concludes with a cohesion-fixing flashback to the messianic age in the summary-restatement of 39:21–29 (cf. chs. 34:11–37:28; 28:25–26; Deut 30:1–10).[80] After all this vigorous action and high emotive tension, the victorious community of faith—this new Israel of the heart—can finally rest in peace (chs. 40–48). They can bask in the radiant glory of the LORD's everlasting presence (43:7; 48:35)

---

prophetic rhetoric tends to be passive in nature in that it makes "the hearer rather than the speaker the deciding figure in a rhetorical act" (1992:377; cf. Gitay 1991:4–7).

[79] Block's summary is again apropos: "The presence of his sanctuary *(miqdas)* in the midst of the people will be the ultimate demonstration of his commitment to them ('I will be your God'). His sanctification *(qiddes)* of Israel will be the final proof of them as a holy nation, consecrated to himself for his glory ('You will be my people')" (1998:421).

[80] In keeping with the earlier text material that it summarizes, 39:21–29 is another instance of a neatly patterned pericope: A: The LORD's glory is revealed in his justice ("face hidden," 21–24); B: The LORD demonstrates his holiness by restoring the fortunes of his people (25–26) = B¹: the "nations" are witnesses (27); A¹: The LORD's glory is revealed in his mercy ("face not hidden," 28–29). It may be noted that this segment makes it apparent that *YHWH*'s restoration of "Israel" was not completely "unconditional"—a "unilateral act of God" or an "imposition"—in the sense that absolutely no response or reaction on their part was necessary, or "a future bliss without the precondition of repentance" (as argued by Greenberg 1997:735–737). Rather, the fact of sin and the need for personal cleansing is strongly emphasized (39:23, 26), even in retrospect within the eternal Temple of the LORD's presence (43:7).

within the sacred precincts of his Temple sanctuary, from which the river of regenerative spiritual life continually flows (47:1–12).

7.5.9 Summary

In closing this section, we might display the varied rhetorically captivating, "gospel"-centered—but judgment-confirming—central text portion of Ezekiel 33–37 by means of another (admittedly impressionistic) visual summary of its prophetic "plot" and associated connotative flow. The figure below is a schematic, now "scenic," view of the panoramic display given at the beginning of this chapter (7.2.1):

religious connotation

```
                                                                        >Q
 +|
  |               >E      >G          >J            >M     >O
  |
  |                    >F    >H  >I       >K     >L    >N      >P
 0| >A       >D
  |
  |   >B  >C
  |
  |_____
 -                                                  textual progression
```

A schematic depiction of the rhetorical dramatic movement of chs. 33–37

Unit A = 33:1–20   I-J = 36:8–12
A-B = 33:21–22   J-K = 36:13–15
B-C = 33:23–33   K-L = 36–16–23
C-D = 34:1–10   L-M = 36:24–38
D-E = 34:11–16   M-N = 37:1–8
E-F = 34:17–19   N-O = 37:9–14
F-G = 34:20–31   O-P = 37:15–18
G-H = 35:1–15   P-Q = 37:20–28
H-I = 36:1–7

As shown above, our focal section begins with the connotatively neutral (0) judicial text of A, but this bearing takes a sudden emotive plunge with the news of Jerusalem's fall (A-B). The overall depression continues in the judgment oracles of B-C, but this is relieved to some extent by the just condemnation of the unfaithful shepherds (C-D). The connotation then moves in a decidedly positive (+), upward direction as *YHWH* assumes the role of Shepherd for his scattered flock (D-E), but again there is another perceptible downward trend (yet not really negative or totally condemnatory in tone), as unrighteous oppressors within the external community are rebuked (E-F). This wave-like, positive (blessing) ⇔ neutral (warning), thematic movement continues in rhythmic progression throughout the rest of the unit—right up to its quiet, spiritually consolatory close at the end of ch. 37 (P-Q). This final unit, 37:20–28, constitutes the thematic peak of the entire section spanning chs. 33–37: God dwells within his sanctuary among his people, forever together in a covenantal relationship of peace (37:26, cf. 34:25).

The cleansing mercy of God's gospel message thus stands out more clearly when contrasted with the ugly reality of the sinful human condition, both individual and communal,[81] as evaluated and judged according to the eternal covenantal principles of *YHWH*. A person's faithful obedience or rebellious wickedness, as the case may be, will inevitably be met with either the LORD's abundant grace or his punitive justice. According to the book of Ezekiel, former option is always the utmost divine desire (18:23, 30b–32; cf. Hos 11:8–11). A major implication therefore of this prophet's proclamation to the dry bones of most of what passes for religion nowadays is that a spiritual resurrection is not only a priority from a covenantal "peace" perspective (34:25/37:26), but it also constitutes an essential aspect of *YHWH*'s glorious self-revelation to the entire world—"You (all) will know/acknowledge that I am the LORD!" וִידַעְתֶּם כִּי־אֲנִי יְהוָה (37:13a).

7.6 "Can these bones live again"—in translation?

Thus far, our study of Ezekiel 33–37 has focused on the Hebrew text in an effort to reveal its varied artistic and rhetorical features that make the prophet's communication so compelling in the original. In this section

---

[81] Cf. Alexander 1986:746; *contra* McKeating 1993:84.

we will consider the process of translation, that is, how to re-present the prophet's word from the LORD to his people in a language that contemporary hearers/readers can understand and in a manner that they can appreciate. My discussion of this often neglected topic includes an initial overview of the ministry of Bible translation as it is being carried out in Africa, where the people of God are rapidly increasing in numbers on the one hand, but facing severe threats and challenges to their physical and spiritual vitality on the other. Thus, the powerful visionary messages of Ezekiel are just as necessary today as they were some 2400 years ago. As a case study, we will examine the prophet's vision of dry bones in 37:1–14 as it is rendered oratorically, that is, with an oral-aural, rhetorical flair, in the Chewa language of east-central Africa.

7.6.1 An overview of the development of Bible translation in Africa

Most Bible translations in an African context today are discussed in terms of a literal text and some form of a popular or common-language version. Unfortunately, each of these types of rendering in its own way tends to ignore, under-utilize, or distort the abundant stylistic resources that are available in a Bantu language. Why is this the case and what can be done about it? In this section I make some initial proposals for carrying out a project that is intended to produce a full oratorical translation, the general aim of which is to communicate the essential sense and significance of the biblical text in an idiomatic, rhetorically dynamic, stylistically creative, medium-sensitive, functionally equivalent manner. What are some of the chief pros and cons, possibilities or constraints that are involved in such a manifold effort? The term "oratorical" is used here (not "literary"), despite the fact that for most translators the text of Scripture normally originates in printed form, because of the great influence of the *oral-aural* factor in the text composition and transmission process from beginning to end. After a brief survey of the different types of Bible translation available in relation to their appearance in Bantu Africa, the main features of an oratorical version are outlined, along with the principal steps involved in carrying out a translation project of this nature. This includes a consideration of the *printed format* in which the text is presented for optimal legibility. The significant communicative potential posed by this novel approach to Bible

7.6 "Can these bones live again"—in translation? 395

translation is illustrated by means of a comparative analysis of the well-known "dry bones" vision recorded by the prophet Ezekiel (37:1–10) as it appears in three different Chewa versions—an old, literal translation *(Buku Lopatulika)*, a recent, common-language version *(Buku Loyera)*, and a specially composed "oratorical" text. It is hoped that this paper will stimulate the desire to attempt such a challenging formal and interlingual re-creation of the literature of the Scriptures—at least on a selective, experimental basis—in several of the major languages of Africa.

According to official statistics *(quantity)*, the story of Bible translation in Africa has been one of notable success.[82] By the end of 2009 a total of 335 New Testaments and another 173 complete Bibles were available in various African languages.[83] While it is true that there may be over 2000 distinct languages spoken on the continent, especially in the sub-Saharan region (including some 500+ members of the Bantu macro-family), the Bibles and Testaments that have already been published would be accessible to over 90 percent of the total speaking population. Furthermore, plans have been made by a broad coalition of independent Bible translation agencies to greatly reduce, if not completely eliminate, the number of "have-nots" within the first two decades of this new millennium. That is the good news.

The bad news—over and above the well-known functional literacy factor—concerns the comparatively limited selection, or kind *(quality)*, of translation that is currently available to a large proportion of users. This is of course a rather more subjective and debatable issue. For some, just about any version is acceptable—indeed, desirable—*if* it has been prepared by the "right" personnel (i.e., people who are ecclesiastically compatible and theologically credible). This would be the verdict no matter how literal, archaic, or stylistically unnatural the text may actually sound (since it was probably either composed or strongly guided by foreigners)—hence unintelligible in many places. To provide an alternative, or indeed a complement, to the prevailing literal type of translation in the early 1960s the United Bible Societies (UBS), Wycliffe Bible Translators (WBT), and other such agencies initiated a new strategy and style of translation. This method was oriented more towards conveying the meaning rather than the forms of the biblical text. These versions were often called "common-language," "popular-language," or simply "idiomatic" translations since they

---

[82] For a dated, but still valuable overview of this history, see Schaaf 1994.
[83] Source: United Bible Societies website (http://www.biblesocieties.org/), accessed on 27 Sept. 2010.

were intended to speak the natural language of the masses—ordinary Scripture consumers (whether readers or hearers of the text).[84] Such versions featured certain readability/intelligibility-promoting, content/context-sensitive features such as: a selectively limited vocabulary (e.g., archaic, figurative, colloquial, translational, or technical terms) and reduced grammatical range (e.g., fewer genitives and compound prepositional phrases); a preference for relatively short, non-complex, right-to-left attributive (head-first), active sentences; a greater tendency to express implicit information explicitly in the text (e.g., pronominal referents and noun classifiers); the use of redundancy to prevent conceptual overloading; a reduction in the number of event nouns (transformed into verbal constructions); the avoidance of unusual, highly idiomatic lexical or syntactic constructions; clearly marked sentential and discourse transitions (cf. Wonderly 1968:75–78).[85]

Unfortunately, in the rush to produce and publish such CL or PL versions (perhaps an inevitable outcome of the "one size fits all" approach), some crucial mistakes were made at times, that is, with respect to certain sensitive exegetical matters (e.g., "blood" => "death"), radical stylistic transformations (e.g., the combination of two verses into one), key term usage (e.g., re-expressing "grace"), illustrations (e.g., the Valliton line drawings), publication format (e.g., duplicating the GNT text), and the wording of footnotes (e.g., concerning the relative lack of clarity in the Hebrew text). A number of sad experiences of this nature (not only in Africa, but also in various other parts of

---

[84] A "common-language" (CL) translation is a version that restricts itself more or less to "that part of the total resources of a given language common to the usage of both educated and uneducated [classes]" (Wonderly 1968:3). A "popular-language" (PL) translation, on the other hand, applies more to a situation where the language in question is "spoken by people with [relatively] little specialization along social, occupational, and literary lines" (ibid., *loc. cit.*), i.e., where the society still communicates, for the most part, via oral-aural means. Thus, a PL version reflects "the contemporary language in a form that it shared by the entire population that speaks it" *(loc. cit.)*. Since it is becoming increasingly difficult to find such relatively uncomplicated sociolinguistic settings in today's world, it may be helpful to qualify a PL translation as one that is oriented towards the *younger* generation (15–25 years) with a *spoken* style of language (or "level of formality," or social "register") that tends to be "regular-casual," whereas a CL version would be stylistically more "regular," or generally mainstream, in terms of *written* discourse (here I have modified Wonderly's definition somewhat; ibid., 14, 28–29, 41–46). Two influential early manuals that promote the "dynamic equivalence," or "idiomatic," approach to Bible translation (the central characteristic of either a CL or a PL version) were Nida and Taber (1969); Beekman and Callow (1974).

[85] Wonderly (1968) illustrates the application of these techniques with extensive reference to the Spanish CL version, the *Version Popular*. They are also very much evident in the English counterpart *Today's English Version* (TEV) and more recently in the *Contemporary English Version* (CEV).

7.6 "Can these bones live again"—in translation?

the world), coupled with the irrepressible "King James factor,"[86] has somewhat tempered the original enthusiasm for these meaning-based translations. But the undeniably great need for them remains, and nowadays much greater care is exercised during the production process of most projects (e.g., engaging more competent translators to carry out this work, more extensive pre-project and ongoing staff training, closer consultant supervision and text checking, computerized keyboarding and typesetting, multimedia research and application). It looks promising, therefore, that most of the major translational goals for Africa (at least)—whether new translations or needed revisions for all viable languages on the continent—will be achieved within the span of the first quarter of the 21st century (cf. one target date that has been set [by SIL]: 2025).

7.6.2 Translation goal: A different Bible version for every major variety of user

The subject of style as it pertains to Bible translation brings up the issue of *versions*—that is, different text-types that vary not only according to the nature of the rendering (whether more or less literal or free), but also with respect to the such matters as language dialect, social register, text format, amount of Scripture included (etc.) as determined with reference to the particular receptor group that is being especially targeted.

7.6.2.1 *Many varieties of versions*

In addition to making different types or styles of *traditional* published Scripture translation available to cater to the differing needs and desires of distinct constituencies, as noted in the preceding section, the United Bible Societies has in recent years attempted to be even more audience- and situation-specific, or "pro-choice," in its various outreach endeavors.[87]

---

[86] I am using the expression "King James factor" non-pejoratively to refer to a situation where a significant segment of a particular sociolinguistic population is closely tied—historically, emotionally, and sometimes also dogmatically—to an old(er), literal translation that was prepared by early foreign missionaries. Such attachment, even devotion, in itself is not a problem; the difficulty arises in those cases where church leaders (including contemporary missionaries, not generally the laity) decree that no other, more recent translation is acceptable, especially a meaning-based version (which is frequently referred to negatively as a "paraphrase," i.e., not a "genuine" Bible translation).

[87] As a UBS Translation Consultant, I am most familiar with the guiding principles and established programs of the United Bible Societies, though I do have contact with several other

For some time now it has supported an extensive, post-literacy *New Reader* program, which publishes graded and specially formatted text selections that are designed for people (not just children) who are learning to read their mother tongue. The aim is to progressively train these inexperienced readers to the point where they can manage the text of a CL version without much difficulty. In many parts of the world, especially in Asia, younger readers in particular are responding with enthusiasm to text portions that have been prepared in a typical *comic* book illustrated format. Extensively annotated *study Bibles* have been produced for readers who wish to have more background information available to help them understand and apply the original text. *Audio Scriptures* are a necessity to provide access to the Word of God for "hearers"—either those who do not know how to read or those who for one reason or another prefer not to. The medium of sound is further utilized in song productions that clothe selected biblical texts in a diverse array of appropriate contemporary musical styles. *Video* productions are popular with those who have grown up and become accustomed (perhaps overly so) to this mode of message transmission. Great success is also predicted for recent developments in the *electronic* medium, where a flexible "hypertext" format makes it possible for the computer user to immediately access a wide range of text-related material (e.g., notes concerning the ancient biblical setting, illustrations maps, charts, explanatory diagrams, a topical index, key-term glossary, and more).

7.6.2.2 An oratorical version

My special interest in this chapter is to explore yet another special kind of translation that is aimed at a particular group of receptors, namely, a *literary* (or, as I shall modify the term, an *oratorical*) version for people who appreciate and respond to the full stylistic and rhetorical resources of their language.

What exactly is a literary translation then, and how does it differ from some of those already mentioned, the CL and PL versions in particular? Wonderly broadly defines such literary translations as follows:

---

translation agencies, in particular, the Wycliffe Bible Translators/SIL International. For a survey of some of these new receptor-oriented developments in a Chichewa language setting (the country of Malawi, to be specific), see Wendland 1998:ch. 6.

7.6 "Can these bones live again"—in translation?

> These are fully contemporary, are oriented to the general public (not just the Christian in-group), and vary from regular to formal in their *[sociolinguistic]* functional variety. They make free use of all the resources of the language at all levels which are considered acceptable for published materials, and are thereby not intended to be fully accessible to the uneducated reader. (1968:30)

Obviously, a literary version as defined above is possible to produce only in a linguistic community that possesses a relatively long tradition of *written* literature. Its envisioned constituency, or target group, would be people who are comparatively well-educated, widely read, and who enjoy the challenge of wrestling with the full range of lexical, grammatical, stylistic, and rhetorical usage in the particular language and society concerned.[88]

Does anything correspond to a literary text in the case of a language group that does not have such a long or strong tradition of literature and whose members communicate predominantly by oral-aural means? This situation would characterize most societies in Bantu Africa as well as in many other regions of the world. In such cases, the closest equivalent might be termed an *oratorical* text—that is, oral discourse that makes use of the complete range of genres and styles in the spoken language to convey a message that is widely regarded by listeners as being impressive, eloquent, persuasive, and beautiful. Such semi-formal, oral-rhetorical usage would exclude youthful jargon and foreign-based colloquialisms (e.g., English borrowings and calques) on the one hand and widely unintelligible archaisms or specialist in-group technical argot on the other (e.g., vocabulary pertaining to specific occupations or activities like hunting, fishing, herbalistic medicine, or traditional initiation ceremonies). Nowadays, such an oratorical style is manifested in the main by popular public speakers and radio broadcasters, including skillful oral performers of ancient verbal art forms as well as Christian evangelists and revivalists.[89] Thus, many recognized models of excellent oratory style do exist; however, they must be carefully collected (often by recording, hence requiring transcription), analyzed, and published (or broadcast) for standards of assessment to develop to the point

---

[88] A literary translation is not necessarily the same as a "liturgical" version, although the two types are sometimes confused. A liturgical Bible is often quite traditional and literal in nature, hence not literary at all according to natural TL verbal norms—although it may regarded as being so as a result of long usage and "official" promotion by the user churches.

[89] I present the results of an extensive study of an outstanding representative of the last mentioned group in Wendland 2000. Some politicians too are good orators, but their topical repertory tends to be quite limited and focused on issues of government and social welfare.

where they may be effectively applied in written literature. Of course, the medium of print itself requires certain compositional modifications to be made to any published text, for example, less overt repetition, a more explicit expression of content (to counteract the lack of a situational context), compensation for suprasegmental, intonational, and elocutionary (phonological) significance (e.g., the use of commas to represent dramatic pauses), more precise conjunctive and transitional devices ("function words"), and a lower incidence of informal or colloquial diction.[90]

The use of these oral models and stylistic techniques is particularly appropriate for translations of the Bible, which are much more frequently accessed by the ear than the eye.[91] Furthermore, recent research has tended to confirm the hypothesis that the various documents of the Scriptures were in large measure composed aloud and/or were written down with an oral-aural transmission and reception of their message in mind.[92] Consequently, "[s]ince the acts of both writing and reading were normally accompanied by vocalization, the structure [and style] of [the] text was marked by aural rather than visual indicators."[93] This fact (assumed here to be true) has important implications for both the analysis as well as the ongoing transmission of the biblical text via translation. For one thing, such prominent

---

[90] Compare the set of audio-oriented features noted in the study of Sundersingh 1999:170. I would strongly support Sundersingh's appeal that "[t]he media scene of today's world demands that we be sensitive to the needs of non-literates and non-readers [these two categories overlap, but are not the same] by way of providing them with biblical [i.e., faithfully rendered] Scriptures in media [and *modes*, i.e., distinct verbal styles or varieties] other than print" (ibid., 315; the comments in brackets are my own).

[91] The preface to the *Contemporary English Version* states this point well: "Languages are spoken before they are written. And far more communication is done through the spoken word than through the written word. In fact, more people *hear* the Bible than read it for themselves. Traditional translations of the Bible count on the *reader's* ability to understand a *written* text. But the *Contemporary English Version* differs from all other English Bibles—past and present—in that it takes into consideration the needs of the *hearer*, as well as those of the reader, who may not be familiar with traditional biblical language" (New York: American Bible Society, 1995; original *italics*). This final claim concerning its uniqueness may be somewhat of an overstatement, but for our purposes the point is simply this: An *oratorical* version is meant primarily to be *orally* read, to be clearly understood *aurally*, and to make its impression upon an audience through the message as it is being *heard* by them.

[92] On this point, see Achtemeier 1990:3–27 and Sundersingh 1999:ch. 6.

[93] Davis 1999:11. Similarly, concerning the Old Testament, David Dorsey writes: "[A]ncient texts were written primarily to be heard, not seen. Texts were normally intended to be read aloud.... To study structure in the Hebrew Bible, then, requires paying serious attention to verbal structure indicators..." (1999:16). Such "aural indicators" would include features such as: rhythmic lineation, phonic accentuation, verbal patterning, prominent discourse demarcative devices, lexical recursion, direct speech, graphic diction, and vivid imagery (to promote topical-thematic recall).

aural sonic, stylistic, and structural indicators—the "rhythmic envelope" of discourse, including its audio-punctuation devices—need to be reproduced by means of functionally equivalent techniques in a translation. This oral-elocutionary dimension of meaning is a particularly important consideration in the case of any specifically oratorical version, which is meant primarily to be heard rather than read.[94]

However, a possible objection to an oratorical, or indeed a literary, translation needs to be considered. This concerns a stylistic comparison and evaluation with respect to the original texts of Scripture. Thus, one might question whether an artistic-rhetorical manner of composition constitutes a distortion of—in this case, an intentional improvement upon—the supposed vernacular, common-language, or *koine,* style of the New Testament documents.[95] Are we in danger here of *over*-translation? In other words, to what extent are the biblical books themselves literary (or oratorical) in nature—that is, of recognizable and demonstrable excellence with respect to their compositional and rhetorical quality? In short, there is considerable evidence in support of an affirmative answer to this question.[96]

Thus, the various books of the Bible arguably *do* manifest, by and large, a high literary standard and thus require a correspondingly high quality of translation to maintain a relative balance in terms of functional equivalence, communicative effectiveness, or more specifically "aesthetic parity."[97] Whether the language is Hebrew or Greek, the texts of Scripture over and above their recognized religious and moral content *do* evince a level of compositional excellence that is second to none with regard to both the *macro*structure and also

---

[94] For a discussion of these concepts in relation to a poetic translation of John 17:1–9 into Chichewa and Chitonga (two south-eastern Bantu languages), see Wendland 1994b.

[95] A stylistic assessment of the of the Hebrew Scriptures is of course more difficult to make due to the limited corpus of texts, religious or secular, on the basis of which an adequate analytical comparison may be made (even in cognate literatures). However, the diversity and abundance of "universal" literary features present in the Old Testament greatly reduces the doubt concerning this issue.

[96] See for example, Dorsey 1999, Davis 1999, and Wendland 2004, 2006, 2008b.

[97] With regard to the translation goal of "functional equivalence," de Waard and Nida state: "The translator must seek to employ a functionally equivalent set of forms which in so far as possible will match the meaning of the original source-language text" (1986:36). "Meaning," in turn, is not only "informative" in function; it is also "expressive" and "affective" in nature. Concerning translation effectiveness, Hatim and Mason propose that "one might define the task of the translator as a communicator as being one of seeking to maintain **coherence** by striking the appropriate balance between what is **effective** (i.e., will achieve its communicative goal) and what is **efficient** (i.e., will prove least taxing on users' resources) in a particular environment, for a particular purpose and for particular receivers" (1997:12).

the *micro*structure of discourse organization (e.g., from the skillful selection and combination of complete literary genres to the corresponding usage of figurative language, varied syntactic arrangements, patterns of repetition, rhetorical features such as irony and hyperbole, and diverse phonesthetic combinations).

The preceding claim may be supported whether one analyzes the discourse from a Semitic, a rabbinic, or a Greco-Roman stylistic perspective (or all three literary influences in the case of many NT texts). That being the case (should this assumption be granted), it behooves literary/oratorical translators to at least attempt to reproduce or match this level of stylistic *excellence* in the TL text—to the extent that this is possible (in keeping with their own level of education, competence, experience, and commitment as well as the encouragement and support provided by their translation administrative committee). To do any less would represent a corresponding *reduction* in the overall communicative value of the translation in relation to the original SL text. Thus, the attempt to produce a sonorous and moving "poetic" rendering of at least certain portions of the Scriptures—those of undeniable literary quality to begin with—would seem to be justified, as long as there is a receptor constituency that is either calling for such a translation, or which research suggests would presumably benefit from one.[98]

7.6.3 Principles and procedures: How is a "oratorical" version prepared?

The following is a summary of a literary-oratorical approach to Bible translation. This does not involve a completely new translational philosophy and technique but simply highlights and focuses upon certain components of a standard meaning-based, medium-sensitive methodology. The goal is to produce the closest *artistic* functional equivalent of the original SL message in an oral-aural-oriented TL text, with special reference to both *style* (literary form) and *rhetoric* (communicative purpose). Seven general principles are paramount during the process of *analyzing* the biblical text, and twelve more specific procedures serve as guidelines when *recomposing*

---

[98] The sort of rendition that I am proposing here would be classified as a "homologous" translation by Christiane Nord in her helpful overview of functional approaches to translation (1997:52). She defines this as a version in which "the *tertium comparationis* between the source and the target text is a certain status within a corpus or system, mostly with respect to literary or poetic texts" *(loc. cit.)*. This translation technique, the ultimate in linguistic "domestication" (Venuti), is also known in secular circles as "semiotic transformation" (Ludskanov) or "creative transposition" (Jakobson).

7.6 "Can these bones live again"—in translation?

the essential message in translation. A further four parameters may be used when *assessing* the extent to which the essence of the original message has been successfully captured, or transmitted, in translation. These last topics are outlined in greater detail to underscore the importance of actual audience *testing* in translation studies. What constitutes essentiality or essence here is determined on the basis of the three major criteria of *accuracy* (i.e., with respect to the semantic content and pragmatic intent of the SL text), *relevance* (i.e., interpretive, text-processing efficiency as well as effectiveness in relation to communicative import, impact, and appeal), and *appropriateness* (i.e., in terms of the primary contextual setting of oral-aural text reception and target-group usage).

7.6.3.1 Seven analytical principles

The principles listed below constitute the main pragmatic perspectives according to which an oratorical approach may be applied to the exegesis (analysis) of a particular biblical text (Wendland 2004:84–88). They also underlie the fundamental set of procedures that guides the translation (synthesis) of this same passage in a given receptor/target language. We have:

a. A *discourse-oriented* (top-down ←→ bottom-up),[99] *genre*-based methodology, one analytical perspective and direction of operation being utilized to mutually inform, correct, and develop the other (normally beginning this exercise from the top, or larger, units) to reveal the salient compositional features (or forces) of demarcation, cohesion, progression, and projection within a text.

b. A prominent pragmatic-*functional component*, i.e., message form + content is assumed to convey some simple, compound, or complex communicative purpose (the intentional *[illocutionary]* force == *[locution]* ==> resultant *[perlocutionary]* effect) in an integral act of text transmission that unites an original (implied) author and his (presumed) audience or readership.

c. A perspective that views the primary rhetorical, connotative, and communicative intention(s) of the (implied) author as being manifested either *explicitly*—that is, stated overtly in the discourse— or *implicitly* through his motivated selection of specific L-R forms (i.e., linguistic clues or literary cues, from macro-genres to micro

---

[99] For a concise definition and illustration of the difference between "top-down" and "bottom-up" text processing, see Dooley and Levinsohn 2001:52–53.

stylistic features) and subsequent arranging as well as shaping of the original source text itself according to an overall strategy that includes certain important *presuppositions* as well as *implications*.

d. A concern for the pressure of the overall *contextual setting* upon the interpretation of a given passage or pericope, including both its *textual* (immediate, as well as removed in time and space, i.e., *intertextual* resonance) and also *extratextual* aspects (i.e., a gradient of mutually interactive, situational frames of cognitive, emotive, and volitive relevance, e.g., sociocultural, institutional, ideological, interpersonal, transmissional, environmental, personal).

e. A special focus upon the interrelated *artistic* (textual) and *rhetorical* (interpersonal) dimensions of discourse, which concern the relative appeal (aesthetic attraction) and impact (persuasive power) of the biblical message as it was plausibly conceived, composed, and conveyed in the original act of verbal creation (i.e., the expressive, affective, and poetic functions of communication).[100]

f. A corresponding interest in and concern for also the *oral-aural* attributes of the biblical message, with reference to the process of initial text *transmission* (including its creation and reception) as well as its *transformation,* or recomposition, within the communicative framework of a different language, literary tradition, sociocultural (including religious) setting, media network, and interpersonal situation.

g. A *holistic* conception of both the individual books of the Bible, in their individuality, and also the received corpus as a whole—the Holy Scriptures—consisting of a complete, integrated (both topically and textually), mutually illuminating and interpreting collective canon of sacred literature.

7.6.3.2 Twelve translational procedures

The following 12 guidelines summarize the basic steps that may be profitably followed when one endeavors to prepare an oratorically oriented rendering of a given SL message in another language.[101]

---

[100] Christiane Nord would designate the primary function in operation here as the "appellative," which is manifested in language that is specially crafted or designed to appeal "to the reader's [or listener's] aesthetic sensitivity" (1997:42–43).

[101] An explanation of these 12 steps may be found in Wendland 2004:80–92. Additional guidelines would be helpful when dealing with particular genres and macro-text types—for example, attention to parallel lineal patterning, strophic structure, and "free" accent rhythm in the case of Hebrew poetry, or where narrative discourse is concerned, such features as plot development, character types, event lines, point of view, background information, and shifts in the setting. Already translators must learn to anticipate how the analyzed text will turn out

7.6 "Can these bones live again"—in translation? 405

a. Study the textual, intertextual, and extratextual *context* of the SL portion to be translated.

b. *Read* the entire text (repeatedly—*aloud*) and determine its manifest *genre* and sub-genres.

c. Plot all occurrences of *repetition*, patterned or random, in the pericope under consideration.

d. Record all significant instances of formal or topical *conjunction* or *disjunction* within the text.

e. Isolate the areas of stylistic *concentration* and note their structural *placement* and *purpose*.

f. Identify the major points of discourse *demarcation* and *projection* within the whole text.

g. *Outline* the compositional-thematic structure of the entire pericope in terms of *form* and *content*.

h. Do a complete word/motif/image/symbol study regarding *key terms* and *thematic concepts*.

i. Analyze all major *oratorical* features of the individual verses in terms of *form* and *function*.[102]

j. Note the chief *speech intentions* and their interaction within the text (the *rhetorical* structure).

k. Do a close literary-rhetorical *comparison* (SL–TL) to find possible form-functional *matches*.

l. Prepare a *trial oratorical translation* and *test* this in various settings and for diverse audiences.

These twelve heuristic procedures again emphasize the importance of a careful *analysis* in order to lay a solid, text-based foundation for the translation process. The original pericope must *first* be fully understood in terms of form, content, and function—including all its artistic and rhetorical

---

in the TL and within analogous local sociolinguistic settings, each with its distinctive set of situationally determined speech events.

[102] For some practical suggestions on how to analyze biblical and target language texts with respect to their salient and distinctive *oral-aural* characteristics, see Thomas 1991:39–51. This edition of the *UBS Bulletin* features articles that relate to the general theme, "The Scriptures in Audio Video Format. Another helpful selection is "Audio Video Media Working Group: Final Report at the Triennial Translation Workshop," 65–71. See also Sundersingh 1999:*passim*.

features—before one can even begin to reconceptualize the intended message in another language, literary (or oral) tradition, and sociocultural setting. All of this information must be readily accessible in the translator's mind as s/he undertakes the activity of interlingual text transformation, and it must also guide this re-creative movement through to a successful completion.

To a great extent, this is a spontaneous, intuitive, compositional exercise—one that is greatly dependent upon the ultimate skill and proven experience of the verbal artist (poet) involved. However, once a working draft has been written down (or orally recorded), the tough, sometimes tedious business of text comparison (with the source document) and revision begins. This is to ensure that the translation is not only an artistic reflection of the original message, but also a semantically and pragmatically accurate, or faithful, one. In other words, the translation, though existing now in what is possible a radically different micro- and sometimes also macro-form, does not unduly or inappropriately distort the communicative sense and significance of the SL text. This vital activity of qualitative assessment is described somewhat more completely in the following section.

7.6.3.3 Four evaluative parameters

The relative degree of acceptability of a given *Bible* translation may be determined on the basis of a careful evaluation that is made with respect to four interconnected factors. These primary criteria are shown on the diagram below as they relate to each other within a framework composed of two basic dimensions, namely, with a special focus upon either the "source language" (SL) or the "target language" (TL) on one plane, and textual meaning or form on the other:[103]

Focus—	Meaning		Form	
SL	1. **FIDELITY**	╱accuracy ╲authenticity	4. **PROXIMITY**	╱microstructure ╲macrostructure
TL	2. **CLARITY**	╱intent ╲content	3. **IDIOMACITY**	╱written ╲spoken

---

[103] For a more elaborate version of this scheme, see Wendland 2008:226–230.

7.6 "Can these bones live again"—in translation?

These features are numbered in order of their relative priority, specifically in the case of a Bible translation that is intended to be a dynamic, meaning-centered, oratorical-type version. Other types of rendering would require a re-ordering or a re-weighting of the four criteria.

Fidelity to the meaning of the SL message, as intended by the (implied) author, is of stated paramount concern in most, if not all, versions of Scripture (regardless of whether this ideal is achieved in actual practice).[104] The criterion of fidelity may itself be factored into two important aspects. "Accuracy" (*actual* fidelity) is a quality that may be more or less objectively assessed through various analytical means that relate the SL and TL texts in comparative text-linguistic terms. This must, however, not be considered solely in terms of the so-called propositional content of the biblical document, for the dimension of message meaning also includes important affective, imperative, poetic, and relational aspects. "Authenticity" (*perceived* fidelity) is a more subjective property that is based upon a particular receptor's or R-group's expectations about Bible translation. It thus depends on their estimation of the degree to which the translated text, no matter how accurate or intelligible, is viewed as representing the genuine Word of God and is therefore "a trustworthy version of the original message" (Anderson 1998:1).

The second most important factor in any Bible translation is **clarity**, or intelligibility. This feature, too, pertains not only to the semantic "content" of the original text, but also to its primary pragmatic (illocutionary) "intent"—that is, what the *(implied)* author intended to *do* with his message in terms of communicative function in relation to his *(presumed)* audience.[105] What conceptual, volitional, and emotional effect(s) did he desire to achieve

---

[104] It is in fact *impossible* to be fully 100 percent faithful in communicating the intended meaning of a given SL text—including all of its significant, author-intended implications—via its translation into another language. For this to happen, the entire message context—cognitive, literary, cultural, environmental, interpersonal, etc.—would have to be conceptually available and accessible to the target audience and then also actually comprehended by them (cf. Gutt 1992:65, 67). Such congruence would be difficult to achieve even in the case of texts transmitted in the same language. The more disparate the languages, cultures, and settings, the greater the problems involved in communicating the desired message. Thus, fidelity too is a relative notion (as is clarity), dependent upon a host of textual, interpersonal, and situational factors. A certain amount of "give-and-take" or "gain-and-loss" must always be factored into the process of evaluating any translation. The two formal criteria of assessment are less variable in this respect.

[105] When attempting to analyze the *functional* dimension of discourse *meaning,* one cannot limit one's attention to an inanimate or mindless text. The analyst must rather posit, at least, a hypothetical (or implied) author/speaker and reader/audience to make sense of the procedure. Otherwise s/he is simply analyzing her/himself.

by the words that he wrote with respect to rhetorical impact (e.g., encouragement, admonition, consolation, warning) and affective appeal (e.g., the expression or elicitation of joy, anger, disappointment, sorrow)? The violation or non-realization of either criterion 1 or 2 would render any translation of the Holy Scriptures liable to the judgment of being unacceptable. No distortion of the essential meaning of a sacred religious text (as determined by scholarly as well as popular consensus) is tolerable, no matter how innocently or ignorantly perpetrated. On the other hand, if the message of the Word of God is not clearly conveyed to average (ordinary) receptors of the target constituency, it will do them little good,[106] no matter how correct the text may be from an exegetical point of view. *Koine* (common) Greek (and presumably the basic style of Hebrew employed in the OT) was chosen as the principal mode of message transmission on account of its general linguistic clarity to the masses, despite its artistic overlay and theological foundation. Any translation of this corpus of literature therefore should aim to achieve a corresponding effect with regard to overall understandability.

Although features 3 and 4 are more or less optional elements in the measurement of translational acceptability—since they largely concern the form of the text, not its meaning—they must not be overlooked or ignored by serious Bible translators. **Idiomacity** pertains then to the *naturalness* of the style of the translated text, as it has been verbally expressed in the TL with respect to the linguistic signs used in its transmission—phonological, morphosyntactic, lexical, and also those devices employed on the higher levels of discourse organization. A translation may be relatively clear in terms of intelligibility, but still not sound completely natural in comparison with the normal patterns of everyday speech or the (sub-) genres in which it has (or should have) been composed. In some cases this "foreign accent" may be so strong as to threaten the fundamental perspicuity of the text, let alone its manifest stylistic quality. Furthermore, as was noted above, the naturalness or normality of the message, even when composed in "written" form, must be oriented primarily towards the "spoken" (oral-aural) form of the

---

[106] I am referring specifically to *cognitive* benefit here; I do not wish to imply that literal, relatively difficult to understand translations have no value. Such formal correspondence versions may effect a number of important socio-religious functions within a given community, for example, as *liturgical* texts, suitable for reading in formal worship services; as a close linguistic *reflection* of the biblical languages for use in various text(book)s that pertain to systematic theology; as forms of *ritual* communication, intended to deepen a group's sense of "spirituality" or their emotive attachment to a particular religious tradition.

7.6 "Can these bones live again"—in translation? 409

language since this is how the majority of people will be receiving it—today as also in the original communication event.

Finally, how does the criterion of **proximity** apply to the assessment process? This may be the least important factor, comparatively speaking, yet it too involves the issue of procedural *integrity* with respect to the original (divinely inspired) text. In other words, there is a general principle that obligates Bible translators to stay as close as possible not only to message content, but also to the distinctive textual forms that are found in the SL document. Change for the sake of change—or just for the fun (artistry) of it cannot be allowed. However, the proximity principle must be applied according to the guidelines of a priority scale that has been agreed upon for the specific translation concerned (e.g., to render poetry as poetry, prose as prose—all other factors being equal—or to follow formal consistency where key terms are employed with the same sense in similar co-texts (e.g., sin, slave, sacrifice, mercy), or to seek to maintain the same relative level of literary artistry and/or rhetorical force). Thus, such formal closeness, whether on the macro- or micro-structural level of discourse organization, should definitely *not* be retained where it would result in a clear reduction in either semantic fidelity and intelligibility or situational appropriateness (e.g., in a setting where poetry is deemed suitable only for children or to express love lyrics). There may be some—perhaps considerable—debate, however, when attempting to adjudicate between demands or preferences of idiomacity on the one hand and proximity on the other. Such decisions can be made only with reference to a flexible "form-functional continuum" as this is applied within the particular framework of text and context, or message and medium, that has been established as part of the guiding statement, or *Brief* (that is, regarding the purpose/*Skopos*, principles, procedures, and policies) for the specific translation project as a whole.

In this connection, the particular type of biblical discourse being evaluated with a view toward translation also needs to be considered, e.g., a more prosaic versus a more poetic passage. In the figurative language of a psalmic or prophetic pericope, for example, it would normally be necessary to allow a greater measure of idiomacity with regard to certain lexical designations in order to achieve a functionally equivalent (or appropriate) rendering. But in a historical narrative, such as we find in the Pentateuch, one would have to remain relatively more proximate to the referential forms of the text, even the more difficult ones, in order to uphold the preeminent criterion of "fidelity," with regard to either accuracy (actual) and/or authenticity (perceived). Thus, we see that these four factors of assessment interact (and also conflict) to a considerable degree in practice, and it is not easy to give a pat answer or a standard strategy to cater for every eventuality. This hard fact of Bible translation requires staff of the highest competence, aptitude, experience, and dedication. It also calls attention to the need for a carefully and widely conducted audience educational and testing program to ensure that the project remains on target as far as the will of an informed majority (or at least the project's principal supporters) is concerned.

There is yet a final factor to consider, namely, the typographical *format* in which a text, whether original or translated, is published. This is especially important in the case of a document that is intended primarily to be read *aloud* in public. Which particular features render a printed text more—or less—readable? Most publication design experts cite such important elements as the size and style of type, the amount of interlinear and marginal space, relative line length in relation to column width, the use of standard procedures like justification and hyphenation versus leaving a ragged right margin.[107] Obviously, a pericope that is not very legible will tend not to be orally read well either, and this deficiency will in turn adversely affect all those who are listening to the text. Thus, the judicious use of formatting must always be practiced in any effort that aims promote an appropriate (forceful, dynamic, compelling, etc.) *oral recital* of an oratorically oriented translation text. Under the right circumstances, certain important suprasegmental sounds can be signaled in print, for example: smaller print (soft articulation), capital letters (LOUD SPEECH), repeated letters (vooowel elooongaaation), italics (special *stress, intensity,* or *focus*). Some of the main problems and potentials in this respect will be illustrated when presenting the sample texts below (section 7.6.4.1).

7.6.4 Illustration: A comparative stylistic-functional evaluation of translation technique

The three Chewa texts of Ezekiel 37:1–10 below will serve to briefly illustrate the nature and purpose of an oratorical translation (OR).[108] I begin with a

---

[107] For a more detailed discussion of this subject, see Louw and Wendland 1993.

[108] I chose this particular portion of Scripture on account of its general popularity, its theological significance, its stylistic verve, its rhetorical power—and because I had recently analyzed the original Hebrew text in detail for the present chapter.

pair of control texts—the first as translated in the old vernacular version of 1922 (*Buku Lopatulika* "Sacred Book"—BL); the second reproducing the new popular language version of 1998 (*Buku Loyera*—BY).[109] The third text is a specially prepared semi-poetic, rhetorically motivated rendering of this pericope.[110] The two control passages will be formatted and punctuated as they actually appear in published form (but with enlarged type), while the OR version will be set forth in what I propose is a more readable text design (as noted above).[111] Following the three texts (plus fairly literal English back-translations), I will summarize the main stylistic differences among them with respect to form and function and then suggest how each of these versions might serve to fulfill a different communicative purpose within the religious community.

7.6.4.1 Text Comparison: Three Chichewa versions of Ezekiel 37:1–10

Buku Lopatulika

Dzanja la Yehova linandikhalira, ndipo anaturuka nane mu mzimu wa Yehova, nandiika m'kati mwa cigwa, ndico codzala ndi mafupa; 2 ndipo anandipititsa pamenepo pozungulira ponse, ndipo taonani, anali aunyinji pacigwa pansi, ndipo anaumitsitsa. 3 Ndipo anati kwa ine, Wobadwa ndi munthu iwe, mafupa awa nkukhala ndi moyo kodi? Ndipo ndinati, Ambuye Yehova, mudziwa ndinu. 4 Pamenepo anati kwa ine, Nenera kwa mafupa awa, nuti nao, Mafupa ouma	The hand of Jehovah rested on me, and he went out with me in the spirit of Jehovah, and he placed me inside of a ravine, it was full of bones; 2 and he caused me to go right there going around everywhere, and have a look, it was a multitude in the ravine down, and he caused them to completely dry up. 3 And he said to me, One born of a person you, these bones, say, can they become alive? And then I said, Lord Jehovah, you are the one who knows. 4 Right then he said to me, Speak for [me] to these bones tell them, You dry

---

[109] An overview of these two published versions may be found in Wendland 1998:ch. 5.

[110] The main poetic features of a pure lyric style in Chichewa (called *ndakatulo*) are described and exemplified in Wendland 1998:185–189. This involves a greater manifestation of such devices as ellipsis, reiteration, ideophones, exclamations, emphasizers, demonstratives, independent pronouns, figures of speech, idioms, phonological accentuation, punning, and modifications in the normal, prose word order. This poetic text from Ezekiel is the product of a joint compositional effort involving my seminary Psalms class. I served as the final text "redactor" for this project.

[111] I have used smaller print in the case of the third, oratorical text so that the lines of the English translation will match up more closely with the Chichewa original.

inu, imvani mau a Yehova. 5 Atero Ambuye Yehova kwa mafupa awa, Taonani, ndidzalonga mpweya mwa inu, ndipo mudzakhala ndi moyo. 6 Ndipo ndidzakuikirani mtsempha, ndi kufikitsira inu mnofu, ndi kukuta inu ndi khungu, ndi kulonga mpweya mwa inu; ndipo mudzakhala ndi moyo; motero mudzadziwa kuti Ine ndine Yehova. 7 M'mwemo ndinanenera monga anandiuza, ndipo ponenera ine panali phokoso; ndipo taonani, panali *gobede gobede,* ndi mafupa anasendererana, pfupa kutsata pfupa linzace. 8 Ndipo ndinapenya, taonani, panali mitsempa pa iwo, panadzaponso mnofu, ndi khungu linawakuta pamwamba pace; koma munalibe mpweya mwa iwo. 9 Ndipo anati kwa ine, Nenera kwa mweya, nenera, wobadwa ndi munthu iwe, nuti kwa mpweya, Atero Ambuye Yehova, idza, mweya iwe, kucokera ku mphepo zinai, nuuzire ophedwa awa, kuti akhale ndi moyo. 10 M'mwemo ndinanenera monga anandiuza, ndi mpweya unawalowa, ndipo anakhala ndi moyo, naimirira *ciriri,* gulu la nkhondo lalikurukuru ndithu. 11

bones, hear the words of Jehova. 5 So says the Lord Jehovah to these bones, Have a look, I will put breath into you, and you will be alive. 6 And I will put in for you a tendon, and bring upon you flesh, and wrap you with skin, and put breath into you; and you will be alive; thus you will know that I am Jehovah. 7 In this manner I spoke on [his] behalf as he told me, and while speaking on [his] behalf there was a noise; and have a look, there was a *clatter clatter,* and the bones drew closer together, one bone following its fellow bone. 8 And I gazed, have a look, there were tendons on them, there also came on flesh, and skin covered them on the top; but there was no breath in them. 9 And he said to me, Speak for me to breath, speak for me, one born of a person you, and say to breath, So speaks the Lord Jehovah, come, breath you, from the four winds, and blow into these killed ones, so that they may be alive. 10 In this manner I spoke for him as he told me, and breath entered them, and they were alive, and they stood up *upright,* a very big army indeed. 11...

Buku Loyera

1 Mphamvu ya Chauta idandigwira, Mzimu wa Chauta udandinyamula nkukandikhazikika pakati pa chigwa. Chigwacho chinali chodzaza ndi mafupa. 2 Chauta adandiyendetsa uku ndi uku pakati pa mafupawo. Mafupawo analitu ochuluka kwambiri

The power of Chauta grabbed me, the Spirit of Chauta picked-me up and set me down firmly in the midst of a ravine. The ravine was full up with bones. 2 Chauta moved me about back and forth between the bones. Those bones were really very numerous

7.6 "Can these bones live again"—in translation?

m'chigwa chonsecho, ndipo anali ochita kuti *gwaa* kuuma kwake. 3 Tsono adandifunsa kuti, "Iwe mwana wa munthu, kodi mafupa amenewa angathe kukhalanso ndi moyo?" Ine ndidati, "Ambuye Chauta, ndi Inuyo amene mukudziwa zimenezi." 4 Apo adandiwuza kuti, "Ulalikire mafupa amenewa, uwauze mafupa oumawo kuti amve mau a Ine Chauta. 5 Unene kuti zimene

Ine Ambuye Chauta ndikuwauza mafu-

pawo ndi izi: Ndidzauzira mpweya mwa inu, ndipo mudzakhalanso ndi moyo. 6 Ndidzakupatsani mitsempa ndi mnofu, nkukukutani ndi khungu. Ndidzauzira mpweya mwa inu, ndipo mudzakhalanso ndi moyo. Tsono mudzadziwa kuti Ine ndine Chauta."

7 Pamenepo ndidayamba kulalika monga momwe adandilamulira. Ndikulalika choncho ndidangomva kuti *gogobedegogobede!* Mafupa aja kuyamba kulumikizana. 8 Ine ndiyang'a-

ne, ndidaona kuti pali mitsempha, kenaka mnofu ukuwonekanso, potsiriza nkubwera khungu pamwamba pake, koma munalibe mpweya mwa iwo. 9 Tsono Chauta adandiwuza kuti, "Iwe mwana wa munthu, ulalike ndi kuuza mpweya mau a Ine Ambuye Chauta, akuti, 'Mweya iwe, bwera kuno, bwera kuchokera ku mphepo zinai, dzawauzire anthu ophedwawa, murdered folk,
kuti akhalenso ndi moyo.'" 10 Motero ndidayamba kulalika monga adandilamulira. Tsono mpweya udalowa mwa iwo, ndipo akufa aja adakhala ndi moyo, naimiriria. Linali gulu lalikulu kwambiri la ankhondo.

in that whole valley there, and they were just like *stoney* in their dryness. 3 So he asked me, "Say, child of a person, can these bones
live again?" I said,
"Lord Chauta, it is You who
know these things." 4 Then he told me, "Preach to these bones,
tell those dry bones that they should hear the words of Me, Chauta. 5 Say that the things
that I the Lord Chauta am telling the bones
are these: I will blow breath
into you, and you will again
live. 6 I will give you tendons
and flesh, and wrap you up with skin. I will blow breath into you, and
you will live again. Then you
will know that I, I am Chauta."
7 Immediately I began to preach
just as he commanded me. While
I was proclaiming like that I just heard *clatterclatter!* Those bones began to be knit together. 8 While I was gazing
there, I saw that there are tendons, next flesh also appears, finally, the skin comes on top,
But there was no breath in them.
9 So Chauta told me,
"Say, child of a person, proclaim and tell breath the words of Me, the Lord Chauta, and say, 'Hey breath, come here, come from the four
winds, come and breathe into these

so that they can live again.'" 10 Just so I began to proclaim as he commanded me. Now the breath entered into them, and those dead people became alive, and stood upright. It was a very big army of soldiers.

Oratorical Version

Dzanja lamphamvu la Chauta lidandigwira—*gwi!*	[1] The mighty hand of Chauta grabbed me—*tightly!*
Nyamu! Mzimu wa Mulunguwu wandinyamulatu,	Up and away! The Spirit of God picked me up,
nukandiika pakati pachigwa chachikulu chotakaka.	and put me in the middle of a large, broad valley.
Chinali chodzaza ndi mafupa okhaokha ali *mbwee!*	It was filled up completely with bones all *scattered!*
Uku ndi uku Chauta ankandiyendetsa m'chigwa umo.	[2] Here and there Chauta moved me inside that valley.
Pakati pa vibade vija ndinkazungulira pali ponsepo,	In the midst of those skulls I circled all around there,
ali ochulukadi mafupawo nga' mchenga wapagombe.	the bones were so numerous like sand on a sea shore.
Onsewo anali *gwaa!* pansi mu chigwa choopsacho.	All *dried out!* hard on the ground in that awful valley.
Adandifunsa Chauta kuti, "Iwe mwana wa munthu,	[3] Chauta asked me, "Say you, child of somebody,
kodi angakhalenso m'moyo mafupa ouma onsewa?"	can all of these dry bones become alive again?"
"*Ha!* ine ndingadziwe bwanji munthu wapadziko ine?	"*Ha!* how can I know, a person of this earth like me?
Koma inu nokha, Ambuye, popeza mukudziwa zonse."	But you alone, O Lord, since you know everything."
Adandilamula Chauta nati,"Ulalike kwa mafupa awa,	[4–5] Chauta commanded me, "Preach to these bones,
uwauze kuti amvetse mau onse amene ndidzalankhula.	tell them to listen to the words that I will speak.
Ambuye Mulungu ali ndi uthenga wofunika kwambiri	The Lord God has a very important message.
Iwo achere khutu, amve bwino zomwe ndifuna kunena.	Let'em lend their ear n'listen to what I want to say.
"Mafupa oumanu, nazi zimene ine Chauta n'dzachita:	[5–6] "Y'dry bones, here's what I Chauta 'm gunna do:
Ndidzakuuzirani mpweya, mudzapumanso *wefuwefu!*	I'll blow breath in you, you'll breathe again *puff-puff!*
Ndidzakuikirani mitsempa ndi mnofu, *ah!* khungunso.	I will put tendons and flesh on you, *ah!* skin as well.
Apo mudzazindikira kuti ine Chauta ndilipo ndithu!"	Then you'll realize that I Chauta I really do exist!"

7.6 "Can these bones live again"—in translation?

Nanga ine n'kukana kodi? Ndidayambo-lalika mau, monga momwe adandilamulirawo Chauta Mulungu.	[7] So how could I refuse? I began t'preach the words, just as those he commanded me, Chauta God.
Pamenepo panalidi phokoso lingoti *gobedegobede*!	Right then there was a big noise like *clatterclatter*!
Taonani, mafupa onse ouma aja adachito-lumikizana!	Just look, all those dry bones acted t'join together!
Ndili chiyang'anire choncho, n'dapenya zodabwitsa:	[8] While I'm staring there thus, I saw s'amazing things:
Pa mafupa oumawo paoneka mitsempha ndi mnofu,	On those dry bones appear tendons and flesh,
kudzanso khungu pamwamba, zonse zili bwino *nde!*	and also skin on top, everything's just alright *ready!*
Koma muli *zii!* Munalibe mpweya m'kati mwakemo.	But inside is *emptiness!* There's no breath in there.
Adandilamula Chauta nati,"Ulalikire mpweya tsono, iwe mwana wa munthu, uwuze mau a ine Ambuye:	[9] Chauta commanded me, "Now preach to the breath, child of somebody, tell it the words of me the Lord:
'Bwera kuno, mpweyawe, dzawauzire ophedwawo	'Com'ere, you breath, breathe into these killed ones
kuti akhalenso m'moyo pamaso panga monga kalelo.'"	so that they become alive in my presence as before.'"
Izi zonse ndidachita monga adandiuzira Chauta.	[10] All these things I did just as Chauta told me.
Mpweya udangoti *fiku!* n'kulowa mwa mitemboyo.	The breath *arrived!* n'enter'd right into those corpses.
Pomwepo onse aja adasanduka amoyo naimirira *njii!*	Immediately they all revived and stood up *upright!*
Panali chinamtindi cha anthu m'chigwa chonsecho!	It was a huge crowd of people in that valley there!

7.6.4.2 *Evaluation: A survey of the main compositional differences*

The seven principal stylistic features that distinguish the oratorical version of Ezekiel 37 from the other two are summarized below.[112] Since my focus

---

[112] For the special purposes of this short study, I will not consider exegetical issues, matters of text structure and format, or items of a purely terminological nature, such as, the difference in the rendering of the divine name, the Tetragrammaton—*YHWH*, viz. *Yehova* "Jehovah" in BL versus *Chauta* "[the name-title of the supreme Creator God in traditional Chewa religion]" in both BY and OR (cf. Wendland 1998:115–121).

is upon the OR text, this differential overview will be carried out from that particular textual perspective:

a. The OR poem rearranges the ten verses of the traditional version into nine "stanzas" of four measured lines each These are roughly equal in length for rhythmic purposes, including several "ballast lines" (i.e., those which reiterate certain aspects of content or its main implications, e.g., "The Lord God has a very important message" [4–5]). This would presumably be a much easier text to articulate "oratorically" in a public reading than the others, e.g., in a more dynamic mode of intonational expression.

b. Nine different ideophones and two distinct exclamations accent the dramatic character of the discourse in OR (versus only two ideophones and no exclamations in the other versions). Thus, even the lack of an overt action may be thereby highlighted, e.g., "But inside is *emptiness! [zii!]* There's no breath in there" [7].

c. The average sentence length is the shortest in OR; of longer, but still normal (spoken) utterance length in BY; unnaturally long and grammatically complex in BL (the problem here being compounded through the use of semicolons, e.g., vv. 1–2). Thus, the OR text is the easiest to comprehend as it is concurrently being uttered aloud, since each line is meaningful as it stands.

d. The literary style is clearly (audibly) the most idiomatic in the poetic OR text in terms of both lexical and syntactic usage, e.g., many affixes (pronominal, demonstrative, and intensive), word order variations; colloquial diction, rhythmic expression. The literal BL is the most unidiomatic and hence difficult to understand; on the other hand, BY manifests the clearest, most natural and straightforward manner of speaking, in both direct and reported discourse. The BL is almost unintelligible in places—right at the beginning, for example: "The hand of Jehovah rested on me, and he went out with me in the spirit of Jehovah..." [1]. This suggests that "Jehovah" had a physical "hand" and was accompanied by his personal "spirit," which could be sent out on special missions.

e. Several, more specific lexical-semantic replacements and additions are made in OR in order to embellish the language, to "fill out" certain poetic lines, and also to avoid too much exact repetition, for example: "a large, broad valley" [1] (i.e., to accommodate the many bones, belonging to a huge "army" of people!); "those skulls" [2] (a more picturesque and powerful term than just "bones"); "a person of this earth" [3] (to stress the divine messenger's human nature more than the ambiguous expression "child of a person," i.e., male or female!); "let 'em lend their ear" [4–5] (replacing the simple "hear"); "you'll breathe again *puff-puff!*" [5–6] (a more climactic predication than "you will live again"); "all those dry bones" [7] (for the unadorned "those bones"); "everything's just alright *ready!*" [8] (to bring out the cumulative implication of the awesome description at this point); "alive in my presence as before" [9] (emphasizing Yahweh's implied personal relationship to all the dried up, dead "bones"); "entered those corpses" [10] (in place of the mere pronoun "them"). A *ndakatulo* lyric in Chichewa thus features vivid, highly graphic and evocative imagery to stimulate a complete dramatic, visualizable scene along with its associated physical sensations and psychological feelings in the minds (and hearts) of the listening audience.

f. The dialogue portions of the OR are similarly more abundant (some being refashioned out of narrative report) as well as more colloquial in their manner of expression, e.g., "Y'dry bones, now here's what I, Chauta, 'm gunna do…" [5–6]. This crucial feature automatically renders the account in more immediate, personal, familiar, and memorable terms.

g. The poetic text naturally includes a number of impressive phonological devices, including, wordplay, rhyme, alliteration, and assonance, for example: <u>Nyamu</u>! Mzimu wa Mulunguwu wandi<u>nyamu</u>latu—nukandiika pakati pachigwa chachikulu **chotakata**—chinali **chodzaza** ndi mafupa okhaokha… [1]. Such selective, purposeful sound shaping enables the poet to highlight certain similarities, contrasts, or high points within the text. The conceptual and connotative content being conveyed is correspondingly that much more concentrated and sensual.

A word of caution is in order here: The translator(s) of a lyric version of a given biblical text certainly do(es) not have the "poetic" liberty or license to *distort* either the original essential meaning or its particular areas of thematic focus (in this case, for example, the amazing transformation of dead bones into a mighty company that is effected through the life-giving operation of the word of the Lord). A clear measure of functional equivalence, including exegetical fidelity, in relation to the text of Scripture must be maintained to the degree that this may be determined on the basis of all available, reliable evidence.[113] Critics and reviewers are free to debate this

---

[113] Nord devotes an entire chapter to this crucial issue: "Function plus Loyalty" (1997:ch. 8). She explains: "The loyalty principle…induces the translator to respect the sender's individual communicative intentions, as far as they can be elicited…. [It] limits the range of justifiable target-text functions for one particular source text and raises the need for a negotiation of the translation assignment between translators and their clients" (ibid., 126).

or that specific usage as to whether the OR version has gone too far in its artistry in an attempt to create rhetorical impact and aesthetic appeal. But it should always be remembered that the basis for such a comparative evaluation must be a careful examination and analysis of the Hebrew source text, not some English (or other linguistic) translation.

On the other hand, one ought not to get tangled up in minor details of form or interpretation when conducting an assessment of this nature. The exegete's zeal for precision can easily stifle the poetic muse. In the case of biblical poetry and prophecy (as we have in Ezekiel 37:1–10), it is often not the mere individual image or utterance that is important, but the total conceptual, emotional, and sensory impression that is created by the special literary (oratorical) language that has been used. This may well be the primary intention of the original text (and its implied author), namely, to activate the expressive *(emotive),* affective *(imperative),* and aesthetic *(poetic)* functions of communication to an equal or even greater extent than the cognitive *(informational)* function that so many people mistakenly identify as being invariably paramount in the literature of the Holy Scriptures.

7.6.5 Application: Different translation styles for different types of target group

The preceding remarks raise the issue of a specific translation type as this relates to the needs and preferences of particular segments of the overall target audience. Obviously, each of the three different versions above was either composed for, or may be most comfortably received by, a distinct segment of the larger constituency of Chewa speaker-hearers. The BL is clearly the most popular—despite the unnatural archaic awkwardness of its language—because it happens to be the vernacular "King James Version" that the majority (of Protestants) have grown up with in church, learned by heart, and hence become devoted to. The problem is that for many people many passages are either unclear, ambiguous, misunderstood, or not understood at all. The words may be quite familiar (through long exposure), but the content of the whole text is not clearly comprehended. All too often then, ordinary receptors are forced (if challenged) to reply along with the unnamed but well-known Ethiopian official of Acts: "How can I understand unless someone helps me?" (8:31).

For this reason, the meaning-oriented popular-language BY version was prepared by mother-tongue speakers of the language—not to replace the BL, but essentially to be used alongside it (at least). The purpose was/is to provide readers and hearers alike with a more intelligible, *complementary* text to turn to, if need be, for clarification, or when trying to reach an audience of younger people, new/non- Christians, or even second-language speakers of Chewa. Thus, for many people it is high time that the semantic dry bones of an existing literal version be resurrected in the form of a text that finally makes more sense—both overall as well as in a host of passages that simply did not communicate to them heretofore.

As distinct from the BY then, the oratorical version (OR) was created as a *supplementary* biblical text, intended not so much for general usage, but for a more limited employment on selected *occasions* (e.g., a day of public worship and praise, a popular tract publication), for particular *audiences* (e.g., youth choirs, school Bible-study groups), or for specialized *uses* (e.g., in a dramatic "play" *[sewero]* production, as a radio broadcast, or in an audio-cassette series).[114] Thus, it is not a matter of either-or as far as contemporary Scripture choice or consumption is concerned, but rather one of both-and. In other words, which version best fits the specific human need and situational setting at hand? Of course, some explanatory education and illustration is essential with a view toward facilitating the proper mutually supportive use of these different translational types. However, in many areas of Africa today, that is indeed the lesser problem; the far greater challenge is to provide people with more than one reliable version to chose from in the first place.

7.6.6 Conclusion: Some implications for Bible translation in Bantu Africa

It may be helpful to summarize four major implications for Bible translation that arise from the various issues discussed in this final section of our study of Ezekiel.

---

[114] The great potential of CDs (audio cassettes), DVDs, and radio broadcasts for mass-communicating the Scriptures really needs to be more fully exploited, especially in areas of the world where the Bible is a banned book, where access to more sophisticated means of message transmission (e.g., TV, video, computers) are limited for economic reasons, and/or where the majority of the population is not literate. For a helpful comparative survey of the possibilities as well as the limitations of cassette and radio communication, see Sundersingh 1999:138–150 (cf. Wendland 2005).

a. Concerning *transmission strategy:* As was mentioned above, local Bible societies, national churches, and mission agencies need to plan together and budget for the preparation of different versions which are intended to serve distinct audience groups within the total population by means of diverse media and modes of transmission (e.g., standard-print publication, specially formatted and illustrated portion, a narrativized version, new reader selection, audio [+/- visual] text, musical/sung rendition, electronic hypertext, dramatized multi-media production).[115]

b. Concerning *translation style:* The different versions referred to in (a) will necessarily manifest important stylistic variations in several dimensions and on a number of distinct linguistic levels, such as, the amount of formal correspondence or functional equivalence that is demanded/desired/allowed; the degree of artistry and/or idiomacity that is encouraged in order to promote an oratorical reading of the discourse; the application of TL literary/oral genres for (novel) use in Scripture translation; careful textual adaptations to cater for a primary oral-aural medium, and the amount and kind of extratextual reader's helps which are provided such as footnotes, section headings, illustrations, cross references, book introductions, a glossary of key terms.[116]

c. Concerning *translator training:* The more audience + context-focused versions mentioned in [a+b], coupled with the higher standards of quality demanded, will obviously require translation teams that include, or have access to, personnel who are similarly more competent and creative (oratorically artistic) in terms of their natural literary gifts and technical skills, whether as exegetes, stylists, drafters, illustrators, formatters, media experts, school educators, literacy advisers, PR promoters, or whatever. In addition to more intensive biblical training, the translators of today require supplementary courses in a variety of specific and specialized fields, such as: holistic education, media technology, literary-poetics, and cross-cultural communication.

d. Concerning *audience testing:* A detailed and extensive research survey of the potential human area of reception must be carried out nowadays *before* an expensive translation (+/- multi-media) project is embarked upon. Financial resources are too limited to waste on "educated guesses" or subjective, provincial/denominational preferences. A thorough sociolinguistic, religious, and aesthetic testing of

---

[115] In his survey of the Tamilnadu people of India with respect to the most effective "mode" of audio-cassette production of a selected Scripture portion (Mark 1:21–28), Sundersingh found that a "drama format" (multi-voiced) won out over both a "story format" (modulated intonation) and a straight "reading format" (ibid., 290).

[116] These "readers helps" could also be provided in an oral/audio "text," although they would of course need to be carefully distinguished from the actual words of Scripture, e.g., as "asides" by means of a different speaking voice and/or a physical signal in sound (bell, music, etc.).

7.6 "Can these bones live again"—in translation? 421

> the intended target audience should also be conducted *while* a given project is underway, to ensure that it is hitting the mark, especially with regard to its subjective "felt" and objective "real" needs (physical, social, spiritual). Finally, a sufficient amount of *post*-production surveying is necessary in order to determine a version's relative success in achieving the particular goals that it set out to accomplish in relation to its primary user-group. Past mistakes must be avoided and achieved successes repeated when future Scripture productions are planned and implemented.

While the preceding points relate more or less to all types of Bible translation, they may apply in particular, and with special rigor or intensity, to an *oratorical*-type version. That would be due to several critical factors—in particular, an OR's relative novelty in relation to the envisioned audience, and the difficulty required to do a good job of it. A more positive motivation for such verbal artistry and excellence is this: It concerns the great *communicative potential* that such a literary-poetic rendition has, first of all, in conveying the inscripted stylistic and rhetorical dynamics of the original text in a Bantu language. In addition, a recognizably artful—yet also semantically and pragmatically faithful—interlingual re-creation of this nature has the inherent power to make a corresponding impact on people who probably never realized or expected that the Word of God could speak to them so idiomatically, beautifully, and powerfully in their mother tongue.

8

"The Righteous Live by their Faith" in a Holy God: Complementary Compositional Forces and the Rhetorical Generation of Habakkuk's Dialogue with the LORD

8.1 Introduction

The three Hebrew words of Habakkuk 2:4b (וְצַדִּיק בֶּאֱמוּנָתוֹ יִחְיֶה) constitute the best-known and theologically most significant statement in the poetic book of this late seventh century (BCE) prophet. However, as set within its original textual environment, the utterance appears to be not much more than an aside, a fleeting positive contrast that occurs within a strong word of divine denunciation. My aim of this chapter is to advance the proposal that, contrary to its surface appearance, this concise expression forms the thematic nucleus of Habakkuk's entire message. It thereby functions as the semantic kernel from which the complete text may be "generated," that is, organized and interpreted with respect to structure, style, content, and purpose.

Two principal complementary and integrated compositional forces are involved in this complex process of discourse generation, namely, *progression* and *cohesion*.[1] While very little is known about the prophet himself or the precise social, political, and religious situation in which he ministered, a considerable amount of information concerning the past and present import of his intensive dialogue with the LORD may be derived from a careful study of the text he left behind. Accordingly, the progressive development of his prophecy is examined in relation to the two main strands of its larger fabric of syntagmatic organization: the structural-thematic and rhetorical-dramatic movements. This is followed by an examination of the complementary cohesive bonds, primarily topical and paradigmatic in nature, that serve to tie the composition together into a harmonious whole on several levels or spans of discourse arrangement.

This text-oriented investigation provides one with an overview of the architectonic framework and broad poetic style of the book of Habakkuk as a unit and the panegyric hymn of chapter three in particular. The intricately fashioned, composite structure is then discussed with specific reference to its central thematic core in 2:4b (i.e., the faithful life of a just, though tormented person) as this relates to the wider *theodicy* in which it is contextualized (i.e., the justice of a holy God in a wicked world). The formal arrangement of the work is also considered in relation to its manifold pragmatic function as a dynamic piece of rhetorically motivated artistic communication. It is a vital message that had great theological significance in its assumed original setting, and one which continues to "live"—to have a corresponding relevance also in a contemporary context—both in visual form (print) and as an audio rendition (i.e., a modern oral-aural articulation).

8.2 How clear—the "vision" of Habakkuk?

"The book of Habakkuk is a composite unity" (Peckham 1986:617).

In keeping with this equivocal assertion, Peckham's typically disruptive source-critical analysis of the book of Habakkuk contradicts the unity that it

---

[1] These are roughly analogous to *centrifugal* (outward moving) and *centripetal* (inward moving) physical forces, respectively; *progression* moves the discourse forward along its intended thematic pathway, while *cohesion* ties the present text material into what has preceded it in the discourse as a whole, in particular, its thematic core.

8.2 How clear—the "vision" of Habakkuk?

might appear to uphold. Thus, in the process of describing the discourse as "a composition of text and commentary," the analyst engages in a great deal of imaginative and usually unsubstantiated speculation as he attempts to demonstrate how this alleged "commentary changed the lament into a book by modifying some stanzas and adding others" (ibid., 618, 621). Even the discerning reader soon becomes lost in the effort to untangle the complex network of sources which the analyst posits as underlying both the initial artistic lament as well as the subsequently composed ponderous prophetic commentary (ibid., 635–636). Unfortunately, the overall impression that one is left with after plowing through such a study is anything but unity!

The supposedly disparate compositional quality of the text that has come down to us as "Habakkuk" is even touted as a positive stylistic feature by some redaction critics. Marks, for example, draws attention to the "suggestiveness" of the opening dialogues, which he claims "depends largely on the dramatic inconsistencies which result from the composite structure" (1987:219). The lack of a "unified scenario for [this] section" is not a detracting feature at all, for "it is precisely the disjunctions—the fact that prophetic complaint and divine response appear to be at cross purposes—that account for its resonance" (Marks *loc. cit.*). However, the dramatic dissonance being referred to here would appear to be a product of the divergent presuppositions of the prophet in relation to the revealed purpose of Yahweh, not the form and content of his message per se. Various hypotheses regarding the supposed disparate, multi-authored nature of the book are usually supported with reference to chapter 3. Hiebert, for example, asserts that this "hymn in Habakkuk 3 is an archaic composition, added to the corpus of Habakkuk in the post exilic period in order to emphasize God's final victory over evil."[2] As if the prophet himself could not have conceived of such a glorious outcome!

A methodological error that is almost as great as that of presuming to recompose the original work (via source/redaction criticism), is the more subtle one of freely offering to alter its received form. Thus, in an effort to show how "inclusion functions to mark the discrete sections of Habakkuk 3 and to give shape to the poem as a whole," Hiebert finds it necessary to emend the Masoretic text 41 times in 18 verses (1987:120–122). Albright is not far

---

[2] Hiebert 1996:626; the unlikelihood of this thesis will be demonstrated in the following text-rhetorical analysis.

behind in "proposing some thirty-eight corrections of the Masoretic text" of this chapter (1950:3) while Margulis offers an almost complete reconstruction of the same psalm (1970:412). This is not to say that all such proposals for improvement have no merit and are not worthy of consideration. The point is simply that "the Masoretic Text, especially its consonantal framework, should not be abandoned without good reason" (Bruce 1993:835). Thus, other things being equal, the credibility of a close discourse study of the original Hebrew stands in inverse proportion to the number of changes that are made to it in one's analysis and interpretation, especially those which affect the consonantal text (MT). Any critical alteration in this respect, no matter how valid on its own or theoretically, always weakens one's argument in relation to the textual organization as a whole and verse-level exegetical decisions as well.

The difficulty inherent in many of these older studies is that they are founded on a faulty assumption, namely, that of the supposed metrical regularity of the original Hebrew text. Thus, Albright claims that "the utility of the inner Hebrew literary and metric evidence has pointed the way to numerous corrections and amplifications of the text" (1950:10). Conversely, according to Margulis, "metric imbalance is often the tip-off that produces a diagnosis of textual corruption or disturbance" (1970:412). But it is not only a flawed, misleading theory that guides many modern analysts; often worse is a cavalier attitude of disregard for the integrity of the MT, coupled with the presumption that the current expert knows precisely how the original was—or should have been—composed. A typical example is the following assessment of the Masoretic reading of 3:2:

> Despite the theoretical possibility of a tristich (or tricola) the final hemistich is suspect, if for no other reason than its being impossible Hebrew. No classical Hebrew author—as the prophet-psalmist shows himself to be in every passage free of textual disturbance—would have expressed the thought "in wrath remember mercy" in this manner. Cp. Ps 25:6, Lam 2:1.[3]

This critic then proceeds to put things right by means of six different modifications of the Hebrew text.

---

[3] Margulis 1970:412; in this manner, the contemporary critic is able to freely rewrite the Hebrew text in order to "improve upon" the work of the original prophet-psalmist.

8.2 How clear—the "vision" of Habakkuk?

It is clear that a proposed exploration of what I am calling compositional forces is a gratuitous exercise if it is carried out on a text that is either made up of an edited patchwork of sources or one that requires generous external emendation in order to raise it to an acceptable literary standard. However, this is not the case as far as Habakkuk is concerned. On the contrary, the Hebrew text of this book appears to be in fair shape as it stands, exhibiting just a few places where a possible alteration is worthy of serious consideration (Smith 1984:96). But more than that, as will be demonstrated in the analysis below, the entire book displays an intricately fashioned artistic unity as it makes a profound theological statement on the holiness of God (1:12; 3:3) as he demonstrates the true meaning of righteousness/justice (1:4, 13; 2:4) by executing judgment (1:4) and deliverance (3:13, 18) on behalf of his faithful people (2:4).

There are two principal compositional factors that contribute to this essential integrity of the Hebrew text. One, *progression*, is in Grossberg's terms "centrifugal" (outward/forward-moving) in nature, the other, *cohesion*, is "centripetal" (inward/backward-moving) (1989:5). Though different in their discourse operation, these forces are not antithetical or contradictory with respect to one another. Rather, they are fully complementary, and though existing in dynamic tension within the poetic text, their effect is that of mutual reinforcement or enhancement. By their interaction they serve both to organize the structural forms of biblical poetry and also to promote its primary communicative objectives as intended by the original poet.

In this chapter I will first examine the two major compositional constituents of syntagmatically oriented progression in much Hebrew poetic discourse. These are the *thematic*, which is highlighted by a text's overall structural arrangement, and the *dramatic*, which realizes its various rhetorical motivations, both large and small. Progression, in turn, is balanced and defined by the accompanying paradigmatic forces of textual cohesion, which is effected largely by various types of repetition, both formal and/or semantic. As far as the prophecy of Habakkuk is concerned, the compositional interaction of progression and cohesion is viewed as being generated and governed by the work's thematic nucleus, namely, the final three words of chapter 2 verse 4: "the righteous man—by his steadfast faithfulness—he lives!" (וְצַדִּיק בֶּאֱמוּנָתוֹ יִחְיֶה). This brief utterance is crucial in pointing toward a resolution of the great theodicidic debate in which the prophet is engaged: How and why does a just and holy God continue to do business in an unjust, iniquitous world? And what significance or implication does the answer have for those who put their steadfast trust in him? These are issues of timeless relevance, hence a message which needs to be communicated also today in the most dynamic manner that modern media make possible.

8.3 Progression—the forward, climactic movement of discourse

Most recognized works of literary significance tend to manifest some sort of temporal, topical, spatial, or logical progression. This is perhaps not as obvious in non-narrative texts, but such development and its communicative consequences are normally present there as well. Thus, in addition to an intelligible plan or a natural sequence of selection, ordering, and arrangement, there will always be a certain goal, culmination, point, or purpose that is achieved once the end of the composition is reached. This essential forward movement of a text is not amorphous. Instead, it is carefully measured and shaped in order to present the reader/listener with a series of bite-sized mouthfuls, as it were, so that s/he can properly process the material and in turn respond appropriately.

In order to effect the desired progression in a given discourse, it must be segmented, or divided up, into a sequence of integral units.[4] This operation creates the necessary discrete steps or stages that give the illusion, at least, of continuity and purposeful advancement. This also makes it possible for the author to modify or even to change the main thrust of his message en route as he moves from one section to another in the text. Normally, such a rhetorically controlled advance builds up to an implicit or explicitly marked *peak* of significance or intensity either at or near the close of the composition. These segments are created by introducing points of *discontinuity* into the text—places where there is a definite gap or shift in the flow of form and/or meaning.

There are a number of ways in which such syntagmatic disjunction is brought about in Hebrew poetry. Most of these involve some type of modification in the nature or material of the message, e.g., topic, speaker,

---

[4] For some practical details concerning how to carry out a structure-functional manner of discourse analysis, see Wendland 1995:chs. 1–3.

addressee, time, mode of speaking (direct/indirect), connotative tone, functional type, or utterance mood (declaration/ affirmation, question, request/ command). Frequently, linguistic/literary markers also appear, serving to reinforce the relevant discourse break. Five common signals of a beginning *(aperture)* in biblical poetry are these: a formulaic opening (e.g., "thus says the LORD..."), an imperative, a vocative, explicit mention of the divine name, and/or a rhetorical question.

The markers that distinguish the corresponding close of a textual unit *(closure)* are less definitive. At these junctures one usually finds some manner of intensification or specification, which may be manifested by any of the following devices: direct speech, vivid imagery, a condensed utterance, asyndeton, exclamation, a reversal in word order, repetition, a verbless clause, monocolon, or a sharp contrast. However, a diagnostic *convergence* of such features may also appear at an aperture or indeed at some point of segment-internal climax (peak). For this reason, the structure of a given text must always be considered in its entirety, that is, by examining the various correspondences and contrasts of the discrete parts in relation to one another and the compositional plan of the discourse as a whole.

The dominant characteristic of Hebrew poetry—typically cumulative, rhythmic, line-coupled (paired) *parallelism*—is a crucial factor in the process of segmentation. But the disjunction inherent in this mainly binary, incremental mode of literary composition must also be bridged or traversed in order to create structural units of larger, varied scope. Accordingly, this outstanding instance of the so-called poetic principle of equivalence/similarity (paradigmatic clustering) superimposed upon contiguity/combination (syntagmatic progression) is periodically supplemented by spatial displacement to effect what is sometimes termed distant or remote parallelism.[5] This is not done arbitrarily or haphazardly, however. Rather, the deliberate recursion, or paralleling, of form and/or content is employed as a bounding technique in order to effect the marking of a certain textual border: the close of the same unit *(inclusio),* the corresponding beginning of a subsequent unit *(anaphora),* the corresponding ending of a subsequent unit *(epiphora),* a juxtaposed ending plus new beginning *(anadiplosis),* and various lengths of reversed parallelism *(introversion).* This multifaceted structural function of distant parallelism must always be examined and evaluated in conjunction

---

[5] On the notion of the "poetic principle" in literature, see Jakobson 1985:42, 144.

with the diverse means of segmenting a progression that were mentioned above. I will now carry out this analytical operation with reference to the text of Habakkuk, focusing in particular upon the book's several distinct but related macrostructures, along with their respective constitutive compositional forces.

8.3.1 The overall, structural-thematic progression of the discourse

The macrostructure of Habakkuk is one of the most clearly defined of all the prophetic books. This is because the textual organization is demarcated throughout by rather obvious changes in the speaking voice and associated subject matter, as shown in the following figure. The way in which these constituent units of content are related to one another in terms of form and function is not so easy to discern, however, and this has given rise to a great deal of scholarly debate. I am under no illusion that my own study will turn out to be any less controversial, but it will hopefully present the major aspects of exegetical evidence in a manner that is both interesting and credible, if not fully convincing in every respect.[6]

The place to begin is with the discourse as a whole as shown on the following outline, which indicates certain structural-thematic parallels by means of corresponding degrees of indentation:

```
[I]  A. Superscription: Introduction of the prophet and his message (1:1)
     |
     B. Habakkuk's first complaint: Why does injustice in Judah (or anywhere) go
        unpunished by Yahweh? (1:2–4)
     |
     |  C. God's response: The fearsome Babylonians will punish Judah
     |     along with the rest of the nations of the world (1:5–11)
     |  |
     |  D. Habakkuk's second complaint: Why pick the wicked Babylonians
     |     to execute a just judgment upon Judah? (1:12–17)
     |  |
     |  |  E. Habakkuk rests his case (transition):
     |  |     How will God respond to me and I to him? (2:1)
------|---|---|--------------------------------------------------------------------
```

---

[6] I will restrict myself to a consideration of the complete text as it has been received and will not speculate concerning "the redactional process which brought [the various units of discourse] to their present order"; nor am I in a position to say much here about "the role and identity of the 'prophet' Habakkuk himself" (Mason 1994:61).

8.3 Progression—the forward, climactic movement of discourse

[II] F. God's <u>response</u>: I will provide a vision pronouncing a verdict of condemnation upon proud, unrighteous Babylon (2:2–5)

G. A <u>taunt</u> against Babylon: Five judicial "woes" declared against the unjust nation and its wicked citizens (2:6–20)

H. The <u>psalm</u> of Habakkuk: A poem in praise of Yahweh's just and mighty deliverance of his faithful people in the past, concluded by Habakkuk's calm, faith-filled acquiescence to the divine will

---

If the superscription (A) is combined with section B, we are left with seven major form-functional divisions (or forensic moves) in the book, perhaps a significant number. A pair of short, but foregrounded, segments in the middle, i.e., E (2:1) + F (2:2–5), act as a structural pivot between the two unequal, but thematically balanced halves. Part I clearly reveals the theological and practical *problem* as far as Habakkuk was concerned—first of all, grave injustice in the land of Judah and second, Yahweh's apparently unjust plan to deal with the situation by means of the evil Babylonian empire. Clearly, the righteousness of God and the justice of his dealings in the world were at stake as the prophet positions himself for a satisfying answer (2:1).

Part II provides a just *solution* of the entire matter, beginning with a promise of divine certainty (F). A typical compound, prophetic woe oracle of judgment upon all oppressors (G) then functions overtly as Yahweh's response to Habakkuk's second complaint about God's chosen means of justice (C-D). A psalmic prayer (H) concludes the divine oracle that Habakkuk saw (A). It appropriately incorporates a powerful theophanic vision (3:3–15) coupled with the prophet's personal reaction (3:16–19), which together provide a soul-satisfying resolution to the issue of widespread wickedness in the world (B). This psalm also puts to rest (for the believer) the book's central theological-moral controversy concerning the manifest holiness and power (3:3–4) of the invisible but almighty Sovereign LORD (3:19).

8.3.2 The center of the macrostructure

It is important at the outset to note the elaborate manner in which the bifid medial bridge of the composition (2:1 + 2–5) is demarcated. The prophet is portrayed in his conventional role as a "watchman—standing guard"

(וָאֶצְפֶּה) standing high on the city wall (cf. Isa 21:8–12; Ezek 3:17–21; Hos 9:8). But there is a surprising reversal here—something which suggests that things are not what they may at first appear to be in terms of underlying significance. Instead of a proclamation to the nation, whether good or evil, on behalf of Yahweh, Habakkuk is preparing himself to *receive* a personal message from the LORD (2:1), a further answer to his ongoing complaint about proper standards of "judgment" on earth (מִשְׁפָּט; 1:2–4, 12–17). Moreover, he fully expects to respond in turn to what Yahweh is going to say. Thus, he anticipates another occasion when he can press his case with God further, that is, to reply again to his "[my] complaint/rebuke" (תּוֹכַחַת—a term that is probably ironically ambiguous in this context). Habakkuk's eventual public response turns out to be quite different from what the prophet (or his audience) anticipates at this juncture; it takes the form of an ancient psalm in solemn praise of his "Savior-God" (3:18).

Yahweh's climactic (second and final) answer is preceded by the book's only explicit quote margin, literally: "and-he-replied-to-me Yahweh and-he-said..." (2:2). This appears to mark the onset of the second, resolutional half of the debate. The LORD announces a certain "revelation" (חָזוֹן, repeated 2:2, 3) that will clarify things not only for Habakkuk, but also for the entire nation—and for every subsequent receptor (group). This follows starting in 2:4 (appropriately, with הִנֵּה "just look!"), namely, a complete denunciation and condemnation of the wicked, especially all unjust oppressors. The vision here is in fact what Habakkuk declares that "he has seen" (חָזָה) as the prophecy ("the oracle" הַמַּשָּׂא) opens (1:1), hence a prominent instance of structural *anaphora*. The intervening material, i.e., 1:2–17, constitutes a rhetorically motivated *flashback,* as it were, a dialogue between the prophet and God, which both provides the essential background for what Habakkuk says in 2:1 and also leads up to the second half of the book, the larger portion beginning in 2:2.

Part II is considerably more difficult to demarcate with certainty than the first half of Habakkuk. The latter is fairly straightforward, consisting of four relatively homogeneous poetic units, or stanzas, the middle pair containing several included strophes: [B] 1:2–4; [C] 5–11 (5–6, 7–8, 9–11); [D]12–17 (12–13, 14–17); and [E] 2:1. But a complete and detailed subdivision of the discourse is necessary if we are to correctly follow the book's rather subtle structural argument, which reinforces what we read on the surface of the text, and thus to fully experience the cumulative rhetorical impact of both the overt and the underlying levels of communication.

8.3.3 The problem of 2:5

The first major hermeneutical difficulty that one encounters with regard to the book's compositional organization arises in verses 4–5 of chapter two. Are the words of five to be read as a unit *closure* (e.g., N/RSV, NIV), an *aperture* (e.g., GNT, JB), or as neither (e.g., NEB, TOB)? To be specific, does this verse function together with four as part of the promised "vision" denouncing Babylon (cf. 2:2)—or only as a prelude to the revelation, which then begins in v. 6? Alternatively, does it constitute an introduction to a completely independent segment, namely, the compound judgment oracle of five woes? Related to this is the question of who is actually speaking the words of verse six—Yahweh, Habakkuk, or some unknown redactor?

After a careful weighing of the structural evidence, it seems best to adopt a mixed perspective on this problem, which in the end provides the most natural solution. Accordingly, 2:2–5 should be viewed as a complete discourse unit, one in which Yahweh himself takes up his prophet's bold challenge (2:1) and confronts the text's central controversy, that is, concerning the subject of *divine justice*. After this forceful introduction to the matter, the theme of righteous judgment is then panegyrically elaborated upon starting from verse 6 and continuing on to the end of the book.

This transitional section may then be divided into two strophes: The first (vv. 2–3) acts as a prologue which gives the contextual background, namely, to the vision that Yahweh is about to reveal, especially its complete certainty of fulfillment. The emphasizer הִנֵּה "behold" then fittingly announces an onset to the introductory portion (vv. 4–5) of that compound vision, which fully replies to both of Habakkuk's complaints (ch. 1)—but in reverse order. The woe oracles of the remainder of ch. 2 thus ostensibly summarize and intensify the basic content of the LORD's answer to the prophet's *second* complaint expressed in 1:12–17. This pericope, a graphic indictment and judgment of a rapacious but mortal Babylonian nation, also effectively neutralizes the impact of the shocking divine prediction of 1:5–11 and reverses its ultimate communicative function. Then in the closing prayer of ch. 3 Habakkuk himself, under inspiration of the divine theophany (vv.

3–15), quietly responds to his initial complaint with regard to the manifest injustice of his own society (1:2–4). Both constituent elements of this dual vision (i.e., 2:6–20 + 3:1–19) therefore serve to uphold the "faith" of those righteous individuals who remain forever "faithful" to their covenant vows with Yahweh (2:4b).

Several commentators (e.g., Bruce 1993:858; Craigie 1985:94; Hiebert 1987:640) and major versions (e.g., GNT, CEV) separate verses 4 and 5 and begin a new pericope with the latter. However, there are a number of reasons for keeping these two crucial passages together. First, they are linked by the triple transitional expression וְאַף כִּי, literally, "and-furthermore indeed! [asseverative]," i.e., "And what is more, to be sure…!" Second, a censorious description of the proud, greedy person (or group/nation) proceeds from v. 4 (itself a response to the prophet's final protest of 1:17) into its expansion in v. 5. This is signaled by the repeated polysemous term נַפְשׁוֹ "his soul (life, desire, greed)." Associated with this lexical continuity is the central thematic contrast between the "righteous person" (צַדִּיק) and someone whose "soul" is "faithless" (עֻפְּלָה)[7] and not "upright" (לֹא־יָשְׁרָה). The former "will live" (יִחְיֶה) before the LORD "by his faith/steadfast trust" (בֶּאֱמוּנָתוֹ), but the latter will not "abide/endure" (יִנְוֶה).[8]

This initial portion of the divine apologetic discourse concludes at the end of v. 5 with several structural indicators (a distinct concentration) of closure. First, there is a final bicolon in strict formal and semantic parallelism, literally:

| and-he-gathers | to-himself | all = the-nation |
| and-he-collects | to-himself | all = the-peoples |

This grave divine indictment further contains two key terms, "nations" (הַגּוֹיִם) and "peoples" (הָעַמִּים), which appear in boundary positions elsewhere in the book, notably, at the end of the next strophe (2:8, i.e., compositional *epiphora*; cf. 1:5–6). The condemnation, though somewhat muted here, is about to be spelled out in detail in the following series of "woe" (הוֹי) oracles. The preliminary word of judgment found in vv. 4–5 is a pointed reply to the several unit-closing rhetorical questions of 1:13 and 17 (another instance of *epiphora*): Indeed Yahweh does not "tolerate the

---

[7] For text critical comments on this difficult word, see HOTTP 1980:356; cf. Bruce 1993:860. My understanding of v. 4a views נַפְשׁוֹ as being the subject of both verbs, עֻפְּלָה and לֹא־יָשְׁרָה.

[8] Notice the rhyme here, the phonological similarity perhaps highlighting the semantic antithesis between this focal pair of finite verbs in vv. 4–5 יִחְיֶה and יִנְוֶה.

treacherous" (cf. 1:3), and he will not allow them to keep on "destroying nations without mercy." The (lit. "my") "Holy One" (קְדֹשִׁי; 1:12; cf. 2:20) will surely deal in punitive justice not only with unrighteous Babylon but with any other nation on earth that impiously displays such pride-filled "babylonian" characteristics.

8.3.4 A taunt of five "woes" against the wicked

The preceding decision regarding discourse demarcation helps in the interpretation of the following principal text unit, 2:6–20. First of all, it is necessary to determine who speaks these mocking words of "woe"? Many commentators and versions do not mention the issue (e.g., Bruce 1993:863–865), while others are equivocal or non-committal. After a discussion of the various issues involved, Smith, for example, concludes that "we cannot be certain about the speaker in this section" (Smith 1984:646) and the GNT distinguishes the unit from "Habakkuk's complaints and the Lord's replies 1:1–2:4" with the unattributed title, "Doom on the unrighteous 2:5–20." Some scholars see a "new speaker" and a different perspective here, namely, that of "the nations who have been overrun and who now break their silence to address their oppressor" (Hiebert 1996:646). Others, however, posit a continuation of the divine speech begun in 2:2 (e.g., Armerding 1985:510; cf. NIV: "The LORD's Answer" [2:2–20]). Robertson comments on the possible incongruity here (1990:185):

> It might appear beneath the dignity of God to embarrass the proud before the watching world. But a part of his reality as the God of history includes his public vindication of the righteous and his public shaming of the wicked.

There are several pieces of literary evidence that would support this last construal, which assumes a cohesion of speaker throughout chapter 2 (except for v. 1).[9] First and most obvious is the fact that no shift in speaker is indicated, that is, after the prominent quotative margin at v. 2 (the book's structural midpoint): "And Yahweh answered and he said." On the contrary, the third plural pronominal references of v. 6a—emphasized by "all

---

[9] This is one of those relatively rare instances where a chapter break in the traditional text cannot be structurally supported in any respect, i.e., ch. 2 should begin at 2:2.

of these" (אֵלֶּה כָלָּם)—find their natural antecedents at the end of v. 5, i.e., "the nations/the peoples." It is most logical to assume, therefore, that the LORD carries on in v. 6 with a formal sentence that follows naturally after the initial accusation of v. 5. In ironic fashion he puts a judgment oracle into the mouths of those who had previously been themselves ravaged by the Babylonians (cf. 1:6)—and probably did not live to be able to enjoy the present period of divine retribution. Thus, this sequence of woes acts forcefully as a rhetorical elaboration in the form of a judicial consequence of the introductory summary statement given in vv. 4–5. It announces the public verdict, as it were, to the preceding indictment of this worldwide oppressor. However, the entire section, starting from v. 2, is all part of the LORD's instructive and consolatory revelation to Habakkuk (2:2).

The literary form manifested here is quite unusual, for such "woes" of warning were normally pronounced on behalf of Yahweh by his prophet (e.g., Isa 5:8–23; Amos 5:18–20; Mic 2:1–5; Zeph 3:1–5). But Habakkuk had asked for an answer (2:1); so this time the LORD gives him a revelatory oracle both in reply and also to proclaim in turn. The twist occurs in that the message is supplied indirectly through the words of those whom the prophet himself should have been preaching to. However, the same prophetic pattern of *accusation* alternating with *condemnation* is followed (e.g., A = vv. 6, 8; C = v. 7), for the decree is surely Yahweh's own. His authority and the guarantee of certain fulfillment backed up every word (2:3). It is no wonder then that the subdued prophet responds as he does in Job-like fashion when he takes up his final turn in the basic dialogue that structures this book (3:2).[10] It is true of course that it is frequently not possible in the Hebrew poetic literature to clearly distinguish between the words of Yahweh and those of his prophets; they typically speak "with one voice." But in this case, a deliberate variation seems to have been introduced—in keeping with both the rhetorical organization of the work as a whole and also to allow the message being conveyed to make a greater communicative impression.

The prophecy of judgment, or proverbial "dirge" (Baker 1988:62), which comprises the remainder of chapter two, thus consists of five distinct

---

[10] The correspondence here to the arrangement of the *theodicy* that drives the book of Job is probably no coincidence. In a similar chastened manner Job responds to the two speeches of the Sovereign LORD, Creator of the universe (38:1–40:2 = > 40:3–5; 40:6–41:34 = > 42:1–6; cf. Hab 2:18–20, which enunciates the ironic inversion of creation with reference to the lifeless gods of paganism.

8.3 Progression—the forward, climactic movement of discourse

woe oracles which follow a typical discourse-introducing rhetorical question (2:6a): 6b–8, 9–11, 12–14, 15–17, and 18–20. They all display a similar pattern which includes four basic elements: an opening, genre-signaling *"woe"* (or "ha!"; cf. NRSV: "alas!"; GNT: "you are doomed!") + a participle describing some typical *crime* + a word of *denunciation* + "for/indeed!" (כִּי) specifying a divinely ordained *reason* for the punishment to be meted out. The structural reiteration serves to underscore the inevitability of the prediction being made. There is some stylistic variation in the individual composition, especially in the final, climactic stanza, which begins in reversed fashion with the denunciation instead of the woe (2:18–20). Here Yahweh derides the underlying motivation for all unrighteousness, namely, idolatry, which was the driving force behind Babylon's ruthless wickedness, as figuratively described in the earlier parable of the fishermen (1:14–17).[11] There is thus a sarcastic tone that accents this last portion: The Babylonians seek revelations from speechless idols (v. 18), lifeless wood and stone (v. 19)—all in sharp contrast to God's people who receive a concrete and certain revelation from the LORD himself (2:2–3, forming an implicit *inclusio* for this section).

The taunt speech as a whole is divided into two by an elaborate pattern of recursion. Part one consists of the first three woe oracles and part two by the final pair. An accusatory refrain concludes the first unit of each half *(epiphora):* "For you have shed man's blood; you have destroyed lands and cities and everything in them" (2:8b, 17b, NIV). More significantly, the close of each of the two larger portions is marked by a prominent theological affirmation, both of which proclaim the awesome majesty (glory + holiness) of the almighty "LORD of Armies" (יְהוָה צְבָאוֹת, v.13):

> For the earth will be filled with the knowledge of the glory of the LORD. (v. 14, NIV)
> But the LORD is in his holy temple; let all the earth be silent before him. (v. 20, NIV)

---

[11] It is important to observe the double level of application that is implicitly conveyed by the accusations of these woe oracles in ch. 2. The primary plane of reference is undoubtedly the Babylonian imperialists (e.g., 2:8–9, 10, 17), but the language that is used, especially at the beginning of each segment, clearly suggests an underlying level of significance, namely, with regard to the local social and religious injustices that Habakkuk lamented in his opening speech, e.g., the greedy accumulation of power and wealth through extortion (6), profiteering (9), violent crime (12), exploitative oppression (15), and worst of all, the self-serving pursuit of personal spiritual security (18; cf. Mason 1994:91).

Verse 20 then forms an appropriate transition to chapter three and the "prayer (תְּפִלָּה) of Habakkuk" in joyous celebration of the "Holy One" of Israel (קָדוֹשׁ; 3:3, cf. 1:12). The righteous person who requires some explanatory answer from the LORD can but "hush" (הַס 2:20) and wait in faith for his God to act (cf. 2:1, 4; 3:3–15).[12]

It is interesting to observe the verbal symmetry that heightens the poetic nature of the original Hebrew and helps to distinguish its compositional arrangement. Each of the two utterances of closure cited above consists of six "words" (accent groups)—the first (v. 14) ending with the divine name יְהוָה, the second (v. 20) beginning with it. More important perhaps is the relative "weight" of the LORD's "burden" (מַשָּׂא, cf. 1:1) against his enemies: Each half of the taunt, i.e., vv. 6b–14 (excluding the final monocolon of similitude) and 15–20, is balanced in terms of the number of lexical units that compose it, namely, 71 apiece. Thus, the second portion of this larger judgment speech (2:15–20) builds upon and intensifies the first (2:6–14), much in the same way as the "B" line of a poetic couplet elaborates upon and/or enhances its counterpart in "A"—in effect, a discourse level manifestation of the poetic principle of parallelism.

8.3.5 Chapter 3 in relation to the rest of Habakkuk

The final third of the book, the psalm of trust in 3:1–19 (cf. 1:1–2:1, 2:2–20), presents the core of the argument concerning the primary issue that Habakkuk had raised with Yahweh. How does divine justice relate to human injustice, on the one hand, and the righteousness of God's faithful people on the other? Though a psalm-like "prayer" (תְּפִלָּה) may seem to be a rather strange way to end a prophetic work—indeed, it is unique in the Hebrew corpus—this is no reason to consider it a later accretion or worse, an unwarranted addition to the text.[13] On the contrary, due to its prominent theological content it forms a fitting liturgical response to the revelation of "the LORD...in his holy temple" (2:20). Furthermore, Habakkuk here provides a divinely-based, albeit indirect, answer to the questions that he raised at the very beginning of the book (1:2–4). It is a profound lyric reply that verbalizes the result of his intervening leap of faith. We might also view

---

[12] Mason suggests that הַס "was a familiar cultic cry for 'silence' before a theophany" (1994:62) (cf. Zech 1:7, 2:13 [17]). But this proposal, if granted, does not support his further conclusion that v. 20 is an "addition" to the original text (ibid., 91).

[13] Proponents of deletion include: Marks 1987:218 and Peckham 1986:635.

8.3 Progression—the forward, climactic movement of discourse

the psalm as being the chastened prophet's rejoinder to his own challenging complaint registered against Yahweh in 2:1 (at the close of Part I). Similarly, these words fittingly express his awe-filled reaction to the LORD's mighty vision of the great woes that will most certainly topple proud Babylon—after the fall of his own nation. Therefore, from any of these logical or literary perspectives, it is clear that some fundamental compositional forces firmly integrate chapter three into the rest of the work.

There is also a form-critical argument that would lend support to this conclusion. Claus Westermann, for one, considers the first chapter of Habakkuk to be a good illustration of what he terms "the community psalm of lament" (Westermann 1980:29). It is rather strange, however, to observe that both of the prophet's complaints in ch. 1 (1:2–4, 12–17) manifest only the first several of the typical constituent elements of such a composition. In fact, it is clear that one needs to incorporate the entire book in order to fit the organizational pattern that is proposed. Indeed, it is striking to observe how close the overall correspondence is. These may be summarized as follows (using Westermann's proposed genre categories, ibid., 35):[14]

   a. the opening **address**, here combined with an initial appeal to help (1:2)
   b. the **complaint**, with all three of its primary components being included:
      i- a "you" facet, directed against God (e.g., 1:3, 12–13a)
      ii- a "we" facet, detailing the suffering of the righteous (e.g., 1:4, 13b)
      iii- a "they" facet, depicting the cruel acts of the enemy (e.g., 1:15–17)
   c. a **profession** or recital of God's past deeds of deliverance,
      a slot admirably filled by the theophanic-military eulogue of 3:3–15
   d. the **petition** or request for divine intervention, in this case focally placed in 3:2, a verse which serves as "an encapsulation of the message of the book" (Baker 1988:70)
   e. the divine **response**, an element which Westermann observes is only rarely incorporated into community laments of the Psalter, but which is uniquely expressed in incremental multiples within the framework of Habakkuk, i.e., 1:5–11, 2:2–20, 3:3–15 (thus a double-duty constituent, cf. [c])
   f. the **vow** to praise or to serve God, characteristic of individual-laments but rare in their communal counterparts (Westermann 1980:43), acts as the conclusion of both the prophet's prayer (ch. 3) and the book as a whole, i.e., 3:16–19

The preceding generic evidence, when considered together with the structural analysis presented earlier, leaves little doubt that chapter three

---

[14] As Mason notes, there is no *confession of sin* in the book, but this is not a diagnostic feature of the "lament psalm" (Mason 1994:89).

functioned as an integral and indispensable part of the rhetoric of Habakkuk from the very beginning of the book's compositional history. His prophecy would simply not be the same—either without it or with it being regarded as some sort of a later appendix.

8.3.6 A closer look at the prayer of Habakkuk

The psalm-prayer of Habakkuk 3 is the most difficult portion of the book to delineate structurally and hence also to integrate in terms of its progression of content. That is shown by the diversity of schemes which are displayed in the various translations. As Clark and Hatton observe: "It is not easy to make paragraph divisions within the chapter, and modern versions are all different in this respect" (1989:114). However, this is not to say that our current problems in this regard stem from either an artistically inferior or a textually corrupt discourse. Thus, while welcoming the "new approach" toward analysis offered by Margulis, for example, I do not agree with his reason for proposing it, namely, "that the text of this poetic composition is seriously disturbed" (1970:411). The difficulties are due rather to our lack of an adequate contextual background to be able to interpret its many archaic allusions and unfamiliar lexical usages, on the one hand, and our inability to fully delineate the compositional complexity of the work on the other. As a result, several ways of demarcating the psalm and interrelating its parts are possible, depending upon how one chooses to handle the data. The following proposal for segmentation makes use of the diagnostic criteria outlined above as well as the structural evidence to be discussed yet below within the framework of the entire discourse.

Though it is usually classified generally as a lament,[15] the lyric of ch. 3 freely incorporates stylistic elements from other psalmic genres, such as a historical recital, a royal eulogue, a profession of trust, and a hymn of divine praise-thanksgiving. In its broad outline, the organization is not difficult to perceive, but the internal segments are rather more controversial. The psalm begins with a typical editorial superscription (3:1) and ends with a corresponding subscription, or colophon (v. 19d). These musical notations thus circumscribe the whole within a liturgical frame of reverent

---

[15] For example, Margulis 1970:437; Armerding 1985:523; and Sweeney 1991:78. This characterization may be due to the fact that the terms "prayer" (תְּפִלָּה) and "shigionoth" (שִׁגְיֹנוֹת) in v. 1 are employed in the Psalter to refer to other psalms of "lament" (e.g., 7, 17, 86, 90, 102, 142).

8.3 Progression—the forward, climactic movement of discourse

worship. This perspective is possibly reinforced by the rhyming technical terms שִׁגְיֹנוֹת *shigyonoth* (v. 1) and נְגִינוֹתָי *negiynothay* (v. 19), which despite their uncertainty in meaning, serve to heighten the devotional atmosphere of the entire pericope.

The psalm proper opens with a short strophe which enunciates the work's only explicit petition (or prayer) in a balanced cadence of rhythmically uniform utterances (i.e., 5 tri-accented cola in v. 2). This is a general plea based upon Yahweh's covenant commitment, namely, that as in the past in times (cf. v. 2c-d) of trembling, or agitation and turmoil (cf. vv. 7, 16), he will "remember mercy" (רַחֵם תִּזְכּוֹר—the final, climactic utterance of this verse) by intervening both to deliver and to vindicate his afflicted and suffering people. It is a humbled Habakkuk who is speaking here, that is, in contrast to the bold but frustrated complainant of chapter one. These words characterize the man of faith who was highlighted in 2:4; it is he who should now "live" (חַיֵּיהוּ "enliven him," 3:2c) according to the prophet's request of Yahweh (a secondary, but possible interpretation of this verb + suffix).[16] Therefore, his present prayer—on behalf of the nation (first person singular and plural references)—typifies a "righteous" response to both the historical truth and also the future potential of the awesome works (פָּעָלְךָ "your deed") of an active, almighty LORD God (cf. the divine promise of 1:5—"I will surely do" כִּי־פֹעַל פֹּעֵל, i.e., an instance of remote *anaphora* with 3:2).

Habakkuk proceeds to praise that memorable past by means of a composite synopsis and compilation of the LORD's manifestation of his glorious nature and wonderful deeds of deliverance on behalf of his covenant people (vv. 3-15). In effect, through this eulogy the prophet is divinely inspired to respond to his own plea of the preceding verse (2). This large central portion demonstrates in itself the altered perspective which the prophet has been led to adopt, that is, a shift away from provincial concerns, whether personal or national, to a preoccupation with "God...the Holy One" (אֱלוֹהַּ...קָדוֹשׁ; cf. 1:12, 2:20). The pericope may be divided into two constituent sections, or stanzas, the second of which (vv. 8-15) complements the first (vv. 3-7) in the style of additive heightening within poetic parallelism to rise to a peak of intensity, significance, and relevance for the people of God. Both units portray Yahweh in a conventionalized figurative stance by means of a complex *theophany,* or divine appearance,

---

[16] This is suggested in Robertson 1990:218.

first of all (3–7), in a vividly graphic piece which displays the transcendent majesty of Deity via the visible medium of nature (e.g., a thunderstorm, earthquake, volcanic eruption). This is closely associated with traditional heroic military imagery that depicts a cosmic battle between storm and sea (8–15). Both stanzas, which combine familiar poetic images from the spheres of creation and combat, serve as a dramatic reflection and remembrance of some of the prominent events associated with Israel's salvation history.[17]

The opening stanza consists of two tightly interwoven strophes. The first (vv. 3–4) describes the initial appearance of Yahweh in a radiance that permeates the entire universe, surpassing even the brilliance of lightning (in a reverse fulfillment of 2:14). The LORD's glorious splendor is lauded in a series of seven trimeters, which recall his frightening revelation during the giving of his "covenantal instructions" at Mount Sinai (cf. Deut 32:2). The progression ends "there!" (שָׁם) in a dramatic monocolon that personalizes the locus of God's surpassing "power" (עֻזֹּה) as anthropomorphically emanating from his hand. This divine might is then manifested in the second strophe (vv. 5–7) as God rocks the earth with his devastating movements which announce the onset of divine judgment for all covenant violators as well as the contemporary persecutors of his people (cf. Ezek 14:21). There is another swift progression of seven trimeters which lead up to a final bicolon that brings the strophe and the stanza to a chilling conclusion—with terror written in the faces of Yahweh's foes (v. 7). Closure is marked by the shift in rhythm (i.e., a longer 5 + 4 bicolon), the introduction of a first-person reference ("I saw," i.e., this "vision," cf. 2:2), and an *inclusio* formed by the rhymed pair of parallel proper names, all of which are in some way associated with the wilderness of Sinai where the theophany is set (i.e., v. 3: "Teman/Paran"—v. 7: "Cushan/Midyan").

The second stanza, starting in v. 8, may be divided into three strophes. They are all closely connected by means of a common allusion to Yahweh who, as the Warrior-Lord, is coming out to fight on behalf of his defenseless people (cf. v. 13). A sudden shift to direct address coupled with a threefold rhetorical question in synonymous parallelism with an emphasis on the LORD's "anger" (אַף, etc.) announces the beginning *(aperture)* of this

---

[17] Hiebert's comment is appropriate: "By employing the imagery of this traditional [creation] motif and interweaving it with the political imagery of the warrior, the poet has founded God's control of historical affairs within God's control of cosmic orders" (1996:654).

8.3 Progression—the forward, climactic movement of discourse

section in v. 8. Why is the almighty LORD on the move (vv. 3–7), a one-man demolition army as it were? The answer becomes increasingly clear as this climactic stanza unfolds. Another strong *inclusio* delimits its external boundaries and establishes a probable historical setting, namely, God's rout of the hostile forces massed at the (Red) sea—against which "you (O LORD) rode with your horses" (cf. vv. 8, 15).

The initial strophe of stanza two (vv. 8–10) is held together (cf. "cohesion" below) by repeated references to various bodies of water into which the poem's first martial imagery is introduced. Whether or not this has a mythic background or origin, e.g., to the unruly waters at creation or to the pagan god of the ocean,[18] is beside the point—which is to evoke familiar scenes of the LORD's sovereign intervention into human history, for universal judgment during the Flood, and to deliver his chosen people at the Nile (i.e., by the plagues), the Red Sea, and the Jordan River. Yahweh's saving faithfulness in the past will surely encourage the faith of his people in the present about their certain blessed future (cf. 2:4b; 3:3, 13, 19).

The salvific theme of cosmic warfare initiated by Yahweh is prominent in strophe two (vv. 11–13a) which leads off with a highly condensed allusion to an eclipse, literally, "sun moon it-stood-[still] [in-the]-heavens" (v. 11a; cf. Josh 10:12–13). This segment (and perhaps the psalm as a whole; see below) peaks out in the triumphant affirmation of v. 13a with its rhyming pair of key soteriological terms: "you came out to deliver *your people*, to deliver *your anointed one*!" (מְשִׁיחֶךָ אֶת מָשַׁחְתָּ; = Israel/Moses/ the reigning Davidic monarch/the future messianic king?—or probably, all of the preceding).[19] Here at last we have an explicit divine answer to Habakkuk's agonized complaints of 1:3–4, 13, and 17, all of which are amplified by the psalmist's challenge in 2:1 and his rhetorical query at the head of this stanza (v. 8, forming an *inclusio*): The purpose of the LORD's mighty battle—of his furious charge against all his enemies, as epitomized by the "sea" (cf. v. 15)—is to save the covenant nation, thus vindicating the fervent faith of his righteous people (1:2; 2:4) according to promise (2:3, 14, 20).

---

[18] Bruce aptly comments that all these mythological terms functioned as mere "figures of speech" in Hebrew heroic poetry (1993:886). Their only religious significance was to underscore the total superiority of Yahweh over all pagan deities.

[19] For a discussion of the various hermeneutical possibilities, see Armerding 1985:531 and Robertson 1990:238.

The third strophe (vv. 13b–15) then acts as a denouement that sketches in the details of God's past and promised deliverance. It foregrounds the smashing defeat and devastation inflicted by the LORD upon "the head of the house of wickedness," a prediction of the certain fall of the oppressor Babylon (like its analogue Egypt at the original exodus event)—along with any foe who dares to oppose Yahweh or his covenant people. As is the case in strophe two, this third segment consists of seven lines, but several of these are longer tetrameters, notably at its very beginning. The strong literary marks of closure for this strophe and the entire stanza have already been noted. The deeply introspective, sensual, first-person speech of v. 16 is another clear indication of a new discourse beginning.

The final stanza of the song (vv. 16–19) is a fitting reply to its prologue and the psalmist's petition in v. 2. Furthermore, it is a cumulative response to everything that has been said (and seen) in the book as a whole. At the onset of his action-packed "prayer," Habakkuk's faith is incipient, as it were: "I heard your report" (שָׁמַעְתִּי שִׁמְעֲךָ), and he asks that the LORD's works would be renewed—or made to live—in the experience of his people (v. 2). Now, as a result of the confirmatory theophany, his trust is confidently anticipatory: "I have heard" (שָׁמַעְתִּי; i.e., the intervening divine vision), and he reacts with fear and trembling to what he now knows will certainly come to pass (cf. vv. 2, 7 = an instance of structural *exclusio*). The lengthy v. 16 would therefore best be construed as constituting a transitional strophe on its own, while the following material acts as a commentary on the positive nature of Habakkuk's commitment to "patiently waiting" (lit. "I will be quiet"—אָנוּחַ). Verse 16 also complements 2:1 as faith finally overcomes frustration in the prophet's steadfast hope for the LORD to act in the best interests of his people (cf. also 1:13). "Habakkuk obtained what he had prayed for—the assurance that the vindication of divine righteousness was on its way" (Bruce 1993:893).

A series of chiastically arranged syntactic constructions (four paired bicola, but only one sentence in Hebrew) is begun in v. 17. This builds up to the second, now an emotive, climax of the psalm in the rhyming trimeter of v. 18 (marked by emphatic cohortative verbs; cf. v. 13a for the initial, theological peak). The key term "my salvation" (יִשְׁעִי) resonates not only with religious significance (e.g., Pss 62:1–2; 88:1; 89:26; 118:14, 21; 140:7), but also with literary import as an echo of structurally parallel forms in vv. 8 and 13. It would be possible then to regard the prayer's final tricolon in v. 19 as another independent strophe, especially due to its clear dependence upon Ps 18:32–33. Here we have a firm indication in turn of the psalmist-prophet's renewed dependence for his strength (lit. "my might") not only upon God, but also on his Word (cf. "your report" שִׁמְעֲךָ, v. 2). These closing words are a resounding proclamation of unwavering trust on the part of the righteous supplicant and an unshakable confession of his/her faith in the ultimate justice of the Sovereign LORD (יְהוִה אֲדֹנָי). Yahweh makes it possible for the believer to endure the depths of despair in anticipation of an ultimate enjoyment of the "heights" of blessing (v. 19c). The theodicy of Habakkuk is thus complete in the utter contentment expressed here by its lyric voice—no matter who happens to articulate it.[20]

8.3.7 Rhetorical-dramatic progression in Habakkuk's poetic-prophetic discourse

The compositional force of progression may be viewed as including several other basically linear literary arrangements which are interwoven with and run parallel to the structural-thematic (ST) organization of Habakkuk discussed above. They are of course part of one all-inclusive and comprehensive syntagmatic formation. But it is helpful for the purposes of analysis to distinguish what we might term the "rhetorical-dramatic" format (RD) from the structural-thematic framework because, while an ST (structural-thematic) development focuses upon the form and content of a literary work, its RD counterpart concerns the pragmatic communicative aims and dynamic effects of the discourse—its principal constituent units as well as the work as a whole. In its most basic form, the RD configuration realizes the three nuclear elements that underlie every "hortatory" text, namely, problem => appeal => motivation. In Habakkuk, these rhetorical constituents may be expressed in dual form as follows:

---

[20] The structural-thematic overview of the preceding section forms the basis upon which all of the following analyses are built. In other words, it acts as the overarching architectural framework into which each of the other parallel, text-spanning constructions may be fitted to form a single, multi-layered and mutually reinforcing compositional arrangement.

a. <u>problem</u> = i - the prevalence and predominance of evil
in a world created and controlled by "God" (3:3);
ii - the wicked continue to persecute the "righteous"
followers of "the Sovereign LORD" (3:19).

b. <u>appeal</u>   = i - initial—to the ultimate justice of "the Holy One" (3:3), i.e.,
"Do something about it!";
ii - final—to the "faithfulness" of his righteous ones (2:4b), i.e.,
"Put your complete trust in the just judgment of Yahweh!"

c. <u>motivation</u> = i - who our God is—the "Rock," the "almighty LORD"
(1:12b, 2:13, i.e., his theological credibility);
ii - what he has done for his people as their eternal "Savior"
(1:12a, 3:18, i.e., his historical reliability).

In the following overview of more detailed aspects of this hypothetical RD construct, I will try to avoid undue repetition with what has already been said about the larger fabrication of the book. However, I will draw special attention to several crucial points where the ST and RD progressions strongly converge and interact to convey the prophet's message in an especially significant way.

As noted above, the overall prophecy (or "oracle" מַשָּׂא) of Habakkuk assumes the basic literary form of the traditional lament, or prayer, genre which provides the formal and semantic backbone for the entire discourse. Though this structure varies from psalm to psalm, the key compositional elements appear to be seven in number: invocation, plea to God for help, complaint(s), confession of sin [or] protestation of innocence, imprecation upon enemies, reaffirmation of faith in God, and a joyous response to the Lord's (assumed) deliverance, e.g., words of praise, vow of service.[21] Each of these specific motivations finds implicit or explicit expression in Habakkuk, most evidently at the very beginning (1:2–4 + 1:12–13) and again at the close of the book (3:2 + 16–20), thus forming a generic *inclusio*. Coinciding with these two framing liturgical sections, a succession of other poetic types is artistically introduced to dramatize and give a more varied and compelling dimension to the discourse, i.e., a prophetic prediction (1:5), descriptive panegyric (1:6–11), parable (1:14–17), preface to revelation (2:2–3), oracle of censure/indictment (2:4–5), woe/taunt oracles of judgment (2:6–19), liturgical chorus (2:14/20), and finally, a complete psalmic prayer,

---

[21] For a discussion and illustration of these poetic compositional elements, see Wendland 2002:34–36.

consisting of a lament (3:2/16–18), theophanic hymn (3:3–7), salvation-history/royal recital (3:8–15), and a concluding confession of faith (3:19).

Within this shifting arrangement of poetic-prophetic genres as outlined above, the overt message of the book of Habakkuk is projected on several literary planes within the overall framework. This formation involves three closely interrelated sequences or patterns of structural development: narrative, disputational, and emotive. These three elements are skillfully interwoven so that they continually resonate off one another, both semantically and pragmatically as well. They may be described in terms of a narrative, disputational, and emotive progression.

8.3.7.1 Narrative progression

The presence of narrative, or story, is perhaps not immediately apparent in this prophetic compilation, but a careful consideration of the book as a whole clearly reveals the characteristic sequence of a simple plot, at least in rudimentary form: problem/conflict => complication => climax => resolution/outcome. The initial predicament confronting the prophet was local and social in nature, namely, an unbounded oppression of the poor and weak by the nation's rich and powerful. Yahweh's proposed international solution in the form of a punitive invasion by the Chaldean army which would destroy the Judean state along with its land posed an even greater moral and spiritual dilemma for Habakkuk. For all its faults, Judah was still more righteous in comparison with the pagan, imperialistic nation of Babylon (1:13)—and besides, the simple plan seemed to be unfair in that it failed to provide for either a reprieve or an ultimate restoration. So Habakkuk boldly seeks to back Yahweh into a moral corner, as it were, over what now seemed to be an irreconcilable difficulty—a fundamental contradiction in the divine nature/person and behavior/purpose (2:1).

The basic, now prophetically anticipated narrative thread goes on in chapter two to build up to a climax of intensity as the LORD proceeds to reveal, in vivid visionary detail, the ultimate and total destruction of Babylon, the world's violent, idol-worshipping arch-enemy (symbolic of any and all such anti-theistic forces; cf. Rev 14:8; 16:19; 17:5; 18:2). This progression reaches its peak in 2:20 with Yahweh appearing majestically in his holy temple, obviously in complete sovereign control of the cosmos. Habakkuk's psalm then acts as a lyric denouement that celebrates God's great and glorious victories in the past on behalf of his people. The central core of this hymn (3:3–15) contains its own mini-narrative development (complete with a climax [14a] and a flashback [14b]) in which the leader of the land of wickedness (v. 13b) is utterly vanquished by the omnipotent Warrior-God, invincible Ruler of heaven and earth.

8.3.7.2 Disputational progression

The second and more apparent thread of the syntagmatic cord of discourse organization is the text's uniquely (for the prophets) dialogic manner of construction. In fact, the narrative or plot line discussed above is manifested in its entirety by the reverent debate between Yahweh and his prophet, with a heterogeneous gentile chorus suddenly introduced (by Yahweh) for dramatic effect in 2:6–20. This interlocutory pattern is realized in a series of speech "moves" which follow the regular alternation of speakers as outlined in the figure below:

HABAKKUK			YAHWEH	
A. 1:2–4	(3a)	→	B. 1:5–11	(6a)
Ca. 1:12–17	(13c/17a)	←		
Cb. 2:1	(1c)	→	Da. 2:2–5	(4)
E. 3:1–2	(2b)	←	Db. 2:6a [= >] 6b–20 (14/20)	
		→	F. 3:3–15	(13a)
G. 3:16–19	(16c/18a)	←		

This type of interactive construction effectively keeps the discourse moving forward as each speech incorporates a certain peak or challenge (sometimes twofold) that calls for a response from the other party. These key elicitative and responsorial passages, or triggers, are indicated in parentheses on the table above. At the structural pivot, or midpoint, of the whole, i.e., 2:1 (cf. the earlier ST analysis of the discourse), an extended turn on the part of each of the interlocutors is interjected. This takes the form of an extended speech event that is compound in formation and complex in functional intent, i.e., Yahweh (2:2–6a + 6b–20) = = > Habakkuk (3:1–2 + 3–15 + 16–19).

The penultimate pericope, 3:3–15, is particularly interesting in that although it is uttered, or prayed, by Habakkuk, it actually represents Yahweh's reply to several triggers that have preceded it in the discourse, namely, the prophet's challenge in 2:1, God's promise in 2:3, and Habakkuk's contrastive petitions in 1:2 (confrontational) and 3:2 (confessional). Thus, on one level of communication, Habakkuk provides in these words his own, faith-based resolution for the problematic theological issue that he raised at the very beginning of the book (1:2–4). But from another, more significant perspective, it is really the LORD who is doing all the talking—and the teaching. Thus, this divine epiphanic segment consists of a verbal tapestry, or pastiche, of various interconnected quotations, allusions, and reflections taken from the sacred tradition of Scripture, probably both oral and written—God speaking in effect through his own prophetic Word (see the intertextual documentation below).

8.3.7.3 Emotive progression

In addition to the individual peaks that appear as the discourse unfolds, there is also a cumulative progression of dramatic tension and emotive intensity as one exchange builds upon and augments that which has gone before. Indeed, the technique of dialogue serves to heighten the sequence of illocutionary (intentional) forces and their associated psychological attitudes which are manifested as the text develops from point to point. Since this aspect of the text is not often considered, it may be worth a somewhat closer look.

Habakkuk leads off with a bitter complaint—including an implicit rebuke for the LORD—as he sees blatant injustice, involving both social corruption and spiritual apostasy, go unpunished all around him in the land of Judah (1:2–4). This is followed by Yahweh's shocking revelation that he is going to make use of the pagan Chaldeans to exercise divine discipline (1:5–6). It is indeed ironic to hear God himself intone what amounts to a descriptive paean in praise of an ungodly enemy (1:7–11).

This unexpected revelation throws Habakkuk into serious emotional turmoil, and in a string of emphatic, vocative-initial utterances (which could all be interpreted as rhetorical questions, 1:12) he accusingly draws the LORD's attention to the incongruity of the situation: the divine end does not justify a diabolical means (1:13)! The prophet's incredulous dismay coupled with "righteous" anger (from his own biased perspective) is further intensified by his barbed little parable of the ravenous net of a rapacious enemy (1:14–17). He closes on a note of peevish pique as he throws up an even more defiant challenge to the LORD to go ahead and demonstrate his holiness (2:1; cf. 1:13).

In apparent acquiescence and accommodation to the distressed state of his prophet, Yahweh solemnly prepares Habakkuk for a special vision with the reiterated assurance that a day of retribution for the enemy and vindication for his people will most surely come (2:2–5). This ultimate revelation is preceded, however, by an invectively uttered prediction of punitive reversal which is so awesome in its rhetorical force, international repercussions, and theological implications (2:6–20) that it leaves the divine spokesman temporarily speechless (2:20). This graphic woe-sequence gradually ascends to its own internal apex with the graphic liquid imagery of total condemnation in set four (2:15–17). The final segment of this oracle-set defuses the emotive tension somewhat by means of a more reasoned, didactic approach expressed as a sarcastically barbed homily against the utter foolishness of idolatry (2:18–19).

Recovering his composure, so to speak, after Yahweh's terrifying pronouncement of judgment upon the wicked, Habakkuk realizes that he has been dealing with a divinely controlled destiny that he has no right to delve into. He therefore responds appropriately in humble worship. His psalm evinces an attitude and tone which is completely different from that of his previous speeches; indeed, his opening words sound almost Job-like in their penitent chagrin (3:2a–b; cf. Job 42:2–6). But he quickly rises to the occasion to fulfill his prophetic role as a mediator between God and his people with a plea on their behalf for mercy (3:2c). The brilliant, highly evocative scenes of an ancient theophany follow as Yahweh first displays his wondrous creative majesty (3:3–7), which is then manifested in a fierce and furious defense of his people (3:8–15). The colorful but incisive imagery must strike a powerfully responsive chord in the hearts of all those who know its deep literary, historical, and religious background as set forth in the sacred redemption history of Israel. The emotive high point of this picturesque divine vignette cannot be missed; it comes with the crushing of the supreme adversary and epitome of iniquity along with all his proud forces of oppression (3:13b–15).

8.3 Progression—the forward, climactic movement of discourse 451

This moving portrayal of God's trembling anger (3:12b) manifested in judgment, in contrast to the mercy of his deliverance (3:2c, 13a), stimulates such a profound physiological and psychological reaction within the prophet (and those in the audience who empathize with him) that he too starts trembling (3:16)—now in fear of the awesome majesty of the Holy One and Sovereign LORD (3:3, 18). But this shaky feeling is quickly dispelled and replaced by a paradoxical calm which leaves Habakkuk's serenely at peace (16b) despite the threat of impending war and total economic disaster (17). The troubling issue of the theodicy is thus settled at last in a personal resolution of patient trust in the ever-relevant and reliable word of the LORD (i.e., what he heard, 16a). At last, the final emotive peak of the psalm, and indeed the entire book, is reached in the two closing verses with their strongly optimistic affirmations of rejoicing (18) and a triumphant faith in the gracious provision of Yahweh (19). Though expressed in the singular, the obvious implication of the prophet's message is plural, a joyous invitation to all listeners (readers) to join in—that is, intellectually, emotionally, volitionally, and spiritually.

8.3.8 Theodicy realized in theophany

In a number of important ways the urgent issues raised in Habakkuk's initial lament (1:2–4) are ultimately resolved in his devout prayer of chapter three—a word of worship that was stimulated by the LORD's twofold revelation of himself as an almighty God of just judgment (2:6–19 + 3:3–15). There is no doubt that a dramatic alteration has occurred in the prophet's thinking and outlook on life, as expressed, for example, in polarities such as the following:

Habakkuk's initial situation	→	His final situation	
he has no apparent answer	(1:2a) →	he has been answered	(3:2, 16)
salvation is lost	(1:2b) →	salvation is assured	(3:13, 18)
injustice goes unpunished	(1:3a) →	wickedness is defeated	(3:8–12)
conflict is everywhere	(1:3b) →	he is at peace	(3:16b)
no hope of justice	(1:4) →	restoration will come	(3:2, 17–18)

Thus, the main message of the oracle of Habakkuk is simply, but most significantly, this: The same sort of worldview transformation (or confirmation, as the case may be) awaits every one of those righteous individuals—past, present, or future—who faithfully live out their faith (2:4) in life-fellowship with their Savior, the Sovereign-LORD (3:18–19). It depends on their recognition (and acceptance) of the fact that, despite all appearances to the contrary, God's immutable justice continues ever to operate in a world that is seemingly filled with evil and bent on self-destruction. Even partial explanations of the events of personal or corporate (national) history, especially the disasters, are not always possible or desirable. For the most part, then, the LORD's will and his manifold ways must remain shrouded in mystery—yet with the assumption that they are ultimately always right and graciously soteriological in relation to every believer. Accordingly, the following four central principles of divine justice, as poetically enunciated and dramatically visualized in the book of Habakkuk (especially in its second half), stand inviolate forever:

i. God's judgment upon the proud and wicked of this world will inevitably be carried out in just accordance with his perfect holiness (2:2–5; 3:3–7);

ii. the faith of the righteous people of God will be ultimately vindicated when earth's oppressors are punished once and for all (2:6–19; 3:8–15);

iii. the Holy Sovereign LORD (Yahweh) is also a merciful God, who will finally deliver all those who put their trust in him, if not in this life, then most certainly in the life to come (2:4b; 3:2b, 13a);[22]

iv. the "righteous believer" is one who lives his/her faith in joyful, confident, and reverent expectation that the future is secure in a living, loving God who cares, in keeping with his eternal covenant promises (2:4b, 14, 20; 3:2, 16–19).

For those who trust in the God of timeless Scripture, the appropriate response to the troubling vicissitudes of life will be that of the prophet recorded in 3:16–19, or rephrased in modern theological prose (Packer 1988:679):

---

[22] The belief in a life (after death) in eternal fellowship with the LORD God is of course not explicitly stated in the book of Habakkuk, but it seems to be definitely implied within the universal, cosmic, and everlasting framework of divine justice that is so poetically expressed in chs. 2–3, for example, in passages such as 2:3, 2:14, and 3:17–18. As is typical in Hebrew prophetic literature, the notion of a future afterlife is conveyed in concrete, down-to-earth imagery, so common, for example, in the prophecy of *Isaiah:* 2:1–5; 9:6–7; 11:1–16; 25:1–12; 27:1–13; 42:1–9; 49:1–7; 54–56; 60–62; 65:17–25 (note: throughout this clearly *unified* text). The "good news" of Habakkuk was undoubtedly based upon and presupposed the more elaborate message of his prophetic predecessor (e.g., 3:18 = > Isa 61, esp. vv. 1, 8, 10–11).

> Thus through God's sovereign goodness evil is overcome, not theoretically, so much as practically, in human lives. This [perspective] leaves with God the secret things (cf. Deut 29:29)…glorifies God for what is revealed, calls forth wonder and worship, and resolves the feeling, "This ought not to be," into the contented cry, "He does all things well!"

The basic point and purpose of Habakkuk's *theodicy*—his prophetically expressed justification of the justice of God to mankind—thus foregrounds a fundamental message that has equally as much relevance for people today, wherever they may happen to live, whatever their sociocultural background may be, and however they may be living in terms of economic standing or political status. This is true whether they happen to realize it or not, for the book deals with a matter of universal human concern, namely, the relationship between good and evil in the world, with reference to the past, present, and future. It also proposes a solution of lasting validity, that is, in the glorious, revelatory *theophany* of saving LORD who is ever ready, willing, and able to fight on behalf of his faithful flock (3:3–15).

8.4 Cohesion—the internal, connecting tissue of discourse

If the compositional forces of syntagmatic progression are necessary to move a text forward in manageable portions so as to accomplish an author's specific goals of communication, then some corresponding means are also needed to bind the discourse together so that it does not fragment and result in a message that is disparate, diffuse, or obscure. Thus, in order for the whole to be effective, each of the individual structural-thematic and rhetorical-dramatic constructs discussed above must manifest its own internal unity, a coherence that for the most part meshes harmoniously in turn with that of the others. This essential task of conjunction is carried out largely through *recursion*—that is, reiteration of all types: exact, synonymous, and contrastive; macro- and micro-structural; phonological, morphological, semantic, and syntactic. The placement of familiar transitional connective particles (including conjunctions) and phrases on structural boundaries is the second important method of producing such *cohesion*, although these are frequently omitted in poetic discourse.

The judicious use of repetition in one form or another always functions to provide a text with a certain perceptible degree of unity and wholeness, whether or not it is complete with regard to a particular theme or purpose, that is, whether it contains a discernible development of ideas and implications or not. In significant literary works, the two forces of progression and cohesion will of course mutually enhance and balance each other, and such a convergence of function is evident also in the book of Habakkuk. Having taken his message, apart, so to speak, through an analysis of its syntagmatic organization (i.e., the various compositional units and their interrelationships), we now want to put it back together again—that is, to work towards a meaningful "synthesis." We will do this by considering a number of the ways in which repetition in particular effects such connection or bonding on the various strata of discourse.

The cohesive structures formed by recursion in literary, and especially poetic, discourse are primarily *paradigmatic* in nature. In other words, they are based upon analogy or some overt correspondence (similarity/contrast), rather than on spatial juxtaposition and linear development as in the case of purely syntagmatic structures. Of course, these two principles and their textual outputs cannot really be separated, for they invariably depend upon and invisibly impinge upon one another. The techniques of cohesion provide a progression with its integrity, unity, and harmony, while the diverse elements of a progression simultaneously help to forge several types and levels of cohesion within a text. A number of important reiterated features have already been pointed out during the preceding consideration of the major discourse progressions in Habakkuk. In this section then I wish to focus upon the recursive process itself and how it helps to convey as well as to highlight some of the prophet's main theological motives and notions. It is convenient to separate the different forces of cohesion into two types: intratextual, which is of primary importance, and intertextual, which is secondary, but strongly supportive in its discourse operation.

8.4.1 Intratextual cohesion

This type of text-internal connectivity is most commonly generated by means of a linguistic recursion based on some crucial similarity with respect to sound, sense, and/or syntax. Such repetition may perform one or more of three overlapping functions in the text: *demarcative,* i.e., it is used to segment a given progression, as was noted earlier (especially inclusio, anaphora, epiphora); *intensive*, i.e., it may emphasize or foreground a certain concept; or *integrative*, that is, it serves to lend a greater measure of coherence to the content within a specified textual unit. The latter type of lexical recursion plays an especially important role in the book of Habakkuk—in fact, it is one of the dominant features of his poetic style. Though it is prominent throughout the entire discourse, I will focus my attention upon the prophet's prayer in order to illustrate how this portion forms a distinct text-within-a-text.[23] Chapter three is by no means detached structurally (nor was it composed in isolation) from the two initial chapters, as the wider pattern of verbal reiteration itself will also demonstrate. But the psalm is clearly distinguished as being a special constituent of the work in its totality.

The following chart provides a cumulative summary of the main aspects of recursion as considered from the perspective of Habakkuk 3. In other words, the sample presented is only illustrative and not exhaustive in nature. The key reiterated lexical items, both exact and synonymous (i.e., terms within the same lexical field) are given in literal English translation for the sake of convenience. The inventory is organized sequentially, that is, roughly according to the verbal order of occurrence (in literal Hebrew) and following the line-up of strophic units which constitute the psalm. Three types of repetition with regard to scope or distribution are noted, namely, that which is found: within a given strophe, elsewhere in chapter three, or earlier in the preceding two chapters (only a selective listing of exact matches is recorded). This reflects the three basic hierarchical levels at which integrative, or cohesive, recursion operates in poetic-prophetic discourse, i.e., strophe => stanza => psalm/oracle. An asterisk denotes those instances of reiteration which appear to have an additional, locally intensive purpose or a significant demarcative function with reference to a distinct discourse segment.

Verse(s) from ch. 3		Other, strophe-external references	
strophe	recursive concepts	inside-----CHAPTER 3-----outside	
2	Yahweh...Yahweh	8*, 18*, 19*	1:2*, 12*; 2:2* 13, 14*, 16, 20*
	I heard your hearing	16*	1:2*
	your deed		1:5*

---

[23] In addition, Armerding points out how the verses of 1:5–11 "echo focal concepts from vv. 2–4" in the first dialogic exchange (1985:502).

	in midst of years...in midst of years		
	make him/it live		2:4
	make him/it know		2:14
	in trembling	7*, 16*	
3–4	God...even the Holy One	18*	1:11, 12*
	he came		2:3
	his glory...and splendor		2:14
	it filled the earth		2:14
5–7	before him...before his steps		
	he saw...I saw	10*	1:3, 5, 13, 2:1*
	plague...pestilence		
	earth...mountains...hills... land	3, 9, 10, 12	1:6; 2:8, 14*, 17, 20*
	long ago...eternity...eternity		
8–10	rivers...rivers...sea... rivers...torrent of waters...the deep... waves (hands)	15*	1:14; 2:14*
	you rode...your riding things (chariots) he raged...your anger... your wrath	12	
	salvation	13*, 18*	
	uncovered it is uncovered		
11–13	sun...moon...light...flash...lightning		
	your arrows...your spear...	9, 14	
	to save...to save	8, 18*	
	nations...your people	6, 7, 16	1:5, 6, 7, 17*; 2:5*, 8*, 10, 13, 16*

8.4 Cohesion—the internal, connecting tissue of discourse

12–15	head...thigh...neck...head		
	your horses	8*	1:8
	the sea...the waters	8*	1:14; 2:14*
16	it trembled...I trembled	7*	
	my belly...my lips...my bones		
17–18	not...there is no...not...there is no		
	fig tree...fruit on the vines... crop of olives...fields... food...sheep...cattle		1:16
	I will rejoice...I will be glad		1:15
19	Yahweh my Lord	2*, 3*, 18*	
	he makes me walk upon	15*	

The preceding chart gives one an approximate idea of the considerable amount of recursion that binds together the several compositional units (strophes/stanzas) of Habakkuk three both formally and semantically into a cohesive and coherent whole. Furthermore, it indicates the extent to which this psalm is integrated on a purely lexical level with chapters one and two. It is also interesting to observe the multifunctionality of this extensive reiteration: Not only does such recursion serve to unify the text and its constituent segments, but it also helps to delineate structural boundaries and to emphasize important aspects of the prophet's message.

In addition to the manifold semantic recurrence exhibited by the verbal reiteration noted above, the text displays several other types of cohesion-creating repetition that are characteristic of Hebrew poetry. First of all, there is a significant amount of *phonological* recursion, including paronomasia, present to complement the lexical variety. An outstanding instance of this occurs in 2:18 where in contrast to Yahweh, the only true "God" (אֱלֹהִים, left implicit throughout the strophe), pagan idols are pejoratively described as "dumb dummies" (אֱלִילִים אִלְּמִים). Habakkuk likes to link together qualifiers that are close sound-alikes, for example, to characterize the wicked Babylonians, i.e., a "fierce" (הַמַּר) and "impetuous" (הַנִּמְהָר)

people (1:6) who "make [others] drunk" (מַשְׁקֵה), "pouring out" (מְסַפֵּחַ) "mixed drinks" (שְׁכָר) unto their destruction (2:15).

At other times, only certain key morphemes are reproduced to make the connection across a stretch of text, often forming emphatic assonance and/or alliteration, e.g., "Will these [peoples] not all take up a taunt against him with ridicule...?!" הֲלוֹא־אֵלֶּה כֻלָּם עָלָיו מָשָׁל (2:6). Such oral-aural accentuation is particularly effective in the several instances of divinely initiated *lex talionis* that are manifested in the "woe" oracles, e.g., (2:8):

| כִּי אַתָּה שַׁלּוֹתָ גּוֹיִם רַבִּים | Because you plundered many nations, |
| יְשָׁלּוּךָ כָּל־יֶתֶר עַמִּים | they will plunder you all the peoples who are left! |

Usually, such sonic repetition is manifested in pairs, but a number of longer patterns also occur, for example, in the strophe covering 2:12–14 which is stitched together by this alliterative rhyming sequence: ...בְּדָמִים...עַמִּים...לְאֻמִּים...כַּמַּיִם...עַל־יָם... "with bloods...peoples...to nations...like waters...upon the sea." A number of passages are quite saturated with such phonological play which, in addition to its connective function, undoubtedly also had an engaging connotative effect upon listeners even as it amplified the prophetic message, e.g., with respect to the boundless greed of the oppressor (2:9):

הוֹי בֹּצֵעַ בֶּצַע רָע לְבֵיתוֹ	Woe to the one gaining evil gain for his house,
לָשׂוּם בַּמָּרוֹם קִנּוֹ	to place it in the heights of his nest
לְהִנָּצֵל מִכַּף־רָע	to deliver himself from evil.

Or the utter confused folly of idolatry, since an image is nothing more than the inert product of its maker (2:18): פֶּסֶל...פְּסָלוֹ יֹצְרוֹ...יֵצֶר יִצְרוֹ "a-carving...one-forming-him he-carved-him...his-formation one-forming."

In addition to these varied lexical-semantic and phonological means, cohesion in poetic discourse is often produced also by the symmetrical syntactic structures created by manipulating the word order within adjacent cola. This is an especially prominent feature of the psalm of Habakkuk, where such patterned parallelism serves to demarcate as well as to unite certain strophes, e.g., 3:5–7, given in literal translation below:

8.4 Cohesion—the internal, connecting tissue of discourse

```
Before him
                    it went a plague,
                    and it followed a pestilence
before his steps.
He stood            and he measured           [the] earth,
he looked           and he startled           [the] nations.
And they crumbled   the mountains of long ago,
and they collapsed    the hills of eternity.
                    The ways of eternity [are] his!
In distress I saw                             the tents of Cushan,
they were trembling                           the tent curtains
                                              of the land of Midian.
```

In tightly constructed poetic passages of this nature, a (mono)colon that stands outside the overall pattern is usually of special significance, like the utterance of divine attribution above (italics). A combined chiastic-terraced sequence distinguishes the text's penultimate strophe, which itself peaks both formally and semantically in the final bicolon (3:17–18):

Though [the] fig tree	it does not blossom,	
	and there are no grapes	
	[though] it fails	
on the vines;		
the crop of olives,		
	and fields not	
they produce food;		
	[though] he cuts off	
from the fold flocks,		
	and there are no	
cattle in the stalls;		
nevertheless I	in Yahweh	I will rejoice,
		I will be joyful
	in the God of	
my salvation.		

Sound may be combined with syntax to create an especially emphatic linkage, such as the passage which brings the first stanza of chapter two to a rousing conclusion (2:5, *closure*). The total unrighteousness of Babylon is thus foregrounded just before Yahweh begins his righteous condemnation of that wicked nation (and all others like it):

```
...he enlarges
                    like sheol
                                      his soul,
                                      and he himself
                    like death
he is never satisfied.
And he gathers      unto himself      all the nations,
וַיֶּאֱסֹף           אֵלָיו             כָּל־הַגּוֹיִם
and he collects     unto himself      all the peoples.
וַיִּקְבֹּץ           אֵלָיו             כָּל־הָעַמִּים
```

Recursion on a much more generic, conceptual level may be evident in the reversed construction that encompasses Habakkuk's prayer of ch. 3. In this case, the linear syntagmatic development of the discourse (i.e., progression) simultaneously articulates a concentric paradigmatic recycling of the psalm's principal structural-thematic units (i.e., "cohesion") as the text unfolds. This symmetrical compositional construct, which exhibits a special focus at its center and conclusion (i.e., vv. 13a, 18–19) is illustrated in the diagram below:

```
A performance margin (1):
|
|   B lament introduction-----petition
|   |       fear—"I heard" (2a) + anticipatory faith (2b)
|   |
|   |   C theophany--Yahweh marches to battle
|   |   |   revelation: Yahweh displays his glory (3–4)
|   |   |   result: fear on the part of the ungodly (5–7)
|   |   |
|   |   C' theophany--Yahweh engages in battle
|   |       revelation: violent imagery of water/warfare (8–12)
|   |           => purpose = peak: SALVATION! (13a)
|   |       result: violent imagery of water/warfare (13b–15)
|   |
|   B' lament conclusion-------profession
|           fear—"I heard" (16) + confirmatory faith (17–19b)
|
A' performance margin (19c)
```

Whether or not the preceding structure is a completely valid representation of the development of ch. 3, it does serve to highlight the primary semantic

8.4 Cohesion—the internal, connecting tissue of discourse 461

and pragmatic nodes of the poem. Verse 13a with its highly poetic style and cluster of key words, i.e., "deliver," "your people," "your anointed one," and vv. 18–19a with its concentration of terms referring to the Deity, would certainly appear to represent the twin emotive-thematic peaks of the prayer as whole. This profession of faith in Yahweh's power to perform saving works lays the foundation, as it were, for the psalmist's personal faith, as expressed in the similarly emphasized borders of the psalm, i.e., B and B', the latter in particular, which obviously is rhetorically "heightened" (cf. v. 19c) in comparison with the former. The LORD's actions demonstrate his glorious nature on the one hand (C) and his commitment to do justice on the other, namely, through his punishment of the ungodly and vindication of all the "righteous" ones (cf. 2:4b) who rely upon him (C').

8.4.2 The "thematic polarity" of Habakkuk

The foregoing observations apply to the rest of the book of Habakkuk as well as to the concluding psalm. The charts given below provide a rough indication of the text-spanning cohesion that is generated by the book's principal thematic polarity, one which befits its classification as a "theodicy." The two paradigms concerned contrast the manifold *injustice* of humanity with the constant *justice* of Yahweh. In other words, the chart lists those verses that express the various concepts pertaining to righteousness and unrighteousness which cluster around the divine-human axis of attitudes and activity in the world.

These two antithetical categories are generalized for the purpose of this exercise in order to incorporate all concepts that belong to their wider semantic domains. For example, "[they] seize dwellings that are not theirs" (1:6) and "they are a law to themselves" (1:7) both fall within the field of injustice, while "my Holy One" (1:12) and "you cannot tolerate wrong" (1:13) belong with justice. An asterisk marks the occurrence of a topical *reversal*, that is, an expression that refers either to human justice/righteousness (e.g., 2:4b), on the one hand, or to an apparent (humanly perceived) instance of divine injustice, e.g., "why do you tolerate wrong?" (1:3). There are several instances of passages that incorporate a double or combined reference. In 2:7–8, for example, there is a prophecy that those who "plundered" (שַׁלּוֹתָ) others will be transformed into the booty, as it were, of their victims, who will in turn "plunder" them (יְשָׁלּוּךָ). A reversal of this nature is typical of the *divine irony* often expressed in such judgmental woe oracles. In the interests of space, only the verse references are included on the following figure:

chapter	INJUSTICE (man)	versus	JUSTICE (God)
I	2, 3, 4, 6, 7, 9, 10, 11, 13b, 17		2*, 3*, 12, 13a, 13b*
II	4a, 4b*, 5, 6, 7, 8, 9, 10, 11, 12, 15, 17		7, 8, 10, 13, 16, 17
III	13b, 14		12, 13, 14, 15, 16, 19

The preceding summary reveals a general topical development within the book of Habakkuk that moves from an initial emphasis on unrighteousness (even seemingly divine!), through the more spatially balanced, almost antiphonal, presentation of chapter two, and on to the text's predominant focus upon the justice of Yahweh in three.

Now what about the gaps—the verses which were not included—how do they fit into this dominant thematic framework? If considered in isolation, these passages might be construed as having a different emphasis. But situated as they are in this particular discourse, it is not difficult to relate virtually all of the verses not listed above to the book's chief polarity. They may be less obvious or explicit perhaps, but in one way or another they manifest some aspect of (or association with) either human injustice/unrighteousness or divine justice/righteousness. The following listing is a summary of this interactive manner of interpretation:

passage	relationship to the thematic polarity
1:1, 3:1	metatextual: an "oracle" of Yahweh's judgment upon injustice; the "prayer" of a just person in praise of God's holy/righteous being and salvific action
1:14–16	a parable depicting the ravenous appetite of the wicked/unjust/unmerciful person or people
2:1–3	preparation for the revelation of Yahweh's just condemnation of human injustice and his vindication of the righteous victims
2:14, 20	despite the apparent power of the wicked, a holy Yahweh reigns supreme in heaven and on earth in glorious majesty—attributes that presuppose his essential righteousness

8.4 Cohesion—the internal, connecting tissue of discourse

2:18–19   idolatry is both the source and a symptom of base human unrighteousness in relation to God and man

3:2, 17–18   a fitting response of God's righteous people to a revelation of divine vindicating justice in action

3:3–7   God's righteousness is implicit in his glorious, omnipotent being

3:8–15   God's righteousness is active in the deliverance of his people throughout history

The two charts above which delineate the pervasive recursion found in Habakkuk, when considered together with the structural-thematic arrangement discussed earlier, clearly demonstrate how tightly the book's three chapters are bound together. They suggest in particular the need for including the psalm of ch. 3 within the larger framework of the whole. Many commentators regard the latter as being an obvious product of later redactional activity and hence little more than a liturgical addendum or a pious theological afterthought to chs. 1–2. However, a careful study of the internal compositional dynamics of the discourse reveals that this psalm is indeed the climax of the entire work and the culmination of its fundamental line of argumentation. Without it, the vital message of the prophetically uttered oracle of Yahweh through Habakkuk would not really be complete, either formally, semantically, or pragmatically in terms of its overall rhetorical effectiveness or communicative relevance. The supreme righteousness of the holy LORD as evidenced in the deliverance of his people will naturally evoke a similar prayerful response on the part of the faithful who recognize their own unrighteousness and hence rely completely upon his merciful provision to meet their spiritual needs.

8.4.3 The "compositional core" of Habakkuk (2:4b)

The preceding discussion provides a good perspective from which to view the thesis that 2:4b constitutes the thematic nucleus of the entire book of Habakkuk. In other words, one may consider the discourse as a whole to be the product of a paradigmatic generation of its covenantal compositional core—the three words: וְצַדִּיק בֶּאֱמוּנָתוֹ יִחְיֶה "and-[the]-righteous-one by-his-faith(fulness) he-will-live." Within the context of this particular work—and indeed, the complete corpus of Old Testament literature—this proposition carries a great deal of implicit meaning. For one thing, it is a profoundly *relational* statement. In other words, it can be properly understood only in relation to the person and character of its divine author, Yahweh (יְהוָה). Second, the utterance presupposes its polar opposite, namely, the concepts of unrighteousness, infidelity, death. Third, the declaration is ethical as well as theological; it concerns one's life as well as her/his faith. And finally, there is also a crucial *forensic* component, a normative principle, and a norm-evaluator, or judge, involved—that is, the LORD God and the *torah* of his gracious covenant with all people.

The deep-structure theological kernel of Habakkuk may therefore be provisionally expressed as follows:

> The person who is regarded as being righteous by Yahweh, based on his/her faith, or steadfast trust in the "Holy One," lives her/his life in this world accordingly, that is, characterized by faithfulness to the demands of a divine covenant of righteousness, and s/he will ultimately live in holy fellowship with God eternally solely as a result of the just salvation worked by the all-powerful, but merciful, Sovereign LORD.

Thus, although the descriptive statement of 2:4b appears at first glance to focus on man--the righteous individual in contrast to the unrighteous—it is really based upon a much more fundamental proposition. This is a spiritual axiom which foregrounds the righteous being and behavior of the supreme Holy One (1:12, 3:1), the almighty Yahweh of Armies (2:13), the Sovereign LORD (3:19). It is the latter presupposition which gives the former passage its credibility, or truth, as well as its reliability, or trustworthiness. Religious currency (a system of theological and moral principles) is only as good as the divine standard that backs it up. The rest of Scripture attests to the fact that Habakkuk 2:4b has enough in reserve to stake one's eternal life upon.

As we observed in connection with our discussion of the thematic polarity of righteousness/justice versus unrighteousness/injustice above, the discourse is developed with an initial stress on human injustice in the prophet's complaint of ch. 1, an emphasis that evens out in the "revelation" of ch. 2, and then is strongly counterbalanced by the hymnic proclamation of divine justice in ch. 3. There is thus a definite progression in religious force from beginning to end as the critical issues pertaining to the theodicy, both personal and national, are first introduced in ch. 1 and then resolved in the remainder of the book. The ultimate answer is given in 2:4b—an anticipatory apologetic response which is immediately substantiated in the series of woe oracles of ch. 2 and finally by the theophanic vision coupled with the heroic ode in praise of Yahweh in ch. 3.

There is also an implicit, but multifaceted cohesion that complements the linear, progressive movement generated by the syntagmatic forces of the overt structural-thematic and rhetorical-dramatic levels of organization. As we have seen, this essential connectivity operates on both the micro- as well as the macro-level of discourse, radiating out, as it were, from the compositional pivot or content core at 2:4b in ever-widening circles of co-textual relevance with respect to the heart of the message. The major implication then of Habakkuk's prophecy, stated in figurative terms, is simply this: the Cosmic Creator and Divine Warrior so wonderfully portrayed in 3:3–15 is an infinitely greater source or basis of faith than the wicked idol-worshipping enemy host about to overrun the land (1:5–17) was a cause for disbelief. And the rank socio-political injustice that seemed to prevail within the prophet's own country (which is nowhere named in the book, e.g., 1:2–4) would one day pale to insignificance as the righteous LORD instituted irrevocable judicial proceedings against the wicked of all nations (2:6–20).

The promised reply (2:2–3) to Habakkuk's complaint (2:1) comes specifically in Yahweh's pronouncement of the basic principle of righteousness in relation to faith and life (2:4b), and in contrast to a godless, self-sufficient pride that ends in temporal and spiritual death (2:4a, 5). The supreme significance of this vital proclamation is both established and emphasized by a subsequent twofold response: one from the divine perspective (2:14, 20), the other from the refined and renewed point of view of the prophet himself (3:2, 16–19). For a man so profoundly struck by his perception of the divine majesty (3:16), Habakkuk certainly did a magnificent job of conveying the essence of his awesome experience for the future edification and encouragement of generations of similarly life-querying, often querulous, believers.

8.4.4 Intertextual cohesion

It is quite obvious that the text of Habakkuk was not generated in a literary vacuum. On the contrary, as might be expected in the work of a later prophet, one detects a great deal of dependence on the prior religious traditions of Israel in the form of a complex weave of direct citations, mixed paraphrases, and multi-leveled allusions. These theological references, whether strong or weak—historical, hortatory, or lyric in nature—operate in concert to integrate the book firmly into the developing canon that was later to emerge in the text of the Hebrew Scriptures.

Here then we have a unique, divinely motivated and guided (or, to risk the term, inspired) compositional force in action, one that was generating a long-transpiring communication event having much greater magnitude and significance, in terms of religious principles and spiritual values, than the book of Habakkuk would ever have on its own. This was a Spirit-led literary movement possessing both progression and cohesion that culminated in the composition of the Greek (New) Testament. Verse 2:4b, the preeminent text in Habakkuk, for example, continued to manifest considerable influence within ongoing Jewish rabbinical hermeneutics and later peaked in its theological relevance through its citation by several apostolic writers. Both aspects of its thematic import (discussed above) were applicable in early Christian thought: Paul stressed the *forensic* appropriation of righteousness by the believer through faith (Rom 1:17, Gal 3:11, Eph 2:8), while the writer to the Hebrews highlights its *ethical* aspect in the faithful perseverance of the righteous according to their faith (Heb 10:26–39, esp. v. 38a).

It is not possible to consider or even to list all of the citations, partial references, and allusions which permeate this book. I will therefore first present a selection of some of the main cross-scriptural semantic connections that underlie the chief discourse segments of the first two chapters, in particular, those which concern the basic thematic polarity of human injustice versus divine justice:

HABAKKUK verse	semantic category of injustice <=====> justice	intertextual cross-reference
1:1	oracle/burden	Num 1:1; Ezek 12:10; Zech 9:1; Mal 1:1
1:2	violence	Ps 55:9; Jer 6:7
1:3	injustice...evil	Num 23:21; Ps 7:14
	destruction...violence	Ezek 45:9; Amos 3:10
	strife...conflict	Prov 15:18; Jer 15:10
1:4	no law...justice	Exod 18:16; Num 15:16; Isa 1:17; Mic 6:8
1:6	I am raising up a ruthless and impetuous people...	Amos 6:14; Jer 5:14–17; Deut 28:49–50

8.4 Cohesion—the internal, connecting tissue of discourse

1:7		feared and dreaded...	Jer 5:15–22
1:8		like a leopard/wolf...	Jer 5:6; Deut 28:49
1:9		swift as a desert wind...	Jer 4:11–14
1:10		they capture cities	Deut 28:52–57
1:11		their strength is their god	Zeph 2:15; Isa 47:8

[Note: many of the references of ch. 1 deal with human injustice, but they apply in principle to the so-called covenantal curses that Yahweh promised would justly befall Israel if that nation repeatedly violated his holy *torah* (cf. Lev 26; Deut 28–32); thus passages depicting Chaldean aggression are listed under the category of divine 'justice'.]

1:12		for judgment you appointed them...to punish	Isa 11:3–4
1:13		Yahweh does not tolerate evil	Pss 5:4–5; 34:16, 21
	why is God silent in view of the wicked?		Isa 42:14
1:15		a fishhook and a net of divine judgment	Amos 4:2; Ezek 32:3
	wicked Babylon rejoices and is glad		Ps 14:7; Joel 2:21
1:16		sacrificing/burning incense to idols	Hos 4:13–14; 11:2; 2 Kgs 12:3; 14:4; 15:4
1:17	the enemy destroys without pity		Deut 28:50; Jer 6:23

HABAKKUK	semantic category of		
verse	**injustice** <=====> **justice**		intertextual <u>cross-reference</u>
2:1		the prophet as a watchman of the LORD's just judgment; Yahweh will "rebuke" his prophet to establish justice	Ezek 3:17; Mic 7:4, 7; Isa 21:8; Jer 6:17 Prov 1:23, 25, 30; 3:11
2:2		Yahweh commands his just "revelation" be written down so Habakkuk can run with it	Deut 27:1–8; Isa 30:8 Jer 23:21
2:3		Yahweh's righteous judgment about "the end" will surely be revealed at the right time so the righteous must "wait"	Dan 8:19; 11:27, 29; Isa 58:11 Isa 8:17; 30:18; 64:4
2:4	the unrighteous are greedy and proud	the righteous have/are faith/faithful before God	Num 14:44; Prov 14:12 1 Sam 26:23; Ps 33:4–5 Isa 26:2, 5; Gen 15:6
2:5	drunken injustice, like the grave, never stops taking the innocent captive		Prov 30:15–16; 31:4–7; Isa 5:11–12, 14, 22
2:6–8		Yahweh's sentences of "woe" upon the wicked— extortioners and exploiters; former victims will become victors and "plunderers"	Isa 5:8, 11, 18, 20–22; Jer 22:13; Am 5:18 Deut 23:19; 24:10–11 Jer 50:9–15; 51:6–9

2:9–11	those who "build a house" by injustice; Babylon cannot escape the just judgment of Yahweh	Jer 22:13–17 Isa 14:4, 13–15; Obad 4
2:12–13	Babylon will go up in smoke; the God of justice is Yahweh,	Jer 51:58 Num 14:21; Isa 6:3;
2:14	whose glory fills the earth	Isa 11:9; Ps 57:5, 11
2:15–17	Babylon also ravaged plant/animal life; Yahweh will make Babylon drunk from the cup of his wrath	Isa 14:8 Jer 25:15–17; Lam 4:21; Isa 29:9–10; 51:17–22
2:18–19	the unrighteous seek guidance from idols, but they receive no revelation	Ps 135:15–18; Isa 44:6–20 Jer 51:17–8, 47
2:20	the righteous LORD alone can reveal what is the truth	Ps 11:4; Mic 1:2

Beginning in ch. 3 with Habakkuk's thanksgiving psalm, the pertinent intertextual threads really become thick—closely attached as they are to the liturgical corpus and salvation-history of Israel. This is particularly true in verses 3–15. There are four pericopes which provide an especially large number of parallels to some of the key segments of the prophet's prayer, namely: Exodus 15 (= the *historical* source) and Psalms 18, 68, 77 (= the *liturgical* source). The thematic pole of unrighteousness greatly diminishes in overt importance as all attention is focused upon the awesome revelation of Yahweh, the invincible Soldier-King who is coming to fight for justice on behalf of his persecuted people.

As was noted earlier, the poetic discourse takes the form of a mini-narrative, one that has its roots firmly planted in the epic-religious tradition of ancient Israel. Only the primary elements in this lyric story of the LORD's manifestation of glory are listed below, along with their intertextual cross references for the sake of comparison.[24] The following then is a summary of the principal intertextual links that occur within the psalm of Habakkuk in ch. 3.

verses	topic—narrative motif	cross-references
2	**prologue** to the poetic-narrative revelation of the "deeds" of Yahweh, righteous in "anger" but great in mercy	Pss 68:28; 77:5–12
3–4	Yahweh appears on the scene from the desert south/Sinai in all his splendor and might	Exod 19:16–19; Deut 33:2; Judg 5:4a; Ps 68:7–8

---

[24] For similar listings, see Armerding 1985:520–521; Baker 1988:70–75; Patterson 1987:176.

5–7	the effects of Yahweh's advance are felt in the shocking/shaking of nations and nature	Exod 15:13–16; 19:18; Judg 5:4–5; Pss 18:7, 12; 77:18; 78:43–51
8–10	Yahweh vents his anger against the seas (= superiority over all pagan deities) as he rides to war on a chariot of clouds	Exod 15:8; Pss 18:9–12, 15; 68:4; 77:16–19; 89:9–10; 104:3–4
11–13	**climax:** Yahweh, armed with the weapons of nature, battles and completely routs the enemy to deliver his people and anointed one Deut	Pss 18:14; 68:7, 11–14, 17–18; 74:13–14; 77:14–15, 17–18; 32:23, 40–42
14–15	**denouement:** with a flashback to the prior time of oppression; all enemies, both natural and supernatural, are impressively defeated	Exod 15:2–5, 9–10; Deut 32:43; Pss 68:21; 77:19; 144:6–7
16–19	**conclusion:** a personal, meditative response to the narrative; patient and joyful hope for future deliverance and vindication	Deut 26:17–18; 32:13, 32–33, 41–43; 33:29; Joel 1:7–12; 2:23–24; Pss 4:7; 18:32–33; 28:6; 31:7–8; 32:11; 35:9–10

Thus, Habakkuk and his righteous compatriots need wait no more (2:1). His/their faithfulness has been fully vindicated as well as strongly reinforced (3:18–19) by this captivating vision of the Sovereign LORD and his mighty host in saving action.

8.4.5 "Mythopoetic" allusion in Habakkuk 3

One could logically posit another, deeper level of intertextuality with respect to the theophany-victory song of 3:3–15, namely, an ancient mythopoetic corpus that forms the basis for a number of the archaic references, figurative allusions, and even certain terminology to be found in this section. Sawyer, for one, claims that "the brilliant imagery of chapter 3 has a long literary history, going back to pre-Israelite Canaan" (Sawyer 1987:119). A number of scholars have made this particular feature the focus of their analysis of Habakkuk ch. 3.[25] Accordingly, they identify and attempt to elaborate upon the central motifs which were common in Canaanite and Ugaritic epics, which is summarized by Hiebert as follows (1987:132):

---

[25] For example: Albright 1950; Cross 1973; Eaton 1964:144–171; Irwin 1942:10–40.

> This ancient pattern is made up of two segments or genres within which the theophany of the storm god is described in formulaic fashion. [First], the storm god marches out from his mountain to do battle with Sea [i.e., a major deity], in response to which nature is devastated. [Second], the storm god returns victoriously from the battle to take up kingship on his mountain, in response to which nature is renewed.... The victory of the storm god celebrated in Habakkuk 3 reflects not only the victory of Israel's divine warrior over Israel's historical enemies but also, and fundamentally, the victory of Yahweh over Sea, the ancient dragon of chaos.

From this point of view then, what we have in Habakkuk's psalm is not only an instance of heavy intertextuality, but also a significant re-contextualization within the cognitive framework of the pagan mythic and/or secular-heroic worldview. It does not seem likely, however, that at the prophet's time in Israel's religious and literary history, the influence of such an alien and archaic conceptual environment would be nearly so prominent or prevalent in an apologetic work of this nature, namely, a theodicy on behalf of one God, Yahweh.

This is not to deny the considerable presence of ancient epic influence upon the composition of Habakkuk 3. Such a background is reflected in the archaic poetic style, which differs notably from that of chapters 1–2. For example, there are supposedly instances of internal defective spellings, absence of the definite article, the occurrence of an old pronominal suffix in ה- and the enclitic מ, frequent use of the preterite prefix conjugation in variation with suffixed verbals, climactic tricola in key structural positions (e.g., vv. 4, 8, 11, 13b–14a), and word-pairs common to Ugaritic and older Hebrew poetry.[26] In addition, there is a certain amount of thematic correspondence of a largely indirect and general nature, as was noted earlier.[27] But all this, whether pertaining to form or content, is utilized by the present author only in a secondary sort of way, that is, for the rhetorical purposes of illustration and embellishment to create added impact and appeal. Such material was necessary on purely literary grounds because it was characteristic of the poetic genre which the author was clearly trying to evoke to provide a fitting climax to his work. Besides, it was undoubtedly familiar to his audience, having already been de-mythologized and extensively re-focused

---

[26] See, for example, Patterson 1987:175–176 and Barre 1988:186–187. Bruce attempts to deal with some of the textual difficulties presented in ch. 3 with reference to "The Habakkuk commentary discovered in Qumran Cave 1 in 1947" (1993:835).

[27] See also Cassuto 1973:99–101.

in favor of Yahwist orthodoxy by numerous texts in the corpus of Hebrew religious literature, both oral and written (even in a relatively old poem such as Exod 15).

There may or may not have actually been an ancient Hebrew religious epic on the familiar salvation-history theme concerning the nation's movement, under God (Yahweh), from Egypt (slavery) to Canaan (freedom), that is, from the Red Sea (via the exodus) to Sinai to the promised land across the Jordan.[28] The point is that the prophet Habakkuk obviously did make extensive use of the extant literature of Scripture in other parts of his text (as shown in the diagram on pp. 466–469) in order to found his theophany upon the very word of the LORD (cf. 2:1). So why not also in the climactic portion of his prophecy to contextualize his concluding "prayer," specifically verses 3–15, with reference to the well-known and proven past of Yahweh's great deeds of deliverance on behalf of Israel? The former pagan myths were probably no longer a viable spiritual currency as far as their thematic or pragmatic (motivational) "buying-power" goes. That had been supplanted—not merely superimposed—first of all, in the liturgical tradition of worship (the Psalter, e.g., Ps 74:13–14). Heathen religious notions were also rendered impotent and useless by the messages that Yahweh communicated through his prophets, who revealed a monotheistic and merciful covenantal theology that was unique among the nations, both then and now. This dynamic tradition of a Savior-God actively moving in world history for the redemption of his chosen people provided, and still furnishes, the most viable frame of reference according to which Habakkuk 3 (and similar passages) may be understood and hermeneutically applied.

Within the very boundaries of his own prayer of thanksgiving then, Habakkuk's request that the LORD mercifully renew his works of salvation (3:2) is granted in an anticipatory, but deeply satisfying, sort of way before his very eyes in the theophanic vision of vv. 3–15. The latter is also an initial fulfillment of the LORD's promise to provide him with a certain revelation (2:2–3). The epic or heroic manner of composition, with its significant soteriological core (v. 13), epitomizes the central theme of the book as a whole, namely, Yahweh's unfailing faithfulness to his people throughout the ages. This existential truth in turn provides the only sure foundation for

---

[28] As argued by Patterson (1987:186–187); on the great differences between Near Eastern mythology and Hebrew narrative, cf. ibid., 189–190.

the faith of the righteous, who live according to it (2:4b) and who patiently, yet joyfully, wait for the divine plan of deliverance to be worked out in their own lives (3:16–19). This essential literary and religious connection with the past provides an ever-present hope for the future.[29]

Thus, the prophet's extensive use of the rhetorical technique of intertextuality itself becomes an important aspect of the theme of his message—stylistic form transformed into theological significance. The redemptive deeds of Yahweh, whose very name (יְהוָה) connotes continuity, reliability, permanence, and presence, provide that cohesive bond which gives sure meaning and purpose to the ongoing progression of human history. In specific terms, the exodus salvation event (gospel) lays the groundwork for the declaration of the LORD's covenant will at Sinai (law; cf. Exod 20:2), and this pattern of divine revelation continues throughout the Holy Scriptures, for example, in the life of Abraham (Gen 15:6; 17:1–14), in the teachings of Christ (Luke 7:39–50), and the writings of the Apostle Paul (Eph 2:8–10). Indeed, such steadfast continuity amid discontinuity, cohesion underlying progression—the promise (and even realization) of salvation despite endless world crises and catastrophes—is a powerful compositional force and a crucial theme not only of Habakkuk and the two Testaments, but it remains a vital aspect of personal experience for all who by faith are integrated into the transgenerational, multicultural, and polylinguistic family of God. It is also a valuable nugget of biblical truth that continues to inspire a verbal response on the part of the Lord's singing prophets throughout the ages, for example, in the well-known words of Isaac Watts (1719; cf. Ps 90):

> Our God, our Help in ages past,
> Our Hope for years to come,
> Our Shelter from the stormy blast,
> And our eternal home!

---

[29] Among a number of helpful applications of Habakkuk's message to the present age, Hiebert has this to say about the special relevance of the "apocalyptic hymn" of ch. 3: "According to the apocalyptic point of view, the injustices of history, such as those about which Habakkuk so eloquently complained, could be rectified only through a decisive intervention of God that would end history and inaugurate an age in which God's reign would be absolute.... The perspective from which the problem of injustice is viewed has been significantly broadened to include a new sphere of existence beyond this earthly life. In this context, the affirmation that 'the just shall live by...faith' takes on a new sense. It becomes an admonition not only to remain faithful within the injustices of this world but also to await the vindication God has promised the righteous in the next world" (1996:655).

8.5 Communicating crucial aspects of the rhetoric of an ancient biblical text today

8.5.1 "May the whole world hush in his presence!" (Hab 2:20b): From silence to psalmody

In this section I will focus on the practice of Bible translation from a more practical, rather than a theoretical, perspective. I discuss the problem of how best to convey some of the crucial structural and rhetorical features of the biblical text through its translation today. This is very much a contextualizing process that must pay sufficient attention to both the contemporary setting of communication and also the particular needs, limitations, and desires of the target language community. Three general techniques for achieving this objective are considered in greater detail: the use of appropriate textual markers in the translation itself, employing a functionally equivalent vernacular mode (genre) of composition, and adopting a more listener-friendly, oral-aural medium of transmission, including a restructuring of the printed format. This discussion is exemplified with reference to some of the prominent rhetorical features of the book of Habakkuk, especially the prophet's psalm of chapter 3. I suggest that the use of one or more of these meaning oriented translational strategies can help to convey a greater measure of the dynamic impact and aesthetic appeal of the various literary texts of Scripture in situations where the preparation of such a rendering is both possible and appropriate.

A general call to universal "silence" (הַס) surprisingly perhaps, but most appropriately concludes the dialogic portion of the book of Habakkuk (Hab 2:20b). The prophet's vigorous debate with YHWH (chs 1–2) thus comes to a quiet end with the reiterated assurance that justice will be done and wickedness will be punished. The twofold divine response (1:5–11, 2:2–20) silences an extended series of bitter prophetic complaints (1:2–4, 1:12–2:1). It is somewhat ironic, however, that in contrast to the strongly worded threats that are predicted for Babylon and similar oppressors in the five woe oracles of chapter two, the Lord of vengeance (2:16–17) is described in rather passive proclamations of trust that extol his "glory" (כְּבוֹד– 2:14) and "holiness" (קְדֶשׁ– 2:20; cf. 2:4). But such quiescence is simply the rhetorical calm before the storm that immediately breaks out then in the prophet's action-packed panegyric psalm of chapter 3 (3–15). Later, another dramatic contrast in literary style occurs as the pivotal silence of 2:20 is reflected in Habakkuk's trembling response to the divine theophany that he has just proclaimed (3:16–18). Here we have a realistic, but also positively optimistic personal confession that brings his stylistically diverse message to God's persecuted people to an encouraging close.

These dynamic expressions of anger and frustration, of warning and rebuke, of awe and humility, of worship and testimony must be correspondingly conveyed to the righteous as well as the wicked of every world age (Hab 2:14). This inevitably necessitates a process of text conversion into one of the 5000-plus tongues of those who need to know about the LORD's deliverance (3:13). Bible translation presents one of the most complex acts of communication imaginable—involving a transfer of time, place, language, culture, and religious ideology. The constant challenge, whatever the passage, is to convey sacred Scripture as accurately as possible, yet at the same time with at least some of the great power, appeal, persuasiveness, beauty, and grandeur that it possesses in the original language. To more fully accomplish these challenging communicative objectives requires a rigorous literary-rhetorical approach to the task of both rendering and representing the translated text.

8.5.2 The rhetoric of discourse and performance

Every well-formed literary composition, including those collected in the diverse corpus known as the Bible, embodies several distinct levels of rhetorical significance. Each of these needs to be analyzed initially on its own terms and then in relation to any other levels that have been identified. Two crucial aspects of literary communication, which together manifest the original author's efforts at artistic persuasion, operate on the perceptual planes of *discourse* and *performance*. I will explore the practical relevance of this twofold structuralist notion by considering it in the light of certain principles of modern translation theory and with reference to the book of Habakkuk, the prophet's psalm in particular.

The scope of discourse lies within and is limited to the referential plane of the biblical text itself. Messages are uttered, received, responded to, or repudiated by the internal participants, in the case at hand, the primary players: YHWH and Habakkuk. Then there are the secondary roles that are referred to or interact with the principals: Babylon the aggressor versus all persecuted nations. The dynamics of this area of message signification must be thoroughly studied first in order to surmise the likely impact of the work as a whole on the level of "performance"—that is, its effect upon the initially intended audience in their particular situational circumstances and ancient Near Eastern sociocultural setting. To be sure, our current lack of contextually derived background information makes this a rather tentative exercise, on both levels of rhetorical composition. Such intensive exegetical investigation is necessary nevertheless—and indeed possible to different degrees, using modern techniques of discourse-based and anthropological analysis, including various literary, linguistic, and social-scientific approaches.

Having thus arrived at a basic understanding of text's assumed meaning, its denotation as well as connotation, one is prepared to undertake a contemporary performance event—that is, a representation of its semantic essence and emotive significance on behalf of a present-day constituency. Several new efforts along these lines are briefly described below, with special reference to the practice of a meaning oriented, rhetorically shaped rendition of the Scriptures.[30]

8.5.3 Some basic issues in Bible translation

How can we best transmit today the intricate compositional dynamics of structure, cohesion, progression and climax to be found in such an artfully shaped poetic work as that of the prophet Habakkuk, specifically with respect to its thematic density, tectonic arrangement, illocutionary intent, emotive force, and stylistic beauty? Or is one not really responsible for these less perceptible or tangible aspects of the biblical message? To begin with, it is obvious that some sort of a translation is needed, in other words, an interlingual, cross-cultural *re-composition* of the original text using all the verbal resources of a contemporary language. Anyone who has made a serious attempt at producing a meaningful translation—even that of a

---

[30] I do not mean to suggest that this is the only type of translation possible. There are a wide variety of choices available, as determined by the situational setting and the communicative circumstances ("frames of reference") of the project being undertaken (see Wilt 2003:ch. 1). I am simply presenting my case for one of the least chosen, but in my opinion, most needed options—that is, for much of Africa.

simple narrative, let alone one of the prophetic oracles—has undoubtedly come to realize the utter impossibility of the task. One simply cannot effect a total or complete reproduction of the message as it was first given. It is possible, in fact, to convey only certain selected aspects of the initial communication event, and therefore a studied choice must be made: Where should the priority lie and the emphasis rest with respect to the translation at hand—on the verbal *form* of the source language (SL) document, on its basic semantic *content*, on the supposed functional *intent* of the message, or on its assumed *effect*(s) in terms of audience impact and emotive appeal?

For the past several decades, much more consideration has been given in the practice of translation to the exegetical, or referential, meaning of the Scriptures. This is a decided shift away from the focus on a literal, formal correspondence rendering which dominated the procedure of previous generations. Some theorists have gone even farther, pursuing aspects of meaning other than pure cognitive content, and have defined the translation task more broadly in terms of communicative *function,* for example:

> The translator must seek to employ a functionally equivalent set of forms which in so far as possible will match the meaning of the original source-language text...[so that] the receptors of a translation should comprehend the translated text to such an extent that they can understand how the original receptors must have understood the original text. (de Waard and Nida 1986:36)

Such a translation therefore aims to reproduce the closest natural equivalent of the biblical message in functional terms, either on a literary or a common level of style in the target language (ibid., 41–42).

More recently, proponents of the cognitively oriented linguistic theory of *relevance* have drawn attention to some complicating factors involved in determining just exactly what constitutes the "closest natural equivalent" for a given translation constituency. One of these issues concerns the fundamental matter of initial feasibility:

> [The] cause-effect nature of communication means that the first question in translation is not what we...*want* to communicate by our translation but what we reasonably...*can* communicate. (Gutt 1992:67)

According to this perspective, ostensive (i.e., overtly intentional) communication must be defined in terms of the "principle of relevance,"

8.5 Communicating crucial aspects of the rhetoric of an ancient biblical text today 477

which assumes that a message will be completely and/or correctly processed by a text's consumers (readers or hearers) only to the extent that they perceive it to "yield adequate contextual effects, without requiring unnecessary processing effort" (ibid., 25).[31] Such an approach highlights the all-important factor of conceptual *context*—in all its diverse, and often discordant, complexity: historical, cultural, sociological, ideological, ecological, situational, and experiential. Thus, communication depends upon both what is expressed, whether explicitly or implicitly, in a given text (along with any associated para-/extra-linguistic features) and also on the level of contextual background knowledge that is available and accessible to its envisaged audience. To the extent that this latter cognitive environment is either partial or deficient, any translation—no matter how good exegetically or linguistically—will correspondingly fail in conveying the intended sense and significance of the original composition.

Recently, Pilkington (2000) has extended the discussion of "relevance" and applied it to a study of stylistic effects in literature. He suggests that the use of figurative language, rhetorical techniques, and various other poetic devices (e.g., meter, alliteration, parallelism, rhyme, strophic structure) encourages a semantic comparison and contrast of the componential and encyclopedic information that is conceptually attached to the lexical items that are thus foregrounded. In the actual context of usage then, certain cognitive assumptions and emotive associations are made more prominent, thereby stimulating a mental search for possible relevance. These constitute the poetic effects, or communicative clues, that form the basis for conveying either "a range of weak implicatures" (i.e., over and above the literal denotation of the text) or "a new concept forming part of the proposition expressed by the utterance" that has been stylistically activated (ibid., 141). Such features contribute greatly to the impact, appeal, and import that is generated by good literature, including many portions of Scripture, by serving "to broaden context, and make both thoughts and feelings richer, more complex and more precise with regard to actual situations or states

---

[31] The term "consumers" is used here to emphasise the conceptually active role that the intended reader- or listener-ship plays in the communication process. They are not passive receptors; nor are they merely an inert target to be shot at with the translated text. Rather, they significantly influence, even as they are normally influenced by, the ultimate message that is transmitted. Due to my emphasis on the orality of Scripture communication, I will refer to this group as the "audience" in the following discussion, but will retain the commonly used term "target language" (TL) simply for convenience.

of affairs" (ibid., 161). Some general aspects of this complex interpretative process will be illustrated below with reference to a rhetorically reformatted version of Habakkuk 3.

8.5.4 Bridging the contextual gap

Bible translators obviously need to take the total situational setting of the audience into greater consideration as they plan and carry out their work. As noted above, the principal medium activated during most Scripture use is *oral-aural* in nature. Thus, translations that are even more hearer-oriented or reader-friendly in orientation are required if this communication process is to succeed in raising the overall quality of message transmission, that is, by increasing the amount of the originally intended meaning actually made textually available to its processors. People cannot accurately, or even adequately, respond to the source message if they have just a minimal knowledge about either the biblical composition itself or the manifold extralinguistic setting out of which it arose. Translators must therefore attempt to represent in their language not only the essential contents, the stylistic beauty, and the rhetorical dynamics of a given Scripture pericope, but also the manifold resonance of theological significance that may be associated with or evoked by it, for example, the ancient allusions attached to the psalm of Habakkuk. The problem is that most contemporary Scripture users, even those who are functionally literate with a high level of biblical education, have little or no inkling of what really lies behind a poetic masterpiece such as this.

Such a knowledge deficit applies also to the prophecy of Habakkuk as a whole. Few "average" readers, let alone more resource-limited listeners, have any notion of its larger point and purpose. Nor do they have any idea of what a "theodicy" is all about in its original Jewish cultural and socio-religious context. Therefore, they will probably not see much point to this sort of elaborate disputative rhetorical work that seeks to justify (i.e., to defend, but not necessarily to explain) the ways of God in view of the ubiquitous problem of evil and suffering in the world. But surely this larger apologetic theme, and its religious function, is an essential part, if not the heart, of the prophet's message. It is an element that needs to be conveyed to current receptors, in one form or another and in the most relevant (convincing

8.5 Communicating crucial aspects of the rhetoric of an ancient biblical text today

and compelling, appropriate and applicable) way possible. This is the stimulating challenge of enhanced communication—of assisting people to read or hear behind the lines of the original text—that I wish to briefly consider now in terms of literary compositional forces and rhetorical techniques, both past and present.

In his helpful overview of some of the principal factors involved in successfully communicating the Bible via printed translations, E-A. Gutt concludes (ibid., 68):

> It must be clearly recognized that the final objectives of Scripture translation cannot be realized by translation alone.... Translation projects need to be seen in the wider context of communication, rather than book production. In particular, they need to provide strategies that will enable the audience to eventually bridge the contextual gap.

I would like to suggest three possible techniques that pertain to contextually relevant ways of helping contemporary audiences bridge this ever-present situational gap—some might even call it a chasm. These methods are intended to counteract or compensate, as it were, for the lack of sufficient background knowledge necessary to make possible an adequate (yet by no means ever complete) interpretation on the part of participants on the performance level of the communication process today. Thus, we may be able to facilitate this goal through the provision of:

- Appropriate translational *markers* of the structural organization, rhetorical strategy, and sociocultural background of the original document;
- A functionally equivalent, local poetic *mode* of literary composition; and/or
- Use of more natural oral-aural and more nuanced visual *media* of transmission.

Each of these procedural categories will be selectively overviewed and illustrated in the next sections, the last in somewhat greater detail. The ideas presented here are merely suggestive of some of the innovative, non-traditional techniques that may be considered and tried out on an experimental basis (along with more extensive vernacular educational ministry), if the local circumstances allow. These methods must therefore always be carefully evaluated in conjunction with one another and within the framework of a comprehensive communication strategy; this would be an explicit set of principles, procedures, and goals that have been developed for a particular audience in relation to their overall sociocultural context.

8.5.4.1 Text markers

This category includes a variety of procedures for highlighting significant structural and rhetorical features to be found within a given biblical book or pericope. These may be applied either intra-textually or extra-textually, depending on the nature of the SL literary device involved, the particular problem it presents in the TL, the vernacular resources available for resolving this difficulty, and the level of literary competence and biblical background knowledge of the intended audience/readership.

The use of *intra-textual* markers in a translation to distinguish significant discourse boundaries and peaks, namely, those actually present within the biblical composition, is not really an optional procedure. Rather, it is clearly required as part of a broader text-oriented, communication-centered method of interlingual message transmission. All too often, however, we find that this essential text shaping and shading operation is carried out only intuitively and haphazardly, if at all. In other words, it is not strategically planned and formulated by the translation team *before* they begin their work. Neither is it based upon an explicit set of translation principles or transfer procedures derived from a systematic comparative discourse analysis of the SL document or related TL genres and compositional features.

The results of such research should make it possible to suggest the various stylistic markers that typically introduce particular literary genres—"woe" oracles, for example (2:6–20; see Zogbo and Wendland 2000:ch. 4), or those which are commonly utilized to signal such crucial junctures as aperture, closure, and peak (e.g., at the prominent theological affirmations of 2:14, 20, and 3:18–19). Also necessary are natural ways of indicating a topical transition (e.g., at 2:17–18, violence = > idolatry), a shift in emotive tone (e.g., 2:16b–16c, reverent awe = > patient hope), or a new speech "turn," for example, in the dialogic exchanges of Habakkuk 1, especially at verses 4–5 (i.e., prophet = > LORD) and 11–12 (i.e., LORD = > prophet). Similarly, the sharp changes in content, perspective and attitude at the close of each of the first two chapters (i.e., 1:17–2:1, 2:19–20) also need to be

8.5 Communicating crucial aspects of the rhetoric of an ancient biblical text today 481

verbally (orally and aurally) highlighted in an appropriate TL manner, not simply left to the visual signals of verse numbers and the printed format. Finally, the intensely personal reflective framework that bounds the divine victory hymn of chapter 3 (i.e., vv. 1–3 and 16–19) may require some extra differentiation by means of linguistic markers so that its borders are immediately apparent (audible) to listeners as the poetic text is being read aloud.

The use of additional, *extra-textual* educative helps does not obviate the need for the discourse internal devices just mentioned. Rather, the two types of auxiliary aid should be closely integrated in order to reinforce each other as part of a cohesive and coordinated program of text re-presentation. This second category of markers is meant to compensate for the lack of knowledge that characterizes most contemporary audiences, that is, with regard to the entire biblical communicative setting—discourse as well as performance (cf. 7.5.2). Such supplementation includes the use of familiar features like explanatory footnotes (that is, keyed to the principal historical, social, literary, cultural, political, ecological, and religious aspects that underlie the biblical text), maps, structural diagrams, illustrations, cross-references, book introductions, section headings (with optional content synopses), text-critical or translational comments (in footnotes), and so forth.

During this procedure a judicious selection must be carried out, for there is always a considerable amount of additional information that ought *not* to be supplied in order to preserve the efficiency and effectiveness of the translation (in keeping with the principle of communicative relevance). In short, this refers to whatever was not linguistically implied, referentially presupposed, or connotatively conveyed by the original text in its own contextual setting (e.g., possible allusions to aspects of the ancient mythological worldview). This is not an easy differentiation or decision to make, but the important thing is that the issue of inclusion or exclusion is thoroughly dealt with by mother tongue speakers in relation to the primary cultural context of usage and target group envisioned for the version being prepared (Gutt 1992:70–74; Wendland 1987:ch. 8).

One final point needs to be noted again in connection with the provision of extratextual aids, and this concerns the possible danger of overdoing it. Such helps must always be carefully tailored to meet the specific needs, limitations, requests, and expectations of the consumer constituency, based upon a systematic program of research and pre-testing, along with ongoing inquiry and assessment. At times too much information is worse than none at all, for instance, in the case of detailed structural, etymological, redactional, or text-critical footnotes. A related, potential problem area concerns the inclusion of cross-references to supposedly parallel texts and key terms of Scripture. All too often one finds only a very slight (at times a debatable or even dubious) connection between the verse at hand and the one(s) listed in the note or text margin. It certainly does not seem to justify the time or effort required to look such citations up, and a negative outcome of this nature, when compounded, quickly discourages readers from making further use of this valuable resource. Therefore, in an intertextually dense prophecy like that of Habakkuk, which does make considerable reference and allusion to other portions of Scripture, especially in chapter 3, it would be wise to limit the designated passages to those for which most readers will be able to readily notice the relevant biblical pre-text or correspondence, some valid exegetical implication, or a clear contemporary application.

8.5.4.2 Literary mode

The strategy of localized contextualization also pertains to the use of a functionally equivalent literary rendering of the original message on the generic level of discourse, beginning with the broadest possible distinction, namely, that between prose and poetry. As many scholars have pointed out, however, these are not really two clearly differentiated categories or macro-genres of literature in Hebrew religious composition, and the same may be true also for the language of translation. Thus, the situation may be more like the nature of a progression or continuum featuring more as opposed to fewer poetic/prosaic features, which need to be applied in accordance with the content and intent of a particular biblical text and its TL rendition.

Other important stylistic variations, either with or without functional implications, would be those that involve direct and reported or formal and informal speech patterns. These too are probably not manifested in a strictly polar opposition in most languages, but instead there may be a gradient of discourse types that manifest greater versus lesser directness, markedness, or formality (syntactic freedom, lexical idiomacity, deictic precision, referential politeness, etc.), perhaps even including certain specialized styles that allow a great deal of mixing (i.e., so-called "free indirect" discourse or oratorical prose). It would be helpful to signal such a prominent shift

8.5 Communicating crucial aspects of the rhetoric of an ancient biblical text today

in discursive mode, distinguishing in the TL for example the central, formalized theophanic vision-report of 3:3–15 from the more informal and personalized responses of the psalmist which contrastively surround his thanksgiving prayer (3:2, 16–19).

As is obvious from a perceptive survey of little Habakkuk, his oracle, or burden (1:1), incorporates a rather large variety of Hebrew literary genres in relation to its size, and these textual diversities should ideally be reflected in a serious translation, if at all possible. Translators would need to discover, for example, whether or not there are any indigenous generic equivalents to the prophetic lament (see 1:2–4, 12–13), the incriminatory and ironic use of parables (see 1:14–17), pronouncements of accusation-condemnation (see 2:6–19), or ancient heroic poems in praise of deity (see 3:3–15). Such local literature, no doubt originally oral in nature (orature), may or may not be helpful to use as discourse models, depending on the current connotative, sociolinguistic, and possibly negative traditional religious associations connected with them. For instance, the poetic declamatory song-chant *(ciyabilo)* in Chitonga, or the popular expressive lyric *(ndakatulo)* in Chichewa (two south-central Bantu languages), would appear to fit the common psalmic lament form quite closely (e.g., Ps 22; Hab 1:2–4, 12–17; Klem 1982:*passim*; Wendland 1994b:19–43).

Perfect form-functional *matches* on this larger level of composition are not to be expected, but if the local genre overlaps sufficiently in terms of sociocultural function, then an attempt at least might be made to either reproduce or adapt it in a translation. The more formal correspondences that happen to exist between the two types of discourse, the better the ultimate functional parity, or communicative fit, will be. This is because artistic form always carries its own distinct overlay of significance, for example, the typical exclamatory (woe) introduction to the Hebrew judgment oracle. In the Chichewa language of Malawi, for example, we find a rather close correspondent in the exclamatory noun *kalanga* ("regret, remorse") which is used in both literary and ordinary discourse as an expression of great grief that arises from sorrowful circumstances, e.g., a bad accident or news of someone's death. However, if the indigenous genre turns out to be noticeably different in style and usage, then it is likely that a corresponding amount of semantic or pragmatic distortion will be introduced into the translation as a result. But this may be the communicative price that one has to pay in order to achieve an acceptable level of meaning equivalence with respect to other vital aspects of the message, such as emotive intensity, rhetorical force, thematic credibility, connotative tone, or pure esthetic attraction. In any case, this too must necessarily be an issue for trained and perceptive local critics to decide in consultation with competent representatives of their respective speech communities.

8.5.4.3 *Medium of transmission*

In many world settings today, in so-called developed as well as the developing countries, a transposition of the text of Scripture out of print and back into its original oral-aural medium may be necessary in order to permit relevant (in the full technical sense) communication to take place. In some regions an adequate level of *functional* literacy is not widely attained at all (Malmstrom 1991:13), while in others it is being progressively lost due to intense competition from more popular media: audio alone (cassette, CD, radio), audio-visual (video, TV), and increasingly in this computer age, the electronic text (or hypertext). The last mentioned category is not nearly as alien or improbable for Bible usage as it may at first seem. In fact, it may be the most malleable of all in terms of the degree of flexibility and need-related interaction that it allows the individual participant during the act of communication. The great disadvantage of course, especially in an African setting, is the individuality of its performance; computer use does not promote a sense of corporate unity, or interdependent community.

So-called "hard" media are those that are most rigid or concrete in their format and presentation. They also require a certain level of media literacy on the part of those who make use of them, e.g., books and films. "Soft" media, on the other hand, are malleable—that is, they may be adapted to meet the needs of the immediate situation, they allow for interaction among participants, and they do not require any type of education or literacy other than basic literary/linguistic competence in the language-culture and oral tradition concerned. The softest media are found in traditional oral-aural performing arts and are strongly interpersonal in nature, involving customary dialogue and debate patterns, storytelling, improvisational drama, balladeering, sapiential repartee (i.e., with proverbs, riddles, enigmas), and spontaneous musical production.

8.5 Communicating crucial aspects of the rhetoric of an ancient biblical text today 485

The use of a soft medium of presenting one's message is generally more effective due to the greater degree of individual as well as community participation that it makes possible. Most communication in the world occurs in this personalized way to begin with. But is such a flexible, immediate, and interactive approach really feasible where Bible translation is concerned? An increasing number of modern communicators feel that this is where the future lies and that some real breakthroughs can be expected specifically in the area of the traditional performing arts on the one hand and in the field of computer technology on the other. As one media expert has remarked: "God has given us electronic communication and the possibility of forming a world-wide communications community in order to save us from ourselves" (Boomershine 1990). But in such a sophisticated modern endeavor, we must not lose sight of the ancient oral genres and familiar oratorical techniques, e.g., popular public dramatic peformances, that many traditional societies continue to cultivate and value most highly.

Whether this electronic potential will be turned into reality depends on many factors. But it is clear that specially designed computer programs, interactive connections, and databases are able to provide an immediately available resource for filling in gaps with regard to many different facets of a biblical text even *while* it is being read, for example: its larger discourse structure, rhetorical features, stylistic devices, parallel passages, sociocultural and environmental setting, theological and religious implications, both ancient and contemporary. Additional informational access is often made possible in terms of a Bible concordance, dictionary, and a selection of commentaries and related scholarly works. The future development of electronic, computer-based telecommunications networks (e.g., Bitnet, Internet) will make it possible to dialogue or interface with a given pericope of Scripture to increasing levels of sophistication and depth (Kraft 1993).

For public communication in today's world, however, more conventional audio and print media are still necessary, especially in regions where the more complex machinery and methods of modern technology are beyond the financial means of most people. The worldwide channel of satellite television and radio is one of the newest to be explored as a possibility for transmitting the Bible to the many who otherwise, either by choice or by chance, have no ready access to God's Word. However, adding a visual dimension to the spoken word, as in a video recording, presents linguistic translators and media transpositors with special obstacles and difficulties that pertain to the issue of *fidelity* to the original message. As Boomershine (1990) points out:

> The transmediazation of the Bible into television will require that the biblical tradition be presented as sounds and images rather than as printed marks on a page.... This process will require new methods of exegetical study that will focus, first of all, on identifying the oral characteristics of the text in its original context.... The investigation of the images of the texts is even more difficult. What are the appropriate visual components of biblical texts?

Due to limitations of space, we must leave the final question unanswered (see the essays in Hodgson and Soukup 1997). One thing is certain: in addition to providing future communicators with a challenge, the varied and variable visualization of Scripture will inevitably provoke controversy due to the degree of implicit information covertly present in the biblical text that simply has to be made explicit in any video production. The problem is that such explication, no matter what the medium being used, "always has the potential for distorting the original meaning" (Gutt 1992:73), in particular, through an overly localized transculturation of the message. Unfortunately, more often than not in modern productions, such negative hyper-domestication is realized, and the task is to see how best to overcome or counteract it.

Of the contemporary media, the purely *audio* channel, via a simple cassette tape recording or a mass media radio broadcast for example, remains the safest for use as a vehicle for conveying Scripture translations to people who cannot, or who prefer not to, read the text for themselves. But this endeavor too requires a level of exegetical analysis that goes beyond what is normally performed. This is done in order to determine—to the extent that this is possible with an ancient written text—the oral units of speech, for instance, or the major and minor pause points, any special mnemonic or emphatic structures as indicated by repetition, chiasmus, parallelism, rhythm, alliteration, assonance, and so forth. Such formal cues provide vital clues to readers with regard to how they ought to modulate their vocal presentation in terms of tempo, tone, volume, stress, melody, and emotive paralinguistic shading. Indeed, a battery of special procedural controls is essential in helping producers to remain faithful both to the content, intent, and import of the original text and also to the potentials and limitations of the audio medium itself (see Malmstrom 1991:ch. 11; Sogaard 1991:ch. 14). However, the various complexities and difficulties that are confronted in these productions need to be evaluated in relation to a simple but highly significant fact: The proportion of this world's population that can/will receive the Bible only in audible form is as large as it ever has been, and this percentage is constantly increasing as modern technology creates hardware that is getting ever smaller in size, hence more portable, and also less expensive.

The preceding survey does not mean to imply that the Scriptures in print are, like dinosaurs and phonograph records, doomed to eventual extinction. That would happen only if the entire world lapsed into illiteracy, which is not likely since most people—those who read well at any rate—still, and probably always will, prefer to engage the sacred text in a more tangible, published form. There is also a certain amount of prestige, authority, and permanence associated with a printed text, even by those who cannot read it, and these are undoubtedly important values with respect to the *written* Word of God. There may even be some critical theological considerations to be further debated in this regard (e.g., Exod 31:18; Josh 1:8; Ps 102:18; Luke 10:20, 18:31; John 20:31; Rev 22:18–19). Since there will always be at least some call for printed editions of the Word, it is necessary to address the legitimate communication concerns that certain modern media and translation specialists have raised on an *intra*textual level, that is, within the actual published texts of the Bible. One major issue here relates to attempts to provide a more legible text that will enable public lectors to perceive and comprehend the printed message at first sight so that they can in turn articulate it orally in a more meaningful (also hearable) manner.

8.5.4.4 *Formatting the text on the printed page*

One prominent media expert has put the challenge facing publishers in this way: "We need to develop a whole new series of translations of the Bible for recital rather than for study"; as an essential part of this goal, "we will also need to develop new ways of printing the texts that will indicate the units of sound in the translation" (Boomershine 1990). Various degrees of modification in the primary variables of typography and page formatting from the norm for Scripture publications will surely be necessary in order to accomplish such an objective. This includes, for example, the use of more legible typefaces, different print styles (to signal different discourse functions), additional interlineal and marginal space, a ragged (vs. justified) right-hand margin (to ensure minimal hyphenation), lines comprised of or at least ending in complete sense units, and indentation to highlight important textual parallels and correspondences (Louw and Wendland 1993). Initial tests have shown that not only are such reformatted versions—"audio texts in print form" (Newman 2001:11)—more legible and comprehensible, but they are also more enjoyable (and instructive) to read. These are significant factors that motivate a more serious and sustained engagement with the Scriptures, whether one happens to be reading silently to oneself or before a public gathering, as in a worship service.

The use of variations in typography as part of a larger strategy of discourse design is also needed in order to make it easier for readers to grasp, at a glance as it were, the overall structural organization of the pericope they happen to be viewing. To simply ignore the issue and carry on with Bible publication in the conventional manner solely for economic reasons is not really satisfactory. In addition to detracting from readability, such a policy may operate in contradiction to what one actually wishes to communicate via a certain text. This is because the discourse arrangement is an integral part of the total meaning-package of a biblical composition, and every printed framework, even the supposedly neutral, unadorned one, characterized by large neat blocks of small type on the average page, inevitably conveys its own distinctive message. This semantic significance is generally both denotative in nature (i.e., all of the material in one chunk deals with the same topic/theme or episode/event), and it also has important connotative (emotive, attitudinal, value-related) associations as well. Such a traditional print style, often ceremoniously adorned with all sorts of artistic flourishes, may be deemed scholarly or possessing the appropriate religious decorum—hence suitable perhaps for public display on a pulpit. Unfortunately, however, such texts are not very serviceable in terms of promoting either better comprehension of the biblical text or more widespread and well-informed Scripture use.

The problem too with a more conservative, cost-saving approach is that "the wrong typeface and format can seriously undermine or distort the meaning of a discourse" (de Waard and Nida 1986:184). This is what often happens in cases where the text is not formatted so as to reflect its underlying discourse structure. In the case of poetic material, for example, whether

8.5 Communicating crucial aspects of the rhetoric of an ancient biblical text today

of a prophetic (e.g., didactic, hortatory, admonitory, predictive) or lyric variety (e.g., of lament, thanksgiving, praise, confidence, or instruction), the seemingly elementary matter of paragraphing can produce some serious problems in conveying the intended meaning of the original text. The book of Habakkuk is perhaps one of the least controversial in this regard, but even here some major differences of opinion appear, for example, at the onset of the series of judgment oracles in chapter two, i.e., with a diagnostic marker placed at v. 5 (GNT), v. 6 (NIV, NRSV), v. 7 (LB, REB), or having no indication in this section at all (Tanakh). Certainly, the paragraph placement here will affect one's reading and understanding of the pericope on either side of the boundary. Similar difficulties of segmentation presented by the prophet's psalm may be noted in any critical commentary; for example, the stanzaic break after 3:7 (cf. NIV) is ignored completely by NRSV and is misplaced by GNT, i.e., put before v. 7. Thus, we see that form has consequential meaning even in these largely implicit respects.

8.5.4.5 The rhetorical typographical display of a prophetic text

A newly formatted example of Habakkuk 3 to illustrate the preceding point is shown below (based on Wendland 1999:601–606). The English translation follows in large measure the moderately literal, but poetically phrased *New Jerusalem Bible* (NJB), including its helpful section headings. However, this text is spatially reset in order to overcome, at least in part, some of the deficiencies outlined above. Accordingly, the two major objectives of this experimental display are:

- To present a clearer indication of the dynamics of the Hebrew discourse structure, i.e., its organization and movement in terms of progression, cohesion, as well as the principal compositional units and their relationships.

- To provide a text that is more reader-friendly and aurally attuned, i.e., one that facilitates oral elocution and is at the same time more easily perceived and accurately interpreted—by the eye as well as the ear.

This format makes use of such basic techniques as a single column of print, measured degrees of indentation (cf. Clark and Hatton 1989:123), lineal utterance units, right hand displaced verse numbers, selective spacing to indicate major discourse breaks, and the use of italic print and capital letters to show (possibly) distinctive content and special emphasis, respectively. More specifically, we note that in the panegyric middle of the psalm the more left-placed indented units of the formatted text call visual attention to the mighty attributes and actions of the YHWH, the Warrior King, while the more righted indented units describe the fearful reaction to this theophanic display on the part of creation and humanity (including Habakkuk himself). Probably the best way for such an illustrative format to be evaluated and, where necessary, corrected and improved is through a professional oral recitation—or perhaps even a dramatic performance—of the text before a live audience. After all, that is one of its primary purposes, namely, to encourage a more accurate, decisive, and dramatic reading of the written text of Scripture.

III. A PLEA TO YAHWEH FOR DELIVERANCE

Title: A prayer of the prophet Habakkuk: with a tune as for dirges.   1

Prayer

> *Yahweh, I have heard of your renown;*   2
> *your work, Yahweh, inspires me with dread.*
> *Make it live again in our day,*
> *make it known in our time;*
> *in wrath remember mercy!*

Theophany: Yahweh's approach

> Eloah comes from Teman,   3
> the Holy One from Mount Paran. *[Pause]*
> > His majesty covers the heavens,
> > and his glory fills the earth.
> > His brightness is like the day,   4
> > and rays flash from his hands,
> > that is where his power lies hidden.
>
> Pestilence goes before him,   5
> while Plague follows close behind.
> > When he stands up, he shakes the earth,   6
> > with his glance he makes the nations quake.
> > The eternal mountains are dislodged,
> > the everlasting hills sink down—
> > but his movements are everlasting.

> I saw the tents of Cushan in trouble, 7
> the tent-curtains of Midian shuddering.

Yahweh's battle

Yahweh, are you enraged with the rivers, 8
are you angry with the sea,
that you should mount your chargers,
your rescuing chariots?
You uncover your bow, 9
and give the string its fill of arrows. [*Pause*]
You trench the earth with torrents.

> The mountains see you and tremble, 10
> great floods sweep by,
> the abyss roars aloud,
> lifting high its waves.
> Sun and moon stay inside their dwellings, 11
> they flee at the light of your arrows,
> at the flash of your lightning-spear.

In rage you stride across the land, 12
in anger you trample the nations.

YOU MARCHED OUT TO SAVE YOUR PEOPLE, 13
YES, TO SAVE YOUR ANOINTED ONE!

You wounded the head of the house of the wicked,
you laid bare his foundation to the very rock. [*Pause*]
With your shafts you pierced the leader of his warriors 14
who stormed out with shouts of joy to scatter us,
as if they meant to devour some poor wretch in their lair.
With your chargers you trampled through the sea, 15
through the surging abyss!

Conclusion: human fear and faith in God

> When I heard, I trembled to the core, 16
> my lips quivered at the sound;
> my bones became disjointed,
> and my legs gave way beneath me.
> Yet calmly I await the day of anguish,
> which is dawning on the people now attacking us.

> For the fig tree is not to blossom, 17
> nor will the vines bear fruit;
> the olive crop will disappoint,
> and the fields will yield no food;

> *the sheep will vanish from the fold,*
> *no cattle left in the stalls.*
> *But I shall rejoice in Yahweh,* 18
> *I shall exult in God my Savior!*
> *Yahweh the Lord is my strength,* 19
> *he will lighten my feet like a doe's*
> *and set my steps upon the heights.*

For the choirmaster; played on stringed instruments.

While this translation is certainly not an instance of poetry in English (in mimicry of the Hebrew original), it does give evidence of a number of poetic features that distinguish this pericope from those that have preceded it in Habakkuk. We observe, for example, the relatively balanced lineation, some rhythmic cadences (e.g., v. 17), a bit of rhyme, variety in word order, and of course the original imagery that speaks for itself. Whether this text would be viewed as a functional equivalent of the original would depend on the audience concerned and the purpose for which the version is intended. In my opinion, this translation as it has been formatted is comparatively easy to read and also pleasing to listen to. To what extent the special typographical features such as indentation and italic print are meaningful to readers remains to be tested; surely the use of capital letters (v. 13a) would call for more vocal stress and/or loudness at that point.

As for an application of the relevance principle, the obvious divergence from usual printing techniques would cause readers to pause at those points in order to determine their functional significance—for example, the use of italics at v. 7, where the shift in speaker and perspective might be noted, thus suggesting some sort of modulated articulation.[32] What this contributes to a person's overall understanding of this pericope would no doubt vary according to one's level of print-literacy and understanding of the content and purpose of this passage as a whole. In any case, a sectional introduction or

---

[32] In this case, updated Relevance Theory builds upon the old Russian Formalist poetic principle of "defamiliarization" (*ostraneniye* 'making strange'), whereby an effective literary device causes a delay in the automatic conceptual processing of a text (cf. Pilkington 2000:18). Its meaning, whether local or global, and aesthetic-emotive effect is thereby highlighted, thus enhancing the communication process: "The technique of art is to make objects 'unfamiliar,' to make forms difficult, to increase the difficulty and length of perception because the process of perception is an aesthetic end in itself and must be prolonged.... [T]he author's purpose is to create the vision which results from that deautomatized perception" (Victor Shklovsky, in Lemon and Reis 1965:12).

localized footnote explaining the significance of the novel typography and format would certainly be an essential extra-textual addition.

8.6 Conclusion—A hush in His presence

This study has illustrated the importance of progression and cohesion, not only in the discourse of Habakkuk the prophet, but also in the general methodology that one adopts in any discourse analysis. Starting from the basic assumption that the original text is an *integral* and *cohesive* unity, we applied a progressive sequence of different analytical approaches aimed at giving us a clearer, more comprehensive picture of the compositional organization of the book in its entirety. We observed that while this work follows the pattern of the prophetic corpus as a whole; it is considerably more complicated rhetorically and more artistically constructed than is often supposed. The simple dialogic arrangement which appears on the surface of the text masks a discourse that is composed of several integrated syntagmatic and paradigmatically constituted structures. These were found to complement one another as the prophecy unfolds in a mutual reinforcement of its principal theme, which is developed throughout in relation to the unified central core found in 2:4b: Yahweh is invariably just and righteous in his dealings with mankind—but only his righteous and pious people can fully appreciate the significance of that fact or indeed benefit from it in a world that surrounds them with injustice and iniquity on every hand.

From an *analysis* (exegetical interpretation) of the discourse, we moved to a brief consideration of its *synthesis* (applied transmission) as embodied in a contemporary communication of its essential message. How can the plaintive "How long" (1:2) of believers today best be answered on the basis of this short prophetic book? What form should the crucial "revelation" take in translations today "so that a herald [or a communicator of any sort] may run with it" (2:2, NIV) in order to proclaim its meaning just as forcefully to others? One could hardly ask for a more relevant and timely theme, with wickedness seeming to run rampant in a world that often appears to be devoid of divine presence and control. Translators everywhere face the challenge of accurately and effectively trying to convey in a rhetorically heightened, but natural style in their language the substance of what

Yahweh wants all people, the unrighteous as well as the righteous, to know about him personally and about his immutable principles of dealing with the human race—both as Sovereign LORD (3:19) and as merciful Savior (3:2, 18).

This study has merely been able to touch upon a few of the many salient rhetorical features that made Habakkuk such a powerfully persuasive prophecy—the diversity of genres that this short book incorporates, the vivid imagery and dynamic dialogue that distinguishes its development, and the ever-relevant thematic issue that it gives expression to (theodicy). My purpose has been to suggest that some new translational techniques are required in order to convey this ancient text more dramatically to a contemporary audience. The goal is to achieve, where possible, a greater measure of literary functional *equivalence* through the use of local genres and stylistic markers, oral/aural-sensitive compositional techniques, and a typographical format that promotes readability. This will hopefully result in a message that has increased significance with respect to both efficiency of transmission and also effectiveness of communication. In other words, the translated text will prove to be easier to comprehend in terms of content and intent; furthermore, it will produce more of a cognitive and emotive impact that makes it more readily applicable in turn to a believer's life in the 21st century.

As was noted earlier, the issue of current relevance pertains to the *medium* of communication as well as to the message itself. Certainly, a silent reading of the printed text is not the most helpful way to convey such a dramatic discourse, with respect to either its form or its content. An oral-aural presentation, if well composed and executed, would do a great deal to impress the prophet's point more strongly on the listener's mind. And then, what about all of the graphic imagery that contributes so much to one's perception of the ruthless injustice of the destructive Babylonian hordes in contrast to the holy righteousness and omnipotent glory of the saving LORD? To be able to comprehend and appreciate a bit more of this dynamic aspect of Habakkuk's vision, one requires a complete audio-visual production in technicolor, cinemascope, and the highest quality quadraphonic sound. But such details are perhaps best left to the unfettered vision of one's imagination.

Christian communicators are thus engaged in an ongoing, progressive process which involves the transmission of a formally and semantically

8.6 Conclusion—A hush in His presence

diverse, but in essence also an amazingly cohesive, literary-religious text, namely, the Holy Scriptures. This "Bible" presents a vital, life-giving message which continues to have the greatest relevance for all humanity, but especially for God's faithful, believing communities of every age, place, language, and culture—no matter how far they may have progressed technologically (or otherwise?) since the times of canonical composition. Are things that much different in our supposedly enlightened society from the spiritual and moral situation that prevailed during the days of Habakkuk? Indeed, the prophet could be preaching this very same message in pulpits throughout the oppression-ridden earth today:

Destruction and violence are before me;
there is strife, and conflict abounds.
Indeed, the law is paralyzed,
and justice never prevails. (1:3b–4a)

But Yahweh's firm commitment to the preservation of his people remains the same today as it was during the days of Habakkuk. Divine justice will surely prevail, and although an outworking of God's righteous revelation may await his appointed time, it will certainly come without fail (2:3). And in the meantime?—"the righteous continue to live by their steadfast trust" in a righteous, holy LORD—the Rock (צוּר; 1:12b). That is their fundamental philosophy of life now as well as their hope for the future. So as was the case for the prophet of old, the best answer to all of our just questions concerning the issue of theodicy may be simply to stand at our watch in faith as we look to see how Yahweh is going to sooner or later work things out (2:3) according to his good purposes (cf. 1:5). That is Habakkuk's enduring contribution to the theology of faith for the faithful. The most appropriate reaction to whatever mode whereby the message is communicated is that of the prophet himself: Having heard—more clearly perhaps through an oratorical rendition of the Word—the biblical report about Yahweh's wonderful works in behalf of his anointed ones (3:13), one can only respond in steadfast humility and joyful expectation (3:16, 18):

Renew them in our day,
in our time make them known;
in wrath remember mercy...
The Sovereign LORD is my strength! (3:2, 19—NIV)

9

The Drama of Zephaniah:
A Literary-Rhetorical Analysis of a Proclamatory Prophetic Text

9.1 Introduction: What is so "dramatic" about Zephaniah's discourse?

The Hebrew prophetic literature presents some of the most dynamic and dramatic preaching to be found in the Scriptures—intensely personal, pastoral proclamation. The relatively small text of Zephaniah is certainly no exception; in fact, his book offers instances of some of the most powerful hortatory discourse of the entire prophetic corpus. In this chapter, a structure and function oriented analysis is applied in support of the preceding assertion. Thus, the literary-rhetorical nature of the book's textual organization is closely examined with special reference to its prominent poetic features and overall thematic development, including its vibrant oral-aural (oratorical) characteristics. This study emphasizes the skillful manner in which stylistic form is used to effectively shape theological and ethical content in order to dramatize the prophet's message so that it is conveyed with a greater measure of persuasive force. In the final section, I will challenge contemporary translators to communicate the lively dynamics of Zephaniah's discourse in their own language using a similar measure of impact, appeal, and life-shaping relevance.

So why is a new look at the structure of the little book of Zephaniah called for? Zephaniah certainly ranks in the lower half of any popular rating of the twelve prophets as far as recognition or usage goes. Furthermore, its structure is a matter of considerable controversy, as the Hebrew scholar Adele Berlin notes in the introduction to her own commentary on this text (1994:17–19):

> The Book of Zephaniah is a short book, and, aside from the superscription which introduces it, there are no editorial insertions to suggest how it is to be subdivided.... Modern translations and commentaries differ considerably in their subdivision into sections.... The lack of agreement in dividing so small a body of text is truly amazing.

Reliable interpretation of a text normally begins with an accurate reconstruction of its larger organization, for that will influence the subsequent construal of all of the embedded units, thus affecting one's understanding of the discourse as a hierarchically composed whole. I take this whole to encompass the entire book, right down to the individual word units and lexical combinations, for these derive much of their specific sense and significance from the larger structures in which they are implanted. I will not engage in exploring the compositional history of Zephaniah, for "[t]he book as it stands...now presents itself rhetorically and structurally as a unified work (with the possible exception of the superscription) and in its canonical form it was apparently intended to be interpreted as such" (Berlin 1994:20).

During the course of my literary-rhetorical analysis, the salient aspects of its title will be progressively unfolded—that is, how does an artistic, combined with what we might call an "oratorical" (oral-aural oriented), style of composition contribute to a better understanding of the dramatic thematic concepts being expressed? In this effort, I would agree with Berlin that (1994:20):

> [A] prophet's power is in his rhetoric, and words ascribed to a prophet must not be trite or trivial. He must be saying something

9.1 Introduction: What is so "dramatic" about Zephaniah's discourse?

meaningful, and saying it in a manner that will have impact. Many prophets have a similar message, but each expresses it differently. A literary approach tries to get at the distinctiveness of a prophet's rhetoric and to explain how it achieves its impact.

The text of Zephaniah commends itself as a worthwhile object of such a study for the following reasons: (1) its vigorous, continually alternating dialogic construction that features dynamic prophetic sayings in response to equally forceful divine declarations; (2) the vividness and vigor of the language that is used, especially by the persona of YHWH; (3) the undivided attention that the discourse devotes to the theme of the "day of the LORD" and its contrasting punitive and salvific implications for all mankind;[1] and (4) as already suggested, the masterful arrangement of the book as a whole, in which the form of the text makes a significant contribution to its ultimate "meaning" (pragmatic as well as semantic, including the rhetorical qualities of impact, relevance, and appeal).[2]

An accurate construal of the discourse structure is especially important for Bible translators, for in many ways it affects how they will render the original document, that is, its major as well as minor aspects of composition. The relevance of this concern will be noted with respect to such important features as these: perceiving the textual cohesion and thematic coherence of the composition; outlining its overall topical organization; and making precise paragraph and sectional breaks (including where to place section headings). The issue of who is speaking any given passage (i.e., the prophet, God, or someone else) is also crucial, for this influences to a considerable degree how one interprets the rhetorical dimension of any given passage—its sense, significance, implications, and implicatures.[3] After an

---

[1] "The day of the Lord (יוֹם־יְהוָה *yom-Yahweh*) is the central referent around which the final canonical shape of the collected oracles is formed.... 'day of the Lord' or simply 'day' recurs cascade-like or as a thundering avalanche in practically every verse" (Bennett 1996:664).

[2] I do not discuss questions of authorship or date since I have no quarrel with the traditional assumption that this text was authored during the reign of Josiah or its accepted ascription to a prophet called "Zephaniah." The critical nature of the discourse would suggest that it was composed prior to King Josiah's reform movement, after the "Book of the Law" was discovered (2 Kgs 22), i.e., sometime before 622 BCE. I will not engage in debating text-critical issues either since these do not seriously affect the essential aspects of my analysis; for such concerns, consult the latest online edition of the NET Bible (2003).

[3] *Implications* refer to information that is linguistically implied, but not overtly expressed by an oral or written text (e.g., "Do not take away my soul along with sinners; [do not take away] my life with bloodthirsty men"—Ps 26:9, NIV). *Implicatures* refer to unstated information derived from the contextual setting that permits the correct interpretation of a certain linguistic utterance (e.g., with dark clouds on the horizon and thunder in the background, A says, "It's

extended overview of the form and function of the original text, I conclude by offering some suggestions as to how a manifold discourse analysis of this nature can assist translators in their effort to represent the closest functional equivalent of that same text today in a different language, culture, and communicative setting.

9.2 Overview: The dialogic structure of the discourse

In any thorough discourse analysis, it is first necessary to look closely at the text itself and try to see what the linguistic forms show about the structure, before considering how this may impact the meaning of the prophecy. Previous studies in prophetic material have identified a number of discourse-marking formulae (see for instance Clark 1992:23; Parunak 1994:499). Some of these occur in Zephaniah also, but in this book they do not seem to stand in a hierarchical relationship with each other, or to be distributed in a clearly patterned overall manner. So it appears that some structuring principle other than, or in addition to, such markers must be sought. In other words, the strongly interactive, semi-dialogic nature of Zephaniah would seem to indicate that like Habakkuk 1–2, it belongs to a proclamatory genre (or sub-genre) within the prophetic Book of the Twelve distinct from that of, say, Haggai or Zechariah.

Thus, the most striking formal feature of Zephaniah is the frequent alternation of first person pronouncements and third person responses. This at once suggests the likelihood of a dialogue or, more accurately, an antiphonal text, with different parts spoken by different participants. Indeed, the exchange is often quite dramatic in terms of both form and content, as will be pointed out especially in my discussion of the rhetorical discourse structure of this book. The obvious candidates as interlocutors are the LORD and the prophet, and there appears no reason to propose any other speakers, except those that have been cited by one of the two primary participants (e.g., in 1:12 and 2:15). Although some of the utterances of the speakers are rather short, others are relatively lengthy, long enough to contain formal

---

time to go home [because it will soon rain]"; B replies, "Yes, let's get going!). Implicatures often involve a "violation" of one of P. Grice's so-called "cooperative maxims" that pertain to the quality, quantity, relevance, and/or manner of communication (e.g., with dark clouds on the horizon and thunder in the background, A says, "What a beautiful day—just perfect for golf!" [violation of quality plus irony]; B replies, "You're right, we'd better postpone our match.").

9.2 Overview: The dialogic structure of the discourse

indications of subdivision. There is the possibility that in some cases an utterance-response pair (or even more than one such pair) may together form an even larger section of discourse structure, for which "paragraph" may not be the most useful label. On the other hand, certain short speech segments seem to interrupt a longer unit (e.g., 1:11), thus complicating the organization, but at the same time manifesting the text in a more dramatic and audience-engaging format.

It seems clearest to present the outline arising from the analysis first and then explain the rationale for these divisions, along with any alternative possibilities, in the more detailed literary-structural text examination that follows.

Superscription 1:1

	YHWH	Zephaniah
Dialogue 1	1:2–6	1:7
	1:8–10	1:11
	1:12–13	1:14–16
	1:17	1:18
Dialogue 2		2:1–5b
	2:5c	2:6–7
	2:8–9	2:10–11
	2:12	2:13–15
Dialogue 3		3:1–5
	3:6–7b	3:7c
	3:8–13	3:14–17
	3:18–20	

The reasons for dividing the text of Zephaniah into three major units, or Dialogues (which just happen to correspond nicely with the traditional chapter arrangement), will be given in the following discussion. In short, I posit principal structural breaks in the text between 1:18 and 2:1 as well as between 2:15 and 3:1, despite the fact that the speaker does not change at these points.

The alternation of speakers within the three Dialogues assumes the following arrangement: In the first (1:2–18) and third (3:1–20) Dialogues, the participants have an equal number of turns, four each in the first, and three each in the third if the attribution of 3:7c to the prophet is accepted, or two each if it is not. In the first Dialogue, the LORD (Yahweh) speaks first, and in the third Dialogue the prophet speaks first. The effect of this alternation is that the LORD has both the opening and closing utterances of the book as a whole. In the second Dialogue (2:1–15), the turns are asymmetrical, with the prophet having four and the LORD having three speeches. Thus, the middle Dialogue is an inversion of the pattern of the whole book, with the prophet having both the opening and also the closing utterances. In terms of the amount of words, the LORD clearly dominates in the first and third Dialogues, while Zephaniah speaks more in the second. In any case, we are obviously dealing with a very dramatically expressed prophecy, one in which the LORD himself enunciates the dominant voice and plays the lead role.

9.3 The rhetorical function of Zephaniah—A literary-structural analysis

9.3.1 Zephaniah as dramatic prophecy

Is Zephaniah a "prophetic drama" or a "dramatic prophecy"? The former proposal (as argued by House 1988:94–116) is intriguing, but unsubstantiated in the literature of Israel and rather too lax in its interpretation of certain aspects of the textual data. The latter, "dramatic" perspective, on the other hand, is evident everywhere in the Hebrew canon, wherever the text is encoded in the form of direct speech. The interpretation of any verbal composition, in particular one that is presented in the form of direct discourse, can benefit from the insights that are afforded by a speech act analysis. In this approach, one carefully examines the specific communicative purpose of the text—what the speech is doing (pragmatically) over and above what the words are actually saying (semantically). Such a functional methodology provides the implicit basis for the following structural survey of Zephaniah. The principal rhetorical implications of this organization will be pointed out more precisely in a later section (9.4).

As a guide to an analysis of the persuasive purpose of a literary text, one relies heavily upon its compositional structure and style.[4] The aim of the

---

[4] As we embark upon this detailed text analysis, the following caveat by Ehud Ben Zvi seems apropos: "There are several possible ways to outline the book of Zephaniah, each pointing to a particular but partial reading that emphasizes certain aspects of the book and de-emphasizes others. These partial readings inform each other, and all together create a meaning much richer than any of them separately" (in Berlin and Brettler 2004:1235).

9.3 The rhetorical function of Zephaniah—A literary-structural analysis

present review of the discourse of Zephaniah is to demarcate its principal textual units into functionally related strophic and oracular segments (with "strophes" being combined to form "oracles",[5] e.g., 1:2–6 = 2–3 + 4–6). This will require a precise formal de-construction of the text so that its purposeful arrangement and movement from beginning to end can be more closely observed. A Literary-Structural (L-S) analysis is carried out by noting delimiting and highlighting features such as these: significant patterns of *repetition* (exact and synonymous), *formulas* of aperture and closure, pronounced *shifts* in terms of form-content-function, and special *concentrations* of literary devices. In a study of this nature one also observes any distinct stylistic usage as a text-marking device, including the positioning of major/minor peaks of extra semantic or pragmatic import.

In the following summary, I call attention to an assortment of major stylistic devices (or discourse markers) of Zephaniah. Essentially, two macro-genres are recognized, largely on the basis of content in relation to assumed function: Divine oracles of judgment present, in the LORD's own words, an indictment of the people's sinfulness and a prediction of punishment in the form of disaster and destruction upon individuals, groups, and nations. Oracles of salvation, on the other hand, vindicate God's faithful people and announce divine blessing and salvation to individuals, groups, and nations (cf. Sweeney 1996:22–25). In Zephaniah we also have a variety of prophetic exhortations, which act as reflective comments or asides for the purposes of explanation, specification, description, personal reaction, and the like. These are regularly inserted in apparent reply to the preeminent utterances of YHWH, even in 2:1–3, which is clearly a response to what the LORD has said in chapter one about his dreadful day of determination.

9.3.2 Discourse markers in Zephaniah

In Zephaniah we find a diverse array of literary features that may be utilized for the purpose of such discourse marking—that is, for both structural *definition*

---

[5] According to Bennett, "[t]he literary form called 'oracle' is the biblical prophets' stock-in-trade. It is the vehicle through which the prophet proclaims the divinely inspired word of God to God's covenanted people.... Although the idiom of the law court was the chief social setting or institutional context of the prophetic oracle of judgment or that of promise, language of priestly ritual and wisdom advice was also borrowed to drive home the statement of charges and impending judgment" (1996:662–663).

(i.e., text organization, or disposition) and also rhetorical *punctuation* (i.e., text argumentation or persuasion). These include the following stylistic techniques, which are common to the prophetic corpus as a whole:

> Graphic, evocative imagery (e.g., 1:5, 8–9, 10–11, 12–13, 15; 2:6–7, 14; 3:3, 5, 19)
> Local reiteration of key terms (e.g., "sweep"—1:2, "earth/human"—1:3, "day"—1:7–2:4)
> Quoted discourse (embedded direct speech; e.g., 1:12; 2:15; 3:7)
> Exclamatives and intensifiers—words, phrases, and complete utterances (e.g., 2:5; 3:1)
> Rhythm, wordplay, and other phonic features (e.g., 1:2, 9, 14; 2:2–3, 4, 4–15 [3 + 2 *qinah* meter])
> Imperative and other types of directive speech (e.g., 1:7a, 11a; 3:14)
> Unexpected shifts in form-content-function (e.g., 1.2 [sweepingly sweep away], 1:12, 3:9)
> Enigma and deliberate ambiguity (e.g., 1:3, 5b, 7b, 9; 3:1, 10–11)
> Allusion and intertextuality (e.g., 1:2–3 = > Flood/Creation undone; 3:9–10 = > Babel unbound)[6]
> Irony, hyperbole, and sarcasm (e.g., 1:7, 12–13, 15–18 [cf. House 1988:51–2, 66]; 3:8)

In addition, the preeminent device of extended, or displaced, repetition may also be employed in a diagnostic way within a text to highlight the boundaries of larger discourse units. These range from the strophic level (i.e., a poetic structure consisting of a number of conjoined bicola, analogous to a paragraph in prose) to that of a distinct oracle (a combination of strophes having a distinct theme and rhetorical function) and even larger prophetic units, i.e., a conflation of related oracles.[7] There are several types of such demarcative parallelism, all of which are found in Zephaniah (and pointed out in the structural summary that follows in 2:3). These may be defined and represented in formulaic terms as follows:

> **Inclusio** (aX [Y, Z], a¹) There is a significant recursion of form, content, and/or function (a) at the beginning and ending of a recognized discourse unit (X), which may or may not be composite in nature (+/-Y, +/- Z). [Note: a "discourse unit" is an integral structure at the level of the "paragraph/strophe" or higher.]

---

[6] Periodically the blessings and curses of Deut 28 resonate within Zephaniah's prophetic words, e.g., 1:13 = > 28:30; 3:30 = > 28:1; cf. 26:19.

[7] A distinct term for the sub-unit is required because a "strophe" is more formally marked in its structure than the typical prosaic paragraph, where often content is enough to delimit its outer boundaries.

Exclusio	(ya, X, a'Z) In this case, the relevant recursion (a) occurs at the end of one unit (y) and at the beginning of another (Z), thus enclosing or circumscribing a distinct unit in the middle (X).
Anaphora	(aX, a'Y, [a'' Z]) Here the recursion comes at the beginning of distinct discourse units, at least two but sometimes more in number; they may be non-consecutive.
Epiphora	(Xa, Ya', [Za'']) The focal recursive item (a) is now found at the end of distinct, consecutive or non-consecutive discourse units.
Anadiplosis	(Xa, a'Y) The salient recursion occurs at the end of one unit and the beginning of the next distinct discourse unit.
Chiasmus	(abc...X...c'b'a') The recursive items are found in inverse order at the end of the same discourse unit; a strict chiasmus consists of only four consecutive elements (abb'a'), while a concentric *ring* structure consists of just three (aba').
Terrace	(ab, b 'c, c'd, d'e...) This is essentially an extended pattern of *anadiplosis*, although it normally occurs within the same larger discourse unit.
Reflection	(abcd..., a'b'c'd'...) This is a parallel sequential image set in which the same inventory of recursive elements occurs in the same order within two distinct discourse units.

Contrary to what these formulas might suggest, the units of discourse cannot always, or even as a rule, be posited unambiguously. Thus, the same data, even exact repetition, may be interpreted differently, depending on where and with what they co-occur in the text. Therefore, other prominent markers, such as typical unit-initial transitions, exclamations, vocatives, and imperatives to signal an *aperture,* are often needed to support one structural construal as being more probable or plausible than another (realizing that absolute certainty is impossible in any case).

9.4 Overview of the L-S organization of Zephaniah

Two larger levels of internal structure are indicated below by the degree of indentation: clusters and strophes: A *cluster* consists of two or more closely related strophes, whether attributed to the LORD in direct speech (an oracle) or to his prophet (a proclamation). A *strophe,* the lesser (more indented) unit, is the equivalent of a poetic paragraph, usually consisting of from two to four closely related bicola (analogous to the relative number of lexical units in the typical poetic line, or colon). The general breakdown of the book into three macro-sections (Dialogues) is assumed; the boundaries of seven included strophic clusters are indicated by means of dotted lines.

Verses	L-S Structural Markers
1:1	This is a variant of the standard prophetic discourse introduction (i.e., "aperture," an instance of structural *anaphora* on the intertextual level)—the divine word or messenger formula (cf. Jer 1:4; Hos 1:1; Mic 1:1). There must be some reason for the extraordinary length of the prophet's genealogy here, but there is nothing that we can discern in the text itself. In rhetorical terms, it must have had to do with establishing the prophet's *ethos* at the very outset of his message on behalf of the LORD. Three of the prophet's ancestors incorporated the name of YHWH within their own names. The fact that Zephaniah was of royal blood (the renowned, God-fearing King Hezekiah) would certainly enhance his credibility and authority—hence also the reliability of his prophetic proclamation.

1:2–6   This dramatic opening to Zephaniah's "word of the LORD" against the world of the "wicked" (3b) is distinguished by being constructed in the form of a concentric "ring structure" consisting of 7 sub-strophic segments: A – A' – A'' // C // B – B' – B''. The core (C) of this purposeful arrangement (the first strophic cluster) is the unsettling revelation that Judah/Jerusalem also stands under the LORD's universal condemnation (4a; cf. Amos 2:4–5). Three distinct sets of affected parties are arranged on each side of the center. In the case of group A, each set begins with a verb denoting total destruction, i.e., "I will completely sweep away"—"I will sweep away" + "I will sweep away"—"and I will cut off" (vv. 2 + 3a + 3b). Group B begins with "and I will cut off" (i.e., *exclusio* around unit C) and includes three sets of prominent apostates who are dishonoring YHWH in Judah/Jerusalem (vv. 4b + 5 + 6).

    1:2–3   Strong internal lexical and phonological cohesion unifies this initial strophe, the general, all-inclusive one—even "birds" and "fish!" Key repeated creation-reversing concepts are: "I will sweep away," "man/ground," "from upon the face of" (the last forming an *inclusio*—2b/3c). Closure is marked by the formulaic "oracle of YHWH" (reiterated from 2b).

    1:4–6   The second strophe leads off with a distinctive aperture: "And I will stretch out my hand against..." This is reinforced by the reiterated "and I will cut off" (4b, cf. 3c—*anadiplosis*), coupled with mention of the specific nation affected, the rhetorically focal "Judah" (4a). Internal connectivity is generated by the recurrent mention of various syncretistic practitioners (all designated as the object of *hikratti*

9.4 Overview of the L-S organization of Zephaniah

by the syntactic marker *'eth*). End stress is created by the twofold mention of "LORD," coupled with two occurrences of an overt negative particle *(lo')*.

1:7–18   An emphatic interjection (the ritual invocation *has* "hush!") initiates the second strophic cluster of the book (cf. Hab 2:20), which acts as a confirmatory message of judgment to the first. It is further defined strophically by the first mention of, and then repeated reference to, "the day of the LORD" ("day" in vv. 7, 10, [12 = "time"], 14–16, 18). The rhetorical function of this section is to further build the indictment against the people of Judah by introducing the cosmic motif of the apocalyptic day (7), coupled with a listing of more of the religious (8–9) and social (10–13) sins that brought God's judgment upon the whole land. This lays the thematic foundation (rhetorical motivation) for the prophetic appeal (2:1–3) that leads off the next major dialogue section; it "serves as the premise by which the prophet demands a decision from the audience" (Sweeney 2000b:498).

After the initial, ironic priestly pre-sacrificial invitation that introduces the almighty "sovereign LORD" (*'adonay* YHWH), the first half of this divine oracle (7–13) is clearly structured into four strophes of unequal length. This is effected by means of the anaphoric reiteration of the discourse opener "and it shall be" in 8, 10, 12, 13 (cf. the skewed arrangement of Dorsey 1999:311). The strophic midpoint of this first half is punctuated by a taunting prophetic call in 11.

Onset of the second half of this strophic cluster (14–18) is signaled by an instance of structural *anaphora* in the repeated key phrase "the day of YHWH is near" (14a, cf. 7a). There is obvious heightening in this section, perhaps suggested already at its beginning by the attribution of "great" and "(coming) very quickly" to "day." There is also an ironic anaphoric contrast in the mention of "sound, voice, cry" (*qol*, cf. v. 10 and the "silence" of v. 7).

The sub-unit is divided into two by the introduction of a segment of divine speech (17) at the end of the prophet's apocalyptic description of the horrors that will be manifested on "the day." We find here a shocking juxtaposition of images—terrestrial and celestial, historical and cosmic, particular and universal, of light and darkness (e.g., vv. 12a, 15b)—all to make the prophet's prediction all the more memorable. A twofold iteration of a "sudden, complete consummation" (*te'akel kal-...kalah...nivalah,* alliterative wordplay) of the whole earth at the end brings this mixed (prophet ⇔ YHWH) pronouncement of judgment to a fiery, exclamatory conclusion. The reference to the total destruction of mankind is also an epiphoric recall of 1:3b. The thematic macro-construction of this cluster reverses that of the first, i.e., (1) general (world, 2–3) => specific condemnation (Judah, 4b–6); (2) specific (7–13) => general condemnation (14–18). Even the people's "gold" *zehabam* (18) will become part of the LORD's total "sacrifice" *zebah* (7–8, ironic *inclusio*).

1:7 A distinct speech act by the prophet in response to YHWH's announcement of punishment for the idolaters of Judah/Jerusalem (vv. 4–6) begins a series of judgment (crime and consequence) oracles concerning what will come to pass on the day of the LORD. This ironic aperture (i.e., generically a call to worship)[8] is distinguished by the initial exclamation, by the formulaic expression "for the day is near", and by a threefold mention of the divine name YHWH.

1:8–9 This is the first segment of the compound "day of the LORD" oracle, each of which begins: "And it shall be on [the] day..." (i.e., *anaphora*). This unit also refers to "on that day" near its close *(inclusio)* and features a double mention of YHWH's authoritative action, "and I will punish". Alliteration in /m/ highlights a climactic pejorative ending to this strophe, which is colored by intense dramatic irony: the sacrificial animals to be offered to the LORD (7) are none other than the human "fat" of the land, the elite among God's own rebellious and spiritually syncretistic people (8–9). The invited, "consecrated" *(hiqdish)* guests to this cultic celebration would be the unnamed heathen enemies who will carry out a great slaughter on behalf of the great High Priest. Thus he, *'adonay* YHWH (7), would surely punish all those who were presently serving so many false "masters" (*'adonehem,* 9).

1:10–11 This strophe begins with a word of YHWH and ends with a comment by Zephaniah (11). However, it is held together as a discourse unit through repetition of the verb "wail" (no more "silence!", v. 7) and by common reference to another specific class of people who will be affected by God's imminent punitive action, namely, the wealthy merchant-trading community of Jerusalem. This included "Canaanites," obviously a term with more than one meaning in Zephaniah: here "they were people of the LORD, but in business they had become [no better than pagan] Canaanites!" (Motyer 1998:920). The wailing here perhaps foreshadows their ultimate end (2:4).

1:12–13 A slight formulaic variant marks the start of this strophe (i.e., from "day" to "time"), as the LORD resumes his oracle against Jerusalem. The opening image is ominous: in contrast to the ancient Greek philosopher, Diogenes, who searched the great city of Athens with a lamp to seek out a single honest man, a vividly personified YHWH will examine his city "with lamps" to eliminate all the skeptical and boastful, seemingly self-made men. In parallel with the LORD's comment in v. 11, the prophet utters another reflective aside in v. 13. This is a "prediction

---

[8] The onomatopoeic imperative *has* "presupposes the setting of the Temple, and apparently functions as a call to silence in preparation for some liturgical representation of YHWH's action in the world.... [T]he cultic action of sacrifice represents YHWH's intentions to bring judgment against those who have acted improperly [in violation of his covenant]" (Sweeney 2000b:504, my added comment is in brackets).

9.4 Overview of the L-S organization of Zephaniah

of frustration" in fulfillment of some of the covenantal "futility curses (cf. Lev 26:25, Deut 28:29–30) that directly responds to the sacrilegious quote of the intoxicated and idle rich at the end of v. 12. We note again the significant sonic structure: the rhythmic sequence of final /m/ sounds reinforces their undoing. Their entire existence has been thoroughly cursed by the very One whom they utterly disregard, and so they will never profit from any of life's endeavors, no matter how basic (13).

1:14–16 The pronounced aperture that begins this segment has already been noted.[9] The unit presents a graphic, eschatologically toned description of the terrors that will occur on "the day" *(dies irae)* as YHWH the righteous Divine Warrior metes out his frightful justice. This key temporal term is reiterated nine times to form an elaborate instance of an overlapping, cumulative terraced construction that spans the second half of this strophe. The atmosphere is that of creation undone as the repeated "days" of the LORD's activity bring only deeper darkness and greater fear, even for mighty armies (the military motif recurs at the beginning and end of this strophe).[10] These frightful terms also appear in other theophanic texts of the Old Testament (e.g., Am 5:18–20, Isa 24:21–23, Eze 32:7–).

1:17–18 The awful impact of the climactic day's events upon a wicked world are graphically portrayed to make a powerful, hence very memorable visual impression that affects the entire sensorium. In an apparent continuation of the discourse that was broken off at the end of v. 13, the divine "I," agent of all the predicted destruction, is reintroduced with a narrative construction at the onset of v. 17. This is immediately and rather unexpectedly followed (roughly in the middle of the section 14–18) by a simple statement of the reason *(kiy)* for this comprehensive punishment that will be meted out upon them all: "they sinned against YHWH." The LORD's fiery, angry judgment is given a universal scope—affecting "the whole land"—as this lengthy strophic cluster (as well as the first "Dialogue") is brought to an all-inclusive end (cf. 1:2–3, *inclusio*).

---

[9] Motyer (1998:917) feels that the expression "the day of the LORD is near" marks an *inclusio,* and hence extends this section to include v. 14a. This does not seem to fit the facts of the actual discourse structure very well. Such skewing, however slight, is a common occurrence in analyses that depend too heavily on the delimiting function of a single device, the *inclusio*. By utilizing the additional demarcative forms of *anaphora* and *epiphora* (among others) in conjunction with other recognized structural markers, I hope to offer a more nuanced perspective on the organization of prophetic texts.

[10] Other possible echoes to reflect un-creation include *'ebrah* (cf. *'ereb* Gen 1:5 and elsewhere), *hoshek* (15, cf. Gen 1:2, 5, 6) *mar* (cf. *merahepet* Gen 1:2), *teru'ah* and *he'arim* (cf. *raqia'* Gen 1:6, 7, 8), *sho'ah umeshu'ah* (cf. *deshse' 'esheb* Gen 1:11), *haggadol* (cf. *haggedol(im)* Gen 1:15, 16), *'al hapinnot* (cf. *'al pene* Gen 1:2).

2:1–3   This brief strophic cluster (consisting of just seven bicola) occurs both dramatically and also rather unexpectedly in the prevailing sequence of judgment passages (note also the lack of any direct semantic or syntactic connection with 1:18). It is a pronounced hortatory text, the "basic exhortation address" of the book (Sweeney 2000b:510), in contrast to the preceding proclamatory material. This prophetic speech gives the first indication—a limited "perhaps" (v. 3b)—in the text that any hope of averting the imminent universal disaster is possible, namely, through the gathering of a public convocation of corporate repentance. It answers the crucial theological question: What can we do to be "covered up" (s-t-r, 3d; cf. Lev 17:11) in the day of disaster? Answer: "Seek" (b-q-s) the LORD in keeping with his covenantal requirements—that is, justice + righteousness + humility (cf. Deut 10:12–20).

This centrally placed rhetorical unit gives evidence of an internal bifid structure consisting of two short strophes in parallel (vv. 1–2 and 3). Each of the text internal bicola begins with the letter /b/ in Hebrew, with three instances of *beterem* and three of *baqqeshu* on either side of the midpoint between the two strophes. Both units begin with a liturgical imperative (i.e., *anaphora*) and end with a pointed reference to "the day of the wrath of YHWH" (i.e., *epiphora*). However, the overt addressees for these segments contrast markedly: The first characterizes the shameful majority (v. 1), the second, a humble minority (the righteous remnant, v. 3; cf. v. 7).

Thus, as was the case with the prominent opening cluster of Dialogue One, so also the cluster that begins Dialogue Two features some elaborate lexical patterning (cf. Motyer 1998:926). Such oratorical discourse construction is not simply artful or gratuitous; it is also thematically purposeful (helping hearers to focus upon the key issues) as well as being an effective mnemonic device in a primarily oral-aural society.

    A   General *summons* to assemble—the whole insipid nation (1)
        B   Three specific *grounds* for urgency ("before..."; 2a-c)
        B'   Three specific *commands* for action ("seek..."; 3a-c)
    A'   General *motivation*—a "possible" hope for the "humble" (3d)

2:1–2   Considerable lexical repetition defines the boundaries of this strophe and gives it inner cohesion: "gather yourselves together." The reiterated verb *q-s-s* refers to the gathering of "straw," *qas*, for burning (note the initial irony and anaphoric phonic reinforcement, cf. 1:2). There is also an intensive recursion of the concepts "before" (3x), "it comes upon you" (2x), and "the anger of YHWH" (2x).

2:3   Selective lexical recurrence is also a prominent feature of this short strophe, which encapsulates the theological heart of the entire book. These words forcefully as well as poetically specify the action as well as the attitude that is required of the truly penitent: worshipfully "seek" (3x) YHWH (cf. 1:6), who is righteousness and humility

9.4 Overview of the L-S organization of Zephaniah

personified (2x). For this is how he also wants his people to be—and there is no time to waste!

2:4-15   The fourth strophic cluster leads off emphatically with a consequential, explanatory *kiy* "to be sure",[11] which clearly links it with the preceding hortative unit.[12] Here we have a most pressing reason for the audience to "seek the LORD"—their closest neighbors (and possibly also political allies at this time) were about to be devastated by YHWH due to their wickedness. Could the people of Judah then be far behind? Here was clear evidence that that day of the LORD destined to punish sin was no joke; this would soon become evident on their very doorstep. The unstable history of the region should have taught them that any military conflict involving both Egypt and Assyria was bound to affect Judah.

This section follows a familiar prophetic pattern, belonging to the topical genre known as oracles against the [pagan] nations. The wrath of the LORD against wickedness on his chosen day of judgment will encompass the entire world. Each of the four major sections of this set has particular reference to a geographical area that lies in a different (idealized) direction from Judah: Philistia (4–7, *west*); Moab/Ammon (8–11, *east*); Cush (12, *south*); Assyria (13–15, *north*). "The number four, linked with the four cardinal points of the compass, is a motif for coverage of the whole earth" (Motyer 1998:931). The predominant metrical rhythm of this entire section is 3 + 2, often referred to as the *qinah* "lament" pattern, which is appropriate to the message. Zephaniah is the principal speaker and the LORD enters the discourse briefly to reinforce this prediction of destruction (i.e., vv. 5c, 8–9, and 12).

---

[11] *kiy* normally indicates that what follows in the text is a direct *consequence* of what has just been stated. At times this consequence is so crucial to the structural and thematic development of the larger discourse that a meek "for" does not give the necessary impact (at least not in English). For this reason, translations often render the connection more dynamically (i.e., as an asseverative, e.g., "indeed, surely"), thus leaving the causal linkage implicit.

[12] Those who interpret the *kiy* as closely conjunctive "for" link v. 4 grammatically and logically with v. 3 "as an illustration of the fate awaiting wayward Judah" (Bennett 1996:685). This is certainly a possibility, for the following unit would then begin more naturally with an initial "Woe!" accompanied by a vocative (5). However, the concluding nature of the final utterance of v. 3 (closure) coupled with the shift in topic ("shameful nation"/Judah = > Philistine city-states) and elaborate sonic and metaphoric structure of v. 4 also allows for a break between the two. Thus, verse four's staccato rhythm along with alliteration, punning, and a chiastic phonology all connected with the four city names, the abandoned wife imagery underlying the four associated verbs, as well as its obvious semantic connection with what follows—the "Kerethite people"—leads me to posit v. 4 as an independent segment—a "Janus"-type passage that may be connected both with what has gone before it and also what comes after. There is the possibility that it was shifted out of its expected (oral) position in order to create a special effect. Thus, Roberts suggests "that Zeph 2:4 has been transposed from its original position [i.e., after 5b] as a part of the *hoy*-oracle in order to create a bogus link with 1:2–2:3" (1991:196; my addition in brackets). The link surely is not "bogus," however; 2:4ff. provides the rhetorical motivation for the forceful appeal which has just been made in 2:3.

2:4   The intensely poetic character of this verse, involving parallelism, ordered naming,[13] multiple paronomasia, condensation, figurative language, and enigma, calls immediate attention to its special rhetorical function in the discourse, namely as a distinct structural and thematic bridge. The unit is linked semantically to what follows, but there is a formal barrier that also isolates it, namely, the initial "woe" *(hwy)* of v. 5, which is a diagnostic marker of a discourse aperture *(anaphora)*.

2:5–7   The initial "woe" is an obvious verbal harbinger of disaster; it immediately cues the audience in on the nature of the discourse to come. Zephaniah utters most of this first strophe against the land of the "Kerethites" (Philistia), with just a snatch of direct speech by the LORD (5c) to dramatically mark the boundary as it were between the two constituent strophes. The second (6–7) makes a surprising response to the preceding message (4 + 5ab), effectively transforming the overall connotation and implication from negative to positive in a word of blessing for "the remnant of the house of Judah" (7a).[14] The two contrastive units are linked by common mention of "land of the sea," "Kerethite[s]," and "Ashkelon." Their respective endings feature contrastive *epiphora*: complete destruction for the Philistines (5b) as opposed to a "restoration of the fortunes" of Judah (7b).[15] Thus, a nation of "shepherds" will replace those who lived by the "sea."

2:8–11   YHWH again leads off by announcing the first strophe (vv. 8–9), while Zephaniah concludes this oracle against Moab and Ammon (vv. 10–11). The two strophes are conjoined through the occurrence of some key vocabulary at the beginning of each one (i.e., *anaphora*): "insult" and "taunt" (vv. 8 and 10). Strophe One features an emphatic self-reference to the divine speaker: "Therefore, as I live, utterance of YHWH of Hosts, God of Israel, surely..." on the border of the shift from indictment (8) to punishment (9a). "YHWH of Hosts" is also mentioned in the second strophe (10b), which begins with a foregrounded anaphoric demonstrative "This..." *(zo'th,* 10a), pointing

---

[13] "[T]he order of the Philistine cities is Zeph 2:4 is significant, in that they are presented in the order that one would encounter them from south to north, i.e., from the direction of Egypt [moving towards Assyria, the principal world aggressor of the age]" (Sweeney 2000b:514). This south to north direction would actually have been the direction taken by Pharaoh Neco in 609. Sweeney also provides a good summary of the punning that is involved with these four names (ibid., 513).

[14] "As so often in the Old Testament, and not least in Isaiah and Zephaniah, the note of hope is sounded unexpectedly" (Motyer 1998:932–933). While such dramatic suddenness ought to be reproduced in a Bible translation, it also should be clear to receptors that the connotation and implication of the text has thus shifted from woe to weal. An additional discourse marker or two may be necessary in the TL in order to prevent any misunderstanding.

[15] The attempt to make a chiastic arrangement can at times obscure a more satisfactory construal of the organization of a given prophetic unit. For example, the chiasmus proposed by Dorsey 1999:312) appears to put special emphasis only upon the destruction of Philistia (5c).

9.4 Overview of the L-S organization of Zephaniah

back at the judgment that has just been announced. "This" also links the preceding with the underlying reason for the LORD's condemnation—namely, "pride" (*ge'onam,* in contrast to the attitude enjoined in 2:3). Strophe Two culminates in a blessed prediction of awesome implications—this time for nations of the entire earth (11b), not only the remnant of my people (9b, i.e., augmentative *epiphora*).

2:12 What could be the point and purpose of this oracular fragment, as it seems? The LORD (my sword) is clearly speaking these words, which are marked by heavy consonance (from final /m/ to initial /ch/). Scholars wonder what to do with this "seemingly intrusive mention of Ethiopia" (Dorsey 1999:312; literally "Cush"—NE Africa by metonymy), but this place is clearly required in the locative scheme of the careful arrangement of this set of oracles—i.e., a reference to the south. There could also be an element of contrastive foreshadowing, as Cush is the only one of these nations that is mentioned later, namely, in the positive half of the oracle that is found in 3:8–10 (3:10a; there is also a prominent *Cusi* listed in Zephaniah's genealogy, 1:1). Furthermore, this short segment of divine speech combines "three characteristic aspects of the day of the Lord theology:… There is a threefold 'no-escape': no escape for any people, no escape from the wages of sin, no escape from divine confrontation" (Motyer 1998:936).

2:13–15 Zephaniah himself has the honor of predicting the utter ruin of Assyria and its capital Nineveh—probably a case of saving the *worst* till last. Significantly perhaps (cf. vv. 9–11), the LORD is not even mentioned at all, perhaps as a foretaste of the rhetorically motivated ambiguity that is about to enfold Jerusalem in the same net of judgment as Nineveh (2:15–3:1). However, there can be no doubt as to whose "hand" is being "stretched out" in various acts of judgment "against the north" (v. 13a; cf. 15c, *inclusio* with "his hand"— see also 1:4, *anaphora*).[16]

A portrait of complete desolation, like a desert scenario, unifies the first strophe (13–14), including a masterful juxtaposition involving tokens of nature with a ruined urban setting (14b). What a shocking visual contrast that must have presented, especially for those in Zephaniah's audience who had actually seen (or even heard about) the magnificent Nineveh of that day. Strophe Two leads off with another spotlighted "This…" (cf. v. 10a, *anaphora*) coupled with

---

[16] Motyer argues that the full jussive force of the initial verb *(weyet)* ought to be rendered in translation: "and, oh, may he stretch." "It is as if Zephaniah were himself caught up in the divine program and was urging it on to completion. Note the same excited prophetic involvement in Zechariah 3:5…" (1998:936). Such an interpretation would certainly fit the dramatic perspective that I have adopted with regard to the discourse of Zephaniah. It is little stylistic touches like this, and there are many of them, that make his prophecy such a memorable and rhetorically moving message, one that is designed to make a strong impression upon the ear as well as the heart.

intensive adjective "exultant" *('allizah)*. Vividly contrastive utterances and images that summarize Nineveh's chief sin (rampant pride, contra 2:3) and her downfall distinguish the second strophe (15). We note in particular: a boastful attributed quote of self-ascribed divinity (15b); the prophet's exclamation of what the city will become (a wasteland of "ruin," 15c); and some final climactic gestures of defiant condemnation on the part of passers by (perhaps former captives and victims, 15d). Indeed, the popular joy and celebration that accompanied Assyria's shameful demise should have included the people of Judah (i.e., a curse upon my enemy is a blessing for me), but as the next oracle indicates, with considerable shock effect, this would not be the case.

3:1–7 This strophic cluster, the fifth, which begins the third and final Dialogue section of the book, assumes the shape of an A-B-A' ring structure: The two [A] segments are additional declarations of condemnation, first upon the "city" of Jerusalem (implied), then (A') universally upon "all nations" with a final implicit reference to Jerusalem again (v.7). In the center (B, v. 5) we find a word in defense of the LORD's righteousness and just judgments.[17] The initial exclamative *hoy* both initiates a major new unit and suggests a significant continuity with what has gone before (cf. 2:5, *anaphora*), namely, the oracles against the nations. The prophet plays with a certain measure of enigma here as part of his persuasive rhetorical technique.[18] This draws his audience into the discourse, and before they know it, they are mentally entrapped to face the LORD's incriminating charge directly: "in YHWH she (the city of Jerusalem) trusts not!"

3:1–4 At first hearing, the characteristic warning of woe would seem to be directed against the same pagan city that was mentioned in the preceding strophe, namely, Nineveh (2:15; cf. 2:13).[19] As the strophe progresses, however, it is clear that, instead, the rebellious, defiled, and oppressive (1a) city of Jerusalem is being addressed with this ironic indictment by the prophet. This dramatic revelation (an instance of intratextual recursion, cf. 1:4–6, 2:1–3) is reinforced when

---

[17] Dorsey (1999:312) proposes another chiastic arrangement for this section; unfortunately, this structure is rather skewed or unsupported in its suggested topical parallels and hence on the whole misleading.

[18] Sweeney calls attention to several other aspects of the terminology used to characterize the "city" in verse 1 that is potentially ambiguous, thus suggesting a double entendre which would captivate the audience (2000b:519–520). "Like Amos, Zephaniah uses the rhetorical device of condemning surrounding nations, but all the while—unannounced to his hearers—bringing their own condemnation ever closer" (Motyer 1998:941). Ehud Ben Zvi puts it well: "This type of ambiguity shows the artistry of the book's composition and also points to the use of ambiguity as a rhetorical device to capture the readers' attention, and then lead them to a central issue: the identity and main characteristics of the city" (in Berlin and Brettler 2004:1240).

[19] Fee and Stuart point out that the initially disguised oracle against Jerusalem extends for nine poetic lines, just like the invectives against each of the preceding nations, all except for the short segment incorporating Cush in v. 12 (2002:250–251).

9.4 Overview of the L-S organization of Zephaniah

YHWH is referred to as being actually "within her" (5a). Along with secular leaders (3), even the holy men of God (prophets and priests) are totally corrupt as they profane the sanctuary and violate the law (4, = negative end stress upon a cluster of key theological terms). Because she paid no heed to the divine "voice" *(qol)* of "correction" *(musar)* (2), Jerusalem would soon hear the "bitter" *(mar)* "voice" of the "warrior" *(gibbor)* YHWH on a day of distress (1:14, distant structural *anaphora*).

3:5 It is indeed a surprise to find the "righteous YHWH" (juxtaposed initially both for emphasis and to mark a unit aperture) in the very midst of so much corruption and shameful evil. The striking spiritual contrast that is forged here by the prophet is highlighted by other reiterated items from verse 3: "judges/judgment" + "in the morning." Here we have a wonderful prophetic confession of the constant (morning by morning) upright nature of YHWH and the justice of all his works, qualities that are highlighted in contrast to the shameful deeds of the unrighteous leaders of Jerusalem. By way of anticipation, this distinctly faith-confessional strophe lays the groundwork for later thematic development in 3:8ff.

3:6–7 Seemingly in response to the prophet's testimony (5b) about dispensing "his justice" *(mishpato)*, YHWH breaks in here (I) with his own declaration concerning destruction ("cutting off"—a perfect of certainty) for all godless nations, including all their cities (v. 6, with much lexical recursion; cf. 1:3–4, 16; 2:5). Once more, the focal city (implied) of Jerusalem is tarred with the same brush of severe condemnation (7b). This is because they defiantly continue to act corruptly (7c) despite the LORD's personal appeal, in a self-quote intensified by the exclamative *'ak*, to "accept correction" (7a). The term "correction/instruction" *(musar)*, borrowed from the didactic rhetoric of the wisdom school, helps to forge a rough *inclusio* with the beginning of this oracle (v. 7, cf. 2), while the verb "cut off" *(k-r-t)* forms a similar inclusive boundary with the beginning of the book (3:6–7 = > 1:3–4).

This unit-concluding strophe also reflects the book's central appeal of 2:1–2 in several key respects: first and foremost, the LORD's passionate desire for his people's repentance, God's fiery anger against covenantal infidelity, and the certainty of a thorough destruction of all the unrighteous in accordance with the judgment curses of the Law. He would surely visit them with punishment (note a prominent epiphoric contrast with the same verb *p-q-d*, used in the sense of a positive "visitation" in 2:7). Would the intended audience listen? The prophet himself is skeptical, as we hear in a final brief and pessimistic comment, initiated by the contrastive particle *'aken*. Indeed, "all" *(kol)* the people's evil deeds seem to keep calling for "all" of the LORD's just deserts.[20]

3:8–13   This complex strophic cluster is thematically diverse, but unified as well as segmented by means of renewed references to the day of the LORD (last directly referred to in 2:3): "on the day" (8a), "then" (9a), and "on that day" (11a, all instances of structural *anaphora*). Each of the three oracles that comprise this unit is uttered directly by YHWH, who begins with a dramatic call to attention: "Therefore wait for me, oracle of the LORD..." That a new section begins here is intimated by the attention-calling initial conjunction *laken*, which "indicates that YHWH's future actions follow as a consequence from those outlined in verses 6–7" (Sweeney 2000b:522). Normally, this particle introduces "a pronouncement of divine punishment based on a preceding accusation of wrong" (Motyer 1998:948). But here, the LORD says, somewhat enigmatically, "Wait for me!" But wait for what? In this case, there will be not only the expected meting out of judgment (8), but YHWH will also institute an amazing outpouring of blessing for the faithful (9).

A major unit aperture at v. 8 also suggested by the sudden shift from a particular (Judean) to a universal perspective and scope in terms of the message of condemnation (until a return to the specific national addressees again in v. 11). This compound oracle is unexpectedly interrupted (hence concluded) by a thanksgiving psalm, sung by Zephaniah in response to a wonderful prediction of blessing for the remnant of Israel (v. 13 => 14–17, the psalmic Interlude).

3:8   In this opening strophe of the conjoined set, the LORD solemnly proclaims another judicial "assembly" *(le'ad...le'esop)* of all nations, apparently only to make it easier to pour out his (note the reiterated personal pronoun) just punishment upon the whole world. There is a cohesive sequence of sustained blazing imagery in the second half of this pivotal unit: "my wrath" => "my anger" => "my jealous indignation" (cf. 1:18), as well as intratextual links with a number of other passages (e.g., 1:17; 2:9; 3:15, 19–20). This is coupled with "the harvest terminology of Zeph 1:2 (cf. 1:3; 2:1), [which] aids in conveying the imagery of sacrifice that appears especially in Zeph 1:2–18" (Sweeney 2000b:522).

3:9–10   The onset of this strophe presents us with what is perhaps the most unexpected of the many surprising shifts that punctuate the topical progression of this varied and variable prophecy. It begins (9a) with another emphatic consequential *kiy* "so indeed", which duplicates that of the preceding line (an instance of *anadiplosis*; cf. 2:4, *anaphora*).

---

[20] Motyer calls attention to the progressive build-up in dramatic suspense, initiated in the preceding Dialogue (2:3, 6–7, 9, 11), that is maintained in this section (3:7a-b, 8a)—namely, concerning the possibility of a reprieve, and more, for the penitent (1998:947).

9.4 Overview of the L-S organization of Zephaniah

In this case, the consequence is coupled with the prominent temporal deictic "then" *('az)*, which refers forward to the expression "on that day" of 11a *(anaphora; 'az* is repeated in 11b), and thus arguably also back to the ambiguous time when YHWH calls upon everyone to "wait..." (8a, more *anaphora).* Thus, instead of yet another prediction of punishment for the wicked (which the *kiy* would lead us to expect from v. 8), there will also be an amazing "purification" and a spiritual unification of all peoples (9a).

The initial verb of v. 9 also prepares us for a message of doom, "I will overturn" *(h-p-k),* for it is used in reference to such paradigmatic cases as Sodom (Gen 19:25) and Jonah's Nineveh (Jon 3:4). But here the verb must have a drastically different sense, being coupled as it is with "pure speech" (lit. 'lip') intended to call upon the name of the LORD in worship and joint service shoulder to shoulder. There is a strong allusion here to the complete overturning of the linguistic, ethnic, and religious confusion of Babel (Gen 11:1–9) that will be characteristic of the messianic age (9b; note also the reversal in the connotation of verb "call" compared to 1:7b—contrastive, displaced *anaphora).* This fellowship pointedly (albeit somewhat obscurely in terms of the Hebrew) includes a vivid extreme instance—namely, those worshipers living in far-off Africa (beyond the rivers of Cush—a clear connotative reversal in relation to 2:12; cf. the allusion to Isa 18:1, 7). Zephaniah's rhetoric as well as the subject of discussion is clearly reaching a peak in terms of intensity and salience, as we observe in the pronounced personal pronouns that designate the positive sphere of YHWH's influence (10b, in sharp contrast to their negative correspondents in v. 8).

3:11–13 "In that day" is a clear anaphoric reference to YHWH's ultimate day of reckoning (3:8, 9). The addressee(s) of the present divine strophe are not immediately apparent—not in English that is. In Hebrew, however, the second person feminine singular pronouns of verse 11 would suggest that the inhabitants of a particular city are intended. That this would be Jerusalem is clarified finally by the reference to "my hill of holiness" at the end of the verse.

An internal contrast between the self-righteous proud (11b), whom the LORD will remove, and the spiritually humble (12, cf. 2:3), whom he will renew, provides this strophic unit with cohesive unity, which is given additional lexical substance by a repetition of the root *s-'-r* ("and I will leave behind"... "a remnant of Israel"; cf. 2:7, 9). This select group, including Gentiles (9–10) as well as Jews (11–12) is described in terms of heart-attitude (humility, trust—12), behavior (do no evil—13a), and speech (no lies, deceit—13b; cf. 3:9). As a result (another *kiy* consequential) "they" (emphatic)—the united "remnant of Israel"—will be blessed with a return to Edenic bliss at the divine eschaton (Isa 11:6–9; Ps 23). Surely a powerful motivation, whether for constancy or change, is made by this compelling rhetorical appeal.[21]

3:14–17 YHWH's oracle of salvation (vv. 8–13) is so awesome, so earth shaking in its implications, that his prophet cannot, as it were, contain himself. In Isaianic fashion,[22] Zephaniah suddenly breaks into a standard thanksgiving genre of psalmody (with "royal" overtones) as he exhorts the Daughter of Zion to rejoice in the LORD's gracious attitude and saving activity towards his people. From a linear perspective, there are two strophes that comprise this song of joy (14–15/A-D and 16–17/D'-A'), the latter announced by explicit mention of "that day" of the LORD's judgment/deliverance. Both units highlight the covenantal actions of YHWH.

This sixth strophic cluster of the book gives evidence of a cohesive chiastic lexical and topical arrangement; the joyous, reassuring message for Jerusalem is repeated twice, as it were—first in the words of the prophet, second in reversed order through the direct acclamation of an unnamed source (the nations?):[23]

A—Zion/Israel/Jerusalem is called to sing and rejoice (14)
  B—reason: YHWH's forgiveness and protection (15a)
    C—*King* "YHWH is within you" [city] (15b)
      D—"you will never again fear" (15c)
        E—focus again on "that day" (16a)
      D'—"do not fear" Jerusalem/Zion (16b-c)
    C'—*Warrior* "YHWH is within you" (17a)
  B'—reason: his salvation and love (17b-c)
A'—[YHWH] himself will "rejoice" and "sing" for you [Zion] (17d)

3:14–15 A series of four imperatives and three vocative expressions announce the onset of this initial strophe, which is then taken up with the salvific activities of YHWH (explicitly named twice) on behalf of a Zion/Israel/Jerusalem that is ruled by a messianic King of Israel.

3:16–17 Jerusalem and Zion are again referred to as this strophe begins *(anaphora),* and there are other lexical reduplications as noted in the chiastic structure above, which closely link the two strophes

---

[21] "[T]he exhortational character of the book must be considered, as it aims to convince its hearers or readers that they should be a part of the poor and humble remnant of Israel that will be reestablished in Zion" (Sweeney 2000b:523).

[22] "Zephaniah is nearer in literary spirit and talent to Isaiah than any other prophet" (Motyer 1998:956).

[23] We observe some difference of opinion as to how this chiastic structure is manifested (Baker 1988:87; Dorsey 1999:313; Motyer 1998:956). Readers must test such disparate proposals against the original text, following careful structural controls (e.g., the more *form*-based the arrangement, the more credible the proposal), and come to their own conclusion. There is obviously an underlying organizational pattern here; the question is: how can it best be represented so as to reveal its pertinent contours? On the other hand, some commentators do not recognize this passage as being a distinct psalmic segment at all (e.g., Bennett 1996:702–703).

9.4 Overview of the L-S organization of Zephaniah

that comprise the oracle as a whole. The second might well be considered a "parallel" to the first, a macro-structural equivalent of the A-B parallelism that is found on the utterance level of Hebrew poetic discourse organization. It even manifests the typical "heightening" effect, i.e., "[A] and what is even more, [B]". The "loving" bridal imagery of v. 17 (= > "Daughter of Jerusalem" in v. 14, metaphoric *inclusio*), uniquely coupled with the picture of YHWH as a "mighty Savior," clearly distinguishes this as a major (as distinct from a minor) thematic peak in the book as a whole.

3:18–20   A fronted nominal phrase, "sorrowful ones for/from/because of the appointed feasts," initiates this final strophic cluster (#7). Though difficult to interpret, this expression clearly introduces a provisional conceptual and connotative contrast in relation to the last line of the preceding strophe: "he will rejoice over you with singing" (v. 17d). The LORD resumes his salvation oracle and the beatific vision that was broken off at v. 13 by the prophet's song of praise (i.e., an instance of *exclusio;* "I" refers only to YHWH as speaker in Zephaniah; "you" [fem. sg.] only to the personified Jerusalem). This concluding segment is distinct, however, in that it features a series of eight actions on the part of YHWH to completely deliver his faithful fellowship—five in the first and longer strophe (18–19, note the "perfects of certainty"), three in the second and final strophe (20). The crowded stage that YHWH gathers here within the scope of this reassuring promise of blessing makes it both a rhetorically powerful as well as a theologically fitting conclusion to the book as a whole.

3:18–19   Verse 18 could be viewed as another Janus-like transitional passage, one that has structural connections in both directions, anaphoric as well as cataphoric (cf. 2:4). Thus, were it not for the first person pronoun, it might easily link up with v. 17 as a positive-negative restatement. This would allow the strophe to begin with a clearer aperture, such as is found in 18: "Behold-I...at that time." As the text stands, however (and there seems to be little support for emendation), the verb "I will remove" (18a) definitely initiates the first person action sequence that characterizes this oracle, which also appears to shift in its prevailing setting from the royal court to the priestly cult. This first strophe ends on a minor thematic peak at the end (19c), with the final term "shame" *(b-s-t)* reflecting contrastively with the strophe ending at 3:5 (structural *epiphora*).

3:20   A number of lexical links tie this ultimate strophe to the preceding one, especially to v. 19: "at that time...I will gather...for praise and for a name in every land"; v. 20: "at that time I will gather...for a name and for praise among all the peoples of the earth." These form connections also with other important motifs in the book as a whole, thus distinguishing this unit as a (arguably, *the*) major climax of Zephaniah. There is a prominent recurrence of the notion of a universal "gathering" (*a-s-p*, 20a; cf. 19b and 3:8—*inclusio*), one that encompasses the whole earth (1:2–3/3:19–20—*inclusio*). Another verb for "gather" (*q-b-ts*) overlaps with the end of the preceding strophe (also with 3:8, reinforcing that *inclusio*), along with the temporal marker "at that time" (with reference of course to the "day" of the LORD, cf. v. 16). The minor thematic peak found at the end of v. 19 is heightened here with reference to "my restoring your [pl.] fortunes"—a key eschatological concept throughout the prophetic literature (cf. 2:7). YHWH has the last word in Zephaniah, both literally ("...Yahweh has spoken!") and conceptually (cf. 1:1a—*inclusio*), for the powerful divine Word has been in focus throughout the text. As we have seen, this is as true stylistically as it is semantically in the development of this dramatic defense of his "day."

9.5 Summary of the literary-structural analysis

There are seven composite strophic clusters that appear after the introduction (1:1), not counting an included interlude of praise (3:14–17). These appear to manifest a broadly chiastic thematic arrangement:[24]

→ 1:1 Prophetic <u>aperture</u>
I. 1:2–6 (Jerusalem/Judah destroyed along with all nations for their sin)
  II. 1:7–18 (day of the LORD—punishment of J/J and the whole world)
    III. 2:1–3 (seek the "righteousness" of YHWH within a doomed nation)
      IV. 2:4–15 (judgment of nations to the W + E + S + N)
    V. 3:1–7 (the LORD alone is "righteous" within a corrupt society)
  VI. 3:8–13 (day of the LORD—purification of the nations along with J/J)
→ 3:14–17 (psalmic <u>interlude</u>)
VII. 3:18–20 (Jerusalem/Judah blessed and gathered from among all nations)

Thus, the standardized set of "oracles against the nations" forms a middle structural bridge from the first portion of the book, where predictions of judgment prevail, to the third in which there is a movement towards the surprising message of a blessed future for the faithful remnant of YHWH's covenant people. On either side of the center then are oracles that declare that deliverance is possible—that there is still hope—but only for those

---

[24] See Dorsey (1999:311) for a different macro-chiastic construction and hence also a somewhat different thematic organization for the book as a whole.

9.5 Summary of the literary-structural analysis

who "humbly seek righteousness" (2:3) and "fearfully accept the LORD's correction" (3:7).

In fact, the decision to divide Zephaniah into three progressively unfolding macro-sections, or Dialogues, is supported in terms of the implied answer that is given to a key thematic question: "On the day of the LORD, will there be any hope?" Three different answers are proposed in each Dialogue:

> I—"Not at all!"
> II—"Maybe?"
> III—"Yes indeed!"

After hearing part I (1:2–18), a perceptive audience would conclude that there is absolutely no hope. Everything seems completely dark with despair due to the destruction that is predicted for the whole wicked world. Part II (2:1–15) presents a glimmer of hope at its beginning (i.e., "perhaps," 2:3) and ending, as well as in three passages that clearly single out a human "remnant" for whom things will be different (2:7, 9b, 11). The identity of these people is more fully revealed in part III (3:1–20). They are the humble and righteous few (2:3; 3:12a) who depend on the LORD (3:12b) and who live according to his covenantal discipline (3:7). The third Dialogue overlaps with the second, just as the second does with the first. However, after an initial negative transition (3:1–8), Part III suddenly shifts to a universally positive, salvific and all-inclusive perspective (9–13, 18–20). This incorporates the joyful song (14–17) in celebration of a hope that is not only possible, but also one that has been fully realized as a result of the purifying and protective actions of YHWH.

Structurally marked (e.g., by a chiasm or end stress) and/or artistically highlighted peaks of salience in terms of either judgment/punishment or of blessing/salvation occur periodically throughout this rhetorically arranged progression, even within the darkest of judgment oracles. The following is my tentative proposal (minus [–] = *punishment*, plus [+] = *blessing*); all the positive, favorable or complimentary, peaks are especially foregrounded against the harsh background of the grim judgment oracles that predominate in the first two Dialogues.

1:6 (–), 1:9 (–), 1:13 (–); 2:3 (+), 2:7b (+), 2:9b (+), 2:11b (+), 2:15 (–); 3:5 (+), 3:8 (–), 3:9—10 (+), 3:12—13 (+), 3:17 (+), 3:20 (+)

This cumulative thematic development thus manifests an inexorable movement towards a climactic conclusion, one that is lyrically marked by Zephaniah's penultimate thanksgiving psalm. The relevance of such an artfully constructed text for Bible translators is simply this: These peaks of major structural, semantic, and emotive significance must be made manifest also in the target language translation, along with an adequate representation of the discourse organization outlined above (or some defensible alternative proposal).

9.6 Deconstructing a crux interpretum—2:4

As was noted earlier, at the book's medial compositional hinge we find a Janus-like verse (2:4), that is, a passage which semantically links up in both directions—formally as a consequential conclusion to 2:1–3 and rhetorically as the emphatic onset of strophe 2:4–7. As further evidence of this verse's architectonic importance, we note that it stands at the center of a tripartite discourse unit (2:1–7) that acts as a structural-thematic microcosm of the entire prophecy. Thus, this medial segment (2:4) presents a strong motivation for people to heed the preceding divine warning-appeal (2:1–3) and also functions as the dramatic opening of the LORD's case against all nations in terms that were contextually very real and most relevant to the original audience. In terms of the organization of Zephaniah as a whole then, the following parallels are manifested (following Ball 1987:164):

> **2:1–3** (cf. 1:2–18)—the LORD's warning indictment against the world and Jerusalem/Judah for their sinfulness [parallels: opening double root for "gathering"; "near"-ness of "the day of YHWH"; imagery of burning to represent the LORD's anger; turning towards/from "seeking" YHWH]
>
> **2:4** (cf. 2:8–15)—the LORD's judgment upon the pagan nations stands as a testimony to what could happen to Judah and Jerusalem if the people do not change their behavior [parallels: 4 cities/nations in focus; complete "destruction"/ *lishmamah* of all four; puns on the proper names]
>
> **2:5–7** (cf. 3:1–20)—the LORD's transformation of the situation from utter "woe" to a final restoration for a "remnant" incorporating all nations, including Judah and Jerusalem [parallels:

begin with a "woe"; end with "restore fortunes"; use of key terms in the same sequence; predicted deliverance and restoration of the LORD's "remnant"]

The central, linking position of 2:4 in this crucial structural movement therefore suggests why it causes so much consternation in the ranks of commentators as well as variation among the versions. My proposal has certainly not fully resolved the problem of how to handle this verse hermeneutically, but I hope that the preceding overview at least explains why there is so much scholarly disagreement over it. More positively perhaps, I would simply affirm Ball's conclusion that "a correct understanding of [such] rhetorical features enables us more clearly to understand the meaning of specific words or units and thus the overall meaning of larger [structural] units" (1987:165).

9.7 A rhetorical-argument analysis of Zephaniah

9.7.1 The rhetorical situation

It is difficult to posit a precise historical setting (i.e., the rhetorical exigency) for the prophecy of Zephaniah. That is because, as in the case of the work of his illustrious predecessor, Isaiah, "[t]hroughout the book there is a sense of distance from historical events" (Motyer 1998:899). In any case, it is clear that Zephaniah's prophetic ministry is overtly represented as being carried out "during the days of Josiah, son of Amon, king of Judah" (1:1). It is tempting to suggest then that Zephaniah's messages regarding the need for serious change had a significant influence in the young king's life (cf. 2 Chr 34:3). At any rate, it is highly probable that this prophet did play an important role in the radical Yahwistic reform movement which King Josiah supported, though the evidence of that is not strongly reflected in this text (except perhaps by way of anticipation at the end, 3:8–20). The call for total repentance and spiritual renewal is the thematic kernel that underlies the vigorous prophetic appeals and proclamations of the first two-thirds of the discourse. The glorious results of such a reform movement, when accomplished, act as the motivating force for the salvation oracles of the final third of the book.

9.7.2 A speech-act perspective

The central speech act of any prophetic text is normally a directive *appeal* (prohibition or exhortation) of some sort—that is, for people to repent and refrain from evil or to affirm and follow what is good in YHWH's eyes. This central appeal, or a closely related set of appeals, is regularly prefaced by a simulated judicial indictment that specifies the prophetic *condemnation*. This concerns the underlying spiritual problem—the wicked behavior (moral, social, political, and religious) that made such public reproof and serious warning necessary. In addition, interspersed throughout the typical prophetic text, we also find various types of *motivation* given, both negative (e.g., reminders and threats of divine punishment) and positive (e.g., encouragement, consolation), urging the audience to give heed to the appeal and put it into practice.

Thus, the various general communicative goals and more specific speech acts (each with a particular illocutionary force) that are encoded within a prophetic text's major and minor structural units are all related in one way or another to the following trio of generic macro-functions. These interact in smaller and larger combinations to develop the LORD's line of reasoning (argument) concerning his day of judicial determination and resolution (whether for retribution or renewal).

CONDEMNATION	→	APPEAL	→	MOTIVATION
(1:2–18)		(2:1–3)		(– 2:4–3:8 / + 3:9–20)

As suggested above, the book of Zephaniah appears to follow this simple argumentational dynamic quite closely. The first part of the book (Dialogue I) emphasizes the component of *condemnation*, that is, the LORD's judgment will be meted out upon flagrant wickedness in both the secular and religious segments of any society. The central prophetic *appeal* makes it clear that the only hope for escape or reprieve lay in a penitent seeking of YHWH so that his cleansing action might have its salutary effect in the hearts and lives of those who responded to this entreaty. In the remainder of the book, the LORD through his prophet is concerned to provide sufficient *motivation* to encourage any audience to make the right decision in this regard. *Negative* motivation is present everywhere, every time that the LORD's day

9.7 A rhetorical-argument analysis of Zephaniah 525

of judgment is explicitly mentioned or alluded to. But there is also abundant *positive* motivation for a renewal of the covenant relationship with YHWH. This is highlighted in the eschatological imagery of restoration that is promised to all the humble, those who live their lives in devoted service of their loving Savior-Lord (as stressed in the Interlude of 3:14–17).

There does not appear to be a single central peak of thematic significance in the book of Zephaniah (i.e., in distinction from the obvious hortatory peak of 2:3). Rather, there is a progressive build-up of theological and ethical import throughout the text, climaxing in chapter 3 to reach a final area of *end stress* (3:18–20). This place of closure is preceded and prepared for by a number of major and minor points of special salience along the way (particularly those having a positive implication/blessing), which need to be both interpreted and evaluated as an entire set. Any item that is unexpectedly introduced or made semantically or pragmatically prominent attracts the focused attention of the audience, and as noted above, these passages are structurally and stylistically marked in various ways for the purposes of verbal (especially oral-aural) foregrounding.

9.7.3 The connotative aspect of the discourse

The following chart is an idealized Judean perspective on the variable connotative (emotively negative versus positive) movement of the linear plot of the prophetic argument. This appears to exhibit a semi-narrative progression from a general present towards an indefinite future perceptual focus. We observe a development that shifts in prominence from severe warning and judgment (–), to vindication in relation to the enemy (0, including direct and indirect calls to repentance), and on towards an ultimate gentle consolation coupled with a stirring promise of abundant blessing (+):

```
(–) 1:2–6   1:8–18, 2:1–2                                3:1–4  3:6     3:7c, 8
(0)    \1:7/          \2:3, 4–5, 6  2:8  2:10–11a  2:12, 13–15/  \3:5/ \3:7ab/   \\
(+)                         \2:7/ \2:9/     \2:11b/                              3:9–13, 14–17, 18–20
```

As this impressionistic schematic outline would suggest, words of terrible judgment prevail in Zephaniah through chapter one. Chapter two is for the most part connotatively neutral from Judah's perspective, especially where the merciful "righteousness" of YHWH shines through to give some hope in a very dark discourse, namely in the several eschatological transformative passages of chapter 2. The minatory message for God's people resumes at the beginning of the third Dialogue until it is finally and permanently extinguished by the various predictions of surpassing blessing that come after verse 8.

9.7.4 Overview of the argument

The following is a rhetorical overview of the prophetic-divine argument of Zephaniah as it unfolds according to the book's literary structure (i.e., seven major strophic clusters plus an interlude). The entire message has been dramatized with a particular focus upon the momentous coming day (a decisive divine intervention in human history) so as to create greater impact and appeal. It therefore functions as a more effective instrument of artistically fashioned persuasion in relation to a diverse audience, both then and now:

Cluster	Summary
I.	YHWH proclaims a universal message of judgment against all the wicked of the world—one that is earth-shaking in its scope and implications. But there is a sting in the tail: this divine indictment includes all the apostates and syncretists among the chosen people Judah! This is the primary problem that motivates the rhetorical argument and message of Zephaniah: the universal condemnation apparently offers no possible reprieve. [1:2–6]
II.	The sins of Judah that provoked the LORD's anger (the outstanding judicial issue) are here specified in considerably greater detail, and now this anger is seen to involve the whole nation, especially the rich and powerful who live in Jerusalem. This condemnation is again contextualized in terms of a much wider setting: the "day of YHWH" will bring an awful judgment upon all evildoers, wherever they may be found in the world. [1:7–18]
III.	The fundamental appeal and central core of the prophetic argument is unexpectedly introduced. Those who were ironically invited to the LORD's sacrificial celebration of condemnation (II) are mercifully given an option—all individuals who are prepared to seek YHWH in humble repentance and righteous living may perhaps be spared. New hope is thus motivated within the overall discourse development. [2:1–3]
IV.	The pessimistic setting of total doom is renewed in this selective set of illustrative "oracles against the nations." The LORD is in a punitive mood, and here is the evidence of his power to punish. But there are several surprising snatches of blessing that are predicted for the faithful remnant of believers

(2:7, 9b), including—amazingly enough—those who are found among the pagan peoples (2:11b). The appeal of III is thereby confirmed as being completely genuine—on the one hand, totally frightful; on the other, almost too good to believe. **[2:4–15]**

V. The general, external judgment by a righteous LORD upon sin predicted in IV is now made specific again with reference to the corrupt and polluting leadership of Jerusalem (secular and religious, cultic and nonconventional, including the prophetic corps). Blindly oblivious of the righteous God who dwells among them, they will bear the responsibility for their shameful behavior. Their fate will be no different from that of the ignorant heathen that their corrupt lives imitate. **[3:1–7]**

VI. An angry LORD God announces a third "gathering" for judgment (cf. II and III), one that embraces all nations. But wait—there is a totally unexpected turn of events: instead of punishment, a miraculous purification of the peoples is predicted, not for the proud oppressors among them, but for a humble, trusting "remnant" of the repentant. The implicit "appeal" is that at least some among the prophet's audience would follow along in penitence and join this blessed company. **[3:8–13]**

INTERLUDE: The prophet breaks into a typical communal psalm of thanksgiving in order to celebrate the wonderful acts of restoration that the LORD has worked on behalf of Jerusalem. The people are to rejoice—and YHWH along with them—as if full salvation were already theirs. Zephaniah puts words into the mouth, as it were, of his formerly fearful audience, namely, those who accept his loving message of forgiveness and deliverance in faith. **[3:14–17]**

VII. The prophetic argument is resumed from the end of oracle VI. Further motivation for accepting the prophet's appeal on behalf of the LORD, a profound reversal involving aspects that are both negative (punishment of oppressors) and positive (vindication plus promotion of the oppressed), concludes Zephaniah's dramatic word of prophecy. A final gathering of the redeemed remnant will most certainly take place, a public endorsement that culminates in a declaration of their total transformation (lit. 'turning their turnings') to a position of honor and glory in the presence of all those who did not accept YHWH's gracious invitation. **[3:18–20]**

9.8 Conclusion

9.8.1 Of what relevance is this study for Bible translators?

The preceding analysis has shown how one skillfully crafted poetic structure reflects and reinforces another to dramatize Zephaniah's manifold prophetic proclamation concerning the day of the LORD. In closing then, I wish to make a few suggestions as to how this type of **literary-rhetorical (L-R)** text study serves to clarify the larger compositional organization as well as certain important stylistic and oratorical features on the micro-level of discourse in the interest of producing a more effective Bible translation.

To be sure, from a relevance theoretical perspective this particular multi-staged method of analysis will cost translators more in terms of the conceptual as well as creative effort that is required to apply it—first, when interpreting the original text of Scripture, and then also when applying the results to produce the closest possible functionally equivalent version in their language. However, given a suitably qualified and trained translation team, the potential gain in terms of actual communicative benefits for both themselves as well as their intended target audience is indeed great. These may be summarized as follows with regard to four distinct aspects of the biblical text:

9.8.2 Summary of practical implications

a. **Structural**: An L-R approach gives translators a more complete and accurate picture of the discourse as a whole and how its various parts function in harmony and hierarchically to develop a unified prophetic-divine argument around a particular theme (or teaching, e.g., "the day of YHWH") and/or appeal (e.g., the exhortation "seek the LORD/righteousness!"—2:3). This could be reflected, for example, in the judicious placement and wording of section headings that are used to demarcate the text into its major compositional units (such as the seven constituent strophic clusters). Titles that are overly general or misleading in their scope or application must be avoided, e.g., "The Great Day of the LORD" (NIV) at 1:14 (is "great" good or bad, and for whom?); "Judgment on Israel's Enemies" (NRSV) at 2:1 (thereby obscuring the distinct appeal for repentance in 2:1–2); "A Song of Joy" (GNT) at 3:14 to mark the book's final portion (the "song" itself ends at v. 17).

b. **Typographical**: An L-R analysis provides readers with a visualizable picture of certain critical aspects of the text's structure and points of emphasis which may be displayed in print through the use of selected typographical and formatting techniques, such as: changes in the type or font style, indented lines and blocks of parallel text patterns, use of white space, capital letters. Translators might decide, for instance, to formally distinguish the sequence of dialogic exchanges between YHWH and his prophetic voice, or to graphically highlight 2:4 as a key textual linchpin ("the central cohesive element"—Webster) in the discourse by printing it separately, perhaps in

9.8 Conclusion

italics. They might go even farther, if the argument above is accepted, and set off the entire tripartite unit at the beginning of the second Dialogue (i.e., 2:1–3, 4, 5–7) and use accompanying marginal text references and explanatory comments to indicate how this section seems to epitomize the book of Zephaniah as a whole.[25]

c. **Exegetical**: An L-R method helps translators to better understand a given biblical discourse conceptually, especially its periodic problem points, where a thorough macro-study might direct them more readily along one path of interpretation rather than another. The vital, but paradoxical relationship between verses 8 and 9 of chapter three, for example, needs to be clarified for readers at least by means of a succinct footnote, if not within the translation itself. This might involve such measures as these: selecting a transitional expression at the onset of v. 8 that suggests its wider consequential implications (and applies to discourse units of larger scope in the TL); rendering the subsequent imperative "wait!" in such a way that gives the term larger, as distinct from just local, structural and semantic significance; employing a similar strategy at the start of verse 9 so that the message clearly relates to and contrasts with (but does not contradict) what is said in v. 8.

d. **Translational**: An L-R technique enables translators to more accurately represent in the target language what has been ascertained to be the original text's communicative macro- and micro-functions, including the various areas of thematic importance as well as points of recognized pragmatic significance. In such passages it is necessary to manifest a corresponding level of "poetic" impact (rhetoric) and appeal (artistry) in the TL. This concern would include the *oratorical* dimension of the discourse, as key aspects of the phonic fabric of the biblical text are composed specifically for oral-aural presentation before a live audience.[26] Special attention in terms of this translational technique thus needs to be given to those places that have been identified as obvious "peaks" in the original Hebrew with regard to both rhetorical impact and esthetic appeal, e.g., 1:7; 2:3, 4; 3:5, 9–10, 14–17, 20.

The following, for example, is a dynamic, literary functional equivalence (*LiFE*) poetic rendition of 2:4 in Chewa. The intricate wordplays of the Hebrew cannot be reproduced, but they are replaced by some dramatic devices indigenous to a Bantu language: rhythmic diction, alliteration, ideophones, exclamative particles, deictic sharpeners, and graphic figurative language.[27]

---

[25] Of course, if translators (and their publishers) agree to adopt typographical devices of this kind, they need (a) to carefully explain them in a general introduction and (b) to be consistent from book to book in the way they use them. Since different biblical books have diverse structures, different formatting strategies may have to be adopted accordingly. The text structures so depicted should also be those that have received some recognized (published) scholarly support.

[26] Ehud Ben Zvi rightly draws attention to this vital oral-aural dimension of the biblical text: "As a written work, [Zephaniah] was composed to be read (and reread) by those able to do so and to be read aloud to those (by far the majority) who were not" (in Harrelson 2003:1327).

[27] I suspect that this vernacular rendition can be appreciated even by those who do not know the language. One might try reading the text aloud to gain an impression of how it "sounds." Every syllable in Chewa ends in one of five open vowels; some vocalic stress may be placed on

Ku mzinda wa Gaza kudzakhala zii!	At the city of Gaza there will be SILENCE!
Asikeloni adzasanduka dzala zeedi!	Ashkelon'll be transformed into a complete dump!
Adani adzapitikitsa okhala ku Asidodi	Enemies will chase the inhabitants of Ashdod,
onse adzathawa padzuwa mwadzidzi!	all will flee under the [hot] sun SUDDENLY!
Adzazula a ku Ekironi ngati udzutu!	They will root out those of Ekron like mere grass!

The preceding efforts must of course be made language-specific and multiplied many times over in relation to complete books so as to maximize our current translational goal of persuasively communicating the urgency, relevance, forcefulness, and beauty of Zephaniah's compact message about YHWH's decisive day of judgment—or deliverance—with all the worldwide audiences that need to *hear* it in corresponding fashion also today.

---

the penultimate syllable of longer words. For further information on the *LiFE* approach to Bible translation, see Wendland 2004, 2006.

10

Linear and Concentric Patterns in the Rhetorical Structure and Style of Malachi

10.1 Introduction

> The element of beauty [in the prophecy of Malachi] is almost wholly lacking, there being but slight attempt at ornamentation of any kind. The figurative element is very limited.... Neither in spirit, thought, nor form has it the characteristics of poetry. (Smith 1961:4–5)

> Unlike Zechariah, Malachi does not employ any particular literary structure in order to convey his meaning. The subjects with which he deals follow one another apparently haphazardly.... (Baldwin 1972:214)

In this chapter I will adduce various types of evidence, based on a literary-structural analysis of the Hebrew text, which would contradict the two scholarly opinions stated above. In the first place, the style of Malachi is as beautiful as it is forceful, manifesting a rich diversity of rhetorical ornamentation, including figurative language, which has much in common with the poetic forms to be found in other prophetic literature. Second, the discourse structure of Malachi is in fact quite elaborate, for it features two distinct, yet overlapping types of formal organization, linear as well as concentric in nature. These textual arrangements complement one another in expert fashion, both to demarcate meaningful units within the prophecy as a whole and hence also to persuasively convey the burden of Yahweh's urgent message to his errant people of Judah.

10.2 Aspects of Malachi's rhetorical style

Most commentators are quick to classify Malachi's prophecy as being essentially prose in character.[1] While this may be true, it is important to specify the reasons why such an evaluation is made, especially if the implication is also given that this more prosaic manner of writing is somehow less artistic or effective. In fact, the distinction between prose and poetry in ancient Hebrew literature is not as obvious as the general lack of discussion on the subject (or evidence given to support one's assertion) would suggest. Rather than being an either-or situation, we are dealing with a continuum of possibilities, ranging between pure narrative prose and lyric poetry (e.g., hymnic psalms). It is not uncommon to find varied blends of style even within the same document, all being the product of a single creative author (not a patchwork of sources), skillfully using the available literary resources of his language within the register of religious discourse (e.g., Zechariah 8–9).

A careful analysis reveals that the book of Malachi incorporates a wide range of poetic forms. The following is a selective sample of some of the more prominent and characteristic examples.

10.2.1 Parallelism

Many instances of parallel phrasing occur in the rhetorical argumentation of the text's opening verses, e.g., 1:2, which leads off the LORD's case against his wayward people:

---

[1] Stuart, for example, "finds clear evidence of poetic parallelism only in the following parts: 1:2–5...1:6–9...2:6–9...2:10" (1998:1251). However, even within this opening section of the book, parallel expressions are arguably present also in 1:10–14 as well; it all depends on one's definition (and consequent recognition) of "parallelism" (cf. Wendland 2007) and "poetry" as well (Wendland 2004:110). Other instances of parallelism are evident in the examples from Malachi that follow.

10.2 Aspects of Malachi's rhetorical style

"I have loved you," says Yahweh. And you say, "How have we loved you?"	אָהַבְתִּי אֶתְכֶם אָמַר יְהוָה וַאֲמַרְתֶּם בַּמָּה אֲהַבְתָּנוּ

A longer example, 1:6 marks the onset of the next dispute in the sequence:

A son honors [his] father, And a servant [honors his] master. Now if I [am] a father, where [is] my honor? And if I [am] a master, where [is] my fear?	בֵּן יְכַבֵּד אָב וְעֶבֶד אֲדֹנָיו וְאִם־אָב אָנִי אַיֵּה כְבוֹדִי וְאִם־אֲדוֹנִים אָנִי אַיֵּה מוֹרָאִי

A number of parallel pairs occur also in the later sections of Malachi, which some commentators (e.g., Stuart 1998:1252) view as being virtually devoid of it—for example, the very last verse (4:6):[2]

And he will turn the heart[s] of the fathers to their sons, And the heart[s] of the sons unto their fathers... lest I come and I strike the land with a curse.	וְהֵשִׁיב לֵב־אָבוֹת עַל־בָּנִים וְלֵב בָּנִים עַל־אֲבוֹתָם פֶּן־אָבוֹא וְהִכֵּיתִי אֶת־הָאָרֶץ חֵרֶם׃

Of course, the last two half-lines (cola) do not exhibit typical parallelism with regard to form and function, but Yahweh's climactic warning does break into two in terms of the number of words, and the overall pressure of poetic symmetry does exert at least some motivation for this interpretation. In any case, it would seem that there is enough parallelism present to classify the prophet's style as being clearly poetic to enhance the rhetorical purpose of his discourse.

10.2.2 Chiasmus

Reversed parallel constructions also appear rather frequently in Malachi. Two typical examples follow, one from the book's beginning (1:2d–3a; cf. 1:2, which is also contrastively chiastic), the second from its middle portion (3:1):

---

[2] All verse references are based on the English text, which follows the Septuagint tradition.

And I loved
  Jacob,
  and [but] Esau
I hated.
	וָאֹהַ֖ב
	אֶֽת־יַעֲקֹֽב׃
	וְאֶת־עֵשָׂ֣ו
	שָׂנֵ֔אתִי

"Behold, I am sending
  my messenger,
  and he will prepare the way
before me.
	הִנְנִ֤י שֹׁלֵ֙חַ֙
	מַלְאָכִ֔י
	וּפִנָּה־דֶ֖רֶךְ
	לְפָנָ֑י

And suddenly he will come to his temple the Lord
  whom you are seeking
    namely, the messenger of the covenant,
  whom you are pleased (with).
Behold he comes," says YHWH Almighty.
	וּפִתְאֹם֩ יָב֨וֹא אֶל־הֵיכָל֜וֹ הָאָד֣וֹן ׀
	אֲשֶׁר־אַתֶּ֣ם מְבַקְשִׁ֗ים
	וּמַלְאַ֨ךְ הַבְּרִ֜ית
	אֲשֶׁר־אַתֶּ֣ם חֲפֵצִים֮
	הִנֵּה־בָ֔א אָמַ֖ר יְהוָ֥ה צְבָאֽוֹת׃

More extensive parallelistic and chiastic text patterns will be displayed later in our discussion of some of the larger poetic structures of Malachi.

10.2.3 Simile and metaphor

These two figures of comparison frequently appear in conjunction with each other, e.g.:

> For he (is) sits <u>like fire</u> of the refiner and <u>like soap</u> of the fuller.
> And he will sit <u>(like) a refiner</u> and a <u>purifier</u> of silver,
> and he will <u>purify</u> the sons of Levi,
> and he will <u>refine</u> them <u>like gold</u> and <u>like silver</u>. (3:2b–3a)

> For behold, the day (is) coming, <u>burning like an oven</u>,
> and all the arrogant ones and every doer of wickedness will be <u>stubble</u>,
> and it will <u>set</u> them <u>ablaze</u>, the coming day...
> And you will <u>trample</u> (the) wicked,
> and they will be <u>ashes</u> under the soles of your feet. (4:1...3a)

Such extended figures are highly poetic; they are also emphatic tools in the rhetorical arsenal of Malachi. Notice that in each case the imagery serves to focus upon one of the key thematic elements of his prophetic message, namely, the events concerning "the coming day of the LORD." In addition to similes and metaphors, we also find a number of important

10.2 Aspects of Malachi's rhetorical style

comparisons, which express the covenantal relationship between Yahweh and his people in intensely personal terms, e.g., father-son (בֵּן...אָב), master-servant (...אָדוֹן עֶבֶד) (1:6).

10.2.4 Synecdoche and metonymy

Metonyms are figures of speech that are based on some conventionalized semantic and/or pragmatic association between a certain focal or key concept (the target) and a word that is used figuratively to refer to it (the source). The latter is thus used to express the former in the oral or written text at hand. Common associations forged between target and source are time, location, entity-attribute, and cause-effect. When a part-whole relationship is involved, the figure is termed a *synecdoche*. These figures are sprinkled throughout the book of Malachi, often combined with metaphoric language and situated at points of increased semantic significance and/or emotive tension in the prophet's words, for example, to lead initiate Yahweh's accusation against his covenant nation:

> Judah (= the people living there) have acted treacherously,
> and an abomination (= divorce/adultery/idolatry) has been done in Israel...
> for Judah has profaned the holy thing (= the sanctuary/Temple/people) of YHWH...
> and he married the daughter (= women who worship) of a god of foreignness
>   (= pagan) (2:11).

10.2.5 Rhetorical question

The rhetorical question, whether used to initiate a new topic (often termed a "leading question") or to highlight some crucial attitude or emotion, was a mainstay in the Hebrew prophet's repertory of stock poetic devices. Rhetorical questions abound also in Malachi as part of the disputation genre that the book features overall. These pointed, confrontational queries occur with notable frequency in the speech of Yahweh himself as he takes his people and their priests to tasks for their various spiritual and moral failings, for example:

> Was not Esau the brother of Jacob? (1:2)
> And if I am a father, where is the honor due me? (1:6)
> Go ahead and bring it to your governor—will he be happy with you? (1:8)
> Am I to accept (such offerings) from your hand? (1:13)

Indeed, these few examples indicate that the rhetorical question is the keystone of the dialectic style that animates and empowers the admonitory message of Malachi.

10.2.6 Antithesis

Malachi is replete with emphatic contrasts that serve to foreground the wicked attitudes and behavior of the Jews of his time by comparing this either with what Yahweh demands in his Law *(torah)* or with what will be the case in the future Messianic age. The latter idea is prominent in the glorious prophecy of 1:11, which acts as a climactic antithesis to everything that has been said thus far in the discourse unit (disputation) spanning verses 6–11:

<u>Positive</u> *(v. 11)*   <u>Negative</u> *(vv. 6–10)*
a. all nations...   a. corrupt priests of Judah...
   great name of YHWH   despised name of YHWH (6)
b. pure offerings/worship   b. polluted offerings/worship (7–8)
c. accepted by/pleasing to   c. rejected by/hateful to YHWH (9–10)
   YHWH *(implied)*

On the discourse microstructure, emphatic (independent) pronouns are also employed in typical poetic fashion to effect a sharp contrast in participants as they relate to one another in the prophet's argument, for example:

For I (אֲנִי) Yahweh do not change;
thus you (אַתֶּם), sons of Jacob, you have not been consumed! (3:6).

10.2.7 Exclamatory utterances

Malachi is a messenger who is thoroughly taken up with his message. He functions as the mouthpiece of the LORD of Hosts, and his preferred method is to allow God to speak for himself (of a total of 55 verses, 47 record the first-person address of Yahweh). Here is a righteous and all-powerful Deity who is paradoxically (especially in comparison with pagan gods) also a merciful and loving Father, continually calling his delinquent children to repentance in order to restore a ruptured familial (covenant) relationship. Such a combination of tense interpersonal factors is emotively combustible, and hence it is not surprising that the language periodically bursts into

10.2 Aspects of Malachi's rhetorical style

flame with a dramatic power that equals anything recorded elsewhere in the Hebrew Bible. The gamut of emotions is expressed—from the intimate, poignant "I have loved you" (אָהַבְתִּי אֶתְכֶם), which opens the dialogue, to the concluding blanket prediction of "holy destruction" (*cherem* חֵרֶם) upon all those to obstinately close their hearts to the passionate appeals of their gracious, but also righteous Savior-Lord (4:5).

The language of Malachi is intensified in various ways, for example through a repetition of sound and sense, as we see in the following passage (1:8a–b) where assonance focuses the hearer's attention upon the "you" being addressed (note also the sound similarity between the bounding words "sacrifice" and "hosts"):

When you bring blind animals for *sacrifice*, <u>is that not wrong?</u>	וְכִי־תַגִּשׁוּן עִוֵּר לִזְבֹּחַ אֵין רָע
When you sacrifice crippled or diseased animals, <u>is that not wrong?</u>	וְכִי תַגִּישׁוּ פִּסֵּחַ וְחֹלֶה אֵין רָע
Try offering them to <u>your</u> governor! Would he be pleased with <u>you</u>?	הַקְרִיבֵהוּ נָא לְפֶחָתֶךָ הֲיִרְצְךָ
Would he accept <u>you</u>?" says the <u>Lord</u> of *hosts*.	אוֹ הֲיִשָּׂא פָנֶיךָ אָמַר יְהוָה צְבָאוֹת׃

This passage also illustrates the biting *irony* that characterizes much of the first chapter of Malachi as well as other parts of his prophecy. This rhetorical figure, too, automatically intensifies the thoughts being expressed.

In addition, Malachi exhibits other emphasizing, oral-aural appealing devices that are commonly found in the oracles of the more poetic prophets (e.g., Hosea, Joel): vocatives (e.g., 1:12), forceful pronouns (e.g., 3:12), rhetorical questions, word order variations, and, of course, the familiar exclamatory particles of visionary, convicting, and/or confirmatory discourse, such as הִנֵּה "look!" (e.g., 1:13), נָא "please!" (e.g., 1:8), וְעַתָּה "and now!" (e.g., 3:9), and the asseverative כִּי "surely, indeed, in truth!":

> כִּי־הִנֵּה הַיּוֹם בָּא *Surely*, just see—the day [of the LORD] is coming…! (4:1).

10.2.8 Graphic diction

This literary feature is often associated with the preceding one, for where the language is emphatic, it is also likely to be evocative, that is, capable of conjuring up vivid images in the listener's mind. Figurative language contributes much to this effect as has already been shown. Hyperbole, too, may be involved, as well as a certain aptness of lexical choice and placement—putting the right(-sounding) words in the proper places. This is evident in the following passage (2:3) which, were it not for the dead seriousness of the situational setting, might strike the audience as being rather humorous (also in contemporary times as people confront an occasionally corrupt or corrupted clergy):

> Look, I will punish your seed (זֶרַע) (metonym, i.e., children);
> I will spread (זרה) **dung** on your faces—the **dung** of your animal sacrifices,
> and you will be carried away with it (i.e., to the dunghill)!

Frequently, Malachi couples his colorful choice of words with apt allusions to outstanding aspects of Yahweh's prior revelation to his messengers. Such intertextual connections may refer to earlier prophetic oracles (e.g., 1:11—cf. Isa 56:6–7; Zeph 2:11) or occasionally also to familiar historical narrative events, e.g., 2:15:[3]

> Has he [i.e., YHWH] not made (them) [i.e., Adam & Eve] one (אֶחָד),
> even a remnant of <u>spirit</u> (רוּחַ) for him [i.e., Adam]?
> And what was the One (הָאֶחָד) [i.e., YHWH] seeking?
> [It was] the <u>seed</u> (זֶרַע) of God [i.e., godly seed].
> So take care for your <u>spirit</u> (רוּחַ)—
> and do not be unfaithful to the wife of your youth!

This is one of the most difficult passages to interpret in the entire Old Testament. Whether it is taken as referring to the original creation of man and woman (as I think the context, e.g., v. 14, seems to support more strongly) to Abraham and his wife (Sarah, not Hagar), the imagery, including wordplay, is both incisive, suggestive—and critical, namely, of husbands who are not totally faithful to their (first) wives. My interpretation has been

---

[3] "This verse has proved impossible to interpret to everyone's satisfaction.... Because the syntactic interpretations vary so much, the translations of the lexical items also vary" (Pohlig 1998:111). See Pohlig (ibid., 11–120) for an excellent survey of the various exegetical and hermeneutical possibilities.

10.2 Aspects of Malachi's rhetorical style

guided also by a literary perspective on the semantic (chiastic) arrangement of this verse.

10.2.9 Verbal shifts

As is common with the other prophets (and Hebrew poetry generally), Malachi frequently capitalizes on the Hebrew language potential for significant variations in word order. This positional fluency normally has a focusing effect which throws information that the prophet considers to be important into a foregrounded location within the clause (or sentence), i.e., either in front or in back of where it would be expected. Shifting in both directions appears in the next passage (3:9), as the LORD indicts his people for gross neglect; an emphatic initial noun-verbal cognate construction sets the tone, while the principal participants are highlighted by the word order of the next clause:

| With a curse you are cursed, for <u>it is me</u> [whom] you are robbing me— <u>the whole nation of you</u>. | בַּמְּאֵרָה אַתֶּם נֵאָרִים וְאֹתִי אַתֶּם קֹבְעִים הַגּוֹי כֻּלּוֹ׃ |

The topic at hand ("the law of Moses") is underscored in 4:4 by a more specific restatement ("the statutes and the judgments") situated at the end of the verse:

| Remember <u>the law of Moses</u> my servant, which I commanded him at Horeb for all Israel— <u>the statutes and ordinances</u> | זִכְרוּ תּוֹרַת מֹשֶׁה עַבְדִּי אֲשֶׁר צִוִּיתִי אוֹתוֹ בְחֹרֵב עַל־כָּל־יִשְׂרָאֵל חֻקִּים וּמִשְׁפָּטִים׃ |

Thus, already on the microstructure of the discourse we see *linear* (forward-moving) lexical-syntactic patterns being overlaid with *concentric* (recursive) ones to heighten impact and of intensity of the Lord's message of rebuke and warning to Judah.

10.2.10 Closure

Closure, sometimes termed "end stress" in poetry, is a rhetorical technique that is employed to bring a certain unit of discourse to a memorable conclusion. It is comprised of a variety of individual literary devices, usually in combination, such as asyndeton, abbreviation/ellipsis, attributive juxtaposition, figurative language, and verbal shifts. A good example of closure occurs in 1:6 as Yahweh begins his second dispute with the Jews of Malachi's time. Notice how the prophet leads off his highly structured indictment with general truths which, though potentially incriminating, must be accepted as most certainly valid by all in the audience. The real truth, that is, concerning the specific *addressees* of Malachi's words, does not strike home, however, until the very end of the utterance when the clergy, who must have surely agreed up to this point, are now trapped as the guilty ones in this shocking accusation:

> A son honors (his) father, and a servant (honors) his master.
> Now if I (am) a father, where (is) my honor?
> And if I (am) a master, where (is) my respect?
> says YHWH of Hosts—*to you, O priests, despisers of my name!* (לָכֶם הַכֹּהֲנִים בּוֹזֵי שְׁמִי)

Verse 3:5 illustrates a somewhat different type of *climactic closure*. It utilizes the enumeration of specific examples to conclude a larger segment of text. Then, at the very end of this pointedly lengthy list of sins and sinners is placed a concise summarizing statement that simply, but forcefully, expresses the root of all Judah's problems:

> ...and I will be a swift witness against the sorcerers and against the adulterers, and against those swearing deceitfully, and those extorting the laborer, and (oppressing) the widow and the orphan, and those turning away the alien, *and they do not fear me* (וְלֹא יְרֵאוּנִי)!, says YHWH of Hosts.

The preceding survey of poetic devices by no means exhausts the rich inventory of rhetorical features that embellish the disputational oracles of Malachi. Other literary forms that could be mentioned, in addition to those having a wider range of application in the discourse (to be discussed below), are: personification (e.g., 4:1), proverbial citation (e.g., 4:1), alliteration (e.g., 2:12), idiomatic speech (e.g., 1:8–9), panegyric appellation (e.g., 2:16), lexical interlocking (e.g., 2:17), and repetition, both exact (e.g., 2:2) and synonymous (e.g., 3:16). These examples should be sufficient to support the conclusion that the style of Malachi demonstrates considerable artistic proficiency, an expertise that reflects a clear rhetorical purpose, namely, to convey the author's urgent (life-or-death) judicial message with an impact and appeal that enhances its overall communicative effectiveness. This assessment of course applies to the original Hebrew text; the challenge for contemporary communicators then is how to reproduce the essential divine argument with sufficient accuracy of content coupled with an appropriate measure of dynamic verbal equivalence (see 10.4.2).

10.3 Aspects of Malachi's rhetorical discourse organization

In this section we will direct our attention to the larger discourse organization (macro-structure) of Malachi with special reference to a description of two complementary strategies of poetic arrangement. The prophet (speaking on behalf of Yahweh) weaves both of these textual schemas together in order to clearly outline his argument, to give the internal parts as well as the whole conceptual cohesion, to accentuate those aspects of the message in need of extra attention, and to enhance the text for oral-aural articulation as well as apprehension (cf. Wendland 2008:375–381). As a result of this manner of organization, which is at the same time both similar to and also distinct from other prophetic compositions, the thematic points as well as the ethical line of reasoning of this book are conveyed with an obvious transparency and power that is second to none in biblical literature.

10.3.1 Linear patterning

Over and above the individual parallel structures of different length and complexity that appear frequently throughout the book of Malachi, we observe a crucial genre template composed of a quartet of sequential elements which is reiterated six times to organize the prophecy in its entirety. This varied, recursive pattern stems from Malachi's distinctive treatment of his subject, viz. a dialectic style that serves a combined didactic-admonitory-consolatory communicative purpose. That is to say, when instructing his Jewish compatriots, the religious as well as the lapsed, about God's faithful love as well as his righteous judgment to come, the prophet casts the divine argument in the form of a series of intense dialogic mini-debates involving Yahweh and his covenant people. These interactive conversations assume the form of a *dispute,* each of which consists of four essential constituents. These may be defined and illustrated by the first disputation as follows:

a. **Assertion** (A): Yahweh (or, less often, his prophet) leads off with a general statement to introduce his critique concerning the present unacceptable faith-life of the people of Judah, e.g., "I have loved you!" (1:2a).

b. **Objection** (O): The people of Judah, or a particular segment of society (i.e., the priests), respond in opposition to the theological or moral assertion/implication just uttered by Yahweh. This verbal reaction is probably not a direct quotation, but through it God epitomizes a certain attitude or behavior of the people which is contrary to his expressed will and/or the Mosaic Law, e.g., "How have you loved us?" (1:2b).

c. **Response** (R): Yahweh, in turn, answers the objection of the people at length, leading off with a potent accusation, reproof, rebuttal, exhortation, admonition, warning, promise—or a combination of such speech acts (illocutions). Usually, this response is directed toward some specific sin of thought, word, or deed that is being manifested by the Jews, e.g., "Was not Esau Jacob's brother…Edom may say…a people always under the wrath of the LORD!" (1:2c-4).

d. **Implication** (I):[4] As a conclusion to his response, Yahweh directly states or clearly implies the punitive/disciplinary outcome of his errant people's rebellious, impious thinking, speaking, or doing, e.g., "You will see it with your own eyes…Great is the LORD…" (1:5).

(A) and (O) are thus essentially rhetorical devices that focus upon a particular spiritual problem in society and set the stage for Yahweh's pastoral instruction of his people (R) that culminates in a forceful challenge that should get them thinking in the direction of repentance (I). This linear progression, namely, A => O => R => I, though basic to the essential forward thematic or disputational movement of the discourse, is by no means a stereotyped one. On the contrary, more often than not, the pattern is varied in order to avoid monotony (negative effect) and to enhance the quality of

---

[4] I owe the recognition and inclusion of this fourth element to the commentary by Stuart (1998:1248).

10.3 Aspects of Malachi's rhetorical discourse organization

the communication (positive effect)—at least the potential for there to be a more persuasive impact upon the people. This argument cycle is completed in full six times, and Malachi's message concludes with a powerful epilogue from the LORD. I have thus segmented the prophecy into six major sections, termed "disputes," each of which expresses a distinct topical focus that is theological or ethical in nature. There are other, structural reasons for positing these principal discourse units which will be revealed later when discussing the concentric arrangements that are embedded within the text (section 9.3.2).

10.3.2 Structural summary

Below is a table that summarizes the linear (diachronic) ground plan of the "oracle" (מַשָּׂא) of Malachi (1:1a). It includes a citation of some of the chief lexical markers and key speech acts which serve to distinguish the onset and progression of these segments, each of which is assigned a certain theme that abstracts its main content. Numerical subscripts indicate any repeated A-O-R-I element, thus revealing the presence of variations or elaborations in the basic sequence of four elements, while the lower case letters in parentheses under the Unit Description column refer to explanatory notes that are given in the next section (10.3.2.1). These notes comment on certain problem areas in the analysis and attempt to justify the exegetical decisions that were reached. At times, outstanding text critical issues make it difficult to be very sure about a given interpretation, and in these cases I followed the advice given in the excellent guide of Pohlig (1998).

Verse(s)	Unit description	Lexical markers + Speech acts	Thematic summary
1:1	Oracle heading	"...the word of YHWH to Israel..."	Divine introduction to the prophecy
1:2–5	Dispute 1		
2a	A	[assertion] "...says YHWH."	YAHWEH's covenant love
2b	O	"And you say, *how*..." [rhetorical question/RQ of protestation]	For Israel is manifested by his rejection of wicked
2c–4	R	[RQ + assertions, indictment, prediction] "...utterance of YHWH"	Edom

5	I	"Your eyes will see and you will say…" [prediction]	
1:6–2:9	Dispute 2		
6a	A	[RQs + assertion, indictment] "…says YHWH of Armies…"	Judah's priests pollute the worship of YAHWEH
6b	O	"And you say, *how*…" [RQ of protest]	and corrupt the covenant
7a	R = A_1 (a)	[assertion]	of Levi
7b	O_1	"And you say, *how*…" [RQ of protest]	
7c–10	R_1	"When you say…" [RQs + indictments, assertions]	
11	I/I_1	"Indeed … my Name is/will be great… says YHWH of Armies"	
12	$(A_2 + O_2)$ (b)		
12–14a	R_2 (c)	"…when you say…and you said…and you brought…" [RQs + indictments]	
14b	I_2	"Indeed, I am a great King, says YHWH…"	
2:1–9	I_3 (d)	"And now this command is for you, O priests… [admonitions + predictions of punishment] "…says YHWH of Armies…" [vv. 4, 7, 8]	
2:10–16	Dispute 3		
10–11	A (e)	[RQs + indictments by Malachi]	Jewish men become
12	I	"May YHWH cut off anyone… bringing an offering to YHWH of Armies."	Unfaithful to YAHWEH through intermarriage
13	A_1	"And this is a second thing…" [indictment]	To heathen women and by divorce
14a	O_1	"And you say, *why*…" [RQ of protest]	
14b-15a	R_1	"…indeed YHWH acts as a witness…"	
15b–16	I_1	[prophetic admonitions] "…says YHWH God of Israel…says YHWH of Armies"	

10.3 Aspects of Malachi's rhetorical discourse organization

2:17–3:5	Dispute 4			
17a	A (f)		*no marker* [indictment by Malachi]	YHWH will send his
17b	O		"And you say, *how*..." [RQ of protest]	Messenger to purify his
17c	R		"When you say..." [RQ + indictment]	people and to punish all
3:1–5	I		"Behold, I am sending..." [divine predictions] "...says YHWH of Armies..." [vv 1, 5]	evildoers
3:6–12	Dispute 5			
6–7a	A		"Indeed, I YHWH...says YHWH of Armies." [assertion, indictment, exhortation]	YAHWEH longs to bless his people, if/when they repent (return to him)
7b	O		"And you say, *how*...?" [RQ of protest]	
8a	R = A$_1$ (g)		[RQ + indictment, assertion]	
8b		O$_1$	"And you say, *how*...?" [RQ of protest]	
8c		R$_1$	[assertion]	
9–12		I/I$_1$	[warning, assertion, exhortation, promises]	
3:13–4:3	Dispute 6			
13a	A		[indictment] "...says YHWH."	Blessing for God-fearers:
13b	O		"And you say, *what*...?" [RQ of protest]	the contrasting fates of
14–15	R		"You said..." [indictments]	the righteous and the
16–18	I		"Then...says YHWH of Armies... and you will again see..." [narrative, promises]	wicked
4:1–3	I$_1$ (h)		"Indeed, look—the day is coming...says YHWH of Armies..." [4:1b, 3b]	
4:4–6	Epilogue		"Remember the instruction of my servant, Moses..." [exhortation, promises, warning]	The 'prophet Elijah' will come in the day of YAHWEH to preach repentance and judgment

There are several points of a general nature to note in connection with the preceding table. First of all, the theme of the prophecy as a whole might be stated as follows: *The merciful, yet mighty LORD of Armies (Yahweh Almighty) call his people to repentance and promises to bless those who respond ("return")*. Neither this macro-theme nor its six specific sub-parts is unique to Malachi, but the manner in which these hortatory elements are recycled and rhetorically expressed certainly is distinctive within the prophetic literature. The criticism by some scholars that there is no rhyme nor reason in the presentation of the prophecy's key ideas is not supported by the textual evidence offered by the preceding literary-structural analysis.

The major portions of the book unfold its principal theme in this way: Yahweh is not only a holy God of the Law—a righteous Judge and Punisher of covenant-breakers; he is first and foremost a merciful Father of faithful love *(Dispute 1)*. It was this divine characteristic that motivated and maintained his gracious covenant promises with Israel/Judah, despite his people's continued infidelity. Nevertheless, Yahweh's justice cannot be compromised. He will surely punish willful, unrepented sin. But first he always exercises mercy by allowing sinners the opportunity to repent (and receive forgiveness) when he calls their attention to the terrible error of their behavior *(Disputes 2–3)*. However, if—despite repeated warnings—some refuse Yahweh's gracious invitation, he will assuredly come in judgment to punish all the wicked *(Dispute 4)*. After uttering this last severe warning, it is almost as if Yahweh regrets having had to threaten his chosen people, and he quickly reminds them once again of his loving desire to forgive and bless them again *(Dispute 5)*. But in view of the people's self-righteous defiance, the LORD must direct their attention once more to the awful reality of "his day," the final judgment, when both the righteous (faithful covenant-keepers) and the wicked (impenitent covenant-breakers) will receive their just reward *(Dispute 6)*. Malachi's prophecy concludes *(Epilogue)* with a rhetorically heightened recapitulation of the main points of his message:

10.3 Aspects of Malachi's rhetorical discourse organization

Reformation (4:4) – Observe the Instructions ("Law") of Moses (the focus of chs. 1–2).
Preparation (4:5) – There will come a future Day of restoration and renewal for the righteous as proclaimed by the messianic "Messenger of the covenant" (cf. 3:1), who will be preceded by the second "Elijah"—but this will also be a time of dreadful judgment for the unrighteous (the focus of chs. 3–4).
Repentance (4:6a) – Yahweh earnestly desires the conversion of all people;
Punishment (4:6b) – but he will not hesitate to "curse" (condemn) the wicked.[5]

Concluding this overview of the discourse structure of Malachi, we note in passing the chiastic arrangement of the initial "A" (Accusation) markers as they are manifested in the sequence of six disputes:

D1. "says Yahweh" .... D6. "says Yahweh"
D2. "says Yahweh of Armies" ....D5. "says Yahweh of Armies"
D3. *the prophet speaks* ....D4. *the prophet speaks*

10.3.2.1 Structural problem points

When analyzing the structural organization of Malachi (as summarized above), one has to make some decisions that others might analyze differently on the basis of a careful text study. The following paragraphs attempt to explain and/or justify the analysis that was presented in the preceding section. These concern a number of problem areas or complications that developed in my construal of the six disputations that comprise Yahweh's word to the post-exilic people of Judah through the mouth/scroll of his prophet. The salient issues are discussed in order according to the lower case letters enclosed in parentheses as given on the table in 10.3.2.

(**a**) In Dispute 2, 1:7 is a complex verse structurally since it manifests an overlapping of the basic sequence of rhetorical elements. Thus, "(you are) offering defiled food on my altar" is Yahweh's response (R) to the priests' objection (O) given in the previous verse (6). The priests then collectively reply with another impudent query (O_1), perhaps as formulated in essence for them by Malachi: "How have we defiled you?" Their self-righteous

---

[5] Some commentators (e.g., Driver 1913:356; Stuart 1998:1391) regard 4:4–6 [3:22–24] to be part of Dispute 6. "Careful reading of the entire section, however, suggests that these final three verses are not functioning at the end of the previous unit; they broach new topics, and they read like a sweeping epilogue or conclusion to the entire book (cf. Eccles. 12:9–14) rather than the completion of the preceeding section" (Dorsey 1999:322).

complaint clearly carries on, and so Yahweh's initial answer functions also as an added assertion (A_1) in the second series of elements that are incorporated within this same disputation. Due to the obvious semantic and rhetorical continuation here, a new major discourse unit is not proposed. This decision, as well as many of those that follow, is supported by an underlying concentric (recursive) arrangement that coincides with the linear pattern that carries the discourse forward from one point in the argument to another.

(b) The eschatological motif, which is prominently introduced in 1:11 (i.e., I_1), marks the closure of a sub-unit (paragraph) in Dispute 2.[6] What then is to be done with the following material, i.e., 12–14, where this important motif recurs at the close to signal another boundary (i.e., I_2)? Since the content and intent of verses 12–14 is so closely related to that of verses 6–11, and since there are no typical (A) or (O) indicators present at the beginning of v. 12, it seems logical to view this section as simply a continuation of the same dispute—a variation on the current theme. For this reason, I posit the pair of missing structural elements (A + O) as being implicitly expressed in the rhetorical context. Support for this interpretation is found at the onset of the dispute in v. 6. The crucial words here are those of Yahweh sharp accusation: "You priests (are) despisers of my name!" (A). That provokes the retort, "How have we despised your name?" (O). If a corresponding pair of elements (i.e., $A_2 + O_2$) are understood by implication to precede the initial clause of v. 12, "And you (are) profaning it (i.e., my Name)," then the subsequent rejoinder by Yahweh follows quite naturally, "...in your saying, the table of the LORD (is) polluted..." (vv. 12–14a, i.e., R_2).

---

[6] I agree generally with Stuart, who extends the theological significance of the symbolism that is found in v. 11: "[W]e must appreciate the presence of eschatological *messianic universalism*, that is, the common Old Testament doctrine that the true God would one *future* day reign over all peoples, who would have no choice but to acknowledge his sovereignty...Such a view is the consistent outlook of the prophets (Isa 2:2–4; 11:10–12; 42:1–9; 45:1–3, 15, 22–23; Jer 3:17; Mic 4:1–2; Zeph 3:8–9; Hag 2:7; Zech 8:20–23, 14:16; compare the oracles against the foreign nations throughout the prophetic books) and is also widely represented elsewhere in Scripture (e.g., Exod 9:16; Pss. 22:28[27]; 95–99" (1998:1306).

However, I would qualify this perspective to include a *salvific* implication, that is, for those peoples and individuals among "the nations" who not only "acknowledge" the Messiah, but who also become his disciples, his new covenant people, by faith (e.g., Isa 49:6 > Acts 13:46–47; Am 9:11–12 > Acts 15:16–17; Ps 19:4 + Deut 32:21 > Rom 10:18–19; Ps 18:49 + Deut 32:43 + Ps 117:1 + Isa 11:10 > Rom 15:9–12; Isa 52:15 > Rom 15:21.

10.3 Aspects of Malachi's rhetorical discourse organization

(c) The paragraph covering 1:12–14 in Dispute 2 is distinctive for several reasons. For one, it is one of the few larger units in the prophecy that does not manifest some sort of concentric overlay (another being the Epilogue of 4:4–6). However, it does display an intricate linear arrangement that closely matches the structural constituents of verses 6–11. The argument of this second, shorter paragraph thus reiterates the argument of the earlier unit to reveal a rather close point for point correspondence. This type of rhetorical structure, whether realized on an abstract conceptual or a concrete lexical level, is certainly not foreign to the OT prophets (e.g., Hosea 9:10–14, 15–17), though it is not often recognized. A summary of this judicial overlay pattern follows:

Rhetorical Designation	$A\text{-}O\text{-}R/A_1\text{-}O_1\text{-}R_1\text{-}I/I_1$	$(A_2\text{-}O_2)\text{-}R_2\text{-}I_2$
-Result	(6) despise *Name* – O priests	(12a) profane it [*Name*] you (emphatic)
	How have we despised it?	*How*...? (implicit expression)
INDICTMENT-*Means*	(7) by offering *polluted food*	(12b) the *table of YHWH is defiled*
-General	on my *altar*	[by improper sacrifices]
(*you despise Yahweh!*)	thinking that *YHWH's table* may be *despised*	its *food* is *despicable*
-Specific	(8) you offer blind animals, lame, sick	(13a) you bring stolen, lame, sick
		members of the flock
VERDICT	(10) I will not accept an offering	(13b) should I accept [this] offering
(*Yahweh rejects you!*)	from your hand	from your hand?
VALIDATION	(11) Indeed, my Name is great	(14) Indeed, I am a great king; my Name
(*Yahweh is vindicated.*)	among the nations!	is feared among the nations!

(d) At the conclusion of Dispute 2 (2:1–9, I_3) occurs a section that illustrates the freedom of composition that Malachi demonstrated when formulating his prophecy. He certainly did not feel bound to confine himself to a single stereotyped manner of composition. This colorfully poetic and intricately constructed unit (see further below) does not give evidence of any of the markers that distinguish the other disputation sections. Nevertheless, it is included in Dispute 2 for several reasons:

- The addressees are the same, namely, the "priests," who are pointedly specified in the opening verse of each sub-section, i.e., 1:6 and 2:1 (structural *anaphora*).

- The content of 2:1–9 nicely complements that of 1:6–14: in the former, Yahweh attacks the corrupted practices of the priests, while in the latter he censures them for their unfaithful teaching and utter disregard for his Law.

- 2:1–9 also vividly warns of the punishment that awaits all those who exhibit such deplorable behavior, while at the middle portion it highlights in summary (vv. 5–7) the contrastive characteristics of the anti-type, as epitomized by the messianic Levi—the "messenger of YHWH of Armies" (cf. the messenger of the covenant in 3:1).

(e) In Dispute 3, two (A) constituents appear near the beginning of the unit to complicate the basic sequence. Verses 10–12 introduce the prophet's denunciation of a serious family problem which forms the main topic of this disputation, that is, the marriage of heathen women by Jewish men. Malachi leads off with a lengthy indictment of this practice (vv. 10–11) followed by an initial implication (I), namely, a curse upon all those guilty of it (v. 12). This is followed by a reiteration of the accusation (A_1), which is prefaced in v. 13 by some graphic imagery depicting the pathetic result of the men's worship due to their infidelity to their wives and hence also their God. The naïve objection, "For what reason (i.e., have our offerings been rejected)?" (O_1, v. 14a), then sets the stage for Yahweh's forceful condemnation of the sin of divorce.

(f) Dispute 4 begins in v. 17a (A) with the unmarked speech of the prophet, which criticizes the people in general for their wearisome words, i.e., their misguided complaints against Yahweh's justice (the fault really lay with the nation itself, the leaders and common folk alike, for not living according to the principles of the Torah). The remainder of this unit alternates among the discourse segments of Yahweh, Malachi, and the Jews. The quotes of the people are clearly indicated since each one starts off with, "And you

10.3 Aspects of Malachi's rhetorical discourse organization

say…" But there is some uncertainty about where the boundary of the (R) section (or sections) occurs because this appears to incorporate the citation of additional utterances by the people. However, since these words are cited by Yahweh as evidence against them, I have interpreted them as part of the LORD's response, for example:

> You have wearied YHWH with your words.
> (O) And you say, "How have we wearied him?"
> (R) When you say, "Every evildoer is good in the eyes of YHWH…" (2:17).

(g) In Dispute 5, Yahweh's response (R) in 3:8a to the objection (O) of the descendants of Jacob, "How shall we return (repent)?" serves simultaneously as an introduction to a more specific indictment (A_1) of the sin that is being condemned. In this case, the function of the repeated sequential pattern is to emphasize the LORD's accusation by means of a general-specific progression: "…you have turned away from my decrees.." (v. 7) => "You have robbed me!" (v. 8a). The latter provokes another objection (O_1) and an appropriate response by Yahweh (R_1), which surprisingly concludes with an amazing promise of blessing for those who dare to trust his promises and provision (vv. 10–12).

(h) The designated conclusion of Dispute 6 in 4:1–3 (3:19–21 in Hebrew) does not give evidence of any of the normal sequential markers. Therefore, one must either construe it as an independent unit within the book as a whole or attach it to an unambiguous section that has already been established. In this case, the evidence seems to point clearly in the direction of the second possible interpretation. Thus, 4:1–3 appears to be yet another instance of the artistic freedom that we have noted on a number of other occasions in the prophecy of Malachi. Such variety, within limits, avoids monotony and preserves audience interest in the main message being conveyed, namely, the LORD's critical rebuke coupled with his encouraging reassurance for his covenant people. As we saw in the case discussed under point (d) above, it is likely that the present segment is best viewed as a continuation of the preceding Dispute 6 (3:13–18), its divinely-stated climactic closure in fact. Evidence that would substantiate this interpretation is as follows:

- In terms of lexical form, there is a considerable amount of repetition of several important concepts, in particular, reference to a future "day" of judgment (vv. 17, 19), when two groups of people will be distinguished—the doers of wickedness (vv. 15, 19) and the fearers of YHWH/my name (vv. 16, 20).

- Element I (the implication of the disputation) anticipates I$_1$ semantically by alluding to a time when there will be a difference between the righteous and the wicked (v. 18)—a difference that is then elaborated upon in a variety of contrasting images in 4:1–3.

10.3.3 Concentric patterning

As we have now observed, the message of Malachi appears to be meaningfully organized on a *linear,* diachronic plane: One accusation follows upon another as YHWH and his prophet confront the post-exilic community of Judah with their outstanding sins: (a) a neglect of proper, reverential worship in the rebuilt Temple; (b) a failure of the clergy, the priests, to address these issues with a call for repentance; (c) a breakdown of public morality through divorce and intermarriage with pagans; (d) a failure to honor Yahweh and to acknowledge in their lives that he as the righteous Judge would one day punish all evildoers and reward those who were faithful to his covenant requirements. The book's overall organization thus contradicts the opinion of scholars and Bible publishers alike who fail to see the order in the author's passionate, hortatory argument.

It is important to recognize, however, that the prophecy of Malachi is also arranged along another, a *concentric* plane of compositional development. It is especially in these larger chiastic patterns, skillfully superimposed as it were on the linear progression of the book, that the rhetorical genius of the prophet is fully revealed. These reversed parallel structures perform a *cohesive* function in the discourse to knit the discrete units (paragraphs and larger portions) together internally and also to provide a verbal framework that links up related (corresponding or contrasting) sections in the message, as viewed by the prophet (or his scribe/editor). Furthermore, by expressing his (Yahweh's) ideas and concerns in a poetic form that was familiar to the people, Malachi promoted their ease of memorization (*mnemonic* function) and also enhanced their impact on and appeal to listeners (*affective* function), thus heightening their response, whether sympathetic or antagonistic.

Even the latter, hostile type of reaction serves an important communicative purpose, for it gets people to think more seriously what is being said, whether they happen to agree or not. After some later reflection then, they might decide that they need to reevaluate, perhaps even revise their initial opinion and attitude towards the message.

The basic formula for the concentric, or chiastic, pattern is this: **A-B-(C-... n...-B')-A'**. The items in parentheses indicate those elements that are optional in any given realization of this arrangement in the text. The simplest pattern is the basic A-B-A' ring construction, while the most complex rarely extend to more than seven elements in a palistrophe (i.e., A-B-C-D-C'-B'-A'). It is normally the case that special thematic and/or pragmatic emphasis is manifested in the central unit of this formation and oftentimes also at the end. The perspicuity, validity, and significance of any such structure varies in context according to how well it coincides, or meshes, with any existing linear arrangement in the text, the degree of correspondence in the parallels used to establish the structure (exact lexical repetition being the strongest evidence), and on the number of other literary features that appear to support it (e.g., prophetic formulas, word order, balance in size, phonological correspondences, and so forth). It must be granted then that in some cases a concentric pattern exists only in bare outline, whereas elsewhere its presence cannot really be doubted. However, the presence of so many clear chiastic structures in the book of Malachi does tend to give certain questionable cases the benefit of the doubt (i.e., a poetic principle known as the "pressure of symmetry" within the artistic whole).

Three other rhetorical devices based on *repetition*—exact, synonymous, or contrastive—occur in the discourse of Malachi to assist the analyst in delineating the various unit boundaries and their interrelationships within the Hebrew text. These features may be described as follows:

- **Inclusio** – This refers to the occurrence of clear formal and/or semantic correspondences at both the *beginning* and the *ending* of a particular discourse unit, e.g., section, paragraph, strophe, whether this is included within some larger segment or itself incorporates one or more smaller segments. As a rule, every type of concentric arrangement employs at least some form of *inclusio*.

- **Anaphora** – This device is similar to *inclusio*, but instead of the formal or semantic correspondences being found at the onset and end of the *same* unit, in the case of *anaphora*, they occur at the respective beginnings (only) of *different* discourse units, whether adjacent or separated in textual space.

- **Epiphora** – This device is similar to *anaphora*, except that the formal/semantic correspondences appear at the respective endings of distinct discourse units. As in the case of *anaphora*, the number of segments similarly marked by *epiphora* are not limited to two within a larger span of text.

I will outline below in sequence the main concentric structures that I (or others) have noted in the book of Malachi. These are presented only in summary schematic fashion, except for the section 2:1–9, which is displayed in more detail to illustrate the complexity with which such patterns are manifested in the poetic-rhetorical oratory of the prophetic literature (orature).

10.3.3.1 Dispute One (1:2–5)

Verse 2 of chapter one leads off with a double chiasm: A: "I love you" – B: "says Yahweh" = B': "and you [people of Israel, cf. v. 1] say" – A': "how have you loved us?"[7] There is also a chiasm of personal names within the verse: Jacob – Esau = Esau – Jacob. This construction perhaps sets the stage for a general chiastic arrangement of the first dispute as a whole:

(A) Yahweh refers to Israel (v. 1) in blessing (rejected): "I loved you!" but "you [Jacob] say" (2)
   (B) Yahweh's judgment of Esau: "I have made his mountainous land a desolation…" (3)
      (C) Edom's lack of repentance: "we will rebuild the ruins!" (4a)
   (B') Yahweh's judgment of Esau: let them rebuild—I will tear down…the wicked land…!" (4b)
(A') Yahweh refers to Israel in blessing (affirmed): "you [Jacob] will see and you will say…" (5)

We observe how appropriately the reversed structure mirrors the prevailing theme, which deals with Yahweh's contrasting treatment of the two brothers/nations. The core element (C) is significant for it suggests that the Lord's dealings with Esau/Edom were not the result of a purely a random choice or arbitrary favoritism. Rather, apart from Yahweh's universal mercy

---

[7] "The language of love evokes the rich covenant tradition of the theology of Deuteronomy, with its attendant themes of election, obligation, and loyalty…Deut. 7:7–8…7:12–13; 10:15; 23:5)" (Schuller 1996:854). "In the diplomacy of the ancient Near East, the language of 'love' and 'hate' was employed not to indicate personal emotion or affection, but routinely to convey the concepts of alliance or enmity among nations" (Stuart 1998:1284).

10.3 Aspects of Malachi's rhetorical discourse organization

(also a theme of Malachi), his relationship with Edom was at least partly determined by the latter's response to God's will (cf. Obadiah) and past revelations and/or opportunities given to them (cf. Num 20:14–21).

10.3.3.2 Dispute Two (1:6–2:9)

This disputation is the longest and most complex in the entire book, as was shown in its linear structure discussed in 10.3.1. The syntagmatic organization is complemented by its various included, paradigmatic (concentric) patterns, which are outlined below. The latter serve to reinforce the internal cohesiveness of the former development as well as to highlight selected salient topics within the whole.

Part 1: (1:6–11)

(A) the priests dishonor the Name of Yahweh: "my/your name"(2x) – "says YHWH of Armies" (6)
  (B) the priests sin during worship: "my altar" + "offer" + "food" + "sacrifice" = defective, unacceptable offerings (7–8a)
    (C) Result$_1$—no mercy!: "governor" will not "lift up your face"–"says YHWH of Armies" (8b)
    (C') Result$_2$—no mercy!: "God" will not "lift up your faces" – "says YHWH of Armies" (9)
  (B') the priests sin during worship: "my altar" + "meal offering" – "says YHWH of Armies" (10)
(A') BUT (כִּי) Yahweh's name will be honored everywhere!: "my name" (3x) – "says YHWH of Armies" (11)

The divine "verbal signature" ("says YHWH of Armies"—אָמַר יְהוָה צְבָאוֹת) occurs near or at the close of each chiastic constituent, except the long second one where it is missing. The peak of this sub-section clearly occurs at its conclusion in v. 11.

Part 2: (1:12–14)

As was pointed out in section 10.3.2, the organization of this unit is basically linear since it manifests an overlay structure that duplicates the essential elements of the preceding sub-section. After the initial link (i.e., "But as for you, you are polluting it [my name]"—cf. 1:6), the three chiastic constituents of Part 1 reappear, but in an altered order:

(B") the priests sin during worship: "table of the Lord" + food" + "fruit" + "meal offering" = defective, unacceptable offerings – "says YHWH of Armies" (12–13a)
(C") result—no mercy!: "I will not accept it from your hand" + "cursed" – "says YHWH" (13b-14a)
(A") BUT (כִּי) Yahweh is a "great king" and Yahweh's name will be honored everywhere!: "my name" – "says YHWH of Armies" (14b)

We again observe the prominent Messianic refrain which recurs to conclude *(epiphora)* the major segments of chapter one, thus tying the first two disputes together. This is a most reverent tribute to this self-revelation of Yahweh (his name) and his greatness as well as his intense desire to establish a covenantal relationship with all people (vv. 5, 11, 14).

Dorsey (1999:322) calls attention to a complementary arrangement that joins Parts 1 and 2 of the second disputation into an even larger concentric organization. This chiastic structure clearly highlights an emotive climax in the center that expresses the personified LORD's bitter frustration and disappointment, in particular, over the failures of those whose job it was to serve him in worship as mediators between the people and their holy God:

The priests (and people) have cheated and thus dishonored Yahweh! How have they sinned thus?

(A) As Israel's father and lord (אֲדֹנָיו) YHWH is not honored or feared (מוֹרָא) ...*says YHWH of Armies* (אָמַר ׀ יְהוָה צְבָאוֹת) (1:6a).
  (B) The priests have offered YHWH polluted (מְגֹאָל) food, and YHWH's table (שֻׁלְחָן) is despised (נִבְזֶה)...*says YHWH of Armies* (1:6b–8).
    (C) YHWH will not accept offerings from your hands (מִיֶּדְכֶם)...*says YHWH of Armies* (1:9).
      (D) **Climax**: Close the Temple! ...*says YHWH of Armies* (1:10a).
    (C') YHWH will not accept offerings from your hands (מִיֶּדְכֶם), but his Name will be great among the nations...*says YHWH of Armies* (1:10b–11).
  (B') The priests have offered YHWH unacceptable sacrifices so that YHWH's table (שֻׁלְחָן) is polluted (מְגֹאָל) and his food despised (נִבְזֶה)...*says YHWH of Armies* (1:12–13a).
(A') As Israel's king and lord (אֲדֹנָיו) YHWH has been dishonored by Israel's worship, but his Name will be feared (נוֹרָא) among all nations...*says YHWH of Armies* (1:13b–14).

Part 3: (2:1–9)

This long sub-section exhibits a general A—B—A' "ring structure" arrangement as follows:

10.3 Aspects of Malachi's rhetorical discourse organization

(A) the priests' **perversion** ➔ curse (1–4)
  (B) the pure priestly **prototype** (5–7)
(A') the priests' **perversion** ➔ punishment (8–9)

Each of these three segments is itself intricately arranged in a variety of concentric patterns:

Paragraph 1 (2:1–4)

(A) **Introduction**: "to you this command" + "O priests" (1)
    [Note the anaphoric links: "now" (1:9) and "priests" (1:6).]
  (B) **Judgment**: x- "you don't take it to heart" (2a)
                   y- "I will curse your blessings" (2b)
                   y'- "I have cursed it" (2c)
              x'- "you don't take it to heart" (2d)
  (B') **Judgment**: x- "I will rebuke you" (3a)
                   y- "dung" (3b)
                   y'- "dung" (3c)
              x'- "I will carry you out" (3d)
(A') **Conclusion**: "to you this command" + "*Levi*" (4)

Paragraph 2 (2:5–7)

(A) **Introduction**: "before my name trembled *he*" [*Levi*] (5)
  (B) **Description**: portrait of the priestly life: x- "Law" + "in his mouth" (6a)
                                       y- "lips" (6b)
                                            z- "he walked with me" (6c)
                                            z'- "he turned many" (6d)
                                       y'- "lips" (7a)
                               x'- "Law" + "from his mouth" (7b)
(A') **Conclusion**: "the messenger of YHWH is *he*" (7c)

Paragraph 2 stands in marked contrast to Paragraph 1, though there is an overlap in the reference to "Levi" (לֵוִי) at the end of v.4, being a symbolical designation of the entire priesthood of Israel under the Mosaic Law.[8] Paragraph 2 begins this way (v. 5, literally):

> My covenant was with him, [one of] life and peace,
> And I gave them to him [for] reverence—and he reverenced me...

---

[8] "What would the priests have understood by the term 'my covenant with Levi' ['the covenant of Levi' in v. 8]?...it is likely that they would have understood it to mean the whole arrangement that made them priests in Israel—the entire body of Mosaic law that defined Israel's religion, its national offices including the priesthood, its worship regulations, and its specification of priestly duties..." (Stuart 1998:1315); cf. Deut 33:8–11; Num 25:11–13; Jer 33:20–22; Neh 13:29.

This characterization of the covenantal desire of Yahweh, the ideal priest(hood), is foregrounded in several ways over and above by serving as the subject of this central and focal section. First of all, these two lines occur almost precisely at the midpoint of this entire section, Part 3, viz. 61 words (120 syllables) after the initial "And now…" (וְעַתָּה) (v. 1), and 62 words (114 syllables) prior to the final "…in the Law" (בְּתוֹרָה) (v. 9). Second, the rhythmic pattern of the two lines (a virtual identical 12 and 11 syllables respectively), should this section prove to be metrical, appears to be quite distinct from the utterance lines that occur preceding and subsequent to it. In other words, in the sequence of poetic lines (when construed as such) these two are considerably longer than the average for this section, i.e., approximately seven syllables, and this would be immediately noticeable to anyone listening to this text being recited or chanted. Finally, we observe that the thematic appellation found at the end of this medial paragraph/strophe in v. 7, "the messenger of Yahweh of Armies" (מַלְאַךְ יְהוָה־צְבָאוֹת הוּא),[9] is highlighted at the beginning by the pun on the prophet's name (messenger/Malachi), the greater allusion to the LORD's specially chosen "messenger/angel," and the back-shifted emphatic pronoun "he."

Paragraph 3 *(2:8–9)*

  (A) **Means**: "turned from the way" + perverting "instruction" (8a)
     (B) **Result**—indictment: "you have corrupted the covenant of Levi" (8b)
     (B') **Result**—punishment: "I have made you despised" (9a)
  (A') **Reason**: "not keeping my ways" + perverting "instruction" (9b)

This short unit is semantically linked with Paragraph 2 both anaphorically: "my covenant…with him" (5) – "the covenant of Levi" (8), and also epiphorically: "the Law" (7) – "the Law" (9). All of these concepts are, of course, crucial in the development of Yahweh's case against those who had been entrusted with "the high calling of the priesthood set out in the Pentateuch, from which the priests had fallen far by Malachi's time" (Stuart 1998:1321). Is it any wonder then that the lay people of Judah were not

---

[9] "The dominant semantic background for the term *messenger of Yahweh* as it appears here and as Malachi's audience would have understood it, is surely the fifty times in the Old Testament that it indicates the angel of the Lord, God's supernatural spokesman, and secondarily, the three times that it denotes a prophet, God's human spokesman. By applying the term to priests (here alone in the Old Testament), what this verse is saying is that they, too, were supposed to be spokesman for God just as angels and prophets were—though they had failed utterly in Malachi's time to honor that role" (Stuart 1998:1321).

10.3 Aspects of Malachi's rhetorical discourse organization

far behind, a subject that the prophet turns to in the next Dispute when accusing many Jewish men of violating one of the most sacred precepts "in the [Mosaic] Law" (בְּתוֹרָה) (9b).

10.3.3.3 Dispute Three (2:10–16)

(A) **Ideal situation**—*unity*: "one God" + "one Father"; general sin = "infidelity" (10)
    (B) **Indictment**/specific sin—*intermarriage*: "daughter of a foreign god" + "infidelity" (11)
       (C) **Verdict**: exclusion from Israel + rejection of "meal offering" (12)
       (C') **Verdict**: rejection of "meal offering" (12)
    (B') **Indictment**/specific sin—*divorce*: "wife of your covenant" + "infidelity" (14)
(A') **Ideal situation**—*unity*: "one" + "one"; general sin = "infidelity" (15)

Verse 16 effectively summarizes this unit by restating its theme: "God hates divorce...so do not be unfaithful/break faith." Here repeated once more is the leitmotif which acts as a cohesive thread running throughout the dispute: "infidelity" (בגד—cf. v. 10, *inclusio*).¹⁰ We also find an expression that links the end of the unit with the center of the concentric structure: "... covers (כסה) x with y" (vv. 13, 16). There is yet another chiastic pattern that develops throughout the section in the citation of references to the deity: (A) God – (B) Yahweh, (C) Yahweh, (C') Yahweh, (B') Yahweh – (A') God. This series is rounded out in v. 16 with "Yahweh...God."

At the beginning of Dispute 3, we observe an anaphoric element that recalls the start of Dispute 2, namely, a twofold mention of the term "father" (אב).¹¹ In this way the prophet lexically underscores, as it were, this essential presupposition: Yahweh is the one and only "father" of Israel/Judah (he is also a loving father, cf. Dispute 1, 1:2). There are several other ways in which the opening lines of these two major sections are rhetorically marked—that is, through parallelism of members, sound similarity/rhyme, and rhythm—all prominent characteristics of Hebrew poetry:

---

[10] "Malachi calls for faithfulness between husbands and wives because as Jews they all had one father—Yahweh; because marriage is grounded in a covenant between the husband and the wife and Yahweh; and because God intended for a man and his wife to be one flesh for the benefit of godly offspring. This passage does not seem to be based on Deut 24 but goes back to Gen 1–2 and is the forerunner of Jesus' teaching in Matt. 5:31–32; 19:4–9" (Smith 1984:325).

[11] Stuart (1998:1327) notes a number of "catch words" that also closely link Disputes 2 and 3: "father" (1:6—2:10), "altar" (1:7, 10—2:13), "favor, accept" (1:8, 10, 13—2:13), "covenant" (2:4, 5, 8—2:10, 14), "offspring" (2:3—2:15), "guard, preserve" (2:7—2:15, 16).

(1:6)   A son honors his <u>father</u> (אָב), and a servant his *master* (אֲדֹנָיו).
        And if a <u>father</u> [am] I (אָנִי), where [is] my honor (כְבוֹדִי)?
        And if a *master* [am] I (אָנִי), where [is] my reverence (מוֹרָאִי)? (8:8:10)

(2:10a) [Is there] not *one* <u>father</u> to us all (לְכֻלָּנוּ)?
        [Has] not *one* God created us (בְּרָאָנוּ)? (7:7)

The parallelism within and between these two passages is quite apparent, as is the rhythm in terms of syllable counts. Harmonious phonological patterns are also evident, including rhyme, which is not very prominent in Hebrew poetry and alliteration, which is, e.g., ב/ו in 1:6 and ל/א in 2:10a. This highly poetic type of *oracular/oratorical prose* is typical of the onset of each of the six disputation units. Coupled with the diagnostic question-answer format, the rhetoric thus acts as an effective means of oral/aurally distinguishing the initial boundaries of these crucial stages in the prophetic message as well as foregrounding their principal topics to be developed.

10.3.3.4 Dispute Four (2:17–3:5)

(A) **Warning**—the Day of Judgment is coming: "judgment" + "come" + "says YHWH of Armies" (2:17–3:2a)
   (B) **Means**: a "purification" (2x) of the *priests* ("sons of Levi") (3:2b–3a)
   (B') **Result**: "righteous/acceptable" "offerings" (2x) from the *people* (3:3b–4)
(A') **Warning**—the Day of Judgment is coming: "judgment" + "come" + "says YHWH of Armies" (3:5)

Some scholars might not consider this to be a chiastic structure because it seems at first glance that "only the first and last elements are clearly parallel" (Stuart 1998:1346). However, Hebrew *parallelism* does not only involve *synonymous* elements, but *contrastive* (i.e., "antithetical") as well as *logical* (e.g., "cause-effect") semantic relationships may also constitute the segments considered to be "in parallel" (cf. Wendland 2007). Especially in a text like Malachi which exhibits a penchant for concentric structures, one would naturally be inclined to interpret such doubtful cases in the light of this prevailing mode of organization. In any case, "[t]he way that 3:5 echoes 2:17 leaves little doubt that the majority of scholars are right in seeing 3:5 as bringing to a conclusion the fourth disputation and 3:6 as opening the fifth" (Stuart ibid., 1346; *contra* Dorsey 1999:323).

In this fourth major discourse unit, the announcement of a new and important theme, namely, the coming of Yahweh's "messenger" (מַלְאָכִי —3:1a), either to complement or, more likely, to replace Levi (2:7, or even Malachi himself), is foregrounded by a concentration of rhetorical devices, e.g., the LORD's response (R) incorporates a double direct quote of the recalcitrant people of Judah. This introductory portion of the dispute features some elaborate lexical patterning, which takes the form of an interlocking double chiasmus:

(A) "every evildoer...in them [Yahweh] is pleased"
   (B) Question: "where [is] the God of judgment?" (2:17)
   (B') Answer: "he will come...the Lord whom you are seeking"
(A') "...[in] whom you are pleased" (3:1)

The preceding structure is interwoven with the following one:

(A) "Behold, I am sending"
   (B) "my messenger" (3:1a)
   (B') "namely, the messenger of the covenant"
(A') "behold, he comes!" (3:1b)

Considering this section as a whole, it is important to observe that "in the chiastic arrangement of the book...the fourth and third disputations are loosely linked by their thematic content" (Stuart 1998:1347), for example, lexical catch words such as "divorce/sending" (2:6–3:1), "seeking" (2:15–3:1), "covenant" (2:10, 14–3:1), "offering" (2:12–13–3:3–4), "Israel, Jerusalem, Judah" (2:11–3:4), and YHWH as a "witness" (2:14–3:5).[12]

10.3.3.5 Dispute Five (3:6–12)

(A) **Introduction**—a divine premise: "I [YHWH] do not change!" (6)
   (B) **Contrast**—human rebellion: covenant violations in "turning away" from Yahweh (7)
      (C) **Indictment**—specific: "you have robbed me [YHWH]!" (8)
         (D) **Consequence**: "you are under a curse!" (9a)
      (C') **Indictment**—repeated: "you are robbing me!" (9b)
   (B') **Contrast**—divine grace (for those who repent with the tithe): covenant blessings (10–11)
(A') **Conclusion**—a divine promise: Messianic blessings (12)

---

[12] Dispute 4 also has thematic links with Dispute 2 "with which is shares particular interest in the corruption of the priesthood and the need for a restoration of righteousness. And it shares with all the other pericopes of the book a concern for obedience to the divinely revealed covenant, Malachi's central governing concern..." (Stuart 1998:1346)—though it would seem like now a *new covenant* is in the divinely inspired prophetic view. In any case, the careful composition and underlying thematic coherence of this prophecy as a whole is evident.

The initial and final elements in this concentric pattern (A and A') carry strong overtones of several key motifs that were introduced in the first two disputes and feature prominently in the overall message that Yahweh wishes to convey to his people. (A) recalls the loving father theme of 1:2 *(anaphora),* while (A') reminds listeners/readers of the glorious plan that Yahweh will graciously put into effect in the Messianic Age—an evangelistic program that will embrace all nations (cf. 1:5, 11, 14 – epiphora). Verse six is a divine programmatic assertion regarding the immutable justice of Yahweh that underlies much of the argumentation set forth in the rest of the prophecy, especially in 3:18 and 4:1–3.[13]

The chiastic structure of this dispute is not as transparent as in some of the preceding pericopes due to a relative decrease in the degree of parallel phrasing, though there is a considerable amount of lexical correspondence (Stuart 1998:1362).[14] Nevertheless, the patterns that have been observed elsewhere would influence one to view the unit concentrically, in a way that complements the linear arrangement pointed out in 9.3.1, i.e., $A - O - R = A_1 - O^1 - R_1 - I/I_1$. Thus, the structural turning point (C-D-C') coincides with the emotive climax in vv. 8–9, while the twin thematic theological peak is occurs on the boundaries of the structure, A and A'. The central core (D/9a) is quite dramatic, even shocking in its verbal expression as well as its spiritual implication: "As for you, with a curse you are cursed..." (בַּמְּאֵרָה אַתֶּם נֵאָרִים). This grim pronouncement stands out not only in its immediate context but also within the section as a whole since it articulates the antithesis of the outer constituents of the chiasmus. Perhaps this formal device acts as a rhetorical means of calling attention to the theological truth that a righteous God cannot condone sin;

---

[13] Verse 6 is sometimes assigned by versions and commentaries into the preceding unit, Dispute 4 (cf. Pohlig 1998:125–126).

[14] "In accordance with the overall chiastic structure of the book of Malachi, in which the disputations are arranged in a loosely concentric pattern...[see further below], the fifth disputation is relatively closer in theme to any of the others. Both call for proper offerings in obedience to the law of God.... In spite of these connections, the fifth disputatation is a very different oracle from the second. The second focuses on the priests; the fifth does not even mention them. The second warns of the turning of blessings into curses; the fifth promises blessing instead of curse.... The second warns the priests of judgment for disobedience; the fifth invites the nation to obey and witness the generous benefits of obedience. The second is about worship; the fifth is about temple support" (Stuart 1998:1362). Although there is some evidence for these contrastive features that Stuart outlines, there is actually more similarity between disputes 2 and 5 than he seems to allow for, and it is not quite accurate to claim that "the fifth promises blessing instead of curse" (cf. 3:9). The people's sin still had to be dealt with first (by "turning," v. 7b) before any blessing would materialize.

Yahweh's justice will not be compromised by his merciful desire and will to forgive those who have rebelled ("turned"—vv. 6–7) against him.

10.3.3.6 Dispute Six (3:13–4:3)

(A) **Objection**—Yahweh is unjust: "serve God" + "doers of wickedness" (13–15)
   (B) **Blessing**—a "scroll of remembrance": YHWH "hears" those who "fear" him (16)
   (B') **Blessing**—a "treasured possession": compassionate YHWH will "spare" them (17)
(A') **Refutation**—Yahweh is just: "serve God" + the wicked" (18)

Segment (A) bears a strong resemblance to the initial unit of Dispute 4 (cf. 2:17, *anaphora*). An obvious lexical *inclusio* demarcates the boundaries of segment (B) in the words "those who feared Yahweh" (יִרְאֵי יְהוָה),[15] and the thematically significant parallel expression "those who revere his name" (חֹשְׁבֵי שְׁמוֹ—cf. 1:6, 11, 14) leads to (B'). Segment (B') then reiterates the content of (B) in covenantal terminology, coupling "the day" of judgment/vindication with the focal father-son motif (cf. 1:6). Finally, segment (A') sets the stage for the second half of this dispute (4:1–3), which elaborates upon the different manner in which the LORD is going to treat "the righteous and the wicked" in his righteous judicial process:

(A) **Fate** of the unrighteous: "day" + "wicked" + "ablaze" + "...says YHWH of Armies" (1)
   (B) **Future** of the righteous: "fear my name" + metaphors of healing and happiness (2)
(A') **Fate** of the unrighteous: "wicked" + "ashes" + "day" + "...says YHWH of Armies" (3)

These verses are associated with 3:13–18 by virtue of the fact that they thematically satisfy the anticipation that was aroused in v. 18. The two segments are also linked by a number of salient lexical correspondences, for example: "day" (3:17—4:1, 3), "doers of wickedness" (3:13—4:1), "wicked"

---

[15] The third-person narrative discourse of 3:16 is stylistically quite distinct. The text alludes to a "covenant renewal" ceremony involving the penitent God-fearers in Judah (cf. Nehemiah 9–10; Pohlig 1998:179–180). This "serves to remind us that the inspired prophet has not been straitjacketed by the format he has adhered to. The rhetorical disputation format provides the general structure for each oracle, but the content is far more important than the form and is expressed whether or not it exactly fits an idealized norm. To one extent or another this has been the case throughout the book, so that none of the oracles is a mirror image of any of the others" (Stuart 1998:1375). Thus, stylistic *form* is in service of theological *content* is in service of spiritual *purpose*.

(3:18–4:3), and "those who fear YHWH/my Name" (3:16–4:2). These words, as throughout the prophecy, are not chosen at random; on the contrary, each represents a key concept that the LORD wanted to emphatically convey to the Jews in his passionate appeal for repentance. Appropriate and attractive verbal selection, reiteration, and placement are more instances of stylistic expertise—of the masterful application of rhetorical form to divine content that distinguishes the message of Malachi from those of his rabbinic contemporaries at the close of the Old Testament prophetic tradition of religious discourse.

10.3.3.7 Overview

In closing and for the purpose of summary, we note Dorsey's proposed chiastic arrangement of the entire book of Malachi (1999:323, somewhat modified):

Introduction to the "oracle"(s) of Yahweh (1:1)
(A) **Yahweh is just**: he "loves" (the faithful remnant of) Israel, but will utterly destroy wicked Edom (1:2–5)
- Judgment on the <u>wicked</u> (רִשְׁעָה) nation: YHWH has destroyed Edom and "though they rebuild, I will tear down"
  (B) the priests and people have **cheated Yahweh** in their offerings (1:6–14)
  ○ <u>unacceptable and inferior offerings</u> have been brought
  ○ a <u>curse</u> upon those who have cheated Yahweh in their offerings
  ○ Yahweh wishes someone would <u>shut the doors</u> of his temple to prohibit such offerings
  ○ A <u>five-part introduction</u>, followed by exhortation and promise
    (C) in the **past** Levi served in righteousness, but <u>Levites have turned from YHWH</u> (2:1–9)
    - Levi kept Yahweh's <u>covenant</u> (בְּרִית)
    - the priest is the <u>messenger</u> (מַלְאָךְ) of Yahweh
    - priests have turned aside from the <u>way</u> (דֶּרֶךְ) of Yahweh
    - look back at a <u>time of past righteousness</u>
      → (D) CENTER: **the people/priests must stop being faithless!** (2:10–16)[16]
    (C') in the **future** Yahweh's messenger will come and <u>Levites will be purified</u> (2:17–3:5)
    - he will be the "messenger of the <u>covenant</u>" (בְּרִית)

---

[16] "The book's central unit features the book's call to repentance. Here Malachi appeals to the people to stop being faithless. The theme of this unit is the faithlessness of the people—in their social relations, their spiritual obligations, and their marital relations. The term *bâgad* ('be faithless') ties this unit together; it occurs throughout the unit (2:10, 11, 14, 15, 16) and nowhere else in the book" (Dorsey 1999:323–324).

- he will be the messenger (מַלְאָךְ) of YHWH
- he will "prepare the way (דֶּרֶךְ) before Yahweh"
- look back at a time of past righteousness

(B') people have **robbed YHWH** in tithes/offerings, but if they repent, God will bless them (3:6–12)
  - unacceptable tithes and offerings have been brought
  - "You are cursed with a curse, for you are robbing me!"
  - YHWH wishes people would bring proper offerings so he will open the windows of heaven for them
  - five-part introduction, followed by exhortation and promise

(A') **Yahweh is just**: he will reward the righteous, but will utterly destroy the wicked (3:13–4:3 [3:13–21])
- Judgment on the wicked (רָשָׁע): YHWH will destroy them, leaving them "neither root nor branch"

Conclusion: the Day of Yahweh will surely come—for blessing or judgment (4:4–6 [3:22–24])

To be sure, a number of the parallels suggested above could be questioned or argued against, e.g., the "five-part introduction, followed by exhortation and promise" characterization of sections (B) and (B'). But most of the other correspondences seem to be fairly well supported in more abstract, topical terms, especially the two (C) sections, where some important lexical recursion serves to cement the linkage. If this overall concentric discourse organization is granted,[17] it indicates the central portion (D) is of special significance (2:10–16). I would suggest that this section, which corresponds with Dispute 3 in the linear progression of Yahweh's argument, functions as the *hortatory climax* of the prophecy, where Malachi's persistent and forceful, emotively-toned language carries considerable impact, for example:

- "we profane the covenant of our fathers" (2:10)
- "Judah has profaned the sanctuary that Yahweh loves" (2:11)
- "may Yahweh cut him off from the tents of Jacob" (2:12)
- "you [people] cover Yahweh's altar [with] tears" (2:13)
- "you have been faithless to the wife of your youth" (2:14)
- "guard yourselves in your spirit" (2:15)
- "I hate divorce" (2:16)

The *theological peak* of Malachi then appears to occur in the next unit (C' = Dispute 4, 3:17–4:5). At this point in the prophet's message, there is an

---

[17] Stuart observes, "The chiastic arrangement of the book represents a careful, intentional pairing of the various disputations" (1998:1250), that is: (A) Superscription [1:1]—(B) 1st Dispute [1:2–5]—(C) 2nd Dispute [1:6–2:9]—(D) 3rd Dispute [2:10–16] = = (D') 4th Dispute [2:17–3:5]—(C') 5th Dispute [3:6–12]—(B') 6th Dispute [3:13–4:3]—(A') Summary Challenge [4:4–6].

unexpected prediction of "my messenger…the messenger of the covenant" (מַלְאָכִ֑י ... מַלְאַ֣ךְ הַבְּרִ֗ית), uttered by Yahweh himself (3:1). This Messianic prophecy promising future purification and justification is reinforced and elaborated upon then at the end of the book (Dispute 6, especially in 4:1–3), which is a common, rhetorically significant feature of such unbalanced (odd-numbered) chiastic arrangements in biblical discourse.

10.4 Prophetic rhetoric: On the pragmatic implications of literary style and structure

This chapter, like those which have preceded it, gives an indication how a specific literary-structural analysis as part of a broader historical-linguistic approach can assist Bible scholars in their study of the varied prophetic writings of the Hebrew Scriptures. A *structural* analysis deals with the larger organization of the text as a whole, including its compositional boundaries, strategies of internal cohesion and coherence, its arrangement of major and minor topics, and the foregrounding of points of special thematic and pragmatic significance (i.e., peak and climax). A *literary* analysis, in turn, complements the former by investigating the micro-structure (style) of the discourse with respect to *artistic forms* (e.g., figurative language, phonological features, parallel patterns) and *rhetorical functions* (to create impact, appeal, a sense of unity, harmony, tension, and so forth). In this concluding section, I will summarize some of the main implications of this type of study with special reference to biblical exegesis (interpretation) and translation (communication), which have been my primary areas of interest throughout this book.

10.4.1 Interpreting the text—exegesis

There are several important *caveats* to keep in mind when carrying out a literary-structural analysis of Scripture. To begin with, it must always begin with, and be based upon a thorough verse-by-verse, word-by-word exegesis of the original Hebrew text. A study of the whole without fully understanding the parts is, at best, superficial and probably also highly speculative; a study of the parts without an understanding of the total framework (the "big picture") may be misleading or simply wrong in a number of its conclusions since it fails to distinguish the forest (the overall structure and purpose of the discourse) on account of the trees (being bogged down in the disorganized detail of individual verses). Thus, both types of analysis are necessary, the holistic as well as the specific, for they inevitably serve to complement and correct each other. Included as part of a verse-level examination of the text must be some serious *isagogical* (social-scientific) research into its context, namely, the *extra-linguistic background* of a book (i.e., the particular historical, political, religious, literary, and sociocultural setting) as well as the *interpersonal circumstances* (i.e., the "rhetorical exigency") in which the message first originated as a dynamic communication event involving Yahweh, his prophet, and a designated audience group or the people of God in their entirety, present as well as future.

Second, a literary-structural study must never become an end in itself—a convenient means of demonstrating the analyst's facility and finesse in uncovering and describing all kinds of elaborately constructed patterns, some of which pass beyond the bounds of perception and credibility, even for the trained reader. Rather, the aim should always be to elucidate the text in order to bring out its intended message more clearly and comprehensively. It must be to demonstrate how God in his infinite wisdom employed also the diverse forms of human language (Hebrew and Greek in particular) in order to more effectively and memorably transmit theological truths and ethical principles to humanity.

Finally, one must be careful not to claim or base too much upon such a study. Literary criticism and discourse analysis are simply several scholarly tools among many that the Bible student has at his/her disposal to probe more deeply into the depths of meaning and relevance of these ancient religious documents. Even a thorough literary-structural analysis cannot help us solve all of the outstanding questions and pressing exegetical issues that one might confront when probing the various facets that pertain to the investigation of a communication event of utmost importance that took place several thousand years ago or more, and in a cultural-religious environment that is much different from that of the analyst. Nevertheless, that fraction of increased insight must not be ignored if it helps one to better comprehend today what the biblical writer was saying then, and why—that is, what he presumably aimed to achieve by his message.

What are the main contributions of this type of analysis to biblical scholarship? I see two principal applications of a literary-structural (LS) analysis which have been exemplified in the preceding examination of Malachi. It remains for others to follow up and conduct some parallel research in order to more fully assess the validity and to explore the implications of the following related pair of observations.

An LS analysis helps one to understand the biblical author's message more completely by revealing in a more explicit and comprehensive fashion the *overall arrangement of content* of the text under consideration, in particular, how the subject matter is organized and subdivided into a variety of linear and/or concentric patterns. In short, by knowing the "how," one is in a better position to grasp the "what" of the intended message in terms of its semantic sense and pragmatic significance. Thus, the discourse structure reveals a work's principal and subsidiary themes along with the manner in which these are developed (expanded, sub-divided, reiterated, combined, contrasted, etc.) from one point to another to comprise the text in its entirety. The associated stylistic examination then suggests places where the author employed a rhetorical spotlight, as it were, to reinforce and to highlight his main ideas and communicative goals. In the case of Malachi, we have noted how the major and minor linear as well as concentric arrangements, coupled with a diverse inventory of literary devices, serve both to shape and also to sharpen Yahweh's sincere appeal to repossess the "heart" of his obstinate people.

An LS study has relevance not only for the higher-level meaning of a given book, but it also aids in the *exegesis and interpretation* of individual passages. As we have seen, the whole sheds light on the parts (a "top-down" analysis), even as the parts combine to constitute the whole (a "bottom-up" analysis). In cases where two (or more) valid, text-supported interpretations are possible for a certain verse, knowledge of the encompassing literary patterns may tip the balance in favor of one reading or another—or lead one to conclude that both are likely (i.e., an instance of deliberate ambiguity). In our construal of 1:5, for example, *epiphoric* pressure exerted from 1:11 and 1:14 with respect to the repeated phrases, "my name" and "among the nations," would influence one to see a corresponding pair in 1:5, viz., "Yahweh" and "*beyond* the border of Israel" (rather than *over* the border of Israel," e.g., Keil 1969, Verhoef 1987).[18] Similarly, the fact that 2:15 occurs

---

[18] "This translation is supported by at least some old Jewish commentators, and implies that foreigners will praise the God of Israel. This interpretation is also supported by the Targum and the Peshitta" (Pohlig 1998:33–34).

at a corresponding stage with 2:10 in a chiastic frame would lend support to the NIV interpretation of the former passage—namely, that the subject of the initial verb ('he has made/done' עָשָׂה) is "God" and not "Abraham."[19] As was pointed out earlier, evaluative critical comments based on literary and/or structural criteria are by no means conclusive. Nevertheless, they do contribute additional evidence in favor of one exegetical position over against another—hence providing evidence which must be carefully considered and weighed as to reliability just like any other information that is available to the analyst or translator.

10.4.2 Communicating the text—translation

The results of an LS analysis are normally able to improve the overall *quality* of a Bible translation. Over and above the exegetical insights that it provides, this discourse-oriented approach clearly indicates limited points or broader areas where the original text is marked by some type of rhetorical highlighting—for example, the climactic utterance of unit *closure* in 1:5: "Great is Yahweh even beyond the border[s] of Israel!" (יִגְדַּל יְהוָה מֵעַל לִגְבוּל יִשְׂרָאֵל—note the impressive alliteration). These places of formal and semantic prominence ought to be preserved in a translation if possible, for translation is not merely a matter of transferring, or reproducing, message content from one language to another. It must also, if circumstances allow, be faithful also to the manifest beauty and intended communicative effect of the original text. Often to achieve literary as well as semantic equivalence in the target language, the linguistic forms used to convey the source language message must be modified or even completed transformed.

In Chewa, for example, the theological proclamation above would have to be restated from a literal rendering as follows—that is, in order to duplicate its essential impact in direct speech and unit-ending signaling function: *Ndithudi, ukulu wa Chauta umadziwika konsekonse, ngakhale kunja kwa dzikolino la Israele!* "Indeed, the greatness of Yahweh is known everywhere, even outside of this country of Israel!" In the next verse (1:6), which begins the second disputation, the concluding censure of the LORD, which sets up

---

[19] Such a construal is reinforced by the immediate context, where the specific topic has to do with divorce rather than a second marriage. See a full discussion of the many issues that pertain to this extremely difficult passage in Pohlig (1998:111–120).

the priests' impudent reply, is encoded in the form of a participial construction in the Hebrew. In English, however, the emphasis embedded in these words is more dynamically—and arguably more accurately—expressed by an existential copula construction: "*It is you*, O priests, who despise my name!" (NIV). A similar type of syntactic formation is needed in Chewa: *Ansembe inu, ndinu amene mumanyoza dzina langatu!* "You priests (disparaging vocative), you are the ones who despise my very name!" Many instances of this type of restatement occur throughout the prophecy in a literary functional-equivalence translation (*LiFE*, cf. Wendland 2011). Individually, these modifications might not seem so important, but in relation to the book as a whole they do make a difference, thus transforming the Word of the Lord into a much more worthy verbal representation in another language.

A written translation can also be enhanced *typographically* and through the rhetorical use of *formatting*—produced on the basis of the information derived from a prior LS analysis of the Hebrew text. In addition to the inclusion of precise section headings, such a version would seek to display the various parallel patterns and points of emphasis of the original, as shown in the selection of 1:6–14 on the next page (the NIV reformatted) following the Chewa sample below. Not only does a text display like the following make it easier to observe the important parallels in Malachi's argument at a glance, but it also renders it easier to read, whether silently or aloud, as one moves from one meaningful segment to the next down the page (cf. Wendland and Louw 1993).

One might take the preceding a step further and aim to create an oratorical version, that is, a translation that reproduces the vibrant character of the biblical text with a special emphasis on its *oral-aural* qualities—those phonological features that serve to captivate the ear helping it tune in more closely to the prophet's message. Below is a sample of a more sound-sensitive, rendition in Chewa (i.e., balanced utterance length, rhythmic, euphonious)—covering the didactic Epilogue of the book (4:4–6):

10.4 Prophetic rhetoric: On the pragmatic implications of literary style and structure

Inu nonse, kumbukirani zophunzitsa zanga zonse,	All of you, you must remember all of my teachings,
malamulo ndi malangizo amene ndidauza Aisraele,	the commands and instructions that I told the Israelites,
kudzera mtumiki wanga Mose, ku phirilo la Sinayi.	through my servant, Moses, at that mountain of Sinai.
Dziwani ichinso, kuti lisanafike tsiku lija loopsatu,	Know this too, that before the day arrives, that awful one,
la kudza kwa ine Chauta, n'dzakutumizirani wina.	of the coming of me, Yahweh, I'll send you another one.
Iyeyo adzakhaladi ngati Eliya, mneneri wanga uja,	He will be just like Elijah, that prophet of mine,
motero adzamvanitsa mitima ya atate ndi ana ao;	so he'll harmonize hearts of fathers with their children;
n'chimodzimodzinso adzayanjanitsa ana ndi atate.	likewise, he will reconcile children with [their] fathers.
Zikalephereka izi, n'dzabwera ndi kukantha dziko,	If this fails, I will come and strike the land,
lidzaonongeka n'kuoneka kuti n'lotembererekadi!	it'll be destroyed and look like it's completely cursed!

1:6 "A son honors his father, and a servant his master.
If I am a father, where is the honor due me?
If I am a master, where is the respect due me?"
says the Lord Almighty.
"It is you, O priests, who show contempt for my **name**.
"But you ask, 'How have we shown contempt for your **name**?'
    ⁷ "You place defiled food on my altar.
    "But you ask, 'How have we defiled you?'
    "By saying that the Lord's table is contemptible.
        ⁸ When you bring blind animals for sacrifice,
        is that not wrong?
        When you sacrifice crippled or diseased animals,
        is that not wrong?
        Try offering them to your governor!
        Would he be pleased with you?
        Would he accept you?"
    says the Lord Almighty.
    ⁹ "Now implore God to be gracious to us.
    With such offerings from your hands,
    will he accept you?"
    says the Lord Almighty.
        ¹⁰ "Oh, that one of you would shut the temple doors,
        so that you would not light useless fires on my altar!
        I am not pleased with you," says the Lord Almighty,
        "and I will accept no offering from your hands.

> ¹¹ *My **name** will be great among the nations,*
> *from the rising to the setting of the sun.*
> *In every place incense and pure offerings will be brought to my name,*
> *because my **name** will be great among the nations,"*
> *says the* <u>Lord</u> *Almighty.*
>
> ¹:¹² "But you profane [my **name**]
> by saying of the Lord's table, 'It is defiled,'
> and of its food, 'It is contemptible.'
> ¹³ And you say, 'What a burden!'
> and you sniff at it contemptuously,"
> says the <u>Lord</u> Almighty.
> "When you bring injured, crippled or diseased animals
> and offer them as sacrifices,
> should I accept them from your hands?" says the <u>Lord</u>.
> ¹⁴ "Cursed is the cheat
> who has an acceptable male in his flock
> and vows to give it,
> but then sacrifices a blemished animal to the Lord.
> For I am a great king," says the <u>Lord</u> Almighty,
> *"and my **name** is to be feared among the nations."*

In summary, the effort that is expended in carrying out an LS analysis and translation will inevitably be rewarded by an increased awareness of the *rhetorical and artistic qualities* of a given text of Scripture—the pure beauty as well as the evocative power of the Word of God. Such a heightened response may hopefully stimulate a keener awareness of the literary riches of the Bible, which always complement its theological and ethical content in various ways. This may lead, in turn, to a greater appreciation for the work—to be specific, a fuller realization of the different ways in which the diverse poetic devices of the original language are pressed into the service of a more dynamic, even dramatic, representation of the complete meaning (semantic and pragmatic) of the passage at hand. In their repeated encounters with such a timeless, living discourse, readers and hearers alike will be motivated and moved to more effectively communicate the divine message, contextualizing it first of all for themselves and then for others. The essential idea of the prophet Malachi is this: Let us all together reverence Yahweh and respect his name in our daily lives, for as the Lord of Armies, he is most certainly worthy of our total devotion. It is this truth to which the book's rhetorical style also attests—its concentric patterns of arrangement balancing and harmonizing with its linear organization to produce a text in which theological content is powerfully affirmed by literary form to augment its prophetic purpose.

11

A Case Study in Cross-Cultural Communication

"Do you understand what you are reading (hearing)?" – The example of Isaiah 52:13–53:12 in Tonga[1]

As has already been illustrated in the preceding text studies, Scripture communication via translation is a rather complicated process. Before the exchange of messages can be regarded as being complete, the original biblical document must be correctly understood by its intended readership or audience. It is one thing to produce an accurate exegesis of the biblical text; it is yet another to convey that clearly—with appropriate rhetorical flourish—in the target language. Nevertheless, that is not the end of the translation story. The translators and their associates must go on to ensure that their vernacular version is properly understood. This act of comprehension cannot be taken for granted as the following case study would suggest. It is based on a comparative analysis of two translations of

---
[1] This chapter is a revised edition of ch. 6 from Ernst Wendland and Salimo Hachibamba, *Galu wamkota: Missiological reflections from south-central Africa* (Kachere Series Monograph; Zomba, Malawi: Kachere Series/Lansing: Michigan State University Press, 2007).

the well-known prophetic passage of Isaiah 52:13–53:12 in Tonga, a Bantu language spoken by several million people in Zambia and Zimbabwe.

The point of this study is to encourage readers to think of their own (or some other) non-English language and cultural setting and in that contextual light to consider the following questions:

- Would the same or similar problems of style and/or meaning occur in my language-culture as are pointed out in the Tonga translation(s) below?

- Would rather different translation difficulties arise in my communication setting, and if so, why would they occur?

- Which difficulties previously noted are of a specifically rhetorical nature— that is, they would most likely affect people's assessment of the verbal quality of the translation in terms of its impact and appeal—in short, its power to persuade?

- What would be the most effective way of solving these various problems for a particular target group and type of translation? (Specify these variables.)

- How does the oral-aural factor affect one's evaluation of these issues? In other words, how would the translation in my language (or language X) rank in terms of readability and/or audibility? How can this important (but often neglected) feature of the translation be tested and evaluated?

- When considering a purely aural presentation of this translation, how can one deal with those problem areas that a written version can take care of through paratextual means, e.g., footnotes, illustrations, cross-references, section headings, and the like? For example, what can replace footnotes in an oral presentation of the biblical text?

Introduction: Proclaiming an ancient Hebrew prophecy in a modern Bantu setting

In response to the Evangelist Philip's perhaps unexpected query, the Ethiopian dignitary replied, "How can I, unless someone guides me?" (Acts 8:31a, NRSV). This is the answer that many Tonga Christians must also give as they try to read, or simply listen to, the text of the old Bible written in their language.[2] There is no doubt in their minds that this is indeed the

---

[2] The Batonga people (language: Citonga) inhabit as their traditional homeland large parts of the Southern Province in Zambia and corresponding areas across the Zambezi River in northern Zimbabwe. The Tonga (for short) are a matrilineal, patrilocal people who may be roughly categorized anthropologically as a Southern Bantu, cattle-culture group. Of course,

Introduction: Proclaiming an ancient Hebrew prophecy in a modern Bantu setting

Word of God *(Majwi aa Leza)*, but why did he choose to communicate with people in language that is so difficult at times to understand and that often sounds as if God speaks with a foreign accent? To be sure, it is with great gratitude that we note that by the end of 2008 at least a portion of the Bible existed in over 700 (718) of the estimated 2000+ languages spoken in Africa, including 326 New Testaments and 169 full Bibles.[3] But many of these Scripture texts are old and relatively literal, missionary translations which are often characterized by a form of language that is not completely natural and/or up-to-date in comparison with what is used by the majority of speakers today. In many cases, therefore, Philip's question needs to be seriously repeated, again and again: "Do you *[really]* understand what you are reading or *hearing* (since most people hear the Bible being read rather than actually reading it for themselves)?"[4] And this must be followed by another, equally important query, depending on one's response to the first: If "yes," then, "All right, then what does this passage mean in your own words?" This is to check up on the completeness and accuracy of one's understanding. But if "no," then, "Why not; what seems to be the problem here?" This is to try to determine what has gone wrong with the communication process. Why has God's Word failed to convey its intended meaning, and what can be done to set things right?

The following case study is presented to illustrate the importance of questions such as these when evaluating the *quality* of Scripture *use* in Africa. There is no doubt about the *quantity* of such use, for the Bible in most countries on the continent is an "open book," that is, freely and widely used for a variety of purposes under the broad categories of Christian preaching, teaching, witnessing, personal reading, and private devotion. (Mbiti 1986:chs. 2–4). But what people actually do comprehend from their Bibles in terms of the sufficiency and accuracy of information derived is open to serious question. So we will take a relatively well-known portion of the text—that is, the

---

nowadays many Tonga are urban dwellers and engage in various business ventures to earn their livings, but the majority still practice farming and herding in rural areas, which include some of the most fertile agricultural areas of Zambia.

[3] These statistics are from the most recent online UBS *World Report* published by the United Bible Societies (www.biblesociety.org/index.php?id=22) 2008. This list includes 16 vernacular Bibles and ten Testaments in Zambia

[4] This distinction between hearing and reading is especially important in many countries of Africa where the *functional* (that is, the actual, practical) literacy rate is relatively low (despite published government statistics which seem to deny this fact), that is, less than 50 percent overall and usually less than 40 percent for women.

climactic "suffering Servant" pericope from Isaiah, namely, 52:13–53:12 in the old Tonga version[5]—and interrogate it. In other words, we go through this passage from beginning to end verse by verse and select a number of the major critical questions that the text raises from the perspective of an "average" reader or listener (rural, lay, Christian).[6] We will briefly comment on the nature of the various problems involved and suggest some possible solutions, both textual (translational) and extratextual (supplementary), with special reference to the new "popular-language," meaning-oriented translation of the Bible that was published over two decades ago (1997).[7]

It is agreed that for most Christians a "Philip"—whether in the person of an individual fellow believer or the church at large will always be necessary for the purposes of correction, clarification, instruction, guidance, and encouragement. But the issue that we wish to address here is simply this: What can *reasonably* be done—that is, without compromising either the limitations of publishing resources or the conservative theological character of the Tonga constituency—both inside and outside the printed text to promote a fuller grasp of the Scriptures as they are being read, whether orally aloud or silently to oneself? Due to the limitations of space, the respective old (OB) and new (NB) Tonga versions that are cited as examples will be given in relatively literal English only, except for certain key vernacular words or phrases. Furthermore, it will not be possible to go into details during this presentation; the particular problem in question will simply be pointed out and concisely explained with reference also to one or more available means of resolution. Various difficulties pertaining to language and culture will not be separated in the discussion since in many cases they are very closely related and must be dealt with together within the scope of a given translation text. The specific verse from Isaiah under consideration will be indicated by a bold reference number at the beginning of each section. English Scripture text citations are from the New Revised Standard Version [NRSV] unless indicated otherwise.

---

[5] The old Tonga Bible (OB) was published in 1963, its NT in 1949.

[6] In addition to their Bible translation work, each of the authors has been engaged in a multi-leveled teaching and pastoral ministry in both urban and rural Zambia in several language areas for many years.

[7] For an overview of the basic translation principles and procedures that guided the production of this Bible, one may consult Wendland (1998), which deals with a comparable version in Chichewa of Malawi. See also Nida and Taber 1969; de Waard and Nida 1986.

Hearing Isaiah's text today: How would an ordinary Mutonga respond?

52:13 The first problem for the listener (reader) is one which recurs throughout the Hebrew prophets in particular: *Who* is speaking the words of this verse, as well as those which follow? Is it the prophet, Isaiah, God (or "the LORD"), or some other, unnamed person? It is important to clarify this because the reference of all of the text's first-person pronouns (e.g., "my") depends on this identification. Trained Bible readers can look back to the preceding verse and deduce that the speaker and referent (antecedent) of "my" in v. 13 is "the LORD" of v. 12. But such an inference is not so easy to make for unskilled readers and pure listeners of the passage, for two reasons: (a) the references to God in v. 12 are in the third person, not the first; and (b) a major sectional break occurs between verses 12 and 13, and therefore they are not often taken together in most public readings of the Scriptures. In many cases, a section heading or title does not help since this does not usually reveal the speaker either, e.g., "The Suffering Servant" ([NRSV] and *Good News Bible* [GNB]). In order to resolve this difficulty, the Tonga NB introduces this pericope with the words, "In this way speaks Chief-God saying..."[8]

The OB uses the word *mulanda* to render the key term "servant" for which Tonga does not seem to have an indigenous equivalent. The problem with *mulanda* is its rather negative connotation, i.e., a "slave," a person who was either captured in war or was sold in payment for a personal or familial debt. Why would God, the LORD, engage such unfortunate people in his service? The NB employs *mubelesi* "work-person" (M/F), a loanword from the Lozi language. While this is certainly more appropriate in this context than *mulanda*, it still gives a somewhat misleading impression of the nature and role of this "servant of the LORD". In this case, *mwiiminizi* "representative" (ambassador) would fit even better, also according to biblical Hebrew usage, and it would further serve to heighten the shame of this person's total rejection by the majority of his own people (53:3).

---

[8] The NB in Tonga renders the Hebrew divine tetragrammaton *(YHWH)*, "Yahweh" ("LORD" in most English Bibles), as *Mwami Leza* 'Chief-God' instead of *Jehova* as found in the OB. "Jehovah" has a foreign, sometimes even colonialistic (white-man) sound to it because, as far as most people are concerned, this name comes from the English language. The two terms that comprise the compound designation *Mwami Leza* would be ambiguous as references to "Yahweh" if used alone. But when spoken in conjunction with one another, they constitute a natural, easy-sounding designation of the distinct and personal covenant God of Israel.

In the OB it is somewhat surprisingly reported that this divine "slave" will literally "get lucky" *(-jana coolwe)*. His elevation sounds like it is purely a matter of chance, and God has nothing to do with it. The question that this prediction raises for many listeners is, "How would such an amazing turn of events take place?" In a strictly earthly setting (which is all that is suggested by the present passage) the following references to being "raised up" and "honoured" would seem to denote the miraculous obtaining of a well-paying, executive type of job, perhaps as the head of a major company or manufacturing firm. As already indicated, the NB clearly connects the servant's elevation in status to the LORD's pronouncement and activity; nothing is left to "chance." Instead, he will "be successful in" or "carry through to completion" *(-zwidilila)* some activity on behalf of (implied) *Mwami Leza*.

52:14 This verse, together with v. 15, presents the difficulty of inter-clausal transition and semantic complexity, which is another one of the main challenges presented by Hebrew prophetic writing. The question this passage poses for listeners is simply: How does it all fit together? The Tonga OB, following the RSV, translates vv. 14–15 as a single overly long sentence, one that contains a prominent parenthesis in the middle covering the second half of v. 14. Such a large chunk is indeed hard to mentally "process," or comprehend, as one reads along. Therefore, it is broken up into four shorter, more manageable utterances in the NB, while the disruptive parenthesis is removed and recomposed as an independent unit. That still leaves the problem of clarifying the distinct connections between the various clause (or poetic "colon") segments of the sequence of ideas found in these verses, which has also tested the skills of many commentators.[9] Instead of the comparative notion, "Just as..." (NRSV, OB, NB—*Mbubonya mbuli*) at the beginning of v. 14, a contrastive pair of temporal expressions may be the best way to establish the basic twofold effect-to-cause linkage of ideas in these verses. Thus, v. 14 would begin with "Formerly" *[Kaindi]* or "At first" *[Cakusanguna]* in order to relate to a time prior to the servant's exaltation mentioned in v. 13. Verse 15 would start with "So then" *[Nkaako]* or "As

---

[9] One of the clearest exegetical presentations of this entire segment (52:13–15) is found in Alex Motyer, *The Prophecy of Isaiah* (Leicester: InterVarsity, 1993:424–426). Within the confines of this essay, it is not possible to analyze the structure or hermeneutics of this passage (or any other) on the basis of the original Hebrew text.

a result" [*Aboobo,* NB] with specific reference to the amazing effects of the servant's humiliation recorded in v. 14.

Among the Tonga it is culturally inappropriate to laugh at or call attention to a person's ugliness or physical deformity as seems to be the case in v. 14. The literal equivalent of "Behold!" from v. 13 in both the OB and NB appears to suggest this scenario, i.e., *Amubone!* "May you [pl.] see" (better would be *Masimpe!* "Truly").[10] Such behaviour is in effect despising God *(Leza),* the ultimate Creator of all human beings. If someone were born either deformed, lame, or "with an appearance more ugly than anyone else on earth" (OB), the practice of sorcery would be suspected, e.g., a father magically utilizing the power of his unborn child's body part in order to "energize" a charm for making him wealthy. The guilty party in such cases would be identified by means of divination. However, if a person were disfigured later in life, it would be viewed as being the result of punishment for some personal crime against society, e.g., adultery, or less likely nowadays, as a "scapegoat" to pay for some communally-significant violation provoked by one or more members of an entire family or clan, e.g., stealing cattle.[11] In any case, an explanatory footnote would be helpful (i.e., in a future edition of the NB) to point out that none of the preceding "culturalized" interpretations are applicable with regard to this passage.

52:15 The paradoxical pair of parallel statements found in the second half of this verse are made even more difficult to understand in the Tonga OB due to its literal rendering, e.g., How does someone "see" *(-bona)* a "spoken news report" *(makani)?* The proverbial quality of these last two utterances, which seem to point to some "unique truth" of theological significance (Motyer 1993:426), might be utilized to heighten the enigmatic nature of the preceding verses which juxtapose references to the exaltation (v. 13) and humiliation (v. 14) of the LORD's ambassador. In order to formally mark such usage, the traditional verbal introduction to a riddle *(kalabi)*

---

[10] The structural importance of this Hebrew attention-grabbing particle *(hinney)* is outlined in Motyer 1993:424.

[11] From an indigenous Tonga point of view, it would be much more relevant to present the (life) story of Christ beginning with his passion, which is the most significant aspect of his existence here on earth. One would then work back to his earlier years, including his birth, in order to see how these preceding events led up to, or even caused his death at the hands of his own people. The subsequent story of his resurrection and exultation presents distinct interpretational problems of its own (see below).

might be used in the NB, i.e., *Nkaako* "There it is!" – in place of the present causal connective (*Nkaambo* "for").

53:1 Another problem of pronominal reference leads off this second portion (stanza) of the so-called "Servant Song" (i.e., 52:13–15, 53:1–3, 4–6, 7–9, 10–12): To whom does the "we" of "*our* message" refer? Is it the prophet himself (speaking in the "editorial plural"), the prophet and his prophetic colleagues, the prophet and his fellow countrymen/women in general (if rendered "what we have heard" NRSV, cf. GNB), or even the gentiles (speaking as a distinct group, cf. the preceding verse)? A footnote is probably necessary to designate the second choice, the communal "prophetic voice," as the most likely interpretation (cf. 52:7). And what is this message? Most likely what the prophet reported in stanza one as the NB indicates, "the things we have spoken." This is a matter of "belief" (-*syoma*, NB), not mere assent, as the OB suggests: "So who agreed with (-*zumina*) our story?"

Mention of "the arm of Jehovah" being "revealed" (OB) causes considerable perplexity for most listeners: How can any part of God, who is a *spiritual* being, be physically seen by any human? Like all peoples, the Tonga employ various picturesque anthropomorphic expressions to designate certain prominent characteristics and activities of the traditional God *Leza*, for example, in these praise names which laud God's gracious preservation of his people: *Nacoombe* "Madam Cow" and *Namakolomakolo* "She of many breasts" (note the prominent *female* component in each of these). But nothing of this nature is ever said about God's "arm." The NB clarifies (part) of the intended sense with its rendering, "To whom has Chief-God shown his powers?"[12]

The nature of the two rhetorical questions found in this verse is different. The self-understood answer to the first query is "No-one!" But that will not work in the case of the second, which is probably best construed as an implicit critical comment on the first question. In other words, those who have already witnessed the LORD's powerful deeds of deliverance (2) *should have* believed what the prophetic messengers reported (1). This interconnected relationship will have to be pointed out in future editions of the

---

[12] Motyer (1993:427) makes a good case for understanding "Arm of the LORD" as a metonymic reference to God himself in the person of his chosen Servant (52:13, cf. 51:9).

NB, preferably in the translation itself (e.g., by changing the second question into an emphatic direct statement) or alternatively, in an explanatory footnote.

53:2 The first ambiguous pronoun, "he" (OB), is rendered explicitly in the NB as "that worker/servant of his (God's)," while the second, "him" (OB), is replaced by its referent "God" in order to prevent any misunderstanding. The shoot-root imagery used to describe the LORD's servant may be misleading to some who live in a Tonga environmental setting. The original biblical similes would suggest "the miserable nature of the conditions in the midst of which the servant's life was lived" (Young 1972:342) (cf. Isa 6:13, 11:1). For the Tonga, however, it is only natural to expect a root to spring up out of hard, dry ground, for this is what happens every September before the onset of the annual rains. In fact, such prolific growth is a good sign which points ahead to the promise of another season of life-giving "water from God." Such a clash in connotations would need to be pointed out in a footnote. Another misleading notion that may require a similar mode of correction involves widespread beliefs concerning "witchcraft/sorcery" *(bulozi)*. If a green shoot were to spring up out of the dry ground which constituted the floor of one's house, then this would be taken as a clear sign that the owner was a practicing "witch/sorcerer" *(mulozi)*.

The literal expression "that we should desire him" (NRSV, OB) at the end of this verse must be reworded in order to avoid any unwanted sexual overtones. The problem is that the Tonga verb "want/desire" *(-yanda)* also means "like/love" depending on the context. The NB employed a nice idiom here to circumvent this difficulty, i.e., "to attract our hearts" *(kututolela moyo)*.

53:3 Cultural conditioning again enters in to complicate the sad picture being portrayed by the prophet here. This concerns in particular the average person's understanding of the comment that God's servant was "one from whom others hide their faces." What would this mean? For one thing, "others" (OB: *kubantu* "to people," NB *abantu* "by people") wrongly indicates a group that is different from those referred to by the pronouns "we" occurring both before and after. Second, only a woman would exhibit such behaviour of avoidance, and that would be if she were sexually attracted to the man in whose presence she was or to whom she were talking. Thus, a literal translation, besides sounding out of place in this passage, would give entirely the wrong impression. Finally, even though literalism is avoided, one must still be careful how one conveys the intended idea in Tonga. The OB's *uusesemya* "disgusting" goes too far in suggesting that the servant's body was full of smelly, pussy sores. Thus, the NB opted for *uulisenza* "degraded", that is, somebody whom you avoid looking at because he or she is disrespectable, uncouth, or in some other aspect socially inferior.

53:4 The Tonga OB unfortunately introduces an anthropomorphism into its translation, i.e., "the hand of God brought sufferings to him" (cf. v. 1). But how can this be, the listener might ask? The "hands" (pl.) of God may be used figuratively in a positive sense with reference to his relationship with human beings, e.g., "we are in his hands" (protection), but there is no negative counterpart. God can be said to punish a person by "striking" him/her *(-kumuuma),* but no body part is mentioned in connection with such punitive action, e.g., for disregarding tribal customs or ignoring the ancestral spirits.

Ancient religious beliefs may also need to be elaborated upon in a footnote of some kind. Thus, when an entire family or clan has committed a serious crime against sacred tradition or the ancestors, e.g., failing to offer appropriate worship and thanksgiving after a good rainy season and harvest, then some innocent individual of the younger generation will be afflicted with a life-threatening disease as a warning that things need to be rectified by a communal sacrificial ritual, or death could result. On the other hand, if a person is suddenly "stricken" or made to suffer on account of a certain secret crime that he or she committed against someone else, then this would be construed as some form of magical punishment, inflicted by the wronged party by means of a protective potion or security charm. The NB adds "[struck] *by God*" to eliminate the latter interpretation as a possibility.

53:5 One question that could be raised by the text of the OB in Tonga is caused by a rendering that is overly general. Thus, "the punishment that made us whole" turns out to read "to help us is the reason for his being beaten with a whip/stick." But "help" in what way since there would be any number of possibilities? The NB states this notion as "his suffering is that which brought us peace," for "peace" (*luumuno,* from the verb "to be quiet, at rest") is not too far short of the rich Hebrew term found in the original, *shaloom* "wholeness, well-being."

53:6 Here we are presented with one of the most crucial queries of all: What are "sheep?" These animals are not traditionally herded by the Tonga, and many people have never even seen a sheep because those animals tend to be restricted to the vicinity of large commercial farms and ranches. The word used to translate "sheep," *mbelele,* is strangely related to the expression used to refer to the indigenous "pangolin" *cibbata-mbelele,* the spotted variety of which is believed to bring good luck to a person who happens to find one and bring it home to the village. The association of sheep "going astray" is therefore also unfamiliar to most and hence needs to be commented on in a footnote, along with an illustration (if possible) of a sheep or herd of them. The familiar "goat" *(impongo)* cannot be utilized as a cultural equivalent in this case for two major reasons: (a) because of the importance of sheep in the biblical setting and record and (b) due to the undesirable connotations connected with goats, especially males, i.e., unruly, destructive of crops, very sexually active.

The notion of a "scapegoat" implicit in this verse (cf. the possible allusion to Lev 6:21–22) is well known in traditional Tonga religious practice. Thus, a substitutionary, sacrificial animal bearing the sin[s] and/or disease[s] of society may be prepared by ritual and sent out into the bush and far away from the village to remove from the premises some aggrieved or avenging spirit *(cizwa).* However, the particular creature used for this purpose is quite different, namely, a chicken—because it will not find its way back home to bring a curse back upon the community, like some larger animal (a real goat, dog, or even a cow) would do. Another important variation from the biblical sense in this context concerns the notion of a *human* scapegoat, given in death, to atone for some communal crime or offense before God *(Leza),* a practice which is virtually unknown in Tonga traditional religion. The closest local correspondent unfortunately involves the practice of witchcraft, where a "witch/sorcerer" *(mulozi)* will surreptitiously highjack the "breath/shadow" *(muuya),* that is, the life-force, of a close family member in order to empower a certain charm (e.g., for self-protection) or sorcerous activity (e.g., personal enrichment).[13] In this case of course the innocent "substitute" is unwilling while the agent, and beneficiary, is made guilty by means of such nefarious, anti-social action. Therefore, the true Scriptural concept of vicarious substitution (incorporating the foundational "atonement" ritual of Lev 16) might well deserve some exposition in a note because of its importance to the prophetic imagery which appears especially in this and the following verse.

53:7 It would be helpful for listeners to repeat at the beginning of this new stanza in the lament (as also at vv. 4 and 10) a mention of the primary referent, namely, the "servant of God/the LORD." This was done at least in v. in the Tonga NB, but not thereafter. Such clarification is needed especially in longer passages where there is a shift in subject, e.g., vv. 4, 6, 9, and also in cases where it is likely that only a portion of the pericope will be read, e.g., vv. 4–6, as in a sermon text.

In addition to the sheep-related imagery (silence, slaughtered, sheared), which is unfamiliar to most Tonga receptors, this verse introduces another important picture that is made more difficult (also for the Ethiopian official, Acts 8:32–33) due to its implicit nature. Here then we have the setting of a trial of capital offense before a court of law (cf. v. 8).[14] It is a strange situation indeed, for the individual being accused one who is like a "sheep" (reference here to a "*little* sheep/lamb" in both the OB and NB merely muddies the waters of interpretation) refuses to open his mouth either to protest or to defend himself. Such deliberate silence, appropriately reinforced by an ideophone *zii!* (NB), in a traditional Tonga judicial setting is not only disrespectful; it would be regarded as a clear indication of one's guilt. A person who behaved in this manner would most likely be found guilty anyway by means of divination (i.e., throwing bones). In any case, the whole complex

---

[13] In times of severe famine an uncle could ask the clan for permission to sell a niece or nephew in exchange for food, but this did not necessarily involve a death and, if at all possible, such children were always bought back, or "redeemed" *(kunununa)*. On the other hand, in order to prevent such crises, whether due to the vagaries of nature or to the perceived attacks of sorcerers, at times a family would decide to turn to sorcery themselves. Thus, the senior male elder and his sister would secretly plan together to create, by means of a taboo ritual involving the death of a chosen nephew or niece, a magical "wealth-creator" for the clan that would mystically steal from neighbors' crops and herds. According to popular belief, at the time of death, the person who had engaged in such magic-for-enrichment would be transformed into a dangerous spirit-creature (called *ilomba,* from *kulomba* 'ask for, request'), which could only be exterminated by a competent medicine man

[14] On this point, see Motyer 1993:433; Young 1972:351.

scenario portrayed by this passage is completely missed by the majority of uninstructed listeners. Thus, the intended scene, sense, and significance would have to be explained in a footnote for satisfactory communication of the intended meaning to take place.

53:8 In this instance both the OB and NB give an initial, misleading impression of how the trial of the "servant-lamb" was conducted. OB has "he was denied a good judgment", i.e., a satisfactory outcome with regard to his sentence or fine, while NB says that "they arrested him by force and indicted him." The latter could easily be corrected by the addition of a compound adjectival modifier to give the desired prominence: *uutakwe mulandu kakunyina akaambo* "[he] having no case, without anything objectionable (i.e., against him)" strengthened by *uululeme* "upright" in the next poetic line. The literalism of the OB raises further problems of comprehension for the listener, e.g., "he was carried away" (but to which place?); "who among his agemates" (were only they concerned?); "he was removed from the land of the living" (does this mean he was taken to heaven, for even the remembered ancestral spirits are believed to inhabit the same "land" as their living relatives?); "he was beaten" (is that all that happened to him?). In fact, there is nothing in the OB translation which states that the person being persecuted was actually killed. All these queries are clarified in the NB along the lines (but not exactly the same as) the GNB.

There is one point where the NB may be improved, and that is at the final pronominal reference of this verse, literally, *"my* people," which is rendered as *"our people"* (cf. also GNB). Indeed, the pronoun is problematic, but it is also likely to be significant because a less common singular form is used, one which last appeared way back at the beginning of the pericope in 52:13. There it referred to the LORD, and that is the probable antecedent in 53:8 as well though a weaker case could be made for it being the prophet himself.[15] A less obtrusive way of conveying the first interpretation would be by means of a third-person designation, i.e., "the people of Yahweh/God."

53:9 The entire content of this verse is culturally unfamiliar to Tonga thinking. In the first place, if there is one thing that people do not discuss, it is *death* or being buried so as not to risk angering the newly emergent spirit

---

[15] On this point, see Young 1972:352; Motyer 1993:435.

(*muzimo*) of the person concerned. Such verbal circumspection is all the more important if the person is not dead yet (which would be the case if this passage is regarded as predictive prophecy). Thus, the very words of the first part of this verse cause a certain uneasiness to fall upon the hearer. Second, no person, not even the dreaded and detested "witch/sorcerer" (*mulozi*), is regarded as being "evil" anymore after he or she has died. Hence, it is quite inappropriate to say that someone was "buried together with wicked persons" (both OB and NB; GNB's "evil *men*" is even more strange-sounding; cf. also v. 12). The OB is made more difficult by an overt contradiction in its rendering: In the first line it is stated that "he" (whoever that is) was placed in a grave along with *evildoers,* while the very next line says that "he was buried with *a rich man.*" So which is it one or many? To be sure, the Hebrew text is itself quite difficult at this point, but it would be more helpful (as in the NB) to avoid what appears to be an obvious contradiction in the text and to employ a footnote to explain the key hermeneutical issues involved.

The NB further clarifies this passage by breaking up the single overly long sentence into three shorter ones and by making explicit the semantic relationship between its two distinct halves, i.e., with the transitional expression *Zyakaba oobu nikuba kuti* "Things happened in this way even though..." Thus, the essential theological *enigma* of the divine servant's innocent suffering and death is more patently preserved as a key to one's understanding of this entire pericope.

53:10 The initial conjunction *Pele* "But" in the Tonga OB not only distorts the semantic linkage between verses 9 and 10, but it also blurs the structural fact that a new stanza begins here. Better in this case is to leave the transition unmarked (NB), especially since the compositional links of this stanza are stronger in relation to the first (52:13–15) and third (53:4–6) units within the "servant song" as a whole (Motyer 1993:436–437).

The expression "he will see his descendants" (*uyoobona lunyungu lwakwe,* OB/NB) would be viewed as a good outcome from a traditional Tonga perspective. It means that a person will live to see his grandchildren, which is certainly not the norm in a region where the average life-expectancy was only about 45 years even before the onset of AIDS. However, the underlying spiritual sense in this context needs to be pointed out in a footnote, namely, that this refers to the blessed benefits of the suffering servant's vicarious activities which have been so vividly described in the two preceding stanzas (vv. 4–6, 7–9). Also worth a comment here is the likely reference to life after death (with a resurrection implied) for the martyred servant, i.e., in the expression "[he] shall prolong his days" (NT: *akuyooongolola* "and [he] will [live to] be bent over [in his back]."[16]

The OB's opaque literal translation of the final clause of this verse, "and the plans of Jehovah will go forward in his hands," is another good example of "God's language" *(mulaka wa Leza)*. That is to say, these words must mean something because they are found in God's holy book, but their sense is surely not apparent to most. The NB renders this as, "and so through him the will/love (either sense would fit here) of Chief-God is brought to its completion/fulfilment."

53:11 It would probably be helpful for the sake of listeners to introduce this verse with an explicit mention of the speaker, e.g., "The LORD says…" (cf. GNB at v. 10). Otherwise, the first-person pronouns in this and the following verse might not be understood as referring to God, which would consequently present certain problems of interpretation, e.g., who is doing the "alloting" of v. 12a.

The translation of the OB raises an important, but misleading question: "He will see fruit" *(Uyoobona micelo)*. So what sort of "fruit" is being spoken about here? A literal understanding, i.e., fruit from a tree, is supported by the following verb *uyookuta* "he will be [physically] filled." But how would this fit into the present context? Another possible meaning would be a metaphoric one, namely, "children." While such a construal seems to make sense in the light of v. 10, it is not really supported by the Hebrew text, which appears to be an idiom, as rendered by the NB, "he will see/experience its goodness/benefits *(bubotu,* i.e., of his suffering, etc.), and he will be satisfied *(uyoolamwa).*"

---

[16] There is naturally a strong hermeneutical debate over this issue. The problem is that if the servant does not rise to live again, then there is another direct contradiction in the text, i.e., first the servant dies (v.10a–b), and then he lives a long-enough life to see his descendants (v. 10c, cf. GNB's translation). The Messianic Servant's eternal rule has been clearly prophesied elsewhere in the book (e.g., 9:7), and so it should not be surprising to see another allusion here (cf. Motyer 1993:440; Young 1972:355–356). However, the conceptual difficulty of life after death in an indigenous Tonga thought-world also needs to be briefly addressed. Simply put, this concerns the belief that in order for a vicarious self-sacrifice on behalf of the clan or wider community to be valid and efficacious in the estimation of the ancestral spirits, the martyr would have to remain dead! This is because any sort of personal "resurrection" after death is attributed to the practice of witchcraft, either deliberately on the part of the individual involved or due to someone who had bewitched him/her.

It would be preferable in both the OB and NB to present a chronologically based order of events in the final part of this verse in order to clarify the underlying cause-effect relationship. That is to say, "[my servant] shall bear their iniquities" (means) = > "[he] shall *make* many righteous" (result), which is more accurately rendered "he will *provide* righteousness *for*" (Motyer 1993:442).

53:12 Both the NB and the even more literal OB provoke serious questions in the traditional Tonga listener's mind: What kind of "portion" *(caabilo)* is being referred to here? Who are the "elders" *(bapati)* with whom the LORD's servant is going to have to share his portion? From whom were the mentioned battle "spoils" *(zisaalo)* taken? And who are the "strong ones" *(basintanze)* who will be "divided out" *(-abanya)* along with these spoils? There are too many questions raised by the unexpected military imagery and not nearly enough contextual information available to provide an adequate framework for properly understanding the first part of this verse, which consequently sounds almost proverbial in style (cf. 52:15). Only an explanatory footnote will do.

But at least the NB does indicate the discourse-climactic nature of this verse by breaking it up into five shorter, rhetorically more powerful, utterances. The poem's close is made especially prominent and stylistically pleasing in Tonga by means of a final staccato-like series of asyndetic *waka-* "he did-" verbal constructions. This dramatic sequence neatly summarizes the servant's sacrificial offering of himself for the sake of "many"—which in a Bantu, collectively oriented context would automatically incorporate the entire community.

Conclusion: On the importance of a correct and convincing contextualization

A predominant emphasis in contemporary biblical hermeneutics, especially in non-Western settings, is upon some form of "reception (receptor-oriented) theory."[17] The importance of this particular focus cannot be denied if relevant

---

[17] "Reader response criticism, or reception hermeneutics, has introduced biblical scholars to a reader [or hearer] who is no longer perceived as a passive receiver of authorial or textual meaning, but who is now recognized as an active creator of meaning.... This development is particularly relevant for a rhetorical approach to Scripture analysis and communication. Thus,

Conclusion: On the importance of a correct and convincing contextualization 589

communication is going to be the result, that is, with regard to the two main conditions of obtaining what has been termed "optimal [message] relevance," namely, the relative ease of processing effort coupled with the stimulation of an adequate measure of conceptually based "contextual effects" (Gutt 1991:30) Some years ago a volume of *Semeia* (West and Dube 1996) was devoted to an exploration of this issue as it concerns the communication and interpretation of the text of Scriptures in various settings of reception that featured groups of 'ordinary' African readers/hearers, namely, those who tend 'to read [and hear] the Bible pre-critically' (West & Dube 1996:7). These studies, in the light of our own examination of the Isaiah 53 pericope, helped clarify for us a set of seven basic qualities that should (ideally) characterize the process of contextualization, or familiarization, as it is carried out in many, if not most, contexts of significant Scripture use among the Tonga (and no doubt most other Zambian peoples as well). It is not possible to elaborate on these procedures here. However, they are summarized for reference and possible future follow-up below.

A significantly *relevant contextualization* of the biblical message (the book of Isaiah, for example) is more likely to take place under these conditions:

a. The communication leader/initiator/guide/facilitator (whether in the case of a sermon, Bible study, instruction class, etc.), especially if a cultural 'outsider', must clearly realize that s/he is 'reading [listening] with' a pre-critical, non-academic group of receptors. He or she should therefore make every effort to promote a free expression of their distinctive individual and common hermeneutical perspectives, insights, and feedback.

b. An interactive, conversational, participatory, communal method of instruction ought to be encouraged, that is, to the extent possible in keeping with the specific type of religious setting and purpose concerned. The primary aim is to work towards a general consensus (not necessarily a complete agreement) with regard to the main issue(s) of a particular text and, in addition, to facilitate understanding and the opportunity for each participant to make his or her individual contribution to the overall, group communication event.

c. This interpersonal dialogue with the Scriptures in relation to a particular sociocultural setting should normally be conducted in the principal vernacular language that is represented so that key biblical notions and terms

---

the practice of 'reading with' invites scholarly readers, and their allied 'implied' readers and other surrogates..., to read the Bible with actual readers from poor and marginalized communities [but not necessarily limited to such groups], even when many of these readers are only "readers" in a metaphorical sense" (West 1996:27).

may be isolated, conceptualized, and discussed immediately, directly, and contextually, without any linguistic-semantic interference from another, especially a Western, language.[18]

d. The discussion leader must ensure that a sufficient amount of background material pertaining to the biblical text under consideration is provided, whether all at once as an introduction or periodically as the need arises, e.g., culturally appropriate visual aids and a careful selection of descriptive-explanatory comments pertaining to hermeneutically relevant items and issues found either explicitly or implicitly in the passage concerned, particularly those of an important sociocultural, ethical, and religious nature.

e. Any significant rhetorical and oral-aural features of the biblical text need to be pointed out and discussed critically and comparatively in relation to both the target language and literary tradition as well as the contemporary setting of communication, such as: the original genres (e.g., poetry vs. prose), structural organization (e.g., parallelism), stylistic features (notably repetition), rhetorical shading (e.g., punning and alliteration), typical music (for an evocative background), etc.[19] In keeping with this particular aspect of message transmission, an appropriate mode of verbal instruction ought to predominate in the current setting, that is, orally interactive as opposed to (but not necessarily eliminating entirely) the practice of silent reading and writing (cf. [b] above).

f. Following from [e], all teaching should be effected primarily by means of a traditional, inductive, non-analytical, dialogic method, one that features the integrated and holistic use of familiar indigenous modes and popular artistic models of oral instruction such as proverbs, maxims, folk narratives, riddles, praise poetry, initiation precepts, songs (of various types), and so forth including plenty of pertinent examples and life-related illustrations.

g. A multicultural type of presentation should be encouraged if possible, namely, where participants from diverse ethnic groups happen to be present (including the discussion leader). Such a differential and comparative approach, keeping the biblical setting continually in mind as a source of pertinent similarities and contrasts, can encourage a clearer critical perception of one's own cultural and linguistic idiosyncrasies and may also serve to promote beneficial inter-group awareness and cooperation in religious and other affairs.

---

[18] Surprisingly, this crucial point received almost no mention by contributors to the *Semeia* 73 volume. It was either overlooked or, more likely, simply taken for granted. However, as our examination of Isaiah in the light of Citonga has shown, the vernacular should be used because one's interpretation of the biblical text is greatly affected by the type of translation that one is working with, whether more or less literal/meaning-oriented.

[19] For a good overview of some of the main features of 'a residual oral hermeneutic' in relation to lay interpretation of the Scriptures in South Africa, see: J. A. Draper 1996:67–69.

Conclusion: On the importance of a correct and convincing contextualization

In closing, I wish to emphasize the point that during any contextualizing exercise aimed at 'domesticating' the biblical message, the *original text and context* cannot be ignored or allowed to recede too far into the background of the process as a whole. In other words, the presumed authorial intention, as determined on the basis of a careful analysis of his selection of theological and ethical content as well as the author's rhetorical shaping of the structure and style of his discourse, should always be used as a guide for disclosing what he selected to be the main themes, objectives, and emphases of his message to the saints. These exigetical concerns in turn ought to be accorded due consideration today when the particular passage is studied and applied in any sort of religious communication, whether formal or informal.[20] This principle is important for preserving a 'faithful' (factually accurate) testimony to the inspired text and context of Scripture as well as preventing a subjective, over-contextualization of its message (as were noted in the examples from Isaiah above).[21]

However, all our efforts at contextualizing the biblical message in translation should also be convincing (rhetorically compelling and esthetically pleasing) in the sense that they do the best possible) job of it in the target language. That is to say, there may be better or worse instances of this compositional-communicative process from a purely linguistic (structural and stylistic) standpoint. Thus, it is important that Bible translations (the primary source of information) and other forms of Christian communication are able to stand as artistically *excellent* instances of reproducing/recreating the original text in the target language. This would include the use of possibly a more appropriate media of transmission, e.g., the audio cassette, and a more dynamic style of translation, i.e., oral-oratory (or 'oratorical') created especially for the artistically sensitive and appreciative ear. This high

---

[20] The method of introducing such source-oriented 'scholarly' material into an informal TL setting, as well as the amount of such information needed, will of course vary according to the situation and occasion. The ideal source would be a gifted, previously instructed, fellow member of the particular group concerned, one who knows their specific life-setting and personal needs, aspirations, limitations, gifts, etc.

[21] The purpose of a 'valid' (informed) contextualization is not to blur or 'fuse' the two so-called 'horizons' of interpretation (A. C. Thistleton 1980)—the Scriptural/canonical and the contemporary/secular—thus transculturizing the original message. Rather, the point is to distinguish the principal correspondences and distinctive contrasts in relation to the two contexts based on a thorough understanding of this religious communication event within its biblical setting. In this way then receptors today are drawn closer in their understanding of the text of Scripture, on the one hand, while the text is enabled in turn to speak more directly and relevantly to them within the framework of their actual life and thought-world.

standard of quality should be reflected too, as suggested earlier, in the task of providing descriptive/explanatory notes that get at the heart of contextual problems which relate to both understanding the intended message (SL focus) and also adapting it with respect to the sociocultural and religious setting of the target group. This is not an easy assignment, hence not one for Scripture novices and/or culturally naive enthusiasts. There is an obvious need first of all for competent and creative national-led 'contextualization teams', supplemented (if necessary) by sympathetic and experienced foreign (especially fellow African) assistants to help out in particular areas of hermeneutical or technological deficiency (e.g., biblical languages, contextual [Ancient Near East] background, oral poetics, multi-media expertise, research and testing, etc.).[22]

As this little exercise in translation and interpretation has shown, the understanding of "average" Bible receptors is not a matter that can be taken for granted, even with regard to such a well-known pericope as Isaiah 53. Many different questions are raised by the text when people honestly attempt to assess their level of comprehension based on what they are reading or hearing. The preceding comments on this pericope have also indicated that it is not possible to deal adequately with all of the queries evoked by a particular passage of Scripture within the translation itself, that is, by changing from a literal to a more dynamic, rhetorically expressed, meaning-oriented rendering. This is especially true where issues of a sociocultural, ecological, and historical nature are concerned, whether these pertain to the life and times of the biblical peoples or to south-central Bantu of the present day. Thus, we saw quite a few instances of where the message of the Bible

---

[22] We wish to posit the following scheme of hermeneutical types/aspects pertaining to possible Scripture-based 'contextualization' procedures, as presented above:
   a. *intuitive* (exegetically unacceptable)
      i. *skewed*: influenced entirely by the resident hermeneutical framework provided by ATR (African Traditional Religion) and individualized or localized personal experience;
      ii. *selective*: influenced unsystematically by isolated elements in the cotext of the individual passages concerned, especially if taken from a formally and semantically more difficult, literal translation.
   b. *informed* (exegetically desirable)
      i. *textual*: effected within the actual text of an idiomatic, meaning-based vernacular Bible translation;
      ii. *extratextual*: supplied through perceptive supplementary notes and other paratextual aids (illustrations, cross references) that are conditioned to the principal setting of reception, including the people's worldview and way of life (including their religious beliefs, value system, customs, traditions, social institutions, felt needs, etc.).

may be misunderstood or misinterpreted in the light of a traditional African worldview and way-of-life.²³

What is needed in such cases is a "Philip" sitting beside the reader or hearer, someone who can anticipate potential problem spots and ask, "Do you *really* understand what you are reading?"—and thereafter to offer the needed guidance and enlightenment. It was further suggested that in the absence of such a live on-the-spot commentator (which is obviously the *best* remedy), a more liberally annotated and illustrated translation, or study Bible, may be able to provide an appreciable measure of assistance by opening up the original sense and contemporary significance of the text under consideration. An audio rendition would be needed of course for non-literates. Explanatory footnotes, whether oral or written, are only a partial solution, however, and such supplementary materials still frequently require some willing and capable person (e.g., teacher, pastor, evangelist, Bible study leader) to select and convey the information supplied in these resources to readers—and especially listeners. An accurate, stylistically natural translation in the vernacular is an essential first step. It is then up to language communities and translation agencies to devote themselves to the task of preparing carefully contextualized, culturally sensitive, and locally relevant auxiliary aids to provide for sociologically diverse audiences and settings of use. There are also new media to capitalize on (e.g., satellite radio, the internet, cellphone technology) as the Church moves forward to face new challenges in this 21st millennium of Christian communication.

---

²³ This problem of limited Scripture understanding is not unique to Africa of course. It is rather ironic in this modern age of ever-increasing communication skills and access to various mass media that the average level of Bible literacy appears to be decreasing overall—probably more rapidly in Western nations than elsewhere in the Christian world. To be sure, there is a lot of preaching and teaching going on nowadays, but this does not seem to be contributing to people's overall knowledge of the Bible and its message to a corresponding degree, if at all. While a hard-to-understand translation may explain part of the difficulty, it is certainly not the entire answer. We would suggest, as one possible solution to this worldwide problem, a greater effort to promote in all churches text and context-related, expository Scripture-study programmes that are also aimed at bridging the crucial conceptual gap between the world and culture presupposed in the biblical books and the corresponding situational life-setting of receptor peoples today. Thus, we recognize that the explanatory notes of a study Bible also need to be supplemented. Footnotes must be relatively short by nature, and they are intended to clarify concepts that do not require a great deal of explanation, or those that would be misunderstood in cases where the indigenous group has a similar custom or idea to what occurs in the Hebrew culture or experience. But trying to introduce and teach a totally foreign concept would take more than a footnote: nothing can replace a competent, "Philip-like" instructor for guidance!

12

Analyzing and Translating Haggai

In this chapter, you might apply some of the perspectives, principles, and analytical procedures that were disussed in the preceding chapters as a way of bringing them home in a practical, text-oriented manner. We will use the book of the prophet Haggai as a basis for this exercise. Begin your study of the prophet Haggai by carefully reading through the RSV and GNT translations that are reproduced in the boxes below. You will be comparing these two English versions with each other and also with a translation in your language (YL) as an essential part of your study of this book. In doing so, you will also learn how to ask questions of the text as a way of more fully investigating its intended meaning in preparation for translation. The original Hebrew text (MT) is given in sections under each portion of Haggai being examined; this will be occasionally referred to for the sake of those who can read it (*chapter 5 of this book may also be consulted before, after, or while doing this exercise*).

RSV	GNT
1 *A new prophetic speech formula begins at v. 3.	**1** **The LORD's Command to Rebuild the Temple**
¹ In the second year of Darius the king, in the sixth month, on the first day of the month, the word of the LORD came by Haggai the prophet to Zerubbabel the son of She-alti-el, governor of Judah, and to Joshua the son of Jehozadak, the high priest, ² "Thus says the LORD of hosts: <u>This people say the time has not yet come to rebuild the house of the LORD.</u>"/* ³ Then the word of the LORD came by Haggai the prophet, ⁴ "Is it a time for you yourselves to dwell in your paneled houses, while this house lies in ruins? ⁵ Now therefore thus says the LORD of hosts: Consider how you have fared. ⁶ You have sown much, and harvested little; you eat, but you never have enough; you drink, but you never have your fill; you clothe yourselves, but no one is warm; and he who earns wages earns wages to put them into a bag with holes. ⁷ "Thus says the LORD of hosts: Consider how you have fared. ⁸ Go up to the hills and bring wood and build the house, that I may take pleasure in it and that I may appear in my glory, says the LORD. ⁹ You have looked for much, and lo, it came to little; and when you brought it home, I blew it away. Why? says the LORD of hosts. Because of my house that lies in ruins, while you busy yourselves each with his own house. ¹⁰ Therefore the heavens above you have withheld the dew, and the earth has withheld its produce. ¹¹ And I have called for a drought upon the land and the hills, upon the grain, the new wine, the oil, upon what the ground brings forth, upon men and cattle, and upon all their labors."	¹* During the second year that Darius was emperor of Persia, on the first day of the sixth month, the LORD spoke through the prophet Haggai. The message was for the governor of Judah, Zerubbabel son of Shealtiel, and for the High Priest, Joshua son of Jehozadak. ² The LORD Almighty said to Haggai, "These people say that this is not <u>the right time to rebuild the Temple.</u>"/³ The LORD then gave this message to the people through the prophet Haggai: ⁴ "My people, why should you be living in well-built houses while my Temple lies in ruins? ⁵ Don't you see what is happening to you? ⁶ You have planted much grain, but have harvested very little. You have food to eat, but not enough to make you full. You have wine to drink, but not enough to get drunk on! You have clothing, but not enough to keep you warm. And workers cannot earn enough to live on. ⁷ Can't you see why this has happened? ⁸ Now go up into the hills, get lumber, and rebuild the Temple; then I will be pleased and will be worshiped as I should be. ⁹ "You hoped for large harvests, but they turned out to be small. And when you brought the harvest home, I blew it away. Why did I do that? Because my Temple lies in ruins while every one of you is busy working on your own house. ¹⁰ That is why there is no rain and nothing can grow. ¹¹ I have brought drought on the land—on its hills, grainfields, vineyards, and olive orchards—on every crop the ground produces, on people and animals, on everything you try to grow."

¹² Then Zerubbabel the son of She-alti-el, and Joshua the son of Jehozadak, the high priest, with all the remnant of the people, obeyed the voice of the LORD their God, and the words of Haggai the prophet, as the LORD their God had sent him; and the people feared before the LORD. ¹³ Then Haggai, the messenger of the LORD, spoke to the people with the LORD's message, "I am with you, says the LORD." ¹⁴ And the LORD stirred up the spirit of Zerubbabel the son of She-alti-el, governor of Judah, and the spirit of Joshua the son of Jehozadak, the high priest, and the spirit of all the remnant of the people; and they came and worked on the house of the LORD of hosts, their God, 15 on the twenty-fourth day of the month, in the sixth month.

2

¹ In the second year of Darius the king, in the seventh month, on the twenty-first day of the month, the word of the LORD came by Haggai the prophet, ² "Speak now to Zerubbabel the son of She-alti-el, governor of Judah, and to Joshua the son of Jehozadak, the high priest, and to all the remnant of the people, and say, ³ 'Who is left among you that saw this house in its former glory? How do you see it now? Is it not in your sight as nothing? ⁴ Yet now take courage, O Zerubbabel, says the LORD; take courage, O Joshua, son of Jehozadak, the high priest; take courage, all you people of the land, says the LORD; work, for I am with you, says the LORD of hosts, 5 according to the promise that I made you when you came out of Egypt. My Spirit abides among you; fear not.

The People Obey the LORD's Command

¹² Then Zerubbabel and Joshua and all the people who had returned from the exile in Babylonia, did what the LORD their God told them to do. They were afraid and obeyed the prophet Haggai, the LORD's messenger. ¹³ Then Haggai gave the LORD's message to the people: "I will be with you—that is my promise." ¹⁴ The LORD inspired everyone to work on the Temple: Zerubbabel, the governor of Judah; Joshua, the High Priest, and all the people who had returned from the exile. They began working on the Temple of the LORD Almighty, their God, 15 on the twenty-fourth day of the sixth month of the second year that Darius was emperor.

2

The Splendor of the New Temple

¹ On the twenty-first day of the seventh month of that same year, the LORD spoke again through the prophet Haggai. ² He told Haggai to speak to Zerubbabel, the governor of Judah, to Joshua, the High Priest, and to the people, and to say to them, ³ * "Is there anyone among you who can still remember how splendid the Temple used to be? How does it look to you now? It must seem like nothing at all. ⁴ But now don't be discouraged, any of you. Do the work, for I am with you. ⁵ * When you came out of Egypt, I promised that I would always be with you. I am still with you, so do not be afraid.

⁶*For thus says the LORD of hosts: Once again, in a little while, I will shake the heavens and the earth and the sea and the dry land; ⁷and I will shake all nations, so that the treasures of all nations shall come in, and I will fill this house with splendor, says the LORD of hosts. ⁸The silver is mine, and the gold is mine, says the LORD of hosts. ⁹The latter splendor of this house shall be greater than the former, says the LORD of hosts; and in this place I will give prosperity, says the LORD of hosts.'"

¹⁰On the twenty-fourth day of the ninth month, in the second year of Darius, the word of the LORD came by Haggai the prophet, ¹¹"Thus says the LORD of hosts: Ask the priests to decide this question, ¹²'If one carries holy flesh in the skirt of his garment, and touches with his skirt bread, or pottage, or wine, or oil, or any kind of food, does it become holy?'" The priests answered, "No." ¹³Then said Haggai, "If one who is unclean by contact with a dead body touches any of these, does it become unclean?" The priests answered, "It does become unclean." ¹⁴Then Haggai said, "So is it with this people, and with this nation before me, says the LORD; and so with every work of their hands; and what they offer there is unclean.

⁶*"Before long I will shake heaven and earth, land and sea. ⁷I will overthrow all the nations, and their treasures will be brought here, and the Temple will be filled with wealth. ⁸All the silver and gold of the world is mine. ⁹The new Temple will be more splendid than the old one, and there I will give my people prosperity and peace." The LORD Almighty has spoken.

The Prophet Consults the Priests
¹⁰On the twenty-fourth day of the ninth month of the second year that Darius was emperor, the LORD Almighty spoke again to the prophet Haggai. ¹¹He said, "Ask the priests for a ruling on this question: ¹²Suppose someone takes a piece of consecrated meat from a sacrifice and carries it in a fold of his robe. If he then lets his robe touch any bread, cooked food, wine, olive oil, or any kind of food at all, will it make that food consecrated also?"

When the question was asked, the priests answered, "No."

¹³*Then Haggai asked, "Suppose someone is defiled because he has touched a dead body. If he then touches any of these foods, will that make them defiled too?"

The priests answered, "Yes."

¹⁴Then Haggai said, "The LORD says that the same thing applies to the people of this nation and to everything they produce; and so everything they offer on the altar is defiled."

¹⁵ Pray now, consider what will come to pass from this day onward. Before a stone was placed upon a stone in the temple of the LORD, ¹⁶ how did you fare? When one came to a heap of twenty measures, there were but ten; when one came to the winevat to draw fifty measures, there were but twenty. ¹⁷ I smote you and all the products of your toil with blight and mildew and hail; yet you did not return to me, says the LORD. ¹⁸ Consider from this day onward, from the twenty-fourth day of the ninth month. Since the day that the foundation of the LORD's temple was laid, consider: ¹⁹ Is the seed yet in the barn? Do the vine, the fig tree, the pomegranate, and the olive tree still yield nothing? From this day on I will bless you."

²⁰ The word of the LORD came a second time to Haggai on the twenty-fourth day of the month, ²¹ "Speak to Zerubbabel, governor of Judah, saying, I am about to shake the heavens and the earth, ²² and to overthrow the throne of kingdoms; I am about to destroy the strength of the kingdoms of the nations, and overthrow the chariots and their riders; and the horses and their riders shall go down, every one by the sword of his fellow. ²³ On that day, says the LORD of hosts, I will take you, O Zerubbabel my servant, the son of Shealti-el, says the LORD, and make you like a signet ring; for I have chosen you, says the LORD of hosts."

The LORD Promises His Blessing

¹⁵ The LORD says, "Can't you see what has happened to you? Before you started to rebuild the Temple, ¹⁶ you would go to a pile of grain expecting to find twenty bushels, but there would be only ten. You would go to draw fifty gallons of wine from a vat, but find only twenty. ¹⁷ I sent scorching winds and hail to ruin everything you tried to grow, but still you did not repent. ¹⁸ Today is the twenty-fourth day of the ninth month, the day that the foundation of the Temple has been completed. See what is going to happen from now on. ¹⁹ Although there is no grain left, and the grapevines, fig trees, pomegranates, and olive trees have not yet produced, yet from now on I will bless you."

The LORD's Promise to Zerubbabel

²⁰ On that same day, the twenty-fourth of the month, the LORD gave Haggai a second message ²¹ for Zerubbabel, the governor of Judah: "I am about to shake heaven and earth ²² and overthrow kingdoms and end their power. I will overturn chariots and their drivers; the horses will die, and their riders will kill one another. ²³ On that day I will take you, Zerubbabel my servant, and I will appoint you to rule in my name. You are the one I have chosen." The LORD Almighty has spoken.

Exercises—Haggai as a whole

a. After reading the two translations above, work through the Introduction to the book of Haggai in the NIV Study Bible (NIV-SB, pages 1425–1426) in order to gain some **background knowledge** about the setting of this prophecy from the LORD. *To whom* was Haggai writing and *why* was he writing to them? What was the *religious situation* that called forth this "Word from Yahweh"? **Summarize** the message of Haggai to the people of his day. Mention *three* main things (or more) that you discover in your background reading—facts that probably influenced the divine messages that Haggai had to deliver to his people, as well as their ultimate collection in this prophetic book.

b. Evaluate the following quote, which speaks to the controversial issue of the writing—and subsequent editing—of Haggai's prophecy in relation to its original oral transmission; give your opinion on the matter: "Specialists seem extraordinarily hesitant regarding the prima facie likelihood that the prophets were their own editors. A man conscious of being the vehicle of the word of God will not, in a literary age, leave those words to the uncertainties of oral transmission or to the less informed care of other hands. There is no compelling argument against the view that Haggai—and who better?—was his own editor" (Motyer 1998:967–968).

c. Now study Haggai in the RSV again (in comparison with the GNT) and *draw a line through* the RSV text before each verse where you propose that a **new paragraph** begins. The first division has been made for you. Normally, a new paragraph begins in literature where there is a **shift in content** of some type—e.g., to a *different* speaker(s), addressee(s), chief actor, time, place, topic (or point of an argument), genre (type of discourse), and so forth. The more shifts that occur at the same point, the more likely a new section of the text begins at that place and the more important it is. Along the side of the text, by each line of division that you draw, list the various breaks that you notice there (also note accompanying prophetic **formulas** and discourse **transitions**).

d. It is important to distinguish ***major* breaks** in the text from *minor* ones. How do you do that? It is a matter of evaluating the types of break or shifts that you find at a particular point in the discourse. *How many* are there and *how prominent* are these, relatively speaking? Go through the RSV text again and try to pick out where you think that the major **(section)** breaks occur. Draw *two lines* through the text in these places, or mark the text with a felt-tip marker of a certain color.

e. Normally in modern Bible translations it is common to find a **section heading**, or title, at the beginning of each major break in the text. You have seen these in the GNT translation above. Propose such a title for each of the major sections of Haggai that you have designated. You may use any GNT title if you wish (also see the NIV-SB), or you may improve what is given; you may also need to put headings at any major sections where the GNT does not have one.

f. After you have prepared a section heading at each major break in the text of Haggai, you may move to the next level down and propose a *sub-title* that summarizes the content of every paragraph that you have indicated in the text. Write this out on a separate piece of paper. This will give you a **topical outline** of the contents of the book as a whole. Now *compare* your

Exercises—Haggai 1:1–2 601

outline with that given in the NIV-SB (p. 1426) and any other study Bible that you have available. After this, you may wish to *revise* your own general outline of the book of Haggai.

RSV Haggai	1:1–2 GNT
¹ In the second year of Darius the king, in the sixth month, on the first day of the month, the word of the LORD came by Haggai the prophet to Zerubbabel the son of She-alti-el, governor of Judah, and to Joshua the son of Jehozadak, the high priest, ² "Thus says the LORD of hosts: This people say the time has not yet come to rebuild the house of the LORD."	**The LORD's Command to Rebuild the Temple** ¹* During the second year that Darius was emperor of Persia, on the first day of the sixth month, the LORD spoke through the prophet Haggai. The message was for the governor of Judah, Zerubbabel son of Shealtiel, and for the High Priest, Joshua son of Jehozadak. ² The LORD Almighty said to Haggai, "These people say that this is not the right time to rebuild the Temple."

בִּשְׁנַת שְׁתַּיִם לְדָרְיָוֶשׁ הַמֶּלֶךְ בַּחֹדֶשׁ הַשִּׁשִּׁי בְּיוֹם אֶחָד לַחֹדֶשׁ הָיָה דְבַר־יְהוָה בְּיַד־חַגַּי הַנָּבִיא אֶל־זְרֻבָּבֶל בֶּן־שְׁאַלְתִּיאֵל פַּחַת יְהוּדָה וְאֶל־יְהוֹשֻׁעַ בֶּן־יְהוֹצָדָק הַכֹּהֵן הַגָּדוֹל לֵאמֹר: ² כֹּה אָמַר יְהוָה צְבָאוֹת לֵאמֹר הָעָם הַזֶּה אָמְרוּ לֹא עֶת־בֹּא עֶת־בֵּית יְהוָה לְהִבָּנוֹת: פ

Exercises—Haggai 1:1–2

a. What links these first two verses together as a **separate paragraph**? In other words, what shift or break in content do you note in verse 3 that leads you to begin a new paragraph (or section) at that point? Or perhaps you would prefer *not* to make a break at v. 3; if that's the case, give your reason(s).

b. Compare the RSV and GNT translations and point out a *major* difference (not simply a different word) that you see between them. Can you explain why the GNT starts a *new sentence* within v. 1 and again at v. 2? What is the special difficulty that the RSV presents you with, which is typical of the prophetic literature, especially at the beginning of a major section? How can you deal with it?

c. How does the GNT render the phrase: "the word of the LORD (= LORD/ Yahweh) came by [the hand of] Haggai" (הָיָה דְבַר־יְהוָה בְּיַד־חַגַּי)? Which version do you prefer to follow in your language (YL) and why? However, you must remember that you are dealing with a **prophetic formula** that normally *marks the beginning* of an oracle from Yahweh to the people, whether a word of condemnation and judgment or of blessing and salvation. Therefore, it is good if you can find a distinctive way of signaling this same *discourse function* in YL. What would you suggest in this case?

d. Who does the word "LORD" (יְהוָה) refer to? Explain the meaning of this **key term**. How do you translate this *divine name* in YL (e.g., Chewa: *Chauta*)? How does it differ from "God" (אֱלֹהִים)?

e. What is a "prophet" (נָבִיא)? How do you translate this important term in YL? Evaluate this translation—is it adequate, or can you suggest a better word or phrase? Explain your answer. Carry out the same exercise for the **technical terms** "governor" (פַּחַת) and "high priest" (הַכֹּהֵן הַגָּדוֹל).

f. Who was the "high priest"—"Joshua" or "Jehozadak," and how do you know this? How can you translate so as to make this relationship clear in YL? [NOTE: Whenever you are asked to express something in "your language", YL, be sure to also give a *literal* back-translation into English.]

g. Should you translate "first day" as "Sunday" and "sixth month" as "June" in YL? Explain.

h. How does the GNT translate "Thus says the LORD of Hosts" (כֹּה אָמַר יְהוָה צְבָאוֹת)? This is another important **prophetic oracle opener** in the Hebrew Bible. What is the meaning of "hosts" in this *divine title*? (Check the NET, note 5, plus another study Bible or commentary.) How does the GNT render this title—and what is their justification (do you think) for doing so? How has "the LORD of Hosts" been translated in YL in the past? Evaluate the pros and cons of this translation—can a more accurate and meaningful expression be found?

i. Why does Yahweh quote the people in v. 2—what is the rhetorical purpose of this *incriminating quote*? Do the people of YL debate in this manner, by citing a contentious or objectionable statement by the opponent(s)? If not, how could you render this verse to make its intention clear?

j. "These people" (lit., 'this people'—הָעָם הַזֶּה)—not "my people" (cf. Isa 6:9–10): What is the **connotation** (feeling, attitude) of "these" in this context? How would you convey the same sense of *estrangement* in YL? Can you use a demonstrative pronoun as the Hebrew does? Explain.

k. How does the GNT translate the phrase "house of the LORD" (בֵּית יְהוָה)? Which of these two renderings do you prefer in YL and explain why?

Exercises—Haggai 1:1–2

RSV — Haggai 1:3–11	GNT
³ Then the word of the LORD came by Haggai the prophet, ⁴ "Is it a time for you yourselves to dwell in your paneled houses, while this house lies in ruins? ⁵ Now therefore thus says the LORD of hosts: Consider how you have fared. ⁶ You have sown much, and harvested little; you eat, but you never have enough; you drink, but you never have your fill; you clothe yourselves, but no one is warm; and he who earns wages earns wages to put them into a bag with holes. ⁷ "Thus says the LORD of hosts: Consider how you have fared. ⁸ Go up to the hills and bring wood and build the house, that I may take pleasure in it and that I may appear in my glory, says the LORD. ⁹ You have looked for much, and lo, it came to little; and when you brought it home, I blew it away. Why? says the LORD of hosts. Because of my house that lies in ruins, while you busy yourselves each with his own house. ¹⁰ Therefore the heavens above you have withheld the dew, and the earth has withheld its produce. ¹¹ And I have called for a drought upon the land and the hills, upon the grain, the new wine, the oil, upon what the ground brings forth, upon men and cattle, and upon all their labors."	³ The LORD then gave this message to the people through the prophet Haggai: ⁴ "My people, why should you be living in well-built houses while my Temple lies in ruins? ⁵ Don't you see what is happening to you? ⁶ You have planted much grain, but have harvested very little. You have food to eat, but not enough to make you full. You have wine to drink, but not enough to get drunk on! You have clothing, but not enough to keep you warm. And workers cannot earn enough to live on. ⁷ Can't you see why this has happened? ⁸ Now go up into the hills, get lumber, and rebuild the Temple; then I will be pleased and will be worshiped as I should be. ⁹ "You hoped for large harvests, but they turned out to be small. And when you brought the harvest home, I blew it away. Why did I do that? Because my Temple lies in ruins while every one of you is busy working on your own house. ¹⁰ That is why there is no rain and nothing can grow. ¹¹ I have brought drought on the land—on its hills, grainfields, vineyards, and olive orchards—on every crop the ground produces, on people and animals, on everything you try to grow."

³וַיְהִי֙ דְּבַר־יְהוָ֔ה בְּיַד־חַגַּ֥י הַנָּבִ֖יא לֵאמֹֽר׃ ⁴ הַעֵ֤ת לָכֶם֙ אַתֶּ֔ם לָשֶׁ֖בֶת בְּבָתֵּיכֶ֣ם סְפוּנִ֑ים וְהַבַּ֥יִת הַזֶּ֖ה חָרֵֽב׃ ⁵ וְעַתָּ֕ה כֹּ֥ה אָמַ֖ר יְהוָ֣ה צְבָא֑וֹת שִׂ֥ימוּ לְבַבְכֶ֖ם עַל־דַּרְכֵיכֶֽם׃ ⁶ זְרַעְתֶּ֨ם הַרְבֵּ֜ה וְהָבֵ֣א מְעָ֗ט אָכ֤וֹל וְאֵין־לְשָׂבְעָה֙ שָׁת֣וֹ וְאֵין־לְשָׁכְרָ֔ה לָב֖וֹשׁ וְאֵין־לְחֹ֣ם ל֑וֹ וְהַ֨מִּשְׂתַּכֵּ֔ר מִשְׂתַּכֵּ֖ר אֶל־צְר֥וֹר נָקֽוּב׃ פ ⁷ כֹּ֥ה אָמַ֖ר יְהוָ֣ה צְבָא֑וֹת שִׂ֥ימוּ לְבַבְכֶ֖ם עַל־דַּרְכֵיכֶֽם׃ ⁸ עֲל֥וּ הָהָ֛ר וַהֲבֵאתֶ֥ם עֵ֖ץ וּבְנ֣וּ הַבָּ֑יִת וְאֶרְצֶה־בּ֥וֹ *וְאֶכָּבֵ֖ד (וְאֶכָּבְדָ֖ה) אָמַ֥ר יְהוָֽה׃ ⁹ פָּנֹ֤ה אֶל־הַרְבֵּה֙ וְהִנֵּ֣ה לִמְעָ֔ט וַהֲבֵאתֶ֥ם הַבַּ֖יִת וְנָפַ֣חְתִּי ב֑וֹ יַ֣עַן מֶ֗ה נְאֻם֙ יְהוָ֣ה צְבָא֔וֹת יַ֚עַן בֵּיתִ֔י אֲשֶׁר־ה֖וּא חָרֵ֑ב וְאַתֶּ֥ם רָצִ֖ים אִ֥ישׁ לְבֵיתֽוֹ׃ ¹⁰ עַל־כֵּ֣ן עֲלֵיכֶ֔ם כָּלְא֥וּ שָׁמַ֖יִם מִטָּ֑ל וְהָאָ֖רֶץ כָּלְאָ֥ה יְבוּלָֽהּ׃ ¹¹ וָאֶקְרָ֨א חֹ֜רֶב עַל־הָאָ֣רֶץ וְעַל־הֶהָרִ֗ים וְעַל־הַדָּגָן֙ וְעַל־הַתִּיר֔וֹשׁ וְעַל־הַיִּצְהָ֖ר וְעַ֣ל אֲשֶׁ֣ר תּוֹצִ֣יא הָאֲדָמָ֑ה וְעַל־הָֽאָדָם֙ וְעַל־הַבְּהֵמָ֔ה וְעַ֖ל כָּל־יְגִ֥יעַ כַּפָּֽיִם׃ ס

Exercises—Haggai 1:3–11

a. Compare the RSV and GNT translations above with the NIV and NET with regard to the **discourse structure** of this section covering verses 3–11; point out the major *differences* among these four versions. Then suggest where you would put *paragraph breaks* in this unit and give reasons for each of the breaks that you propose.

b. Why should we begin a major new section at v. 12—what is the *evidence* for this break? On the other hand, do you feel that section 1:3–11 should be divided up to include another major division (e.g., NET)? Tell why or why not. Also explain the importance of paying attention to this larger compositional aspect of the biblical text that you are translating into YL.

c. Which words found in v. 1 are repeated in v. 3? What do you think is the rhetorical *function* of this **repetition**? Does it serve the same communicative purpose in YL? Explain.

d. What is being referred to by the expression "paneled houses" (בְּבָתֵּיכֶם סְפוּנִים) in v. 4? (See the NET and the NIV-SB notes on this verse.) How would you translate this phrase meaningfully in YL?

e. What sort of a question do we have in v. 4? What is the function of this type of question here? What point does it serve to *emphasize?* What personal *emotion(s)* does it also express? Can you use a **rhetorical question** (RQ) in YL for this same purpose—that is, to convey the same forcefulness and feeling? Explain.

f. Why does the RSV add "yourselves" after "you" (Heb, לָכֶם אַתֶּם)—is this not *redundant?* How does the GNT convey this added emphasis, or contrast? How would you do it in YL?

g. What does "lies in ruins" mean (חָרֵב—only one word in Heb)? Note the **position** (location) of this word in the clause/sentence/verse: what is the significance of this *word order?* How would you convey this whole idea naturally in YL?

h. How does the GNT translate the expression "Consider how you have fared" (RSV—Hebrew: שִׂימוּ לְבַבְכֶם עַל־דַּרְכֵיכֶם) in v. 5? How do these translations relate to one another—are they saying the same thing? Explain. This is an **idiomatic** utterance in Hebrew (see the NET for a literal translation); do you have a *corresponding* idiomatic way of saying this in YL?

i. What is the LORD's point in v. 6—what is he trying to impress upon the people with this set of 5 short *contrastive* statements? Does a *literal* translation convey the same effect in YL? If not, what can you do to achieve **functional equivalence** with your rendering? Is a **cross reference**

Exercises—Haggai 1:3–11

to a passage like Deut 28:38–39 (Lev 26:20) necessary here? Explain why (or why not).

j. What is the meaning of putting one's wages "into a bag of holes?" Do you have a similar *idiom* or *proverbial* saying in YL? If so, could it be used here? Why was all this happening to the people—what was the underlying problem (see the NIV-SB not at 1:6)?

k. How does v. 7 compare with v. 5—do you notice any *difference?* Why does Yahweh repeat himself here; in other words, what is the rhetorical function of the *repetition* in this type of prophetic discourse?

l. How does the GNT differ from the RSV in the handling of this verse with regard to the discourse structure? Which version do you think is more correct and why (cf. NIV and NET at this point)?

m. Why does GNT begin v. 8 with "Now…" – what is the sense or function of this *transitional adverb?* Do you need a corresponding word or phrase in YL? Explain.

n. The *quotation* in v. 8 contains 5 main verbs and it is important to discern how they relate to one another so that the *same relationships* are evident in your translation. There are two verbs of command: _____ and _____; one verb of purpose: _____; and two verbs of result: _____ and _____ (fill in the blanks).

o. Was the rebuilt Temple to be constructed of wood? What does your translation imply? Do you need an *explanatory footnote* to clarify this issue? If so, suggest what you would write:

p. How does GNT render the RSV's "that I may appear in my glory" (only one word in Heb.—אֶכָּבֵד)? Which interpretation do you prefer and why (check commentaries)?

q. Which words found in v. 8 has the GNT left un-translated? Can you suggest why it does this? What would you suggest doing in YL and why? Note that the Hebrew **prophetic punctuator**, literally translated as 'says Yahweh' (אָמַר יְהוָה) – cf. 'utterance of Yahweh' (נְאֻם יְהוָה) in v. 9, may add a certain degree of *emphasis* to the preceding utterance or verse. How could you express this same bit of forcefulness idiomatically in YL?

r. Verse 9 develops the ideas presented in which earlier verse? Point out the lexical and semantic **parallels** between verses 5–6 and 7–9.

s. In the first line of v. 9, the GNT first adds a word and then leaves one out in comparison with the RSV translation: Which word is *added* and suggest why? Which word is *omitted* (in Heb it is הִנֵּה)? Should the latter word be ignored? What is its rhetorical *function* in Hebrew and how can you reproduce that in YL?

t. What is the meaning of "[and] I blew it away" (וְנָפַחְתִּי) (see also the NET note)? Can you use a similar idiom or **figure of speech** in YL here? Try to find one!

u. Instead of the single *interrogative* word "why" (יַעַן מֶה) in v. 9, what does the GNT say? Is this necessary also in YL?

v. The Hebrew has another idiom for "while you busy yourselves each with his own house"—which is literally, 'and each of you runs to his house' (וְאַתֶּם רָצִים אִישׁ לְבֵיתוֹ). Do you have an *idiom* that can serve as an *equivalent* here? What *speaker attitude* is implicitly conveyed in v. 9?

w. Instead of "Therefore" (עַל־כֵּן), what does the GNT have? What type of *logical relationship* does this **conjunction** indicate? What is the equivalent indicator in YL?

x. In v. 10, what does the GNT translate in place of "[from] dew" (מִטָּל)? Which translation is more accurate? Explain. Is dew thought to come from "the heavens" (שָׁמַיִם) in your **cultural setting**? Does your dew have the same function as in Palestine (see the NIV note)? Explain. How will you render this part of v. 10?

y. Point out the **poetic parallelism** in v. 10. What special function might this literary feature have here? This parallel phrasing is lost in the GNT. Can you retain it with similar *impact and appeal* in YL? If so, tell how you would do this.

z. Mention three notable *differences* between the RSV and GNT translations of v. 11. Tell which version you prefer in each case and tell why.

aa. What was the *cultural significance* of "the grain, the new wine, the oil" (וְעַל־הַדָּגָן וְעַל־הַתִּירוֹשׁ וְעַל־הַיִּצְהָר) in Bible times (cf. Deut 7:13)? Why is the Hebrew preposition "on" (עַל) repeated so often—what does this *repetition* emphasize?

ab. How did "the drought" (חֹרֶב) adversely affect "all the labor of [the peoples'] hands" (כָּל־יְגִיעַ כַּפָּיִם)? In what sense is this final expression sort of a **climax** to the LORD's speech of *rebuke?* How can you duplicate this same *import, impact,* and *connotative effect* in YL?

Exercises—Haggai 1:12–15

RSV Haggai	1:12–15 GNT
¹² Then Zerubbabel the son of She-alti-el, and Joshua the son of Jehozadak, the high priest, with all the remnant of the people, obeyed the voice of the LORD their God, and the words of Haggai the prophet, as the LORD their God had sent him; and the people feared before the LORD. ¹³ Then Haggai, the messenger of the LORD, spoke to the people with the LORD's message, "I am with you, says the LORD." ¹⁴ And the LORD stirred up the spirit of Zerubbabel the son of She-alti-el, governor of Judah, and the spirit of Joshua the son of Jehozadak, the high priest, and the spirit of all the remnant of the people; and they came and worked on the house of the LORD of hosts, their God, ¹⁵ on the twenty-fourth day of the month, in the sixth month.	**The People Obey the LORD's Command** ¹² Then Zerubbabel and Joshua and all the people who had returned from the exile in Babylonia, did what the LORD their God told them to do. They were afraid and obeyed the prophet Haggai, the LORD's messenger. ¹³ Then Haggai gave the LORD's message to the people: "I will be with you—that is my promise." ¹⁴ The LORD inspired everyone to work on the Temple: Zerubbabel, the governor of Judah; Joshua, the High Priest, and all the people who had returned from the exile. They began working on the Temple of the LORD Almighty, their God, ¹⁵ on the twenty-fourth day of the sixth month of the second year that Darius was emperor.

¹²וַיִּשְׁמַע זְרֻבָּבֶל ׀ בֶּן־שַׁלְתִּיאֵל וִיהוֹשֻׁעַ בֶּן־יְהוֹצָדָק הַכֹּהֵן הַגָּדוֹל וְכֹל ׀ שְׁאֵרִית הָעָם בְּקוֹל יְהוָה אֱלֹהֵיהֶם וְעַל־דִּבְרֵי חַגַּי הַנָּבִיא כַּאֲשֶׁר שְׁלָחוֹ יְהוָה אֱלֹהֵיהֶם וַיִּירְאוּ הָעָם מִפְּנֵי יְהוָה: ¹³ וַיֹּאמֶר חַגַּי מַלְאַךְ יְהוָה בְּמַלְאֲכוּת יְהוָה לָעָם לֵאמֹר אֲנִי אִתְּכֶם נְאֻם־יְהוָה: ¹⁴ וַיָּעַר יְהוָה אֶת־רוּחַ זְרֻבָּבֶל בֶּן־שַׁלְתִּיאֵל פַּחַת יְהוּדָה וְאֶת־רוּחַ יְהוֹשֻׁעַ בֶּן־יְהוֹצָדָק הַכֹּהֵן הַגָּדוֹל וְאֶת־רוּחַ כֹּל שְׁאֵרִית הָעָם וַיָּבֹאוּ וַיַּעֲשׂוּ מְלָאכָה בְּבֵית־יְהוָה צְבָאוֹת אֱלֹהֵיהֶם: פ ¹⁵ בְּיוֹם עֶשְׂרִים וְאַרְבָּעָה לַחֹדֶשׁ בַּשִּׁשִּׁי בִּשְׁנַת שְׁתַּיִם לְדָרְיָוֶשׁ הַמֶּלֶךְ:

Exercises—Haggai 1:12–15

a. Why is it appropriate to put a *section heading* before v. 12? Can you suggest a better title than that found in the GNT?

b. Compare the GNT with the RSV and indicate what the former leaves out in comparison with the latter. Does the *repetition* of the RSV sound all right in YL, or is it confusing or stylistically awkward? What might be the rhetorical purpose of such reiteration in this context?

c. How does the GNT translate "and all the remnant of the people" (וְכֹל ׀ שְׁאֵרִית הָעָם) found in the RSV? What does the expression "the remnant" refer to here (see the NET note)?

d. How does the GNT render RSV's obeyed "the voice of the LORD their God, and the words of Haggai the prophet" (בְּקוֹל יְהוָה אֱלֹהֵיהֶם וְעַל־דִּבְרֵי חַגַּי הַנָּבִיא)? Does the RSV sound strange if rendered literally in YL? Explain.

e. Where does GNT get the words "the LORD's messenger" from (מַלְאַךְ יְהוָה—cf. v. 13)? Do you distinguish this expression from the term "the prophet" (הַנָּבִיא)? Explain. Does it sound good to transfer this phrase to v. 12, as the GNT has done? Explain.

f. What does the expression "and the people feared [from before] the LORD" (הָעָם מִפְּנֵי יְהוָה וַיִּירְאוּ) mean in this context (see the NIV)? Do you have an *idiomatic* way of saying this in YL? Is there any added aspect of meaning in the phrase "their God" (אֱלֹהֵיהֶם)—why is "their" there!?

g. Do you need to break up the single *long sentence* of v. 12 as the GNT has done? If so, explain how you would do this, and tell how the sentence then reads in YL.

h. What is the meaning and *theological significance* of the LORD's assertion "I am with you" (אֲנִי אִתְּכֶם) in v. 13 (cf. Gen 26:3)? Evaluate the GNT rendering of these same words. Notice that they are followed by the "prophetic punctuator" (נְאֻם־יְהוָה)—how is it translated in the RSV? What is the *idiomatic* equivalent in YL? What do you think of GNT's way of handling this?

i. Point out three major differences between the translations of the RSV and the GNT in v. 14. Tell which version you prefer in each case, and give reasons why.

j. Notice that the NIV begins a *new paragraph* at v. 13. Is there any justification for this? Explain why or why not. What about beginning a new paragraph at v. 14—would that be justifiable? Explain your choice in this matter. (Note the *parallelism* in form and content between vv. 12a and 14, as well as between vv. 12b and 15.)

k. How does the GNT translate "YHWH stirred up the spirit of" (וַיָּעַר יְהוָה אֶת־רוּחַ) in v. 14? How would you render this idiomatic expression meaningfully in YL?

l. Explain the difference that you see between the translations of the RSV and the GNT in v. 15. Which version does the NIV and the NET favor? Notice that v. 15 functions as the *temporal heading* for the section beginning in v. 12 and also forms a closing *inclusio* in parallel with v. 1.

Exercises—Haggai 2:1–5

RSV	Haggai 2:1–5	GNT
2		**2**
¹ In the second year of Darius the king, in the seventh month, on the twenty-first day of the month, the word of the LORD came by Haggai the prophet, ² "Speak now to Zerubbabel the son of She-alti-el, governor of Judah, and to Joshua the son of Jehozadak, the high priest, and to all the remnant of the people, and say, ³ 'Who is left among you that saw this house in its former glory? How do you see it now? Is it not in your sight as nothing? ⁴ Yet now take courage, O Zerubbabel, says the LORD; take courage, O Joshua, son of Jehozadak, the high priest; take courage, all you people of the land, says the LORD; work, for I am with you, says the LORD of hosts, ⁵ according to the promise that I made you when you came out of Egypt. My Spirit abides among you; fear not.		**The Splendor of the New Temple** ¹ On the twenty-first day of the seventh month of that same year, the LORD spoke again through the prophet Haggai. ² He told Haggai to speak to Zerubbabel, the governor of Judah, to Joshua, the High Priest, and to the people, and to say to them, ³ "Is there anyone among you who can still remember how splendid the Temple used to be? How does it look to you now? It must seem like nothing at all. ⁴ But now don't be discouraged, any of you. Do the work, for I am with you. ⁵ When you came out of Egypt, I promised that I would always be with you. I am still with you, so do not be afraid.

בַּשְּׁבִיעִי בְּעֶשְׂרִים וְאֶחָד לַחֹדֶשׁ הָיָה דְבַר־יְהוָה בְּיַד־חַגַּי הַנָּבִיא לֵאמֹר: ² אֱמָר־נָא אֶל־זְרֻבָּבֶל בֶּן־שַׁלְתִּיאֵל פַּחַת יְהוּדָה וְאֶל־יְהוֹשֻׁעַ בֶּן־יְהוֹצָדָק הַכֹּהֵן הַגָּדוֹל וְאֶל־שְׁאֵרִית הָעָם לֵאמֹר: ³ מִי בָכֶם הַנִּשְׁאָר אֲשֶׁר רָאָה אֶת־הַבַּיִת הַזֶּה בִּכְבוֹדוֹ הָרִאשׁוֹן וּמָה אַתֶּם רֹאִים אֹתוֹ עַתָּה הֲלוֹא כָמֹהוּ כְּאַיִן בְּעֵינֵיכֶם: ⁴ וְעַתָּה חֲזַק זְרֻבָּבֶל ׀ נְאֻם־יְהוָה וַחֲזַק יְהוֹשֻׁעַ בֶּן־יְהוֹצָדָק הַכֹּהֵן הַגָּדוֹל וַחֲזַק כָּל־עַם הָאָרֶץ נְאֻם־יְהוָה וַעֲשׂוּ כִּי־אֲנִי אִתְּכֶם נְאֻם יְהוָה צְבָאוֹת: ⁵ אֶת־הַדָּבָר אֲשֶׁר־כָּרַתִּי אִתְּכֶם בְּצֵאתְכֶם מִמִּצְרַיִם וְרוּחִי עֹמֶדֶת בְּתוֹכְכֶם אַל־תִּירָאוּ: ס

Exercises—Haggai 2:1–5

a. What is the difference in the **time formula** that begins chapter 2 (v. 1) in the RSV and GNT translations (cf. question [1] above)? Which version do you prefer for YL and why?

b. The remaining words of 2:1 are exactly the same as what you find in which other verse of Haggai? Why is it important for translators to take note of this *exact verbal correspondence?*

c. Notice that the RSV does not actually make a *paragraph break* at the end of v. 5 as the GNT does (see the text given on pgs. 449–450). What are the arguments for and against putting a section break (and a section heading) at this point in the text? [NOTE: the Hebrew letter-marker פ at the end of v. 5 supports the break here.] What is the *structural evidence* then for starting a new major unit at v. 10? (All versions agree on this last division.)

d. What important Jewish festival was being held at the time of year recorded in v. 1? How does this *historical fact* relate to the *theme* of the book of Haggai? Is this worth a **footnote**? Explain.

e. Point out two major differences between the translation of v. 2 by the RSV and the GNT. Which version is a better **model** for the translation in YL and why?

f. What is the **underlying implication** (implicit intention) of the first question of v. 3? What is the meaning of the RSV's rendering "in its former glory", which is a literal translation of the Hebrew (בִּכְבוֹדוֹ הָרִאשׁוֹן)? Is an *explanatory footnote* needed here (cf. NET, NIV)?

g. Do you have an idiomatic way in YL of expressing the 2nd *question* of v. 3 (וּמָה אַתֶּם רֹאִים אֹתוֹ עַתָּה) – lit. 'how you [are] ones looking at it now')?

h. How does the third *RQ* of 2:3 relate to the second one in meaning? What is the best way of rendering this added *emphasis* in YL? Would a cross-reference to Ezra 3:12 help your readers?

i. What is the main difference between the RSV and the GNT translations at v. 4? Which translation would serve as a better model in YL? Tell why. Would you have to make some modifications in order to render the text more idiomatically in YL? Explain what you would do. How can you best deal with the reiterated *prophetic punctuator* – "says the LORD"?

j. The word "yet/but now" (וְעַתָּה – lit. 'and now' – cf. 1:5, 2:15) signals that a *new stage* in the exhortation or argument begins at this point in the text. Do you have a special literary *marker* for that sort of discourse function in YL? If so, tell what it is.

k. How would you express the three-fold command to "take courage!" (lit. 'be strong' חֲזַק) idiomatically, or using a figure of speech, in YL? What does the GNT do here in contrast to the RSV? Does the *repetition* serve an emphatic function in YL, as in Hebrew, or must you follow the *verbal reduction* exemplified by the GNT? Why is a *cross-reference* to 1 Chron. 28:20 needed here?

l. Do you have an idiom to express the command to "work!" (lit. 'do' – וַעֲשׂוּ)? If so, would it be appropriate to use at this juncture? Explain.

m. Point out the difference between the RSV and the GNT at the beginning of v. 5. Which is a more natural way of translating in YL? How do you say "according to" in YL?

n. Who does *"you* [pl. – came out]" actually refer to? Does this affect your translation? Explain.

o. In the Hebrew of v. 5, "promise" is literally 'the word' (הַדָּבָר) and "made" is literally 'I cut' (כָּרַתִּי). Do you have an idiomatic or figurative way of expressing the notion of "[firmly] promising" in YL? Can you use that expression here? Explain.

p. How does the GNT translate "My Spirit abides among you" (וְרוּחִי עֹמֶדֶת בְּתוֹכְכֶם – lit. 'and my spirit [is standing] in/with you [pl.])? Should you refer to the "spirit" or not in this context? Check some reference works and explain your preference here (compare the NIV and NET notes).

q. How does the *command* "fear not!" (אַל־תִּירָאוּ) compare in meaning to "feared the LORD" in 1:12—does the verb "fear" have the same meaning in each context? Explain your answer. If the sense is different here in 2:5, how would you express the correct idea in YL? Do you have an appropriate idiom to use in this place?

r. What meaning does the little particle "so" have in the GNT? In other words, how do the clauses "I am still with you" and "do not be afraid" relate to each other logically? How do you express this same *semantic relationship* naturally in YL?

RSV	Haggai 2:6–9	GNT
⁶ For thus says the LORD of hosts: Once again, in a little while, I will shake the heavens and the earth and the sea and the dry land; ⁷ and I will shake all nations, so that the treasures of all nations shall come in, and I will fill this house with splendor, says the LORD of hosts. ⁸ The silver is mine, and the gold is mine, says the LORD of hosts. ⁹ The latter splendor of this house shall be greater than the former, says the LORD of hosts; and in this place I will give prosperity, says the LORD of hosts.' "		⁶ "Before long I will shake heaven and earth, land and sea. ⁷ I will overthrow all the nations, and their treasures will be brought here, and the Temple will be filled with wealth. ⁸ All the silver and gold of the world is mine. ⁹ The new Temple will be more splendid than the old one, and there I will give my people prosperity and peace." The LORD Almighty has spoken.

⁶כִּי כֹה אָמַר יְהוָה צְבָאוֹת עוֹד אַחַת מְעַט הִיא וַאֲנִי מַרְעִישׁ אֶת־הַשָּׁמַיִם וְאֶת־הָאָרֶץ וְאֶת־הַיָּם וְאֶת־הֶחָרָבָה: ⁷וְהִרְעַשְׁתִּי אֶת־כָּל־הַגּוֹיִם וּבָאוּ חֶמְדַּת כָּל־הַגּוֹיִם וּמִלֵּאתִי אֶת־הַבַּיִת הַזֶּה כָּבוֹד אָמַר יְהוָה צְבָאוֹת: ⁸לִי הַכֶּסֶף וְלִי הַזָּהָב נְאֻם יְהוָה צְבָאוֹת: ⁹גָּדוֹל יִהְיֶה כְּבוֹד הַבַּיִת הַזֶּה הָאַחֲרוֹן מִן־הָרִאשׁוֹן אָמַר יְהוָה צְבָאוֹת וּבַמָּקוֹם הַזֶּה אֶתֵּן שָׁלוֹם נְאֻם יְהוָה צְבָאוֹת: פ

Exercises—Haggai 2:6–9

a. Why does the GNT, in contrast to the RSV, (see actual published version) begin a new paragraph at v. 6? What is the structural support for this *division* of the text? Does a *major* section begin here? Explain your answer.

b. What expression has the GNT left out of its translation of v. 6? Why do you think that they did this? Do you think that these words belong in your translation? Why or why not?

c. What does the expression "Once again" (עוֹד אַחַת) indicate about the events being referred to? How does the GNT translate these words? What do you recommend doing here in your translation? Does the *cross-reference* to Hebrews 12:26–27 influence your decision? If so, why?

d. How would you translate "in a little while" (מְעַט הִיא – lit. 'it [is] little') so that it fits naturally in YL together with the idea of "once again"?

e. What does the LORD mean by saying "I will shake" (וַאֲנִי מַרְעִישׁ)—what kind of a "shaking" is meant here, and how can you express this naturally, even idiomatically, in YL? This is not a "distant future" tense in Hebrew, but an "*immediate* future"; can you put it this way in YL?

f. Why are all these places mentioned: "the <u>heavens</u> and the <u>earth</u> and the <u>sea</u> and the <u>dry land</u>?" What special rhetorical significance is being conveyed? Do you have any difficulties in translating any of the terms underlined above? If so, explain what the problem is and how you propose resolving it in your translation so that the intended idea comes though both clearly and forcefully, as in the Hebrew?

g. What is being "shaken" in v. 7? What verb does GNT use instead? Which verb (or perhaps a different one) is more appropriate in YL and tell why.

h. How does NIV translate the word rendered "treasures" (חֶמְדַּת) in RSV and GNT? How will you translate this word in YL? (See Isaiah 60:5, Malachi 3:1–4, and the note in the *New English Translation* [NET, www.netbible.com])

i. The NIV, RSV, and GNT also differ in their translation of another key term of v. 7—which one (Hebrew כָּבוֹד)? Which version do you prefer? (See the translation of this same term in v. 9.)

j. Translate v. 8 in YL and then prepare a back-translation into English. How does the meaning of this verse relate to what has been said in v. 7? *[Always check how one verse links up with the preceding one because this may require certain specific transitional words or phrases in YL.]*

Exercises—Haggai 2:6–9 613

k. Which words of v. 8 does GNT not translate? Is such a *deliberate omission* a good procedure in YL at this point? Explain why (or why not).

l. What does "latter splendor" (RSV) mean or refer to? How does this rendering compare in meaning to that expressed by the GNT and NIV (see also the NET)?

m. What does "this place" (מָקוֹם הַזֶּה) refer to? (Consult a commentary on this issue.) Can you leave the *reference ambiguous* in YL? Explain why (not).

n. The GNT seems to add an extra *key term* in comparison with the RSV—what is that? There is only one word in Hebrew, namely, שָׁלוֹם – so which translation works better in YL? Refer to a Bible dictionary or commentary and explain the full sense and significance of the important thematic word "peace."

o. Why do you think that the expression "says the LORD of Hosts" is repeated in v. 9? (Note that they are slightly different in Hebrew: אָמַר יְהוָה צְבָאוֹת and נְאֻם יְהוָה צְבָאוֹת—do you *distinguish* these prophetic formulas in YL? Explain how—or why you do not make a difference.)

RSV Haggai	2:10–14 GNT
¹⁰ On the twenty-fourth day of the ninth month, in the second year of Darius, the word of the LORD came by Haggai the prophet, ¹¹ "Thus says the LORD of hosts: Ask the priests to decide this question, ¹² 'If one carries holy flesh in the skirt of his garment, and touches with his skirt bread, or pottage, or wine, or oil, or any kind of food, does it become holy?'" The priests answered, "No." ¹³ Then said Haggai, "If one who is unclean by contact with a dead body touches any of these, does it become unclean?" The priests answered, "It does become unclean." ¹⁴ Then Haggai said, "So is it with this people, and with this nation before me, says the LORD; and so with every work of their hands; and what they offer there is unclean.	**The Prophet Consults the Priests** ¹⁰ On the twenty-fourth day of the ninth month of the second year that Darius was emperor, the LORD Almighty spoke again to the prophet Haggai. ¹¹ He said, "Ask the priests for a ruling on this question: ¹² Suppose someone takes a piece of consecrated meat from a sacrifice and carries it in a fold of his robe. If he then lets his robe touch any bread, cooked food, wine, olive oil, or any kind of food at all, will it make that food consecrated also?" When the question was asked, the priests answered, "No." ¹³ * Then Haggai asked, "Suppose someone is defiled because he has touched a dead body. If he then touches any of these foods, will that make them defiled too?" The priests answered, "Yes." ¹⁴ Then Haggai said, "The LORD says that the same thing applies to the people of this nation and to everything they produce; and so everything they offer on the altar is defiled."

Analyzing and Translating Haggai

```
10 בְּעֶשְׂרִים וְאַרְבָּעָה לַתְּשִׁיעִי בִּשְׁנַת שְׁתַּיִם לְדָרְיָוֶשׁ הָיָה דְבַר־יְהוָה אֶל־חַגַּי
הַנָּבִיא לֵאמֹר: 11 כֹּה אָמַר יְהוָה צְבָאוֹת שְׁאַל־נָא אֶת־הַכֹּהֲנִים תּוֹרָה לֵאמֹר:
12 הֵן ׀ יִשָּׂא־אִישׁ בְּשַׂר־קֹדֶשׁ בִּכְנַף בִּגְדוֹ וְנָגַע בִּכְנָפוֹ אֶל־הַלֶּחֶם וְאֶל־הַנָּ֠
זִיד וְאֶל־הַיַּיִן וְאֶל־שֶׁמֶן וְאֶל־כָּל־מַאֲכָל הֲיִקְדָּשׁ וַיַּעֲנוּ הַכֹּהֲנִים וַיֹּאמְרוּ לֹא:
13 וַיֹּאמֶר חַגַּי אִם־יִגַּע טְמֵא־נֶפֶשׁ בְּכָל־אֵלֶּה הֲיִטְמָא וַיַּעֲנוּ הַכֹּהֲנִים וַיֹּאמְרוּ
יִטְמָא: 14 וַיַּעַן חַגַּי וַיֹּאמֶר כֵּן הָעָם־הַזֶּה וְכֵן־הַגּוֹי הַזֶּה לְפָנַי נְאֻם־יְהוָה וְכֵן
כָּל־מַעֲשֵׂה יְדֵיהֶם וַאֲשֶׁר יַקְרִיבוּ שָׁם טָמֵא הוּא:
```

Exercises—Haggai 2:10–14

a. What evidence is there for a new discourse division at 2:10—what are the *markers* of this break? (Note that the final Hebrew letter פ also suggests that a section of discourse ends *after* v. 9.)

b. The section above ends after v. 14, but many versions and commentaries (including the UBS Translator's Handbook) prefer to begin the next major unit at v. 20—that is, including vv. 15–19 in the present section. What is your opinion on this important issue, and what are your reasons for coming to this conclusion (see also the note in the NET)? We will consider the larger text structure and the LORD's rhetorical "argument" again when we come to v. 15.

c. What is the difference between the RSV and the GNT with regard to the textual arrangement or **format** of the present section covering vv. 10–14? Which method do you prefer and why?

d. Verse 10 is *similar* to which other verse in the book of Haggai? What is the *difference* between these two verses in terms of their structure (not in the details)?

e. Instead of "came by" what does the GNT say? Note that the GNT thereby indicates a slight difference in the Hebrew text—that is, came/was 'to' (אֶל) instead of came/was 'by [the] hand of' (בְּיַד) as in 1:1 and 2:1. Which version do you want to follow in YL (or neither) and why?

f. Why do you think that the GNT includes the words LORD "Almighty" in v. 10 (cp. v. 11)? Do you recommend this procedure of *eliminating redundancy* in YL? Why (not)? Can you see any special reason for the repeated use of the prophetic formula in vv. 10–11?

g. Point out the difference between the RSV and the GNT in how they render the main *imperative* of v. 11? How would you express this *technical* (legal) expression in YL (cf. Lev 10:10–11; Deut 17:8–12, 31:11; cf. Mal 2:7–9)? Do you have an idiom to convey this notion?

h. Point out three differences between the RSV and GNT in the wording of certain *technical terms* in v. 12. Which version do you prefer and why? Tell

Exercises—Haggai 2:10–14

how you will express each of these words in YL: "holy flesh" (בְּשַׂר־קֹדֶשׁ), "skirt" (כָּנָף), "pottage" (נָזִיד).

i. Is there any way that you need to modify the *very long* question of v. 12 in order to ask it in a natural way in YL? Explain the point or intention of this query. Does anything similar occur in the traditional religious rites of your culture? If so, give an example.

j. What does the initial word "Suppose…" in the GNT suggest (contrast "If" of the RSV)? Do you have a similar word in YL that indicates that a *hypothetical example* is about to be given?

k. Why do you think that GNT adds the words "When the question was asked…"—which are not present in the original Hebrew text? Do you need to add these or similar words in YL? Explain.

l. Is it a *polite response* in YL simply to say "No!"? If not, how must you modify the priests' reply to make it polite?

m. Do people become "defiled" by touching a "dead body" in your culture (v. 13)? If so, what must be done to "purify" the person? How was this carried out according to the Mosaic ceremonial law (cf. Num 19:13, 22)?

n. How do you express the concept of being "unclean" or "defiled" (טָמֵא) in YL? Must you use a *euphemism* (term of avoidance) to mention a "corpse" in public speech (lit. Heb 'soul, breath' נֶפֶשׁ)?

o. Why don't the priests simply answer "Yes!"? (Note that their answer is a complete utterance in Hebrew: 'he becomes defiled' יִטְמָא.)

p. Why does the GNT add the words "The LORD says that…" in v. 14—which are not in the original text? Do you need this same sort of a *bridge* (transitional) expression in YL? Explain.

q. What word(s) in the RSV correspond(s) to the GNT's "the same thing applies?" Why is this expression needed in English? Is it necessary also in YL? Explain why (not). (Note the 3x *repeated Hebrew particle* showing a *comparative* relationship—namely: כֵּן.)

r. How does the GNT render "with this people and with this nation"? How will you translate this in YL—and tell why you must express it in this way?

s. Notice the different placement of the expression "says the LORD" (נְאֻם־יְהוָה) in the RSV and the GNT. Which *lexical position* works better in YL from a rhetorical perspective and why?

t. How does the GNT render the word "there" (שָׁם)? Evaluate the correctness of the GNT in the light of what you think that the LORD wished to teach his people through this little object lesson.

RSV	Haggai 2:15–19	GNT
		The LORD Promises His Blessing
¹⁵ Pray now, consider what will come to pass from this day onward. Before a stone was placed upon a stone in the temple of the LORD, ¹⁶ how did you fare? When one came to a heap of twenty measures, there were but ten; when one came to the wine-vat to draw fifty measures, there were but twenty. ¹⁷ I smote you and all the products of your toil with blight and mildew and hail; yet you did not return to me, says the LORD. ¹⁸ Consider from this day onward, from the twenty-fourth day of the ninth month. Since the day that the foundation of the LORD's temple was laid, consider: ¹⁹ Is the seed yet in the barn? Do the vine, the fig tree, the pomegranate, and the olive tree still yield nothing? From this day on I will bless you."		¹⁵ The LORD says, "Can't you see what has happened to you? Before you started to rebuild the Temple, ¹⁶ you would go to a pile of grain expecting to find twenty bushels, but there would be only ten. You would go to draw fifty gallons of wine from a vat, but find only twenty. ¹⁷ I sent scorching winds and hail to ruin everything you tried to grow, but still you did not repent. ¹⁸ Today is the twenty-fourth day of the ninth month, the day that the foundation of the Temple has been completed. See what is going to happen from now on. ¹⁹ Although there is no grain left, and the grapevines, fig trees, pomegranates, and olive trees have not yet produced, yet from now on I will bless you."

¹⁵וְעַתָּה שִׂימוּ־נָא לְבַבְכֶם מִן־הַיּוֹם הַזֶּה וָמָעְלָה מִטֶּרֶם שׂוּם־אֶבֶן אֶל־אֶבֶן בְּהֵיכַל יְהוָה: ¹⁶ מִהְיוֹתָם בָּא אֶל־עֲרֵמַת עֶשְׂרִים וְהָיְתָה עֲשָׂרָה בָּא אֶל־הַיֶּקֶב לַחְשֹׂף חֲמִשִּׁים פּוּרָה וְהָיְתָה עֶשְׂרִים: ¹⁷ הִכֵּיתִי אֶתְכֶם בַּשִּׁדָּפוֹן וּבַיֵּרָקוֹן וּבַבָּרָד אֵת כָּל־מַעֲשֵׂה יְדֵיכֶם וְאֵין־אֶתְכֶם אֵלַי נְאֻם־יְהוָה: ¹⁸ שִׂימוּ־נָא לְבַבְכֶם מִן־הַיּוֹם הַזֶּה וָמָעְלָה מִיּוֹם עֶשְׂרִים וְאַרְבָּעָה לַתְּשִׁיעִי לְמִן־הַיּוֹם אֲשֶׁר־יֻסַּד הֵיכַל־יְהוָה שִׂימוּ לְבַבְכֶם: ¹⁹ הַעוֹד הַזֶּרַע בַּמְּגוּרָה וְעַד־הַגֶּפֶן וְהַתְּאֵנָה וְהָרִמּוֹן וְעֵץ הַזַּיִת לֹא נָשָׂא מִן־הַיּוֹם הַזֶּה אֲבָרֵךְ: ס

Exercises—Haggai 2:15–19

a. What would seem to indicate that a *discourse break* occurs at v. 15? Is this a *major* or a *minor* one? Give textual support for your conclusion. If you think that this is only a minor break, what should be done with the section heading of the GNT?

b. To whom is Haggai speaking in this section (the Heb 'you' is plural)? Cite some evidence for choosing this *addressee* (group) from the text.

c. The expression "now" in RSV (lit. in Hebrew 'and now' וְעַתָּה) indicates that a new stage in the discourse (e.g., a prophetic argument, exposition, or exhortation) is beginning at this point (cf. 1:5, 2:4). Do you have an

Exercises—Haggai 2:15–19 617

        equivalent *text sequence marker* in YL? How do you like the way that the GNT has handled this transition?

d.   The GNT begins v. 15 with "The LORD says..."—which is not found in the Hebrew. Why do you think that these words have been added (cf. v. 17b)? Which *discourse strategy* works better in YL?

e.   The *imperative* "Consider" (Heb 'set to your hearts' שִׂימוּ־נָא לְבַבְכֶם) is strengthened by a particle rendered by the RSV as "Pray" (נָא). How would you express this same function in YL?

f.   How does the GNT translate the RSV's introduction: "Before a stone was placed upon a stone..." (מִטֶּרֶם שׂוּם־אֶבֶן אֶל־אָבֶן)? Do you have a **figurative equivalent** to the RSV in YL?

g.   What in the GNT corresponds to the RSV's "from this day *onward*" (מִן־הַיּוֹם הַזֶּה וָמָעְלָה)? What is the meaning of the time phrase in this context—what does the LORD want to tell his people? (Consult several commentaries or study Bibles, including the NET below.)

h.   The GNT drops the *attributive phrase* "of the LORD" after the noun "temple" ("palace"—בְּהֵיכַל יְהוָה). Why do you think that it does this, and is this procedure a good one for YL? Explain.

i.   What is the meaning of RSV's "how did you fare" in v. 16 (lit. 'from their being'—מִהְיוֹתָם)? Do you have an *idiomatic* way of expressing this idea in YL? If so, explain what this is. Note where the GNT has placed these words. Is this a good model to follow? Explain.

j.   Explain the two *hypothetical examples* that are given in v. 16—what is their meaning and how do they reinforce Haggai's message to the people at this stage?

k.   What does "a heap of twenty measures" (עֲרֵמַת עֶשְׂרִים) refer to? How could you express this *ambiguous* phrase meaningfully in YL?

l.   What is a "winevat" (יֶקֶב), and how will you render this *technical term* in YL? How about the "fifty measures" (חֲמִשִּׁים פּוּרָה)—how can you express that so it makes sense in YL?

m.   Are exact *numerical equivalents* necessary in v. 16? If not, what is the point of these illustrations, and how could you say this more forcefully and idiomatically in YL?

n.   Instead of the literal "smote" (הִכֵּיתִי) to begin v. 17, what verb does GNT use? Which is a better model in YL and why? What does the RSV mean by saying, "I smote you...with blight and mildew?"

o.   How does the GNT express what the RSV translates a "all the products of your toil" (lit. 'all the work of your hands' – כָּל־מַעֲשֵׂה יְדֵיכֶם)?

p. Instead of "blight" for the Hebrew term שִׁדָּפוֹן, GNT more correctly translates "scorching winds". How do you express this sort of plague in YL? Do you have a word for "hail" in YL (בָּרָד)? GNT seems to leave out the middle plague, "mildew" (יֵרָקוֹן). What does that refer to (consult a commentary), and how would you express this concept in YL?

q. The RSV translation "yet you did not return to me" is literally in Hebrew 'and there was not you (pl.) unto me' (וְאֵין־אֶתְכֶם אֵלַי). What does this mean, and how can you best express this idea in YL? Notice how the NET interprets and translates this expression; do you agree?

r. Do you see any special rhetorical purpose for the *prophetic speech punctuator* "utterance/oracle of Yahweh" (נְאֻם־יְהוָה) at the end of v. 17? Can you just leave it out of your translation, like the GNT does? Explain.

s. The words leading off v. 18 *repeat* what is found at the beginning of which other verse? What does this mean for you as a translator? The repetition here, together with the date formula, also serves to *mark the beginning* of a minor division within this section, vv. 15–19. Do you need to put a paragraph break here? Why, or why not? Which *compositional strategy* helps your reader more?

t. What *time reference* is being specified in v. 18 by the expression "from this day onward" (cf. the reference in v. 15 – מִן־הַיּוֹם הַזֶּה וָמָעְלָה)? Notice where the GNT places its equivalent for this expression; which *verse position* is more natural in YL? Explain why, if you can.

u. The RSV translates: "Since the day that the foundation of the LORD's temple was laid" (cf NIV). How do the GNT and the NET express this? Which version do you wish to follow in YL and why? (Consult a commentary on this matter.)

v. Verse 19 is very difficult to translate, as you can see from the different renderings in the RSV, NIV, GNT, and NET (below). The RSV begins with a *rhetorical question* (as in the Hebrew)—what is the *expected answer* to this question (cf. GNT)? What kind of "seed" (הַזֶּרַע) is being referred to here?

w. To make things a little easier, we might simply choose to follow the two versions that seem to present the same understanding of this verse, namely, the NIV and the GNT. Which of these two versions would serve as a better *translation model* in YL? Why?

x. How do you express these agricultural products in YL (the Hebrew terms are *collective* and therefore grammatically singular. In English, the terms require plural forms): "grape vines" (גֶּפֶן), "fig trees" (תְּאֵנָה), "pomegranates" (רִמּוֹן), and "olive trees" (עֵץ הַזַּיִת)?

Exercises—Haggai 2:20–23

y. Which words express the **climax** of this verse as well as that of this section as a whole? How would you *mark* this discourse peak in YL? Notice in particular what the NIV has done.

z. How would you express this final utterance "From this day on, I will bless you" (מִן־הַיּוֹם הַזֶּה אֲבָרֵךְ) in a *forceful* manner in YL? Give an English back-translation of what you have said.

RSV	Haggai 2:20–23	GNT
²⁰ The word of the LORD came a second time to Haggai on the twenty-fourth day of the month, ²¹ "Speak to Zerubbabel, governor of Judah, saying, I am about to shake the heavens and the earth, ²² and to overthrow the throne of kingdoms; I am about to destroy the strength of the kingdoms of the nations, and overthrow the chariots and their riders; and the horses and their riders shall go down, every one by the sword of his fellow. ²³ On that day, says the LORD of hosts, I will take you, O Zerubbabel my servant, the son of She-alti-el, says the LORD, and make you like a signet ring; for I have chosen you, says the LORD of hosts."		**The LORD's Promise to Zerubbabel** ²⁰ On that same day, the twenty-fourth of the month, the LORD gave Haggai a second message ²¹ for Zerubbabel, the governor of Judah: "I am about to shake heaven and earth ²² and overthrow kingdoms and end their power. I will overturn chariots and their drivers; the horses will die, and their riders will kill one another. ²³ On that day I will take you, Zerubbabel my servant, and I will appoint you to rule in my name. You are the one I have chosen." The LORD Almighty has spoken.

²⁰וַיְהִי דְבַר־יְהוָה ׀ שֵׁנִית אֶל־חַגַּי בְּעֶשְׂרִים וְאַרְבָּעָה לַחֹדֶשׁ לֵאמֹר: ²¹ אֱמֹר אֶל־זְרֻבָּבֶל פַּחַת־יְהוּדָה לֵאמֹר אֲנִי מַרְעִישׁ אֶת־הַשָּׁמַיִם וְאֶת־הָאָרֶץ: ²² וְהָפַכְתִּי כִּסֵּא מַמְלָכוֹת וְהִשְׁמַדְתִּי חֹזֶק מַמְלְכוֹת הַגּוֹיִם וְהָפַכְתִּי מֶרְכָּבָה וְרֹכְבֶיהָ וְיָרְדוּ סוּסִים וְרֹכְבֵיהֶם אִישׁ בְּחֶרֶב אָחִיו: ²³ בַּיּוֹם הַהוּא נְאֻם־יְהוָה צְבָאוֹת אֶקָּחֲךָ זְרֻבָּבֶל בֶּן־שְׁאַלְתִּיאֵל עַבְדִּי נְאֻם־יְהוָה וְשַׂמְתִּיךָ כַּחוֹתָם כִּי־בְךָ בָחַרְתִּי נְאֻם יְהוָה צְבָאוֹת:

Exercises—Haggai 2:20–23

a. What marks a *new section* beginning at v. 20? How can you distinguish this point in your translation? Do you need a *section heading* here? If so, what wording do you suggest in YL (also give a back-translation into English)? [NOTE: At this stage, check, revise, and write out all the section headings that you have proposed for the book of Haggai. Does the result give a satisfactory summary of the main messages of this text? Make any additional revisions that are necessary to prepare such a coherent outline.]

b. How does the GNT render the RSV's "a second time" (שֵׁנִית)? Which version serves as a better model for your translation and why?

c. Notice that the sentence of v. 20 carries on into v. 21. Does this make it *too long* for people to follow and understand in YL? If so, what can you do to break this utterance up at the end of v. 20? (Compare the different translations that you have.)

d. What problem do you see in the GNT's wording: "the LORD gave a second message to Haggai?" How would you revise this to avoid any possible misunderstanding?

e. What difficulty is introduced by the RSV's translation of v. 21 (extending also into v. 22): "Speak to Zerubbabel, governor of Judah, saying,...?" How do you propose revising the text to remove the problem presented by this *embedded quotation*—or does it cause no problems in YL?

f. The words of v. 21b are the same as those found in which other verse of Haggai? What is the communicative significance of such *reiteration*—in other words, what pragmatic function does it serve at this point in the text?

g. What is the meaning of the English expression "I am about to?" What is another way of saying this—using words that would translate more easily into YL (note also the NET)?

h. *Who is speaking* these words; that is, to whom does the pronoun "I" (אֲנִי) refer? Is the personal **referent** clear in YL? If not, how can you clarify who is actually the speaker of these words?

i. Verse 22 is rather redundant in Hebrew—the same general idea is repeated in this verse using different words. What is the *rhetorical purpose* of this device in Hebrew poetry? Can the redundancy serve the same function in YL? Explain your answer. Notice what the GNT has done to eliminate this redundancy. Do you think that the GNT has left out any important concept or expression—that is, in comparison with a more literal version like the RSV, NIV, or NET?

j. What is the meaning of the RSV's rendering: "[I am about to] overthrow the throne of kingdoms" (וְהָפַכְתִּי כִּסֵּא מַמְלָכוֹת)? Do you have an *idiomatic* way of saying this in YL, perhaps through the use of an *ideophone*? If so, give your translation as an example of a more vivid rendition that matches the power of the original text.

k. Can you use the same verb "overthrow" (הָפַכְתִּי) with reference to "chariots and their riders" (מֶרְכָּבָה וְרֹכְבֶיהָ)? If not, what do you suggest for YL?

l. What does the text mean by saying that all the horses and their riders "will go down" (יָרְדוּ)—*go down* where? Explain the meaning of the *Hebrew*

Exercises—Haggai 2:20–23 621

     idiom "every one by the sword of his fellow" (אִישׁ בְּחֶרֶב אָחִיו). Do you have an idiomatic way of expressing this same idea in YL?

m.   Should a new paragraph be started at v. 23? Explain why. This verse begins "On that day…" (בַּיּוֹם הַהוּא)—but which day is referred to here? What is the special significance of this "day"? Remember how you have translated this key *eschatological opener* in the past.

n.   Note the threefold repetition of "says the LORD of Hosts" (נְאֻם־יְהוָה צְבָאוֹת) in v. 23. The repetition may actually serve different *discourse functions* here; can you suggest what these might be? Evaluate the GNT translation with respect to this issue. What do you propose for YL and why?

o.   What identifying phrase has the GNT omitted with reference to Zerubbabel? Should the same thing be done in your translation? Explain.

p.   What is semantically significant about the expression "my servant" (עַבְדִּי) in the Hebrew Scriptures (see the NET note)? Is a similar connotation conveyed in your translation? If not, what might be done about this loss of "meaning"? Is a reference note needed here? If so, suggest what this might be.

q.   Explain the symbolical sense of the *simile* of the "signet ring" (חוֹתָם) with reference to Zerubbabel (cf. the NET note). First describe how you can analyze such similes and metaphors. How has the GNT translated this expression? How would you render it meaningfully in YL—do you have a similar concept or custom in your culture? Explain your answer. What important cross reference needs to be put into your translation at this verse? Explain why.

r.   Notice how the GNT has translated the clause "…for I have chosen you" (בָחַרְתִּי). GNT is a better rendering in this case; try to give a reason from a **rhetorical** standpoint (i.e., relating to impact and appeal).

s.   Make a list of the *five most difficult translation problems* that you have encountered in the book of Haggai. Clearly explain each problem along with your proposal for resolving it in YL. Alternatively, specify which difficulty still needs to be explained or clarified for you.

t.   What suggestions can you offer to help your primary target audience to more effectively "engage" with your translation of Haggai? (For some ideas, see Hill and Hill 2008:chs. 16–24 in particular.)

13

Proclaiming Prophetic Rhetoric Today: Promoting its Potential

The Hebrew prophets are certainly not dead today, though that is what some may think based on the paucity of sermons preached from them on any given Sunday, or the number of articles that appear annually about them (especially the so-called "minor" prophets) in popular scholarly journals. However, their vibrant messages as recorded in the Scriptures continue live on in the original language, whether people today happen to access and make use of them via that medium or not. Thus, these ancient divine spokesmen may be misunderstood and ignored, but they still continue to speak just as forcefully in and through the pages of the enscripted Word of God. Our challenge—at least for those who recognize the exegetical riches that lay beneath the surface of the original text—is to promote and continue to proclaim their ever-relevant life-or-death orations. This is accomplished, first of all, by means of more literary-perceptive methods of analysis (the approach demonstrated in my study is just one of many possible models) and, secondly, through new or revised Bible translations. The aim it to represent the text in an idiomatic, situation-sensitive manner so that our contemporaries can better grasp the sense and learn to appreciate the significance of these timeless messages proclaimed to God's people of Israel of old. The articulation of the Scriptures in a vivid vernacular style can act in an analogous way to the illustration depicted on the inside cover of this book. The living Word reproduced meaningfully in a group's mother tongue does indeed have the Spirit-infused power to give life to the "dry bones" of listeners who never had a chance to hear it before in such a direct, immediate manner (Ezek 37:4–5).

In this concluding chapter, I will first consider some possibly controversial issues that pertain to the activity of orally proclaiming the Scriptures to audiences today. This leads to a summary of the major implications of my investigation for the practice of Bible translation, with particular reference to doing this in a way that does more justice to the literary quality and rhetorical force of the original documents. I will conclude with several thoughts about the urgent need also for "contextualizing" the biblical text in order to provide an adequate "frame of reference" for understanding the cultural-historical setting as well as the message of Yahweh's chosen spokesmen, the Hebrew prophets.

13.1 On the drama of prophetic proclamation—or is it "performance?"

Two decades ago, Paul House called attention to the dramatic character of the prophecy of Zephaniah (1988:21):

> The fact is, Zephaniah thinks, moves, and means as drama. It can excite the reader as drama. In short, perhaps Zephaniah *can* rise from the ashes of scholarly neglect.

In one sense I can heartily assent to the preceding assertion—that is, concerning the *dramatic quality* of Zephaniah's composition, which "achieves a vividness and concentration that grips the reader" (ibid.,105)—and more forcefully, the hearer of the text (cf. ch. 9 above). However, I am not able to agree with the further conclusion that House arrives at, namely, the genre categorization that "in classist terms Zephaniah is a drama" (ibid., 116):

> It is apparent that the structure and dialogue of Zephaniah reflect the same basic principles as in drama. Sets of speeches work together to form parts of the plot, thus serving as scenes. Groups of speeches that serve as scenes constitute a section of the plot and therefore create acts.... These scenes and acts fit well with basic dramatic plot theory... (ibid., 97)

13.1 On the drama of prophetic proclamation—or is it "performance?" 625

Now it is one thing to claim that a literary text *reflects* drama; it is quite another to conclude that it *is* drama—that is, in the classical, theatrical sense. Such a conclusion regarding the alleged genre of discourse, namely, as *performance* and/or *character*-oriented can lead to a misunderstanding of the essential nature and purpose of the divine-human communicative event. Thus, it can detract from the complete and undivided prophetic focus on the person and word of Yahweh as well as on the theological and ethical relationship that he wishes to re-establish with his human addressees. We are dealing then not with prophetic drama, but rather with dramatic prophecy—not with *performance,* which focuses the spotlight of attention on the actors, but with *proclamation,* which emphasizes the text and message of the primary speaker, in this case, "the LORD Almighty" (Zeph 2:9–10), "the King of Israel" (3:15).

The preceding caveat leads to a somewhat fuller, comparative discussion of several of the notions put forward in a recent examination of "performance criticism of the Hebrew Bible" by Doan and Giles (2005; hereafter D&G, cf. section 2.6.2).[1] The authors offer a number of important insights into biblical, especially prophetic, text analysis from this performative standpoint, as summarized below (quotations with page numbers from D&G 2005 in parentheses). However, in some instances their various observations and conclusions might be supplemented, while in other cases a critical response from a more conservative textual perspective might be offered. A partial dialogue format will therefore be followed in the remainder of this section, i.e., first the position of D&G is cited, followed by my own reflection on the subject being considered:

> The Hebrew prophets spoke to their audiences.... Embedded in the prophetic literature are echoes of that prophetic performance, now layered over by a scribal performance, that form the prophetic documents as we now know them. (ix)

It is important to recognize the vital oral-aural basis of the original biblical message. However, I do not believe that the subsequent "scribal performance(s)" being referred to above was overly significant in terms of

---

[1] "Performance criticism recognizes the remnants of oral performances in the literature of the Hebrew Bible and gives a conceptual framework for analyzing those performances" (D&G 157). For a more detailed overview and critique of the theory and practice of *performance criticism,* see Wendland 2008b:ch. 1.

either form or content—certainly not with regard to the basic meaning of the prophetic text. Thus, normal scribal activity in ANE times was not really a freely improvised "performance," for that was not the role of the disciple/scribe—not, at any rate, when recording the sacred words of Yahweh. Who, except a false prophet, would dare misquote or alter the words of God?

> "They [the prophets] were originally orators, as can be seen from the expression 'Hear!' with which their speeches begin. We must try and imagine their sayings being uttered orally, and not as they stand on paper, if we are to understand them" (citing Hermann Gunkel). (2) For example: "The abundance of imperatives, and thus the frequency of direct address, marks the urgency of Joel's message and suggests oral presentation" (citing James Crenshaw). (162)

The manifold oratory, or diverse oral-aural rhetorical skills, of the prophets was abundantly demonstrated in the analyses of the preceding chapters of this book. Thus, these Hebrew authors demonstrated an orally derived, "performance mode of thought" (see the following point)—and oratorical style—in their writings, that is, a dynamic literary manner of composition which was clearly written to be read, or better proclaimed aloud, to a listening audience.

> A performance mode of thought is that peculiar type of orality that is still evident in the prophetic literature of the Hebrew Bible.... "Orally derived texts would mean traditional texts conceived largely in oral terms but still produced in writing" (citing Robert Culley). (5) An oral discourse can be transformed into a written discourse or vice versa. When the conceptual profile of a communication that is offered in one medium by the originator can be transferred to a second medium without affecting the "conceptual content of the discourse" (citing Wulf Oesterreicher), that quality is referred to as "medium-transferability" (citing John Lyons). (9)

I assume that such conceptual "medium-transferability" applies also to the prophetic literature of the Hebrew Bible. In most, if not all, cases then, the original author (the human vehicle of divine transmission) or his immediate disciple/scribe was responsible for both the form and also the content of the final document that was attributed to the prophetic name.

13.1 On the drama of prophetic proclamation—or is it "performance?"

> The Hebrew *[d-b-r]* is not a literary notion but is an idea that may be better understood as "utterance, speech, message." (32)

A *both-and* perspective on this point, rather than *either-or*, is more accurate in my opinion. Certainly any reference to a particular "utterance, speech, message" would include a specific genre, and that is definitely a "literary (or oratorical) notion." In any case, a similar complexity of meaning and usage is found in a number of southeastern Bantu languages, in Chewa, for example, where *liu* refers to "voice" or a single written/printed word, while the plural *mau* designates "words" or "utterance, speech, message."

> Marti Nissinen suggests that Near Eastern prophecy was an oral performance that was retransmitted both orally and in written form. The written form was used to communicate to an audience distant from the speaker, both geographically and chronologically, and to assist in the recall of the original prophetic communication. (36)

The written prophetic text thus also served as the authoritative, author-attested control, norm, and point of reference which governed any subsequent oral reproductions of the message, especially where any variants were concerned.

> [T]he hymnic fragments [in Amos] are part of an increasingly drastic set of images of the Lord used as a strategy for enhancing the prophet's project to convince his spectators that divine judgment will befall them [and] support the argument that we are dealing with an intensive mode of drama. (134)

Such a build-up of intensity is typical in the prophetic literature. However, the goal was not to embellish the text for a dramatic performance in view of the live spectators who happened to be on hand. Rather, it was to intensify the *aural* impact and impression made on any audience that would hear such a proclamation—whether sooner or later (also nowadays!) in the history of God's people.

> The application of performance criticism to the vision reports [of Amos 7–9] offers a challenge to the scholarly consensus that accepts a multilayered composition of the book. There is a unity to the visions and a clear rationale to their present placement within the book of Amos. When condensed and placed back-to-back, the dramatic visions flow as a series of acts in a unified dramatic presentation. (155–156)

A discourse-centered literary (artistic-rhetorical) and structural analysis of Amos and the other prophetic texts of the Hebrew Scriptures leads me to the same conclusion with regard to the unity and integrity of the various books included within this corpus. These theological and pastoral messages were all composed and inscribed with a certain thematic unity that centered in Yahweh and his crucial covenantal relationship with the people of Israel. This dynamic interpersonal religious and spiritual focus also rendered the prophetic texts very well suited for an oral proclamatory mode of presentation to their intended audiences, right up to the present day.

The preceding as well as other observations in *Prophets, Performance, and Power* tend to support my selected studies of the prophets above as well as what I have written elsewhere about the "oratorical" nature of the New Testament epistles (2008).[2] However, all too often D&G push their thesis too far with respect to what they view as the performative "drama" of *Amos* (and other OT writings) and the aggressively *creative* character of the scribes who were their text recorders and possibly editors. The following is a sample of some of the more speculative and often misleading assertions (in my opinion) which D&G make about the compositional process of this especially "dramatic" type of Hebrew literature:

> The process of transforming an oral prophetic performance into a text is an exercise of social power. The transformation takes ownership of the performance from the performer [i.e., the prophet] and

---

[2] My assumption, as argued in *Translating the Literature of Scripture* (2004:2–12), is that the prophetic writings along with the Scriptures generally, are instances of genuine "literature," which according to the Concise Oxford Dictionary refers to "written works, especially those regarded as having artistic merit." I reiterate this point in view of a recent study that claims that "there is no biblical literature" (Mazor 2009:21) Mazor reasons as follows: "The primary objectives of the Hebrew Bible—religious, philosophical, historical, moral—are not discrete… but intertwined, and they are all pragmatic, seeking to educate, teach, preach, and impart knowledge, values, and religious instruction. Being devoid of aesthetic objectives, the Bible cannot be considered a literary work but a collection of books with a defined pragmatic goal, making use of an astounding array of aesthetic patterns and devices. These patterns and devices are there only to serve the main purpose" (ibid., 21–22). Such reasoning is obviously flawed. In the first place, why must a particular composition serve only a single communicative function? As Mazor himself observes, the aesthetic-artistic is employed in the service of the "pragmatic" (I would say rather the combined "theological-moral" goal). One might even argue that artistry, or aesthetics, is itself a "pragmatic" goal. Good literature gives evidence of a complex of aims, which may vary in priority according to the particular section in view (e.g., Isaiah 40:1–5, prophetic/revelatory; 9–14, 28–31, theological; 19–20, moral). Second, according to common critical understanding, as reflected in the dictionary definition, a literary work is one that manifests clear "artistic merit," something that Mazor himself presumably grants with reference to the Hebrew Bible (and indeed describes in great detail in his book).

13.1 On the drama of prophetic proclamation—or is it "performance?"

> gives it to the scribe. (4).... By appropriating the character of the prophet, the scribe became, both in speaking and writing the prophetic text, what appeared before his spectators *as* the character of the prophet. (24)[3]

D&G continually over-emphasize this notion of "social power" in their analyses, as if the typical scribe were some sort of major power-broker in ANE society, who used his position as a prophet's recorder for personal gain as a means of social advancement and/or prestige. Even if this might have been the case in secular society, the prophets (as guided by God who initially inspired the words) would have selected scribes who wished to promote the divine message(s) as originally given, rather than to push their own personal and social (or political) agendas. Thus, I take the working relationship between *Jeremiah* and *Baruch* (i.e., speak = > record, more or less precisely) as being paradigmatic of the modus operandi of the typical OT prophet and his scribe (e.g., Jer 36).

> [P]ractitioners of all kinds of performance (in our case, the scribes) assume that some behaviors ("organized sequences of events, scripted actions, known texts") and oral traditions are separate from the performer and can be "stored, manipulated, transmitted, and transformed" (citing Richard Schechner).... Yet it is not a straight line from prophetic performance to literate recording of that performance. The process of recording can change and even undermine the original performative intent of the prophet. (15)

One cannot too facilely or liberally apply the theories of a modern specialist in "theatre and anthropology" (Schechner 1985) to the ancient writings of the Hebrew prophets. "Ancient Israel never, as far as we know, produced any drama..." (McKeating 1993:14). And why, in any case, would the scribe—even a much later one—want to "undermine the original performative intent of the prophet?" There is far too much imaginative speculation here, too many gaps in concretely substantiated logic. In any case, sacred texts (with their *divine sanctions*), like royal decrees, would have surely been transmitted as precisely as possible by their scribal tradents, both immediate and subsequent.

---

[3] What might well be the case with reference to the modern secular stage is arguably (without substantially more evidence than that offered by D&G) *not* necessarily applicable to ancient sacred prophetic proclamation. This would be especially true, I would think, in the case of messages from a "holy, almighty" God like Yahweh of Israel.

> The prophet is a performer who exercises social power through the immediacy of the performance. ...the prophet is not only a messenger but the personification of the message. The message has power because the prophet has power.... Rather than a smooth transition from prophet to literature, it is much more likely that the evolution from prophetic performer to prophetic literature was characterized by a struggle for power. The prophetic scribe (or, perhaps better, the prophetic playwright) is dependent upon the prophetic performer [alias, the prophet of Yahweh] for his inspiration and derives his credibility from an attachment to the prophetic performer but, nonetheless, is bent on replacing the prophetic performer. (21)

The preceding set of quotes gives us, in a nutshell, the two main assumptions of D&G: The production of the prophetic literature of the Hebrew Bible is all about "power"—social power, whatever that meant *then*—and about the prophetic scribe's efforts to attain that power for himself by "usurping the role" (ibid., 21) of his source, the illustrious "prophetic performer," i.e., the Lord's chosen prophet. This sort of self-promotional endeavor was supposedly effected by means of the respective scribes' creative re-shaping and re-situating performances of the original texts—a process that presumably repeated itself until the notion of a "canonical text" began to take hold and these scribal efforts at self-expression were gradually curtailed and finally stopped.

However, there is no convincing evidence of such an internal, interpersonal power struggle recorded in the Scriptures themselves, either in or between the lines. If this had been the case, surely such power-hungry scribes would have sought to have their own names recorded within the biblical text—in contrast to Baruch, who was content to allow his prophet Jeremiah to make a few personal references when necessary. On the contrary, the only promotion of power in the Bible, the New Testament as well as the Old, has uniquely to do with magnifying the supreme and incomparable might, authority, glory, etc. of "Yahweh of Armies," the Lord Almighty. He will surely judge the wicked and vindicate his righteous remnant. This is the keynote of Amos (e.g., 1:2, ch. 9, and elsewhere throughout the book, "This is what the LORD says...") as well as the fundamental message of all his prophetic colleagues.

> The prophets find no conclusion [i.e., in terms of their messages] because the scribes writing the prophetic literature will not allow them to conclude. The scribes create prophetic *characters* out of the prophets themselves (prophetic *actors*). (23)... The scribe, both as a writer and a speaker of the text, engaged in a kind of impersonation. (27)

13.1 On the drama of prophetic proclamation—or is it "performance?"

Surely, to apply a proverbial analogy, this faulty hermeneutical assumption would seem to be a clear case of the tail wagging the dog. While the novelty of this hypothesis might be appealing to a post-modern theorist, it suffers from the fatal flaw of not being supported by facts. As far as any prophetic "impersonation" goes, for what purpose would the dutiful ANE scribe *want* to do that—or, more significantly, why would he *dare* to attempt it when declaring "the word of the LORD" (cf. Amos 7)?

> In the prophetic tradition, it was the prophet through whom God himself was present. In the scribal tradition, it was the scribe who, as actor, created the character of the prophet in order for God to be present. (29) The *scribe*, as both *creator* and presenter of prophetic texts, *takes control* over both the scheme, or mode of presentation, *and the content*. The prophet's power, though given him by the Lord, could only be enacted by the prophet himself until the scribe *appropriated the character of the prophet*. (30, added italics)

Here we have the supposition of a "scribal tradition," one that appears to parallel or replace the "prophetic tradition"—but, again, where is the textual, or even any extratextual support for such a sweeping assertion? Instead of textual evidence, this claim is again made with reference to an elaborate theory derived from the writings of modern theatre and drama criticism. How could there be any credibility, reliability, or authority to the resultant message if it were true that the scribe actually replaced or subverted the called prophet during the ongoing program of Yahweh's exhortatory communication with his people? If these scribes were such important, influential, and tradition-forging individuals in ancient times, why do we not read more about them in the literature of the day, or find their names recorded anywhere in the texts that they allegedly re-created?

> "As a mode of theatrical art, the medium of drama is not language, but human presence. Language, vital as it is to the art of drama, is introduced through the activity of men speaking.... [D]rama differs from other modes of presentation in one major respect: The presentation of drama is a presentation of an imagined act" (citing Beckerman 1979:14, 18). In the case of prophetic drama, it was the scribe who moved the presentation along the continuum of theatrical and dramatic activity. (62–63)... The created reality of the prophet [by the scribe/scribal tradition] allows the certainty of the oracle for the prophet and the power of the oracle for the audience. (111)

Thus, the significance of the prophets allegedly does not have to do with the theological or ethical content of their urgent, life-changing messages, but it rather concerns the polished public performances of scribes and their capacity to profoundly stimulate the imagination of their contemporary audiences. However, something quite vital seems to be missing here—namely, *dabar,* the Word, and the concrete, life-or-death pastoral communicative goals that God aimed to achieve in and through these divinely inspired, but humanly conveyed proclamations. Indeed, one might ask: where does Yahweh fit, if at all, into this speculative theatrical scenario?

My brief survey of what "performance criticism" (at least as formulated in D&G; cf. also van der Toorn 2007:*passim*) has to offer to augment our understanding of *prophetic rhetoric* as manifested in the Hebrew prophetic literature, leads me to an equivocal positive-negative conclusion. Performance criticism does indeed suggest some helpful tools and techniques that Bible translators and communicators can put into practice when transmitting selected texts of Scripture in a more personal and dramatic fashion before a live audience, or when producing a non-print, oral-aural (+/− video) version of the Scriptures. However, in their effort to offer performance criticism as a credible redaction-critical method for determining the compositional history of the original text, D&G are not at all successful, in my opinion; in this respect, the approach is overly conjectural and hence quite unconvincing.

On the contrary, the various literary studies that I have presented in this volume would endorse a much more stable, text-oriented, proclamatory perspective. It is my contention, therefore, that the named prophets (in large measure themselves) composed their works using varied artistic and rhetorical forms essentially as we have them recorded in the Hebrew Scriptures that have come down to us.[4] There is little if any textual support for a theory that posits a prophetically-inclined guild of exceptionally gifted scribes who re-created or resourcefully re-fashioned either Amos's or any other of these prophetic texts in order to recycle and adapt them to address some current socio-political need or simply to further their own personal artistic aspirations as popular dramatists of the day. This assessment certainly does not

---

[4] This is the "conventional wisdom" regarding the prophetic books (Amos at least) that D&G (and certain other scholars) would dismiss, namely, that "[t]he disciples sought to be faithful to their prophetic master, even if the literature they created [??] required that the original material be reworked and altered here and there in order to make it compatible to the new social and political context in which the disciples lived" (20).

detract from the fact that the prophetic writings can indeed be presented in a highly "dramatic" manner in order to communicate more effectively with a particular audience group in a specific, oral-aurally attuned cultural setting. Such vocal as well as other non-print, non-traditional modes of transmission will be briefly considered in the next section.

13.2 How can we proclaim the prophetic text in translation?

Throughout this book, I have had occasion to illustrate some possible ways in which the dramatic discourse of the prophetic literature might be expressed in a corresponding manner in meaning-based vernacular Bible translations. In Chewa, for instance, such an oratorical version might well feature a semi-poetic mode of composition that is based on and adapted to varying degrees from traditional *ndakatulo* lyric verse. The glorious close of the prophecy of Amos (9:13–15), for example, would sound (the ideal medium for this genre) like this:

Chauta Mulungu akutitsimikizira pakunena kuti,	*Chauta (= YHWH) God assures us by saying,*
"Masiku akubwera, zodabwitsazi zidzachitikadi:	*"In days to come these amazing things will happen:*
Adzalephera alimi kukolola madalitso zaozonse;	*Farmers will fail to harvest all their blessings;*
zipatso zambirimbiri zidzalemeretsa otcherako;	*many-many fruits will over-burden their pickers;*
vinyo wokoma wochokera kuminda yakuzitunda	*sweet wine from gardens in the hills*
adzachuluka *nde* ngati madzi oyenda m'mitsinje.	*will abound full-up! like water flowing in the streams.*
Zoonadi, ndidzabwezeranso pabwino anthuanga.	*Truly, I will restore to prosperity my people.*
Adzabweranso ku dziko n'kumanganso mizinda,	*They will return to the land and rebuild [their] cities,*
inde, mizinda yabwinja, ndi kutsegulanso minda;	*yes, the ruined cities, and open up new fields;*
iwo mphesa adzalimanso ndi kumwa madzi ake.	*they will grow grape vines again and drink their juice.*
Ndithu, ndidzabzala anga'anthu m'dziko laolao,	*Indeed, I will plant my people in their very own land,*
ndilo dziko limene ndidawapatsa makolo ao aja.	*that's the land that I gave to those ancestors of theirs.*
Palibe adani alionse amene adzawazulanso, ayi!"	*There is no enemy at all who will uproot them again!"*
akuterotu Ine Chauta, AmbuyeMulungu wanune.	*thus it is I who say so, I Chauta, your Lord-God.*

The poetic nature of the preceding Chewa translation is revealed in stylistic features such as: parallelism, rhythmic lineation, alliteration and rhyme, punning, figurative restatement (e.g., "blessings" for "crops" in v. 13), a graphic ideophone (*nde* "full to the brim!" in v. 14), conceptual reiteration, emphatic word order arrangements, additional lexical intensifiers (e.g., "Indeed!" in v. 15), and occasional conjunctive asyndeton. But care was taken not to over-do the manner of expression so that the discourse register would not sound unbecoming of its divine speaker, Yahweh. A vernacular version exhibiting this more dynamic verbal quality would be especially suitable for an *oral* rendition of the Scriptures, as in a *Faith Comes by Hearing* audiocassette, CD, or MP$_3$ production. The text would also be conducive to a *musical* mode of presentation, using either a modern or an indigenous melody to embellish the song.

Other non-print medium formats are also possible, such as a video production or, more viably in certain parts of traditional Africa (which have not been overly influenced by Western media and technology), as a dramatic public performance by experienced verbal artists (e.g., selected members of a practiced choir or a religious theatre group; cf. Wendland 2005). I would like to explore this second option a little further because it would be highly appropriate for many rural settings in east-central Africa. This would also link my study again with the *practice* of "performance criticism" as advocated in the work of Doan and Giles (D&G 2005; cf. section 10.1).[5] They propose a provocative set of questions to assist a dramatic troupe, as well as a hypothetical audience, in setting a mental stage, as it were, for imagining how the "prophetic script" (i.e., the biblical text) is to be performed. Consider, for example, D&G's suggestions for the onset of the oracles against the foreign nations (1:3–2:6) (2005:117–118):

Explicit Activity	**Implicit Activity**
Opening speech: "The LORD roars…"	Who are Amos's spectators (better, "audience"—ew)? How many are there, and where are they gathered? How does Amos create the roar of the Lord's voice? Do all the spectators immediately pay attention? Is there discussion among them? Does Amos wait for their full attention?

---

[5] I must stress here D&G's *practical application* of performance criticism, that is, with special reference to the prophet Amos. In section 10.1 I indicated my rejection of D&G's particular redaction-saturated *theory* of performance criticism, which posits "distinct compositional layers beginning in the eighth century [BCE] and concluding in the postexilic era" (citing H. W. Wolff 2005:106). Thus, "[t]he process of literary representation of the prophetic event introduces a second level of performance. The scribe, as it were [created by the redaction critic], usurps the performance from the prophet and makes the prophet a character in his new version of the prophetic drama" (107). In my experience, composition by committee does not produce good literature, secular or religious—in any language (on the literary integrity, hence unitary authorship of Amos, see Wendland 1988).

13.2 *How can we proclaim the prophetic text intranslation?* 635

Oracle against Damascus	Does Amos look directly at his spectators when he speaks, "Thus says the LORD"? How long does he pause before speaking as the Lord? How does his voice change from speaking as prophet to speaking as Lord?[9] Who does Amos look at or where does he look when proclaiming what will happen to the gate bars of Damascus? Does he choose a group of spectators who are then transformed into the people of Damascus? Are the spectators pleased at this oracle? If so, how do they show it? What feedback do they give to Amos? Does their response motivate Amos to roar again as the Lord? Or are the spectators skeptical of Amos as prophet? How does Amos transition from speaking as the Lord back to a prophet: "says the Lord?"
Oracle against Judah	The oracle against Judah does not end with "says the LORD," but transitions right into "Thus says the LORD," for the oracle against Israel. How does this rhythmic device help the prophet control the attention of his spectators?. How might the prophet use this as a transition? Does he intensify the pitch and volume of his delivery, preparing to reach the crux, or final climactic point, of these oracles when speaking of Israel's transgressions? How does he alter his physical relationship to the spectators so that he is positioned for the final oracle?...

Certain modifications would be needed, of course, when putting questions of this type to an African audience, e.g., what would the prophet's physical position and body stance be in relation to his audience; how would this compare to that of a traditional oral narrative performer (or "singer," *woimba-nthano*) or a praise poet *(mlakatuli);* how interactive would the audience be as they heard the reproving message of the prophet—or as they heard the Lord condemning them; what sort of gestures and facial features would the prophet display; how onomatopoetic would the lion's roar be uttered for people who have actually heard the dreadful sound? But D&G's questions do serve to prompt contemporary dramatic performers to consider such issues more carefully as they prepare their messages for public presentation.

More detailed still are James Maxey's suggested stage directions for the Vuté oral Bible translators whom he works with in Cameroon; the following is a short sample of an "English script" based on Mark 1:40–41 (from Maxey 2008:221–222):

Paralinguistic	Text	Extralinguistic
	Now there comes to him a leper,	Performer looks up and sees someone approaching
	pleading with him,	Performer can choose to dramatize actions of leper.
	falling on his knees, and saying to him,	
Voice is humble, supplicating, perhaps even fearful	*"If you want to,*	
	you can make me clean."	
	And moved by compassion,	Facial features demonstrate compassion
	stretching out his hand,	Performer stretches out hand firmly, but gently
	he touched him	Demonstrate laying on of hands
Voice is full of compassion	*and he says to him,*	
Phrases said slowly and clearly	*"I want to,*	
Tone of authority	*be cleansed."*	
Pace of speech increases	*And immediately the leprosy went from him*	
	and he was made clean.	Lift the hands from imagined leper in demonstrative fashion
	And becoming harsh with him,	Change of expression from compassion to sternness
	immediately Jesus drove him out	Hand gesture indicating separation of leper from center stage
Tone of sternness	*and says to him, "See that to nobody you say nothing, but go,..."*	Point off stage

Maxey (2008:219, 223) offers the following insightful comments regarding his challenging enterprise:

> Performance Criticism offers a concrete method for testing interpretations as scenes are acted out or lines are spoken.... The theoretical distinctions noted above should inform the methods of translation for performance. These methods extend beyond the implications of

orality to those of performance. How do these implications affect Bible translation? Rhoads [2006] notes some of his observations: the historical present can often be maintained in performance (as it alternates with past tenses) more freely than in print form; word order can be more varied in performance, e.g., fronting for emphasis; replication of onomatopoetic words and sounds; length of sentences; issues of punctuation in relation to pauses and stops; contractions and elisions; lexical consistency functions to maintain echoes of events and motifs; the use of parallelism and chiastic patterns shape the rhythm and pace of performance; presentation of translation for performance on a page that reflects rhythms, pauses and pace of performance; adopting the notation of musical scores for translations to indicate pitch, tempo, and volume; footnotes for suggestions for performance.... The script above underscores that translation is an interpretive action. The personal involvement of the translator accentuates his or her social location. It should be remembered, however, that performance is communal. The actual performance of this script will be influenced by the audience, the setting, and so forth – all the particularities mentioned above in relation to the performance event. Both during the performance and as a result of the performance the script might be changed significantly. The words of the translation might be revised along with the paralinguistic and extralinguistic features. Such revision highlights the cyclical, multiform rhythm of performance-oriented translations.

The preceding advice offers an excellent illustration of the valid, applied use of performance criticism as an *exegetical* and *translational* aid, not as a text-critical tool to discern the hypothetical levels of redactional activity within the biblical documents.

13.3 Conclusion: Contemporizing and contextualizing the ancient prophets of Israel

Bible translation is not only a matter of text-transfer strategy and the medium of communication, but it also includes the *need* (not just an option!) for providing an adequate conceptual "frame of reference" (Wilt 2003, Wendland 2008b) to assist a modern-day audience in understanding and interpreting these ancient sermons and religious discourses. Thus, it is imperative to provide a variety of comparative-contrastive enrichment studies that will accompany the biblical text. Such diverse historical, sociocultural, religious, geographical, literary, etc. contextual guides may be paratextual or *extratextual* in nature. The latter might take the form of a popular-level or scholarly study of the kings of Israel and Judah during whose reigns the prophets worked, or the geo-political history of the Ancient Near East during Bible times, or a topical survey of the prophetic books of the Old Testament.

In this concluding section, I will focus on the *paratextual* expository, descriptive, and explanatory marginal or foot-notes that accompany the translation found in a typical study Bible. These comments must be carefully *contextualized* in a situation-sensitive manner to accommodate to the *communicative purpose* of the translation at hand (e.g., a liturgical version versus a devotional Bible) and the *primary target audience* in view. The following is an English summary of some sample notes and "advisories" (comments on points that need exposition) that have been prepared to accompany Amos 9:11–15 for a mature, educated, urban Chewa-speaking receptor group (to simplify this procedure, the NIV is used as the translation "base text," with reference to which a given note is formulated):

Text of AMOS	Paratextual NOTE
9:11 *In that day...*	*Not a note, but a comment:* A "section heading" (e.g., Yahweh will restore Israel) is needed in order to demarcate and introduce this final, "optimistic" portion of the prophecy of Amos, along with an intra-textual cross reference to 2:16, where this expression has already been explained. It refers to some future time when the LORD's righteous judgment will fall upon the wicked nation of Israel—extending unto the age of the promised Messiah, who will come to bless and to vindicate his faithful people.
David's fallen tent	This alludes to a high point in the history of God's people during the rule of King David, when the nation was powerful, prosperous, and living in obedient fellowship with Yahweh. Since then, however, the people had become idolatrous and divided (Israel-N and Judah-S), while their kings, the dynasty of David, had become mostly wicked and weak, as if they were living in a wretched hut rather than a palace as before. The promised Messiah is often spoken of in the Old Testament in language that refers to King David (e.g., 2 Sam 7:12–13; Isa 9:6–7; Jer 33:15, 17; Mic 5:2).
I will repair...build	Yahweh continues the imagery of building and construction. Now he likens the rebuilt walls and city, which would one day be completely destroyed by enemies, to the future spiritual rule of Messiah, which would begin in a small way (very few people) and grow into something very large (many people).

13.3 Conclusion: Contemporizing and contextualizing the ancient prophets

9:12 *possess the remnant of Edom*	In the coming Messianic age, the fellowship of God's people would incorporate even some of their former bitter enemies, whom the Edomites (descendants of Esau) here symbolize. In Acts 15:17, the Apostle James follows the Septuagint translation of this passage from Amos, reading "that the remnant of people may seek the Lord," rather than "possess the remnant of Edom." James uses this passage to support his apostolic argument for the inclusion of non-Jews (gentiles) in the new covenant people of God.
all the nations that bear my name	This expression denotes the vast, worldwide extent of the Messiah's future rule. To be "called" by the name of Yahweh means that those people belong to him as his chosen possession (see Deut 28:10; 2 Chr 7:14; Jer 14:9, 15:16). Foreigners (non-Jews) will be brought into the Lord's kingdom through peaceful, not military, means by God's powerful saving activity.
The LORD, who will do these things	This is an emphatic expression that marks the end of the short poetic paragraph (strophe) beginning in v. 11. It stresses the fact that Yahweh is in control of all the events of human history, which the prophet Amos has focused upon throughout his book.
9:13 *the days are coming*	This expression of future time marks the start of a new poetic paragraph and refers to the same general Messianic period of abundant blessings that was mentioned at the beginning of the preceding paragraph and section in 9:11. The boundaries of this climactic unit are also indicated by divine speech formulas, "declares/says the LORD (your God)." The NIV misses the paragraph-initial emphasizer "Behold!"—that is, "Consider this!"
the reaper overtaken by the plowman	This paralleled figure of speech calls attention to the unexpected reversal in fortunes that Yahweh will bestow upon his people—not only agricultural bounty, but also physical and spiritual blessings that encompass all of life. These possibly allude to the Garden of Eden and contrast with the disasters depicted in Am 4:6–11. The first imagery depicts ground so fertile and productive that the reapers can hardly finish their harvesting when the plowers must already begin the new crop.
the planter [overtaken] by the grape treader	The second symbolical image set pictures grape vines so fruitful that they bear grapes ready for pressing almost immediately after planting—or they will produce so much wine that it cannot be processed before the next harvest begins!

new wine will drip from the mountains...flow from all the hills	The contrast with past and current conditions in Israel/Judah is continued in more exaggerated imagery depicting agricultural abundance. From the multitude of grapes hanging heavily from their vines to large vats that overflow with newly pressed juice, the overall impression is one of grand, even unlimited profusion. The LORD is indeed most gracious and all-providing—how much so remains to be seen by his expectant people!
9:14 *I will bring back my exiled people...*	Here is another promise of blessing, predicting a return (or a "restoration of the [good] fortune") of the exiled people of Israel to their homeland (reversing the punishment of prior passages like 9:4). This prophecy was fulfilled in a literal sense when the people were allowed to return to Palestine after the 70-year Babylonian Captivity. But it will be ultimately fulfilled by the coming Messiah during his spiritual rule over his new covenant people, composed of all nations (cf. v. 12).
they will rebuild...live... plant... drink...make gardens...eat...	This is a less figurative re-statement of the symbolical images presented in the preceding verse (13; see Hos 2:23; Isa 58:12). The reiteration obviously emphasizes the Lord's promise: He will transform—prosper—and enrich his faithful believers, one day.
9:15 *I will plant Israel in their own land...*	Now the nation/people of God as a whole is blessed. The "land" is a concrete image of a sure and secure place of refuge, safety, prosperity—and ultimate fellowship with Yahweh.
...never again to be uprooted	The positive-negative parallel imagery further underscores Yahweh's point, impressing it upon the hearts and minds of all hearers—a direct address from "the LORD, *your* God!" (end stress)!

So then in conclusion, we might ask ourselves: How powerfully does the "roar of the LORD" resound in our Bibles today—how loudly does his voice "thunder" as these texts of Scripture are being read aloud in the hearing of God's people worldwide (Amos 1:2), language by language, in one location or another? Rendering the *prophetic rhetoric* of Yahweh and his spokesmen in a dynamic, compelling, "oratorical" manner to match that of the original Hebrew text would seem to be an outstanding challenge that many translators, teams, and editorial committees have not yet begun to realistically confront, let alone attempt to realize to a sufficient degree in their work. It is hoped that the different studies of this book will contribute in some small way, first of all, to a renewal of interest in the Hebrew prophets and their magnificent theological-ethical literature—and, second, to motivate at least

13.3 Conclusion: Contemporizing and contextualizing the ancient prophets

some practicing translation teams to do these books more poetic "justice" during their contemporary efforts to proclaim the ever-relevant "word of the LORD" to new niches as well as nations of needy listeners.

The theological relevance and motivational imperative of a rhetorical approach to the text analysis and translation of the Scriptures have been well summarized in a recent essay by Peter Phillips:

> Biblical rhetoric is first and foremost the art of persuading individuals and communities to accept the Bible's world view. This is a rhetoric with immense power in that it assumes that that world view is the only viable one for humanity to accept.... Rhetorical criticism is therefore the analysis of the strategies of persuasion within a text – not just the manipulation of words for effect, but rather the manipulation of a world view and the way in which that world is offered to the reader. It is the study of how the Bible seeks to offer the reader a new way of seeing the world, of establishing a new community, a new way of being human. (2008:259, 261)

A better understanding of the biblical text and its original context, including the author's rhetorical intentions, will serve to sharpen the vision of interpreters and translators alike so that they can more effectively communicate the varied messages of Scripture to a present generation of hearers and doers of the Word (Jas 1:22–25; cf. Am 3:7–10; Mic 6:1–8; Zeph 3:9–13; Hag 1:13–14; Mal 2:7–9).

References

Achtemeier, Elizabeth. 1986. *Nahum—Malachi* (Interpretation Commentaries). Atlanta: John Knox Press.

Achtemeier, Paul J. 1990. "*Omne verbum sonat:* The New Testament and the oral environment of late Western antiquity." *Journal of Biblical Literature* 109(1).

Ackerman, J.S. 1987. Jonah. In R. Alter and F. Kermode (eds.), *The Literary Guide to the Bible.*

Albright, W. F. 1950. The Psalm of Habakkuk. In H. H. Rowley (ed.), *Studies in Old Testament prophecy presented to T. H. Robinson,* 1–18. Edinburgh: T&T Clark.

Alden, R. L. 1994. Haggai. In K. L. Barker and J. Kohlenberger III (eds.), *NIV Bible commentary* (Vol. 1: Old Testament), 1507–1513. Grand Rapids: Zondervan.

Alexander, D. 1988. *Jonah.* Tyndale Old Testament Commentaries. Downers Grove: InterVarsity.

Alexander, R. H. 1986. Ezekiel. In F. E. Gaebelein, (ed.), *The Expositor's Bible Commentary* 6, 737–996. Grand Rapids: Zondervan.

Allen, Leslie C. 1976. *The Books of Joel, Obadiah, Jonah and Micah.* New International Comentary on the Old Testament. Grand Rapids: Eerdmans.

Allen, Leslie C. 1990. *Ezekiel 20–48.* Word Biblical Commentary 29. Dallas: Word Books.

Alter, Robert. 1981. *The art of biblical narrative.* New York: Basic Books.

Andersen, David T. 1998. Perceived authenticity: The fourth criterion of good translation. *Notes on Translation* 12(3):1–13.

Anderson, F. I. and D. N. Freedman. 1989. *Amos*. Anchor Bible. New York: Doubleday.
Armerding, C. E. 1985. Habakkuk In F. E. Gaebelein (ed.), *The Expositor's Bible Commentary* (vol. 7). Grand Rapids: Zondervan.
Armerding, Carl E. 1985. Nahum. In F. E. Gaebelein (ed.), *The Expositor's Biblical Commentary* (vol. 7), 449–489. Grand Rapids: Zondervan.
Armerding, Carl E. 1985. Obadiah In F. E. Gaebelein (ed.), *The Expositor's Commentary* (vol. 7), 335–357. Grand Rapids: Zondervan.
Auld, Graeme. 1986. *Amos*. Old Testament Guide Series. Sheffield: Journal for the Study of the Old Testament Press.
Baker, David W. 1988. *Nahum, Habakkuk, Zephaniah: An introduction and commentary*. Tyndale OT Commentaries. Downers Grove: InterVarsity.
Baldwin, Joyce G. 1972. *Haggai, Zechariah, Malachi: An introduction and commentary*. Tyndale OT Commentaries. Downers Grove: InterVarsity.
Ball, I. J., Jr. 1987. The rhetorical shape of Zephaniah. In E. W. Conrad and E. G. Newing (eds.), *Essays and poems in honor of Francis I. Andersen's Sixtieth Birthday, July 28, 1985*, 155–165. Winona Lake: Eisenbrauns.
Barker, K. L. and Bailey, W. 1998. *Micah, Nahum, Habakkuk, Zephaniah*. The New American Commentary, vol. 20. Nashville: Broadman and Holman.
Barre, M.L. 1986. The meaning of *l"shybnw* in Amos 1:3–2:6. *Journal of Biblical Literature* 105(4):611–631.
Barre, M. L. 1988. Habakkuk 3:2: Translation in context. *Catholic Biblical Quarterly* 50.
Barton, J. 2001. *Joel and Obadiah*. The Old Testament Library. Louisville: Westminster John Knox Press.
Batto, B. F. 1987. The covenant of peace: A neglected Ancient Near Eastern motif. *Catholic Biblical Quarterly* 49.
de Beaugrande, Robert. 1968. *Factors in a theory of poetic translating*. Assen: Van Gorcum.
Beekman, John and John Callow. 1974. *Translating the Word of God*. Grand Rapids: Zondervan.
Bennett, R. A. 1996. *The book of Zephaniah: Introduction, commentary, and reflections*. The New Interpreter's Bible, vol. 7, 659–704. Nashville: Abingdon.
Berlin, Adele. 1983. *Poetics and the interpretation of biblical narrative*. Sheffield: Almond.
Berlin, Adele. 1985. *The dynamics of biblical parallelism*. Bloomington: Indiana University Press.
Berlin, Adele. 1994. *Zephaniah: A new translation with introduction and commentary*. The Anchor Bible. New York: Doubleday.
Berlin, Adele and M. Z. Brettler, eds. 2004. *The Jewish study Bible* (Jewish Publication Society). Oxford: Oxford University Press.

Blenkinsopp J. 1990. *Ezekiel.* Interpretation Commentary. Louisville: John Knox.

Bliese, Loren. 1995. A cryptic chiastic acrostic: Finding meaning from structure in the poetry of Nahum. *Journal of Translation and Textlinguistics.* 7(3):48–81.

Block, Daniel I. 1997a. *The book of Ezekiel, Chapters 1–24.* New International Commentary on the Old Testament. Grand Rapids: Eerdmans.

Block, Daniel I. 1997b. Ezekiel: Theology of, In Wm. A. Van Gemeren (ed.), *New International Dictionary of OT Theology and Exegesis.* Grand Rapids: Zondervan.

Block, Daniel I. 1998. *The book of Ezekiel, Chapters 25–48.* New International Commentary on the Old Testament. Grand Rapids: Eerdmans.

Boadt, L. 1990. The function of the salvation oracles in Ezekiel 33–37. *Hebrew Annual Review* 10.

Boase-Beier, J. and M. Holman, eds. 1999. *The practices of literary translation: Constraints and creativity.* Manchester: St. Jerome.

Boda, M. J. 2004. *Haggai, Zechariah.* NIV Application Commentary. Grand Rapids: Zondervan.

Boomershine, T. 1990. A new paradigm for interpreting the Bible on television. In T. Inbody (ed.), *Changing channels: The church and the television revolution.* Dayton: Whaleprints [photocopy, no pagination given].

Brichto, Herbert C. 1992. *Towards a grammar of biblical poetics: Tales of the prophets.* New York: Oxford University Press.

Briggs, Richard S. 2008. Speech Acts. In D. G. Firth and J. A. Grant (eds.), *Words & the Word: Explorations in biblical interpretation and literary theory,* 75–110. Downers Grove: IVP Academic.

Brown, Jeannine K. 2008. Genre criticism and the Bible. In D. G. Firth and J. A. Grant (eds.), *Words & the Word: Explorations in biblical interpretation & literary theory,* 111–150. Downers Grove: IVP Academic.

Bruce, F. F. 1993. Habakkuk T. E. McComiskey (ed.), *The Minor Prophets: An exegetical and expository commentary, vol. 2: Obadiah, Jonah, Micah, Nahum, and Habakkuk,* 831–896. Grand Rapids: Baker Books.

Bullock, C. Hassel. 1986. *An introduction to the Old Testament prophetic books.* Chicago: Moody Press.

Butler, T. C. 1988. *NIV disciple's study Bible.* Nashville: Holman.

Butterworth, M. 1992. *Structure and the book of Zechariah,* JSOT Supplement Series 130. Sheffield: Sheffield Academic Press.

Cassuto, U. 1973. *Biblical and Oriental Studies 2.* I. Abrahams, trans. Jerusalem: Magnes.

Cathcart, Kevin J. 1973. *Nahum in the light of Northwest Semitic.* Rome: Biblical Institute Press.

Chisholm, Robert B., Jr. 1990. *Interpreting the Minor Prophets.* Grand Rapids: Zondervan.

Christensen, Duane L. 1989. The book of Nahum as a liturgical composition: A prosodic analysis. *Journal of the Evangelical Theological Society.* 32(2):159–169.

Christensen, Duane L. 1992. Impulse and design in the book of Haggai. *Journal of the Evangelical Theological Society* 35:17–32.

Clark, David J. 1991. Obadiah reconsidered. Paper presented to the UBS Triennial Translation Workshop (Victoria Falls, Zimbabwe), 1–17.

Clark, David J . 1992. Discourse structure in Haggai. *Journal of Translation and Textlinguistics* 5(1):13–24.

Clark, D. J. and H. A. Hatton. 1989. *A translator's handbook on the books of Nahum, Habakkuk, and Zephaniah.* New York: United Bible Societies.

Clark, David J. and Norm Mundhenk. 1982. *A translator's handbook on the books of Obadiah and Micah.* New York: United Bible Societies.

Clowney, E. P. 1989. The new Israel. In C. E. Armerding and W. W. Gasque (eds.), *A guide to biblical prophecy.* Peabody: Hendrickson.

Coggins, R. J. 1987. *Haggai, Zechariah, Malachi* Old Testament Guides. Sheffield: Sheffield Academic Press.

Collins, J. J. 1997. *Apocalypticism in the Dead Sea Scrolls.* London: Routledge.

Cooper, L. E., Sr. 1994. *Ezekiel.* New American Commentary 17. Nashville: Broadman & Holman.

Coote, Robert B. 1981. *Amos among the prophets: Composition and theology.* Philadelphia: Fortress Press.

Coulson, S. 2001. *Semantic leaps: Frame-shifting and conceptual blending in meaning construction.* Cambridge: Cambridge University Press.

Craigie, Peter C. 1983. *Ezekiel.* The Daily Bible Study Series. Philadelphia: Westminster Press.

Craigie, Peter C. 1984. *Twelve Prophets.* The Daily Study Bible Series 1. Philadelphia: Westminster Press.

Craigie, Peter C. 1985. *Twelve Prophets.* The Daily Study Bible Series 2. Philadelphia: Westminster Press.

Cross, F. 1973. *Canaanite myth and Hebrew epic.* Cambridge: Harvard University Press.

Crouch, Walter B. 1994. To question an end, To end a question: Opening the closure of the book of Jonah. *Journal for the Study of the Old Testament* 62.

Davis, Casey Wayne. 1999. *Oral biblical criticism: The influence of the principles of orality on the literary structure of Paul's Epistle to the Philippians.* Sheffield: Sheffield Academic Press.

Davis, D. A. 1999. *The literary structure of the Old Testament: A commentary on Genesis—Malachi.* Grand Rapids: Baker Books.

Dillard R. B. and T. Longman, III. 1994. *An introduction to the Old Testament.* Grand Rapids: Zondervan.

Dillard, R. 1992. Joel. In T. McComiskey (ed.), *The Minor Prophets* 1, 239–313. Grand Rapids: Baker.

Doan, William and Terry Giles. 2005. *Prophets, performance, and power: Performance criticism of the Hebrew Bible.* New York and London: T&T Clark.

Dooley, Robert A. and Stephen H. Levinsohn 2001. *Analyzing discourse: A manual of basic concepts.* Dallas: SIL International.

Dorsey, David A. 1999. *The literary structure of the Old Testament: A commentary on Genesis—Malachi.* Grand Rapids: Baker.

Draper, J. A. 1996. Confessional western text-centred biblical interpretation and an oral or residual-oral context. *Semeia 73.*

Driver, S. R. 1913. *An introduction to the literature of the Old Testament.* Ninth edition. Edinburgh: Clark.

Eaton, J. H. 1964. The origin and meaning of Habakkuk 3. *Zeitschrift fuer die alttestamentliche Wissenschaft* 76:144–171.

Ellison, H. L. 1985. Jonah. In Frank Gaebelein (ed.), *The Expositor's Bible Commentary.* Grand Rapids: Zondervan.

Evans, Mary. 1992. *Prophets of the LORD.* Devon: Paternoster Press.

Fauconnier, G. and M. Turner. 2002. *The way we think: Conceptual blending and the mind's hidden complexities.* New York: Basic Books.

Fawcett, Peter. 1997. *Translation and language: Linguistic theories explained.* Manchester, UK: St. Jerome.

Fee, G. D. and D. Stuart. 2002. *How to read the Bible book by book.* Grand Rapids: Zondervan.

Fensham, F. C. 1987. The curse of the dry bones in Ezekiel 37:1–14 changed to a blessing of resurrection. *Journal of Northwest Semitic Languages* XIII.

Finley, Thomas J. 1990. *Joel, Amos, Obadiah.* The Wycliffe Exegetical Commentary. Chicago: Moody Press.

Fishbane, M. 1985 *Biblical interpretation in ancient Israel.* Oxford: Clarendon.

Fishbane, M. 1987. Sin and judgment in the prophecies of Ezekiel. In J. L. Mays and P. J. Achtemeier (eds.), *Interpreting the prophets.* Philadelphia: Fortress.

Foster, S. J. 2004. *An experiment in Bible translation as transcultural communication: The translation of B'RITH 'covenant' into Lomwe, with a focus on Leviticus 26.* Th. D. dissertation, University of Stellenbosch.

Garrett, D. A. 1997. *Hosea, Joel.* The New American Commentary. Nashville: Broadman & Holman.

van Gemeren, W. A. 1990. *Interpreting the prophetic word.* Grand Rapids: Zondervan.

Gerstenberger, Erhard S. 1988. *Psalms [Part 1]—With an introduction to cultic poetry.* The Forms of the Old Testament Literature XIV. Grand Rapids: Eerdmans.

Gitay, Yehoshua. 1991. *Isaiah and his audience: The structure and meaning of Isaiah 1–12.* Assen-Maastricht: Van Gorcum.

Good, Edwin. 1981. *Irony in the Old Testament.* Bible and Literature Series. Sheffield: Almond.

Gowan, D. E. 1998. *Theology of the prophetic books: The death snd resurrection of Israel.* Louisville: Westminster/John Knox.

Greenberg, M. 1986. *Ezekiel 1–20.* The Anchor Bible, 22A. New York: Doubleday.

Greenberg, M. 1987. The design and themes of Ezekiel's program of restoration. In J. L. Mays and P. J. Achtemeier (eds.), *Interpreting the Prophets.* Philadelphia: Fortress.

Greenberg, M. 1997. *Ezekiel 21–37.* The Anchor Bible 22B. New York: Doubleday.

Grossberg, D. 1989. *Centripetal and centrifugal structures in biblical poetry.* Society of Biblical Literature Monograph Series 39. Atlanta: Scholars Press.

Gutt, Ernst-August. 1991. *Translation and relevance: Cognition and context.* Oxford: Basil Blackwell.

Gutt, Ernst-August. 1992. *Relevance theory: A guide to successful communication in translation.* New York: United Bible Societies.

Hammershaimb, Erling. 1970. *The book of Amos: A commentary.* John Sturdy trans. Oxford: Basil Blackwell.

Harrelson, W. J., ed. 2003. *The new interpreter's study Bible.* Nashville: Abingdon Press.

Harrison, R. K. 1969. *Introduction to the Old Testament.* Grand Rapids: Eerdmans.

Hatim, Basil and Ian Mason. 1990. *Discourse and the translator.* London: Longman.

Hatim, Basil and Ian Mason. 1997. *The translator as communicator.* London: Routledge.

Hiebert, T. 1987. The use of inclusion in Habakkuk 3. In E. Follis (ed.), *Directions in Biblical Hebrew poetry.* Journal for the Study of the Old Testament Sup. 40. Sheffield: JSOT Press.

Hiebert, T. 1996. The book of Habakkuk: Introduction, commentary, and reflections In L. E. Keck (ed.), *The New Interpreter's Bible,* vol. VII. Nashville: Abingdon.

Hill, Harriet and Margaret Hill. 2008. *Translating the Bible into action: How the Bible can be relevant in all languages and cultures.* Carlisle: Piquant.

Hillers, D. R. 1964. *Treaty-curses and the Old Testament prophets.* Rome: Pontifical Biblical Institute.

Hirsch E. D., Jr. 1967. *Validity in interpretation.* New Haven: Yale University Press.

Hodgson, R. and P. A. Soukup, eds. 1997. *From one medium to another: Basic issues for communicating the Scriptures in new media.* New York: American Bible Society.

Holbrooke, D. J. 1995. Narrowing down Haggai: Examining style in light of discourse and content. *Journal of Translation and Textlinguistics* 7(2):1–12.

House, P. R. 1988. *Zephaniah: A prophetic drama*. Sheffield: Sheffield Academic Press.

House, P. R. 2000. The character of God in the Book of the Twelve. In J. D. Nogalski and M. A. Sweeney (eds.), *Reading and hearing the Book of the Twelve*, 125–145. Atlanta: Society of Biblical Literature.

Hubbard, D. A. 1989. *Joel and Amos*. Tyndale Old Testament Commentaries. Downers Grove: InterVarsity Press.

Irwin, W. A. 1942. The mythological background of Habakkuk 3. *Journal of Near Eastern Studies* I:10–40.

Jakobson, R. 1985. *Verbal art, verbal sign, verbal time*. K. Pomorska and S. Rudy, eds. Minneapolis: University of Minnesota Press.

Jakobson, R. 1960. Linguistics and poetics. In T. Sebeok (ed), *Style in language*, 350–377. Cambridge: MIT Press.

Jakobson, R. 1966. Grammatical parallelism and its Russian facet. *Language* 42:399–429.

Jemielity, Thomas. 1992. *Satire and the Hebrew prophets*. Louisville: Westminster/John Knox.

Katan, David. 1999. *Translating cultures: An introduction for translators, interpreters and mediators*. Manchester, UK: St. Jerome.

Keil, Carl. F. 1969. *The twelve Minor Prophets* (vol. 2), James Martin, trans. Grand Rapids: Eerdmans.

Kennedy George A. 1984. *New Testament interpretation through rhetorical criticism*. Chapel Hill: University of North Carolina Press.

Kennedy, George A., trans. 1991. *Aristotle—On rhetoric: A theory of civic discourse*. Oxford: Oxford UP.

Klein, Wm. W., Craig L. Blomberg, and Robert L. Hubbard, Jr. 1993. *Introduction to biblical interpretation*. Dallas: Word Publishing.

Klem, H. V. 1982. *Oral communication of the Scripture: Insights from African oral art*. Pasadena: Wm. Carey Library.

Koops, R. 2000. Mapping, mental spaces, and blending in Scripture. Unpublished paper presented at the United Bible Societies' Triennial Translation Workshop (TTW) in Malaga, Spain, 1–15.

Kraft, R. 1993. Offline 40. *Religious Studies News* 8:1.

Kugel, James L. 1981. *The idea of biblical poetry: Parallelism and its history*. New Haven: Yale University Press.

La Sor, Wm., D. A. Hubbard, and F. Bush, 1982. *Old Testament survey: The message, form, and background of the Old Testament*. Grand Rapids: Eerdmans.

Landes, G. M. 1967. The kerygma of the book of Jonah. *Interpretation* 21.

Landsberger, J. 1965. Tin and lead: The adventures of two vocables. *Journal of Near Eastern Studies* 24:285–296.

Lemke, W. E. 1987. Life in the present and hope for the future. In J. L. Mays and P. J. Achtemeier (eds.), *Interpreting the prophets*. Philadelphia: Fortress.

Lemon, L. T. and M. J. Reis. 1965. *Russian formalist criticism: Four essays.* Lincoln: University of Nebraska Press.

Limburg, James. 1987. Sevenfold structures in the book of Amos. *Journal of Biblical Literature* 106:217–222.

Limburg, James. 1993. *Jonah: A commentary.* Louisville: John Knox/Westminster.

Long, V. Philips. 1994. *The art of biblical history.* Foundations of Contemporary Interpretation 5. Grand Rapids: Zondervan.

Longacre, Robert and Shin Ja Hwang. 1994. A textlinguistic approach to the biblical narrative of Jonah. In Robert Bergen (ed.), *Biblical Hebrew and discourse linguistics,* 336–358. Dallas: Summer Institute of Linguistics.

Longman, Tremper, III. 1987. *Literary approaches to biblical interpretation* Foundations of Contemporary Interpretation, vol. 3. Grand Rapids: Zondervan.

Longman, Tremper, III. 1993. Nahum. In T. E. McComiskey (ed.), *The minor prophets: An exegetical and expository commentary,* 763–829. Grand Rapids: Baker Books.

Louw, J. P. and E. R. Wendland, 1993. *Graphic design and Bible reading.* Cape Town: Bible Society of South Africa.

Lust, J. 1981. Remarks on the redaction of Amos V, 4–6, 14–15. *Oudtestamentische Studien* 21:129–154

Magonet, J. 1983. *Form and meaning: Studies in literary technique in the book of Jonah.* Sheffield: Almond Press.

Maier, Walter A. 1980 (reprint, 1959). *The book of Nahum.* Grand Rapids: Baker.

Malmstrom, M. 1991. *My tongue is the pen: How audiocassettes can serve the nonreading world.* Dallas: Summer Institute of Linguistics.

Margulis, B. 1970. The psalm of Habakkuk: A reconstruction and interpretation. *Zeitschrift fuer die alttestementliche Wissenschaft* 82:409–442.

Marks, H. 1987. The Twelve Prophets. In R. Alter and F. Kermode (eds.), *The literary guide to the Bible,* 207–233. Cambridge, Mass: Harvard University Press.

Mason, R. 1991. *Micah, Nahum, Obadiah.* Old Testament Guides. Sheffield: JSOT Press.

Mason, R. 1994. *Zephaniah, Habakkuk, Joel.* Old Testament Guides. Sheffield: Sheffield Academic Press.

Mays, James L. 1969. *Amos: A commentary.* Old Testament Library. Philadelphia: Westminster.

Mazor, Yair. 2009. *Who wrought the Bible? Unveiling the Bible's aesthetic secrets,* 21. Madison: University of Wisconsin Press.

Mbiti, John S. 1986. *Bible and Theology in African Christianity.* Nairobi: Oxford University Press.

McKeating, H. 1971. *The books of Amos, Hosea, Micah.* Cambridge Bible Commentary on the New English Bible: Old Testament Series. Cambridge University Press.

McKeating, H. 1993. *Ezekiel.* Sheffield: Sheffield Academic Press.

van der Merwe, Christo, Jackie Naude and Jan Kroeze. 1999. *A biblical Hebrew reference grammar.* Sheffield: Sheffield Academic Press.

Meyers C. L. and E. M. Meyers. 1987. *Haggai, Zechariah 1–8.* The Anchor Bible. New York: Doubleday.

Miller, Patrick D. 1982. *Sin and judgment in the prophets.* Chico: Scholar's Press.

Morgenstern, J. 1961. Amos Studies IV. *Hebrew Union College Annual* 32:300–313.

Motyer, J. A. 1998. Haggai. In T. E. McComiskey (eds), *The Minor Prophets: An exegetical and expository commentary* 3, 963–1002. Grand Rapids: Baker Books.

Motyer, J. A. 1998. Zephaniah. In T. E. McComiskey (ed), *The Minor Prophets: An exegetical and expository commentary* 3, 897–962. Grand Rapids: Baker Books.

NET Bible. 2003. New English Translation, Second beta edition. www.netbible.com.

Neufeldt, Victoria, ed. 1988. *Webster's new world dictionary of American English* Third college edition. Cleveland and New York: Webster's New World.

Newman, B. 2001. *Bible translation: The scene behind the scenes.* New York: American Bible Society.

Nida, Eugene A. and Charles R. Taber. 1969. *The theory and practice of translation.* Leiden: Brill.

Niehaus, Jeffrey. 1992. Amos. In T. E. McComiskey (ed.), *The minor prophets: An exegetical and expository commentary.* Grand Rapids: Baker Books.

Nord, Christiane. 1997. *Translation as a purposeful activity: Functionalist approaches explained.* Manchester: St. Jerome.

O'Brien, J. M. 2004. *Nahum, Habakkuk, Zephaniah, Haggai, Zechariah, Malachi.* Abingdon Old Testament Commentaries. Nashville: Abingdon Press.

Osborne, Grant R. 1991. *The hermeneutical spiral: A comprehensive introduction to biblical interpretation.* Downers Grove: InterVarsity.

Packer, J. I. 1988. *New dictionary of theology.* S. Ferguson and D. Wright, eds. Downers Grove: InterVarsity.

Parunak, H. van Dyke. 1994. Some discourse functions of prophetic quotative formulas in Jeremiah. In R. D. Bergen (ed.), *Biblical Hebrew and discourse linguistics,* 489–519. Dallas: Summer Institute of Linguistics.

Patterson, Richard D. 1987. The psalm of Habakkuk. *Grace Theological Journal* 8:2.

Patterson, Richard D. 1991. *Nahum, Habakkuk, Zephaniah* (WEC). Chicago: Moody Press.

Patterson, Richard D. and Michael E. Travers. 1988. Literary Analysis and the Unity of Nahum. *Grace Theological Journal* 9:45–58.

Patterson, Richard D. and Michael E. Travers. 1990. Nahum: Poet laureate of the Minor Prophets. *Journal of the Evangelical Theological Society* 33:437–444.

Paul, S. M. 1991. *Commentary on the book of Amos*. Hermeneia. Minneapolis: Fortress Press.

Peckham, B. 1986. The vision of Habakkuk. *Catholic Biblical Quarterly* 48.

Petersen, D. L. 2002. *The prophetic literature: An introduction.* Louisville: Westminster/John Knox.

Peterson, E. H. 2000. *The message: The Old Testament prophets in contemporary language.* Colorado Springs: NavPress.

Phillips, Peter M. 2008. Rhetoric. In D. G. Firth and J. A. Grant (eds.), *Words & the Word: Explorations in biblical interpretation & literary theory,* 226–265. Downers Grove: IVP Academic.

Pilkington, A. 2000. *Poetic effects.* Amsterdam: John Benjamins.

Pohlig, James N. 1998. *An exegetical summary of Malachi.* Dallas: Summer Institute of Linguistics.

Preminger, Alex and T. V. F. Brogan, eds. 1993. *The New Princeton encyclopedia of poetry and poetics.* Princeton: Princeton University Press.

Prior. D. 1998. *The message of Joel, Micah, and Habakkuk.* Downers Grove: InterVarsity Press.

Rang, J. C. 1994. *How to read the Bible aloud.* New York: Paulist Press.

Rhoads, David. 2006a. Performance Criticism: An Emerging Methodology in Second Testament Studies–Part I. *Biblical Theology Bulletin* 36(3):1–16.

Rhoads, David. 2006b. Performance Criticism: An Emerging Methodology in Second Testament Studies–Part II. *Biblical Theology Bulletin* 36(4):164–184.

Roberts, J. J. M. 1991. *Nahum, Habakkuk, and Zephaniah.* The Old Testament Library. Louisville: Westminster/John Knox.

Robertson, O. Palmer. 1990. *The Books of Nahum, Habakkuk, and Zephaniah* New International Commentary on the Old Testament. Grand Rapids: Eerdmans.

Rofe, A. 1997. *Introduction to the prophetic literature.* Sheffield: Sheffield Academic Press.

Rosenberg, J. 1987. Jeremiah and Ezekiel. In R. Alter and F. Kermode (eds.), *The Literary Guide to the Bible.* Cambridge: Harvard University Press.

Russell, D. S. 1994. *Prophecy and the apocalyptic dream: Protest and promise.* Peabody: Hendrickson.

Ryken, Leland. 1992. *Words of delight: A literary introduction to the Bible.* Second edition. Grand Rapids: Baker.

Ryken, L and P. G. Ryken (eds.). 2007. *The Literary Study Bible—ESV.* Wheaton: Crossway Bibles.

Sasson, Jack M. 1990. *Jonah: A new translation with introduction, commentary, and interpretation.* The Anchor Bible. New York: Doubleday.

Sawyer, J. F. 1987. *Prophecy and the prophets of the Old Testament.* Oxford: Oxford University Press.

Schaaf, Ype. 1994. *On their way rejoicing: The history and role of the Bible in Africa.* Carlisle: Paternoster.

Schechner, Richard. 1985. *Between theatre and anthropology.* Philadelphia: University of Pennsylvania Press.

Schuller, Eileen M. 1996. The book of Malachi. In L. E. Keck (ed.), *The New Interpreter's Bible VII.* Nashville: Abingdon.

Semino, E. 2002. A cognitive stylistic approach to mind style in narrative fiction. In E. Semino and J. Culpeper, (eds), *Cognitive stylistics: Language and cognition in stylistic analysis.* Amsterdam and Philadelphia: John Benjamins.

Shead, S. L. 2007. Radical frame semantics and biblical Hebrew: Exploring lexical semantics. Unpublished Ph.D. dissertation, University of Sidney.

Shklovsky, Victor. 1995. Art as technique. In Lee T. Lemon and Marion J. Reis (ed. and trans.), *Russian Formalist criticism: Four essays,* 3–24. Lincoln: University of Nebraska Press.

Sim, R. J. 1992. Notes on Haggai 2:10–21. *Journal of Translation and Textlinguistics* 5(1):25–36.

Smith, B. K., and F. S. Page. 1995. *Amos, Obadiah, Jonah.* New American Commentary. Nashville: Broadman & Holman.

Smith, Gary V. 1989. *Amos: A commentary.* Library of Biblical Interpretation. Grand Rapids: Zondervan.

Smith, Gary V. 1994. *The Prophets as preachers: An introduction to the Hebrew prophets.* Nashville: Broadman & Holman.

Smith, J. M. P. [1912] 1961. *A critical and exegetical commentary on the book of Malachi.* International Critical Commentary. Edinburgh: T&T Clark.

Smith, J. M. P. 1911. *A critical and exegetical commentary on Micah, Zephaniah and Nahum.* Internationa Critical Commentary. Edinburgh: T&T Clark

Smith, Ralph L. 1984. *Micah—Malachi.* Word Biblical Commentary, Vol. 32. Waco: Word Books.

Sogaard, Viggo B. 1991. *Audio Scriptures handbook.* Reading: United Bible Societies.

Sternberg, Meier. 1985. *The poetics of biblical narrative: Ideological literature and the drama of reading.* Bloomington: Indiana University Press.

Stine, Philip C. and Ernst R. Wendland. 1990. *Bridging the gap: African traditional religion and Bible translation.* New York: United Bible Societies.

Stine, Philip. 1980. Cohesion in literary texts—A translation problem. *Journal of Literary Semantics* IX(1):13–19.

Stockwell, P. 2002. *Cognitive poetics: An introduction.* London and New York: Routledge.

Stuart, Douglas. 1987. *Hosea–Jonah.* Word Biblical Commentary 31. Waco: Word Books.

Stuart, Douglas. 1998. Malachi. In T. E. McComisky (ed.), *The Minor Prophets: An exegetical and expository commentary* 3. Grand Rapids: Baker.

Sundersingh, Julian. 1999. Toward a media-based translation: Communicating biblical Scriptures to non-literates in rural Tamilnadu, India. Ph.D. thesis, Fuller Theological Seminary. Ann Arbor: University Microfilms International.

Sweeney, M. A. 1991. Structure, genre, and intent in the book of Habakkuk. *Vetus Testamentum* XLI. Leiden and New York: E. J. Brill.

Sweeney, Marvin A. 1992. Concerning the structure and generic character of the book of Nahum. *Zeitschrift fuer alttestamentiche Wissenschaft.* 104:364–377.

Sweeney, Marvin A. 1996. *Isaiah 1–39, With an introduction to prophetic literature.* The Forms of the Old Testament Literature, vol. XVI. Grand Rapids: Eerdmans.

Sweeney, Marvin A. 1998. The Latter Prophets: Isaiah, Jeremiah, Ezekiel. In S. L. McKenzie and M. P. Graham (eds.), *The Hebrew Bible today: An introduction to critical issues.* Louisville: Westminster-John Knox.

Sweeney, Marvin A. 2000a. *The twelve prophets* 1. Collegeville: Liturgical Press.

Sweeney, Marvin A. 2000b. *The twelve prophets* 2. Collegeville: Liturgical Press.

Taylor, J. B. 1969. *Ezekiel: An introduction and commentary.* Tyndale Old Testament Commentaries, Vol. 20. Downers Grove: InterVarsity.

Taylor, R. A. 2004. *Haggai, Malachi.* The New American Commentary 21A, 21–201. Nashville: Broadman & Holman.

Thistleton, Anthony C. 1980. *The two horizons: New Testament hermeneutics and philosophical description with special reference to Heidegger, Bultmann, Gadamer and Wittgenstein.* Exeter: Paternoster.

Thomas, Kenneth. 1991. Translating for audio and video media. *UBS Bulletin* 160/161.

Thompson, John A. 1956. *The book of Obadiah.* The Interpreter's Bible 6, 857–867. New York: Abington Press.

van der Toorn, Karel. 2007. *Scribal culture and the making of the Hebrew Bible.* Cambridge: Harvard University Press.

Trible, Phyllis. 1994. *Rhetorical criticism: Context, method, and the book of Jonah.* Minneapolis: Augsburg.

United Bible Societies. 1980. HOTTP. *Preliminary and interim report on the Hebrew Old Testament Project* 5. New York: United Bible Societies.

Vanhoozer, K. J. 2000. *First theology: God, Scripture and hermeneutics.* Leicester: Apollos.

Verhoef, P. A. 1987. *The books of Haggai and Malachi.* New International Commentary on the Old Testament. Grand Rapids: Eerdmans.

de Waard, Jan. 1977. The chiastic structure of Amos V, 1–17. *Vetus Testamentum* 27:170–177.

de Waard, Jan, and Willian A. Smalley. 1979. *A translator's handbook on the book of Amos.* New York: United Bible Societies.

de Waard, Jan, and Eugene A. Nida. 1986. *From one language to another: Functional equivalence in Bible translating.* Nashville: Nelson.

van der Wal, Adri. 1983. The structure of Amos. *Journal for the Study of the Old Testament* 26:107–113.

Walton, J. H., V. H. Matthews, and M. W. Chavalas. 2000. *The IVP Bible background commentary: Old Testament.* Downers Grove: InterVarsity Press.

Wardlaw, Terrance R., Jr. 2008. Discourse analysis. In D. G. Firth and J. A. Grant (eds.), *Words & the Word: Explorations in biblical interpretation & literary theory,* 266–317. Downers Grove: IVP Academic.

Wendland, Ernst R. 1987. *The cultural factor in Bible translation.* UBS Monograph Series, no. 2. New York: United Bible Societies.

Wendland, Ernst R. 1988. The "Word of the Lord" and the organization of Amos. *Occasional Papers in Translation and Textlinguistics* 2(4):1–51.

Wendland, Ernst R. 1990. What is truth? Semantic density and the language of the Johannine Epistles (with special reference to 2 John). *Neotestamentica* 24(2).

Wendland, Ernst R. 1992. Temple site or cemetery—A question of perspective. *Journal of Translation and Textlinguistics* 5(1):37–85.

Wendland, Ernst R. 1993a. *Comparative discourse analysis and the translation of Psalm 22 in Chichewa, a Bantu language of central Africa.* Studies in the Bible and Early Christianity, Vol. 32. Lewiston, NY: The Edwin Mellen Press.

Wendland, Ernst R. 1993b. Duplicating the dynamics of oral discourse in print. *Notes on Translation* 7(4):26–44.

Wendland, Ernst R. 1994a. Genre criticism and the Psalms. In Robert D. Bergen (ed.), *Biblical Hebrew and discourse linguistics,* 374–414. Dallas: Summer Institute of Linguistics.

Wendland, Ernst R. 1994b. Oral-aural dynamics of the Word: With special reference to John 17. *Notes on Translation* 8(1):19–43.

Wendland, Ernst R. 1995. *The discourse analysis of Hebrew prophetic literature.* Lewiston, NY and Lampeter, UK: Mellen Biblical Press.

Wendland, Ernst R. 1996. Text analysis and the genre of Jonah (Parts 1 and 2). *Journal of the Evangelical Theological Society* 39(2–3):191–206, 373–395.

Wendland, Ernst R. 1998. *Buku Loyera: An introduction to the new Chichewa Bible translation.* Kachere Monograph, no. 6. Blantyre, Malawi: CLAIM.

Wendland, Ernst R. 1999. "The righteous live by their faith" in a Holy God; complementary compositional forces and Habakkuk's dialogue with the LORD. *Journal of the Evangelical Theological Society* 42(4):591–628.

Wendland, Ernst R. 2000. *Preaching that grabs the heart: A rhetorical-stylistic study of the Chichewa revival sermons of Shadrack Wame.* Kachere Monograph, no. 11. Blantrye, Malawi: CLAIM.

Wendland, Ernst R. 2002. *Analyzing the Psalms.* Second Edition. Dallas: SIL International.

Wendland, Ernst R. 2004. *Translating the literature of Scripture: A literary-rhetorical approach to Bible translation.* Publications in Translation and Textlinguistics 1. Dallas: SIL International.

Wendland, Ernst R. 2005. *Sewero! Christian drama and the drama of Christianity in Africa.* Kachere Monograph, no. 20. Zomba, Malawi: Kachere Series.

Wendland, Ernst R. 2007. Aspects of the principle of parallelism in Hebrew poetry. *Journal of Northwest Semitic Languages* 33:1, 101–124.

Wendland, Ernst R. 2008a. *Contextual frames of reference in translation: A coursebook for translators and teachers.* Manchester: St Jerome.

Wendland, Ernst R. 2008b. *Finding and translating the oral-aural elements in written language: The case of the New Testament Epistles.* Lewiston, NY and Lampeter, UK: Edwin Mellen Press.

Wendland, Ernst R. 2011. *LiFE-style translating: A workbook for Bible translators.* Second edition. Dallas: SIL International.

Wendland, Ernst R. and J. P. Louw. 1993. *Graphic Design and Bible Reading.* Cape Town: The Bible Society of South Africa.

West, Gerald. 1996 Reading the Bible Differently: Giving Shape to the Discourse of the Dominated. *Semeia* 73.

West, Gerald and Musa W. Dube, eds. 1996. Reading with: An exploration of the interface between critical and ordinary readings of the Bible (African overtures). *Semeia* 73.

Westermann, Claus. 1980. *The Psalms: Structure, content and message.* Minneapolis: Augsburg.

Wevers, J. 1967. *Ezekiel.* The New Century Bible Commentary. London: Thomas Nelson.

Wilson, V.M. 1997. *Divine symmetries: The art of biblical rhetoric.* Lanham, NY and Oxford: University Press of America.

Wilt, Timothy L. 1992. Lexical repetition in Jonah. *Journal of Translation and Textlinguistics* 5:3.

Wilt, Timothy, ed. 2003. *Bible translation: Frames of reference.* Manchester: St. Jerome.

Wolff, H. W. 1976. *Haggai, Malachi: Rededication and renewal.* Chicago: Moody.

Wolff, H. W. 1977. *Joel and Amos.* Hermeneia Commentary. Philadelphia: Fortress Press.
Wolff, Hans Walter. 1986. *Obadiah and Jonah: A commentary.* M. Kohl, trans. Minneapolis: Augsburg Publishing House.
Wonderly, William L. 1968. *Bible translations for popular use.* New York: United Bible Societies.
Woodard Jr., Branson L. 1993. Jonah. In Leland Ryken and Tremper Longman, III. (eds.), *A complete literary guide to the Bible.* Grand Rapids: Zondervan.
Young, E. J. 1960. *An introduction to the New Testament.* Revised edition. Grand Rapids: Zondervan.
Zogbo, Lynell and Ernst R. Wendland. 2000. *Hebrew poetry in the Bible: A guide for readers and translators.* New York: United Bible Societies.
Zulick, M. 1992. The active force of hearing: The ancient Hebrew language of persuasion. *Rhetorica* 10.

Index of Subjects

Symbols

7 + 1 literary pattern 44

A

A-B-A' ring
  construction 37, 45, 105, 376, 553
  structure(s) 53, 514, 556
A-B parallelism 519
accentuation 233
accuracy 94, 403, 407
accurate exegesis 219, 573
accusation 72, 436, 547
  condemnation 483
    pattern 47
accusatory pronoun 170
acrostic 159
additive heightening 441
address 439
aesthetic
  appeal 473
  parity 401

affective function 552
affirmation 72
a fortiori 288
Africa 283, 517
African
  audience 635
afterlife 452
agricultural bounty 639
alien conceptual environment 470
alliteration 54, 109, 160, 162, 163, 164, 167, 194, 221, 233, 280, 372, 387, 458, 508, 511, 569
alliterative wordplay 507
allusion(s) 54, 59, 60, 61, 63, 82, 109, 174, 188, 208, 217, 243, 361, 466, 469, 478, 504
alternating parallelism 163
alternation of speakers 448, 501
ambiguity 80, 117, 301, 514
ambiguous pronoun 581
amelioration 205
Ammon 512

Amos 630, 634
anadiplosis 5, 11, 58, 108, 149, 152, 166, 274, 352, 375, 380, 389, 429, 505, 506
analogical
  design 272
  organization 262
analogy 191, 262, 454
analysis 454, 493
analytical
  methodology 132
  principles 36, 403
anaphora 4, 10, 12, 13, 17, 41, 47, 48, 55, 108, 109, 150, 152, 181, 273, 274, 373, 429, 505, 509, 553
anaphoric
  cue 59
  vocative 364
ancestors 214, 582
ancient epic influence 470
and now 182
angel of the Lord 558
anthropomorphically 36
anthropomorphic expressions 580
anthropomorphism 193, 442
anticipation 299, 301
anticlimax 323
antiphonal text 500
antithesis 282, 461, 536
aperture 45, 108, 150, 179, 429, 433, 505, 506, 512
apocalyptic
  day 507
  description 507
  hymn 472
  judgment 348
  language 209
  vision 385
  writing 344
apologetic
  discourse 434
  theme 478

apostasy 59, 449
apostrophe 118, 121, 170
appeal 182, 203, 445, 524
  for repentance 564
appellation 127
applications 567
appropriateness 403
approximation 226
apt allusions 538
archaic
  allusions 440
  poetic style 470
architectonic
  design 340
  structure 388
architectural
  cues 56
  vision 345
argument 524
  cycle 543
  structure 200
    Haggai 199
  text-type 199
argumentation 185, 230
arm 580
arrangement of content 568
art 115, 330
artistic
  code 231
  form(s) 231, 566
  functional equivalent 402
  unity 427
artistry 8, 332
ask questions 595
assertion 542
asseverative 511
associated key terms 311
associative resonance 308
assonance 137, 164, 233, 458, 537
assumptions 210
Assyria 152, 269, 513
Assyrians 145
asyndeton 107, 109, 162, 633

Index of Subjects 661

audibility 574
audience 477
  groups 420
  testing 420
audio
  cassettes 419
  channel 486
  image 171
  medium 270
  oriented features 400
  scriptures 398
auditory
  embellishment 137
  focusing 280
aural
  dynamics 40
  impact 627
  indicators 400
  transmission 400
authenticity 407
author
  implanted gaps 297
  intended meaning 298
authorial
  intent 264
  source 267
authority 205
authorship
  Zephaniah 499
autobiographical
  narrative 363
  references 343
avenging spirit 583
average reader 576

B

Babel 517
Babylon 343, 356, 437, 439, 444, 447, 460, 473, 475
background
  knowledge 117, 599
backgrounding 256
back shift 255
  displacement 257
balanced lineation 137, 492
ballast lines 416
Bantu 395
  language 136, 394, 529
  setting 574
Baruch 629
Batonga 574
battle
  scenarios 173
  scene 163
behold 62, 385, 433, 579
Belial 160
Bible
  as literature 330
  literacy 593
  production process 397
  publication 488
  translation 219, 225, 323, 328, 394, 419, 473, 474, 499, 528, 569, 637
    Africa 395
Biblical
  history 272
  rhetoric 641
bifid structure 6, 155, 510
bifurcation 259
blended (metaphoric) space 21, 26
blend space 22
blessing 190, 521, 525
blessings and curses 125, 504
bonding 4
bones 385
book 158
Book of the Law 69
Book of the Twelve 224, 269, 500
bottom-up
  analysis 351, 403, 568
  text processing 403
boundaries 358, 639
bounding 4
  markers 110
  technique 429

bridge the contextual gap 479
brief 329, 409
broken
  style 163
  syntax 58
Buku Lopatulika 219, 395, 411
Buku Loyera 219, 221, 395, 411

C

cadenced utterances 194
call
  narrative 343
  to attention 516
called 639
Canaanites 508
canon 382, 466
canonical
  rhetoric 104
  text 630
capital letters 492
captivity 168
case stud 575
catch words 559, 561
cause-effect 253
  relationship 237, 250
central
  core 493
  nucleus 38
  storyline 278
centrifugal 427
centripetal 427
challenge-response sequence 448
change of order 251, 252
chapter break 435
character
  flaw 293
  viewpoint 242
characterization 281
characterizing quotation 341
Chauta 220, 415
chesed 292, 311
  principle 313
Chewa 136, 317, 327, 334, 395, 410, 529, 569, 633
Bible 219
  language 394
  lyric style 411
  translation 333
  Malachi 570
chiasmus 4, 38, 55, 107, 155, 184, 251, 505, 533
chiastic
  arrangement 320, 518
    Malachi 564
  construction(s) 191, 197, 275, 384
  formations 360
  organization 49
  pattern 44, 188, 374, 553
  structure 10
    Zephaniah 520
  terraced sequence 459
Chichewa 483
chief participant 278
Chitonga 483
citation formula 346, 382
citation(s) 243, 466
ciyabilo 483
clarity 406, 407
clash in connotations 581
classical rhetoric 120
climactic
  closure 540
  conclusion 522
  image 60
  kiy 160
  positions 369
climax 64, 83, 106, 107, 132, 240, 277, 340, 447, 606, 619
  Zephaniah 520
close reading 299
closest natural equivalent 476
closure 16, 59, 67, 110, 112, 153, 160, 171, 179, 181, 366, 369, 429, 433, 460, 506, 539
clues 268

Index of Subjects

cluster 505
cognate accusative 232
cognitive
  benefit 408
  disparity 218
  environment 477
  frameworks 329
coherence 43, 274
cohesion 42, 60, 159, 179, 237, 274, 424, 427, 453, 460, 555
cohesion and coherence 566
cohesive
  function 552
  structures 454
  unity 493
colon 506
colophon 440
colorful poetry 342
comfort 174
comic book 398
commentaries 55
commentary 57
common-language 401
  translation 396
  version 394
communal lament 385
communication 29, 36
  context 332
  gap 141, 218
  settings 328
communicative
  clue 477
  effect 569
  function(s) 264, 356, 358, 476
  potential 421
  purposes 271
  relevance 481
  significance 132
  value 402
communicatively equivalent translation 331
community
  involvement 225

participation 485
psalm of lament 439
comparative
  analysis 573
  discourse analysis 480
comparison 19
complaint 197, 432, 439, 449, 465
  Habakkuk 433, 439
complementary
  cycles 155
  translation 419
complication 447
composite strophic 520
compositional
  boundaries 157
  components 132
  core 256, 463
  excellence 401
  exercise 406
  forces 424, 453
  framework
    Obadiah 106
  hinge 360
  history 96
  intention 298
  midpoint 320
  strategy 618
  techniques 338
  unit(s) 353, 457
  unity 65
compound speech-opener 384
concentrations 503
concentric
  arrangement(s) 66, 568
  framework 86
  patterning
    Malachi 552
  plane 552
  structure(s) 37, 44, 460, 553, 554, 560
    Malachi 554
conceptual
  barriers 215

blending 19, 20
blends 21
context 477
flashback 261
framework 329
inclusio 61
integration 20
lacunae 298
mediators 328
reiteration 633
concession-contraexpectation 151
condemnation 72, 105, 436, 524
condensation 157, 512
confession of faith 447, 515
conflict 447
conflict and resolution 340
conjunction(s) 229, 453
  laken 516
connective particles 453
connotation 393, 475, 602, 621
connotative
  associations 488
  effect 606
  elements 20
  flow 392
  heightening 137
  movement 525
  progression 362
  tone 304, 484
consecration 214
consolation 72
consolatory imagery 348
constituent focus 17
consumers 477
contemporary
  performance 475
  relevance 298
  significance 212
Contemporary English Version 400
content proportioning 272
context 191, 269, 329
contextual
  background 122, 440
  knowledge 477
  effects 477
  gap 478
  guides 637
  irony 286, 290
contextualization 116, 592
contextualized 219, 314
  translation 638
contextualizing 591
contextual setting 404
contiguity 2
continuity 179, 428, 472
continuity amid discontinuity 472
continuum of translation 332
contraexpectation 107, 197, 320
contrast 35, 171, 183, 237, 253,
  281, 312, 449, 515
contrastive
  analogy 262
  deviation 248
  imagery 18
  irony 326
  literary units 372
  statements 604
convergence 36, 84, 114, 429, 454
cooperative maxims 500
corporate unity 484
corresponding signals 172
cosmic
  motif 507
  warfare 443
cotext 130, 208, 269
counter thesis 155, 185, 364
covenant 52, 69, 123, 215, 344,
  347, 348, 369, 441, 561
  background 158
  community 8
  curse(s) 341, 384
  of peace 367, 370, 389
  relationship 525
  renewal ceremony 563
  violations 365
  with Levi 557

Index of Subjects 665

covenantal
  attributes 149, 315
  catalogue 235
  characteristics 154
  correlates 389
  curses 125, 467
  infidelity 515
  language 187, 208
  motifs 558
  obligations 281
  passages 351
  perspective 370
  principles 361, 393
  qualities 312
  relationship 175, 203, 215, 338, 365, 535, 556, 628
  terminology 366, 563
  terms 159
  violation(s) 43, 346
covert text 195
creation-reversing concepts 506
creedal confession 243
crime and consequence 508
crime-and-punishment 149
cross reference(s) 222, 482, 604
crowded stage 519
crucial junctures 480
crux interpretum 22, 522
cues 268
cultural
  conditioning 581
  setting 606
  significance 606
culturally unfamiliar 585
curiosity 301
curse(s) 69, 550, 562
Cush 513, 517

D

Damascus 635
Darius 209
date notice 352
Davidic-Messianic king 389

Davidic (Messianic) servant 354
day 60, 113, 517, 520
  of Judgment 552, 560, 563
  of the LORD 62, 104, 114, 118, 126, 499, 520, 534
  of YHWH 526
death 587
de Blois, Reineir 26
decoding 174
de-construction of the text 503
deductive 206
defamiliarization 247, 277, 492
defiled 615
defilement 183, 193, 214
definition 172
degree
  of acceptability 406
  of markedness 330
  of subjectivity 245
deictic *kiy* 162
deliberate
  ambiguity 308, 504, 568
  omission 613
deliberative 120
  rhetoric 390
deliverance 355, 474
demarcation 171, 229
demarcative
  devices 352
  features 351
  parallelism 504
  recursion 454
demonstrative pointing 220
de-mythologized 470
denotation 475
denouement 113, 320, 340, 469
denunciation 159, 432, 437
departure from the norm 255
desert scenario 513
desolation 375
Deuteronomy 74, 554
deviation(s) 247, 248, 275
diachronically arrangment 356

diachronic plane 552
dialectic style 536, 541
dialogic
  construction 448, 499
  method 590
  structure
    Zephaniah 500
dialogue(s) 417, 449, 521
  Zephaniah 501
diction 416
didactic
  hortatory purpose 306
  irony 293
  text 315
difference 246
difficult translation 621
dilemma 306
direct
  discourse 157
  speech 149, 173, 190, 279, 283
directive speech 504
dirge 436
disambiguation 172
discontinuity 247, 428
discourse 474
  analysis 33, 131, 171, 271
  artistry 178
  boundaries 480
  break 429, 616
  deictic 150
  demarcation 178, 405
  design 488
  division 614
  dynamics 489
  focus 256
  formulae 346
  function 601
  markers 366, 503
    Zephaniah 503
  marking formulae 500
  organization 65, 349
  peak(s) 182, 619
  segments 178

  structure 83, 216, 323, 568, 604
    Ezekiel 358
    Haggai 178
    Jonah 2 317
    Malachi 541
  transitions 600
  unit 504
disjunction 180, 236, 247, 297, 405
disjunctive
  gap 260
dislocation 129
disputation 361, 363, 364
  format 563
  genre 535
  speech 180, 185
  thesis 364
  structure
    Malachi 555
disputational
  cycles 185
  movement 542
  progression 448
  speech 359
dispute(s) 360, 541
  Malachi 546
disruptive parenthesis 578
distance 328
distant parallelism 429
distinctive
  stylistic features 330
  triadic 236
distribution pattern 240
diversity 248
divination 584
divine
  announcement formula 179, 180
  appellation 361
  argument
    Zephaniah 526
  blessing 205
  direct speech 379
  emotions 207

formlas 34
formulas 96
'I' 391
imperatives 188
indictment 434, 526
inspiration 265, 272
intervention 310, 526
irony 462
justice 373, 433, 438, 495
messenger speech 67
name 44, 255, 277, 320, 429, 602
oath 375
oracle formula 108
quote formulas 73
recognition formula 348, 366,
    378, 385, 389
restoration 368
retribution 436
sanctions 629
speech formulas 31, 33
verbal signature 555
verdict 368
Divine Warrior 159, 465, 509
  hymn 148
  imagery 183
divorce 559
Doan and Giles 625
documentary approach 79
domesticating 591
domestication 212, 328, 402
double
  chiasmus 252, 561
double direct quote 561
double-duty transitional 170
doxologies 80
Doxology 61
drama 387, 484, 624, 631
  Amos 628
  format 420
  Zephaniah 624
dramatic
  demonstrative 152
  devices 529
  discours 633
  enigma 305
  irony 291, 508
  monocolon 442
  movement
    Ezekiel 33-37 392
  narrative 57
  pause 325
  peak 164, 384
  performance 490
  perspective 513
  plot 346
    Ezekiel 349
  power 537
  preaching 497
  prophecy 338, 502, 625
    Zephaniah 502
  public performance 634
  quality 98, 624
  quotation 362
  revelation 255, 514
  reversal 105, 375, 377
  suspense 516
  tension 118, 303
dramatization 173
drought 179, 212, 606
dry bones 384
dynamic
  equivalence 396
  impact 473
  match 335

E

Eden 377
editorial plural 580
Edom 106, 123, 125, 134, 371,
    373, 375, 377, 554
education 327, 419
electronic
  communication 485
  medium 398
  text 484
Elijah 282, 290, 547

elocutionary dimension 401
embedded 104
  direct speech 504
  narrative 39
  quotation(s) 121, 620
  units 498
emendation(s) 129, 181, 425
emic 266
emotions 537
emotive
  aspect 36
  associations 477
  climax 74, 111, 182, 323, 444, 556, 562
  diction 283
  intensity 280
  peak 451
  progression 449
emotively-toned language 565
emphasis 255, 279
emphasizer 433
emphatic
  contrasts 536
  (independent) pronouns 536
  interjection 507
  ki 161
  pronoun 251, 256, 385, 558
enactment 245
enallage 150, 172
encouragement 133
enculturization 305
end stress 38, 323, 507, 525, 539, 640
English script 635
enhanced communication 479
enigma 270, 285, 297, 299, 512
enigmatic
  elements 302
enrichment studies 637
enumeration 540
epideictic 120
epiphora 5, 11, 17, 41, 53, 54, 58, 64, 108, 110, 150, 152, 161, 165, 169, 273, 429, 434, 505, 509, 554
epiphoric
  recognition formula 364
  refrain 71
episode 255
eponymic names 388
equivalence 2, 429
Esau 110, 554
eschatological
  climax 184
  day 84
  framework 391
  motif 548
  opener 621
  reference 353
eschatology 184
esthetic-emotional appeal 30
Ethiopia 513
ethos 207, 390, 506
etic 266
Eugene Peterson 28
eulogy 441
euphemism 193, 615
euphony 137
evaluative parameters 406
eventive enigma 302
event-line 258
event vision 151
evocative
  imagery 504
  irony 286
exceptions 206
exclamation of closure 325
exclamation(s) 50, 137, 138, 169, 375, 416
exclamatory
  particles 537
  utterances 536
exclusio 10, 48, 53, 149, 159, 180, 342, 345, 353, 444, 505, 506, 519
exegesis 226, 566

Index of Subjects 669

exegesis and interpretation 568
exegetical
  fidelity 417
exegetical implications 529
exhortation 72, 199
  address 510
exical-semantic replacements 416
exile(s) 64, 389
Exodus 149, 345, 386, 389, 468
exodus terminology 368
expansion/addition 249
explanatory
  aside 256
  footnote(s) 481, 579, 605
  kiy 511
  notes 141, 332
explication 486
extended metaphor 382
external marking 173
extralinguistic
  background 199, 567
  setting 478
extratextual
  aids 224, 481
  educative helps 481
  influence 329
  publication 223
  strategies 223
extrinsic rhetorical situation 199
Ezekiel 337, 339, 340, 343, 346, 356
  33-37 351

F

facticity 270
faith 434, 452
faithfulness 407, 559
faithlessness 564
father 559
father-son motif 563
fear 276, 611
  of the LORD 304
feasibility 476

fidelity 406, 407, 410, 486
figurative
  language 156, 168, 284, 538
  restatement 633
figure(s) of speech 284, 606
flashback 155, 216, 256, 258, 259, 260, 391, 432
focus 12, 255
footnotes 396
forces of cohesion 454
forecast 245, 263
foregrounding 256, 296, 566
foreign accent 408
foreigners 639
foreignized translation 328
forensic component 464
foreshadow 83
foreshadowed 59
foreshadowing 258, 262, 299, 342, 513
formal
  correspondence 235
  layout 333
  substitution 253
format(ting) 223, 410, 570, 614
  characteristics 93
  techniques 528
  the text 487
form criticism 267
form-functional
  continuum 409
  divisions 431
  matches 405, 483
form-meaning 35
formulaic
  opening 429
  pattern 43
  variant 508
formula of divine proclamation 150
formulas 366, 503
fragments 82
frame(s) 20, 329

of reference 27, 327, 475, 637
framework of interpretation 126
free indirect discourse 482
fronted pronoun 256
fronting for emphasis 637
front shift(ing) 255, 278
function 198
functional(ly)
  approach(es) 271, 402
  dimension 407
  equivalence 171, 329, 401, 604
  equivalent 136, 141, 492
    literary rendering 482
    vernacular 473
    version 528
  literacy 395, 484
  parity 483
  reconstruction 268
  significance 230
functions
  of communication 418
  of irony 295
funeral lament 59
funerary lament genre 49
futility curses 196

G

gap-filling 299
gaps 462
genealogy 506
generic
  equivalents 483
  space 21, 22
    abstract 21
    common 26
genre-based methodology 403
genre(s) 7, 131, 147, 261, 266, 318, 330, 405, 439, 590, 627
  Habakkuk 446
Gentiles 517
geographic(al)
  allusions 117
  relation 354

rhetoric 511
gestures and facial features 635
glossary entries 222
goat 583
God 214
God's
  language 587
  righteousness 463
Gog 353, 391
good news 145, 146
gospel 144, 175, 338, 357, 386, 472
  core
    Nahum 146
grace 393
gradient of discourse types 482
grammatical transformations 252
graphic
  design 318
  diction 538
  discourse 385
  imagery 157, 192, 320
Greek (New) Testament 466
grounds 510

H

Habakkuk 425, 432, 441
  Habakkuk 3 440, 468, 490
Habakkuk's
  message 472
  theodicy 453
Haggai 178, 193, 200, 599
Haggai's prophecy 600
hard media 484
harlotry 166
harvest terminology 516
Hebrew
  narrative style 231
  poetics 130
  poetry 404, 470
  prophets 623
  Scriptures 466
Hebrews 466

Index of Subjects

heightened prose 137
heightening 7, 519
helplessness curses 125
hermeneutical
 approaches 267
 closure 298
 frame of reference 221
 framework 216
 key 217
 question 284
hermeneutics 130
heroic composition 471
hierarchical
 discourse organization 189
 levels 455
 pattern 39
highlighting 480
high priest 602
himself 391
hinge 324, 325
hinneh 106, 150, 153, 161, 165, 169
historical
 background 303
 context 78
 setting 191, 356, 523
historicity 270, 272
holiness 379, 391
Holy Scriptures 404, 495
holy-war 106
homologous translation 402
hope 512, 521
horizon(s)
 of hermeneutics 116
 of interpretation 122, 311, 591
horizontal
 hierarchical 38
 structures 39
hortatory 133
 climax 565
 development 270
 discourse 8, 200, 497
 peak 525

text 315, 445
house 179, 192, 213
 of Israel 347, 358, 387
 of the LORD 602
 of Yahweh 225
House, Paul 624
hoy-oracle 511
human injustice 467
humiliation 579
humor 295
humorous tone 296
hush 438
hymn 440
hyperbaton 251
hyperbole 113, 193, 270, 288
hypertext 484
 format 398
hyphenation 410, 488
hypocrisy 59
hypothetical example(s) 615, 617

I

identification 105
ideophone(s) 137, 221, 416, 584, 633
idiomacity 221, 406, 408
idiomatic utterance 604
idioms 193
idolatry 343, 437, 458, 463
illocutionary
 aims 356
 force 72, 403, 524
 functions 298
 purpose 195
illocution(s) 115, 190, 200
illustrations 223, 396
image complexes
 Joel 17
imagery 8, 27, 64, 163, 166, 167, 192, 193, 350, 417, 450, 534
 of building 638
image sets 17, 59
immanence of Yahweh 214

imperative(s) 429, 518, 614, 617
implication 542, 610
implicatures 477, 499
implicit information 486
implied
  audience 267
  author 267, 339, 407
  readers 589
imprecatory 150
inclusio 4, 13, 14, 16, 41, 46, 58,
    62, 84, 106, 120, 134, 149,
    151, 153, 167, 179, 234, 273,
    342, 354, 362, 369, 374, 429,
    504, 509, 520, 553
inclusion 229, 425
incriminating quote 602
indentation 489
indictment 43, 58, 105, 110, 148,
    152, 156, 160, 342, 364, 549
inductive 207
infidelity 559
initial
  setting 127, 199, 297
  situation 451
injustice 461
inspiration 115
integrative cohesion 455
intelligibility 407, 409
intended target group 335
intensification 6, 279, 429
intensive recursion 455
intentional fallacy 267
intentions 204
interactive instruction 589
intercalation 381
interior monologue 281
interlocking
  arguments 186
  introversions 32
interlude 59, 340, 527
interpersonal
  circumstances 567
  dialogue 589

discourse action 200
  interaction 121
interposed horizon 116
interrogation 230
interrogative(s) 280
  climax 251
intertextual
  allusion(s) 351, 370
  cohesion 465
  connections 538
  contrast 294
  deviations 245
  Habakkuk 466
  irony 289, 368
  links 468
  parallels 322
  recursion 243
  resonance 170, 187
  similarity 329
  web of allusions 195
intertextuality 125, 130, 156, 159,
    168, 208, 222, 242, 244, 275,
    326, 361, 382, 390
in that day 191
intratextual 242
  cohesion 454
  contrast 325
  influence 208
  markers 480
  recursion 165, 277, 351
intratextuality 242, 389
intrinsic rhetorical situation 199
introductory formula 55
introversion 38, 50, 54, 60, 88,
    275, 429
introverted construction 320
inversion 385
  sequence 374
ironic
  contrast 325, 368
  inclusio 507
  intertextuality 326
  overlay 322

Index of Subjects

reversal 165, 252
signification 294
vehicle 287
irony 14, 47, 53, 54, 105, 117, 166, 236, 244, 270, 285, 310, 318, 359, 365, 504, 537
  dramatic 305
  evocative 288
  of reversal 289
  situational 293
Isaiah 159, 170, 173, 371, 452, 512, 518, 523
Ishtar 152
isomorphically equivalent 321
Israel 344
issues in Bible translation 475
iterative style 191

J

Jacob 109, 554
Janus
  function 179
  passage 519
  transition 511
Janus-like verse 522
Jehoiachin 210
Jehovah 577
Jeremiah 371
  Jeremiah 49 125
Jerusalem 514, 518, 519, 527
job
  commission 227
  description (Brief) 222
Jonah 158, 164, 266, 269, 281, 295, 307, 315
Joshua 179, 201
Josiah 523
Judah 447, 506, 511, 635
judgment 149, 170, 175, 190, 339, 355, 432, 451
  motifs 125
  oracle(s) 35, 62, 151, 167, 342, 363, 371, 436

speech 438
judgment and blessing 354
judicial
  dialogues 363
  indictment 363
  reversal 150
  rhetoric 120
justice 73, 134, 393, 461, 466, 515, 562
justification 410

K

Kerethites 512
kerygmatic core 339
key
  term(s) 42, 71, 109, 405
    thematic 108
    theological 515
  usage 396
  words 461
King David 638
King James factor 397
King Josiah's reform 499
kingship 134
kinsman-redeemer 374
kiy 309, 511
  consequential 517
Koine 401
Koine (common) Greek 408

L

lament 59, 170, 318, 440, 446, 447
  psalm 7
land 124, 640
larger-to-lesser progression 193
law 357
  of retaliation 167
leading question 535
legislative discourse 363
level(s)
  of comprehension 592
  of formality 396

of indentation 324
  of meaning 288
  of rhetoric 122
  of rhetorical significance 474
Levi 557
lexical
  center 164
  continuity 434
  enigma 308
  intensifiers 633
  interlocking 540
  overlay 260
  position 615
  recurrence 510
  recursion 112, 274, 359, 364, 515
  resonance 309
  semantic
    recursion 33
    variation 249
  substitution 254
lex talionis 194, 364, 374, 376, 458
Leza 580
life-force 583
linear 83
  concentric 37
  discourse development 56
  pattern(ing) 37
    Malachi 541
  progression 196
  structural units 66
line of argumentation 217
linguistic/literary markers 429
lions 165
literacy rate 575
literalism 585
literariness 331, 332
literary 247
  approach 330
  artistry 272
  composition 479
  correspondence 136
  creativity 181

  cues 403
  devices 540, 568
  features 182
  forking 259
  form(s) 35, 131, 328, 572
  framework 34
  functional equivalence 317, 327, 331, 494, 529
    translation 570
  functional equivalent 139
  markers 338
  marking 172
  oratorical approach 402
  parallelism 181
  processes 41
  rhetorical analysis 498, 528
  structural
    analysis 1, 502, 503, 520, 566, 567
    description
      Zephaniah 505
    features 362
    markers 84
    study 171
  style and structure 566
  translation(s) 329, 398
literature 628
liturgical
  chorus 446
  frame 440
  response 438
  version 399
locust(s) 22, 169
locution 200, 403
logical relationship 606
logos 207, 390
long sentence 586, 608
LORD
  of Armies 167
  of Host(s) 165, 602
love 554
loyalty 417
  principle 417

Index of Subjects   675

LXX 64, 338

M

macro-chiastic 55
macro-genre 266
macro-level of discourse 465
macrostructural (plot) development 340
macrostructure 156, 401
  Ezekiel 339
  Habakkuk 430
macro-theme
  Malachi 546
majesty 451
major breaks 600
major/minor peaks 503
Malachi 206, 532, 558
marginal notes 223
Mark 1:40-41 635
marked 2
marriage 550
Masoretic Text 75, 113, 128, 324, 426
  Ezekiel 338
Maxey, James 635
meaning 35, 132, 225, 232, 283, 311, 327, 349, 395, 401, 476, 499
  field 238
  package 488
meaningful
  translation 475
  version 219
mediator 450
medium
  of communication 494
  of composition 270
  of message transmission 140
  of print 400
  of transmission 30, 484
  sensitive 140
  transferability 626
memory 40

mental space(s) 20
  theory 19, 20
mental stage 634
merismus 193
message 231, 627
  of deliverance 156
  perspective 267
  signification 475
messenger 560
  formula 165, 179, 364, 506
  motif 167, 170, 173
  of good news 343
  of the covenant 566
  of Yahweh 558
Messiah 133, 210, 344
  motif 369
Messianic 369
  age 517, 562, 639
  allusion 209
  descendant 215
  implication(s) 64, 135
  prophecy 566
  refrain 556
  servant's 587
  universalism 548
metaphor 19, 23, 188, 193, 210, 366
metatextual frame 462
method of analysis 528
methodology 128, 264
metonymic allusion 209
metonym(s) 113, 535
metonymy 158, 165, 193
microstructural level 157
microstructure 402, 536
  of discourse 330
micro-stylistic features 333
midpoint 361
military
  imagery 442, 588
  motif 509
mimetic function 73
minatory message 526

mini-narrative 468
missionary translations 575
mitigation 205
mnemonic
  device(s) 486, 510
  framework 40
  function 552
Moab 512
mock
  lament 153, 358
  praise 152
mocking command 169
modes of transmission 93, 420
monocolon 108, 438
morphological skewing 85
Mosaic
  covenant 187
  law 61, 557
  Torah 209
motivation 182, 206, 445, 510, 524
mountains of Israel 372
Mount Sinai 442
Mount Zion 114, 125, 134
multifaceted
  analysis 40
  cohesion 465
musical
  mode 634
  rendering 335
  scores 637
Mwami Leza 577
mythological figures 443
mythopoetic
  allusion 469
  imagery 353

N

Nahum 144, 145, 158, 174
name 348, 378, 380, 389
narrative 232, 245, 259
  complication 300
  dilemma 60
  progression

Habbakuk 447
nationalism 356
nations 112, 113
naturalness 408
ndakatulo 316, 333, 411, 483
  lyric 136, 417, 633
  genre 335
new covenant 370, 379
new exodus motif 381
New Jerusalem Bible 489
new paragraph 600, 601
New Reader program 398
new spirit 379
Nineveh 143, 144, 151, 158, 160,
  165, 171, 234, 269, 303, 307,
  513
Noahic covenant 361
Nominal advancement 278
non-finite clauses 257
non-literal meaning 283
non-print medium 634
non-verbal recursion 242
Nord, Christiane 402, 404
now 180
ntertextual resonance 404
nucleus of the introversion 322
number seven 352
numerical
  equivalents 617
  n/n + 1 formula 43

O

oath 60
Obadiah 123, 372
  Joel 27
objection 542
object lesson 183, 209, 372, 387
omission 251
onomatopoeia 233
onomatopoeic
  imperative 508
  quality 166
onomatopoetic words 637

oppositions 312
or 499
oracle(s) 158, 432, 446, 503, 504, 543
  against the nations 42, 104, 156, 351, 371, 511, 520, 526, 634
  formula 380
  of blessing 63
  of judgment 62, 119, 503, 518
  of Yahweh 151
  punctuator formula 179, 181, 188
oracle-vision 170
oracular
  dates 196
  formula 106
  style 128
oral
  argumentative discourse 218
  articulation 173
  elocution 333, 489
  models 400
  narrative performer 635
  performance 283
  proclamation 39, 65
  proclamatory mode 628
  recital 282, 410
  recitation 490
  rendition 633
  Scriptures 634
  tradition 140
oral-aural
  articulation 541
  aspect 173
  characteristics 405
  communication 29
  devices 537
  dimension 93, 529
  factor 100, 394, 574
  features 590
  medium 478
    of transmission 473
  origional text 625

presentation 494, 529
properties 333
rhetoric 218
orality 40, 271
oratorical 139
  dimension 529
  discourse 628
    construction 510
  features 405, 528
  prose 560
  style 498, 626
  text 399
  translation 394, 405, 410
  version 398, 400, 402, 419, 570, 591
oratory 173, 399, 554, 626
orature 332, 346
ordered naming 512
original language 40
overinterpretation 265
over-translation 401

P

pace of performance 637
pagan
  myths 471
  nations 522
  peoples 275
page formatting 487
palistrophe 275, 553
panegyric
  discourse 159
  psalm 474
panoramic
  imagery 348
  perspective 146
parable(s) 446, 450, 462, 483
paradigm 262
paradigmatic
  recycling 460
  selection 2
  structure 454
paradox 63

paraenesis 199
paraenetic 269
  text 199
paragraph 15
  break(s) 604, 610
  placement 489
paragraphing 489
  procedures 324
parallel
  pairs 533
  paneling 350
  panels 65, 180
  patterning 388
  phrasing 532
  structure 197
parallelism 2, 3, 137, 152, 188, 232, 388, 429, 560, 637
paraphrase(s) 235, 243, 397, 466
paratext 174
paratextual
  aids 29
  means 574
  notes 638
  strategies 221
parenthetical remark 278
paronomasia 194, 234, 457, 512
participant
  characterization 280
  interaction 311
particles 192
passionate appeals 537
pastiche of prophecies 387
pastoral appeal 360
patchwork of sources 427
pathos 207, 390
patterned
  arrangement 33
  parallelism 458
  symmetry 198
patterning 4
pattern of recursion 437
Paul 466
pause points 486

pauses 637
peace 150, 153, 183, 370, 371, 583, 613
peak of thematic significance 525
peak(s) 18, 106, 108, 119, 132, 157, 240, 277, 340, 428, 522
peaks of salience 521
people of God 344
perceptual blend 23
performance 271, 474, 475, 625
  criticism 77, 96, 98, 625, 628, 632, 634, 636
  mode 626
performative
  approach 100
  directions 99
  intent 629
peripeteia 325
perlocution 200, 204
perlocutionary effect(s) 298, 403
personal
  confession 474
  description 281
  oath 360
  references 278
personification 540
perspectival clash 253
persuasion 115, 504
petition 439, 441
Philip 593
Philistine cities 512
phonic features 504
phonological
  accentuation 270
  devices 283, 417
  features 173, 570
  linkage 234
  parallelism 168
  play 458
  pointing 194
  punctuation 157
  recursion 233, 280, 457
  underlining 164

Index of Subjects

phonology 136
plane of communication 122
play
  on sounds 170
  on words 194, 234
plot 278, 281, 447
  design 345
    Ezekiel 339
  dynamics 245
  progression
    Ezekiel 339
pluri-signification 283, 286
poetic(s) 3, 272
  devices 477
    Malachi 540
  diction 157
  effects 477
  features 492
  forms
    Malachi 532
  function 2
  line 506
  parallelism 532, 606
  principle 429
  prophetic genres 447
  prose 194
  rendering 402
  structure
    Joel 5, 6
  symmetry 533
poet laureate 157
poetry 482
  Hebrew 132
Pohlig, James 538
pointing 4
point of view 242, 280, 340
polite response 615
pollution 205, 214, 380
polyvalency 314
popular-language 395
  translation 396, 576
  version 419
possession 375

post-exilic community 552
pragmatic 3
  distortion 483
  functional component 403
  intent 36, 407
  resemblance 331
praise poet 635
prayer 438, 440, 441, 446
  of thanksgiving 471
prayerful response 463
predicate focus 16
prediction 105, 113
prepositions 192
pressure of symmetry 553
presumed audience 407
presuppositions 210, 404
pride 167, 514
priesthood 557, 558, 561
priestly case-law 360
priests 206
primary
  rhetoric 157
  target audience 638
principle(s)
  of divine justice 452
  of parallelism 438
  of relevance 210, 476
  of reliability 331
  of retribution 263
print(ed)
  font 96
  format 172, 394
  style 488
  text 93
probing questions 195
problem 201, 204, 431, 445
  of evil 478
procedural
  guideline 130
  integrity 409
processing effort 477
proclaiming the Scriptures 624
proclamation 43, 625

proclamatory perspective 632
profession 439
  of faith 461
  of trust 440
progression 193, 229, 249, 424, 427, 428, 449, 460
progressive
  movement 127
  prophetic argument 198
projection 229
project job description 222
prominence 3, 194
promised Messiah 638
pronominal
  reference 580
  usage 368
pronouns 577
proof oracle 348
proper names 127
prophecy of restoration 63
prophet 386, 602, 608
prophetic
  actors 630
  antitype 293
  aperture 520
  application 168
  argument 527
  complaints 473
  denunciation 153
  dialogue 57
  discourse formulas 363
  disputation speech 155
  drama 54, 340, 502
  exhortations 503
  formulae 351
  formula(s) 178, 600, 601, 613
  genres 41
  history 269
  interlude 127
  invective 167
  lament 483
  message formula 106, 160, 369, 373, 379
  oracle opener 602
  performer 630
  playwright 630
  plot 348, 392
  polemic 149
  preachment 295
  prediction 446
  proclamation 624
  punctuator 605
  reception formula 362, 372, 378
  rhetoric 145, 391, 566, 632, 640
  scribe 630
  script 634
  sermon 189, 390
  symbolic action 352
  tradition 631
  translation 633
  watchman 352, 358
  word
    formula 352, 363
    saying 366
  writing 349
prose 532
prose-poetry continuum 532
proverbial
  citation 540
  saying 605
proximity 406, 409
psalm 296
  of Jonah 244, 260, 316, 322, 326
  of thanksgiving 251, 317, 527
  of trust 438
  prayer 440
psalmic
  interlude 520
  prayer 431
Psalms 468
psychological engagement 296
publication design 410
public opinion 335
pun 58, 110, 558
punishment 386, 516, 521
punitive reversal 450

Index of Subjects

punning 234, 280, 309, 511
purification 389, 517
purposeful redundancy 191

Q

qal wachomer 273
qinah
  lament 511
  meter 233
quality 369
question-answer
  format 560
  scenario 184
questions 283
quotation 230, 384, 605
quote formula 67

R

rabbinic disputation 190
radio broadcast(s) 419, 486
rain shrine 213
randomness 247
readability 94, 283, 396, 574
reader-friendly 489
reader-response 122
reader(s)
  helps 420
  response criticism 122, 267, 588
reading between the lines 122
reason-result 380
rebuilding 225
recapitulation 389
recognition formula 17, 349, 373, 377, 383
recomposition 475
reconstruction 130
recurrence 2
recursion 3, 35, 86, 132, 156, 179, 230, 231, 239, 270, 317, 382, 453
  Habakkuk 3 455
  with variation 282

recursive pattern 541
recycling 3
redactional history 77
redaction-critical method 632
redaction criticism 425, 634
redemption history 450
reductions 139
redundancy 127, 191, 396, 620
reduplication 279
referential plane 474
reflection 505
reformation 357, 361, 547
refutation 155
register 396
reiterated lexical items 455
reiteration 168, 232, 276, 453, 620
relatedness 130
relevance 28, 141, 212, 329, 331, 403, 589
  principle 492
  theory 329, 476
relevant contextualization 589
religious
  connotation 392
  significance 212
  situation 599
relocation 138
reminiscences 243
reminiscent allusion 195
remnant 50, 64, 70, 71, 82, 113, 123, 158, 196, 211, 341, 348, 357, 382, 517, 520, 522, 607, 639
remote parallelism 429
renewal 386
re-oralize the discourse 271
repentance 70, 304, 542, 547
repetend 245
repetition 3, 34, 191, 235, 246, 368, 405, 427, 503, 553, 604
repetitive sequence 239
report 245
representational rhetoric 357

research and pre-testing 481
residual orality 39
re-signification 327
resolution 380, 447
resonance 156, 237
response 448, 542
restoration 19, 70, 162, 175, 339, 365, 382, 522, 640
  imagery 373
  oracle 383
resurrection 384, 386, 393, 587
retribution 18, 450
retributive justice 368
revelation 432, 464, 493
revelatory
  formula 378
  theophany 453
reversal(s) 18, 51, 64, 164, 168, 189, 306, 369, 382, 432
reversed
  parallelism 197
  parallel structures 552
rhetoric 8, 115, 116, 140, 211, 230, 315, 332, 402, 440, 499
rhetorical
  argument
    Zephaniah 526
  argument analysis 523
  argumentation 532
  characteristics 157
  criticism 641
  dimension 404, 499
  dramatic progression 445
  dynamics 34, 122, 327, 421
  effect 56
  exigency 127, 202, 567
  features 41, 132, 494
    Malachi 540
  figures 284
  function(s) 317, 566, 605
  intent 236
  motivation(s) 427, 507
  organization 436

outline
  Nahum 146
overlay 185
poetic devices 138
point 217
punctuation 504
purpose(s) 133, 355
question(s) 45, 52, 153, 157, 164, 167, 171, 195, 197, 284, 369, 385, 429, 434, 449, 535, 580, 604, 618
significance 198
situation 122, 356, 523
spotlight 568
strategy 237, 339
structural markers 62
structure 136
technique 115
technique of intertextuality 472
rhetorical and artistic qualities 572
rhetorically 137
rhetorician 174
rhetoric of reassurance 377
rhyme 160, 161, 170, 233, 434
rhyming sequence 458
rhythm 560
rhythmic
  accentual patterns 233
  cadences 492
  envelope 401
  lineation 633
  pattern 558
  poetic prose 191
riddle 579
righteous 563
righteousness 52, 70, 520, 525
ring structure 506
ritual
  communication 408
  function of communication 328
role-reversal 105
royal recital 447
Russian Formalist 492

Index of Subjects 683

S

sacrificial ritual 582
salvation 444
  history 468, 471
  oracle 184, 187, 376, 385
sanctuary 387, 391, 392
sarcasm 152, 170
sarcastic tone 168, 437
satire 165, 167
scapegoat 583
scene 232, 272
scope 236
scribal
  performance(s) 97, 625
  tradition 631
scribal-oral 39
scribes 97, 629
Scriptural citation 326
Scripture engagement 225
Scriptures in print 487
Scripture use in Africa 575
seconding 388
sectional introductions 222
section heading(s) 90, 222, 324, 481, 528, 570, 577, 600, 607, 619, 638
segmentation 83, 131, 350, 428
self-incriminatory speech 375
semantic
  accentuation 277
  complexity 578
  content 36, 407
  density 309
  parallels 605
  reduction 127
  reversal 27
semantic-thematic significance 312
semicolons 219, 416
semi-narrative 118, 151, 277, 384
  account 163
  progression 525
  sequence 318
sensory

evocation 368
impression 418
sentence length 416
sermon 263
servant 211, 577, 621
setting 200
  of use 218
setting-sensitive versions 336
seven 64
sevenfold
  structures 31
  structuring 41
sheep 583
sheep-related imagery 584
Sheep-Shepherd oracle 367
shekinah 209
  glory 341
Sheol 322
shepherd 175, 348, 366
shepherd-sheep imagery 369
shift(s) 503
  in content 600
  in perspective 367
  in subject 584
signatory formula 366
significance 298, 311
significant silence 242
silence 343, 473
  to psalmody 473
similarity 35, 246
similarity-contrast 35
similarity-with-contrast 162
simile 19, 621
simile and metaphor 534
situation 202
situational
  gap 174
  irony 286, 293
  setting 202, 268
Skopos 222, 227, 317, 327, 329, 332, 333, 335, 409
Skopostheorie 329
social

admonition 71
  power 629
sociocultural setting 475, 589
soft media 484
Solomon 211
solution 431
Song of Deborah 156
song of thanksgiving 261, 316, 319
sonic
  repetition 458
  structure 509
sorcerer 581, 583
sorcery 579, 584
soteriological terms 443
sound
  markers 40
  pattern 234
soundplay(s) 160, 161, 368, 385
source-critical analysis 424
source criticism 267
source (image) space 21, 25
source-oriented perspective 269
Sovereign LORD 374, 380, 507
so-what? factor 171
spatial
  displacement 363
  layout 318
spatial-syntactic variation 254
speaker alternation 500
speaking voice 430
species of rhetoric 390
specification 429
speech
  event 246
  formulas 191
  intentions 405
  levels 121
  "moves" 448
  punctuator 618
speech act(s) 190, 200, 542, 543
  Malachi 543
  model 198
  perspective 72

structure
  Zephaniah 524
  theory 298
spirit 215, 383, 611
Spirit (of God) 357, 379, 386
spiritual
  problem 542
  reversal 384
spoken oral-aural form 408
SSSS 226
staccato
  rhythm 511
  style 166
stage directions 99, 635
staging 256
stanza(s) 131, 432, 455
step-up device 160
Sternberg, Meir 264, 307
stick 389
story format 420
storytelling 484
stressed pronoun 369
strophe(s) 38, 51, 106, 131, 149, 432, 455, 503, 505
strophic
  divisions 14
  level 504
  structure 10
  units 455
structural
  analysis 75, 114
  anaphora 353, 506
  arrangement 390, 427
  boundaries 457
  breaks 501
  bridge 110, 520
  center 49, 156
  core 62
  definition 503
  description 42, 148
  development 447
  diagrams 481
  indicators 434

Index of Subjects

markers 105
  Zephaniah 506
midpoint 341, 435
organization 127, 172
outline
  Amos 41
pattern 240
pivot 431, 448
placement 405
problem points 547
reiteration 437
significance 324
summary
  Malachi 543
symmetry 273
units 41
  Obadiah 104
structural-thematic
  cycle 165
  framework 445
  outline
    Habakkuk 430
    Nahum 154
  overlap 151
  progression 74
  summit 157
study
  Bibles 398
  notes 96
style 189, 230, 402
  of performance 98
  of writing 217
stylistic
  assessment 401
  clues 132
  correspondences 173
  devices 100, 145
  differences 411
  effects 477
  excellence 402
  features 179, 351, 415
    Chewa 633
  form 133

functional evaluation 410
  naturalness 283
  quality 408
  resources 394
  techniques 504
  variation 437
stylistically marked 330
stylistics 230
subjectivism 298
subjectivity 245
subscription 440
sub-texts 196
sub turn 237
summary 272
summary-and-scene 261
summons 510
superscription 440
supplementary biblical text 419
supportive patterning 196
suprasegmental sounds 410
surprise 300
  factor 73
surprising shifts 516
suspense 163, 300, 301, 304
symbolic
  action(s) 347, 351, 388
  image 58
  meaning 220
symbolical
  blessings 370
  images 640
  image set 639
symbolism 193, 210, 376, 387,
    390, 548, 621
symmetrical
  macrostructure 346
  organization 324
  syntactic structures 458
symmetry 88, 187
synecdoche 161, 162, 164, 168,
    378, 535
synonymy 235, 246
synoptic overview 262

686

syntactic
  advancement(s) 169, 256
  ordering 256
  position 250, 257
  usage 416
syntagmatic
  disjunction 428
  organizatio 424
  progression 2, 453
synthesis 454, 493

T

tail-head lexical construction 149
target
  language 477
  space
    base 21
    topic 25
taunt 152, 512
  song 165
  speech 437
technical terms 602, 614
technique 115
television and radio 485
temple 180, 183, 201, 203, 207,
       210, 323, 341, 345, 392
  vision 345
temporal
  deictic 517
  disjunction 258
  displacement 292
  frame formula 179
  openers 191
  pragmatic variation 257
  setting 362
terrace(d) 505
  construction 388, 509
  pattern 50
testing 403
Tetragrammaton 415
text
  argumentation 504
  characterization 280
  comparison 406
  conjunction 274
  criticism 75, 129
  demarcation 273
  markers 480
  organization 271
  presentation 282
  projection 276
  sequence marker 617
  speaker 499
  transmission 404
text-linguistic study 1
text-rhetorical analysis 358
textual
  adjustment strategies 220
  aperture 383
  architecture 198
  arrangement 349, 614
  cohesion 499
  displacement 303
  foregrounding 361
  highlighting 172
  integrity 326
  irony 286, 287
  markers 473
  organization 146
  re-construction 227
  recursion 40
  strategies 219
texture 355
thanksgiving psalm 468, 516, 518
theatre 629
theatrical art 631
the day is near 508
thematic 241
  center 62
  climax 384
  coherence 499
  contrast 434
  correlates 134
  density 314
  enigma 310

Index of Subjects 687

framework 66
interlude 342
interweaving 367
movement 367
nucleus 235, 277
   Habakkuk 427, 463
peak 7, 113, 127, 161, 323, 393
   Ezekiel 370
polarity 346, 461
pun 57
reversal(s) 119, 160, 183
unity 81
theme 279
   Malachi 546
the nations 378, 389, 548
theocracy 383
theodicy 338, 347, 348, 350, 357, 360, 379, 383, 424, 436, 451, 461, 478, 494
theological
  enigma 586
  hymn 149
  paradox 74
  peak
     Malachi 565
  presuppositions 264
  purpose 281
  significance 338, 424, 478
theology 131, 272
  of fait 495
theophanic
  description 158
  hymn 447
  imagery 22, 181
  refrain 390
  revelation 48
  vision 431
theophany 10, 147, 149, 154, 441, 450, 451, 460
theophany-victory song 469
thesis 155, 185
time 179
  formula 609

reference 618
setting 352
titles 88
Tonga 574
top-down analysis 351, 403, 568
topical
  chiasmus 362
  convergence 65
  inversions 381
  outline 600
  recycling 389
  reversal 461
  selection 390
  shifts 366
  symmetry 359
  transition 480
Torah 69, 124, 135, 158, 361, 467, 536, 550
  Covenant 73
  ruling 190
traddutore, traditore! 226
traditional performing arts 485
tragic-comic resolution 64
tragi-comic account 296
transculturation 486
transition 433, 438
transitional
  adverb 605
  bridge 359, 362, 615
  devices 172
  words 612
translation 137, 140, 327, 328, 331
  comparison 410
  differences 601
  difficulties 574
  evaluation 406
  principles 576
  sound units 487
  style 335, 397, 420
translational
  aid 637
  markers 479

procedures 404
techniques 494
translator training 420
transmediazation 486
transmission strategy 420
transposition 251
treaty curse 167, 169
triggers 448
tructural constituents 56
truncation/ellipsis 250
turning 105
  point 342
typographical
  devices 529
  display 489
  format 410
typography 487, 488, 570

U

un-creation 509
unified dramatic presentation 627
unitary authorship 339
United Bible Societies 395
unity 274, 453
  in diversity 367
universalism 344
unrighteousness 468
utility curses 509
utterance emphasis 256
utterance-response pair 501

V

vagueness 308
variation(s) 230, 242, 246, 247, 278, 317
  from the norm 323
verbal
  cadence 192
  center 187
  cognate construction 280
  irony 287
  parallels 65
  quality 574
  recursion 242, 308
  shifts 539
  structure indicators 400
  symmetry 438
  tapestry 449
verdict 43, 58, 156, 168, 342, 549
vernacular language 589
verse numbers 96
video productions 398
viewpoint 280
vindication 175, 371, 444, 450, 525
vision report 57, 384
vision(s) 55, 60, 106, 143, 144, 153, 158, 424
visual aids 590
vivid images 538
vocal presentation 486
vocative(s) 45, 54, 196, 221, 252, 378, 429, 518, 537
  exclamation 358
vow 439
V-S-O word order 251

W

war
  oracle 105
  poetry 162
  warning 133, 560
  of woe 514
Warrior-God 448
Warrior-Lord 442
watchman 341, 354, 431
waw-consecutive
  construction 261
  wayyiqtol construction 278
wayyiqtol 179
  clauses 255
  construction 261
weʻattah 160
Westermann, Claus 439

Index of Subjects

wicked speech motif 377
wisdom debate 361
witch 586
witchcraft 167, 581, 583
woe oracle(s) 55, 376, 431, 433, 435, 437, 462, 480
woe(s) 54, 152, 165, 366, 436, 512, 522
woe-sequence 450
word of the LORD 31, 67, 72, 75, 205, 346, 506, 601, 631, 641
word of Yahweh 203
word order 604
  variations 537, 539
wordplay(s) 374, 538
worldview 210, 218, 356, 470, 641
  transformation 451
written prophetic text 627
Wycliffe Bible Translators 395

Y

Yahweh 70, 117, 135, 149, 175, 184, 211, 243, 274, 312, 314, 338, 391, 415, 457, 464, 472, 490, 493, 501, 536, 556, 559, 577, 632
  of Armies 464, 555, 558
Yahwistic
  reform 523
  theology 275

Z

Zambia 212
zeal 376
Zechariah 532
Zephaniah 497, 498, 624
  Zephaniah 2:4 522
Zerubbabel 179, 184, 188, 189, 191, 201, 210, 211
Zion 518

SIL International Publications
Additional Releases in the
Publications in Translation and Textlinguistics Series

6. **Orality and the Scriptures: Composition, translation, and transmission,** by Ernst R. Wendland, 2013, 405 pp., ISBN 978-1-55671-298-2
5. **Lovely, lively lyrics: Selected studies in biblical Hebrew verse,** by Ernst R. Wendland, 2013, 461 pp., ISBN 978-1-55671-327-9
4. **The development of textlinguistics in the writings of Robert Longacre,** by Shin Ja Hwang, 2010, 423 pp., ISBN 978-1-55671-246-3
3. **Artistic and rhetorical patterns in Quechua legendary texts,** by Ågot Bergli, 2010, 304 pp., ISBN 978-1-55671-244-9
2. **LiFE-style translating: A workbook for translators,** by Ernst R. Wendland, 2006, 347 pp., ISBN 978-1-55671-167-1
1. **Translating the literature of scripture: A literary-rhetorical approach to Bible translation,** by Ernst R. Wendland, 2004, 509 pp., ISBN 978-1-55671-152-7

SIL International Publications
7500 W. Camp Wisdom Road
Dallas, TX 75236-5629 USA

Voice: +1-972-708-7404
Fax: +1-972-708-7363
publications_intl@sil.org
http://www.sil.org/resources/publications

www.ingramcontent.com/pod-product-compliance
Lightning Source LLC
Chambersburg PA
CBHW052038290426
44111CB00011B/1547